GW01606823

TWENTY FIRST CENTURY NARROW GAUGE

To my wife who has been a tower of strength in innumerable ways, from taking holidays in places she wouldn't otherwise have dreamed of visiting to putting up with my absences on other occasions and the ceaseless support she has offered during the hours I've spent behind the computer writing this book. Without all her help it wouldn't have been possible.

Mount Lyell Railway 0-4-2RT no 1 (Dübs 3369/1896) climbs through the tree ferns as she approaches Rinadeena, Tasmania, on 24th March 2013.

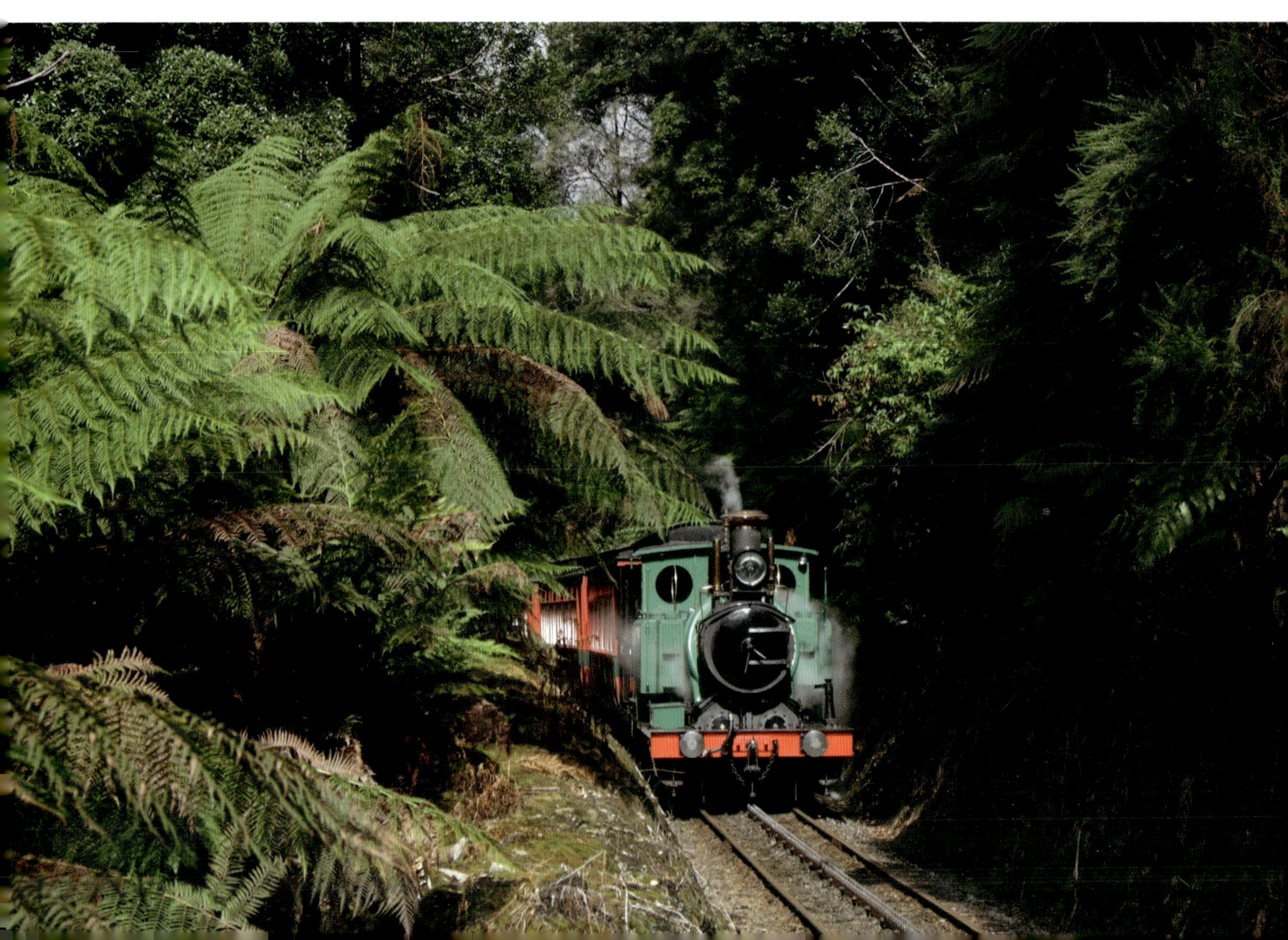

TWENTY FIRST CENTURY NARROW GAUGE

A PICTORIAL JOURNEY

JAMES WAITE

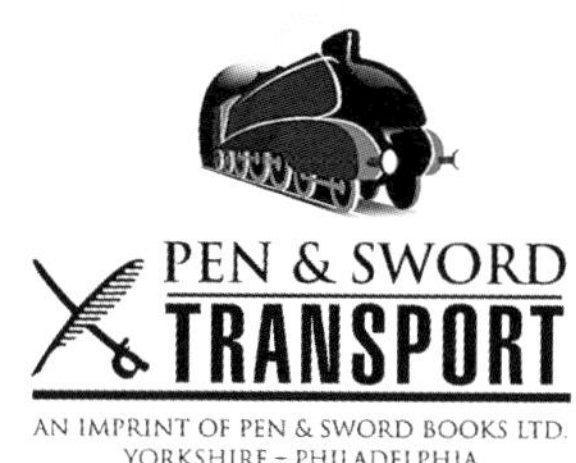

First published in Great Britain in 2019 by
Pen and Sword Transport
An imprint of
Pen & Sword Books Ltd
Yorkshire - Philadelphia

ISBN 978 1 47388 767 1

A CIP catalogue record for this book is available from the British Library.

Typeset in 11.5/14 Palatino
Typeset by Aura Technology and Software Services, India

Printed and bound in India by Replika Press Pvt. Ltd.

Pen & Sword Books Ltd incorporates the Imprints of Pen & Sword Books Archaeology, Atlas, Aviation, Battleground, Discovery, Family History, History, Maritime, Military, Naval, Politics, Railways, Select, Transport, True Crime, Fiction, Frontline Books, Leo Cooper, Praetorian Press, Seaforth Publishing, Wharncliffe and White Owl.

For a complete list of Pen & Sword titles please contact

PEN & SWORD BOOKS LIMITED
47 Church Street, Barnsley, South Yorkshire, S70 2AS, England
E-mail: enquiries@pen-and-sword.co.uk
Website: www.pen-and-sword.co.uk

or

PEN AND SWORD BOOKS
1950 Lawrence Rd, Havertown, PA 19083, USA
E-mail: Uspen-and-sword@casematepublishers.com
Website: www.penandswordbooks.com

CONTENTS

ACKNOWLEDGEMENTS

I've received immense help, friendship and kindness from many people throughout my travels. I've named some of them in the captions to these photos. Of the others, special thanks go to Bernd Seiler from Berlin, whose FarRail Tours operation arranges visits to railways and the use of steam locos against seemingly insurmountable odds, all for little financial return, and does so with such enthusiasm that it sometimes seems the next day's operations are in danger of starting before the previous ones have ended! Increasingly he has also invested in things like stocks of coal, overhauling locos and the maintenance of steam infrastructure.

Bob Turner from British Columbia has been a brilliant travelling companion in many places as well as being immensely knowledgeable about the railways of North America. In the US, Bill Shechter at Fairbanks and James Patten at Wiscasset were most helpful as were James Bane and Pete Lerro at the Sumpter Valley and Doug Cummings both at the White Pass and in Colorado. Pepe Fabregat was very hospitable at Cuautla and was mortified when the mayor wouldn't allow NdeM No 279 to run. Steve Cossey arranged numerous introductions and gave up a great deal of his time in Bogotá. My visits to railways in Brazil wouldn't have been possible without the great assistance of Bruno Sanches, Leandro Guidini, Julio Moraes, Rafael Bordini and José Warmuth. Marcelo Benoit, Fabiana and Alexandra Häberli and Fabian Iglesias all went out of their way to help me in Uruguay.

Christian Cederberg provided great assistance and accompanied me to the Hedelands Veterenbane and Roar Stenersen was most hospitable during visits to the Hamar museum, has provided a great deal of information about his country's railways and has very kindly checked over the Norwegian section of this book. Rune Bergstedt, Stig Gustavsson, Robert Herpai, Karl-Gunnar Karlsson, Lars Olof Karlsson, Kurt Möller, Anders Nordebring, Frank Stenvall, Lotta Sjöberg, Staffan Sjöberg and Håkan Zaar have all been most helpful in Sweden as has Jussi Tepponen at Jokioisten. Sergei Dorozhkov, the director of the Pereslavl museum, has been a tower of strength in preserving Russia's narrow gauge heritage for many years. He and his colleagues at Pereslavl were very hospitable during my visits and Sergei has checked over and provided much of the information about former Soviet locos. Vadim Anokhin was very helpful at Rostov-on-Don as were the late Peeter Klaus at Lavassaare, Toms Altbergs at Gulbene, Zilvinas Urbutis and Udrius Armalis at Panevėžys and Wolfram Wendelin, Dimitri Babarika and Sergei Trouchelle at Haivoron.

In the UK, several of my photos are the results of photo charters arranged by David Williams and Martin Creese, both of whom are experts in their field and work tirelessly in the interests of their customers, always at prices much lower than those charged elsewhere and sometimes for no financial reward at all. Julie Stirland at the Ffestiniog, Lawrence and Jane Garvey at Tywyn, Will Smith at Aberystwyth, Simon Bowden at the Welshpool & Llanfair, David Coleman at Corris, Tony Nicholson at Woody Bay and Bill Best at Bredgar have all offered unstinting assistance and Patrick Keef has taken my unusual, if not outrageous, requests in his stride at Ross-on-Wye and has always offered great hospitality.

In Germany Marcus Dettenberg has arranged visits to some of his country's lesser-known lines and Carsten Gussmann travelled a long distance early on a Sunday morning to open up the Asbach museum for me. Hans Hufnagel has given good friendship and help in his native Austria and many other parts of the world and John Organ guided me through the convoluted history of Austria's 0-6-2Ts. Ľubomír Lehotský runs the Kosice line and was most hospitable, Assen Stoyanov has always been a reliable friend in Sofia, Joan Enguix, the FGC's heritage officer, gave up a whole day to show me around his railway, Zoran Veresic has provided much of the information about his native Serbia and Dževad Hodžić, the transport manager at Banovići, deserves the thanks of many enthusiasts for keeping steam alive there and providing an unfailing welcome. Keith Chester is an acknowledged expert on the railways of eastern Europe and has always responded enthusiastically and unstintingly to my requests for help. My visits to the Greek narrow gauge wouldn't have been possible without the kindness and help of Nikos Kantiris and his friends at the Athens Railway Club.

Tedros Kebbede and the late Amanuel Ghebreselassie were overwhelmingly hospitable in Eritrea as were Christian Marot at Beau Champ, Julian Pereira at Ixopo, Hawkin Hansen, Henry Anderson, Les Reed and Anthony Stanton at the Sappi factory at Umkomaas and Maurice Barasa, John Ashworth, Kevin Patience and Geoff Warren in Nairobi. There would probably have been no recent steam trains in Kenya were it not for the untiring efforts of the late Francis Waweru at the Mawenzi Gardens Hotel in Nairobi who underwrote the financial risk, carried out much behind-the-scenes work - and provided great catering! Ashok Sharma from Real India Journeys has given me great help during both my visits to his ever-fascinating country as have Peter Jordan of Darjeeling Tours and Maria Cook of Ffestiniog Travel. Manfred and Kyi-Kyi Schoeler have been of great assistance in Burma and Michael Whitehouse has helped with information about the Burma Mines Railway. Priyanka Rodrigo was a welcoming host in Sri Lanka as was Ray Schofield in Cambodia and Paul Molyneux-Berry has shared his extensive knowledge of the C2s in China. Nothing was too much trouble for the gentleman I know only as Director Chang at the Alishan Forest Railway. Takahide Yamamoto provided an invaluable introduction to the railways of Japan as well as giving me much detailed information and has been a congenial travelling companion in many countries. Toki Sasaki runs a valuable English-language Japanese steam website and has been very helpful with follow-up information. In Australia Ian Willis was very helpful at the Hotham Valley. Jeremy Browne was most hospitable at the Pichi Richi as were John Browning in Queensland, Jean Clowes at the Puffing Billy and Nigel Day and Tristan McMahon in Tasmania.

To all of them as well as to the many others whom I haven't mentioned by name I offer my heartfelt thanks for all their help and friendship.

LOCOMOTIVE BUILDERS

Addington	NZR, Addington Works, Christchurch, New Zealand
Ajmer	Bombay, Baroda & Central India Railway, Ajmer Works, India
AK	Alan Keef Limited, Lea, Ross-on-Wye, Hereford & Worcester, England
Alco	American Locomotive Company, Schenectady, New York, USA
Ansaldo	Ansaldo SA, Sampierdarena, Genoa, Italy
Atlas	AB Atlas, Stockholm, Sweden
Avonside	Avonside Engine Co Ltd, Bristol, England
Bagnall	WG Bagnall Ltd, Stafford, England
Baldwin	The Baldwin Locomotive Company, Philadelphia, Pennsylvania, USA
Barclay	Andrew Barclay, Sons & Co Ltd, Kilmarnock, Scotland
BB	Brown, Boveri & Cie, Baden, Switzerland
BH	Black Hawthorn & Co, Gateshead, England
Birmingham	Birmingham Railway Carriage & Wagon Co Ltd, Smethwick, Birmingham, England
Borsig	Borsig AG, Tegel, Berlin, Germany (later Hennigsdorf, Germany)
BP	Beyer Peacock & Co Ltd, Gorton, Manchester, England
Breda	Società Italiana Ernesto Breda, Milan, Italy
Budapest	Magyar Királyi Államvasutak Gépgyára (later MÁVAG), Budapest, Hungary
Cail	SA des Anciens Établissements Cail, Paris, France
CEMSA	Costruzioni Elettro Meccaniche di Saronno, Saronno, Italy
ČKD	Českomoravská Kolben-Daněk, Prague, Czech Republic
Chrzanów	Pierwsza Fabryka Lokomotyw w Polsce Sp. Akc., Chrzanów, Poland
Davenport	Davenport Locomotive Works, Davenport, Iowa, USA
ĐD	Đuro Đakovi Đuro Industrija, Slavonski Brod, Croatia
Decauville	La Société Nouvelle des Établissements Decauville Aine, Corbeil, France
Dübs	Dübs & Co Ltd, Glasgow, Scotland
Energie	Société Energie, Marcinelle, Belgium
Esslingen	Maschinenfabrik Esslingen, Esslingen am Neckar, Baden-Württemberg, Germany
Falun	Vagn- & Maskinfabriksaktiebolaget i Falun, Falun, Sweden
FJ	Fletcher, Jennings & Co (later Lowca Engineering Co), Lowca, Cumberland, England
Floridsdorf	Wiener Lokomotivfabrik AG, Floridsdorf, Vienna, Austria
Fowler	John Fowler & Co (Leeds) Ltd, Leeds, England

GE	George England & Co, New Cross, Surrey, England
GNS	Great Northern Steam Ltd, Darlington, County Durham, England
Hagans	Maschinenfabrik Christian Hagans, Erfurt, Germany
Hanomag	Hannoversche Maschinenbau AG, Hannover, Germany
Harbin	Harbin Forestry Machinery Factory, Harbin, Heilongjiang, China
Hartmann	Richard Hartmann, later Sächsische Maschinenfabrik, Chemnitz, Germany
HC	Hudswell, Clarke & Co Ltd, Leeds, England
Heisler	Heisler Locomotive Works, Erie, Ohio, USA
Henschel	Henschel & Sohn, Kassel, Germany
Hitachi	Hitachi Ltd, Chiyoda, Tokyo, Japan
Horlock	A Horlock & Co, Northfleet Ironworks, Northfleet, Kent, England
HSP	SA Forges Usines et Fonderies Haine-Saint-Pierre, Haine-Saint-Pierre, Belgium
Hughes	Henry Hughes & Co, Loughborough, Leicestershire, England
Humboldt	Maschinenbauanstalt Humboldt AG, Cologne-Kalk, Germany
Hunslet	Hunslet Engine Co Ltd, Leeds, England
Ipswich	Queensland Railways, Ipswich Works, Ipswich, Queensland, Australia
Jung	Arnold Jung Lokomotivfabrik GmbH, Jungenthal, Germany
Kawasaki	Kawasaki Heavy Industries, Kobe, Japan
Kisha	Kisha Seizo Co Ltd, Osaka, Japan
Kitson	Kitson & Co Ltd, Leeds, England
KL	Locomotivfabrik Krauss & Co, Linz, Austria
KM	Locomotivfabrik Krauss & Co, Munich, Germany
Kolomna	Kolomensky Zavod, Kolomna, Russia
Kristinehamn	Kristinehamns Mekaniska Werkstad, Kristinehamn, Sweden
Krupp	Friedrich Krupp AG, Essen, Germany
KS	Kerr, Stuart & Co Ltd, Stoke-on-Trent, Staffordshire, England
LEW	Lokomotivbau-Elektrotechnische Werke, Hennigsdorf, Germany (the old Borsig factory)
Lima	Lima Locomotive Works Inc, Lima, Ohio, USA
LKM	Lokomotivbau Karl Marx, Babelsberg, Potsdam, Germany (the old OK factory)
Lokomo	Oy Lokomo Ab, Tampere, Finland
Martin	James Martin & Co, Gawler, South Australia
Meiningen	DB Dampflokwerk Meiningen, Meiningen, Germany
Midland	Western Australian Government Railways, Midland Junction Works, Perth, Western Australia
Mitsubishi	Mitsubishi Heavy Industries Ltd, Hiroshima, Japan
Motala	Motala Verkstad, Motala, Sweden
Munktells	Munktells Mekaniska Verkstads AB, Eskilstuna, Sweden
MÁVAG	See Budapest

MV	Metropolitan-Vickers Electrical Co Ltd, Manchester, England
NB	North British Locomotive Co Ltd, Glasgow, Scotland
Neilson	Neilson & Co, Glasgow, Scotland
Newport	Victorian Railways, Newport Works, Victoria, Australia
Nippon	Nippon Sharyo Ltd, Nagoya, Japan
Nohab	Nydqvist & Holm AB, Trollhättan, Sweden
OK	Orenstein & Koppel AG, Drewitz, Berlin, later Babelsberg, Potsdam, Germany
Porter	HK Porter Inc, Pittsburgh, Pennsylvania, USA
Portland	The Portland Co, Portland, Maine, USA
Price	A&G Price Ltd, Thames, New Zealand
RE	Officine Meccaniche Italiane S.A. Reggio Emilia, Italy
Reșița	Uzinele de Fier și Domeniile Reșița SA, Reșița, Romania
Rogers	Rogers Locomotive and Machine Works, Paterson, New Jersey, USA
RSH	Robert Stephenson and Hawthorns Ltd, Darlington, County Durham, England
SACM	Société Alsacienne de Constructions Mécaniques, Graffenstaden and Mulhouse, France
Sentinel	Sentinel Waggon Works (1920) Ltd, Shrewsbury, England
Schwartzkopff	L Schwartzkopff, later Berliner Maschinenbau AG, Wildau, Berlin, Germany
Shijiazhuang	Shijiazhuang Motive Power Machinery Works, Shijiazhuang, Hebei, China
SLM	Schweizerische Lokomotiv und Maschinenfabrik, Winterthur, Switzerland
Škoda	Škodovy Závody, Plzeň, Czech Republic
SL	Stephen Lewin, Poole, Dorset, England
SS	Sharp Stewart & Co Ltd, Manchester, England (later Glasgow, Scotland)
Swindon	Great Western Railway, Swindon Works, Wiltshire, England
Takatori	Imperial Government Railway, Takatori factory, Takatori, Japan
Tampella	Oy Tampella AB, Tampere, Finland
TG	Thomas Green & Son Ltd, Leeds, England
Thompson	Thompson & Co (Castlemaine) Pty Ltd, Castlemaine, Victoria, Australia
Thunes	Thunes Mekaniske Værksted A/S, Skøyen, Oslo, Norway
Tubize	SA La Métallurgique, Nivelles, Tubize & Le Sambre, Belgium
Valmet	Valtion Metallitehtaat Lentokonetehdas, Tampere, Finland
VF	The Vulcan Foundry Ltd, Newton-le-Willows, Lancashire, England
VIW	Vulcan Iron Works, Wilkes-Barre, Pennsylvania, USA
VS	AG Vulcan Stettin, Stettin, Germany (now Szczecin, Poland)
Walkers	Walkers Ltd, Maryborough, Queensland, Australia
Winson	Winson Engineering Ltd, Daventry, Northamptonshire, England

FOREWORD

Patrick Whitehouse and Peter Allen's book *Round the World on the Narrow Gauge* was published more than fifty years ago and opened the eyes of many enthusiasts to fascinating narrow gauge railways in far-away places. Much more recently I've been fortunate to visit several countries around the world and it has been a pleasure to discover just how many interesting steam-worked lines are still there to be enjoyed. Nowadays the majority are inevitably heritage railways or involve steam locos which have been kept running after they have retired from their everyday work, but they're none the worse for that.

When I was a small child, I won a prize at school and the headmaster was perceptive enough to choose an earlier book by Mr Whitehouse, his *Narrow Gauge Album* which became my introduction to the delights of the little lines. A family holiday in North Wales provided the opportunity to see them for myself and I was well and truly hooked! The trains fitted so well into their surroundings and seemed to complement what nature had to offer rather than intruding upon it. Maybe this is part of the enduring appeal of the narrow gauge. There can be few more peaceful sights than that of a small steam train gently puffing along through beautiful countryside.

I've regarded any line whose gauge is less than 4ft 8½ins as being eligible for inclusion in this book. There are photos of the enormous Garratts in East and South Africa and large conventional locos in countries like Brazil and Australia alongside more obviously small ones. I hope they provide a balanced selection of subjects and will make for interesting reading. In the case of heritage railways, I've tried to concentrate on trains which look at least something like they did when they were running for real. This isn't to criticise the many lines which have built modern carriages or facilities to fulfil their customers' expectations, but it does seem to me that heritage involves the conservation of old material and it's this which makes for the most satisfying photos.

This isn't intended to be a guide to the world's narrow gauge railways as there are just too many which have eluded me. I never got to see the fascinating sugar trains of Cuba and only visited the lines in Java and Zimbabwe some forty years ago. There are many fascinating and scenic railways in countries like Ecuador, Chile, Brazil, Hungary and Russia which I have yet to explore. I've concentrated on locos in steam but have included some static subjects where I thought they had a tale to tell or just looked attractive. Some of the photos at heritage railways are of their everyday trains. Others, mostly of freight trains, involved photographers' specials, either chartered by specialists or arranged directly by the railways. It will be clear from the photos and their captions which these are. Much the same goes for lines whose main business is running everyday services where steam locos are used on only special occasions.

The relatively small number of railways in these photos which were still working for their living became obsolete many years ago and have now mostly stopped using steam locos or closed altogether. It's tempting to think that preserved railways, or steam trains still running on non-heritage lines, have a secure future. This is often so but there have been some sad and unexpected losses. Amongst the railways featured here the East Broad Top in Pennsylvania and, nearer home, the Tralee and Dingle and Penrhyn lines have closed, and steam locos no longer run on the Catalan metre gauge or the Waldenburgerbahn in Switzerland. The loco at the FC Indare in Uruguay needs major overhaul and operations are only spasmodic on much of the Esquel branch in Argentina. Much more widespread tragedies have brought an end to steam trains in Syria and parts of Burma, the suffering of whose peoples eclipses anything to do with railways. If you have the opportunity to visit some of the world's little lines, try to go sooner rather than later!

In order to do justice to this wide-ranging subject, I've drawn information from a great many books, magazine articles and websites. With considerable misgivings I decided not to attempt a reading list as it would just be too long and I hope that their authors will forgive me and accept this collective offer of thanks.

This book is first and foremost a celebration of all the wonderful little railways around the world which continue to provide much enjoyment for many people. I hope it will be as great a pleasure to read as it has been to write.

CANADA AND THE USA

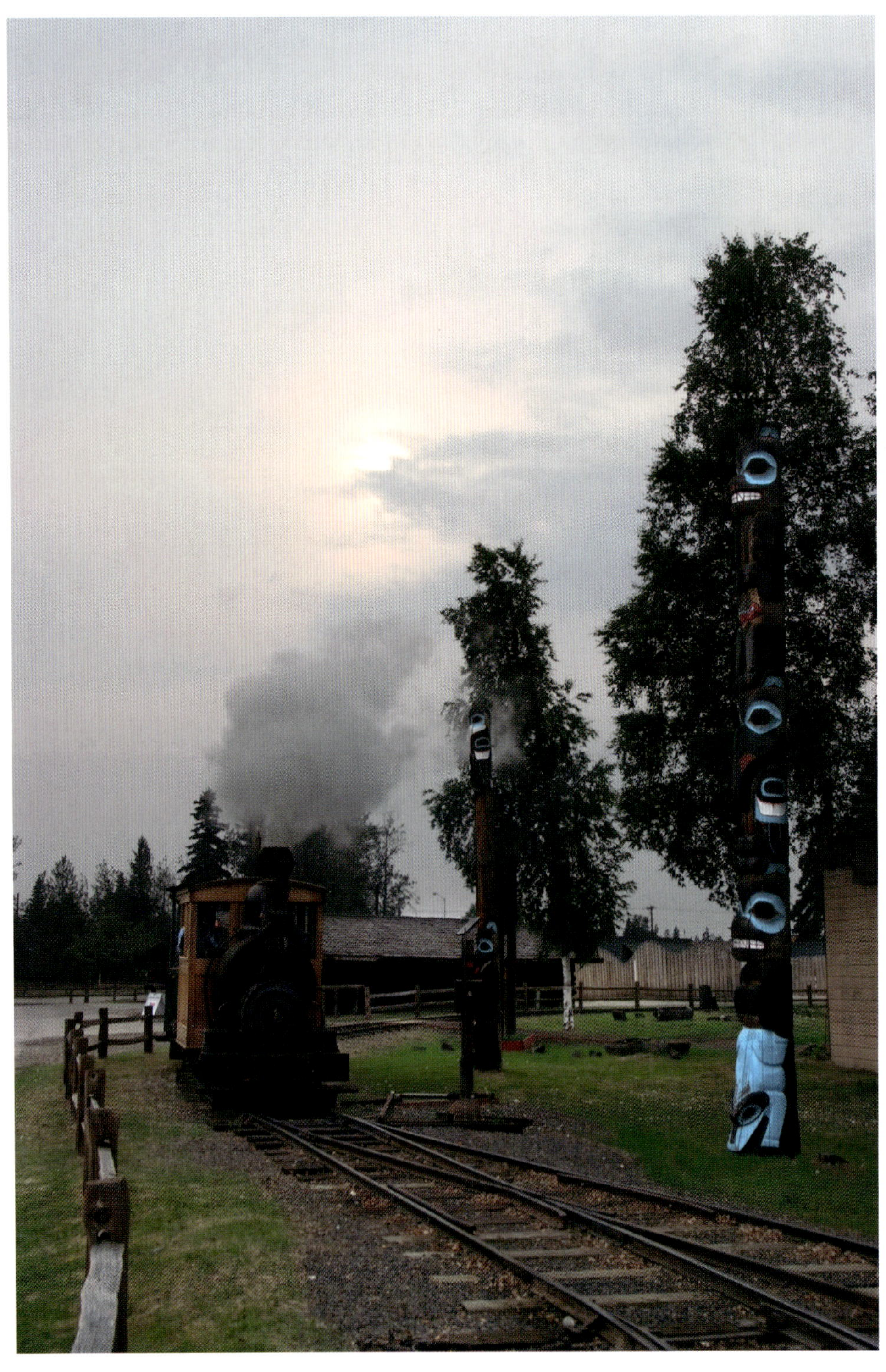

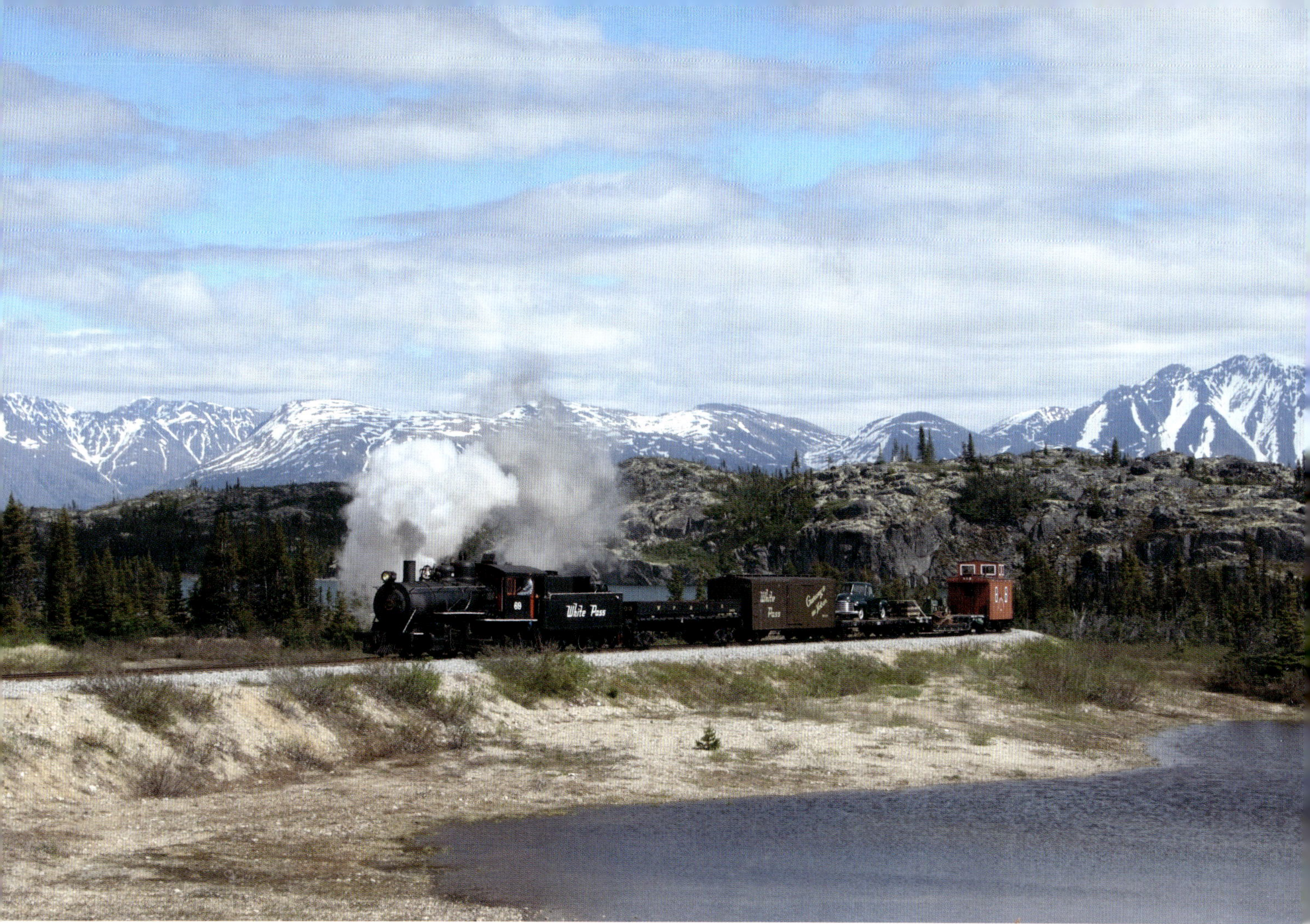

Above: Word of the Klondike find reached the outside world in July 1897 and at once the goldrush was under way. So many stampeders, as they came to be known, headed north that a railway through the mountains became an attractive economic proposition despite the heavy engineering involved. The 3ft gauge White Pass & Yukon RR began at Skagway, Alaska, and headed inland for 118 miles to Whitehorse, now the capital of the Yukon. 2-8-0 No 69 (Baldwin 32962/1908) is one of two steam locos still in working order. Here she takes a freight train around the loop at Fraser, British Columbia, on 12 June 2011.

Opposite: Tanana Valley RR 0-4-0ST No 1 (Porter 1972/1899) approaches her shed at Fairbanks, Alaska, on 8 June 2011 and passes totem poles still being carved, a much-loved tradition in the region. Few locos can deserve to carry the number 1 more than this little 3ft gauge machine! Gold was found in the Klondike River near Dawson City in August 1896 and she arrived in the district during the goldrush years, becoming the first loco to work in the Yukon. In 1903, she moved to the new Tanana Valley RR at Fairbanks as its No 1, the first loco to work in the interior of Alaska. In 1917, the US government bought the Tanana Valley to use its route into the town for the Alaska RR; they operated the narrow gauge for a few years with the little loco as their No 1 and later passed her on for preservation on account of her role in the state's history. Enter the Friends of the Tanana Valley Railroad who started to overhaul her in 1992 and she now makes occasional outings over a circle of track at Fairbanks. They very kindly steamed (and let me drive!) her on what would have been a bright sunny evening but for a forest fire, the smoke from which had got into the upper atmosphere – strange photographic conditions indeed. A great little railway and one that's well worth visiting!

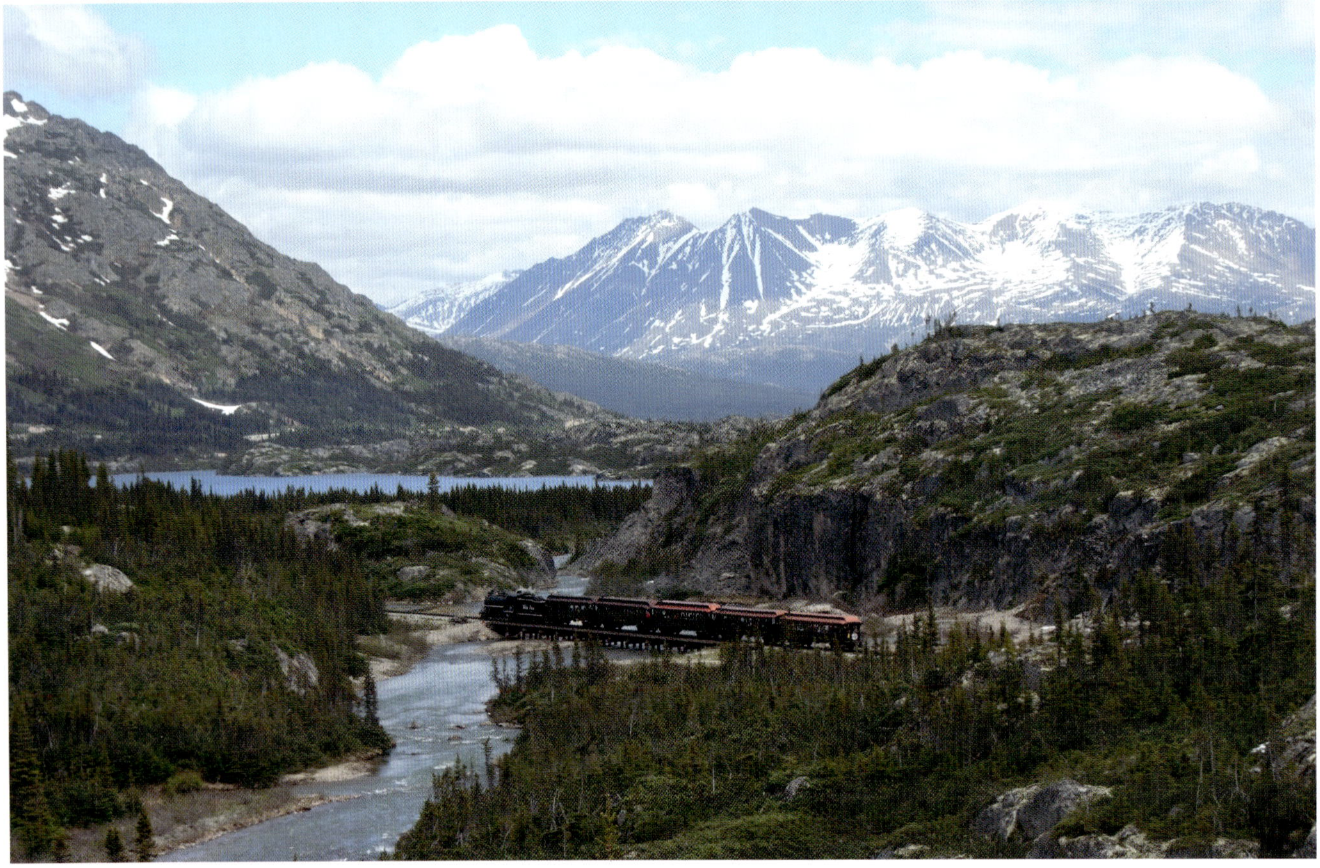

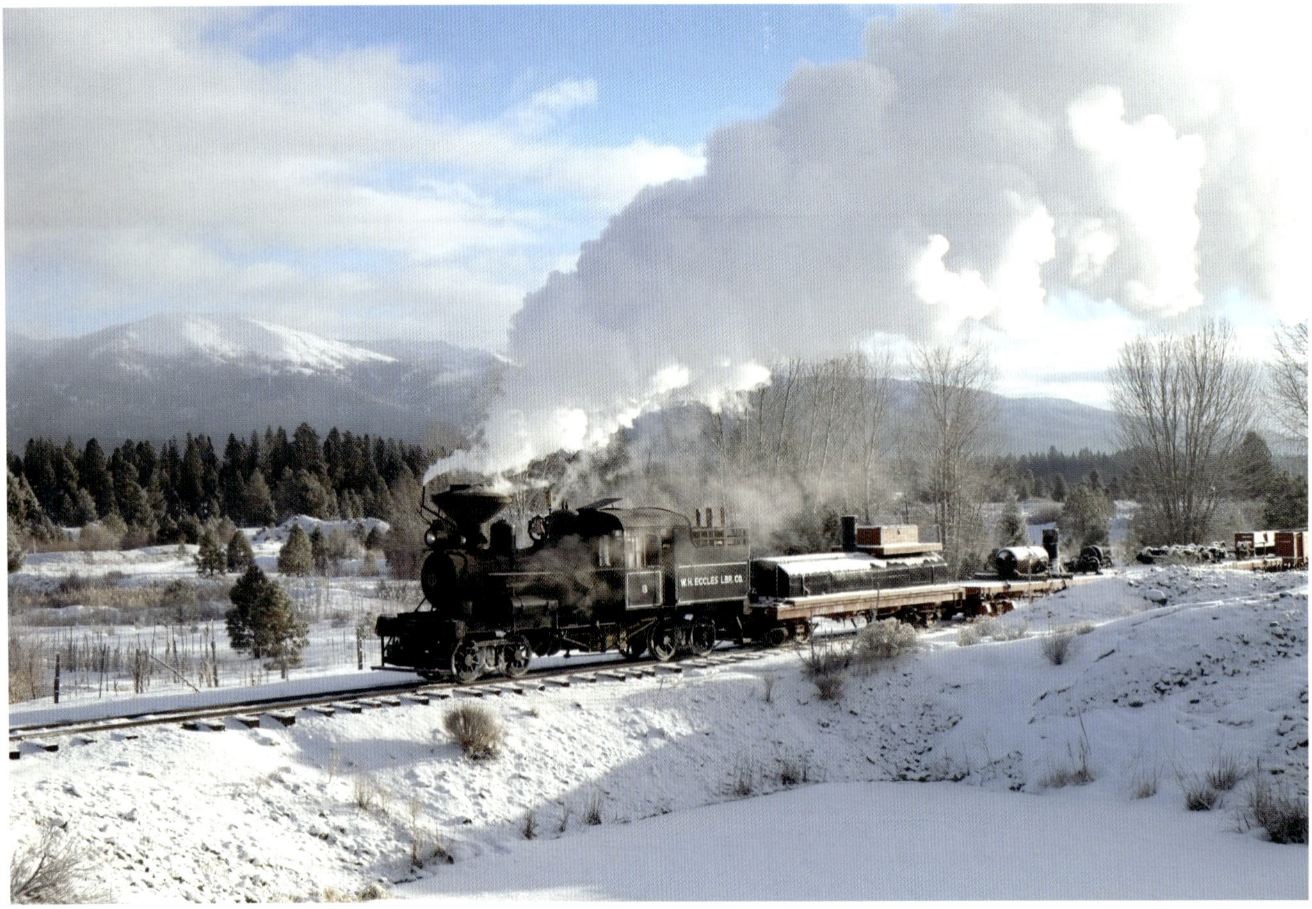

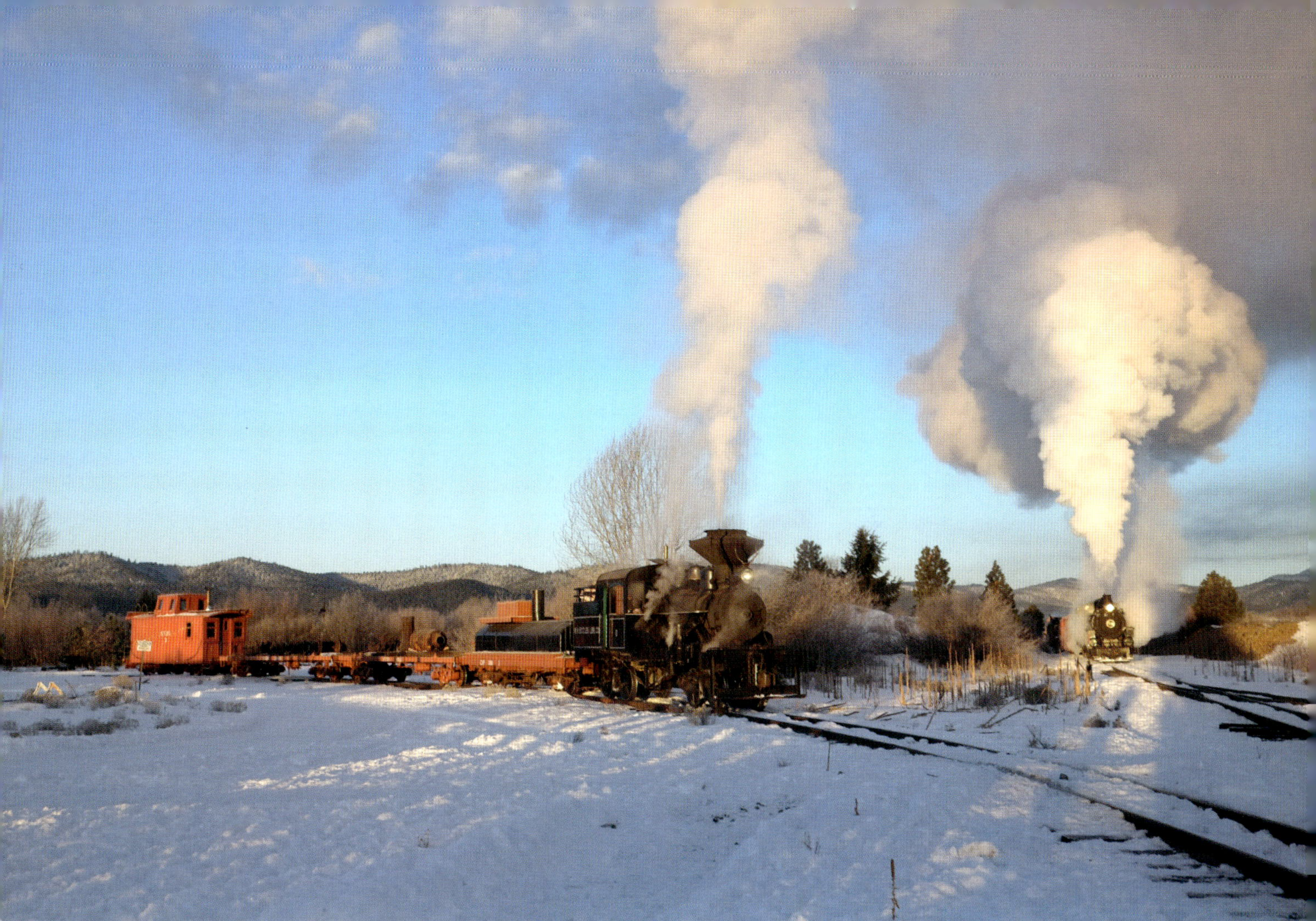

Above: After the gold fever ended, the Sumpter Valley settled down to serve the logging industry until closure in 1947. Enthusiasts began to restore the section between McEwen and Sumpter in 1970, a difficult task since much of the trackbed had slipped away into the pebbly ditches. No 3 stands on a siding at McEwen as 2-8-2 No 19 (Alco 61980/1920) heads along the mainline on the very cold morning of 2 February 2014.

Opposite above: 2-8-2 No 73 (Baldwin 73352/1947), the White Pass line's youngest steam loco, crosses the Thompson's River near Fraser with a passenger train on 13 June 2011. Times became hard for the railway over the years, but it kept going until 1982. Six years later it reopened as a tourist line when Skagway became a popular port of call for cruise ships. Most trains are now diesel-hauled but there's also a steam service.

Opposite below: On 1 February 2014 W.H. Eccles No 3 (Heisler 1306/1915) heads west from McEwen on the 3ft gauge Sumpter Valley Railway in eastern Oregon with the Elkhorn Mountains as a backdrop. The old line ran southwest from Baker City, entered the broad Sumpter valley at McEwen and continued for about five miles to a junction near Sumpter town before heading further west. The valley was dredged from the early 1900s during Sumpter's goldrush, leaving this barren landscape composed of ditches, ponds and pebble banks in place of the old meadows. No 3 was built for Eccles's logging line which connected with the Sumpter Valley. She ended up on another logging railway in Cascade, Idaho, and still carried her original Eccles paint scheme when she entered preservation.

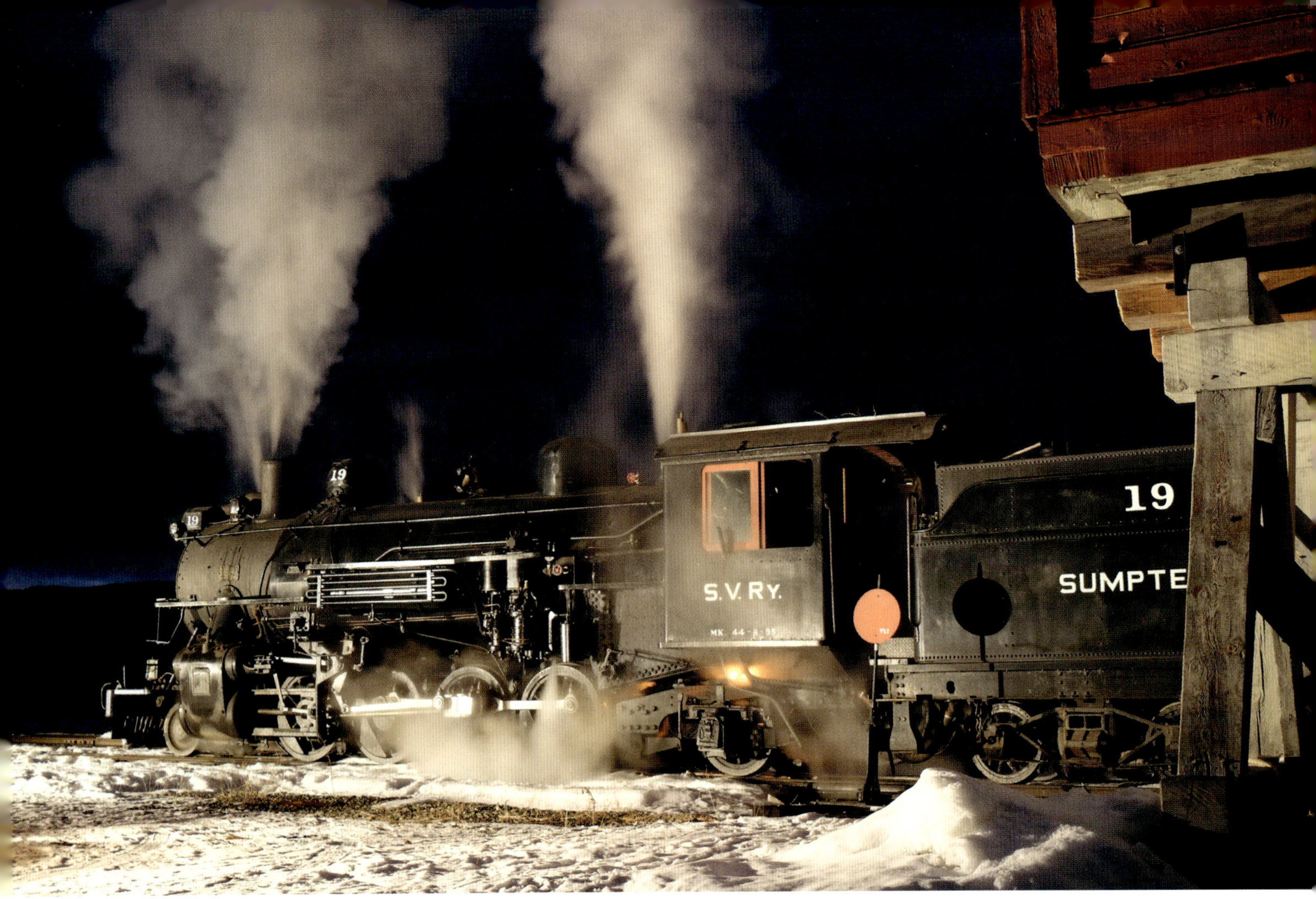

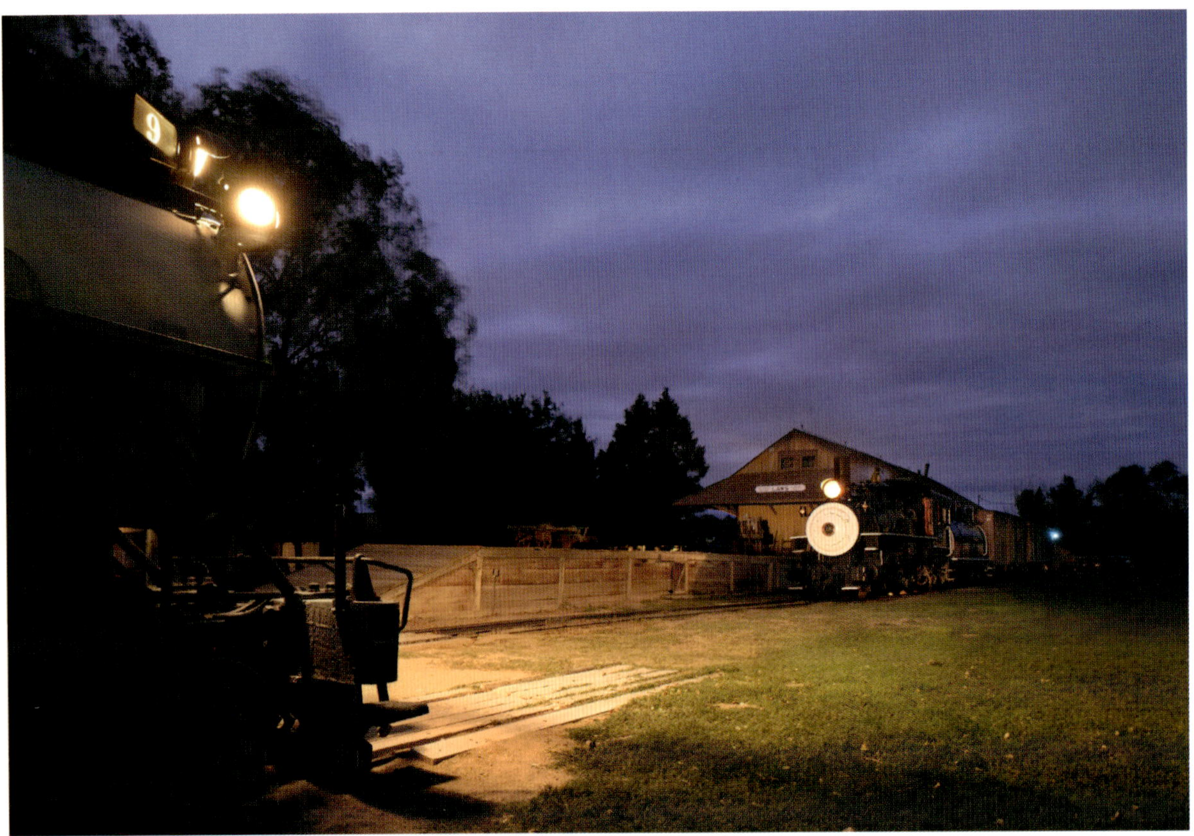

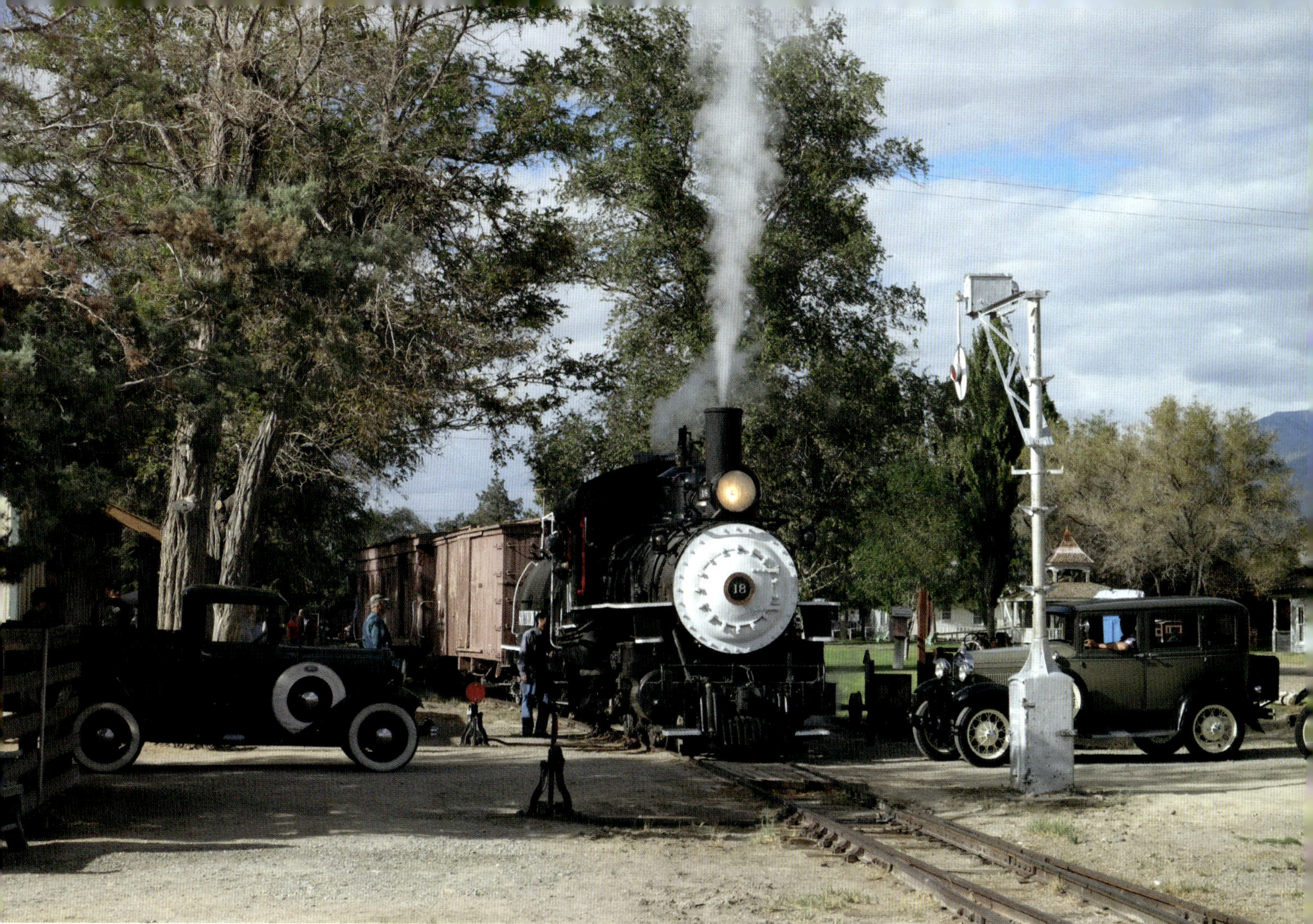

Above: Southern Pacific No 18 and her short freight train hold up the traffic at a level crossing at Laws on 22 September 2017. The Carson & Colorado started as a feeder line for the standard gauge Virginia & Truckee RR but was bought by SP in 1900. A long section became standard gauge, other parts closed and after 1943 the seventy miles through the Owens Valley between Laws and Keeler were all that remained of the narrow gauge.

Opposite above: Sumpter Valley No 19 stands at McEwen water tower on the evening of 1 February 2014. She's one of two similar 2-8-2s which were sold to the White Pass in 1940. Their tenders were retained to run with two Mallets and after 1947 moved with them to the International Railways of Central America in Guatemala. Eventually the Mallets were scrapped but happily the tenders survived to be reunited with the 2-8-2s back at their old home.

Opposite below: Southern Pacific 4-6-0's Nos 9 (Baldwin 34095/1909) and 18 (Baldwin 37395/1918) meet at Laws station on SP's old 3ft gauge Owens Valley line in the early evening of 22 September 2017. This railway was originally part of the Carson & Colorado RR which opened between Mound House, Nevada, and Keeler, California, about 300 miles away to the south between 1881 and 1883. With their distinctive round-topped tenders, marking them out as oil-burners, these were two of its last three steam locos, all acquired by SP when it took over the Nevada-California-Oregon RR in 1927.

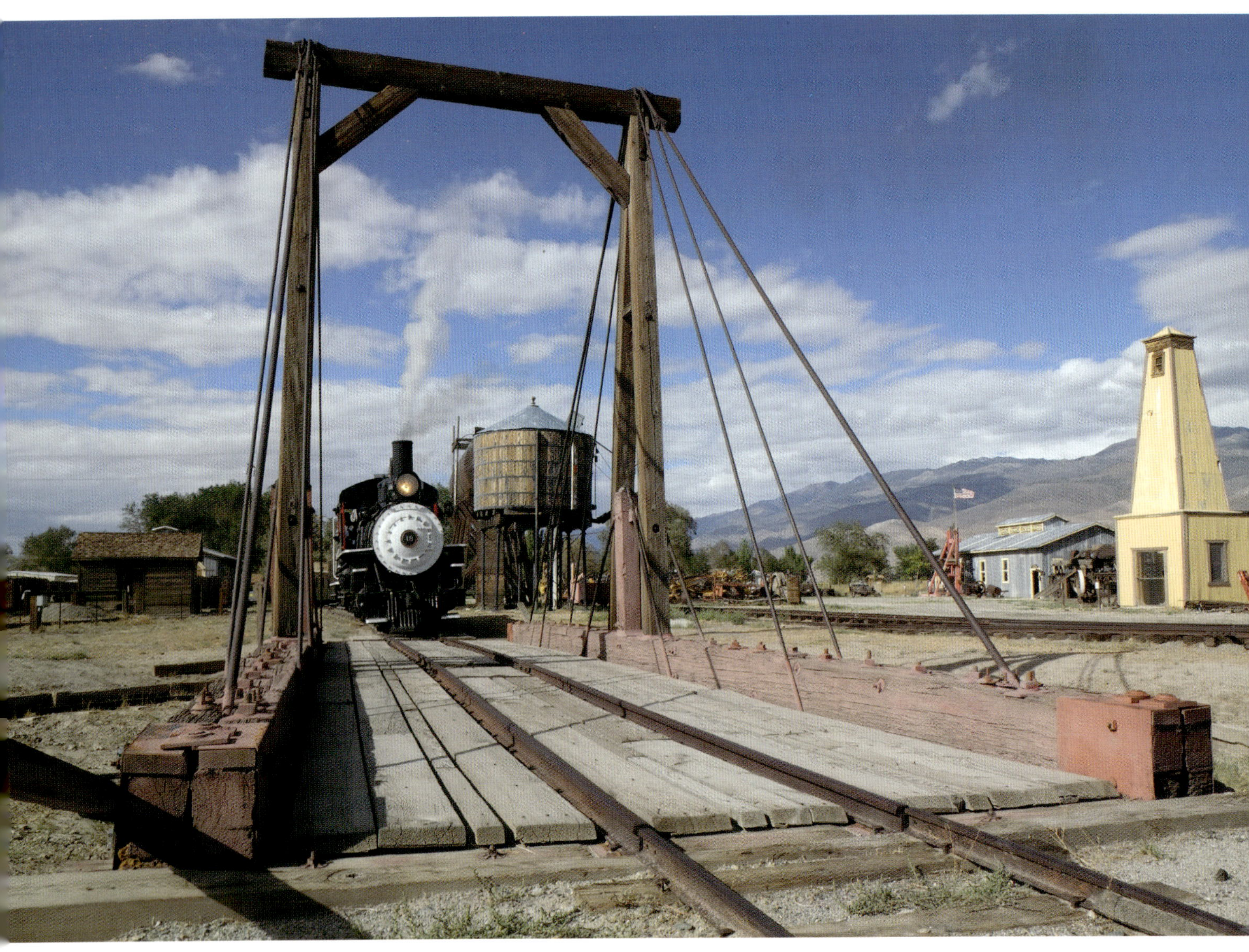

No 18 stands in the loco yard at Laws on 22 September 2017. When the line closed in 1960, SP presented Laws station to the local authority to become a museum, along with No 9 and numerous vans and wagons. No 18 was visiting after being restored to working order. The old wooden turntable, typical of many in the US, had also been restored but rot discovered in one of the main timbers was preventing its use. To the right of the loco are the old water and fuel oil tanks; the cream-coloured building is a water pumphouse dating back to the line's early days.

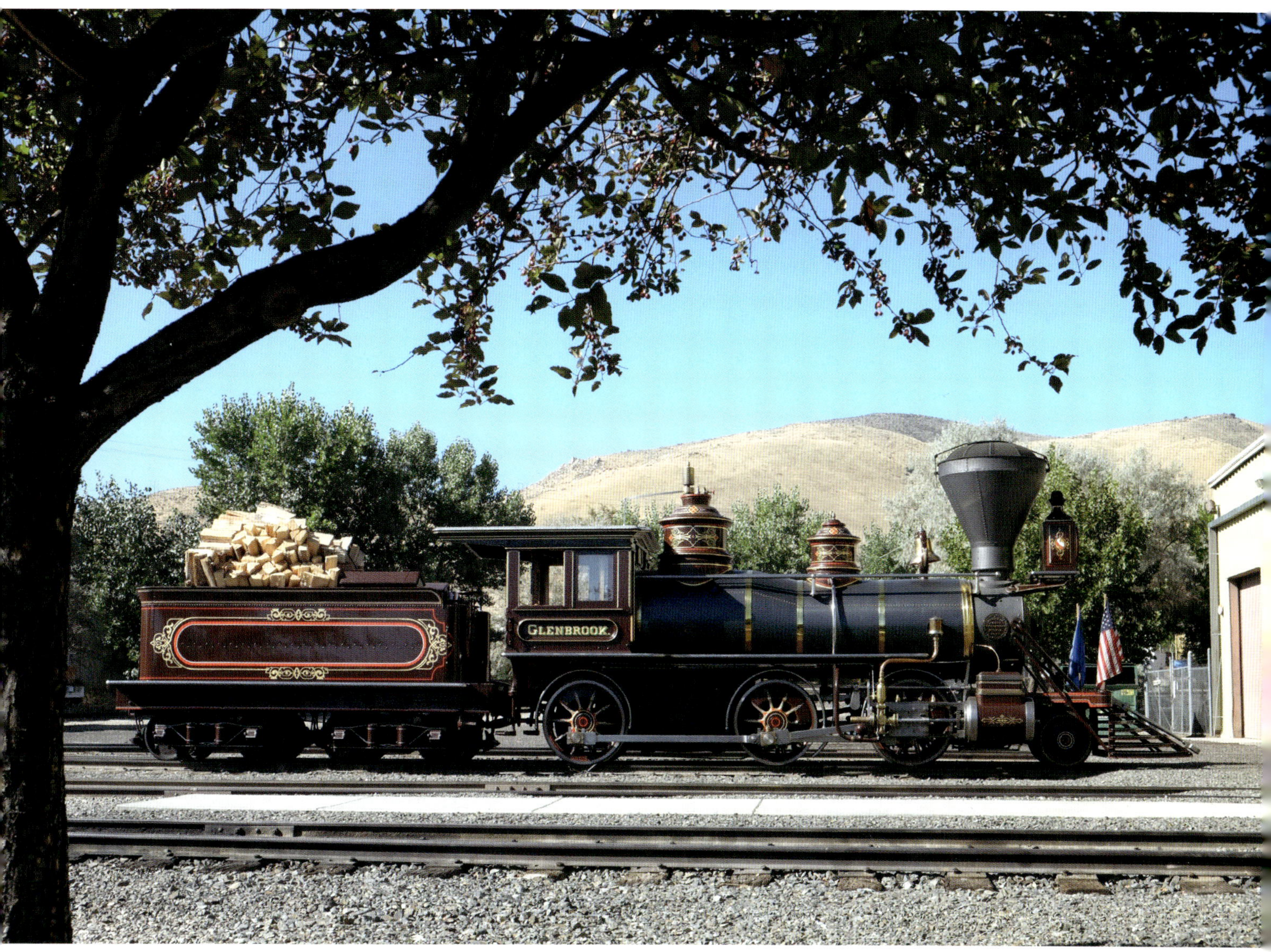

Wendell Huffman, the Curator of History at the Nevada State Railroad Museum has kindly pulled 3ft gauge 2-6-0 *Glenbrook* (Baldwin 3712/1875) out into the morning sunshine on 24 September 2017. She started life on a forestry railway running into the hills to the east of Lake Tahoe from where the logs were transported by a flume down to a yard near Carson City at almost exactly the spot where the museum now stands. She moved in about 1899 to a new line serving Tahoe City and in 1937 was sold on to the Nevada County Narrow Gauge RR but only as a source of spares. She was soon stripped and would probably have disappeared altogether had it not been for the perseverance of the delightfully-named Miss Hope Bliss, her original owner's daughter. She bought her in 1942 and presented her to the predecessor of the Nevada museum. Many of her missing parts were 'rescued' by Nevada County railwaymen and followed her there. Now she's back in working order.

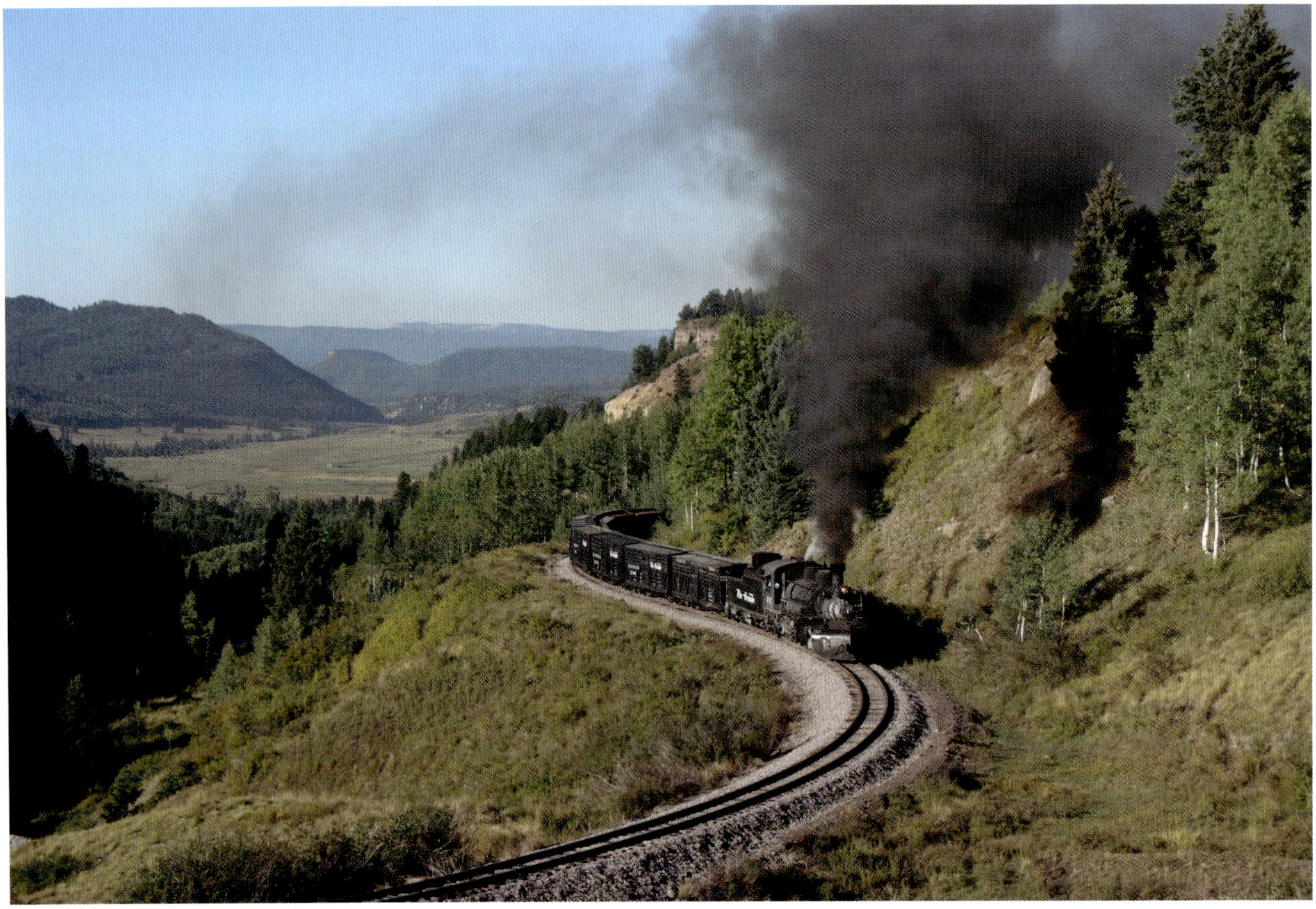

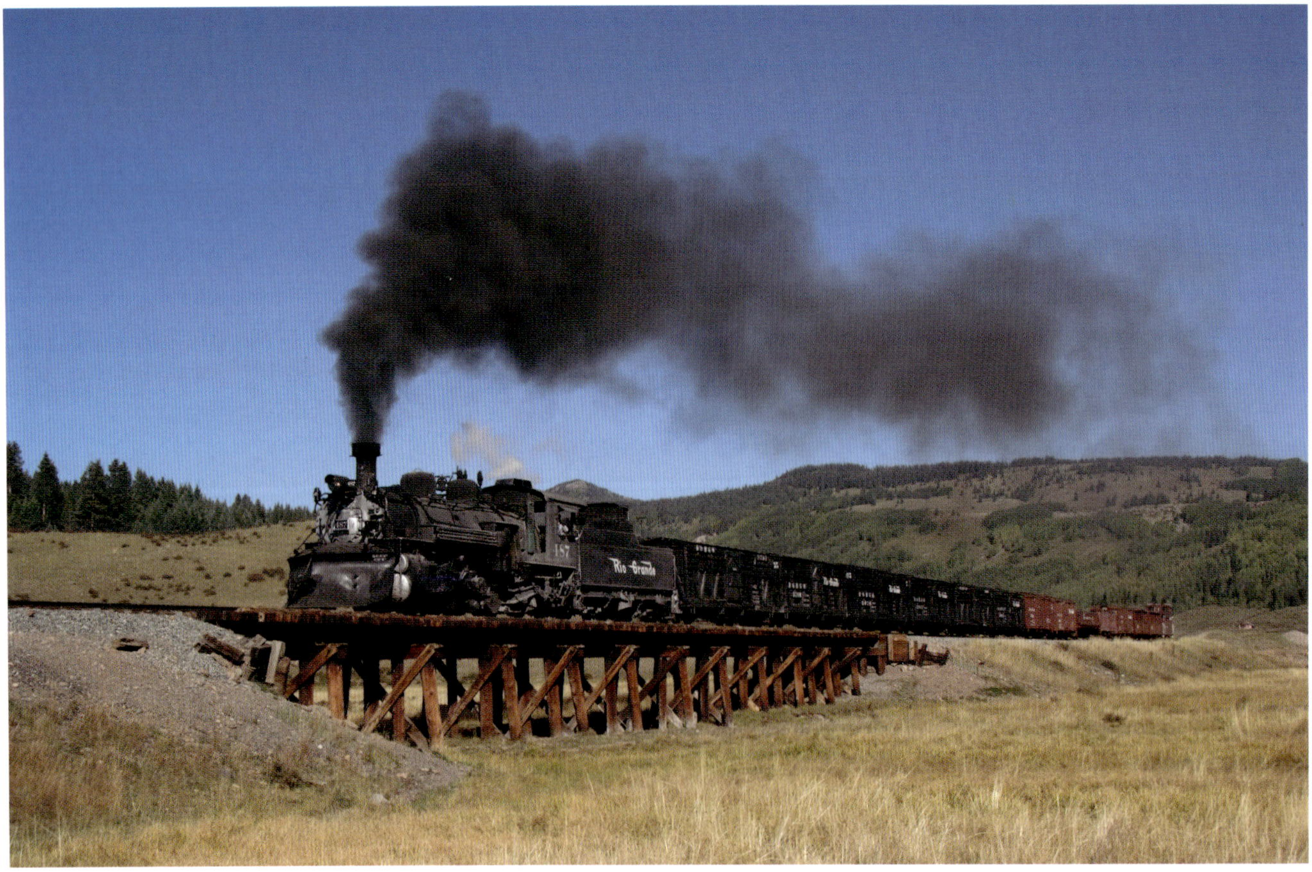

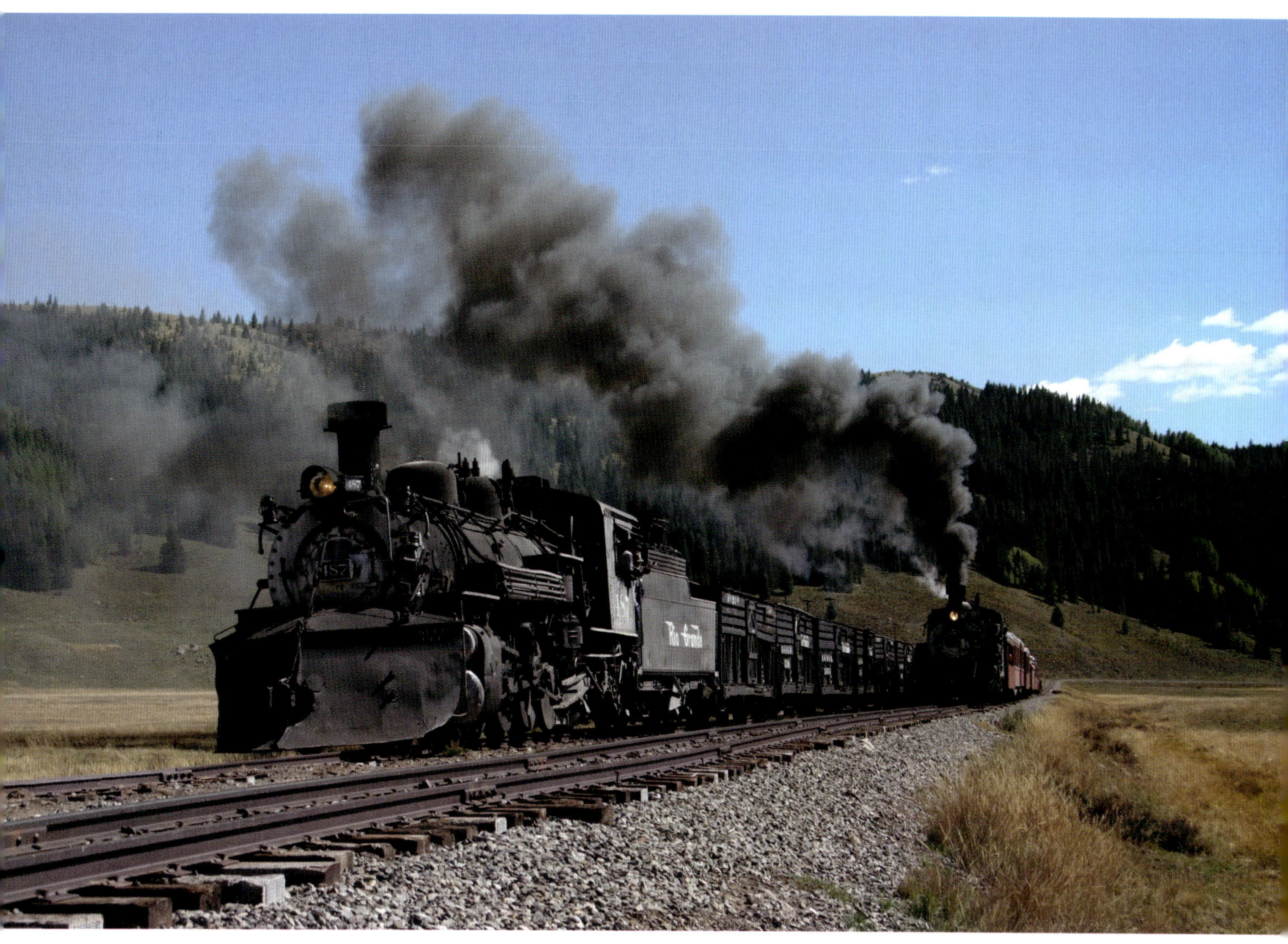

Above: No 487 stands at the wobbly-looking loop at Los Pinos as K-36 No 489 (Baldwin 58590/1925) passes with a westbound passenger train painted in the Rio Grande's pre-1917 crimson. The black-painted vehicles are cattle wagons.

Opposite above: Construction of the Denver and Rio Grande, the first major US 3ft gauge railway, began in 1871. General William Jackson Palmer, its founder, intended that it should run to the Rio Grande and onwards to México City, but this was frustrated by competitors and instead it turned west at Antonito to climb over Cumbres Pass. On 22 September 2011, K-36 class 2-8-2 No 487 (Baldwin 58588/1925) heads a freight train from Chama towards the pass on what is now the Cumbres & Toltec Scenic RR.

Opposite below: The hard climbing is over as No 487 takes her eastbound train over a wooden trestle bridge near Los Pinos, east of Cumbres. By 1968 the long, straggling mainline through Antonito and Chama to Durango and its branches to Farmington and Silverton were all that remained of the Rio Grande's narrow gauge. Most of it closed in 1968 but the most scenic part of the mainline soon reopened as the Cumbres & Toltec.

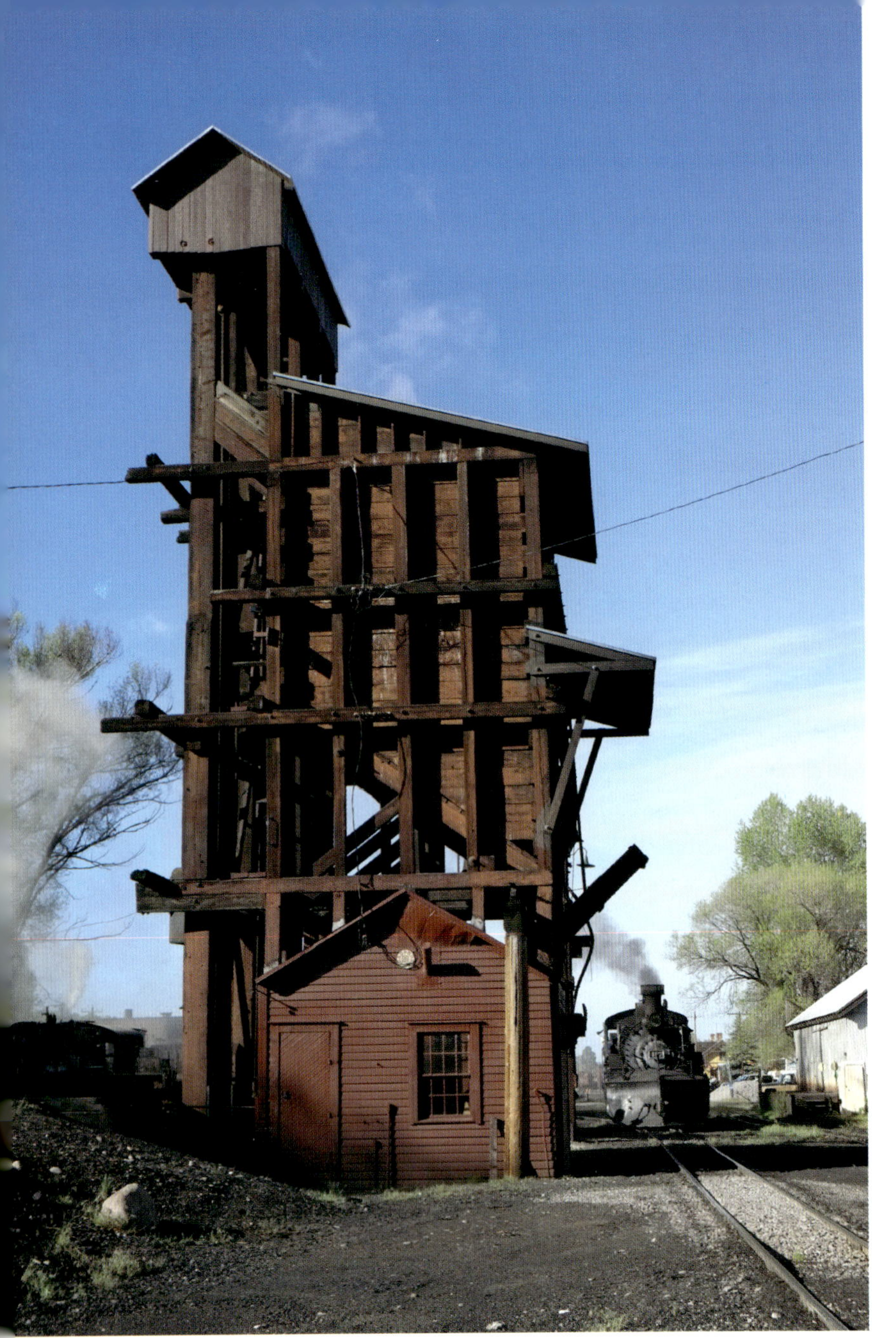

Chama shed, with its enormous wooden coaling tower, serviced locos working over the pass. On 24 May 2014 K-36 No 484 (Baldwin 58585/1925) is on its left and No 487 on the right.

Opposite above: C-18 class 2-8-0 No 315 (Baldwin 14352/1895) and K-27 class 2-8-2 No 463 (Baldwin 21788/1903) stand at Antonito on 24 May 2014 about to set off with the Cumbres & Toltec's first westbound train of the season. No 315 was built for the Florence & Cripple Creek RR as their No 3 *Elkton* and arrived on the Rio Grande in 1917. After many years on static display, she was restored to working order by a Durango-based society and normally lives at Silverton. The fifteen K-27s were the Rio Grande's first 2-8-2s and were originally Vauclain compounds. No 463 is one of two survivors. The mixed gauge track is a relic of Antonito's pre-preservation days.

Opposite below: By 1968, tourists had discovered the Silverton branch. The Rio Grande operated it for several more years but eventually sold it off. K-28 2-8-2 No 478 (Alco 64989/1923) crosses the Animas river on 24 September 2011. The Durango & Silverton, as it's now known, paints most of its carriages in the Rio Grande's diesel-era bright yellow but happily a few of them ran for a brief period in the old post-1917 dark green.

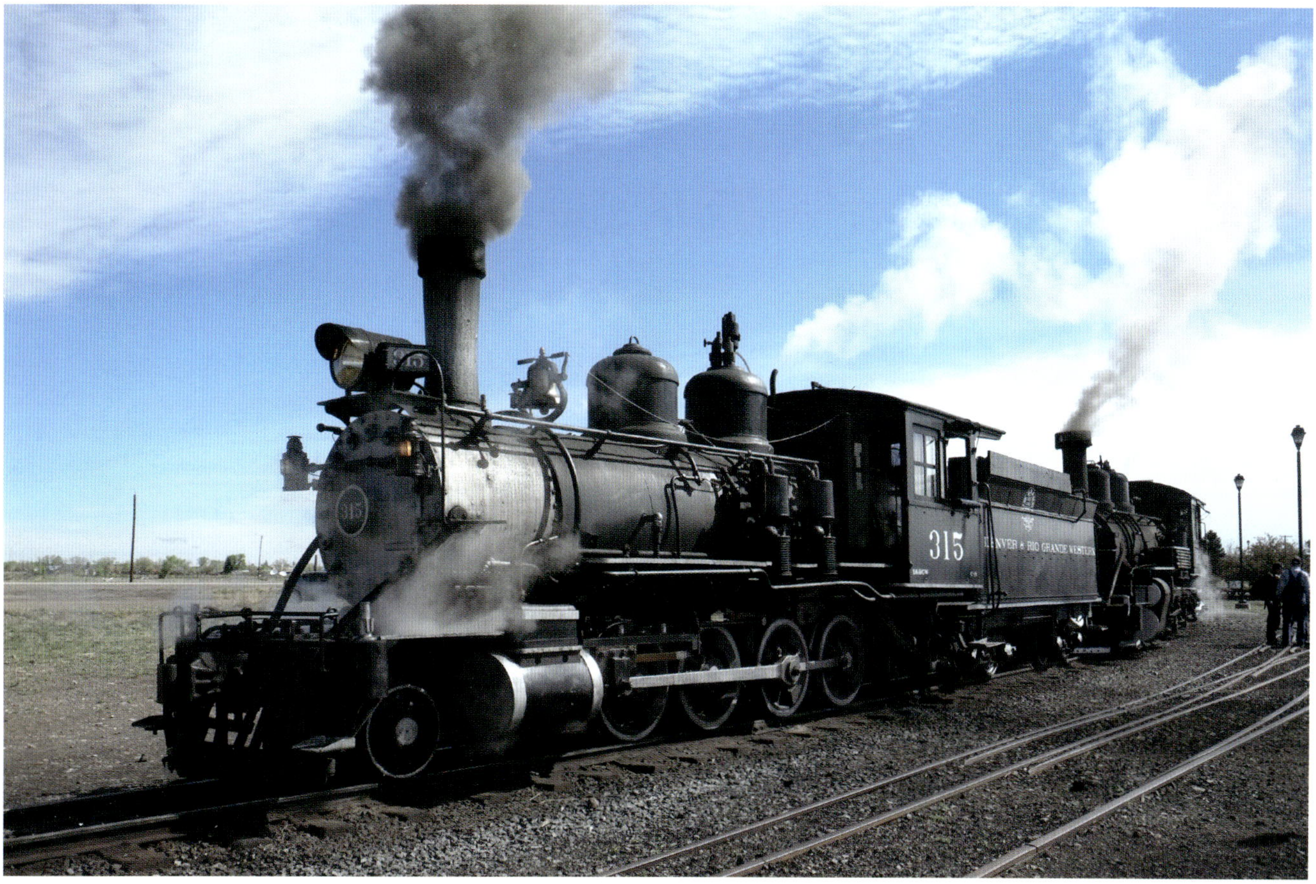

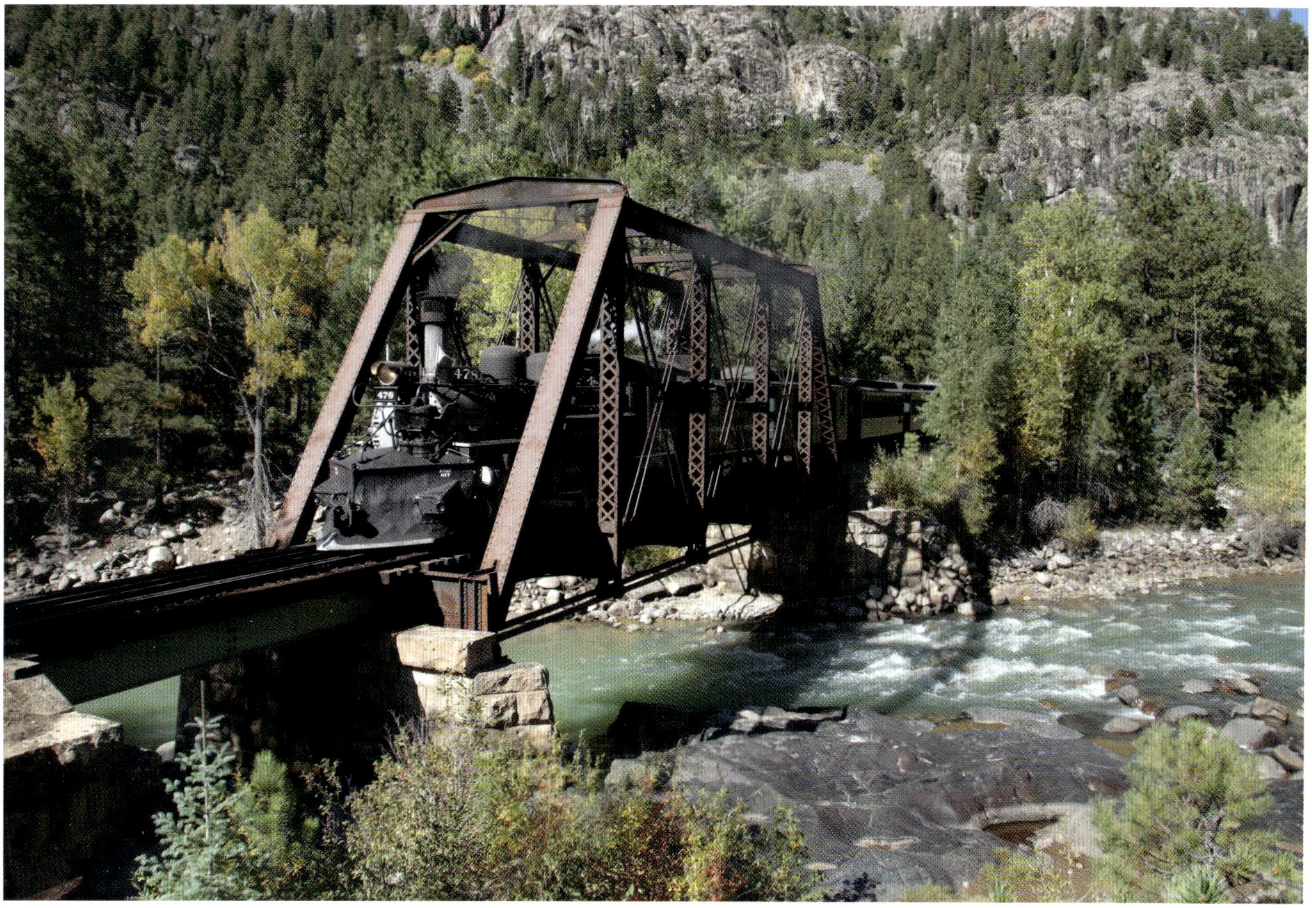

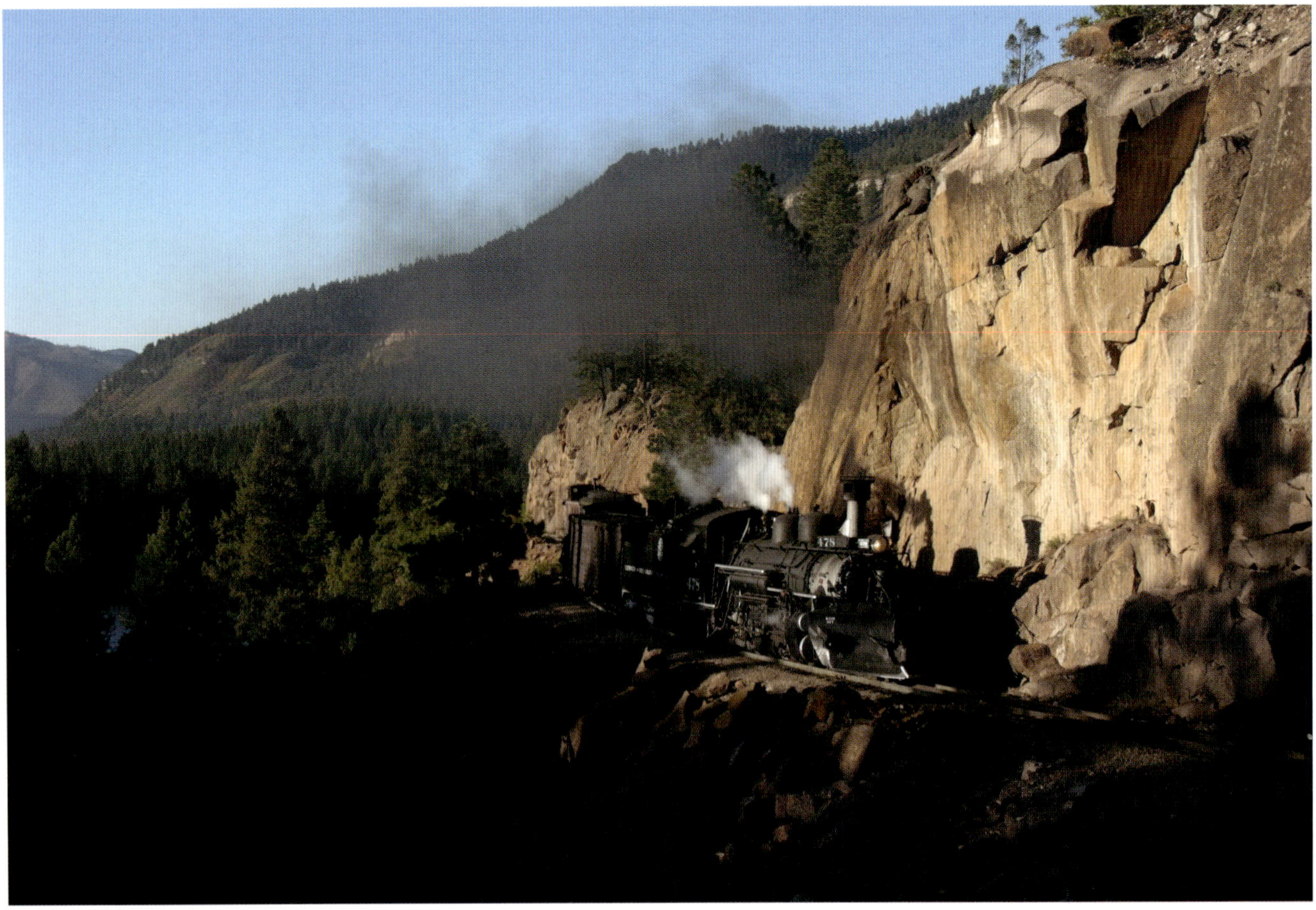

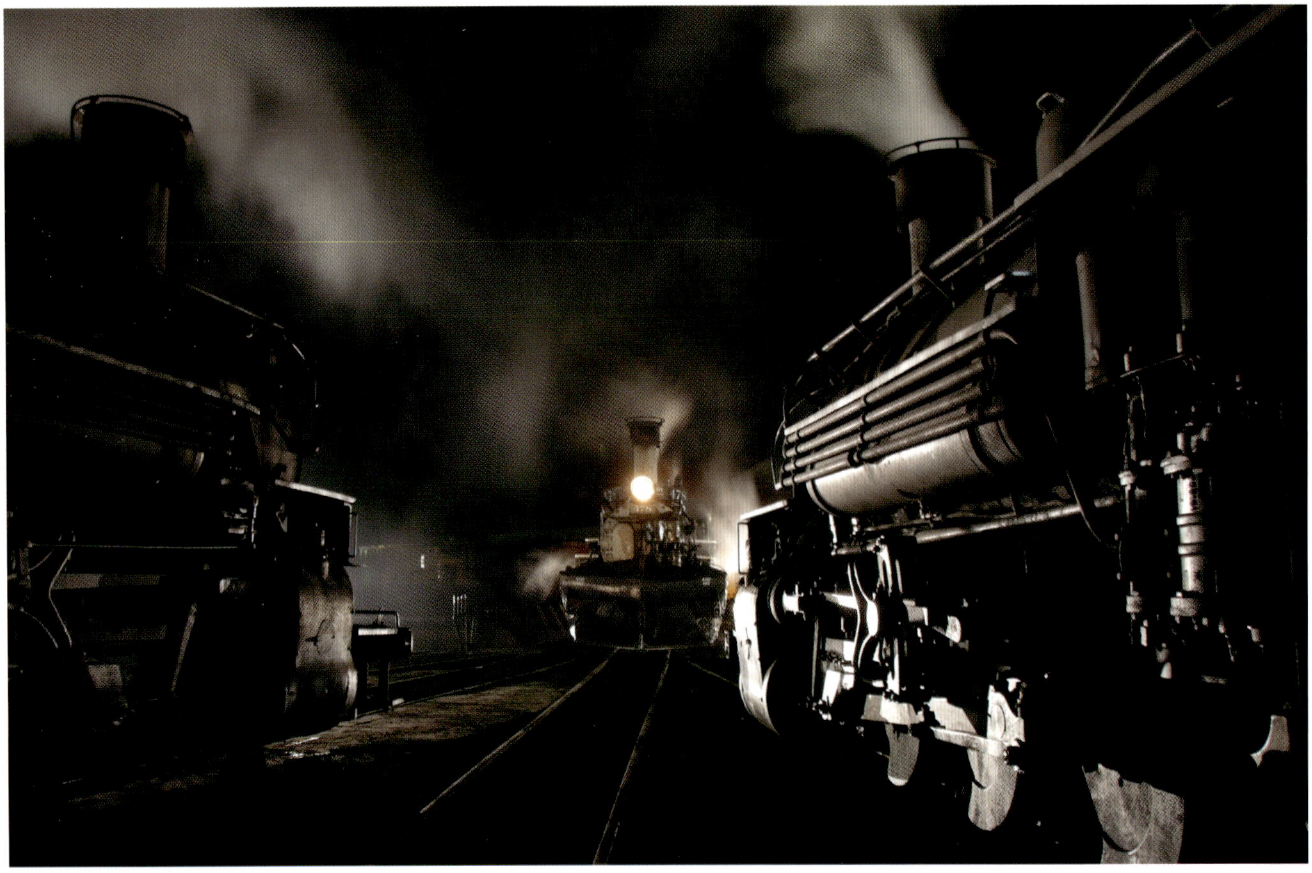

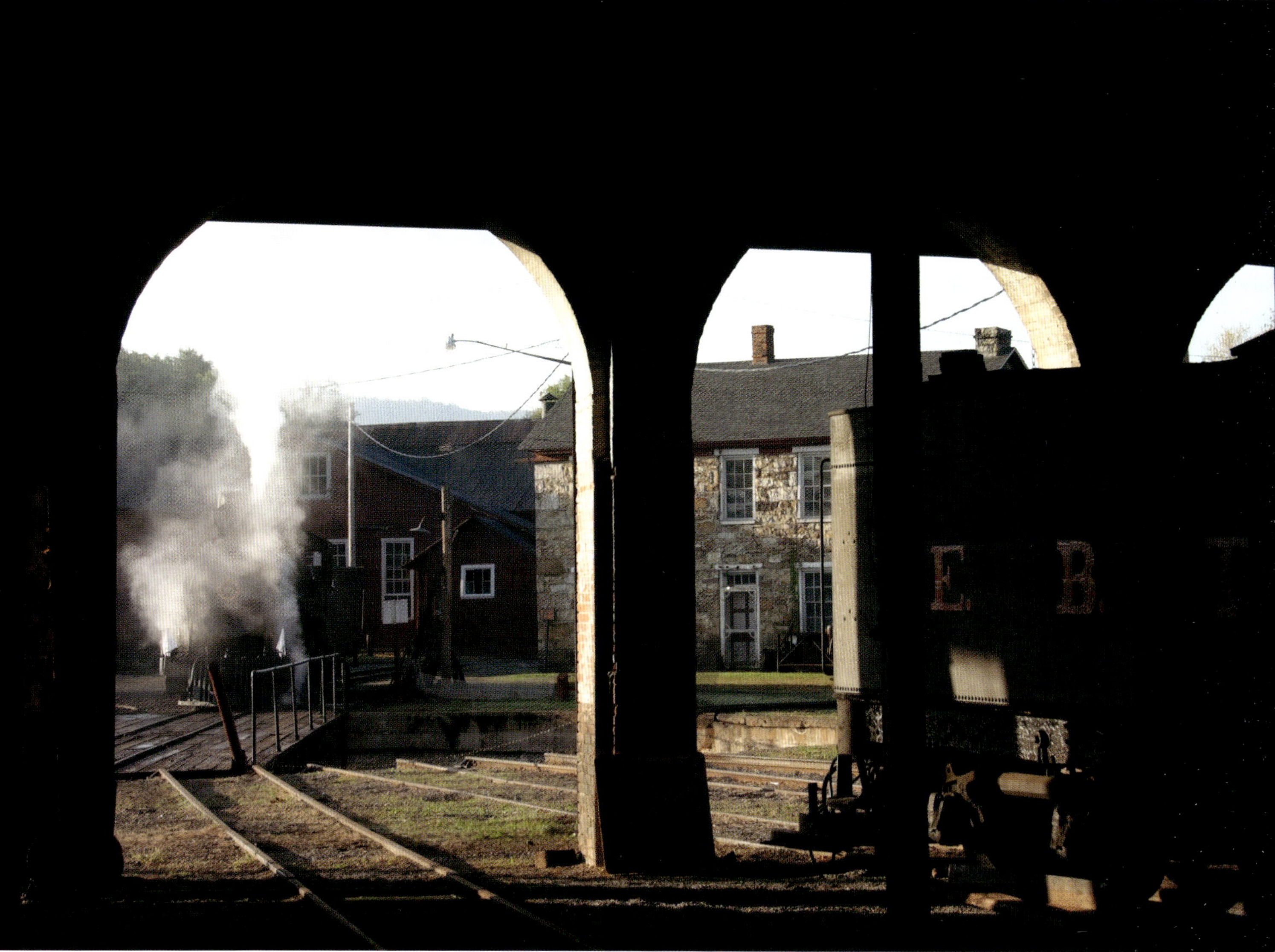

Above: Construction of the 3ft gauge East Broad Top RR began in 1872. It served an ironmaking and coal mining district in Pennsylvania and flourished for many years. Early in the twentieth century it bought six modern 2-8-2s which served it until closure in 1956. One of them, No 15 (Baldwin 41196/1914), stands on the turntable at Rockhill Furnace, seen from the roundhouse in the early morning of 8 October 2011. The stone building is an old farmhouse which pre-dated the railway. It served as its general offices for some years and later became the loco yard headquarters.

Opposite above: It's just after sunrise as No 478 approaches Rockwood on the Durango & Silverton with a mixed train on 25 September 2011. This was an attractive photo spot but the warning signs all around that trespassers would be shot on sight were distinctly unwelcoming! Seven of the ten K-28s were requisitioned by the US military during the Second World War. They were sent to work on the White Pass and were scrapped after the war. The remaining three are at Durango.

Opposite below: A busy evening scene at Durango shed on 23 September 2011. In the foreground are Nos 482 (Baldwin 58541/1925) and 486 (Baldwin 58587/1925), both K-36s, while No 478 stands on the turntable. Nine of the ten K-36s have survived.

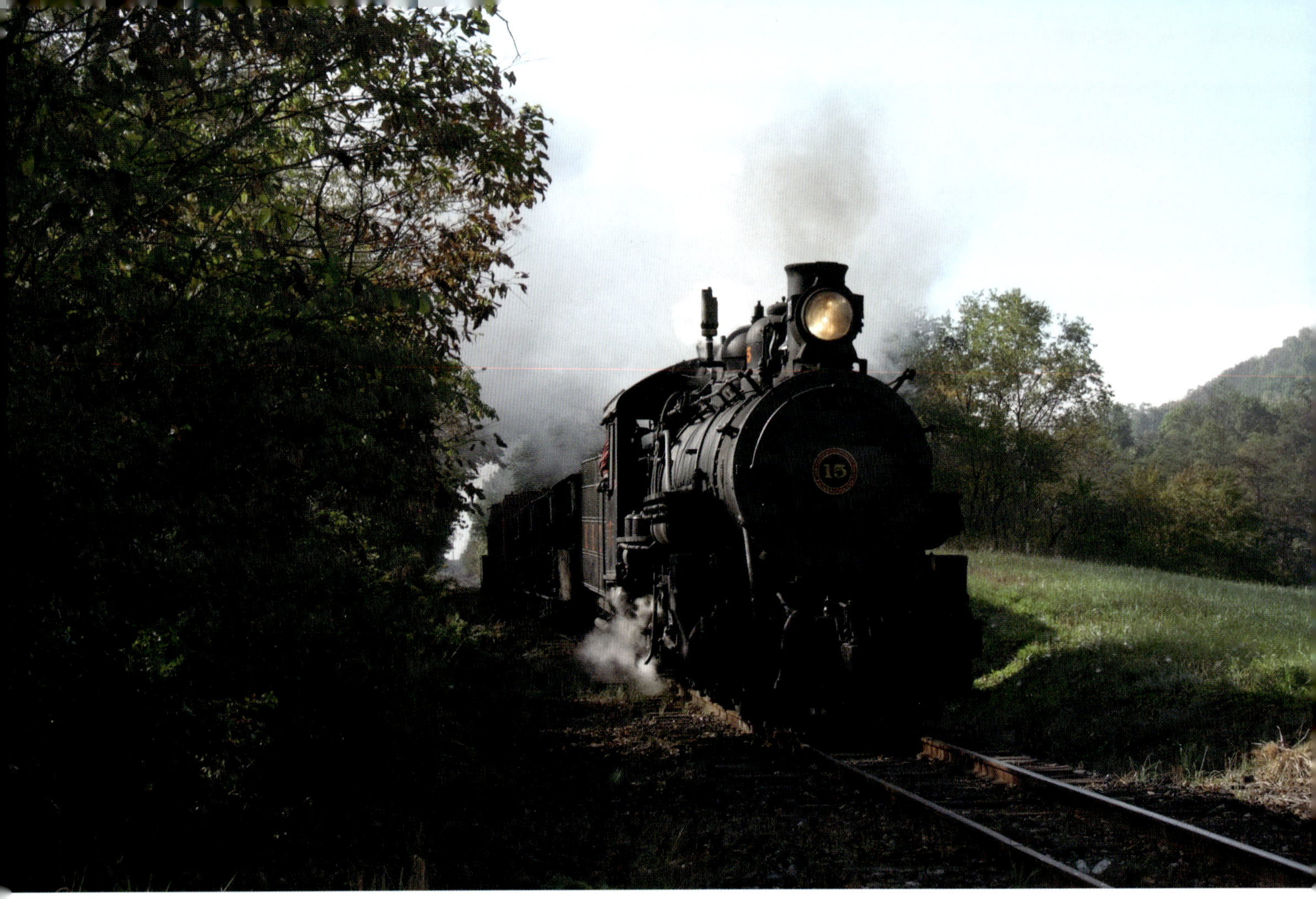

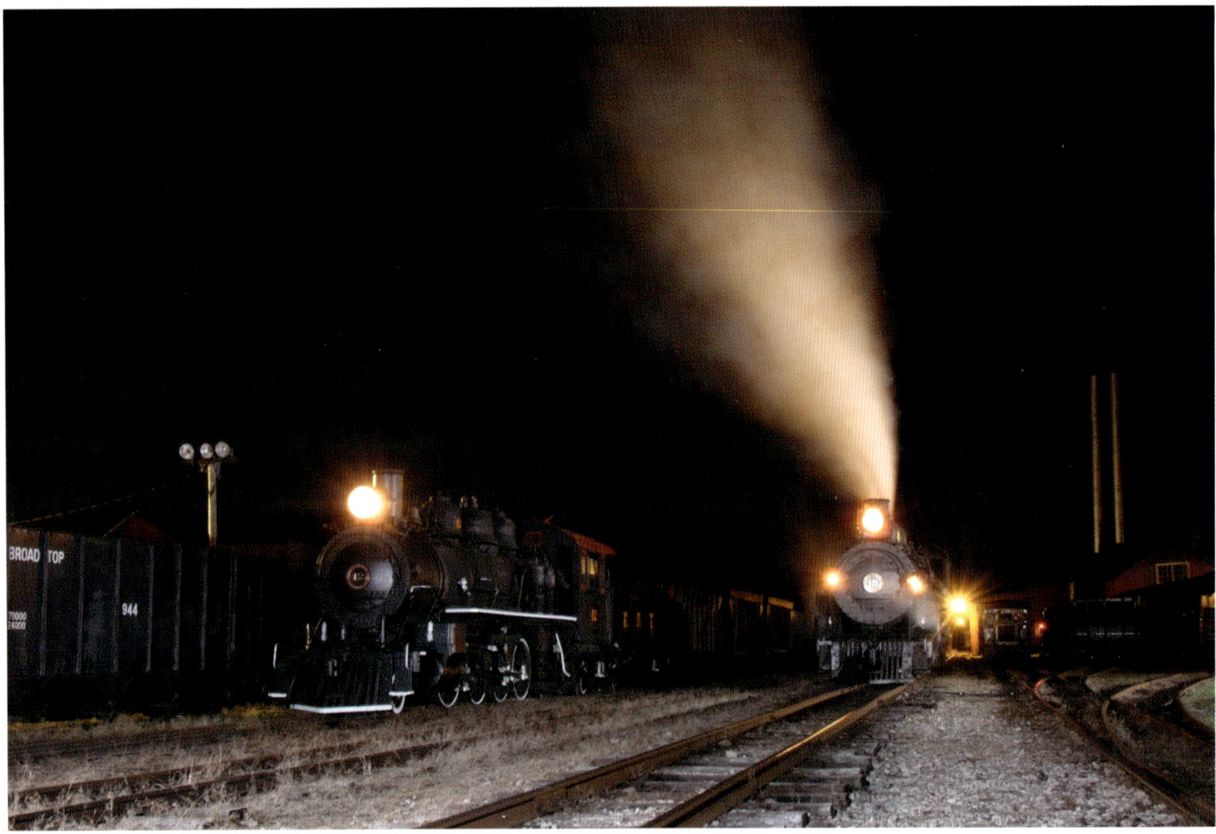
BROAD TOP
944

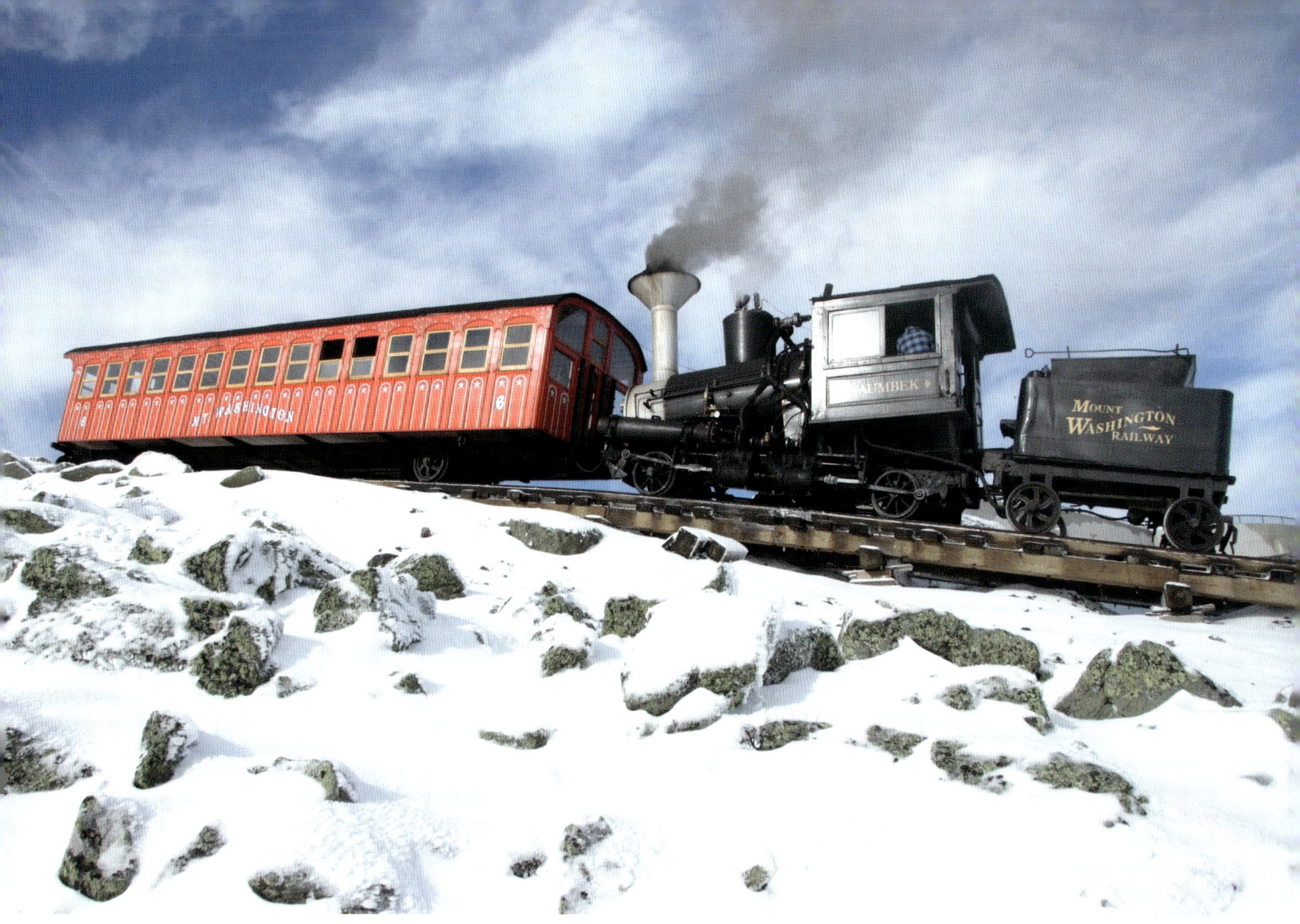

Above: The Mount Washington Cog Railway in New Hampshire was the world's first rack line when it opened in 1869. It is 4ft 8ins gauge, surely the widest-ever narrow gauge railway, and one wonders how its builders managed to miss that extra half inch! Until 2008 this was an all-steam operation. Now six diesels have arrived, though happily the first train of the day is still steam-worked for much of the season. 23 October was the last steam day in 2011. At the summit the sun was shining on the pristine snow which had fallen overnight. 0-2-2-0 No 9 *Waumbek* has stopped short of the station so that the staff can hack ice out of the points. She was built in 1908 by the Manchester Loco Works in New Hampshire and is the younger of the two locos still in service.

Opposite above: In 1956, the East Broad Top was sold to scrap merchants but, to many people's surprise, most of it was left intact and in 1960 they reopened a short section out of Orbisonia station as a heritage railway. No 15 heads a short coal train towards Colgate Grove on 7 October 2011.

Opposite below: No 12 (Baldwin 37325/1911) was the first of the 2-8-2s and here stands alongside No 15 in Rockhill Furnace yard on the evening of 7 October 2011. Sadly, the railway closed a second time at the end of the 2011 season. The six 2-8-2s still slumber in the old roundhouse and the shops, an amazing complex of wooden buildings with machinery driven by overhead shafts and belts, survive almost intact, as do many of the distinctive coal wagons.

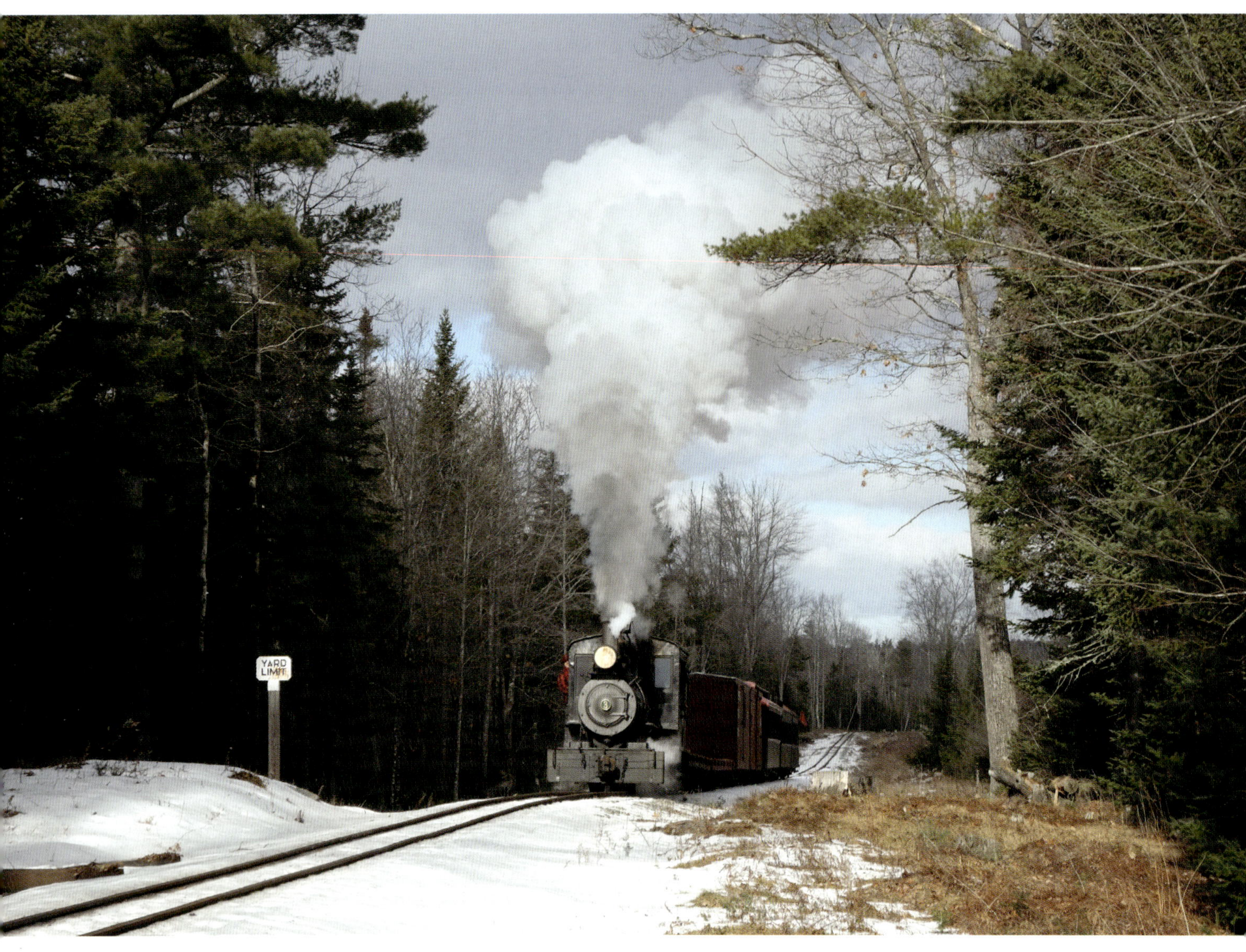

Maine was home to most of the US's 2ft gauge public railways. The last survivor was the little Monson RR, a slate carrying line up in the north east which closed in 1943. Fortunately, its two most recent locos, 0-4-4 Forney-type tanks, have survived. Here No 3 (VIW 2093/1912) recalls the Monson's old days as she approaches Alna Center on the preserved Wiscasset, Waterville & Farmington line on 15 January 2017. The WW&F closed in 1933 but a short section north from Sheepscot is gradually being reconstructed by volunteers.

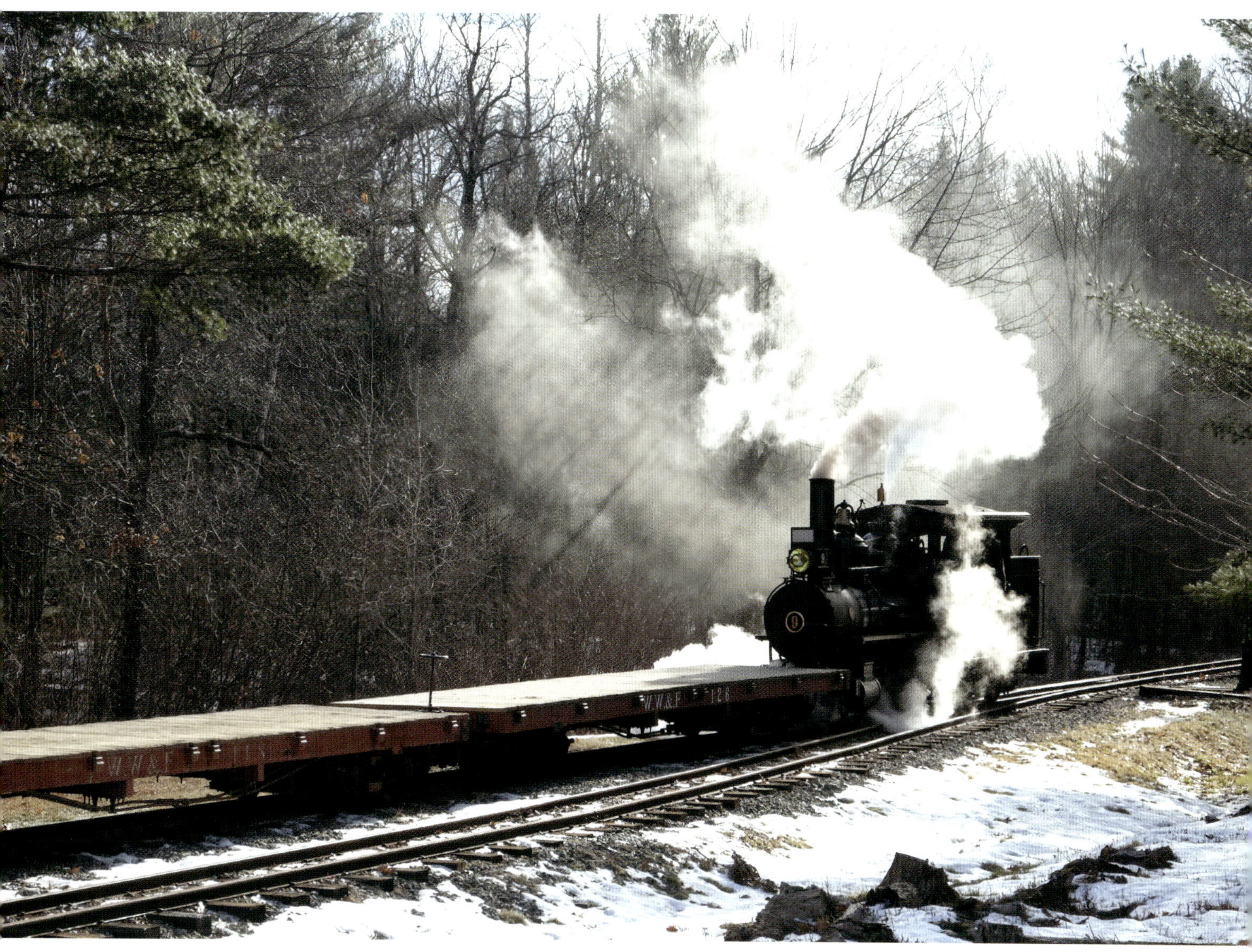

No 9 (Portland 624/1891), the only survivor of the WW&F's 0-4-4 Forney tanks, shunts at Alna Center on 15 January 2017. She served no fewer than three of the old Maine two-footers and was rescued by enthusiasts in 1937. No 118 is an original wagon from the old railway while No 126 is a replica. The Portland company built several Forney locos for the Maine 2-footers and one of its old buildings now houses the superb Maine Narrow Gauge RR Museum.

MÉXICO

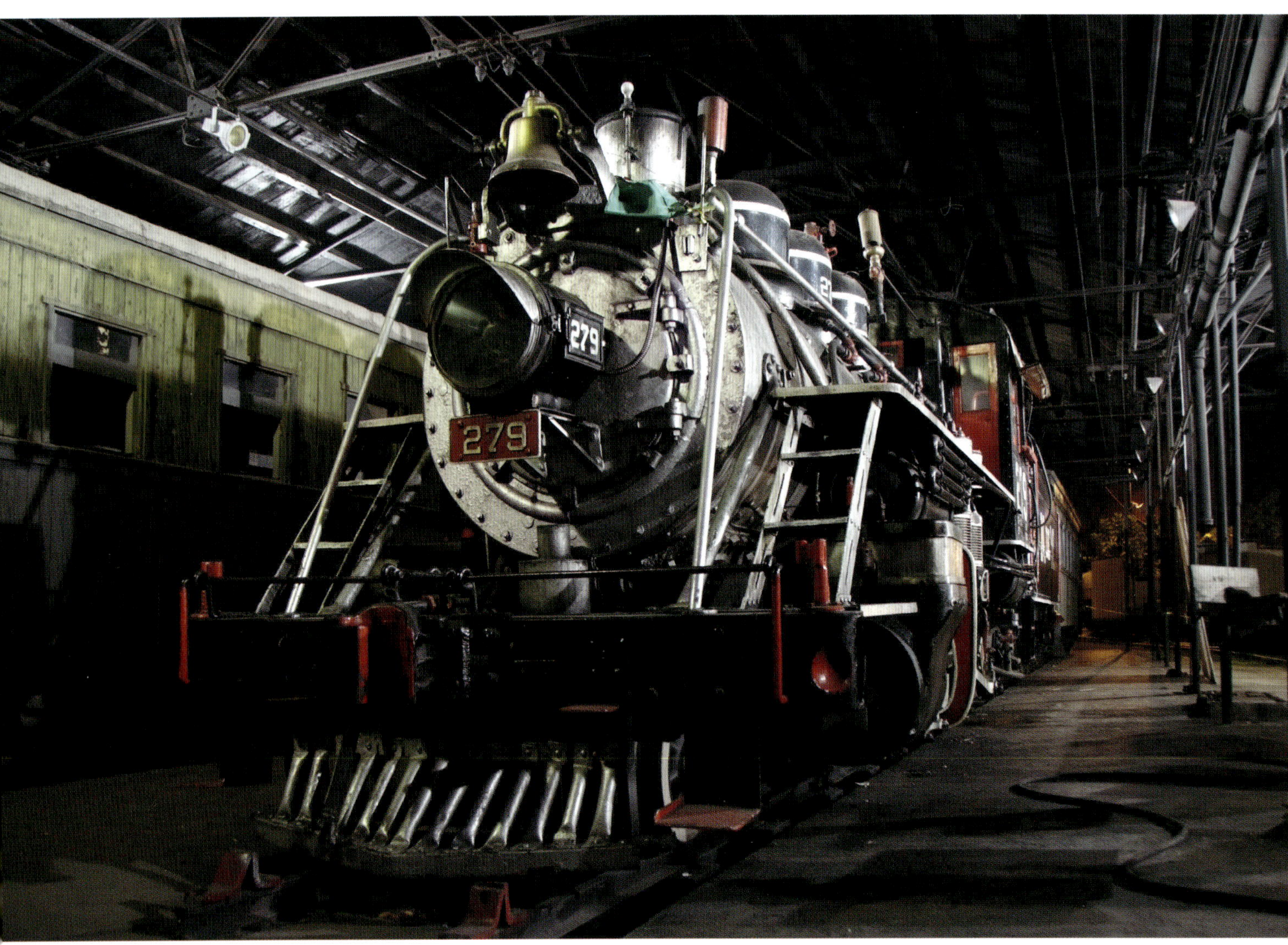

México once boasted many 3ft gauge railways, a legacy of General Palmer's early ambitions for the Rio Grande. The first opened in 1881 from Cuautla to México City and later became part of the Ferrocarriles Nacionales de México. It closed in 1973 but the 20kms section as far as Yecapixtla reopened as a heritage line in July 1986 using the NdeM's G-030 class 2-8-0 No 279 (Baldwin 55110/1921) and four of its characteristic boxy carriages. Most of the operating staff came from the old NdeM narrow gauge. Time wasn't kind to the venture. Gradually the route was cut back and when I visited on 18 November 2012 just a few hundred metres at Cuautla remained. No 279 should have been in steam and had been fired up overnight when the town's mayor cancelled the event. Here the loco is still warm and dripping water at Cuautla shed but definitely not in steam. In 2013 she was condemned. The shed is now a museum with No 279 and her coaches as the principal exhibits.

EL SALVADOR

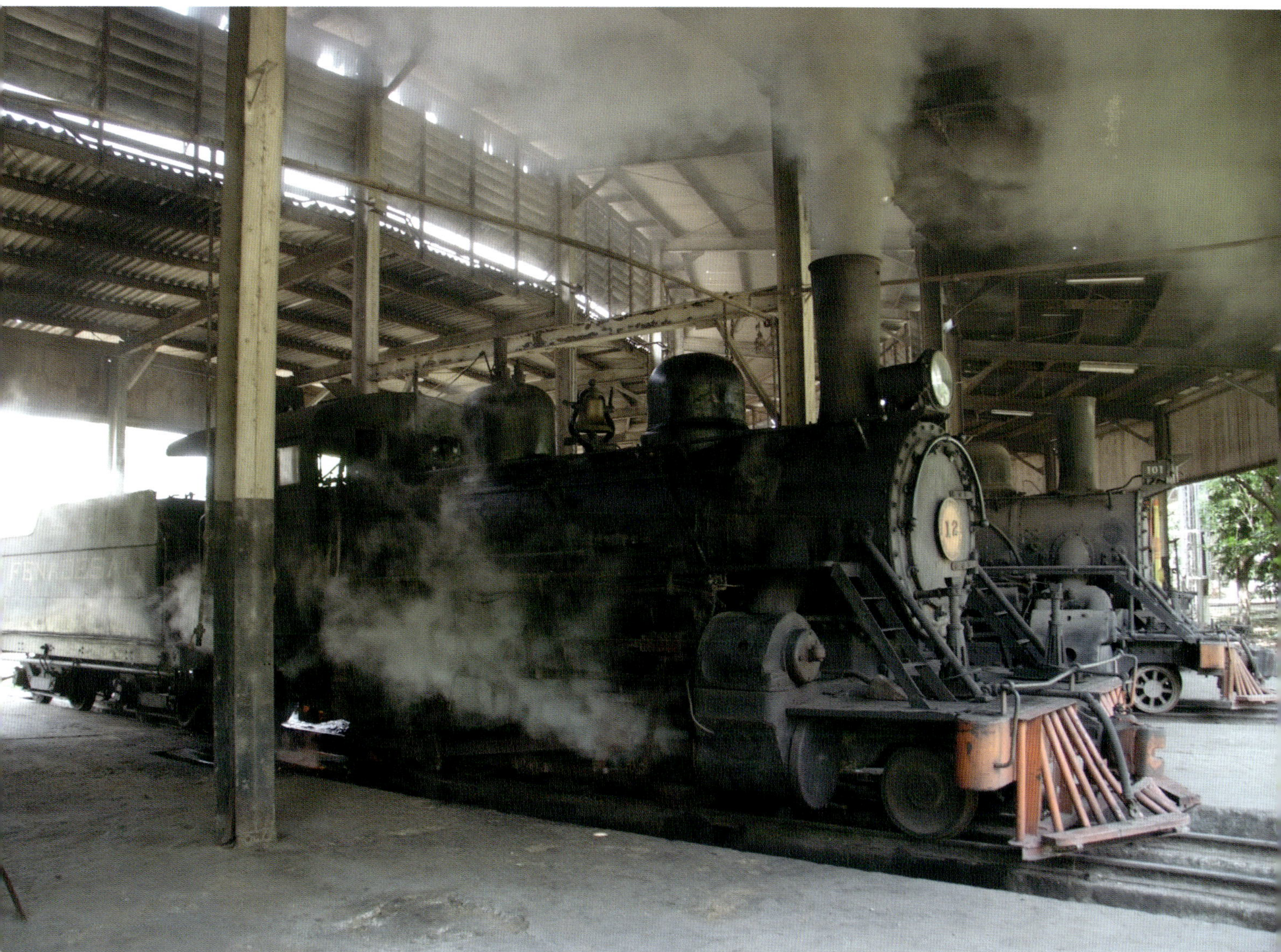

Fenadesal 2-8-0 No 12 (Baldwin 58244/1925) raises steam in the roundhouse at San Salvador on 12th April 2012 with 2-8-0 No 101 (Baldwin 58441/1925) behind. IRCA, a US-owned concern with close ties to the United Fruit business, operated 3ft gauge railways in Guatemala and El Salvador until they were nationalised, the El Salvador operation then becoming Fenadesal. The last Guatemalan line closed in 2005 but part of the railway at San Salvador was refurbished in 2003 to provide commuter services, worked by ex-IRCA diesels.

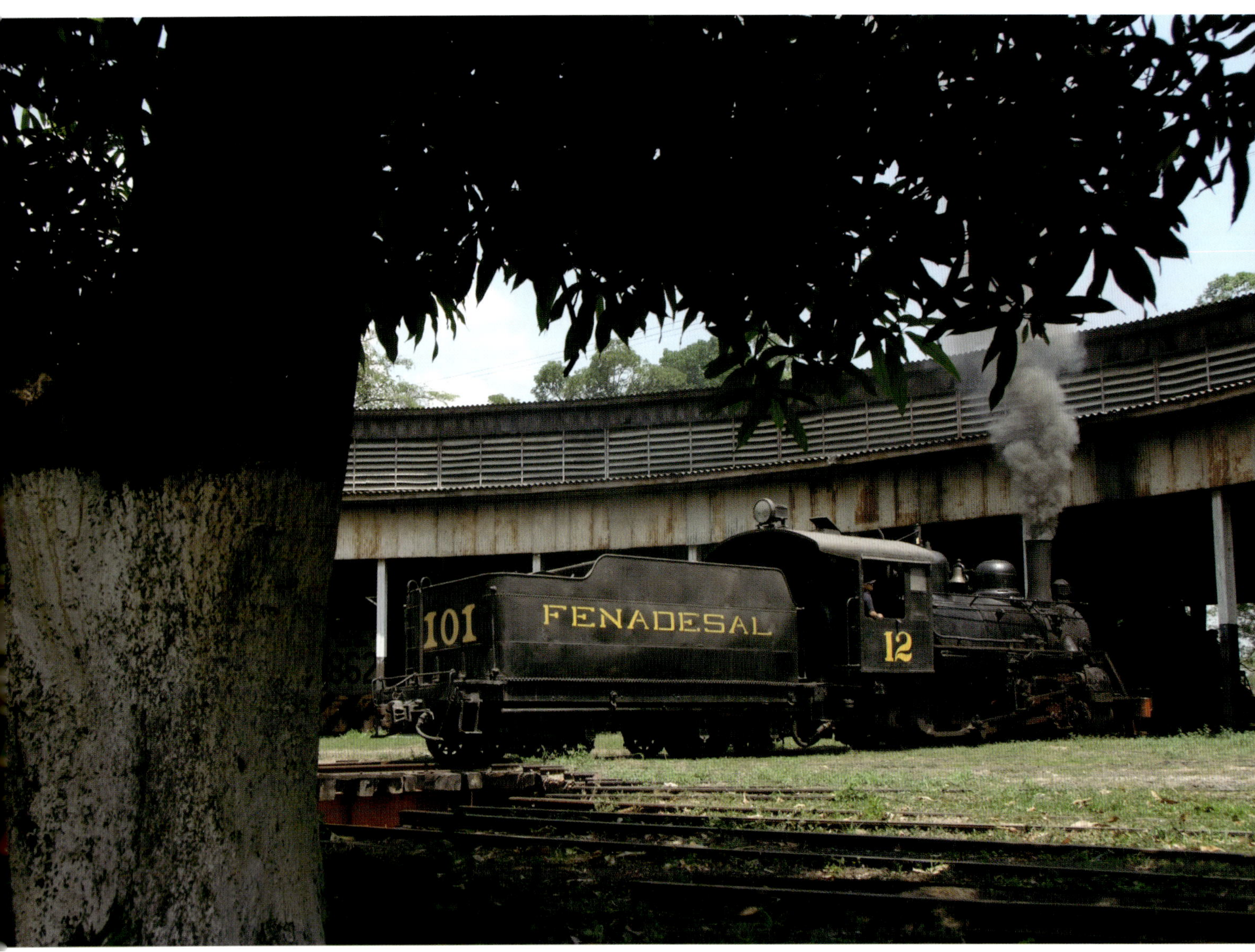

Before my trip Ing Salvador Sanabria Mira, the railway's helpful general manager, told me that the two 2-8-0s were no longer in working order but I would be welcome to visit the shed. Imagine my delight when his assistant Mrs Ingrid de Ceseña greeted me with the news that the staff were raising steam in No 12 and polishing her up. What a treat!! It turned out that several of them were steam enthusiasts and were relishing the opportunity to operate her one more time. Here's another view of No 12, running with No 101's tender, outside the smartly maintained roundhouse. Sadly, the line was condemned as unsafe four months later and all services ceased. The roundhouse and adjoining workshops now house a small museum.

COSTA RICA

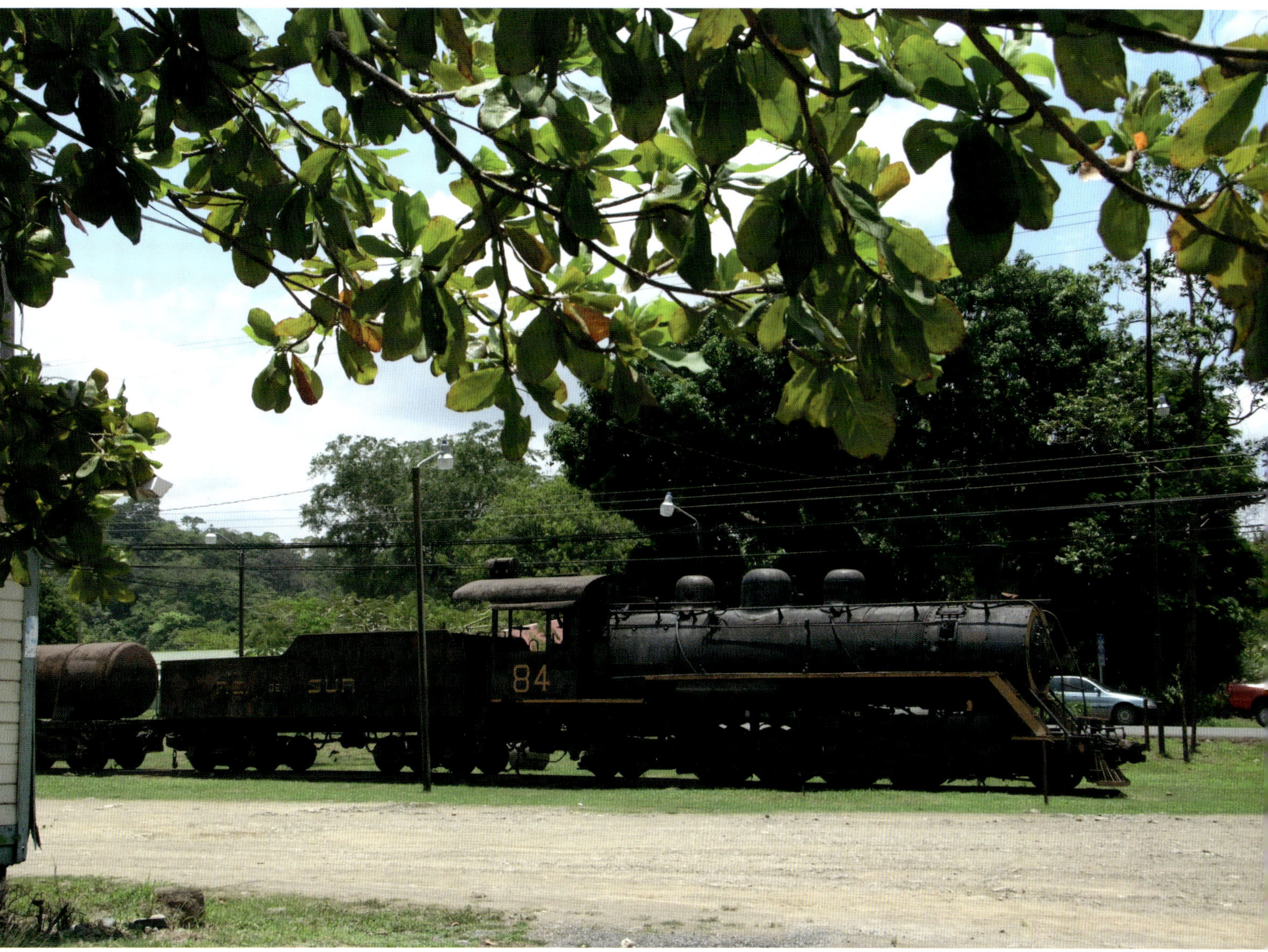

The 315kms-long FC del Sur, an isolated 3ft 6ins railway in southern Costa Rica, was another United Fruit operation, built from 1938 to carry bananas from their plantations near the Pacific coast to the fine natural harbour at Golfito. Baldwin delivered six 2-8-2s between 1940 and 1946. Three were kept on after diesels arrived as the line was prone to flooding and the diesels couldn't cope with this. It closed in 1982 but the three locos are still there, two at Golfito and No 84 (Baldwin 72669/1946) at Palmar Sur where I saw her on 16 April 2012. Behind her is an oil tank wagon still carrying its original US Army paint scheme, probably one of the many vehicles built to help rehabilitate the railways of Japan after the Second World War. In the event they weren't needed there and several found their way to Central America.

COLOMBIA

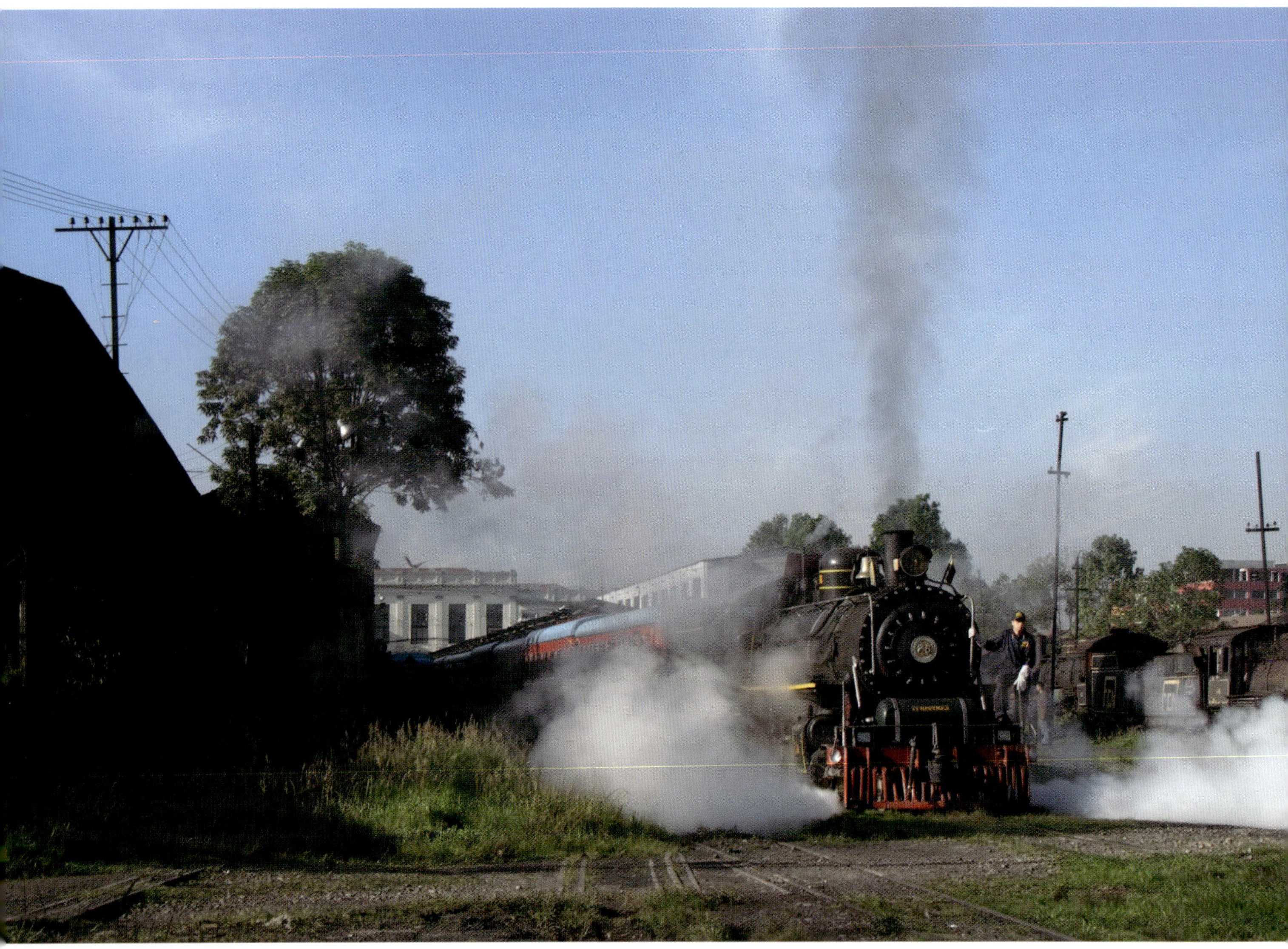

Just after sunrise on 10 December 2011, 4-8-0 No 76 (Baldwin 73095/1947) leaves the Estacion de la Sabana at Bogotá, built in 1917 under the direction of the British engineer William Lidstone, and passes the enormous 4-8-2 No 109 (Baldwin 70893/1944) and 2-8-2 No 44 (Baldwin 60009/1927), both awaiting restoration. Regular steam working on Colombia's 3ft gauge system finished in the early 1970s but returned in 1982 when Dr Eduardo Rodriguez, its assistant general manager, oversaw the repair of several locos for a weekend tourist service, using luxury coaches laying over between trips down to Santa Marta on the Caribbean coast. These 4-8-0s were designed in the 1920s by P.C. Dewhurst, the state railway's talented chief engineer and also a knowledgeable enthusiast. The rear axles have Cartazzi slides and the locos' high adhesion and low axle loading as well as the flexible wheelbase made them ideally suited to the steep, sharply curved and lightly laid Colombian tracks.

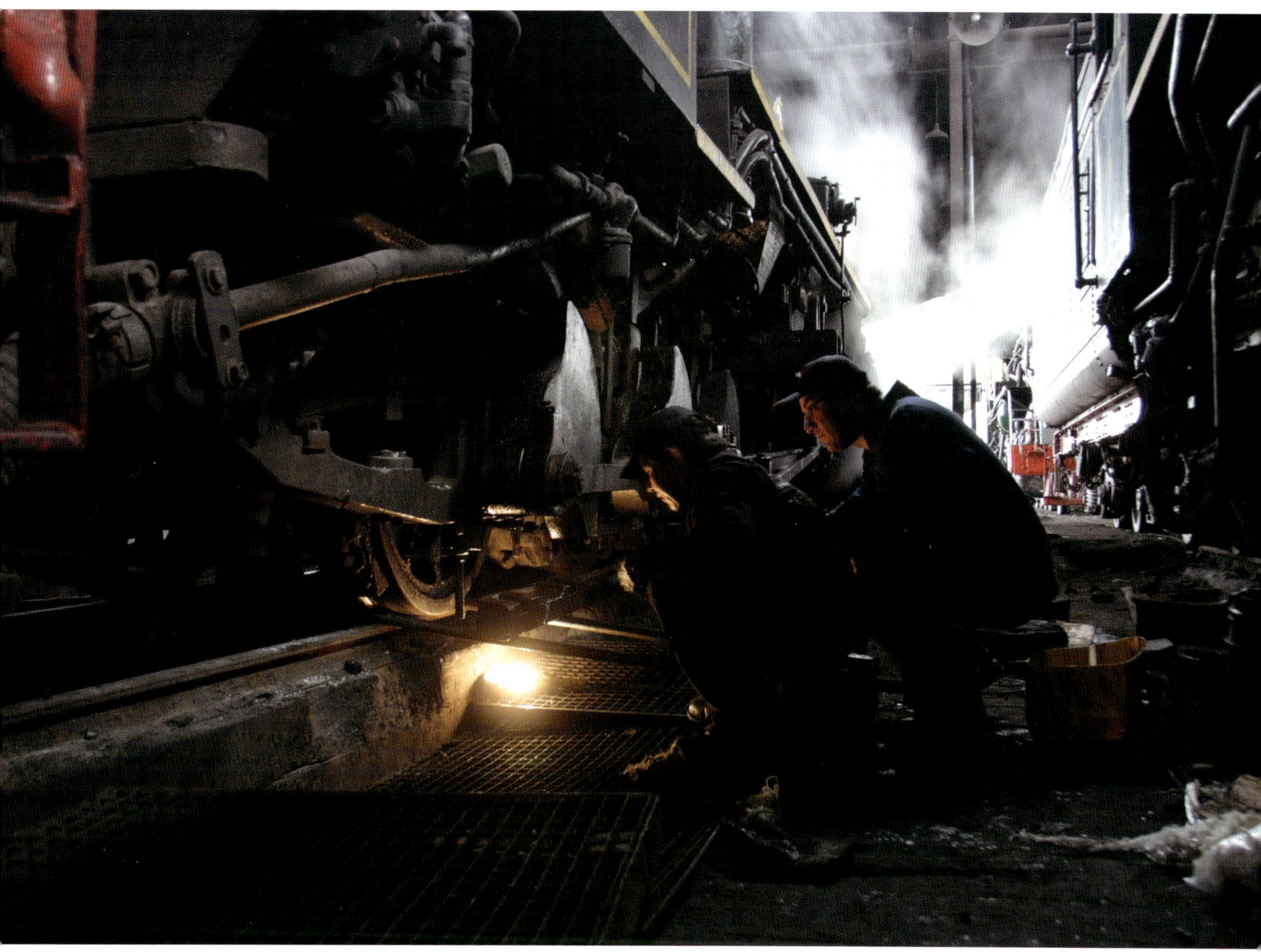

Early the following morning, No 76 receives attention at Bogotá shed. 2-8-2 No 75 (Baldwin 73059/1947) is on the right. The tourist service became a much-loved institution within the city, but its future looked bleak when the railway closed in 1992. Dr Rodriguez and colleagues purchased the coaches and several locomotives in 1993 and restarted the trains. They now run every Sunday throughout the year.

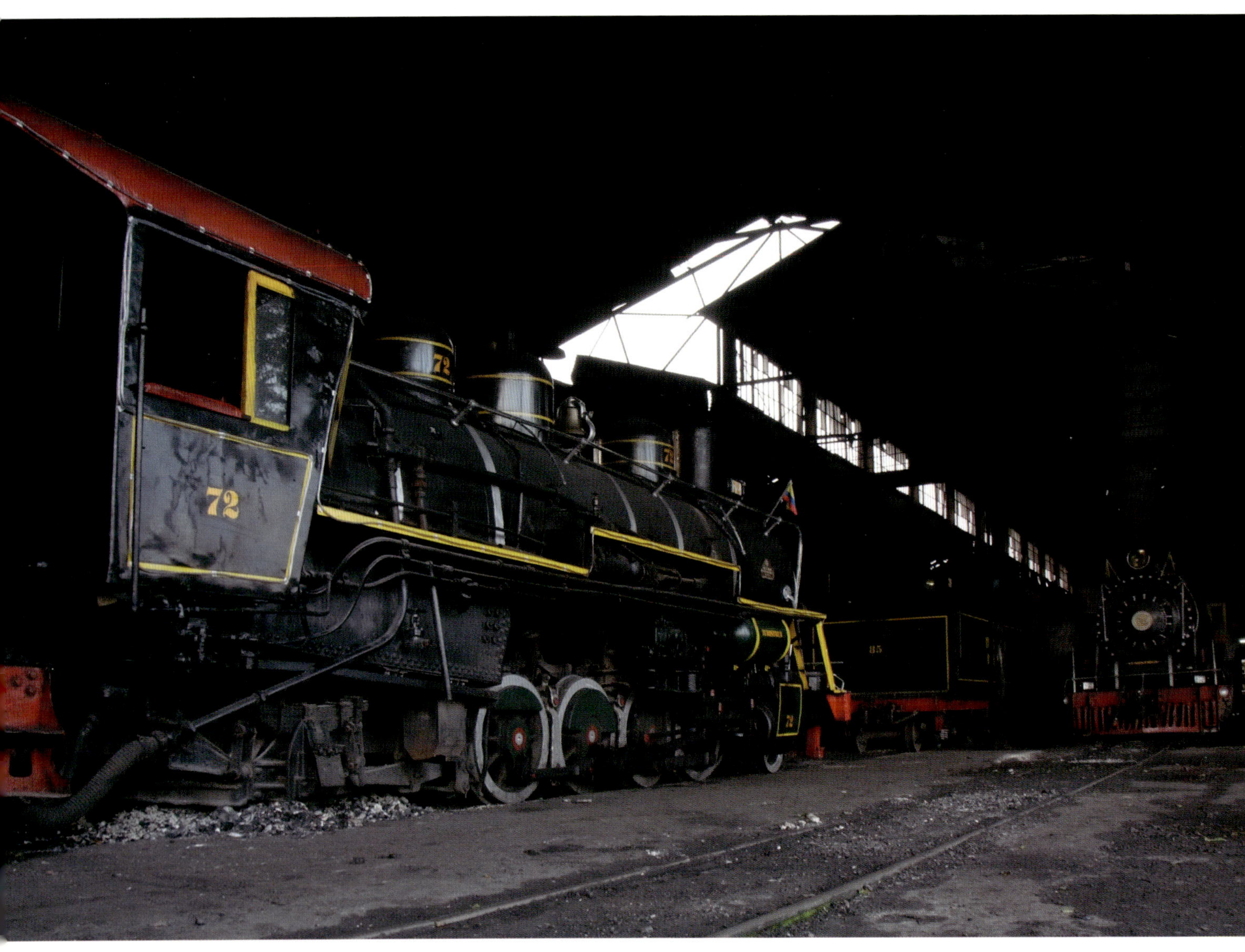

No 76 sets off from the shed, passing 2-8-2s No 72 (Baldwin 73056/1947) and 85 (Baldwin 73051/1947). When friends and I visited the train's fourteen coaches were full. Colombia is a land of music and no fewer than three bands were on board while the restaurant car did a roaring trade in delicious local food. Dr Rodriguez kindly travelled with us and treated us to footplate rides. Great hospitality on a magnificent railway!

BRAZIL

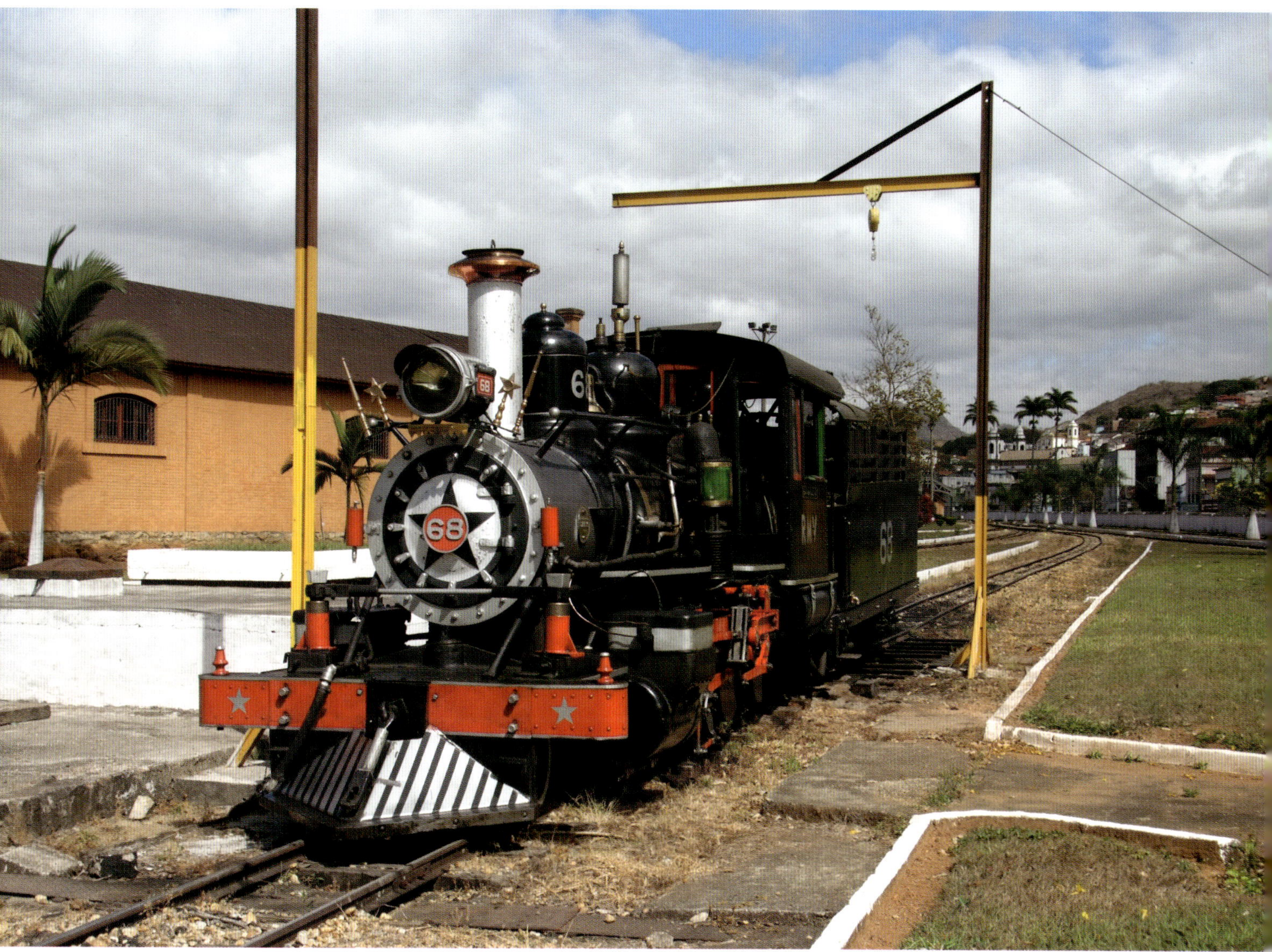

On 23 August 2012 the Rede Mineira de Viação's 2-8-0 No 68 (Baldwin 52256/1919) stands at São João del Rei, a fine old Portuguese colonial city in Minas Gerais. When I first visited in 1977, it was the operating centre of a 2ft 6ins gauge railway running west for no fewer than 202kms from Antonio Carlos on the main line north from Rio de Janeiro. In its heyday the line was much longer still and reached Barra de Paraopeba, 602kms away. No 68 was its youngest loco. Back in 1977 she was even more brightly painted, with many parts picked out in yellow and she now looks positively sober!

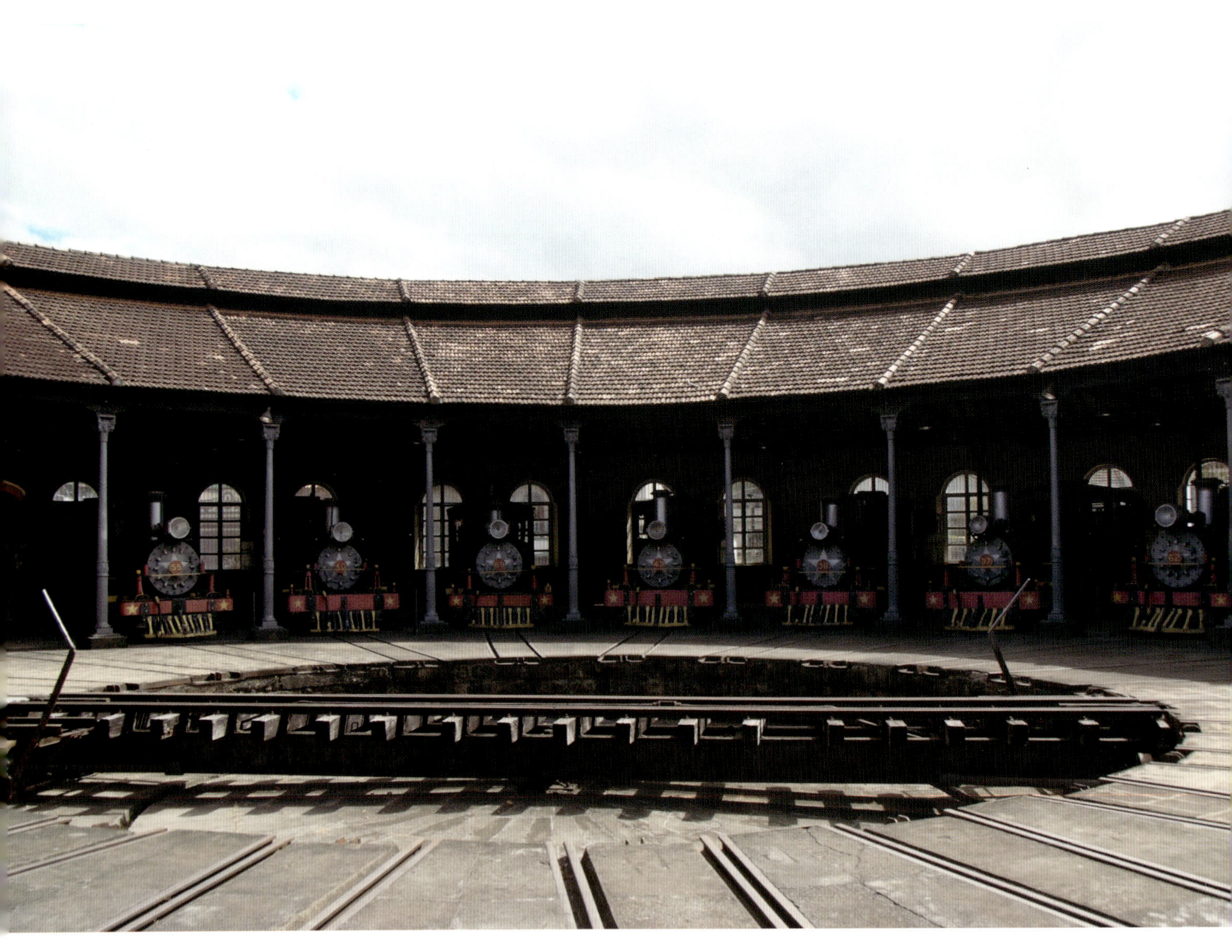

Above: Seven little Baldwin locos stand in São João del Rei roundhouse on 23 August 2012. Nos 37 and 38 (37082-3/1911), 40 (38010/1911) and 43 (38051/1912) are 4-6-0s; 2-8-0s Nos 55 (12934/1892) and 62 (13831/1893) were rebuilt from Vauclain compounds while No 69 (14134/1894) has always been a simple. The RFFSA, Brazil's nationalised railway, retained the 12.8kms section between São João del Rei and Tiradentes as a heritage line after the remainder closed in 1982. The roundhouse burned down in 1972 but was rebuilt to house this museum. Brazil's railways have now been privatised but the concession for the railways in Minas Gerais requires that this line and its museum must be kept open.

Opposite: 4-6-0 No 41 (Baldwin 38011/1912) approaches Tiradentes on 24 August 2012. The railway was built by the Estrada de Ferro Oeste de Minas which went on to run a large metre gauge system. In 1931 it merged with other railways in Minas Gerais, all metre gauge, to form the RMV. No 41 has been restored to her original OdeM condition including a replica of her old wooden pilot.

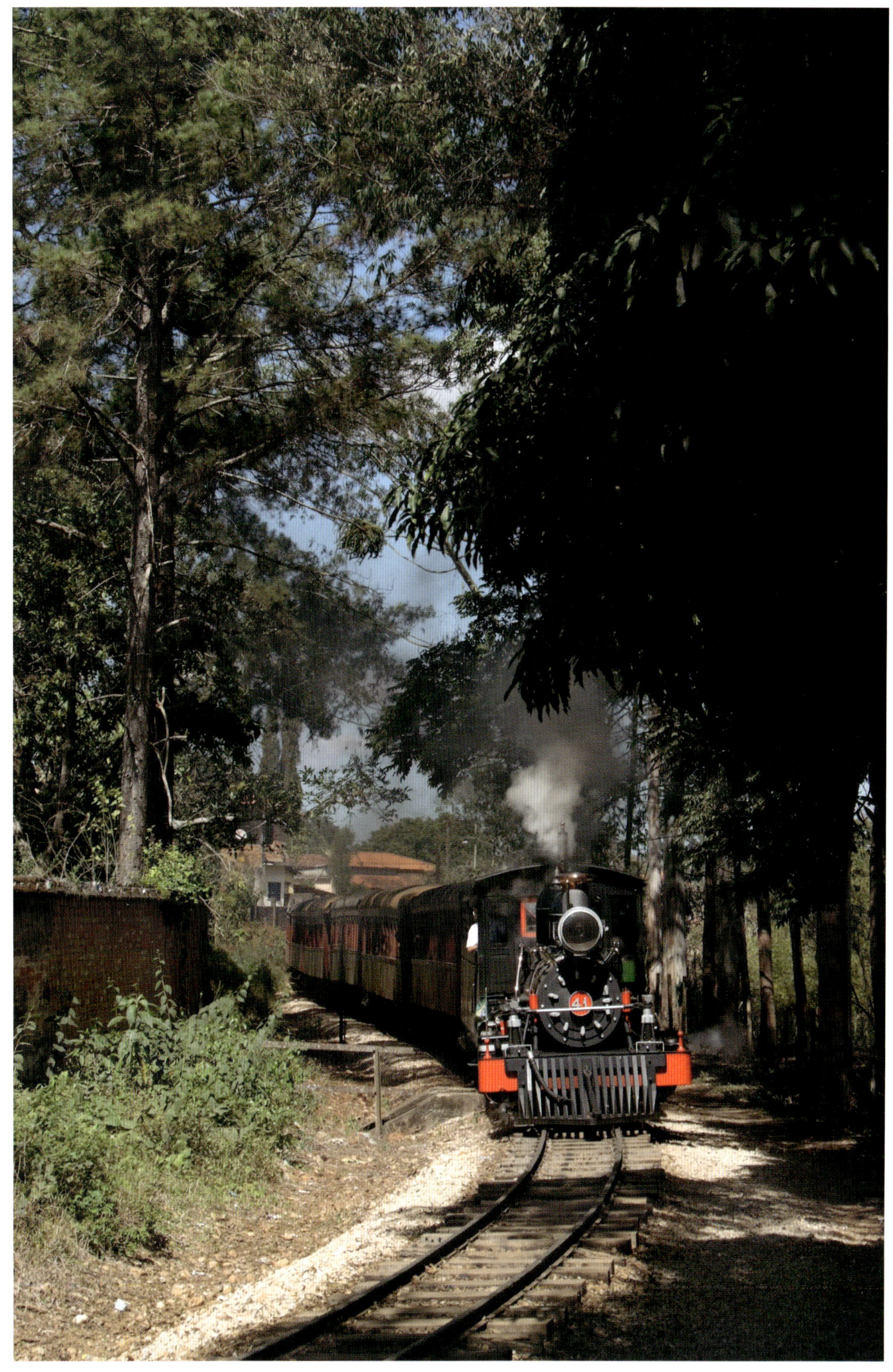

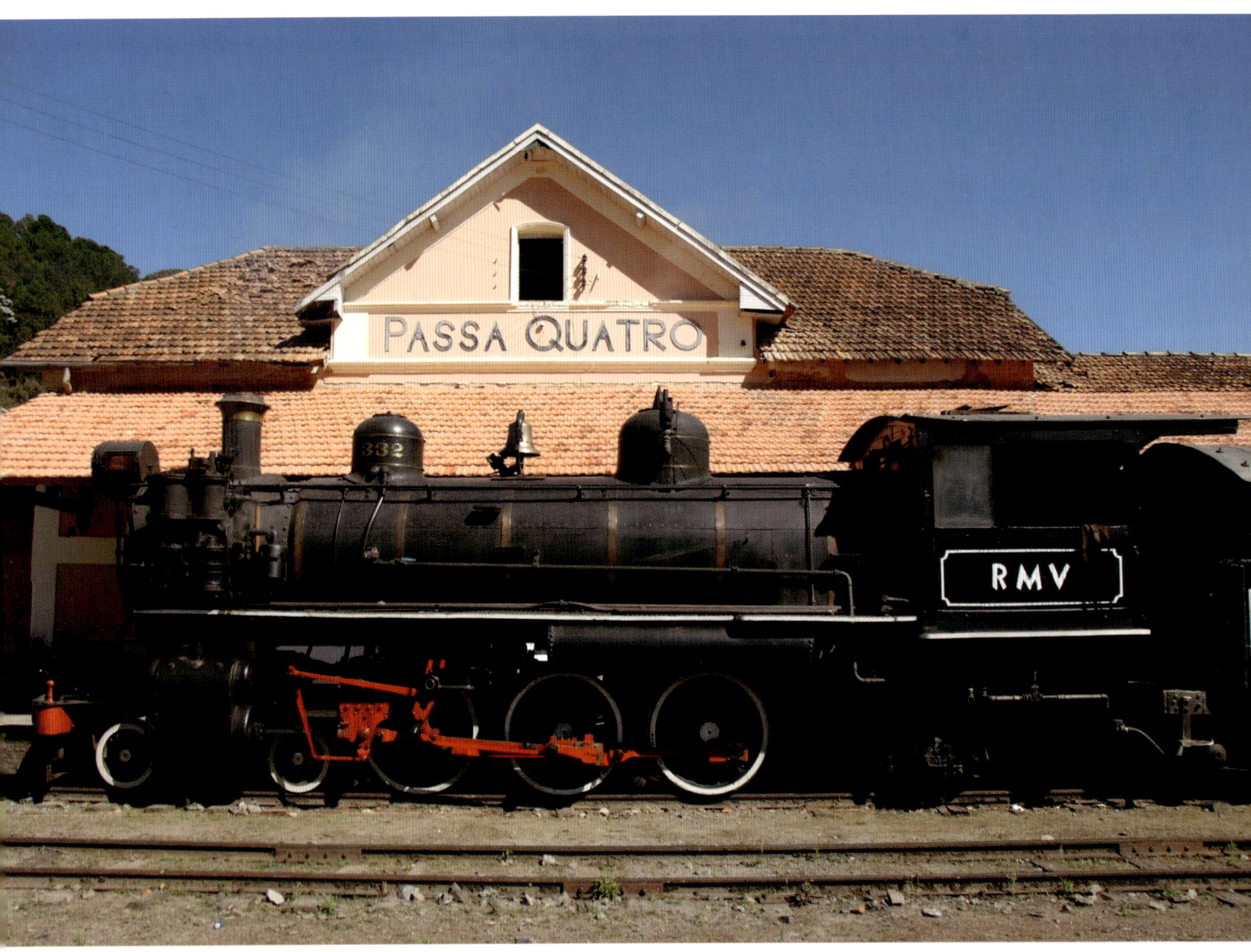

Above: The RMV's metre gauge Pacific No 332 (Baldwin 58552/1925) stands at Passa Quatro station on 19 August 2012. The long line running north from Cruzeiro, originally the British-owned Rio and Minas Railway, closed in the early 1990's. The Sul de Minas chapter of the ABPF, Brazil's main preservation society, looks after 90kms of it and operates trains over two sections, each about 10kms long. This is the more southerly one, between Passa Quatro and Coronel Fulgêncio.

Opposite: On 19 August 2012 No 332 climbs through the Serra Mantiqueira which separates Minas Gerais and São Paulo states as she approaches Coronel Fulgêncio.

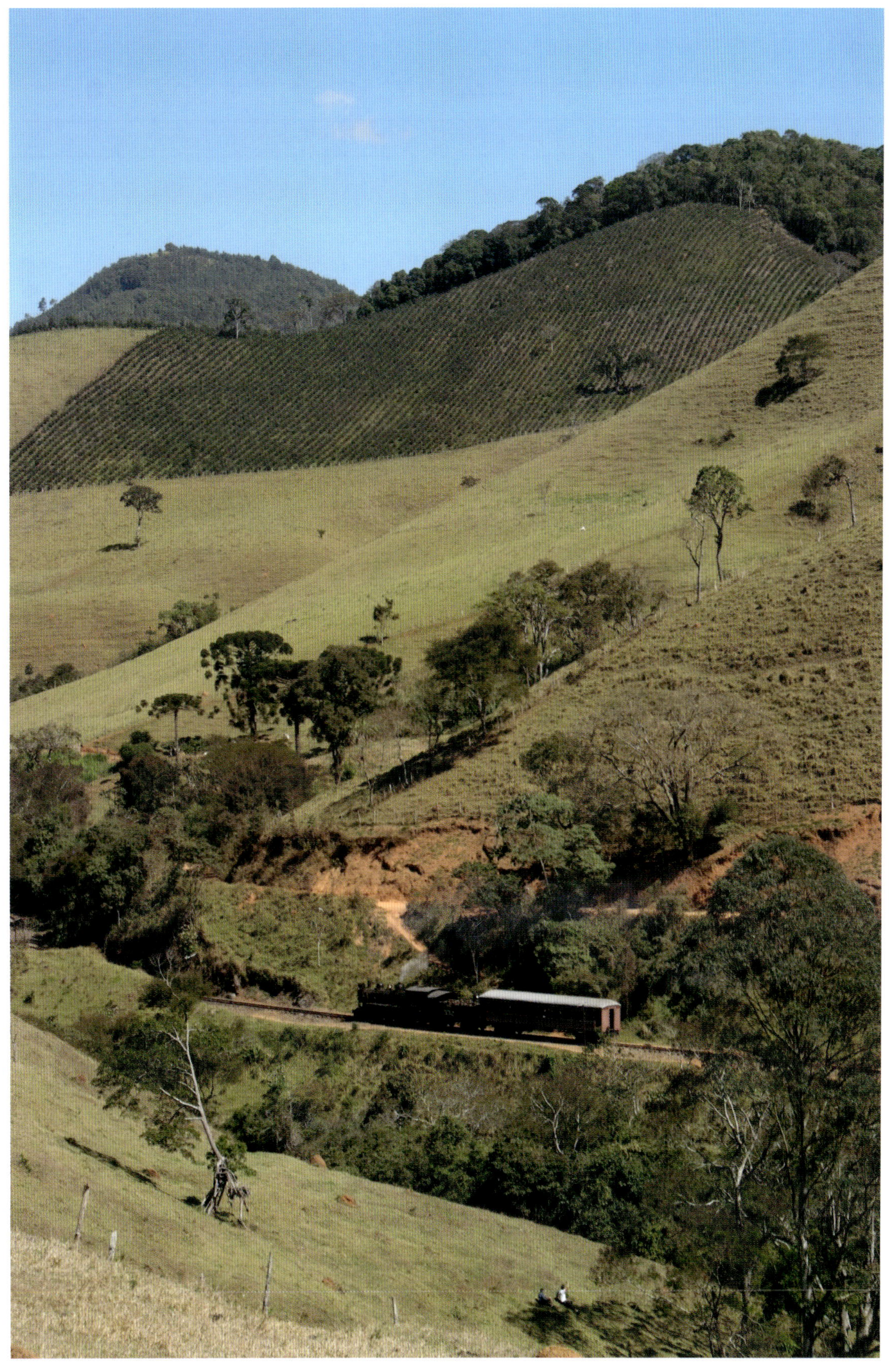

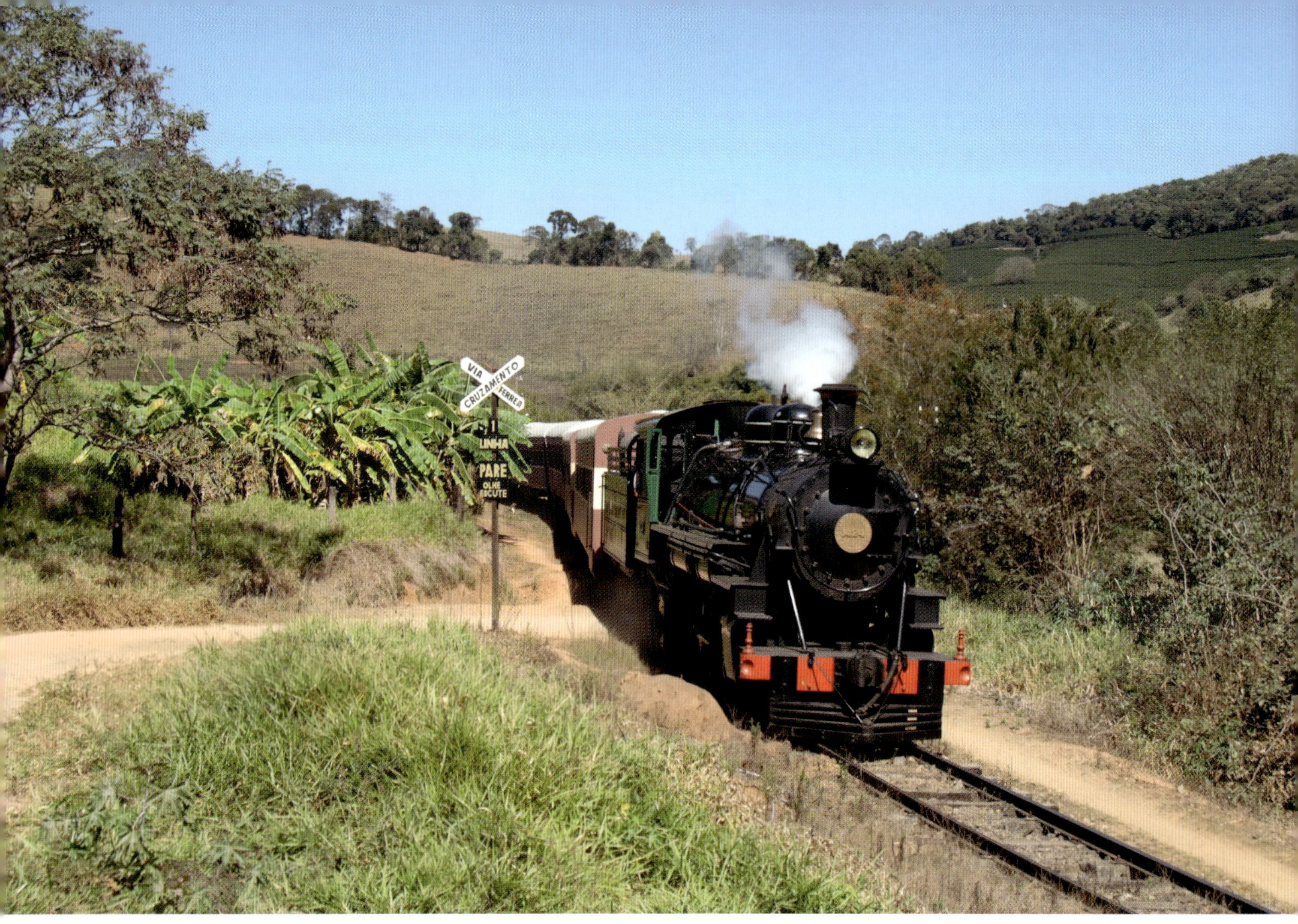

Above: The other working section runs between São Lourenço and Soledade de Minas through a popular tourist district. On 26 August 2012, EF Central do Brasil 2-8-2 No 1424 (Alco 59712/1927) passes a level crossing with a northbound train.

Opposite above: The ABPF's first preserved railway was a section of the old metre gauge EF Mogiana's mainline in São Paulo state between Anhumas, in the outskirts of Campinas, and Jaguariúna and it's still home to most of its steam locos. Here, RMV 2-8-2 No 505 (Schwartzkopff 8904/1927) approaches Carlos Gomes on 25 August 2012.

Opposite below: RMV No 215 (Baldwin 37710/1912), is being wooded up in the yard at Anhumas before working an afternoon train on 9 July 2013. She was one of several RMV 4-6-0s which ran in the south of Minas Gerais until the early 1980s. Their continued existence was unknown to us overseas visitors in the 1970s and so we missed them, even though some worked quite close to the São João del Rei line.

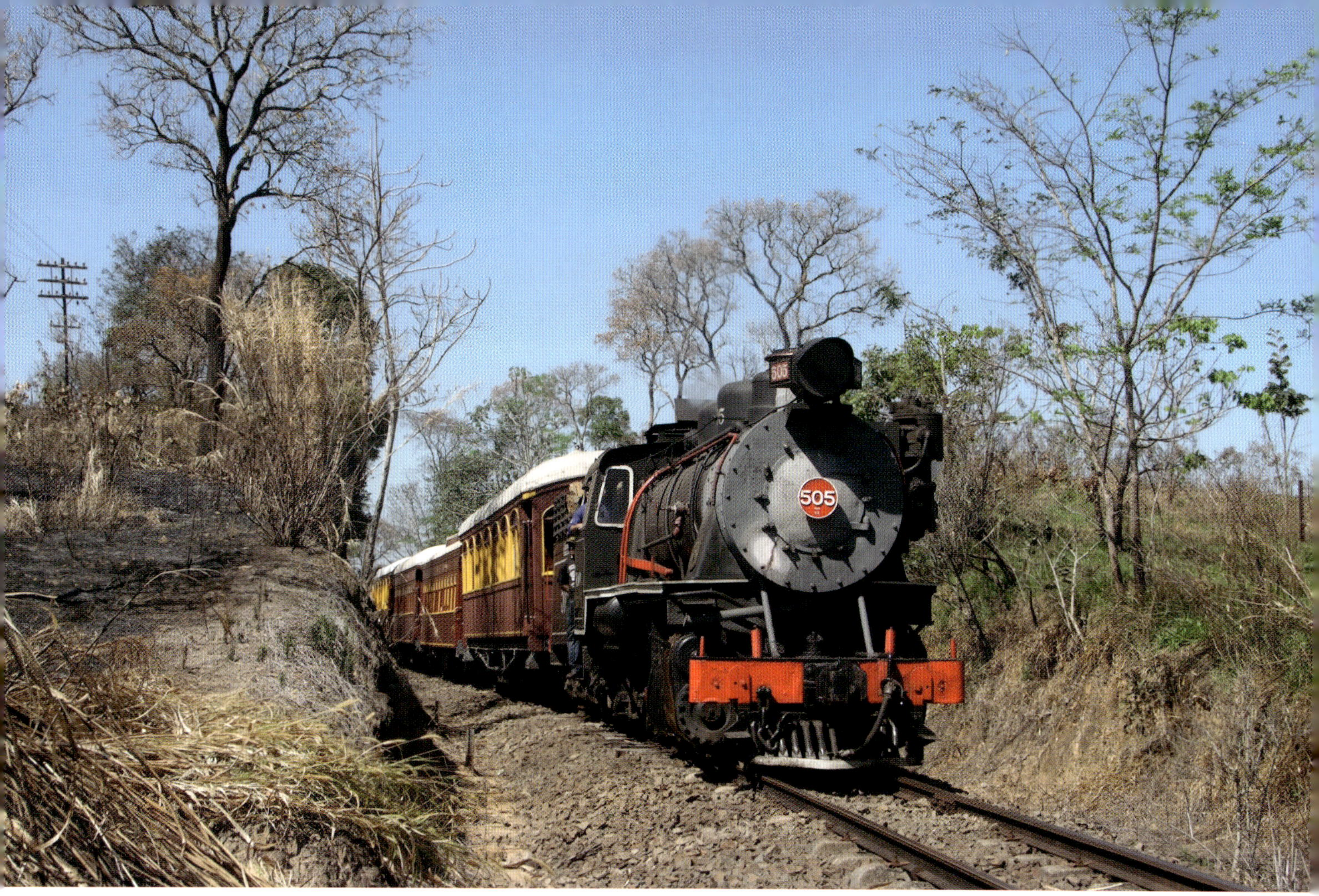

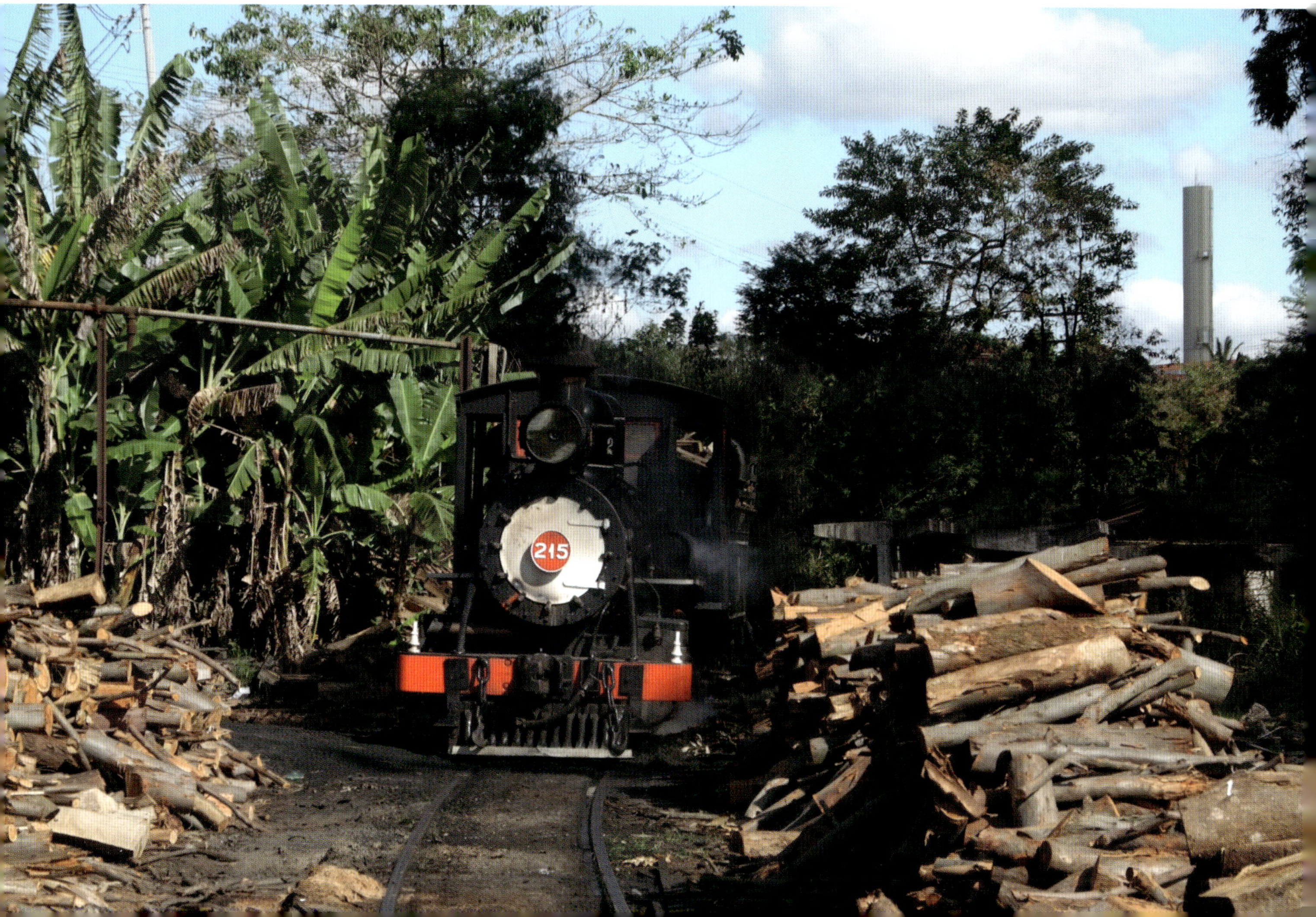

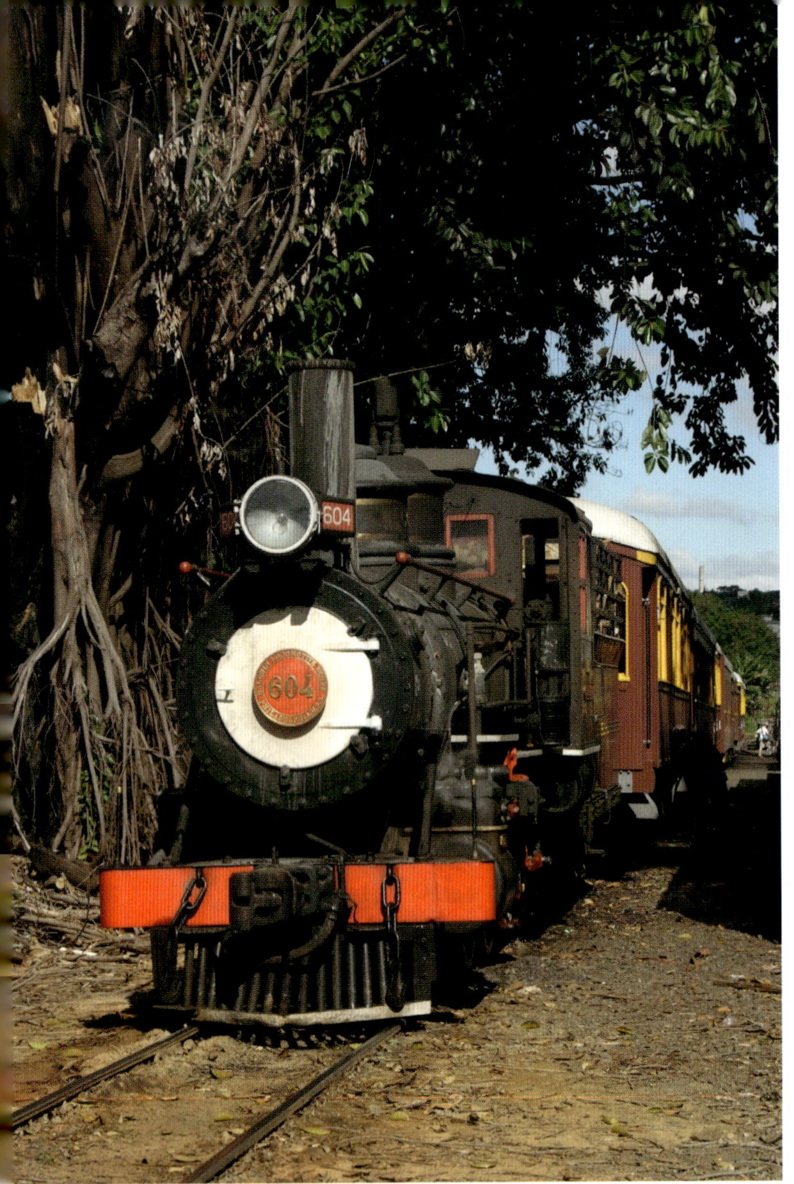

The Companhia Paulista's 5ft 3ins gauge mainline ran from the São Paulo Railway at Jundiai to Bauru, far away in the interior of São Paulo state, and metre gauge feeder lines went even further inland. Its venerable metre gauge 4-6-0 No 604 (Baldwin 14255/1895) was on station pilot duty at Anhumas on 9 July 2013.

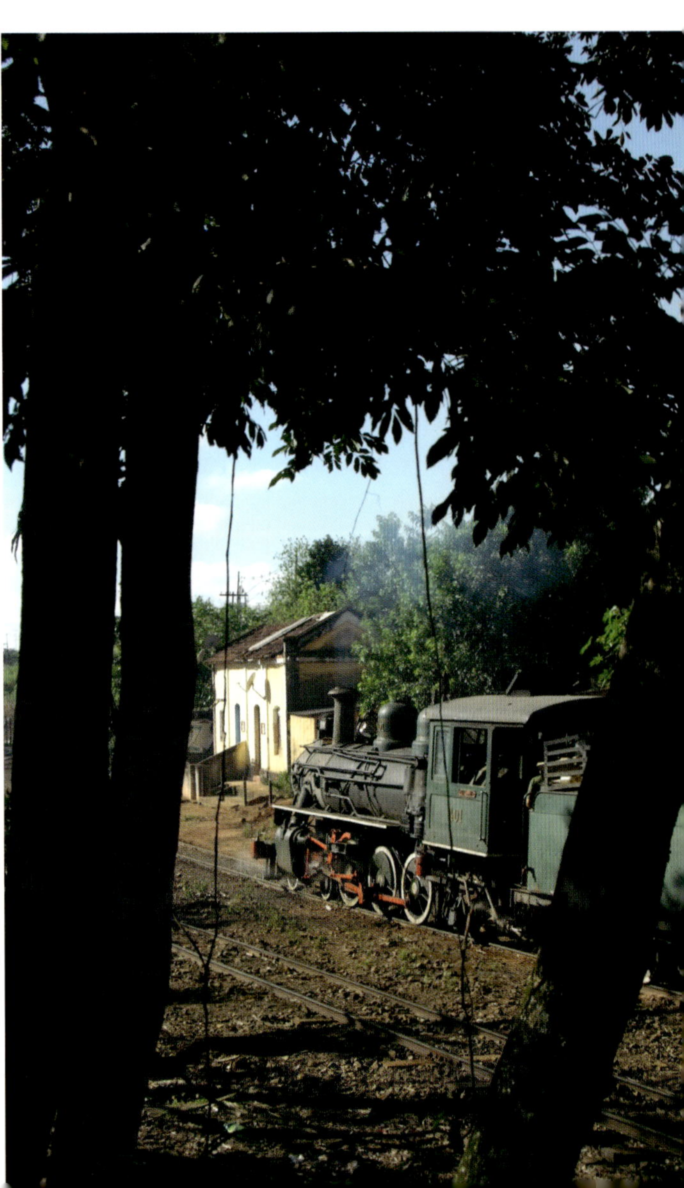

Glimpsed through the trees at Anhumas metre gauge EF Noroeste do Brasil Pacific No 401 (Baldwin 53766/1920) leaves for Jaguariúna on 9 July 2013. The Noroeste headed west from Bauru across the vast marshy Pantanal, today a haven for wildlife but also inhabited by diminishing numbers of pre-Columbian peoples who sometimes attacked trains with bows and arrows in the railway's early days. After many years' construction it was completed to Corumbá in 1952 and now joins the Bolivian railways there.

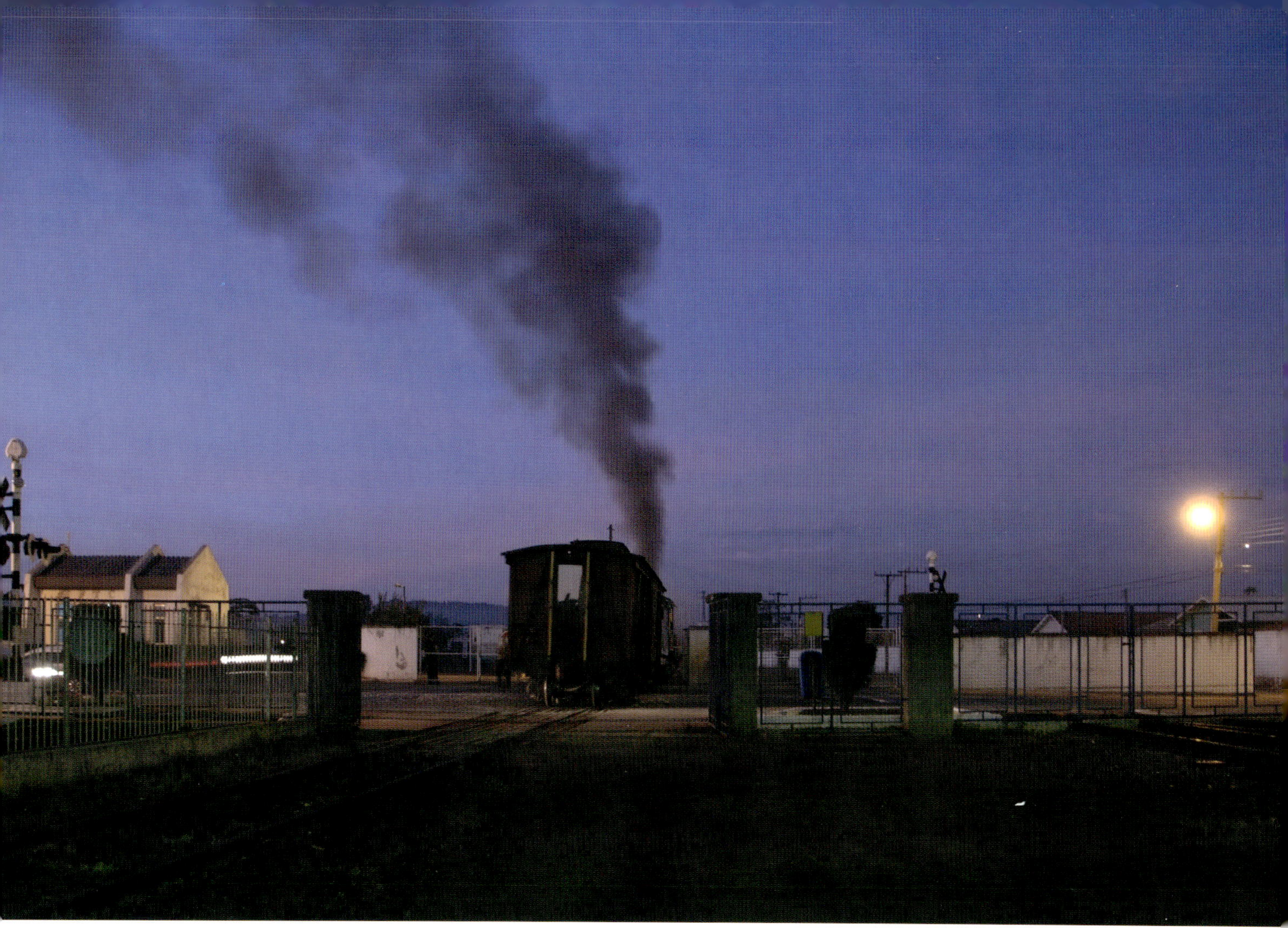

It's before dawn on 6 July 2013 as EF Dona Tereza Cristina 2-8-2 No 153 (Alco 69445/1941) and a van set off from Tubarão. The first section of the metre gauge EFDTC, in Santa Catarina state in southern Brazil, opened in 1884 and by the 1920s had developed into a substantial system serving the country's principal coalfield. It has been an exclusively coal-carrying line since passenger services ended in 1968.

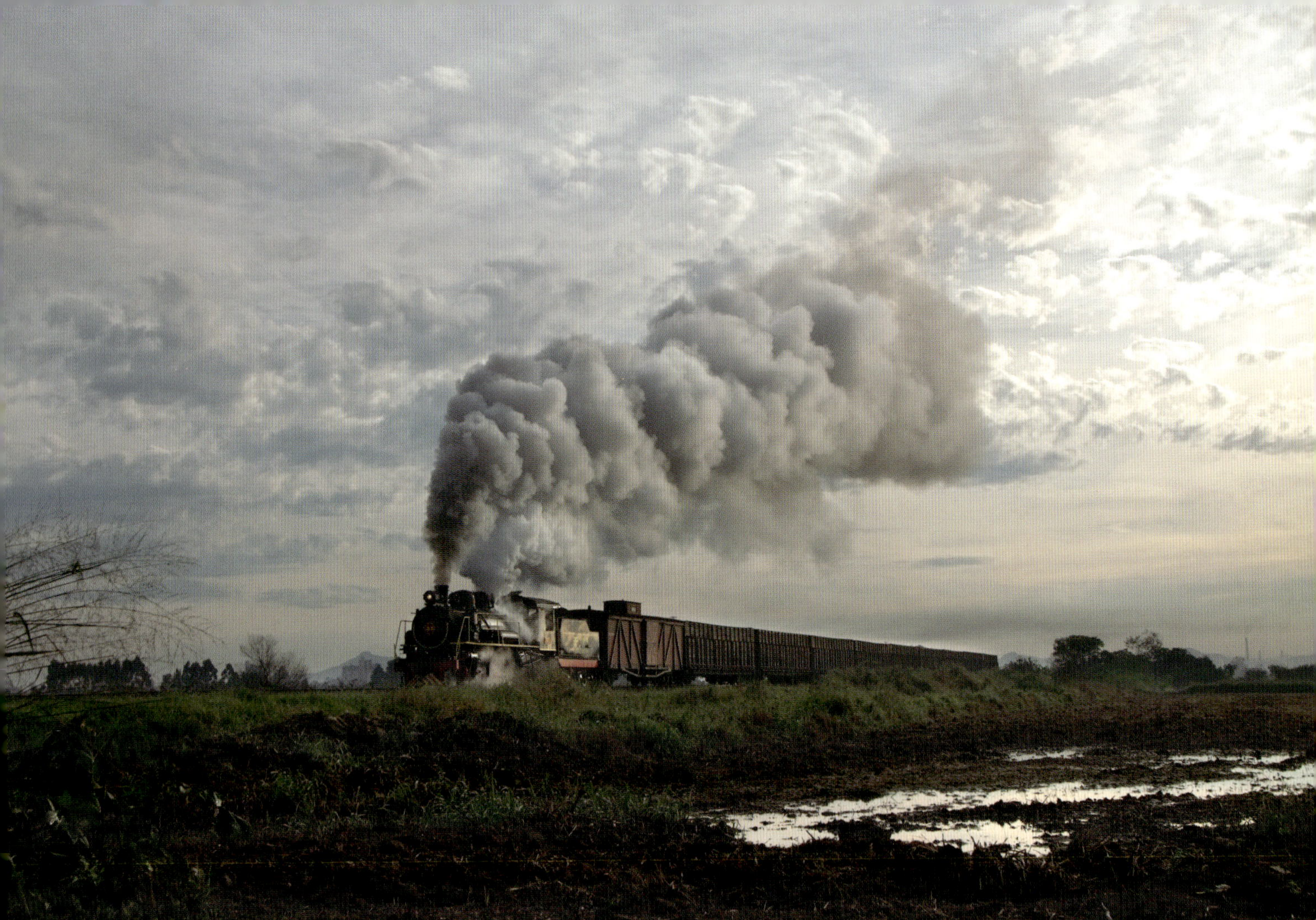

Above: No 153 heads south from Tubarão with coal empties later that morning. The EFDTC has always been isolated from the country's mainline network. Diesels took over in the late 1980s but three steam locos are kept in working order for heritage trains. They are looked after at a purpose-built workshop at Tubarão where there is also an excellent museum with several non-working locos. They include No 300, one of a series of powerful and fast 2-10-4s which all but monopolised the coal trains until the early 1980s.

Opposite above: 2-10-2 No 205 (Skoda 1982/1949), one of fourteen similar locos bought second-hand from Argentina in 1980, stands in Tubarão yard at dusk on 6 July 2013. She was formerly Argentine No 1352 and was modified at Tubarão by LD Porta, the innovative Argentine engineer, to include his advanced exhaust system – easily recognised by the forward-sloping chimney needed for the blastpipe to clear the superheater header.

Opposite below: The 600mm gauge EF Perus-Pirapora opened in 1914 between a quarry at Gato Preto and the São Paulo Railway's mainline at Perus; a cement factory built there in 1925 provided most of its business in later years. It closed in 1983 but thanks to preservationists little was scrapped and a heritage operation eventually began between Perus and Corredor. 2-4-2ST No 2 (Alco 66405/1925), one of six similar locos on the old line, approaches Corredor on 25 August 2012.

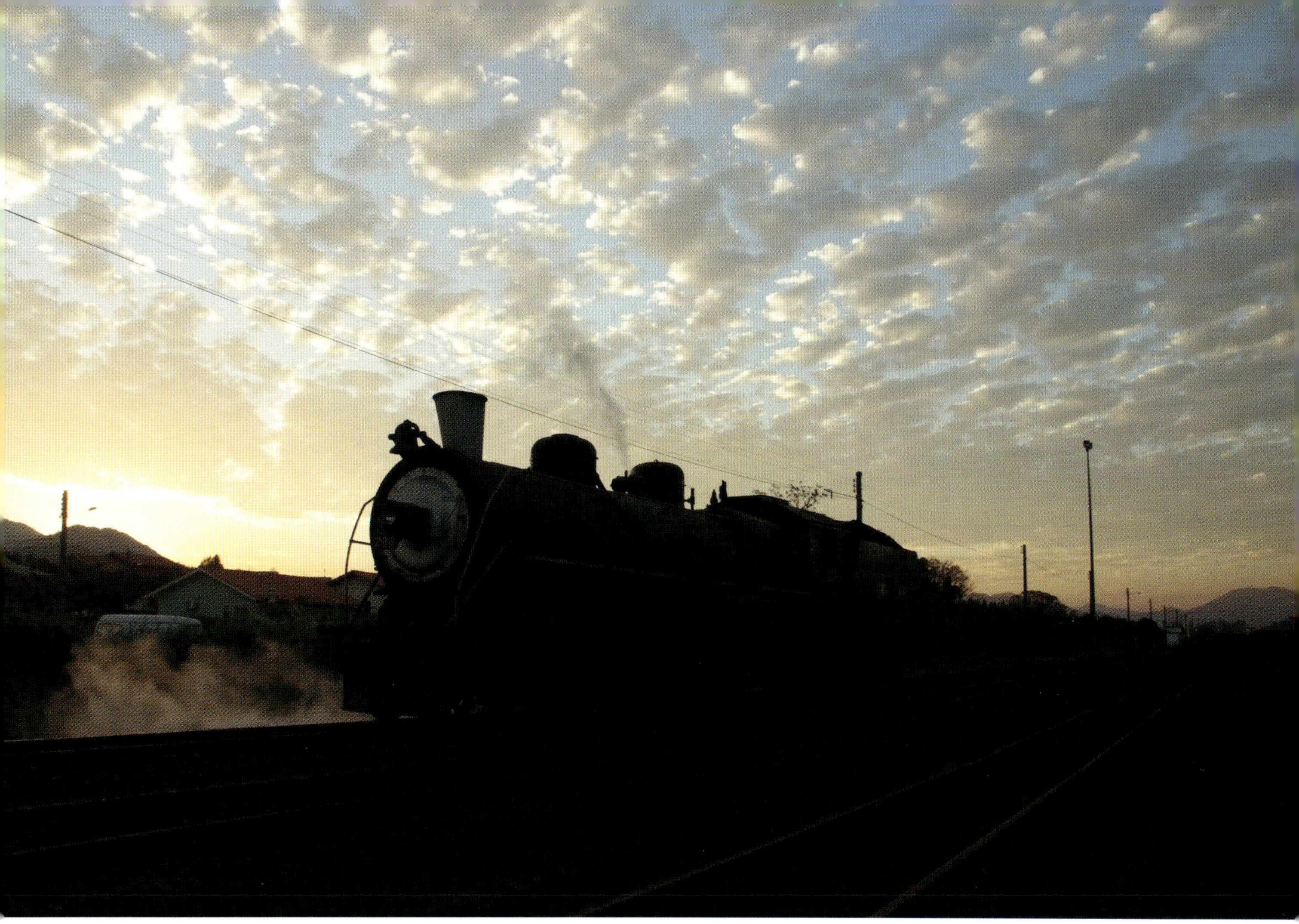

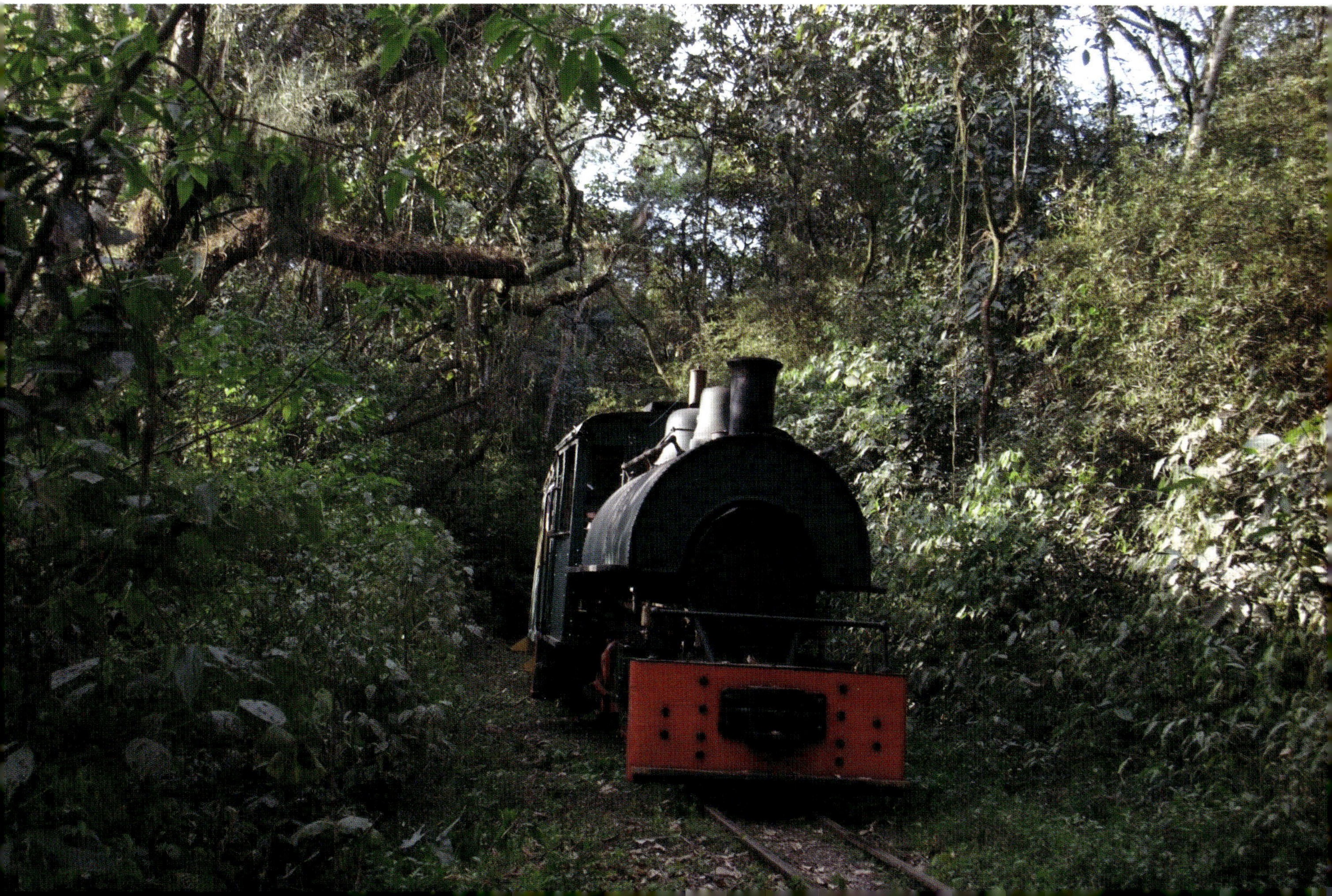

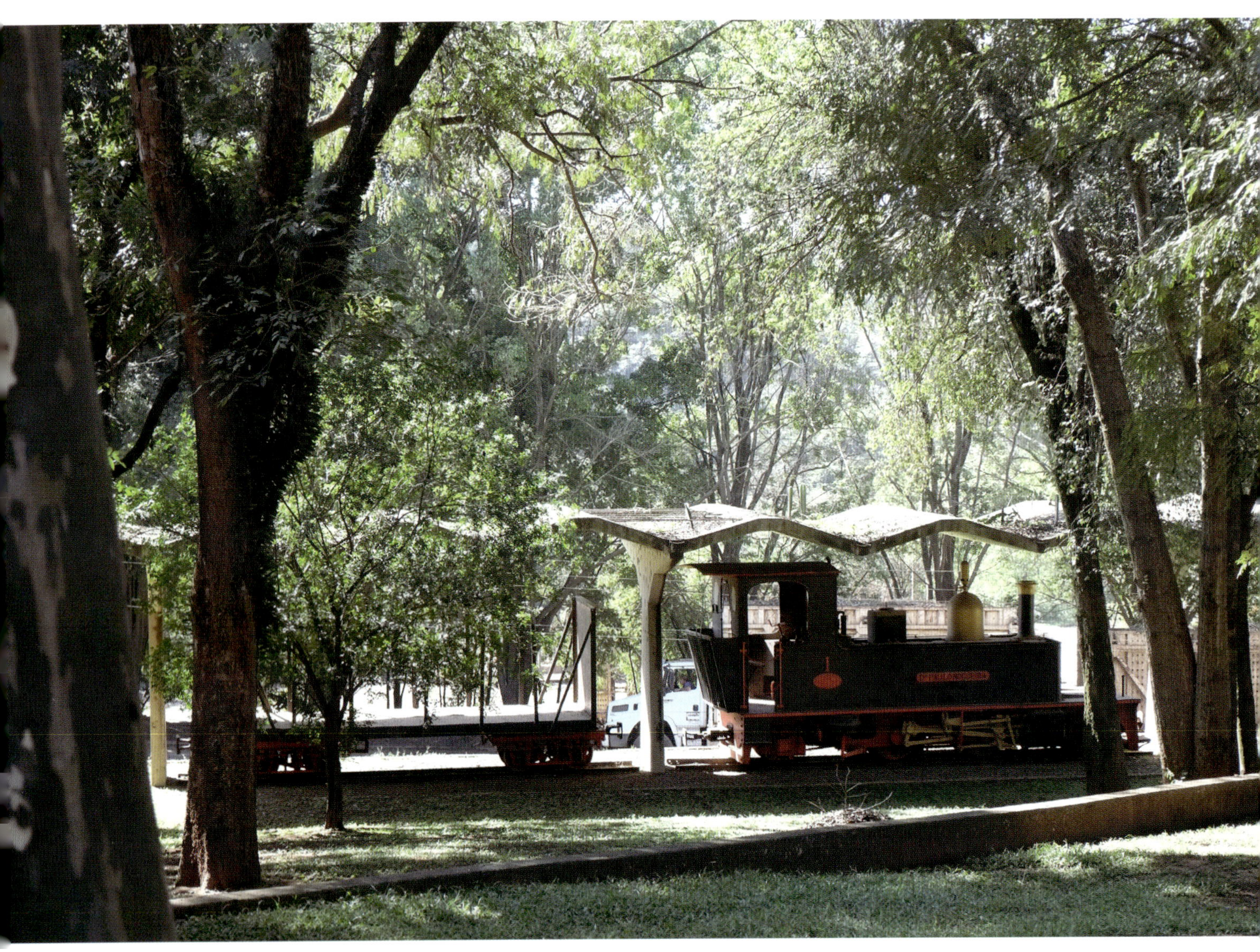

On 28 March 1892, the Mogiana opened a steeply graded 600mm gauge branch from Amparo to Serra Negra, more than 1,200m up in the mountains, and two stylish 2-4-2Ts were supplied for its opening. They proved to be underpowered and were sold to the Carril Funilense, a 600mm gauge line which opened between Campinas and Cosmopolis in 1899, moving later to the Usina Esther, a sugar factory at Cosmopolis. Its railway closed long ago but the locos are still there. No 1 (SS 3484/1888) sits in the shade on 5 July 2013, complete in every way. Even her gauge glasses are intact and she looks as though you could just raise steam and drive her away!

URUGUAY

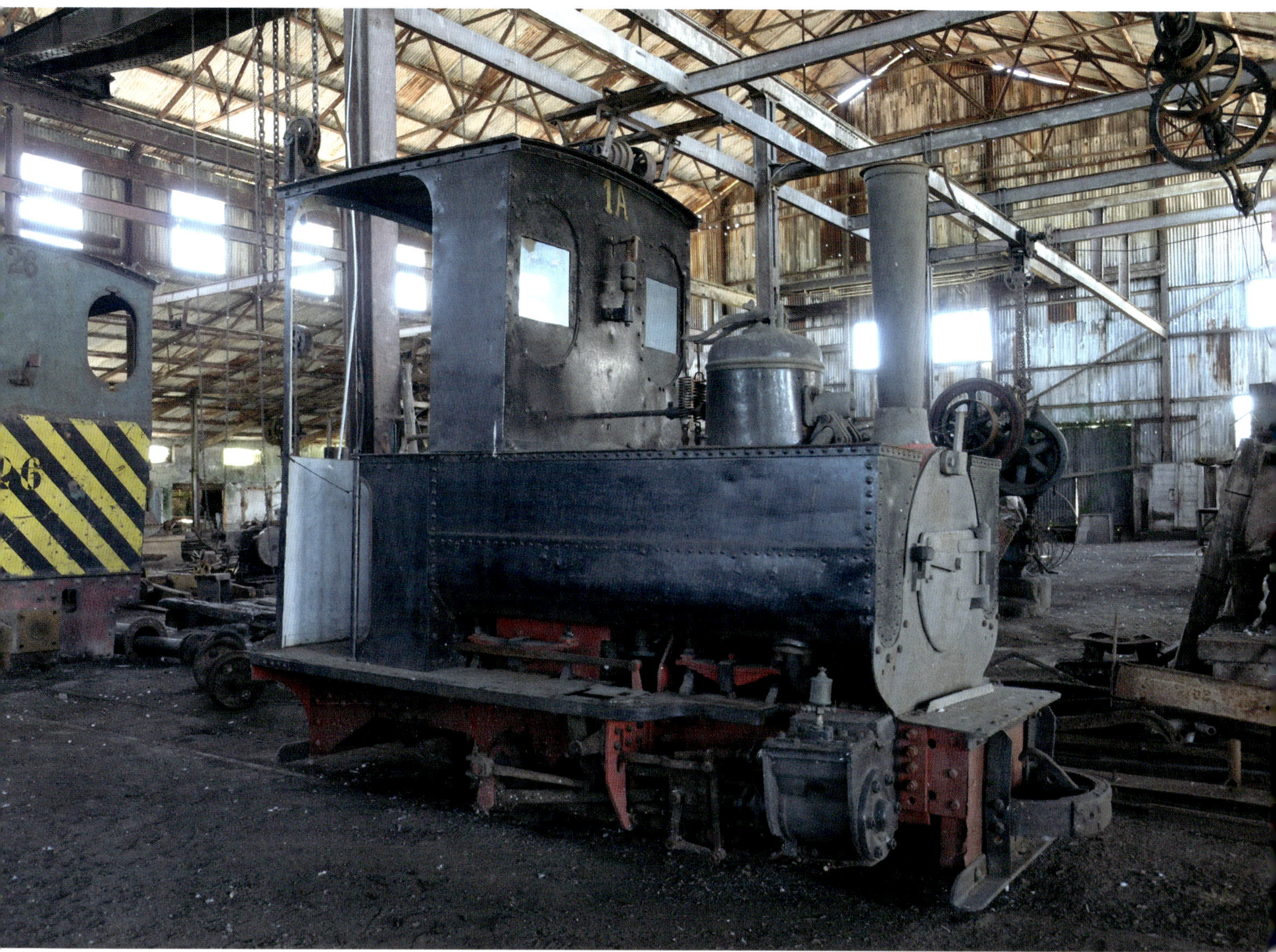

This tiny 600mm gauge loco, 3.5 tonne 0-4-0T No 1A (Decauville 526/1909) stands in the repair shop at the FC Indare on 7 December 2013. She started life at Montevideo docks and later became the smallest of twenty-seven locos at Indare's sand and gravel pits at Boca de Rosario on the Uruguayan side of the Rio de la Plata. Behind her is 0-4-0T No 26 (Henschel 28519/1950), Indare's youngest loco. The pits were worked from 1912 to provide material for construction at Buenos Aires on the other side of the river. The last regular train ran in 1982 and the pits closed soon after.

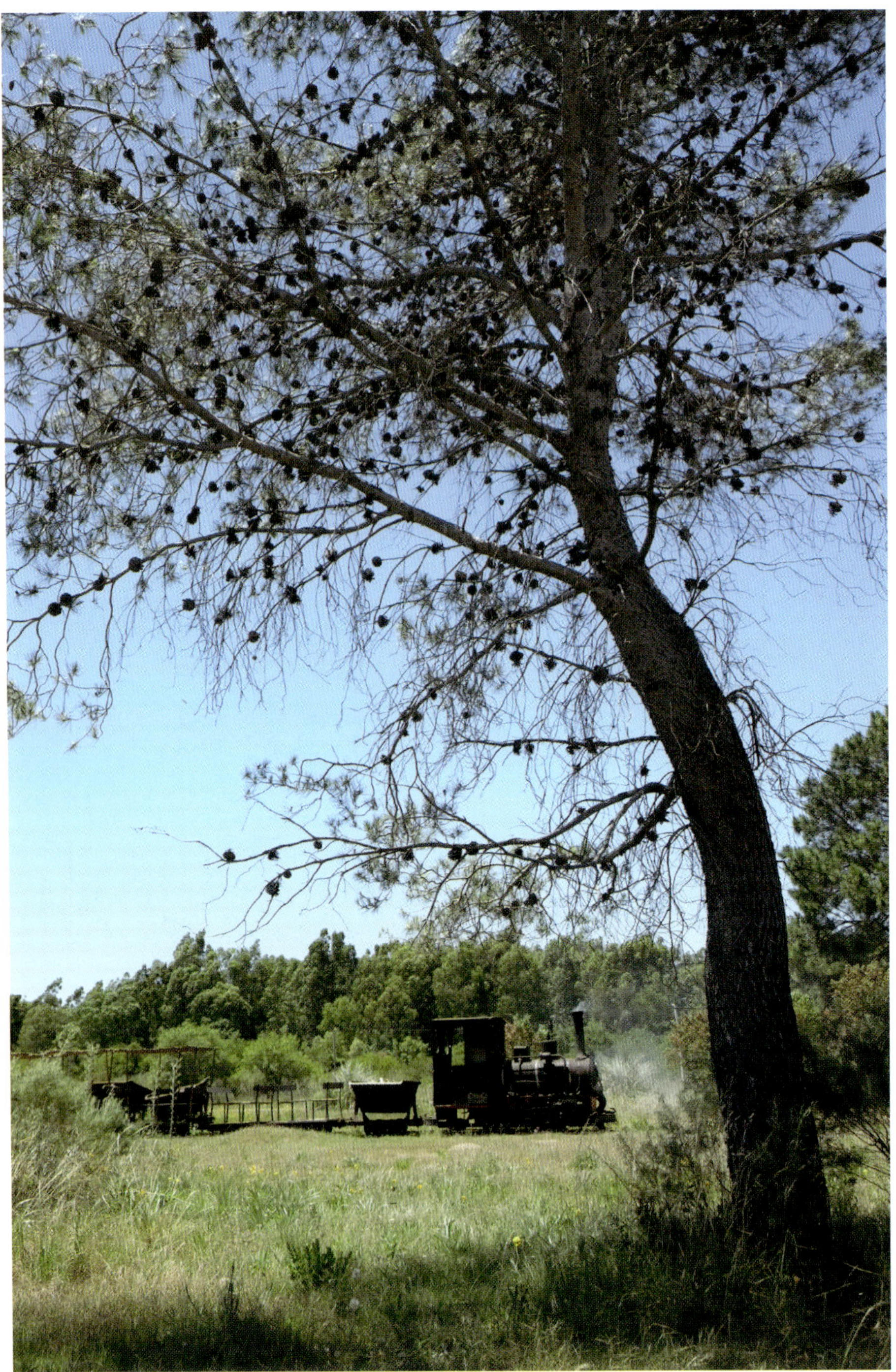

The Indare site has been run as a nature reserve and low-key tourist attraction since 1998. The repair shop and the running and storage sheds, complete with the twenty-seven locos, are still as they were in 1982, as are the stationary steam engines at the old company's power station. They're all looked after by a gentleman named Pepe who has spent his working life there and who put 0-4-0T No 15 (OK 5835/1912) back into working order for a tourist service over about 700m of the old route. She's clearly his pride and joy though for the last couple of years she's needed a more extensive overhaul than he can achieve unaided. Here she has paused out along the line for a visit to the power station on 7 December 2013.

ARGENTINA

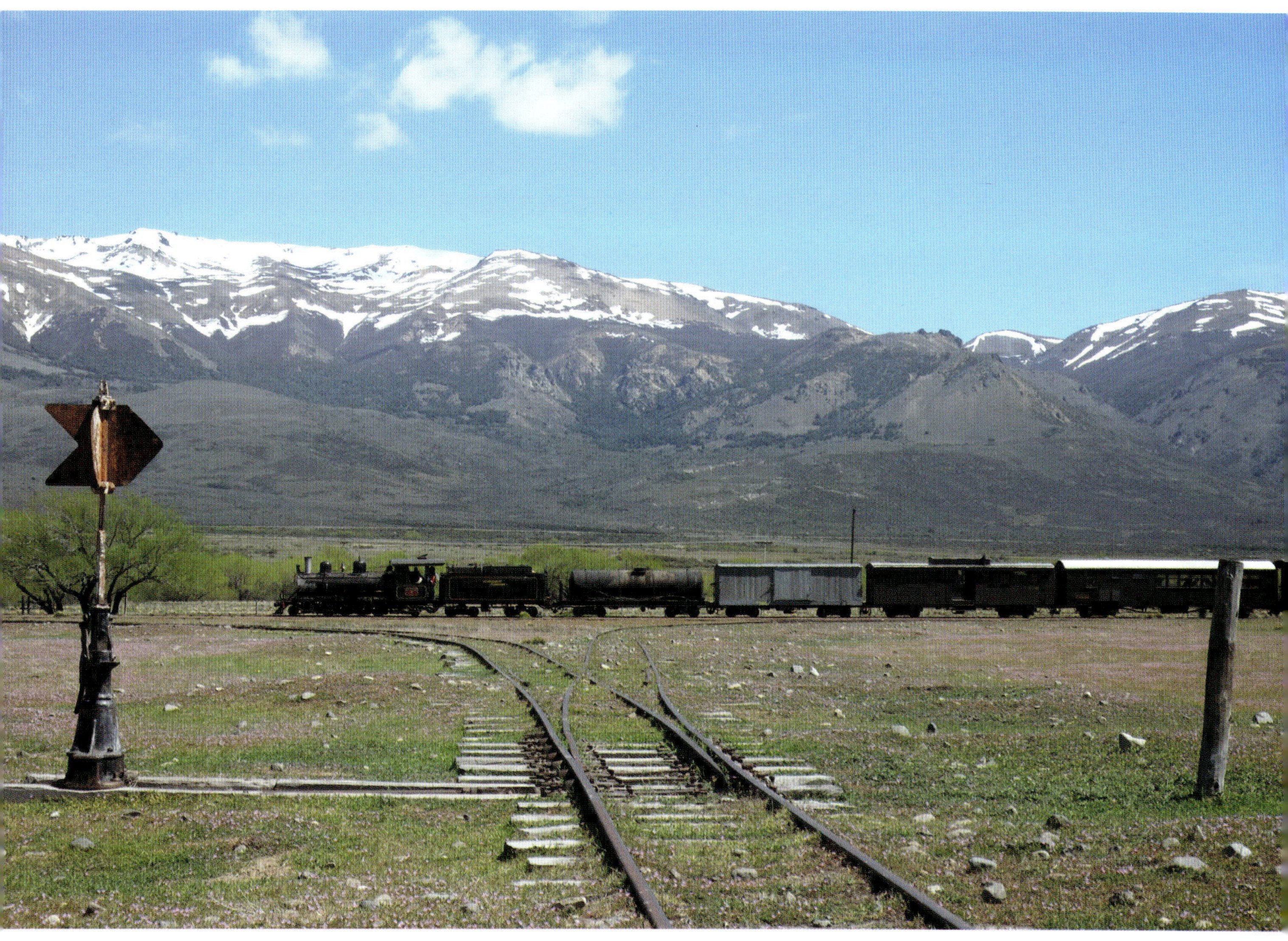

The district around the headwaters of the Rio Chubut near Esquel, in the Argentine part of Patagonia, was settled by Welsh farmers in the 1880s. Their community was an offshoot of the Welsh colony on the coast which had been founded back in 1865. The settlers built a line west from Porth (later Puerto) Madryn which opened in 1889 and being Welsh they of course chose a narrow gauge! The government later took over and converted it from metre to 750mm gauge as part of a scheme to build railways throughout Patagonia. This was to have included an extension of the Welsh line to Esquel and a 750mm branch to the town from the broad gauge mainline further north but only the latter was completed. Ferrocarriles Argentinos 2-8-2 No 4 (Baldwin 55432/1922) and her train pass the turning wye at Leleque, in the barren foothills of the Andes south of El Maitén, on 22 October 2014.

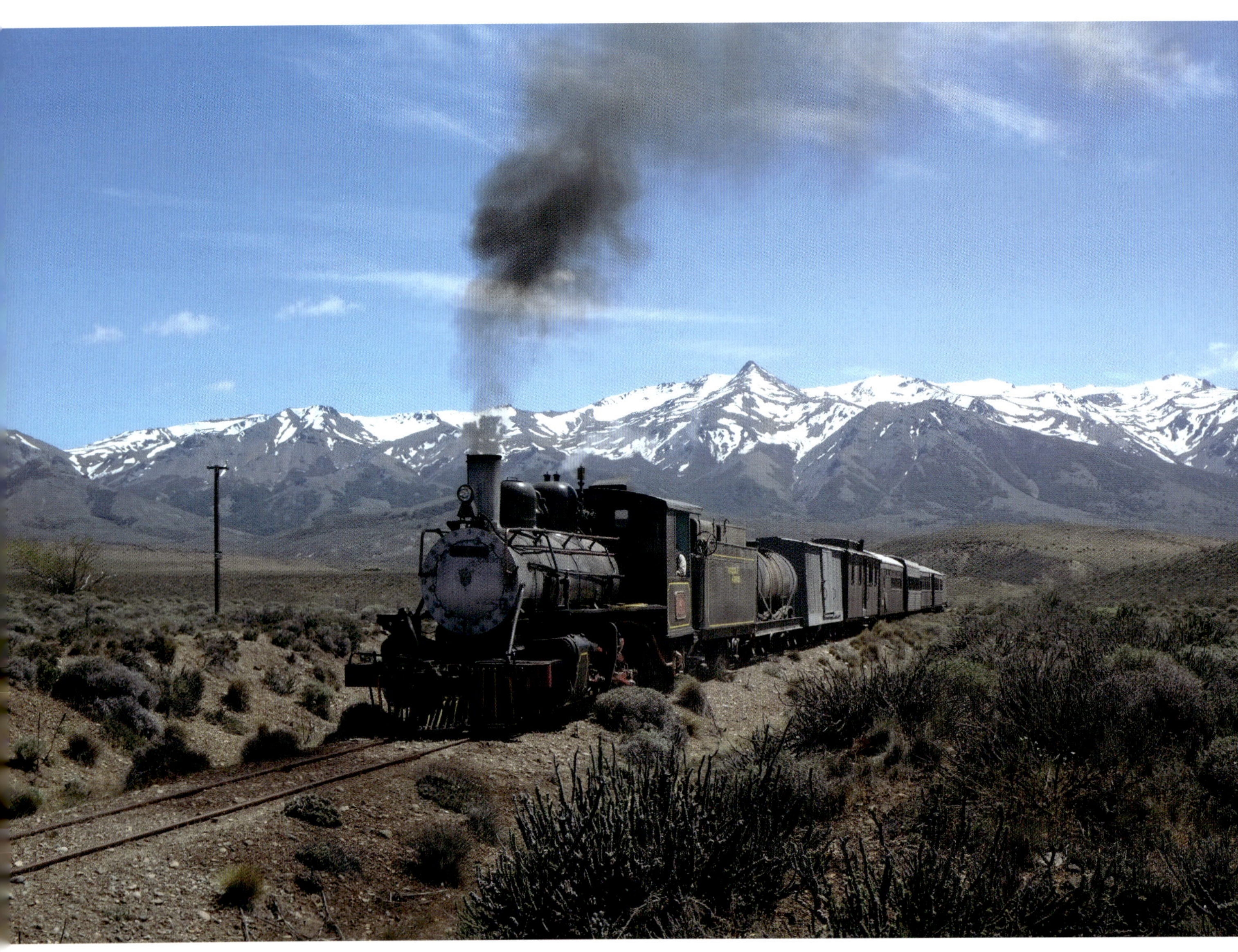

A little later, No 4 heads south from Leleque and the scenery is, if anything, even bleaker. The railway's construction began in 1923 and was completed in 1945. Most of the indigenous people of Patagonia were the victims of genocide in the 1880s. The Welsh seem to have been the only people to treat them kindly and give them shelter and some of their descendants work on the line. One of them, a lady member of the restaurant car crew, took my arm during lunch and gestured towards a condor circling overhead. I'd hoped, but never really expected, to see one of these magnificent though elusive birds! Esquel and El Maitén remain significant centres within Y Wladfa, the Welsh Patagonian community, and Welsh and Mapuche, the indigenous language, can still be heard on and around the railway.

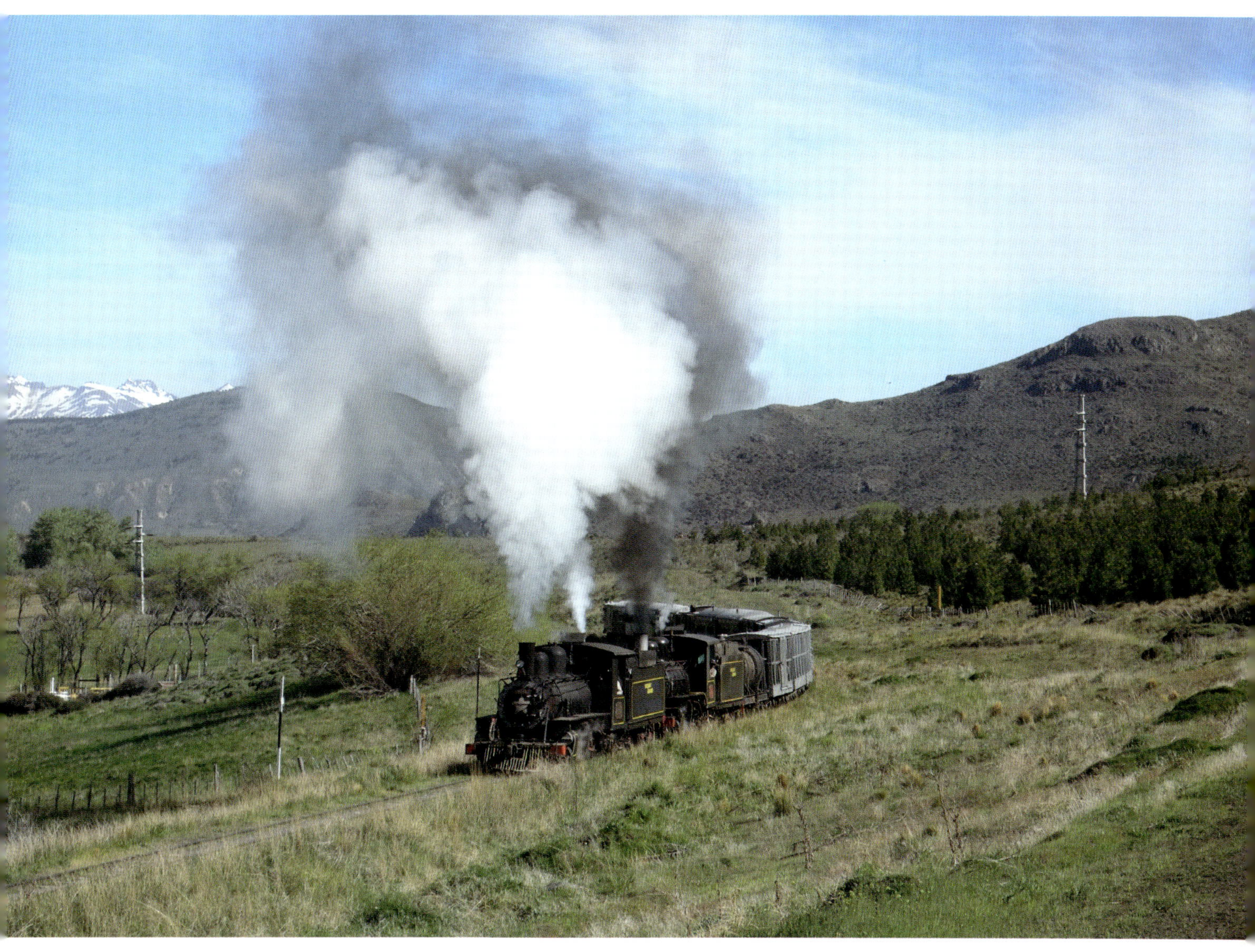

The fertile valley at Esquel is quite different from the arid countryside elsewhere and it's easy to see why the Welsh settled there. Here Nos 16 (Baldwin 55443/1922) and 4 climb away from the town with a long mixed train on 23 October 2014. The seventy-five 2-8-2s built for the original scheme were far more than were needed and some spent many years in store before seeing use. No 16 was originally numbered 15. The foreman at El Maitén shops indulged in a little subterfuge when instructions arrived that No 15 was to be withdrawn. She'd only recently entered service and he swapped her plates with the worn-out No 16 and despatched her for scrapping instead.

ICELAND

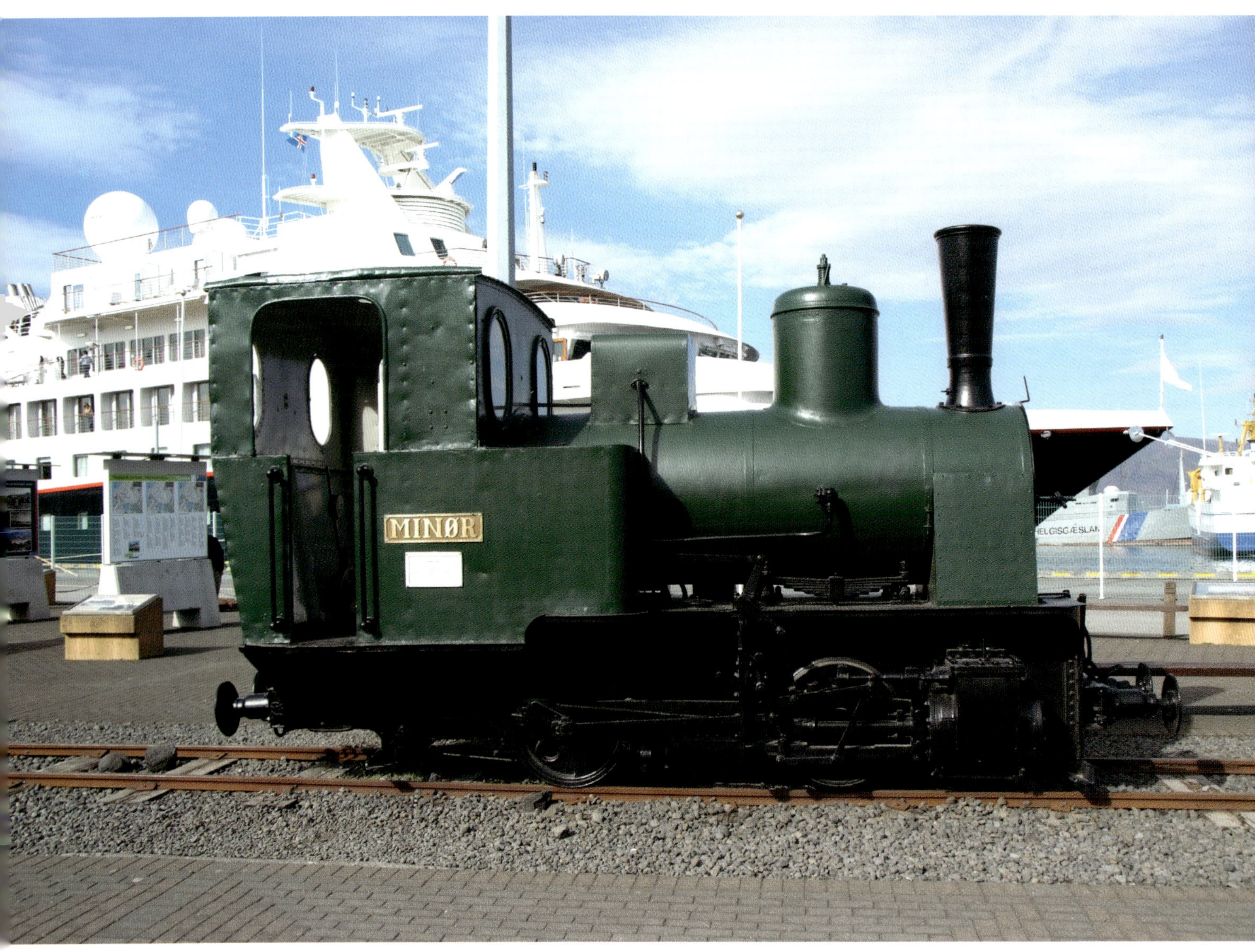

0-4-0T *Minør* (Jung 130/1892) and her companion *Pionér* worked the 900mm gauge Reykjavik harbour railway, built in 1913 to carry stone for breakwater construction. Iceland's only steam locos, they were originally supplied to Rudolph Dolberg, a dealer in agricultural light railway material at Rostock, Germany and later ran in Copenhagen before moving to Reykjavik. The harbour was completed in 1918 but the railway continued to operate on a reduced scale until 1928. Here *Minør* stands on a short length of the old rail on the quayside on 29 July 2008. *Pionér* lives nearby at the Árbæjarsafn, an excellent regional museum. Iceland must be the only country to have preserved its entire steam fleet!

DENMARK

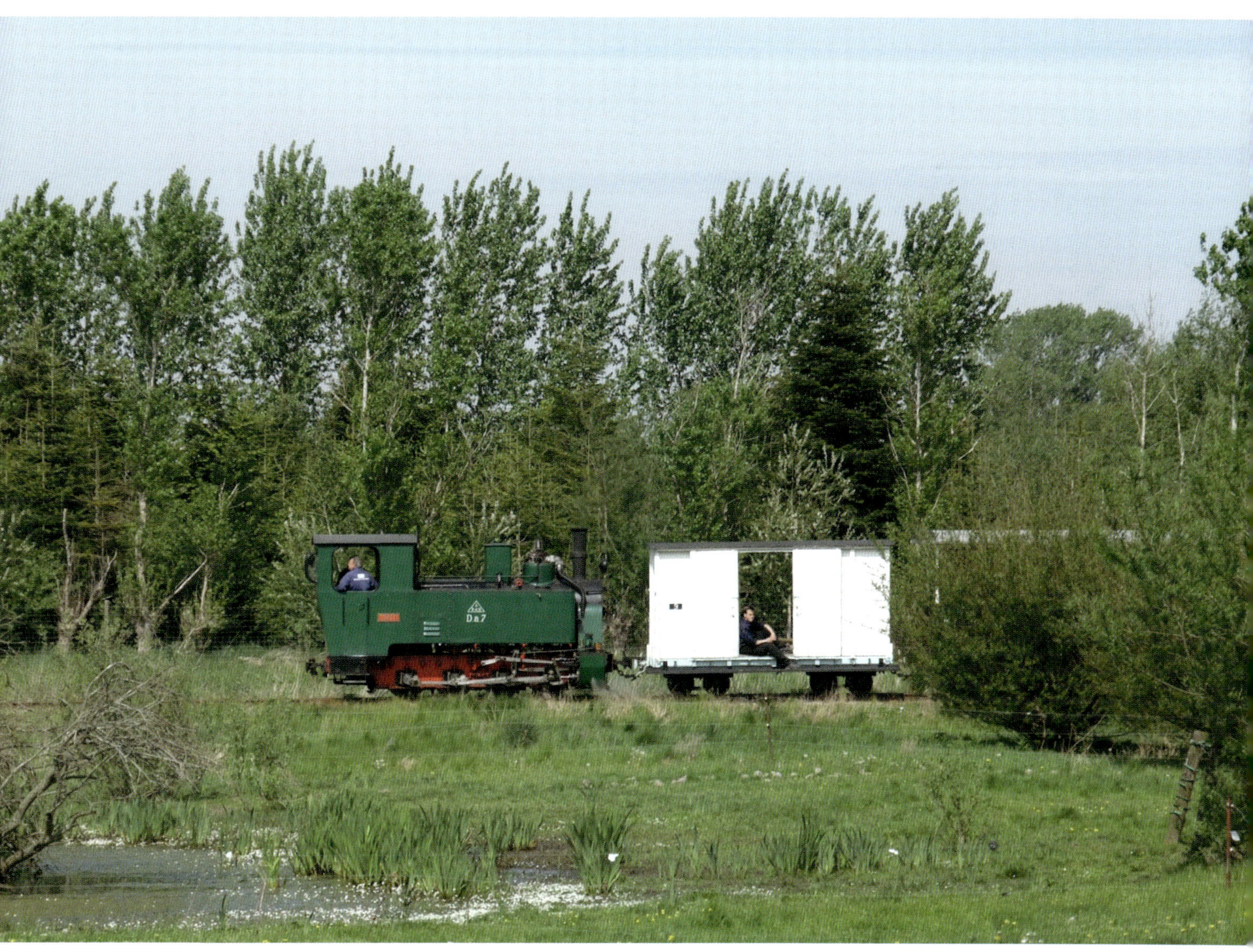

The Danish Sugar Company, founded in 1872, built 700mm gauge railways at several of its factories to bring in sugar beet for processing and to carry away the finished product. Their 0-8-0T No Da7 (Henschel 18449/1921), finely restored in their attractive green paint scheme, now lives at the Hedelands Veteranbane near Roskilde. She worked at factories at Assens until 1934, Maribo for one year and Sakskøbing until the 1960s. Here she is on 12 May 2008. The leading van was once used for transporting bagged sugar.

NORWAY

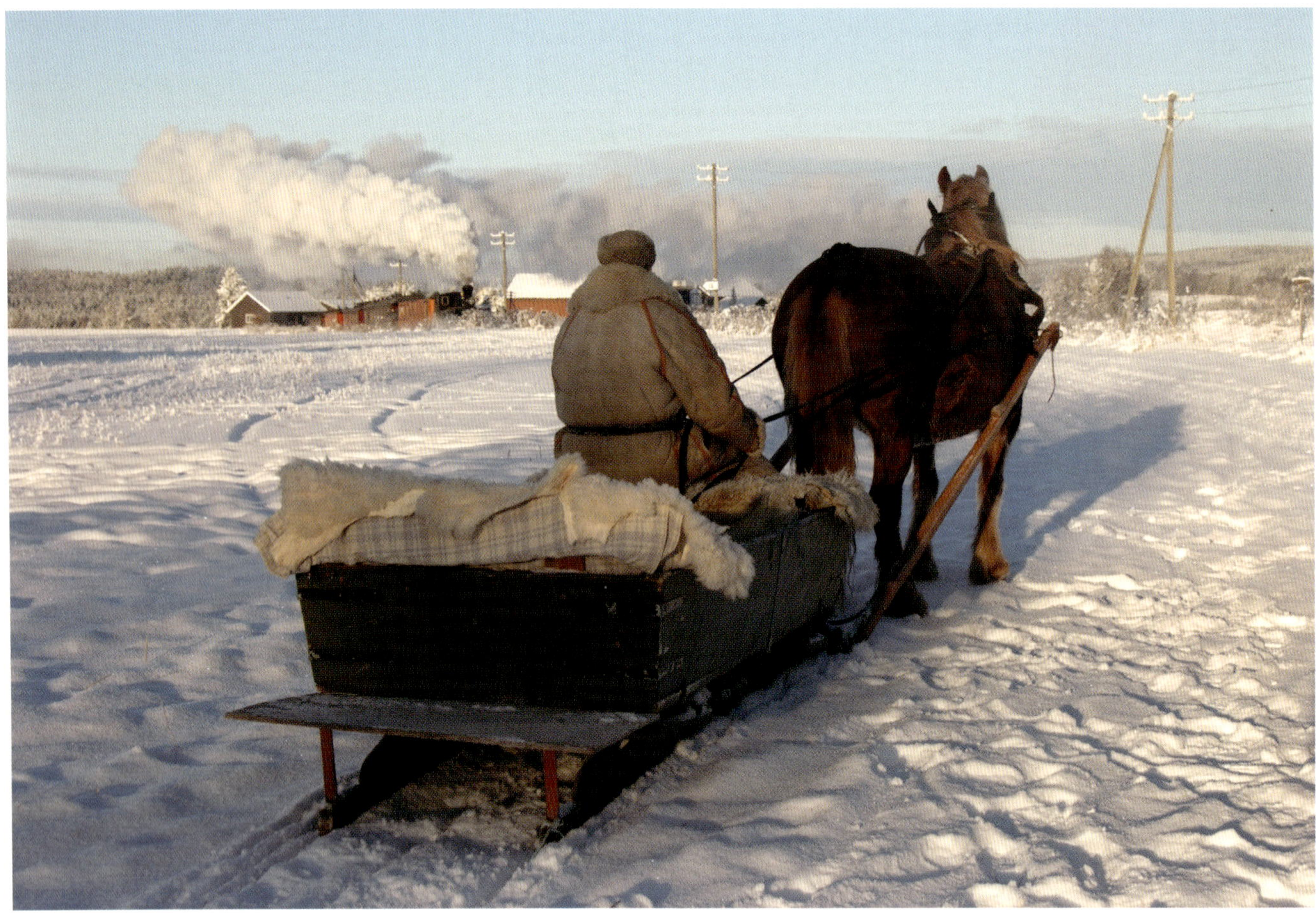

Above: 2-6-2T No 7 (Henschel 28463/1950) of NSB, the Norwegian state railway, approaches Fossum on the Tertitten heritage line on the very cold morning of 12 December 2010 as suitably seasonal connecting transport awaits! She was the youngest of four generally similar locos and the last steam loco of any gauge to be added to NSB's stock. They named her *Prydz* after the line's long-serving manager.

Opposite above: Another view of No 7 approaching Fossum on 12 December 2010. '*Tertitten*' is the Norwegian word for 'tertiary' and under the country's railway classification system means a line, usually an insignificant one, built to the lightest standards. The old Urskog-Hølandsbanen railway which opened in 1895 was one of these and it was probably its insignificance which allowed it to adopt the 750mm gauge at a time when the country was looking towards building a unified, standard gauge system.

Opposite below: No 7 leaves Fossum at sunset on 12 December 2010. The railway ran for 57kms through sparsely inhabited country from a mainline junction at Sørumsand to Skulerud, not far from the Swedish border, and became part of NSB in 1945. Enthusiasts took over a short section after it closed in 1960.

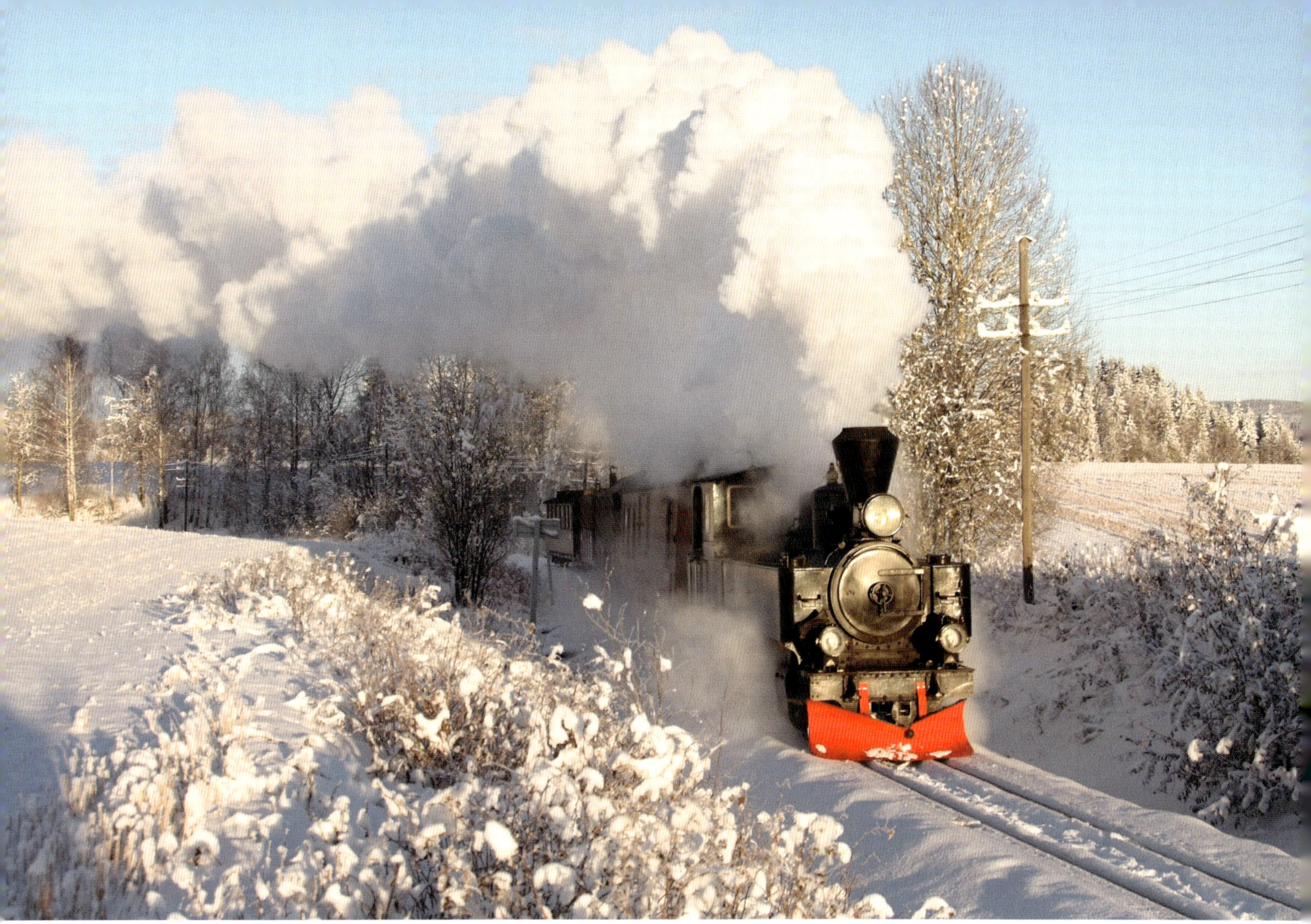

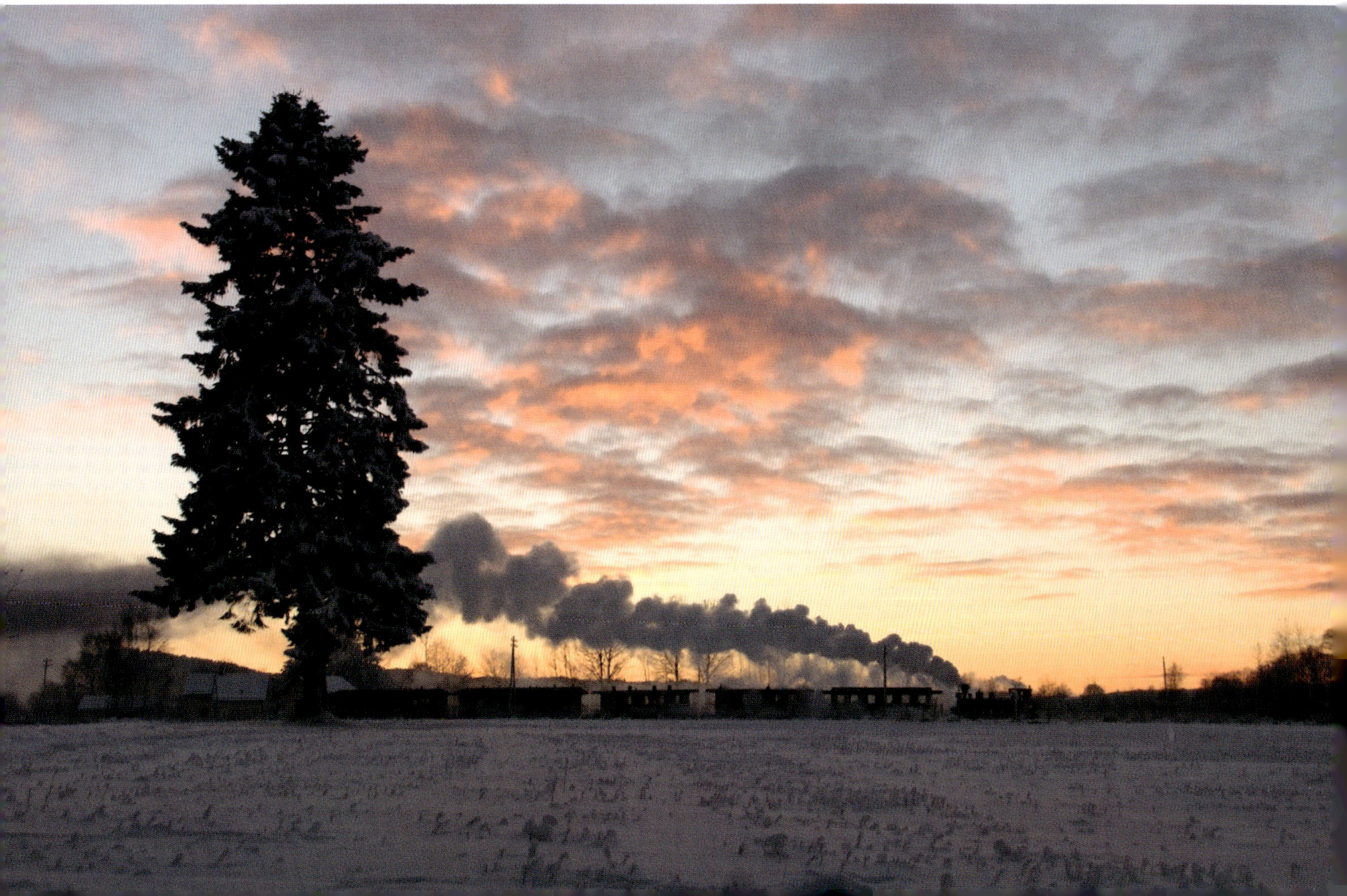

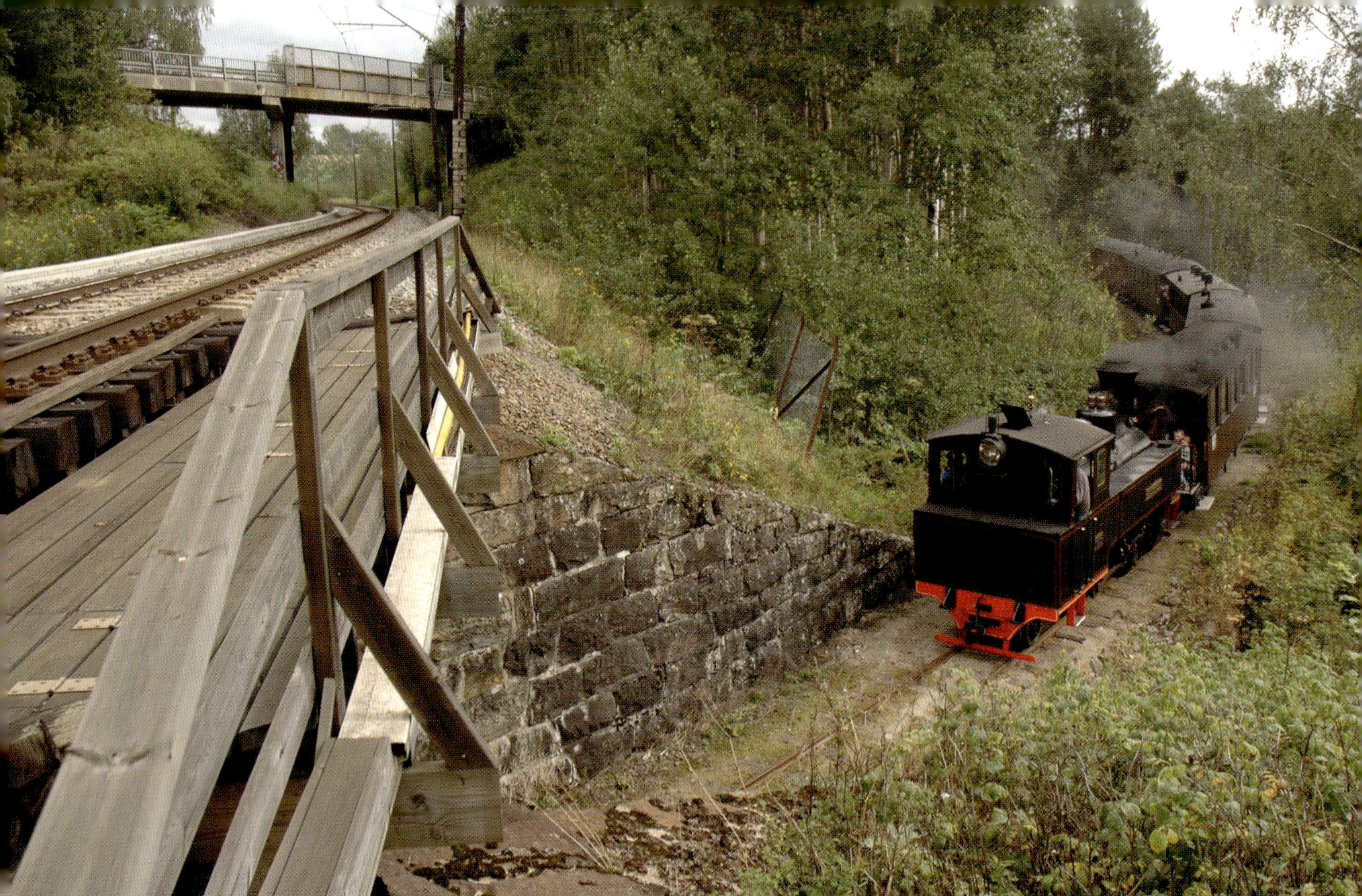

Above: A summer scene as No 4 *Setskogen* (Hartmann 3356/1909), the oldest 2-6-2T, is about to pass under the Oslo-Stockholm mainline between Bingsfoss and Sørumsand on 19 August 2007.

Opposite above: No 2 *Urskog* (Hartmann 2102/1895) was one of two 0-6-0Ts built for the line's opening. Here she hauls a train of Tertitten coaches at the excellent Norsk Jernbanemuseum at Hamar on 4 June 2008. She now burns agricultural bio-pellets and must be about as carbon-neutral as a steam loco can be!

Opposite below: The 3ft 6ins gauge Setesdalsbanen's 2-6-2T No 5 (Thunes 4/1901) catches a glimpse of sunshine as she leaves Beihølen for Røyknes on 24 August 2008. The old line between Kristiansand and Byglandsfjord was 78kms long and opened in 1896. The first locos, two 2-6-2Ts and two 2-4-2Ts, were built by Dübs in Glasgow and the 2-6-2Ts survive at Grovane shed.

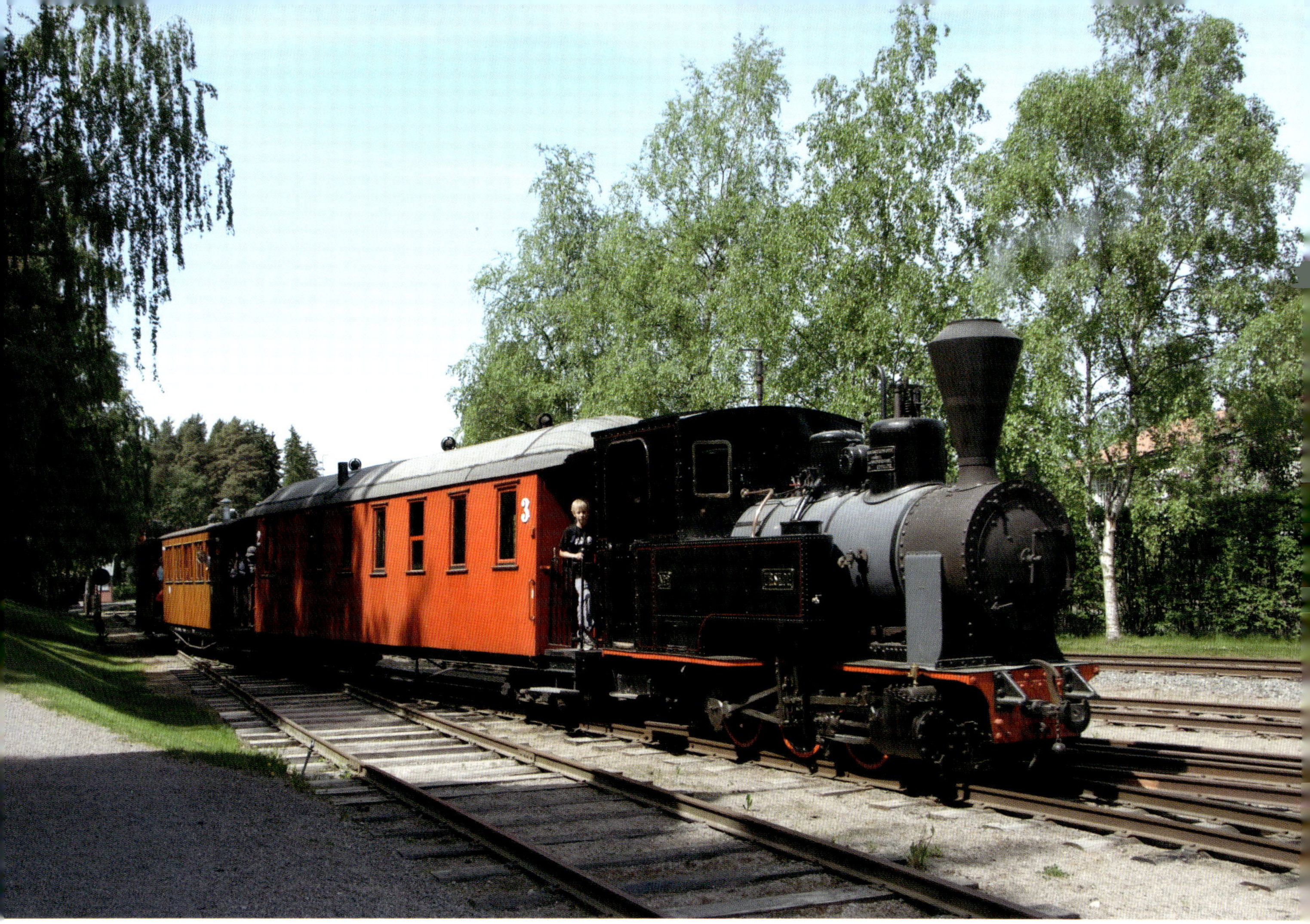

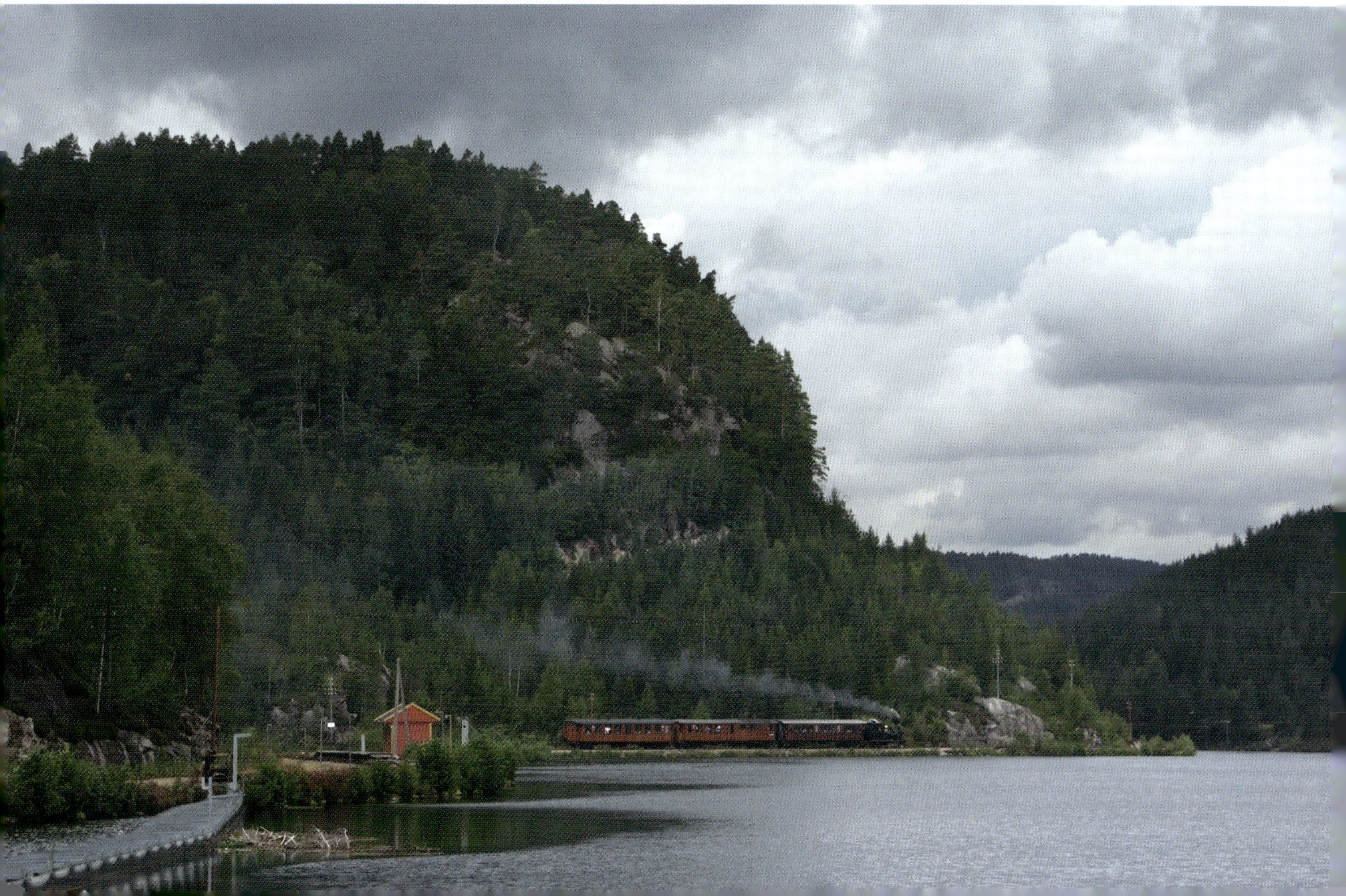

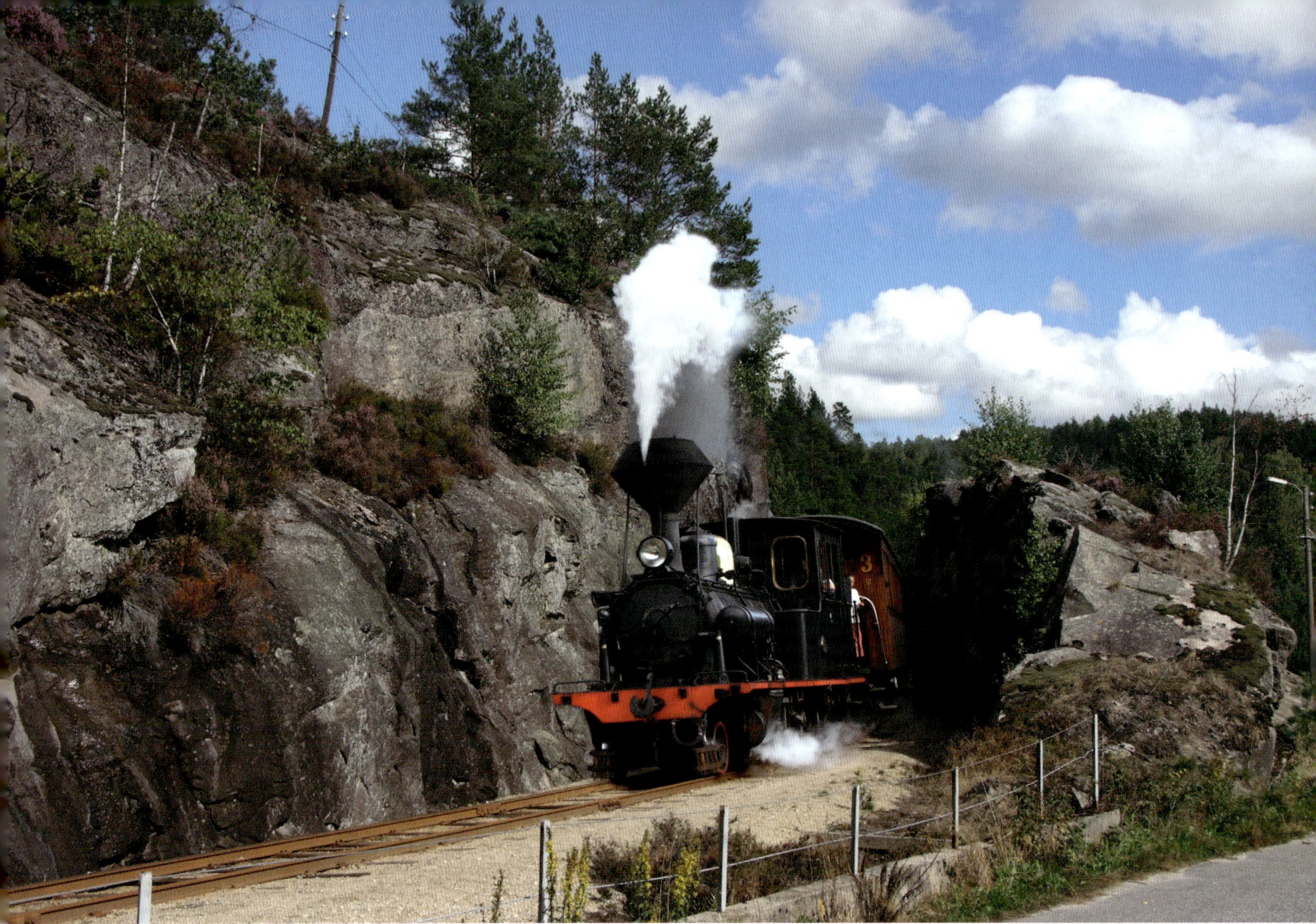

Above: No 5 passes through a rock cutting near Grovane on 24 August 2008. In 1898 Norway adopted standard gauge for future construction. Over the years all the 3ft 6ins lines were widened or closed and the Setesdalsbanen had become the last survivor when services ceased in 1962. A short section north from Grovane reopened as a heritage railway in 1964 and more recently was extended to Røyknes, 8kms away.

Opposite above: No 5 and 2-4-2T No 6 (Thunes 7/1901) stand outside Grovane shed on 24 August 2008. They're copies of the Dübs locos. The section north of Grovane was the only tertiary railway built by NSB and both types have widely spaced wheels to spread the load on the lightly constructed line. In 1861 Norway was the first country in the world to adopt the 3ft 6ins gauge for a loco-worked railway and until 1898 used it for those lines not providing international connections. Eventually 1,055kms were built, some of them short branches but others with a distinctly mainline character.

Opposite below: British enthusiasts tend to think of these Beyer Peacock 2-4-0Ts, with their sloping running plates, as being quintessentially Manx but the type originated on the NSB 3ft 6ins gauge. There were three classes. No 21 *Alf* (BP 992/1870) was one of six class IIIs built between 1868 and 1871. They were NSB's smallest locos with a weight of just 13.2 tonnes. She spent her working life on the Rørosbanen and was withdrawn in 1923. She has been at the Hamar museum since 1928 and still carries the paint applied during her final overhaul in 1915. The second carriage of her short train is a royal saloon, once used to convey King Chulalongkorn, Thailand's great modernising monarch who oversaw construction of his country's early railways. Built in the USA in 1877, it was NSB's first bogie and first corridor vehicle.

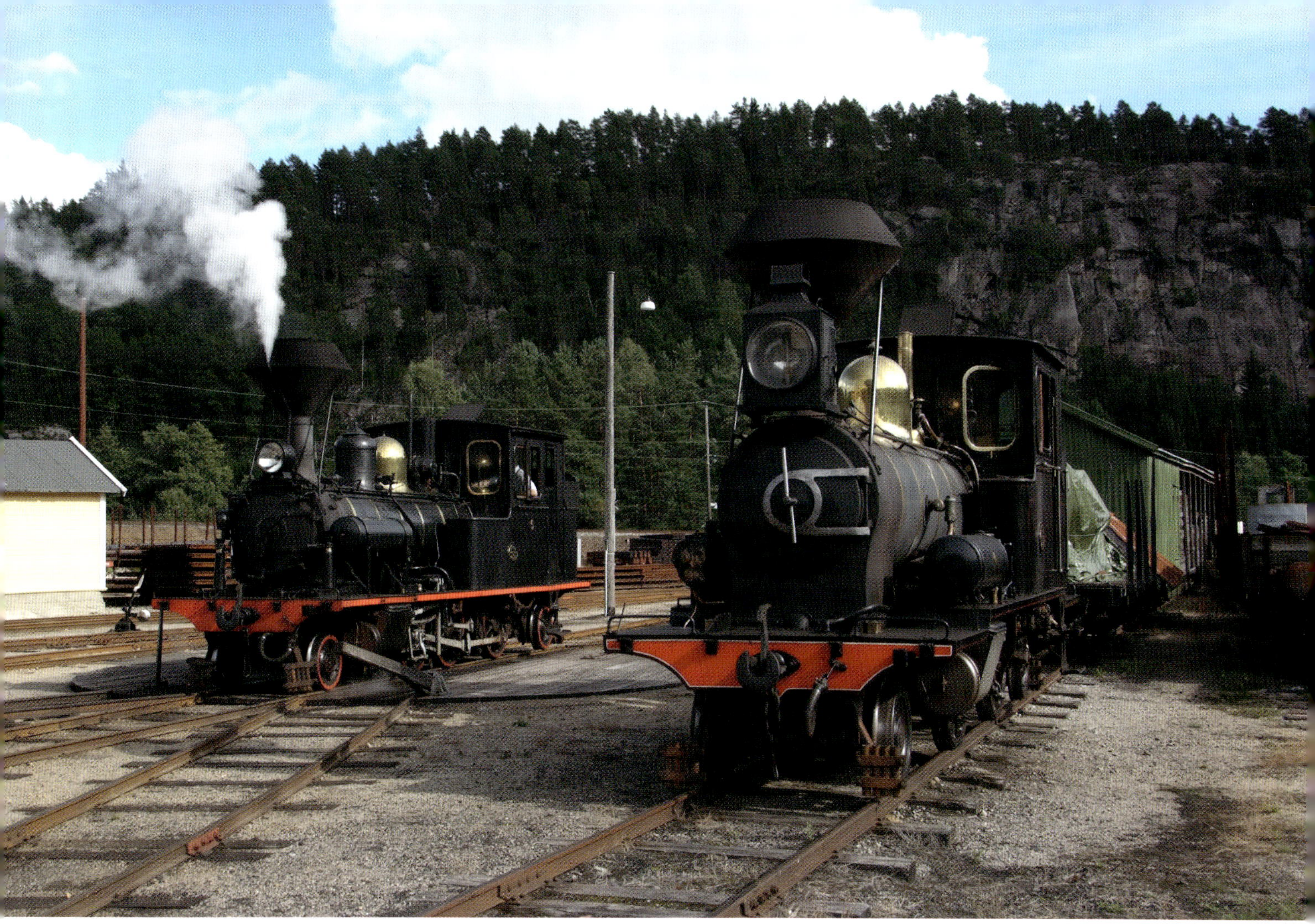

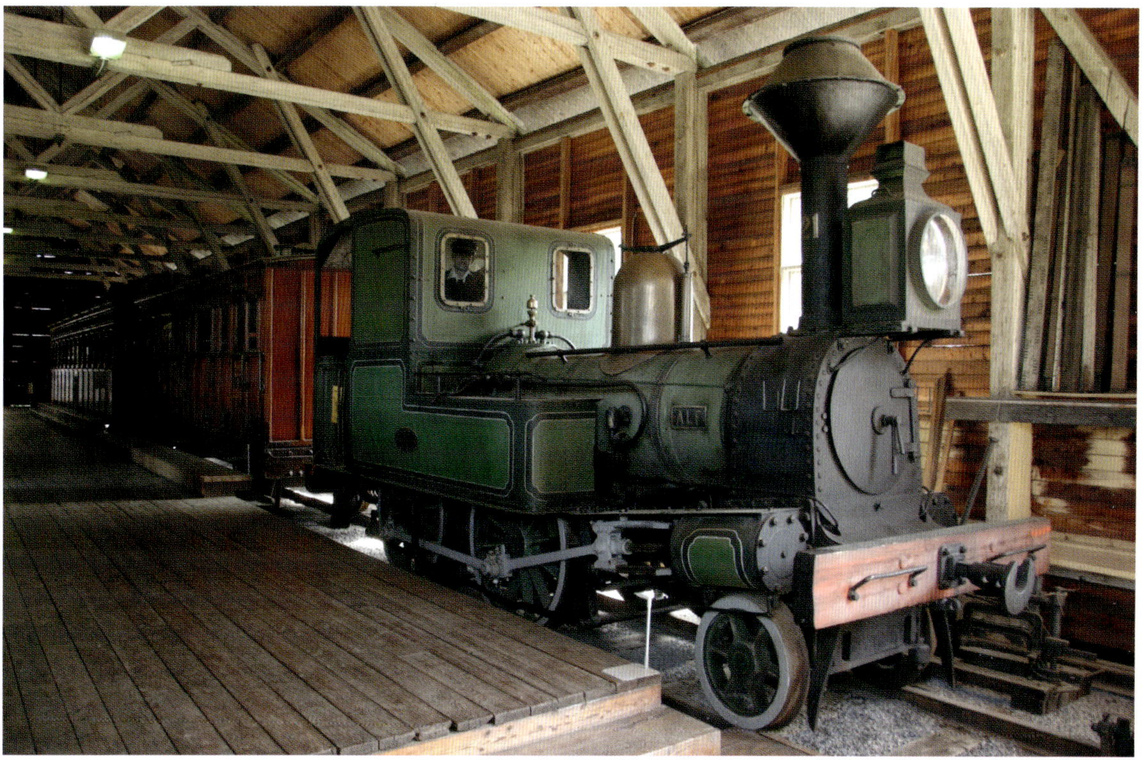

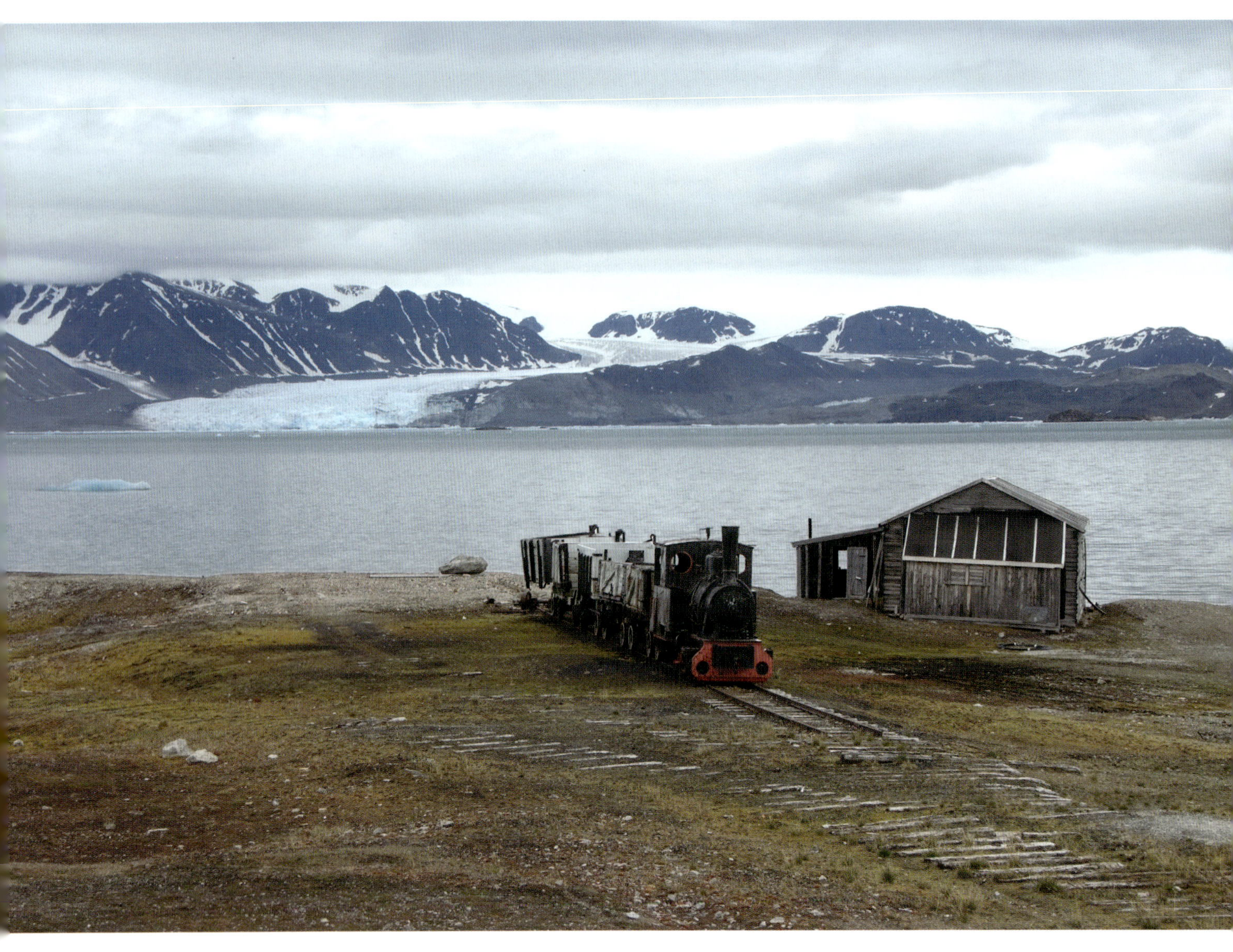

At a latitude of 79 degrees, Ny Ålesund, in north western Svalbard, is the world's most northerly settlement with an all-year-round population. Its old colliery's 900mm gauge 0-4-0T No 2 (Borsig 7095/1909) stands next to the old harbour on 21 July 2008 with its short train and there are remains of other lines all around. There are many 'most northerlies' here including the post office, the North Pole Hotel and the disused colliery as well as the train. The railway operated between 1917 and about 1958. No 2 came second-hand from Salangsverket in northern Norway and was the colliery's first loco when she arrived on 12 July 1917.

SWEDEN

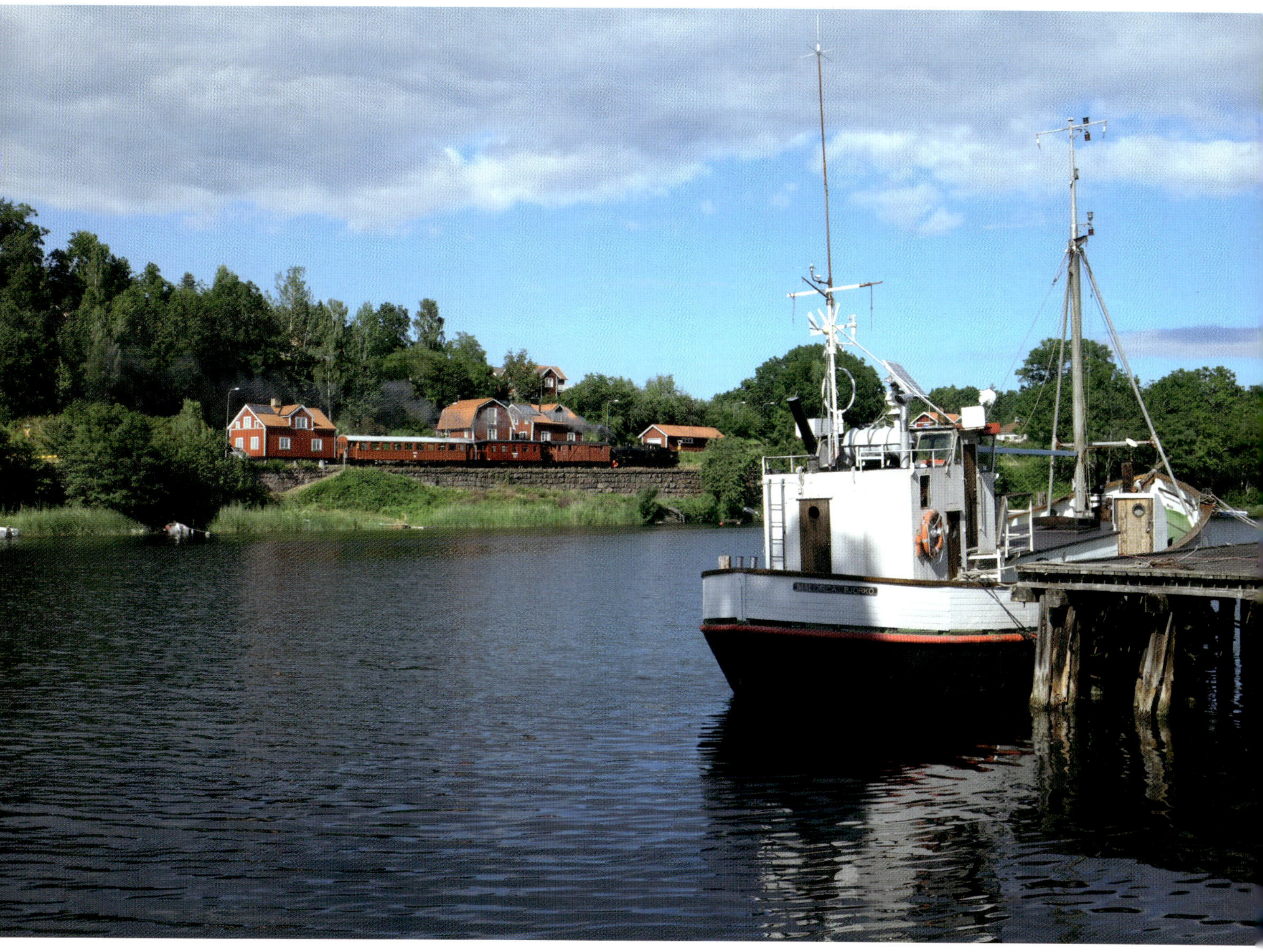

2-6-0 No 3147 (Nohab 848/1907) of SJ, the Swedish state railway, runs beside the estuary at Verkebäck on the 891mm gauge Hultsfred-Västervik Järnväg on 11 July 2015. The line opened in 1879 and was nationalised in 1941. Everyday passenger services ended in 1984. The loco has spent her entire life on the line. She was rebuilt by SJ in the 1950s with a superheated boiler and a winter-friendly cab which considerably altered her appearance so it's right that she's preserved with her SJ number.

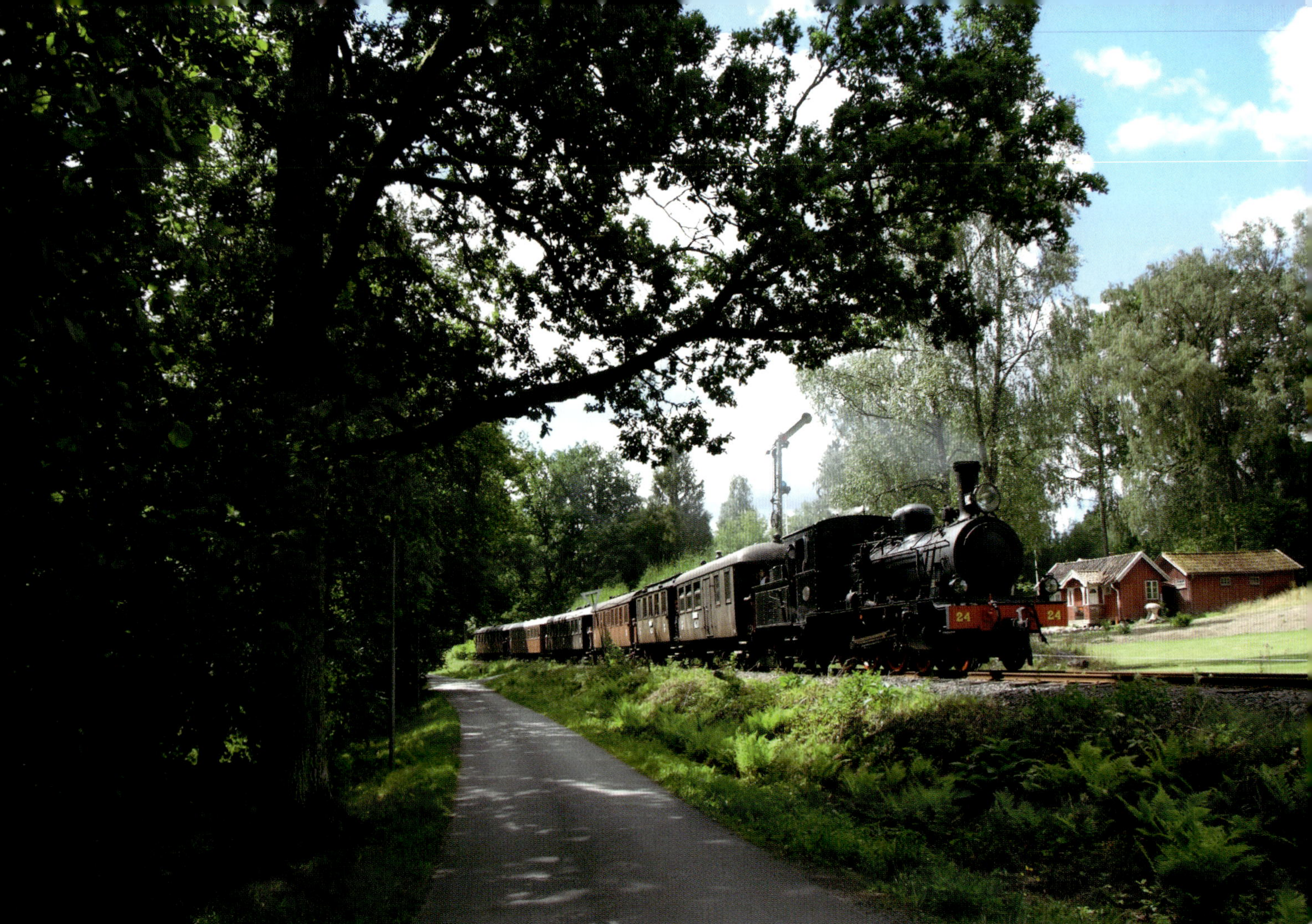

Above: The Västergötland-Göteborgs Järnvägar's 4-6-0 No 24 (Nohab 982/1911) approaches Gräfsnäs on the Anten-Gräfsnäs Järnväg on 17 July 2008. The VGJ ran a secondary 891mm gauge mainline north east out of Gothenburg along with several branches and altogether its system was over 400kms long. After nationalisation in 1948 a steady decline set in and by 1987 the entire network had closed. The AGJ, part of the old mainline, is one of two sections which are now run as heritage railways.

Opposite above: VGJ No 4 (Motala 193/1898) hauls her train along the Skara-Lundsbrunns Järnvägar, the other heritage section, on 17 July 2007. It has the use of the extensive running shed and workshops at Skara, the VGJ's main operating centre. The 891mm gauge, equal to three Swedish feet, was first used on a short line at Hjo on Lake Vattern in 1873. It was soon adopted for most of Sweden's narrow gauge railways and eventually extended for 3,030kms. The only significant exception was in the far south east where a 3ft 6ins gauge network about 600kms long was built from 1874.

Opposite below: The Jädraås-Tallås Järnväg is the surviving section of the 891mm gauge Dala-Ockelbo-Norrsundet Järnväg which ran for 86kms between Linghed and Norrsundet on Sweden's east coast and opened in 1876. Timber and metal ores for export through Norrsundet provided its main traffic. Its motive power included three of these 0-6-6-0 Mallets. No 12 (Atlas 113/1910) crosses the river near Tallås on 22 July 2006.

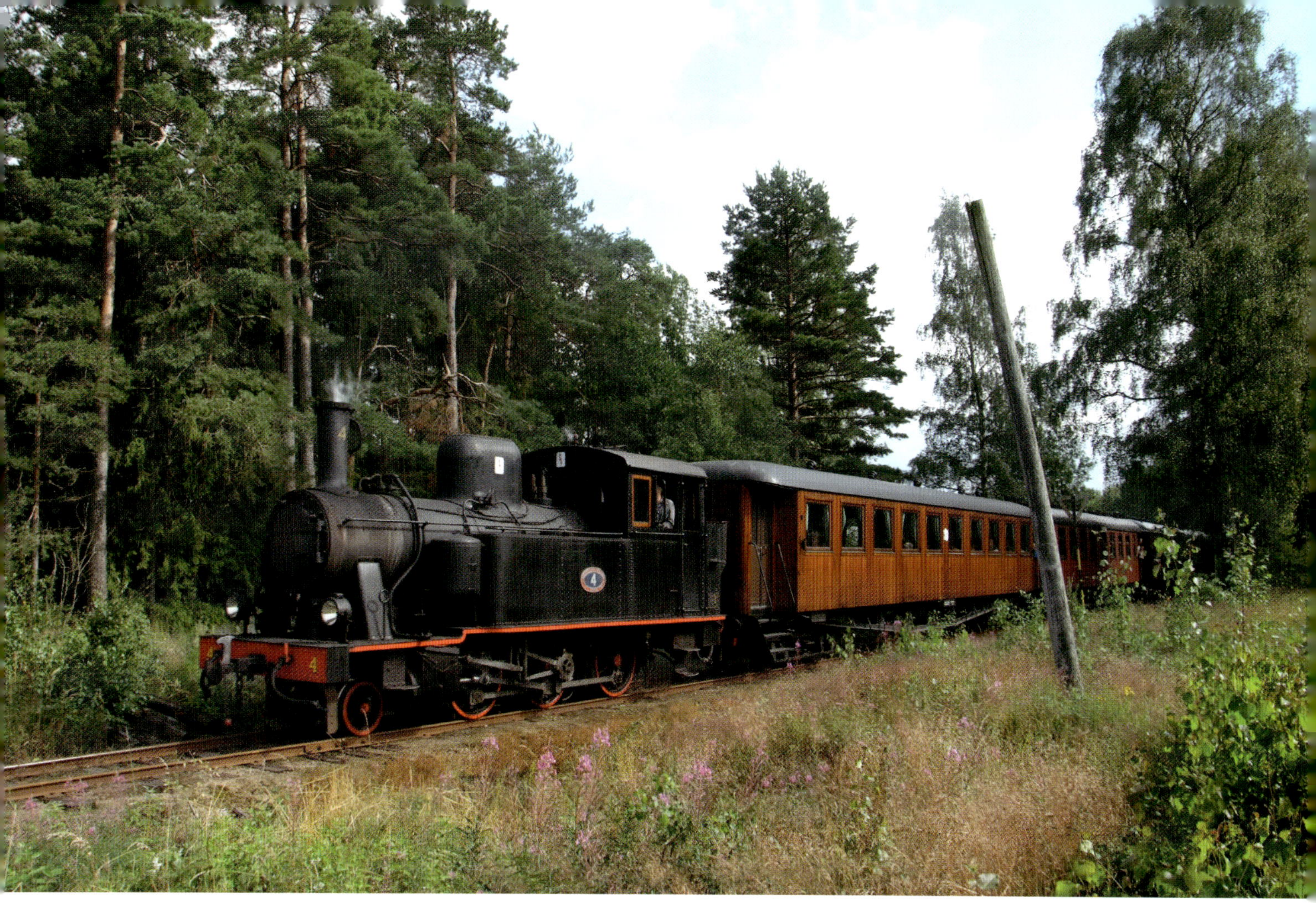

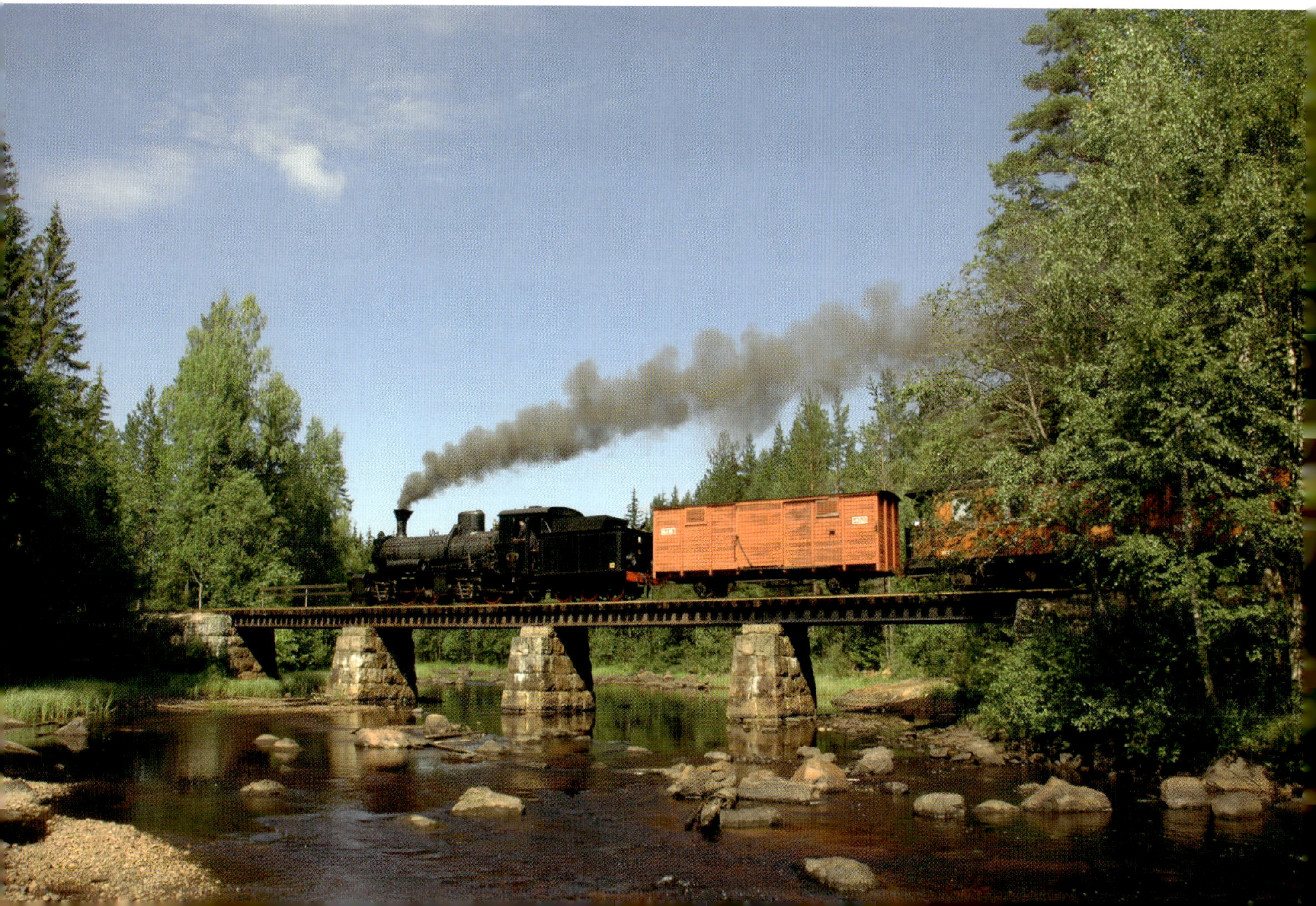

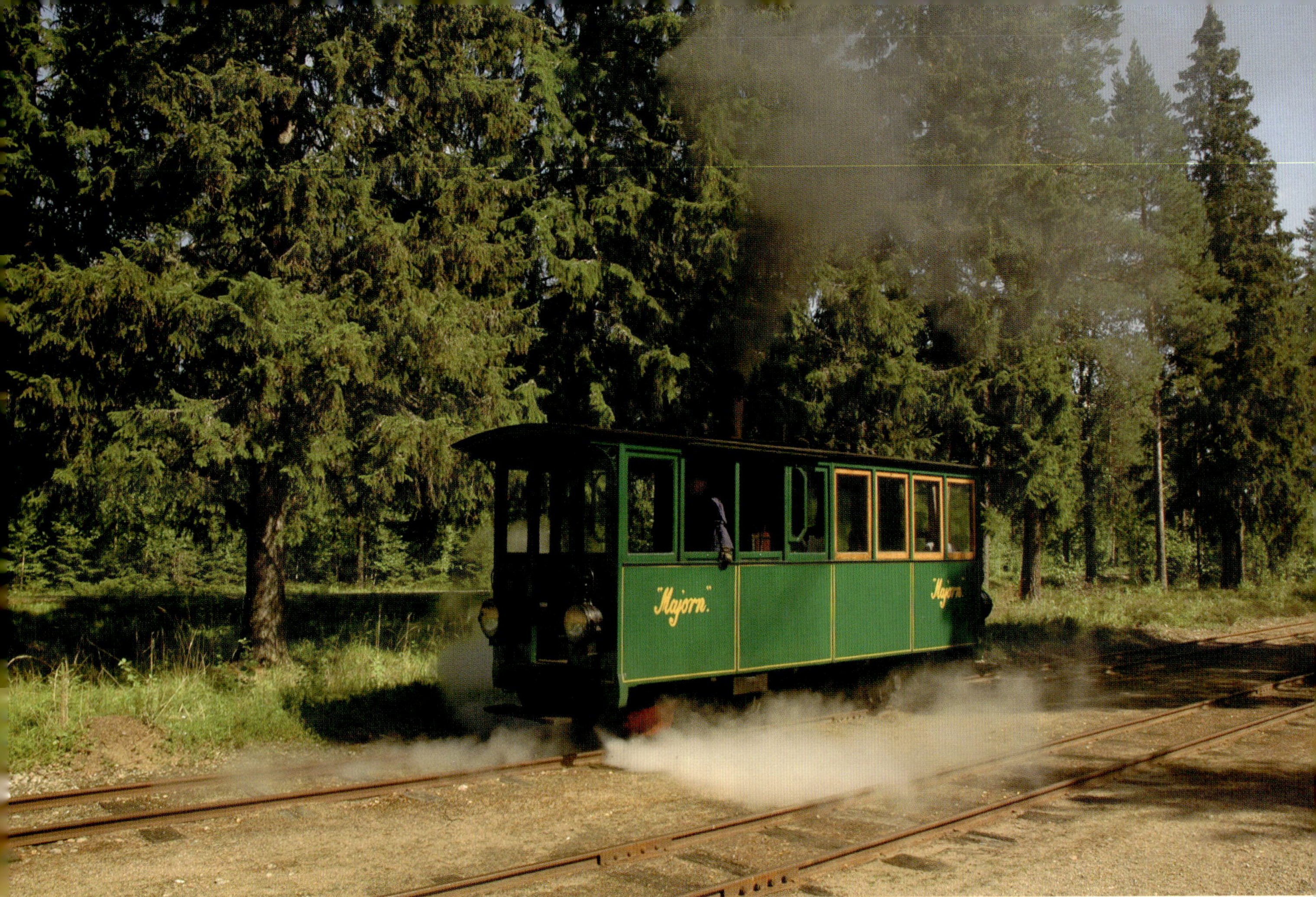

Above: The line closed to passengers in 1959 and to freight in October 1970, after which the JTJ immediately took over the section between Jädraås and Tallås along with much of the rolling stock. In 2004 they extended it for 1.5kms from Tallås to Svartbäcken. Here the DONJ's steam railcar *Majorn* (Atlas 18/1888) sets off from Pallanite on 22 July 2006.

Opposite above: On 14 July 2016 2-8-0 No 5 *Thor* (Falun 107/1909) approaches Faringe, the eastern terminus of the Uppsala-Länna Järnväg. The 891mm gauge ULJ incorporates the oldest part of the Stockholm-Roslagens Järnvägar which opened in 1876. Its network served the district northeast of Stockholm and was once more than 300kms long. It was nationalised in 1951, closures began in 1960 and by the late 1970s it had all been abandoned apart from two lines close to Stockholm which today offer a busy electrified commuter service. The ULJ reopened as a heritage railway in 1977. *Thor* was built for the Byvalla-Långshyttans Järnväg and came to the ULJ in 1974. The SRJ once had a similar loco, its No 10, but she was scrapped in 1961.

Opposite below: This tiny steam inspection car, built in the DONJ's workshops in 1898, stands at Jädraås shed on 22 July 2006. Jädraås was the old line's operating base and the shed is one of several historic buildings which survive there.

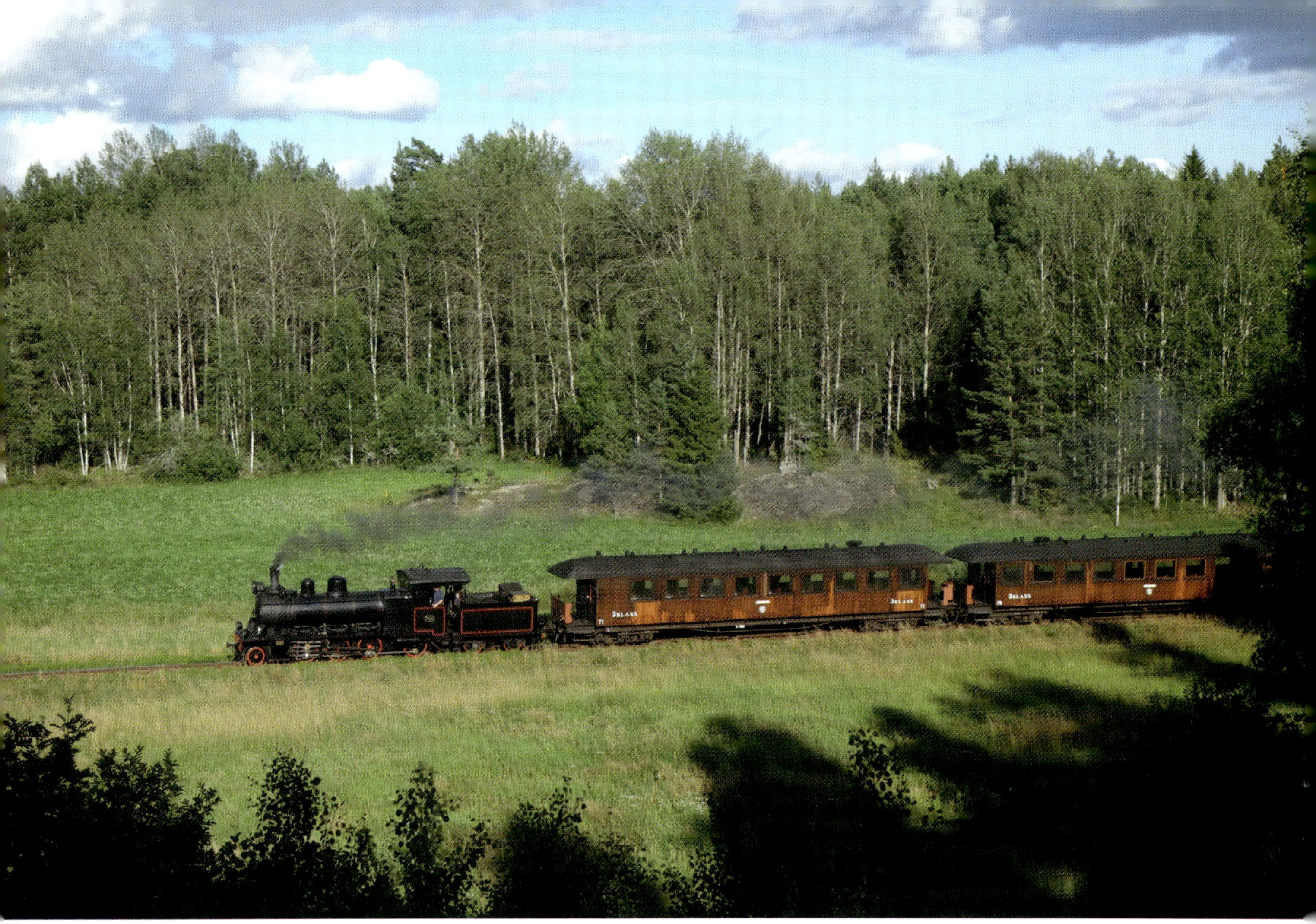

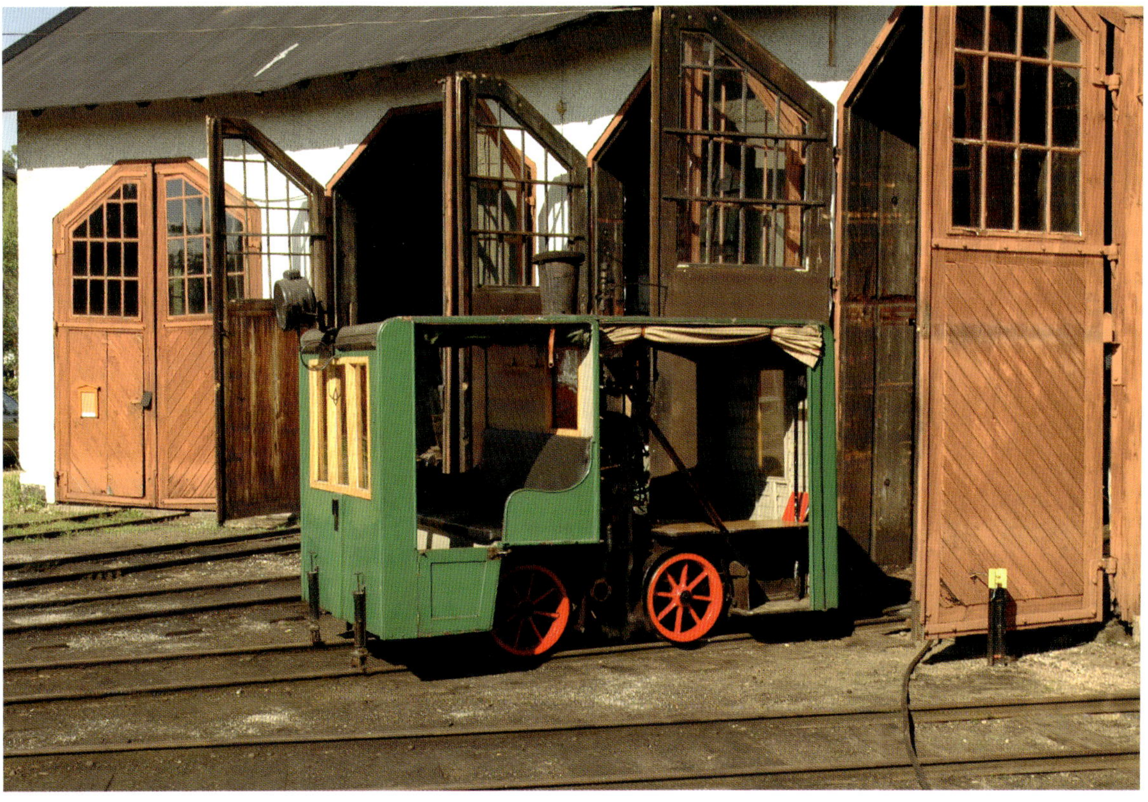

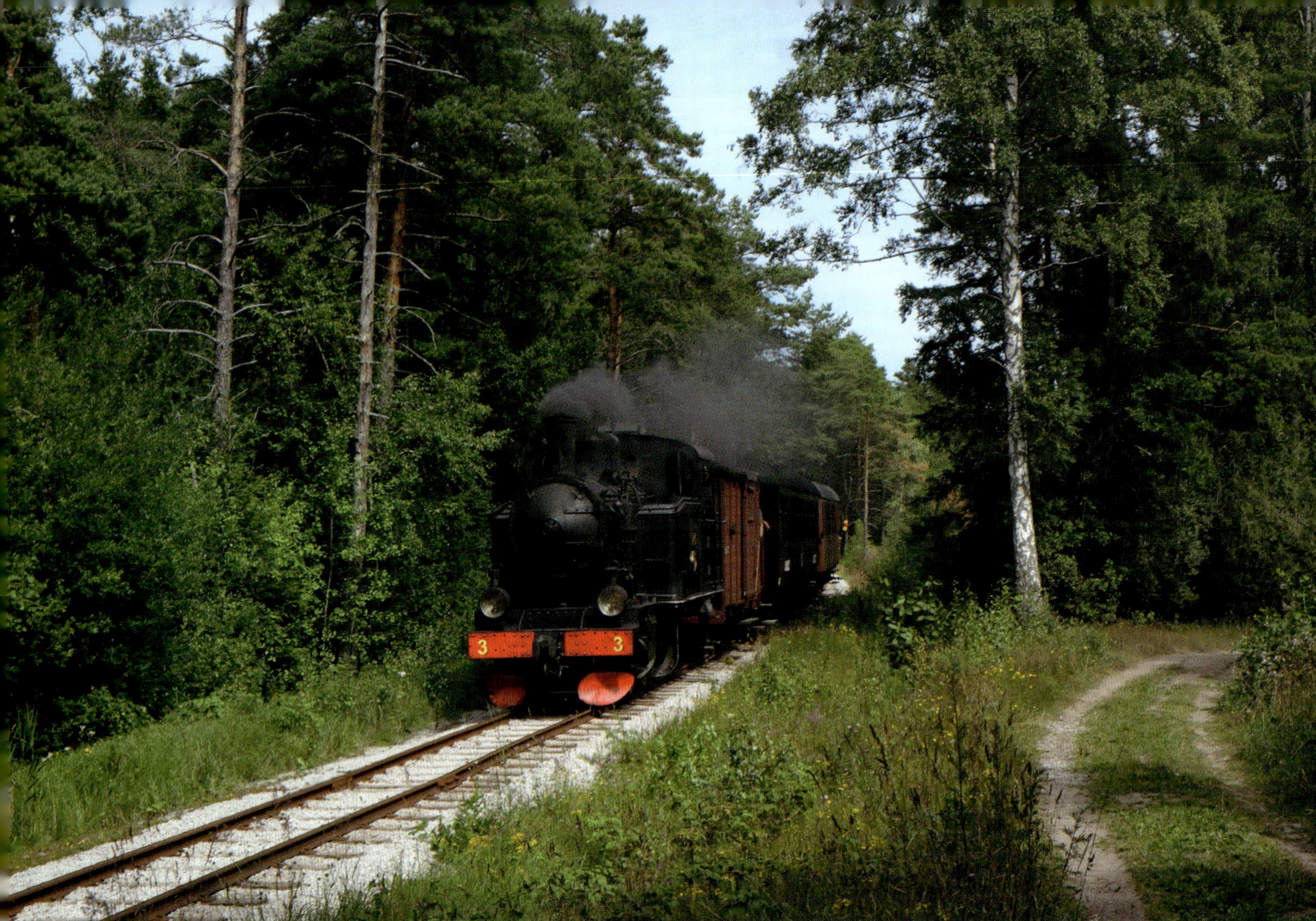

Above: Slite-Roma Järnväg 2-8-0T No 3 *Dalhem* (Henschel 18152/1920) has just left Tule on the Gotlands Hesselby Järnväg on 26 July 2017. Gotland, the large island in the Baltic Sea between the Swedish mainland and Latvia, was once home to several independent 891mm gauge railways which were all nationalised in 1947. Closures began soon after and in 1962 the last section was abandoned. The GHJ began operations on part of the SlRJ's route ten years later. The leading van also came from the SlRJ.

Opposite above: Sweden once possessed several 600mm gauge railways. None have survived but several locos and carriages are preserved at the Östra Södermanlands Järnväg which opened a 600mm gauge museum line in 1964 on the route of the old standard gauge Mariefred branch west of Stockholm. 2-6-2T No 4 *KM Nelsson* (Motala 520/1914) came from the Nättraby-Alnaroyd-Elmeboda Järnväg. No 9 (Motala 568/1915) is similar but came from the Jonkoping-Gripenbergs-Järnväg. Here they approach the harbour station at Mariefred on 26 September 2009.

Opposite below: This 0-8-0T (Hartmann 4290/1919) is a Brigadelok, 2,573 of which were constructed by fifteen builders for the German army between 1905 and 1919. Several found their way into industrial service in Sweden. This one, not completed until peace had returned, worked on the east coast at Emsfors Bruk, near Västervik, probably from new. Here she sets off from Mariefred harbour on 26 September 2009.

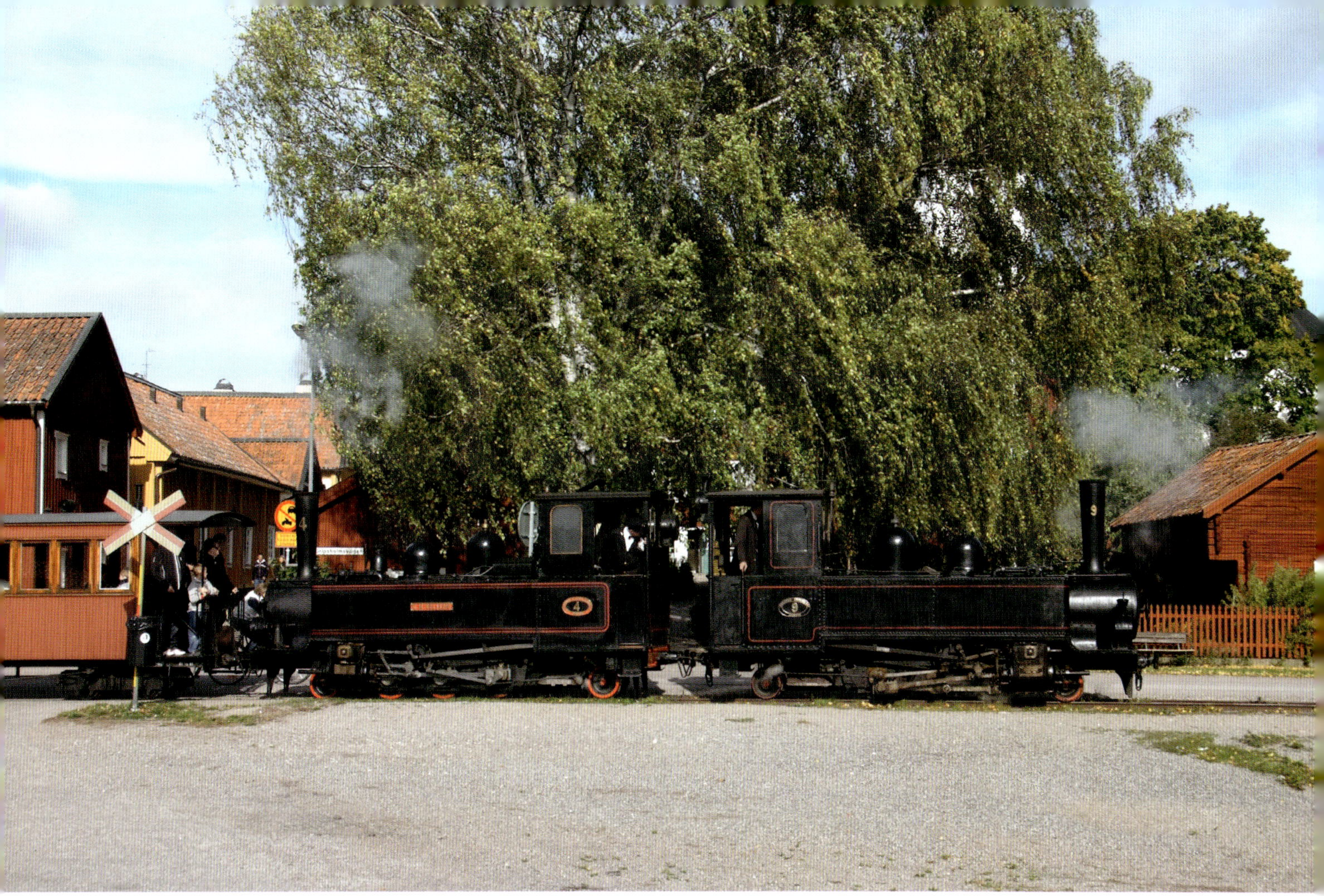

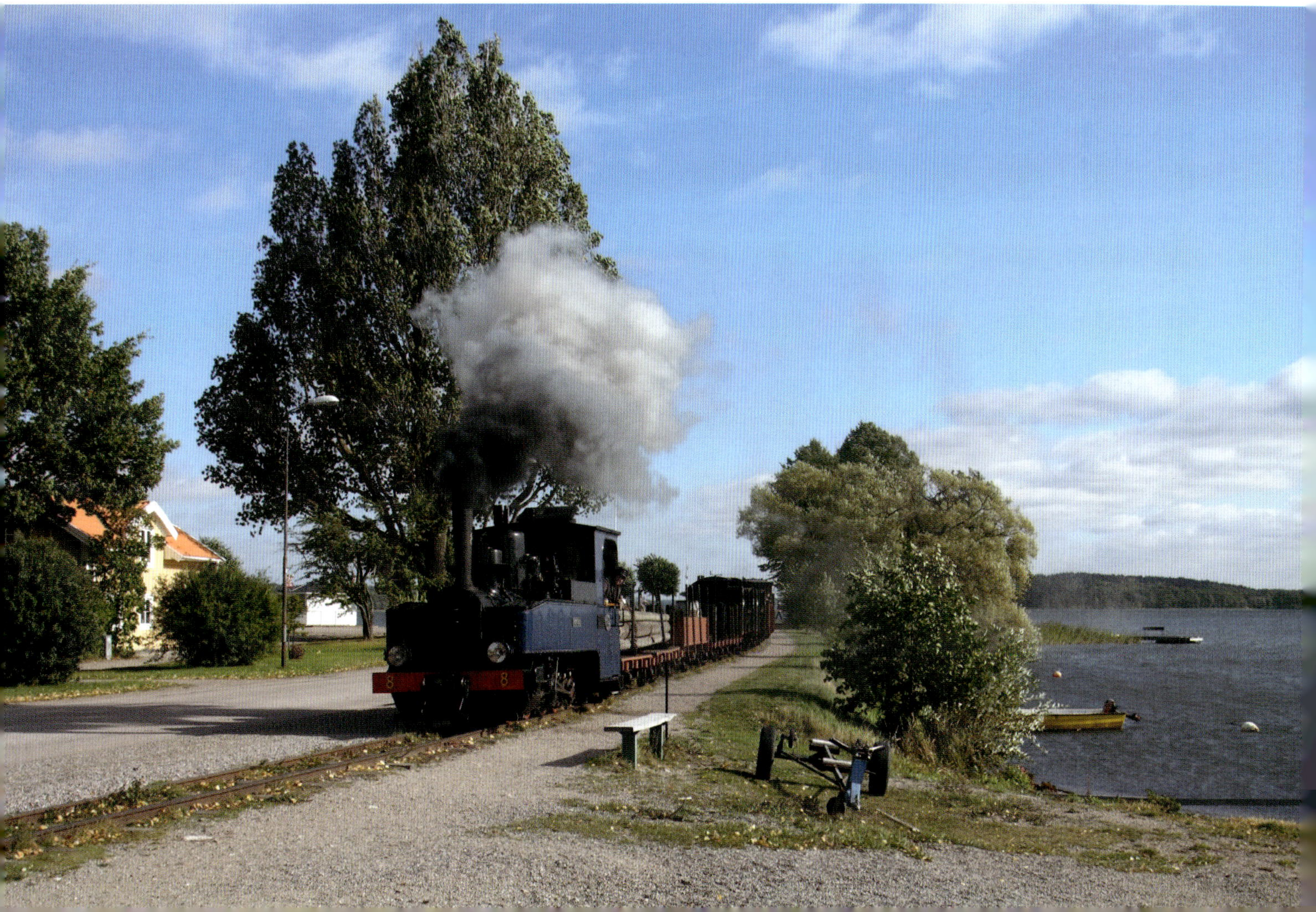

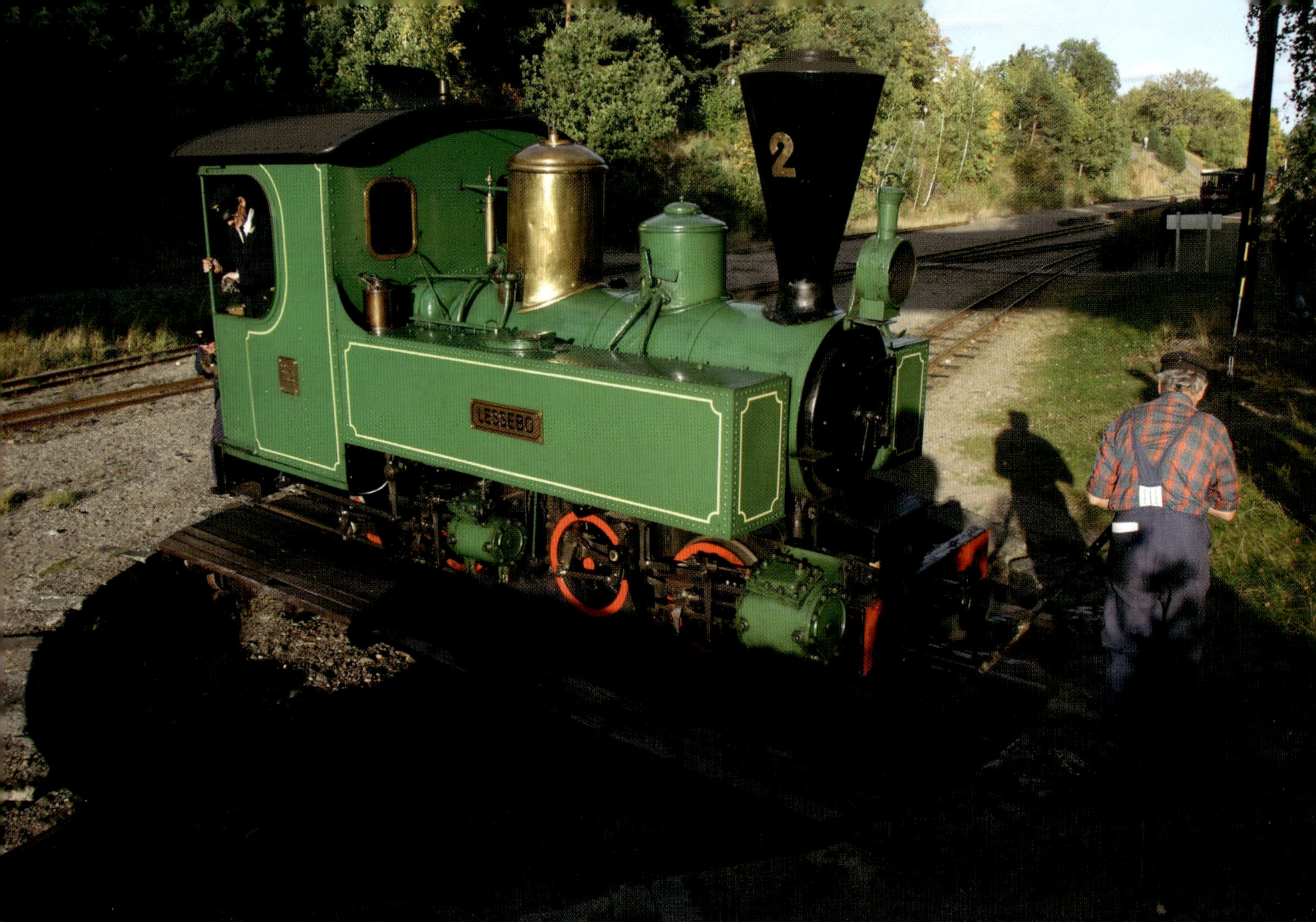

Above: 0-4-4-0 Mallet tank *Lessebo* (Munktells 27/1891) is being turned at Läggesta Nedre on the ÖSlJ on 26 September 2009. She was built to Decauville's pioneer Mallet design and worked for the Kosta-Lessebo Järnväg for many years before moving to the Munkedals Järnväg where she was withdrawn in 1954. She's the only survivor of her type and was on long-term loan from the Sveriges Järnvägsmuseum at Gävle. She has now returned there.

Opposite above: On 21 September 2015 0-4-0T *Vaulunder* (Kristinehamn 17/1876), built for the opening of the Surahammar ironworks railway, stands with her train at the ironworks where they have rested since it closed in the late 1920s. Sweden used several unusual gauges but this one, 1,093mm, must be the oddest of all! It originated on a neighbouring line where it was adopted due to a confusion between British and Swedish feet, the latter being slightly shorter. The ironworks produced carriage and wagon wheels, as its successor in the town still does, and has been preserved as a museum ever since closure.

Opposite below: Many of Sweden's early locos were built in the UK. The 891mm gauge Nordmark-Klarälvens Järnväg's 0-4-2ST No 1 *Ua* (Hughes, 1874) stands at the line's excellent museum at Hagfors on 22 September 2015. Although she has been an exhibit ever since 1931, oil or water seems still to be dripping from her cylinders! Like the Corris Railway's Hughes locos, she started out as a 0-4-0ST and a trailing axle was added after a few years. Behind her are 0-6-2Ts Nos 5 *Lovisa Tranæa* (Avonside 1114/1875) and 7 *Hagfors* (Nohab 175/1883). The NKlJ was electrified between 1921 and 1942 but all of it closed by 1990. Note the typically Swedish turbine spark arresters which in the case of *Ua* probably dates from her reboilering by Nohab in 1918.

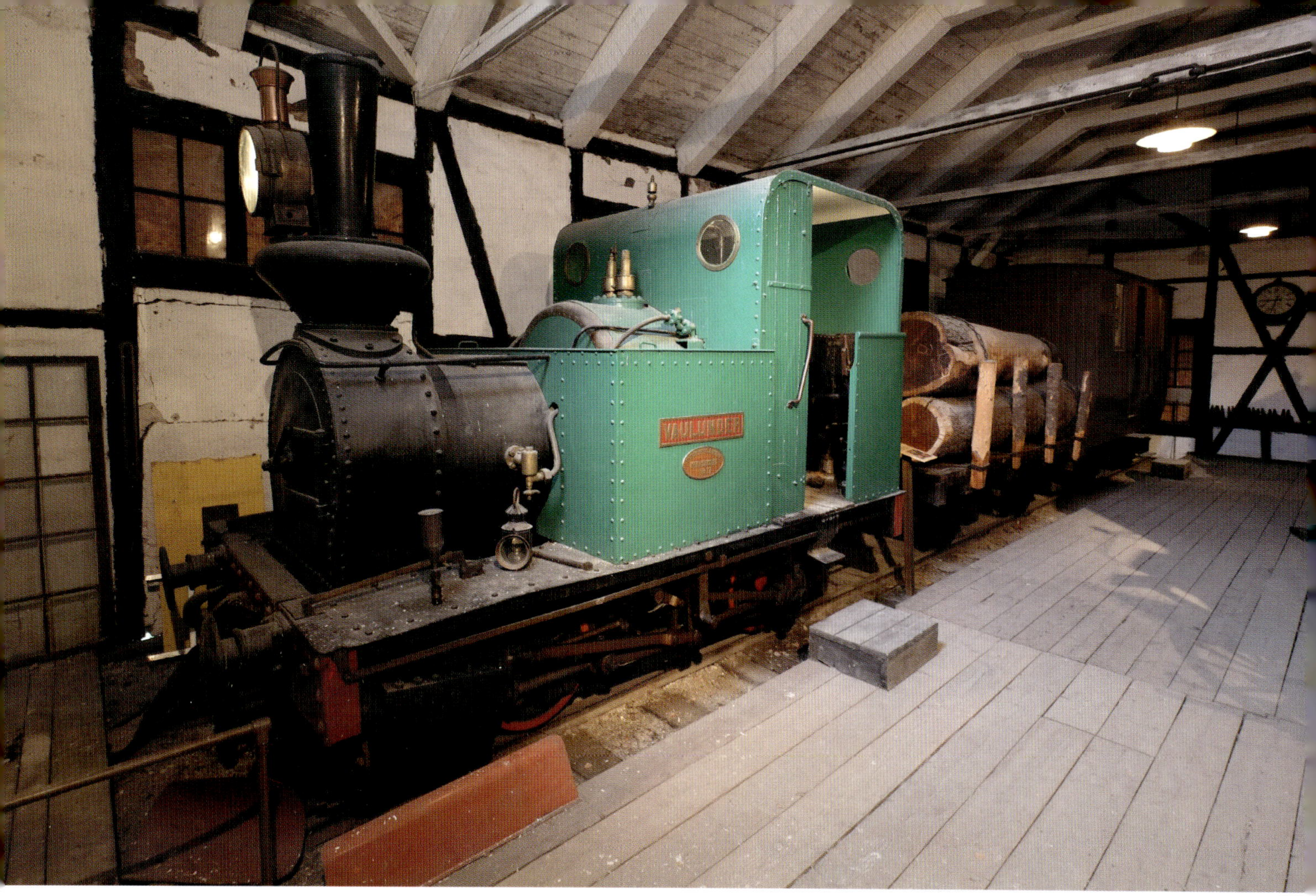

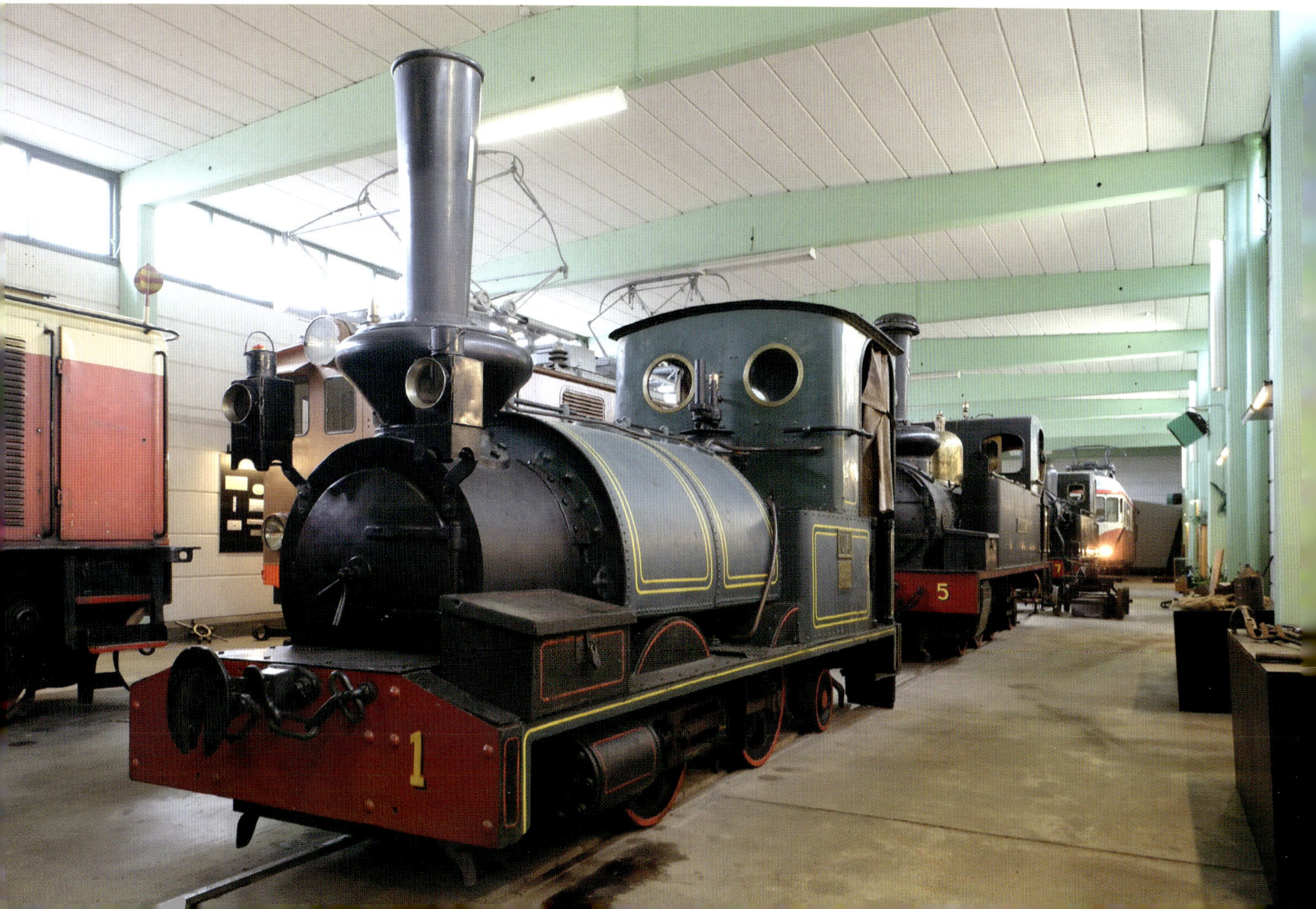

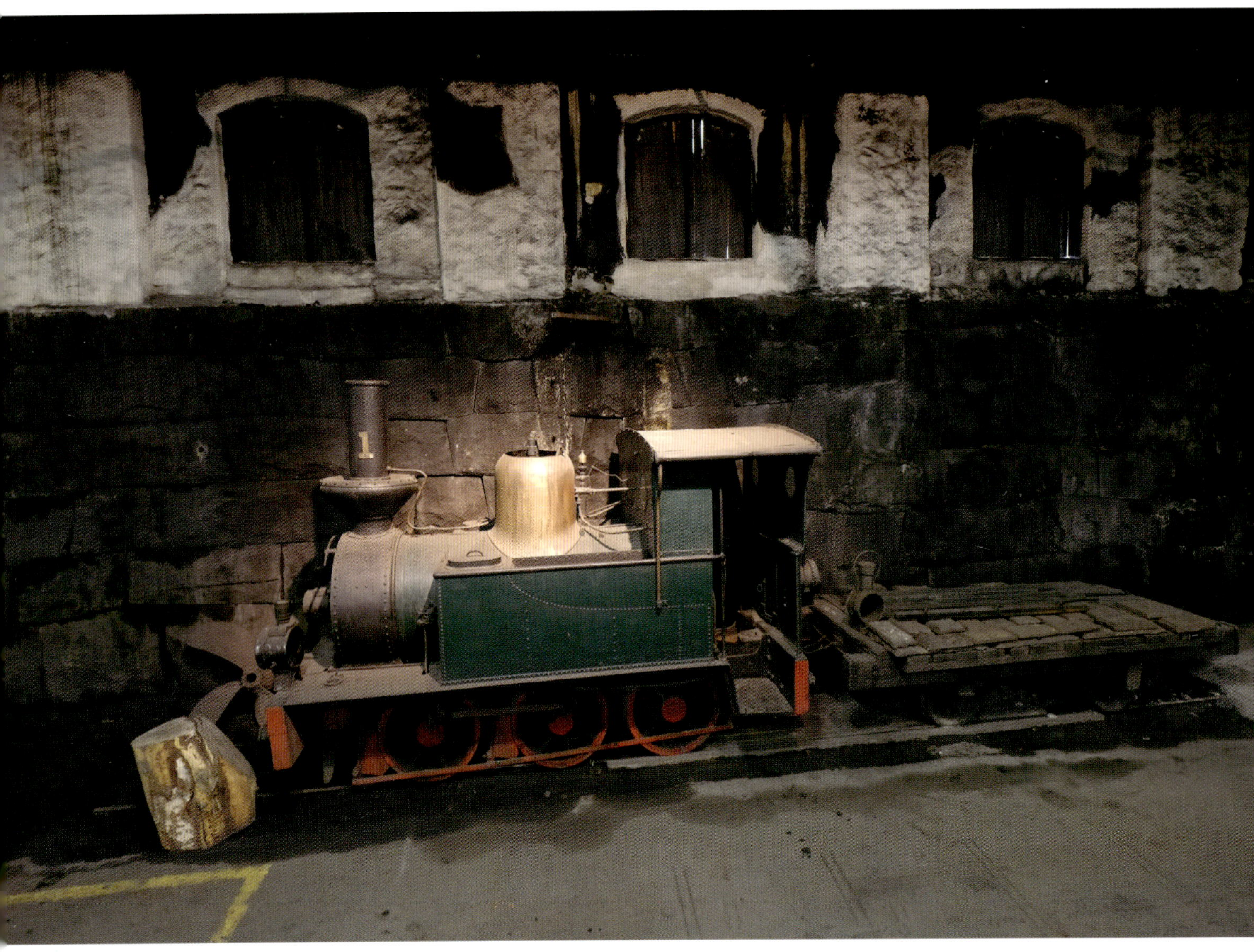

This cumbersome-looking 760mm gauge 0-4-2T is Iggesund ironworks No 2 (Nohab 72/1876), later renumbered 1. After retiring in 1948 she took up residence in the main ironworks hall, built of some of the largest stone blocks I've ever seen! This establishment, on Sweden's east coast, has the unusual distinction of having been destroyed by the naval forces of Peter the Great of Russia in 1721 – and maybe those huge blocks were intended to stop this happening again! Its railway, 8.5kms long, ran from 1874 until 1955, mainly to bring in timber for the furnaces. Here she is on 13 July 2016.

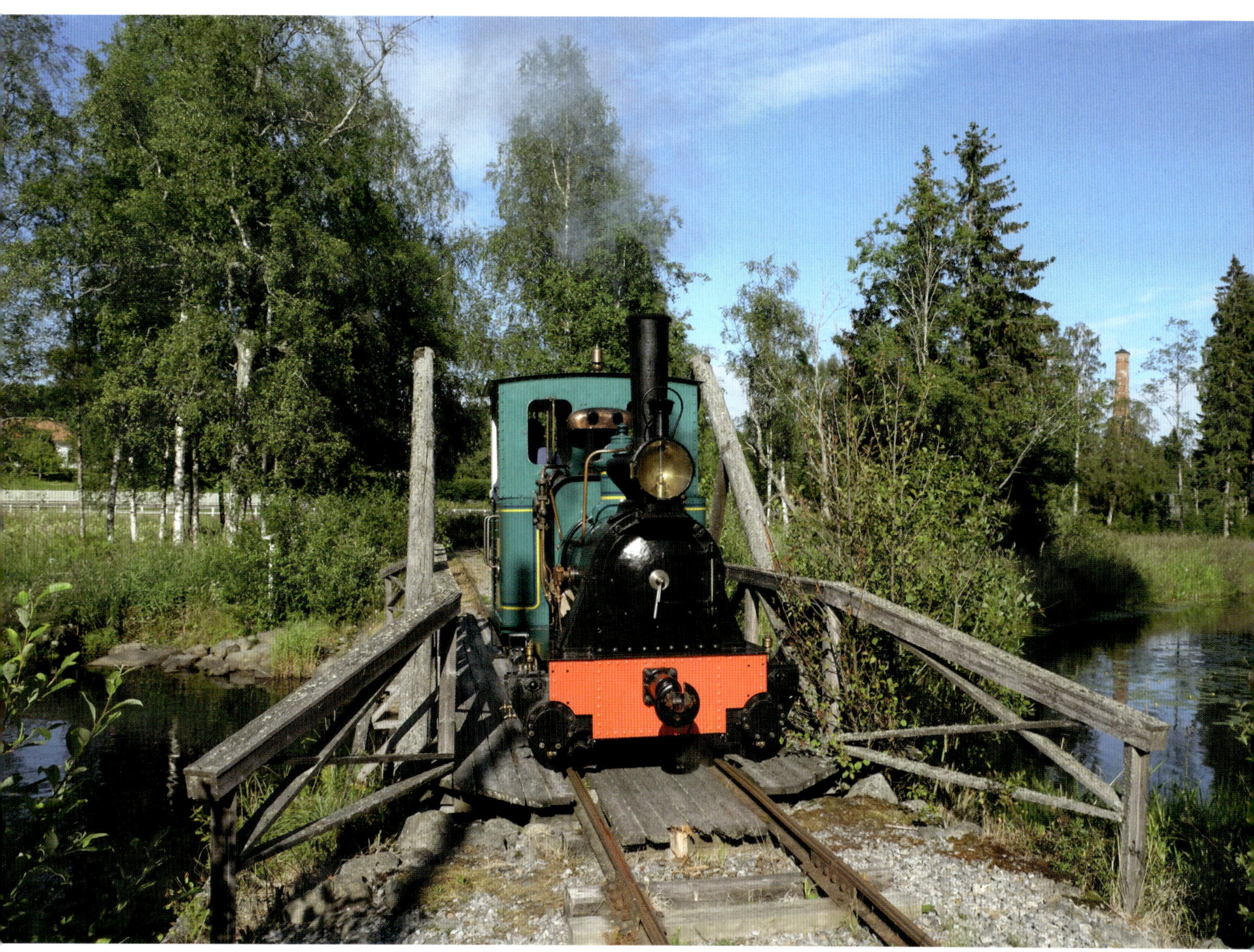

0-6-0T *Loke* (Kristinehamn 45/1887) pauses on a bridge over a small lake to take on water on the sunny evening of 13 July 2016. The Galtströms Bruksmuseum, near the coast about 90kms north of Iggesund, occupies what remains of another small ironworks. A short 891mm gauge railway was built from 1887. *Loke* was its only locomotive and the little line closed in about 1932. I was told that *Loke* only ever had one driver who maintained her in pristine condition. After the closure, he worked hard to ensure her survival, initially by dismantling the track leading to her shed so that the firm scrapping the railway couldn't use her. He kept the key and made surreptitious visits to keep her in good order. She became an exhibit when the Bruksmuseum was set up in 1955 and in 1990 a small group of enthusiasts began to restore her to working order and rebuilt most of the line. Her boiler and some platework are new but otherwise she contains all her original parts. It wasn't difficult to ascertain what her old paint scheme was since she has never been painted in any other way!

FINLAND

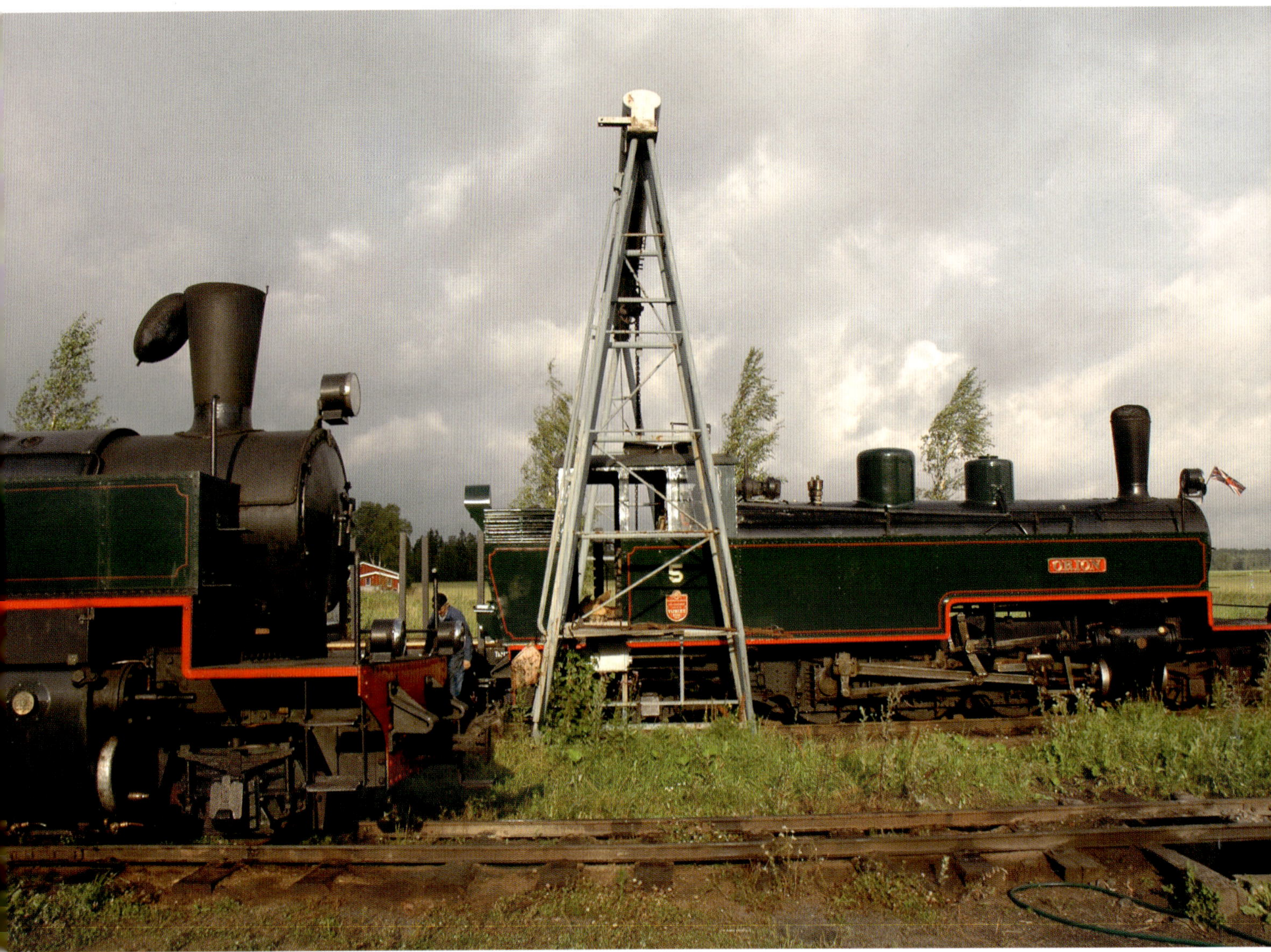

The 750mm gauge Jokioisten Rautatie's Nos 4 (Tubize 2365/1947) and 5 (Tubize 2369/1948) are prepared for service at Minkiö in the early morning sunshine on 29 July 2007, and in the northern summer this means really early! The Jokioisten opened on 25 October 1899. Its first locos, unusually for a European railway, were two Porter Forney-type 0-4-4Ts which weren't scrapped until the Tubize locos had settled in. It lost its previous most modern loco, a 1937-built Henschel 2-6-2T, when the Finns had to provide reparations to the Soviet Union after the Second World War. The railway turned to Tubize because Tampella and Lokomo, the two Finnish builders, were fully committed to building 570 Soviet 750mm gauge PT-4 reparations 0-8-0's.

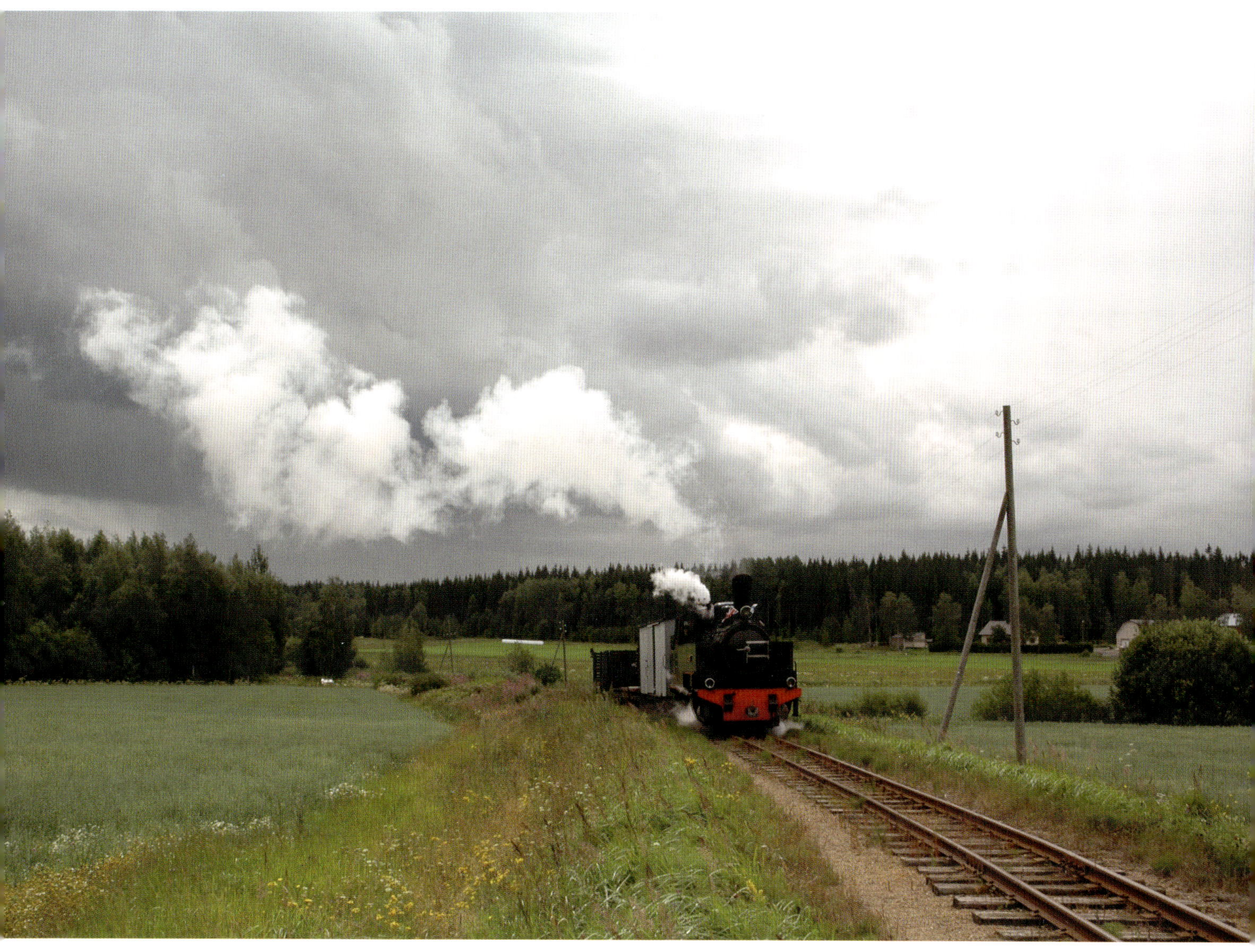

No 5 heads a freight train near Minkiö on 29 July 2007. She was withdrawn in 1964 needing heavy repair but No 4 worked until the old line closed ten years later. Volunteers had run heritage trains since 1971. In 1978, they reopened a section as the Jokioisten Museorautatie and in 1994 extended it back to the mainline junction at Humpilla. No 5 was bought by a UK enthusiast in 1972, mainly to keep her out of the hands of the scrapmen, and ended up on the Welshpool & Llanfair where she was restored to working order in 2000. Six years later, the W&L generously sold her to the Finnish group and here she's still carrying the Finnish and British flags with which she was sent off from Wales nine months earlier.

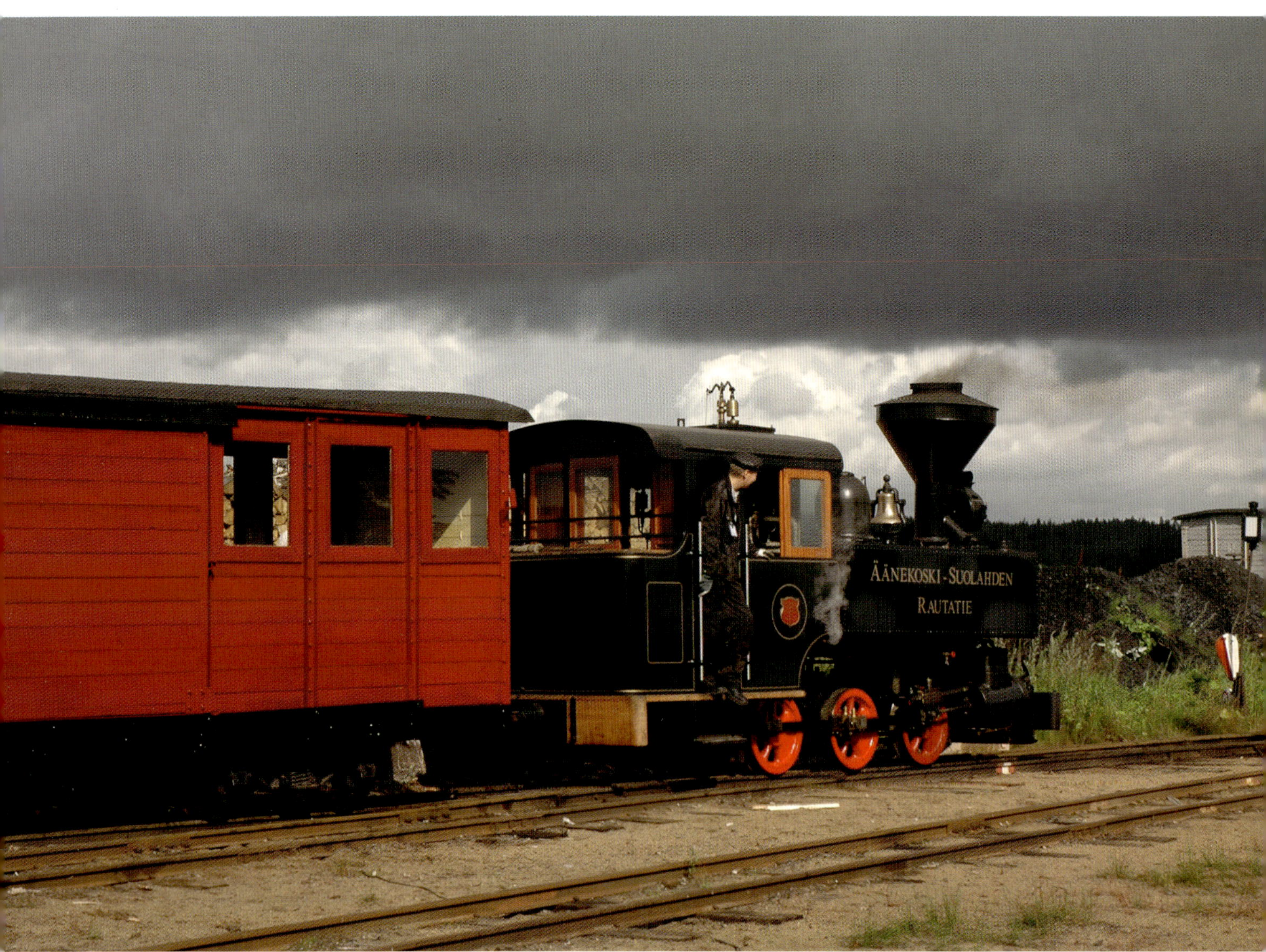

The museum railway is also home to several locos from Finland's other narrow gauge lines. The little Äänekoski-Suolahti Rautatie opened in 1901 and ran until 1943. 0-6-0T No 1 (Porter 2313/1901), the larger of its two Porters, shunts in Minkiö yard on 28 July 2007 just before the heavens opened! In 1943, she moved on to Äänekoski paper mill's internal railway, working until 1964, after which she served for a final two years as a stationary boiler. She was given to the Jokioisten's enthusiast group in 1972 along with locos Nos 3, an OK-built fireless machine, and 4, a diesel, and this rudimentary coach which the ASR converted in 1902 from a German-built van to supplement its only purpose-built one. No 1's bell came from one of the old Porter Forneys as the original was missing. She's now lettered and lined in gold paint but when she was new gold leaf was used, which must have looked very exotic!

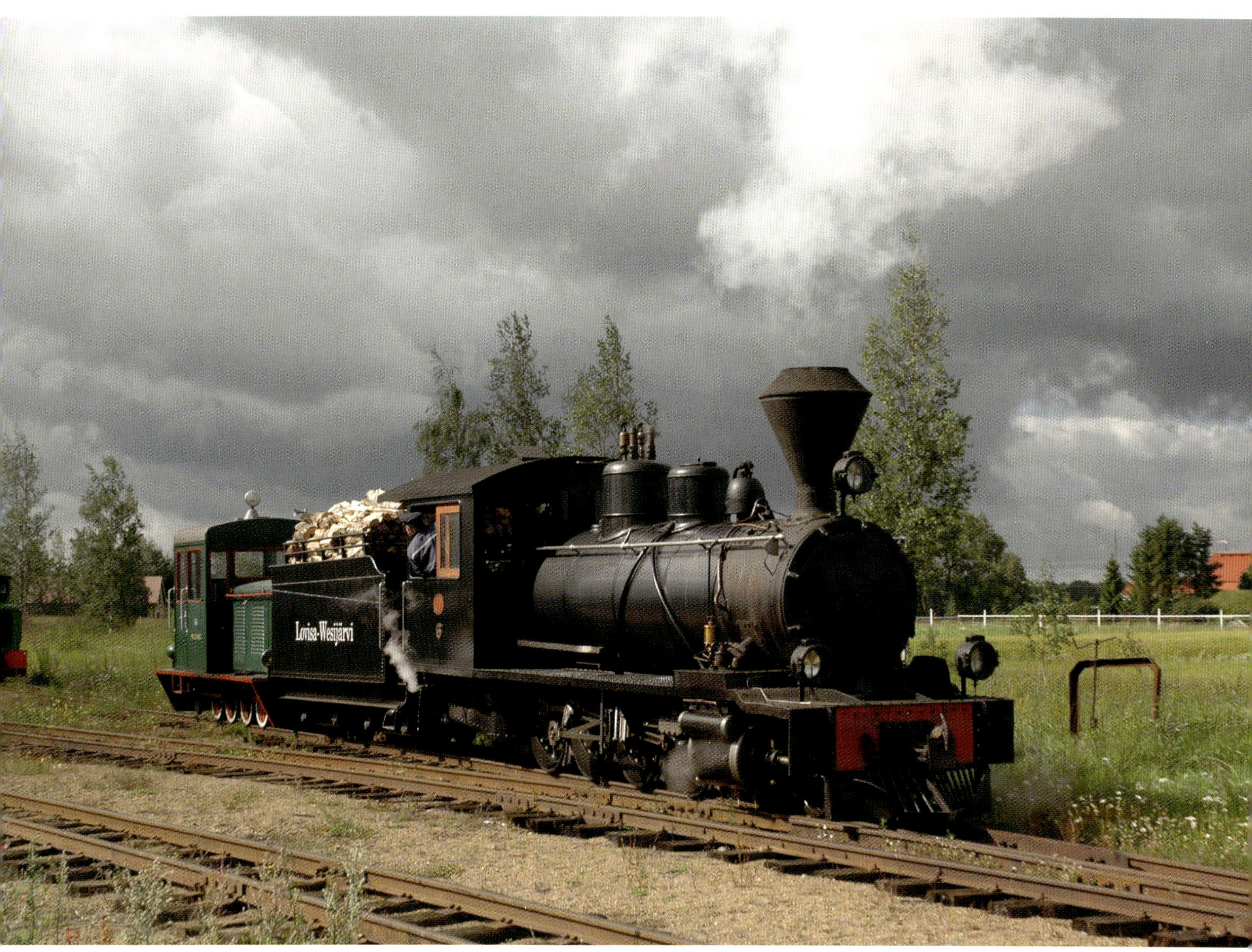

Loviisa-Vesijärvi Rautatie 2-8-0 No 6 (Tampella 141/1909) at Minkiö on 28 July 2007. The loco she's shunting is a Move 21, originally a PT-4 variant fitted with a wood-gas generator feeding an i/c engine. Seventy-six were built between 1946 and 1952 as part of the Soviet reparations commitment. No doubt they promised economical operation in the Russian forests, but few lasted long, mainly because the reparations order didn't include spares for the unusual power system. Ten stayed in Finland, reportedly after failing Soviet quality controls, and were converted to conventional diesels. Three of them served the Loviisa line from 1956 until it was converted to broad gauge in 1960 when they moved to the Jokioisten. In 1967 they were joined by this unnumbered loco (Valmet 63/1948), made redundant when the Hyvinkää-Karkkila Rautatie closed. She moved away into private preservation in 1974 and had only just returned. Now she and two of the former Loviisa locos are the only survivors.

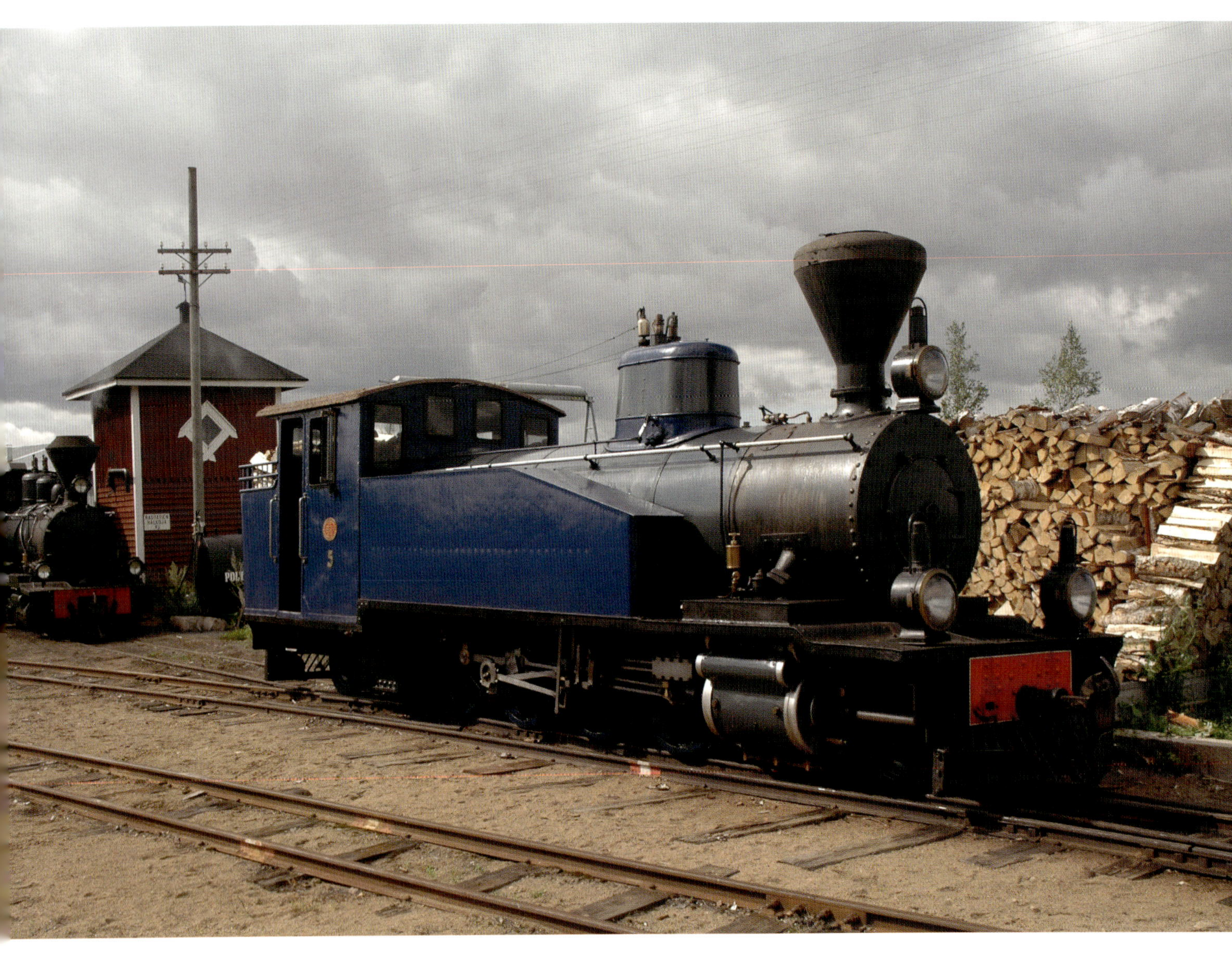

This beautiful blue 2-8-2T, the Hyvinkää line's No 5 (Tampella 289/1917) stands in Minkiö yard on 28 July 2007. She was the Jokioisten group's first loco when they started operations on the old line in 1971. Other locos stored at the back of Minkiö shed awaiting restoration include another Loviisa 2-8-0 and a pretty Tampella-built 0-6-2T which started out on the Lohjan Sähkörautatie and later moved to the Harvialan Metsärautatie. Jokoisten No 3 (Lokomo 22/1922), a generally similar loco, was scrapped after the Move 21's arrived from Loviisa in 1960. Hyvinkää, incidentally, is home to the superb Suomen Rautatiemuseo, Finland's national railway museum and Hyvinkää 2-8-2T No 3 is on show at Karkkila.

RUSSIA

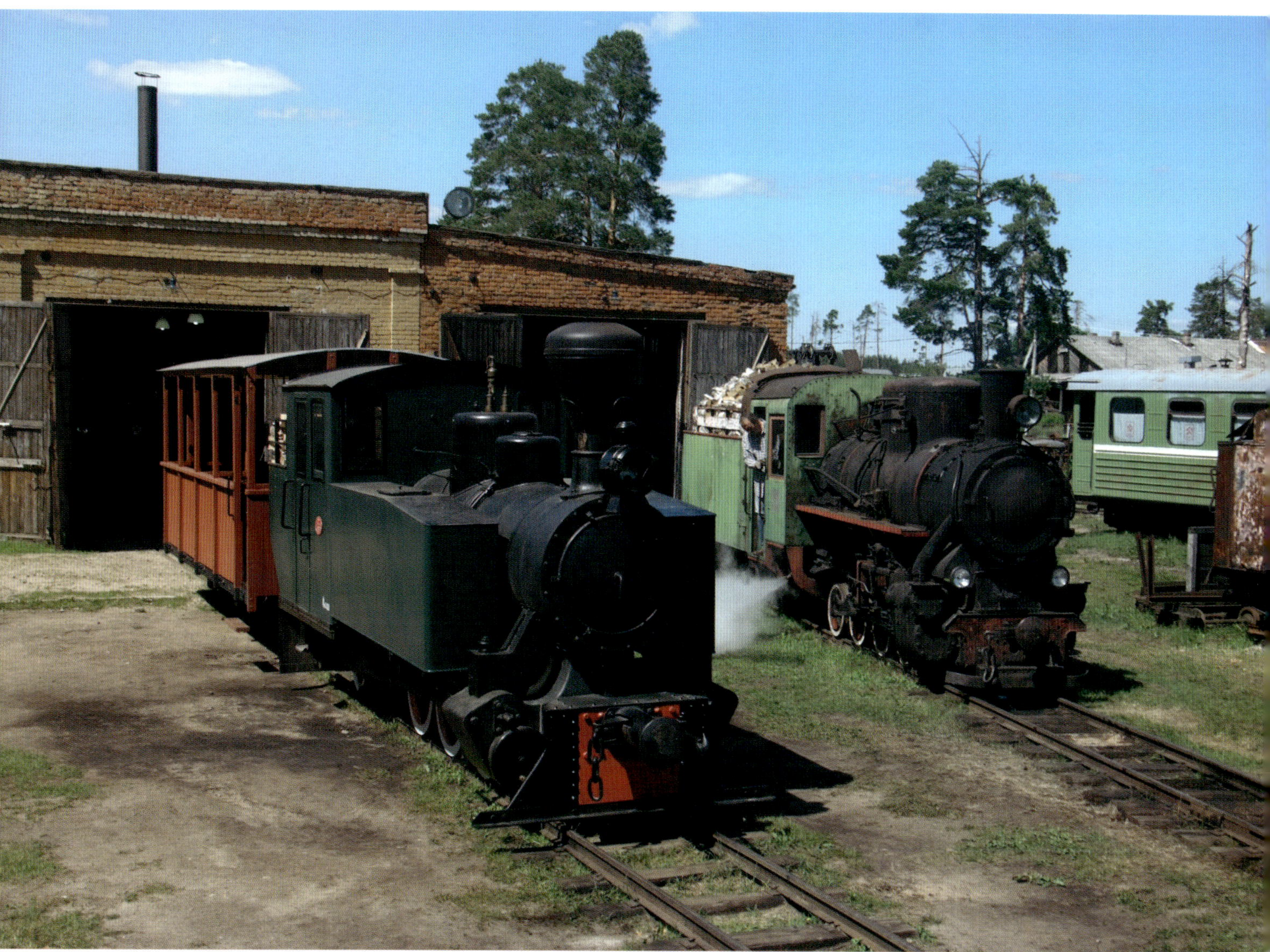

750mm gauge 0-6-2T No F^t-4-028 (Tampella 559/1945), another Finnish reparations machine, and PT-4 0-8-0 No K^p-4-469 (Chrzanów 4384/1957) stand together on 21 June 2012 at the superb Pereslavl narrow gauge museum which occupies the shed and yard built in 1948 at an old peatery at Talitsy, 130kms north of Moscow. The PT-4s were developed from the pre-war 159 class 0-8-0s which had proved to be underpowered. Mass-production got under way with the Finnish reparations locos and the Finns supplied twenty more on a free trade basis. No K^p-4-469 was one of 790 delivered to the Soviet Union by Chrzanów in Poland. She spent her working life at a sleeper creosoting plant at Zeleny Dol in Tatarstan before arriving at Talitsy late in 1990.

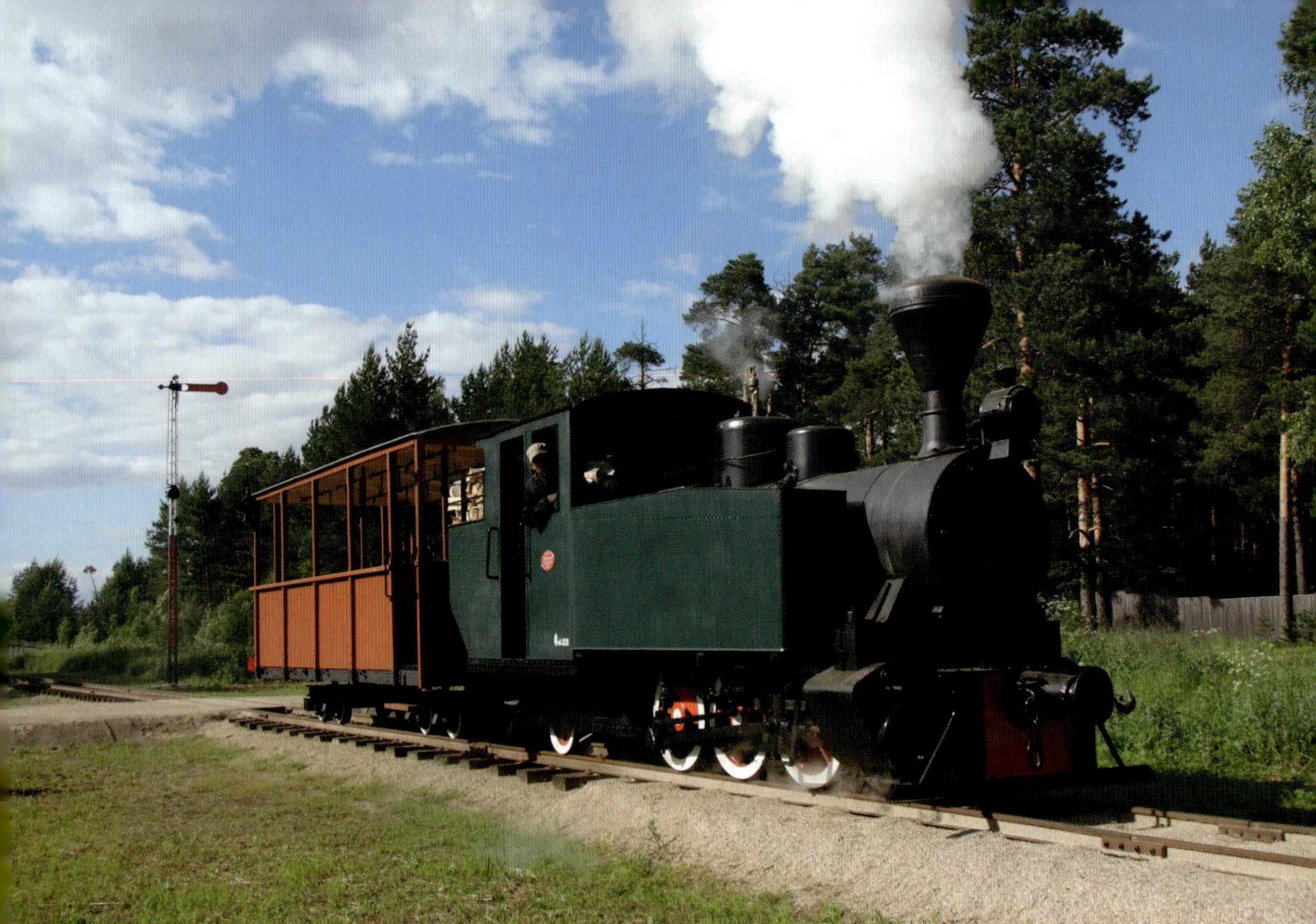

Above: No F^t-4-028 heads away along the old Talitsy branch on 18 June 2012. The thirty F^t-4s were developed from an earlier Finnish design similar to Jokioisten No 3. They seem to have been ordered as a stopgap while the detailed design of the PT-4s was being finalised in the light of experience gained with nine prototypes constructed in 1941. This loco worked in a tufa quarry in Armenia and later went into store at Leninakan where she was lucky to survive an earthquake in 1988 before becoming the museum's first loco in 1990. The Jokioisten society very helpfully supplied the original builders' drawings during a thorough rebuild completed in 2011, along with technical info such as the code for the correct shade of paint – the dark green standard for Finland's mainline steam locos.

Opposite: PT-4 0-8-0 No K^p-4-430 (Chrzanów, probably built in 1957) has spent her entire life on the 750mm gauge Nizhny Novgorod children's railway and here stands at the magnificent station at Rodina on 1 August 2009. Russia's children's railways, or pioneer railways as they were called in socialist days, are intended to enthuse children and to educate them in railway operation. Most are 750mm gauge and differ markedly from the old Soviet Union's many other narrow gauge lines since they need to emulate contemporary mainline practice in order to fulfil their educational function. The Nizhny Novgorod railway opened in 1939 and is one of the finest. It was originally more than 9kms long but is now much shorter.

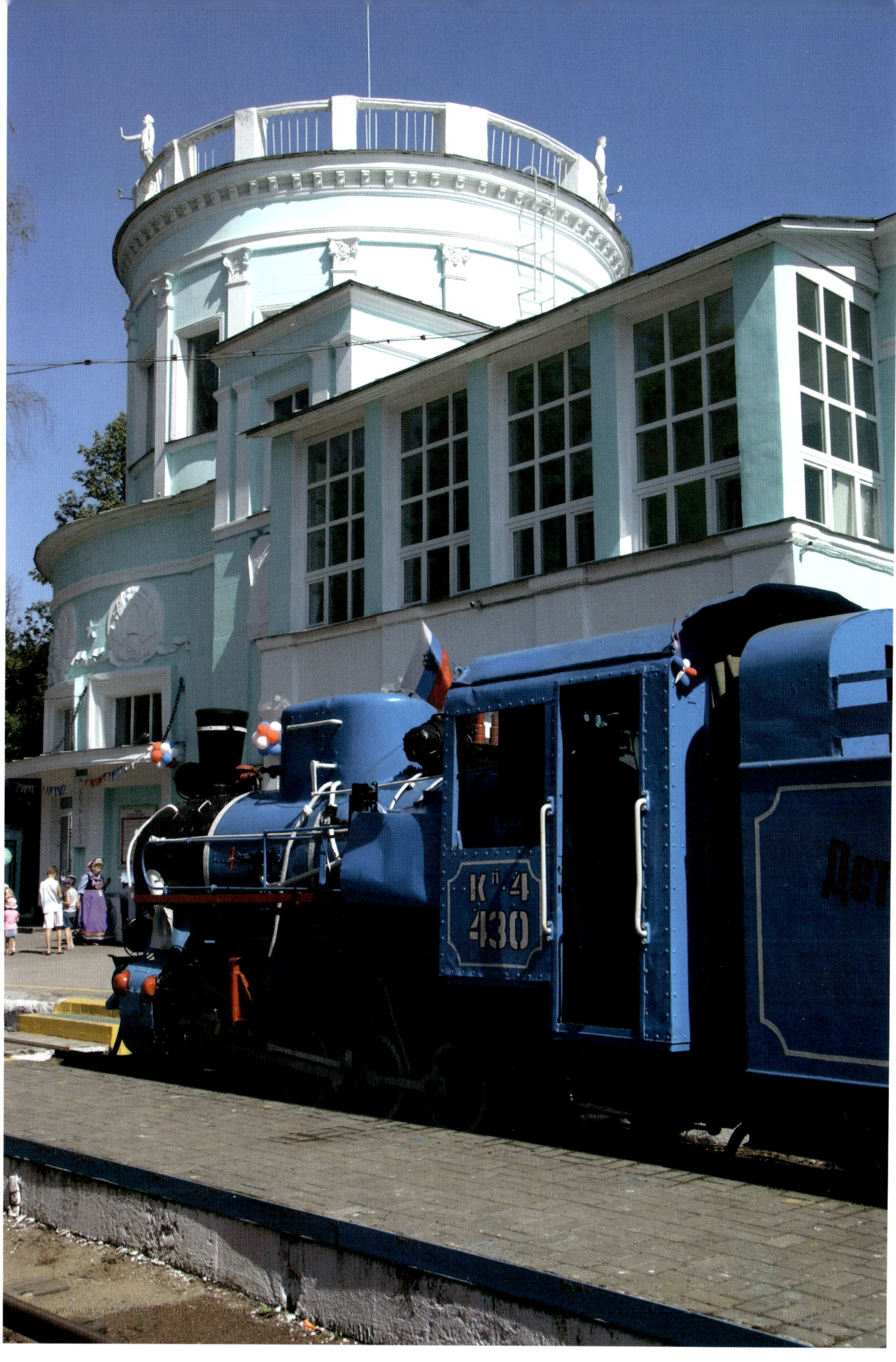
Кп·4
430

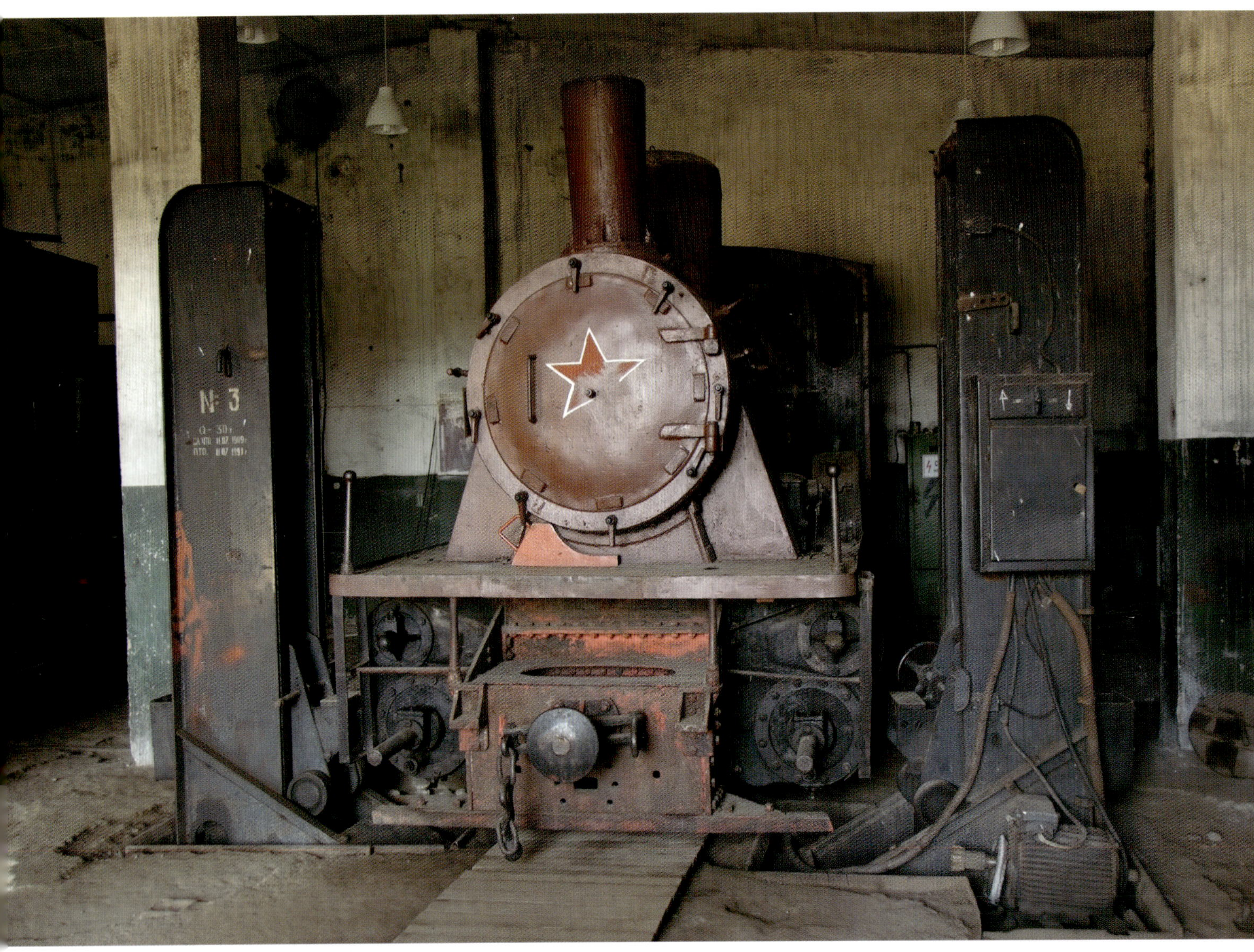

The Soviet Union's 157 class 0-8-0s were larger and heavier than the PT-4s. They dated from 1928 and are widely considered to be the most successful narrow gauge locos the country ever produced. No 157K469 (Kolomna 5674/1928) undergoes restoration in Talitsy shed at the Pereslavl museum on 31 July 2009. The museum once had the use of an old peat and forestry railway which ran into Pereslavl-Zalessky, a historic town popular with tourists. Sadly, political chicanery saw its destruction but the museum owns the branch outright and so its future should be secure.

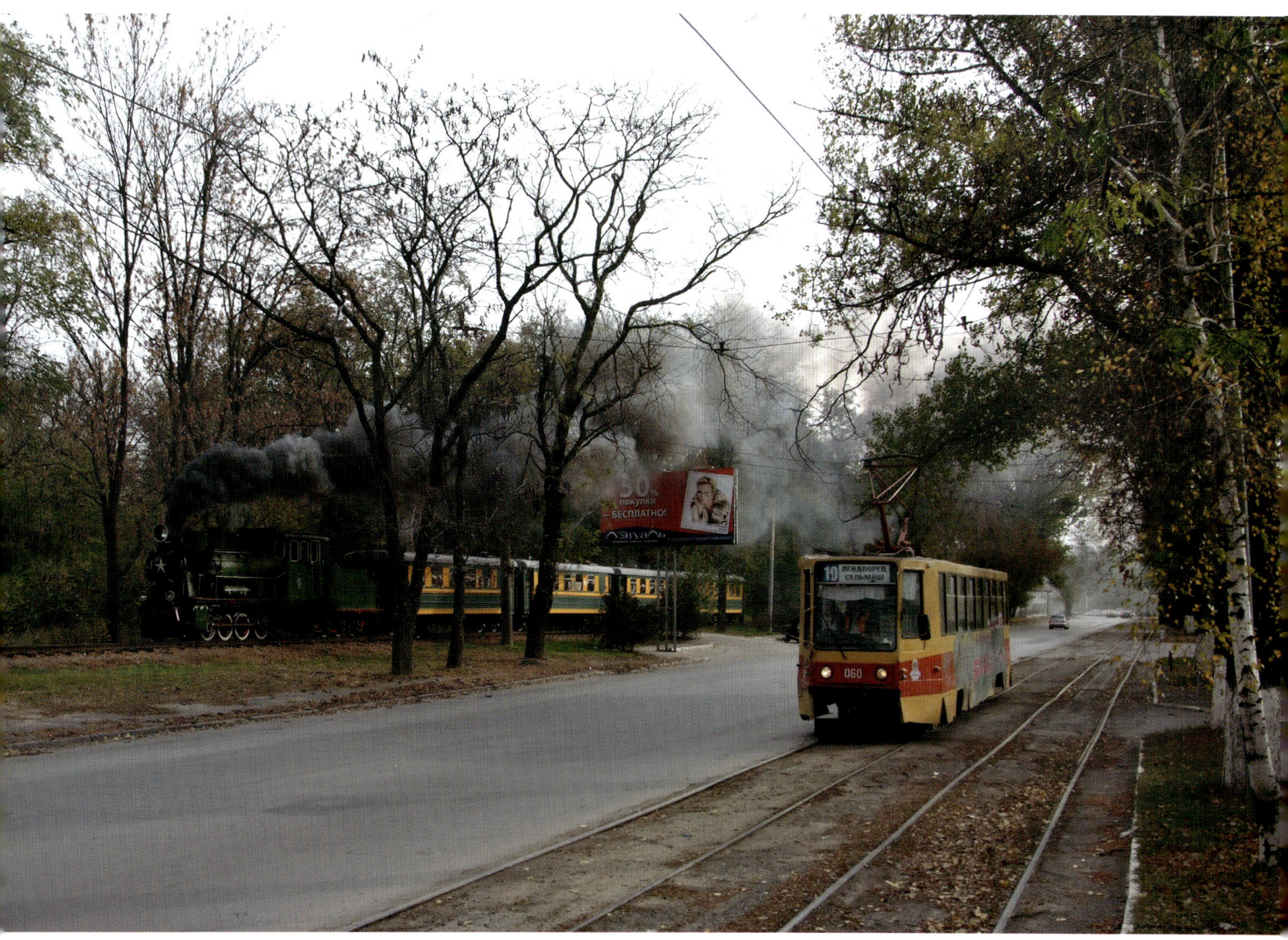

The great race! Thanks to a friendly tram driver I was able to photograph 750mm gauge 0-8-0 No Gr-185 (OK 15285/1949) running alongside his tram at the Rostov-on-Don children's railway, down in the south of the country, on 1 November 2009. The line opened in 1940 and forms a 4kms circuit around a park in the east of the city. Despite a Soviet government decision in 1956 to phase out steam, the last four Grs weren't withdrawn until 1984. They have a 6.5-tonne axle loading like the 157s but weren't liked as much. The 750mm gauge was very much a Russian standard even before the 1917 revolution, both for public and industrial railways.

UKRAINE

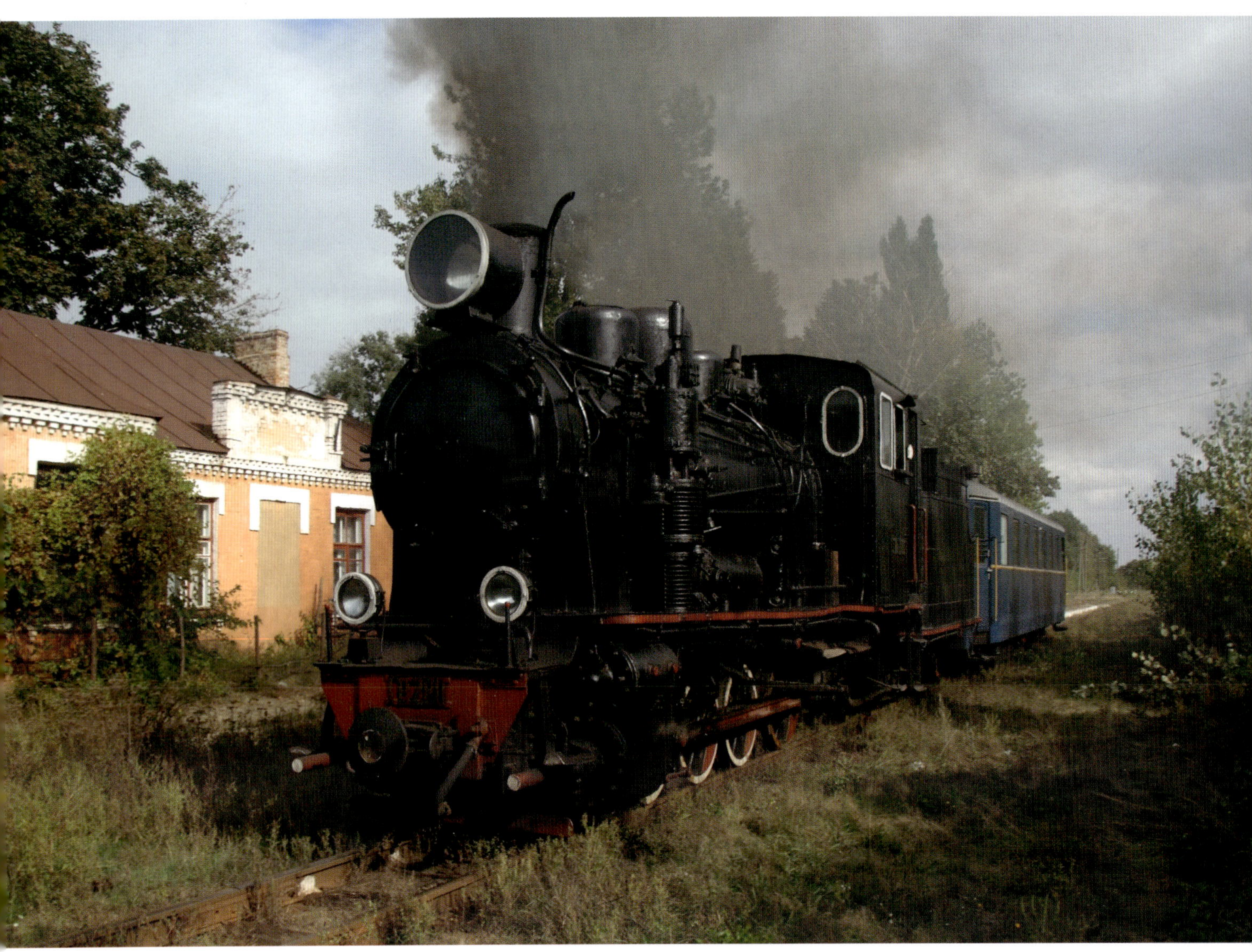

0-8-0 No Gr-280 (LKM 15377/1950) approaches Bershad in central Ukraine on 5 October 2010. More than 800kms of 750mm gauge lines were built in this part of the country from 1896 and this last surviving section, running both east and west from its operating base at Haivoron, opened three years later. The Ukrainian government has made repeated attempts to close the line but it has seen them all off. No Gr-280 was one of the locos withdrawn in 1984. She had worked at Haivoron for many years before being transferred away in 1978 and later returned as a heritage loco.

LITHUANIA

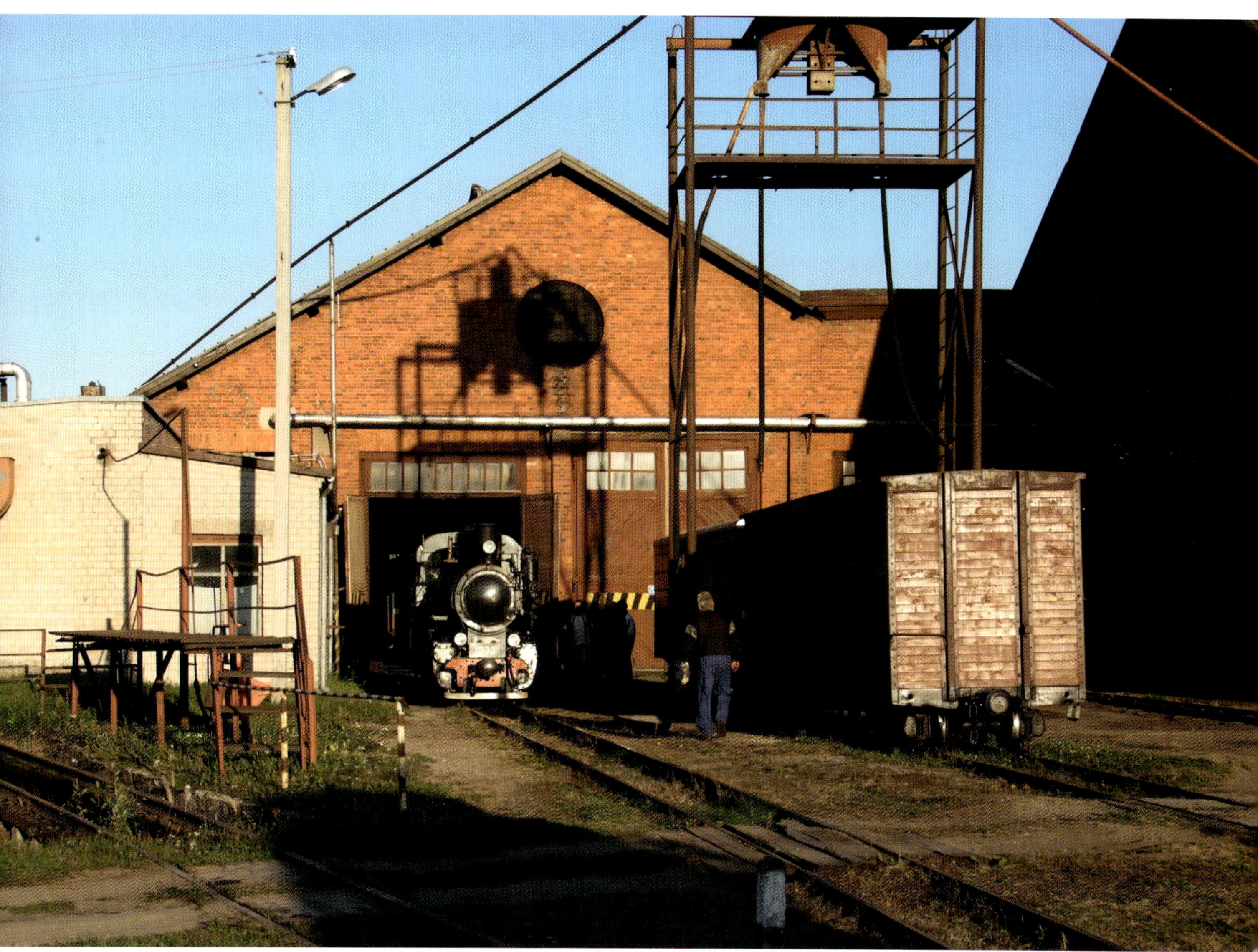

Like Finland and Ukraine, Lithuania was another part of the Russian empire when a 750mm gauge line opened in 1898 to serve the sparsely-inhabited district between Švenčionėliai and Panevėžys. In 1919, a few months after Lithuania became independent, Poland invaded and annexed a part of the country which included Švenčionėliai, where the railway's main shed was located, and the route across the de facto border was closed. The loss caused obvious difficulties and eventually a large new shed and workshop complex was built at Panevėžys in 1937. The line here is now a heritage railway and PT-4 No K^{ch}-4-332 (Škoda 2347/1950), visiting from the Estonian Railway Museum at Lavassaare, waits outside the shed in the evening sunshine on 20 September 2009.

ESTONIA

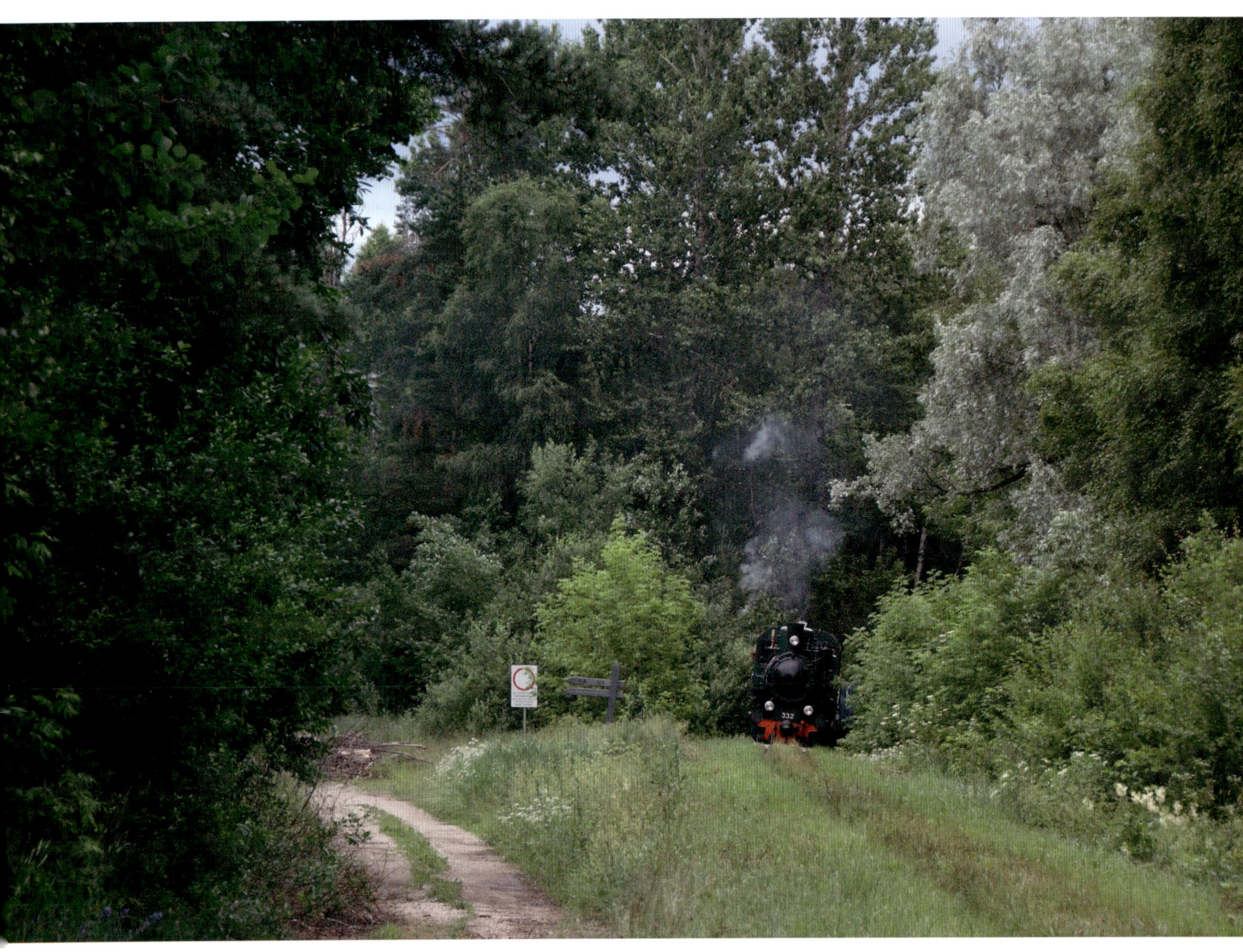

Same engine, different country! As at Pereslavl, the Estonian museum is based at an old peat railway. It has a magnificent collection of Soviet narrow gauge equipment and some dating from Estonia's pre-1939 period of independence. No K^{ch}-4-332 makes her way between Müramaa and Lavassaare on 11 July 2009. No doubt there are rails somewhere under all that grass!

LATVIA

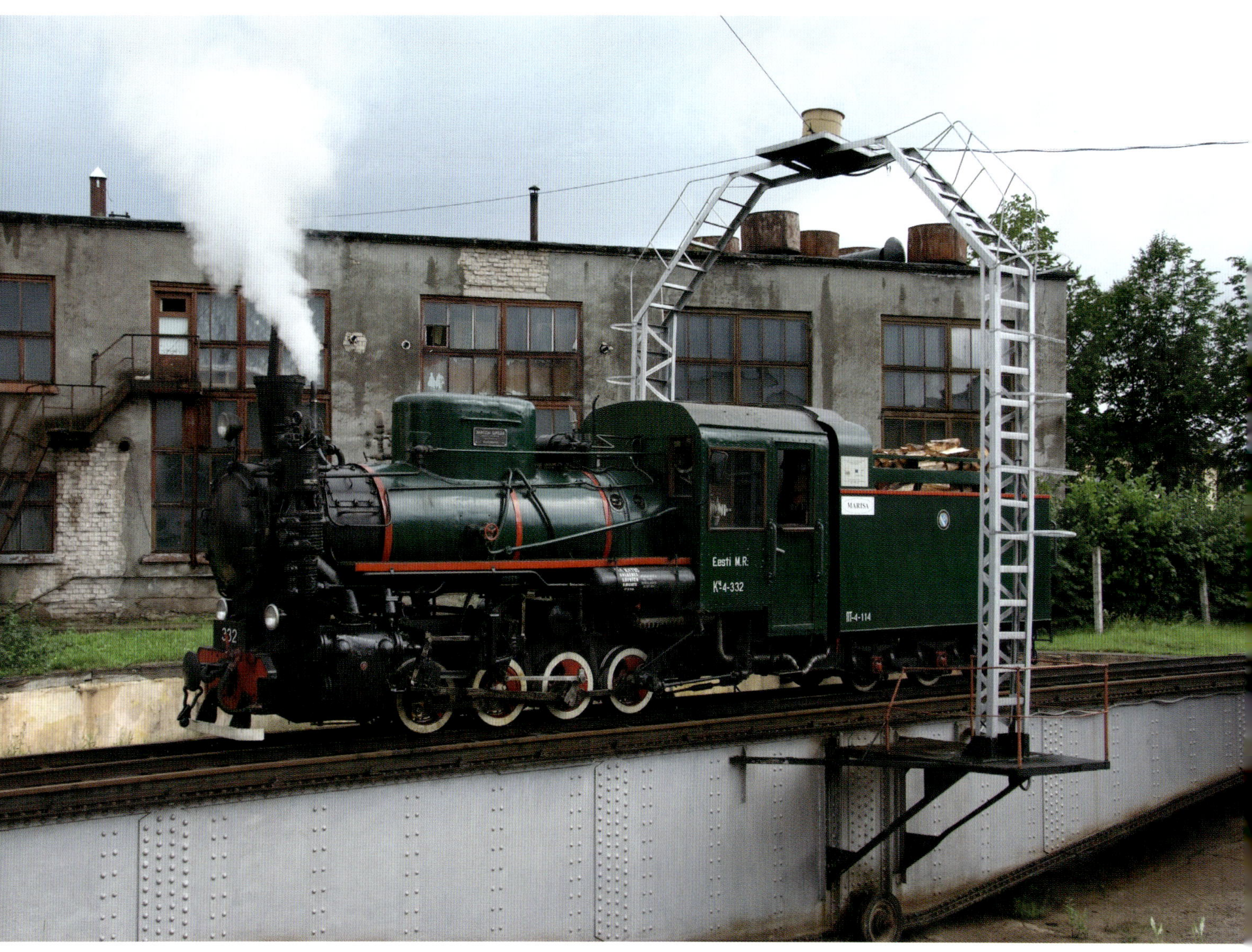

Different country again! On 7 July 2007, No K^{ch}-4-332 looks somewhat lost on the big mixed gauge turntable at Gulbene. She was restored to working order here and remained on loan for several years. In addition to the PT-4s built in Finland and Poland, the Soviet Votkinsk works supplied 2,356 between 1947 and 1960, Škoda 420 and MÁVAG 234. A few more of the Chrzanów, Škoda and MÁVAG locos remained in their home countries, perhaps rejected as substandard like the Finnish Move 21's.

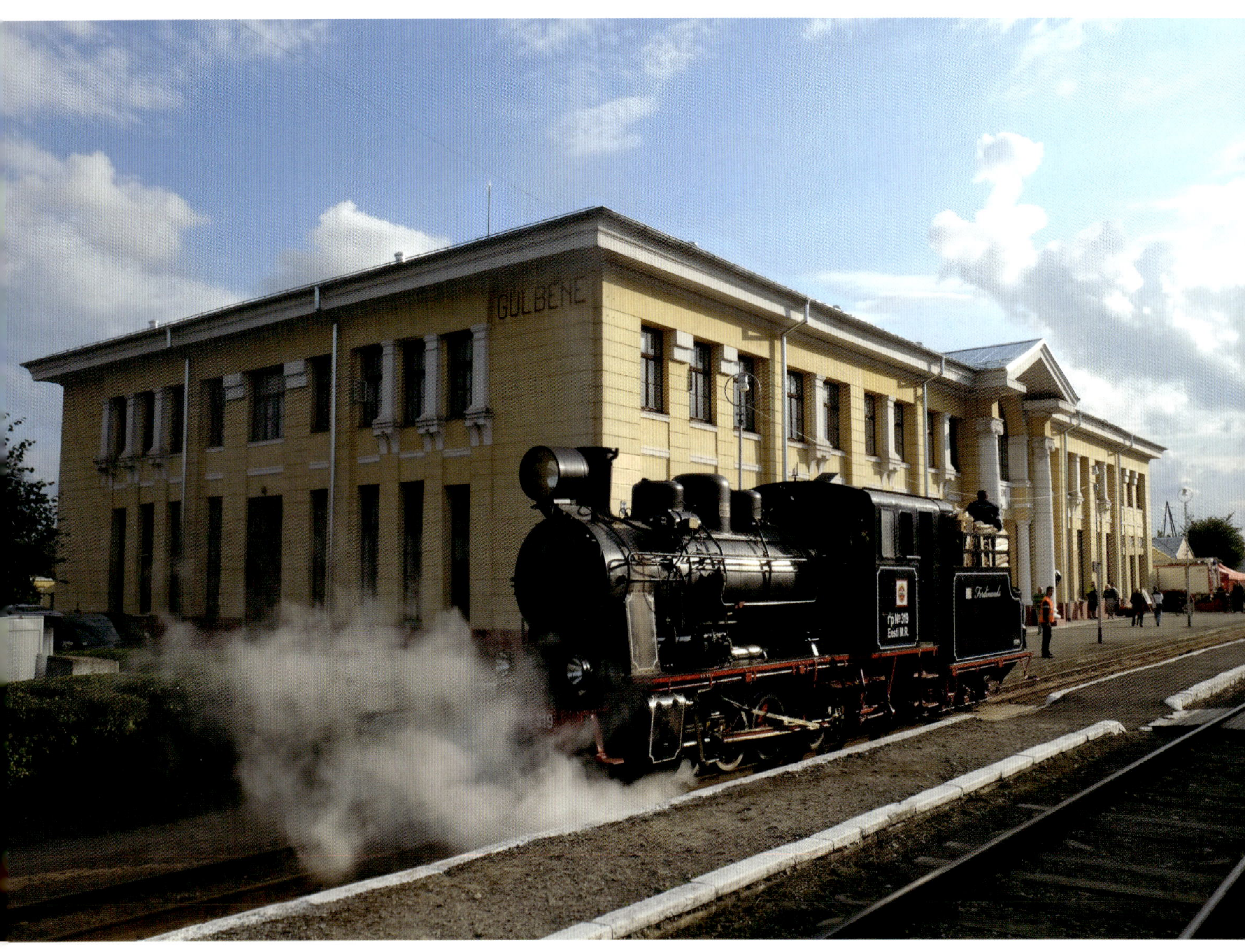

On 5 September 2015, No Gr-319 (LKM 15416/1951), another loco on loan from the Lavassaare museum, shunts next to the splendid main station building at Gulbene, designed in 1926 by Peteris Feders, one of Latvia's foremost architects. The line nowadays goes to Alūksne but was much longer when it opened in 1903. Like the Haivoron railway it still provides an everyday service. About 420 Grs were built in East Germany, mostly as reparations.

IRELAND

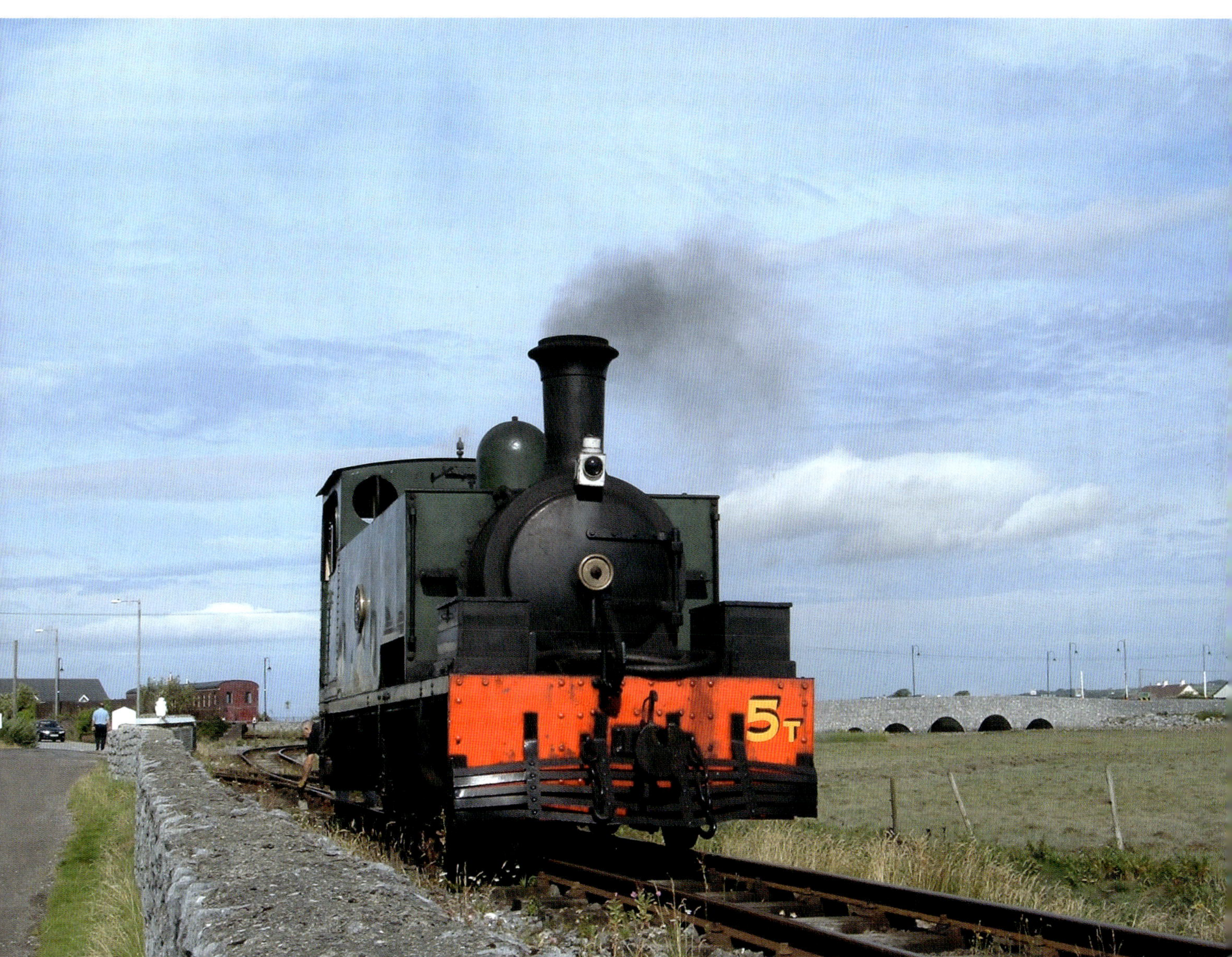

The 3ft gauge Tralee & Dingle Light Railway's 2-6-2T No 5T (Hunslet 555/1892) has just left her shed at Blennerville on 7 August 2004 and is about to back down to the station to collect her train. Construction of the line began in 1888 and took three years to complete. In its final years, it only saw cattle specials in connection with a monthly fair at Dingle. These often required double heading; the locos were very run down and there was more than a hint of a trip into the unknown whenever the trains ventured out from Tralee. By the time it closed in 1953 it had acquired an almost legendary status amongst enthusiasts. The closure wasn't quite the end as several of its locos, including No 5T, went on to lead second lives on the Cavan & Leitrim until it closed in 1959.

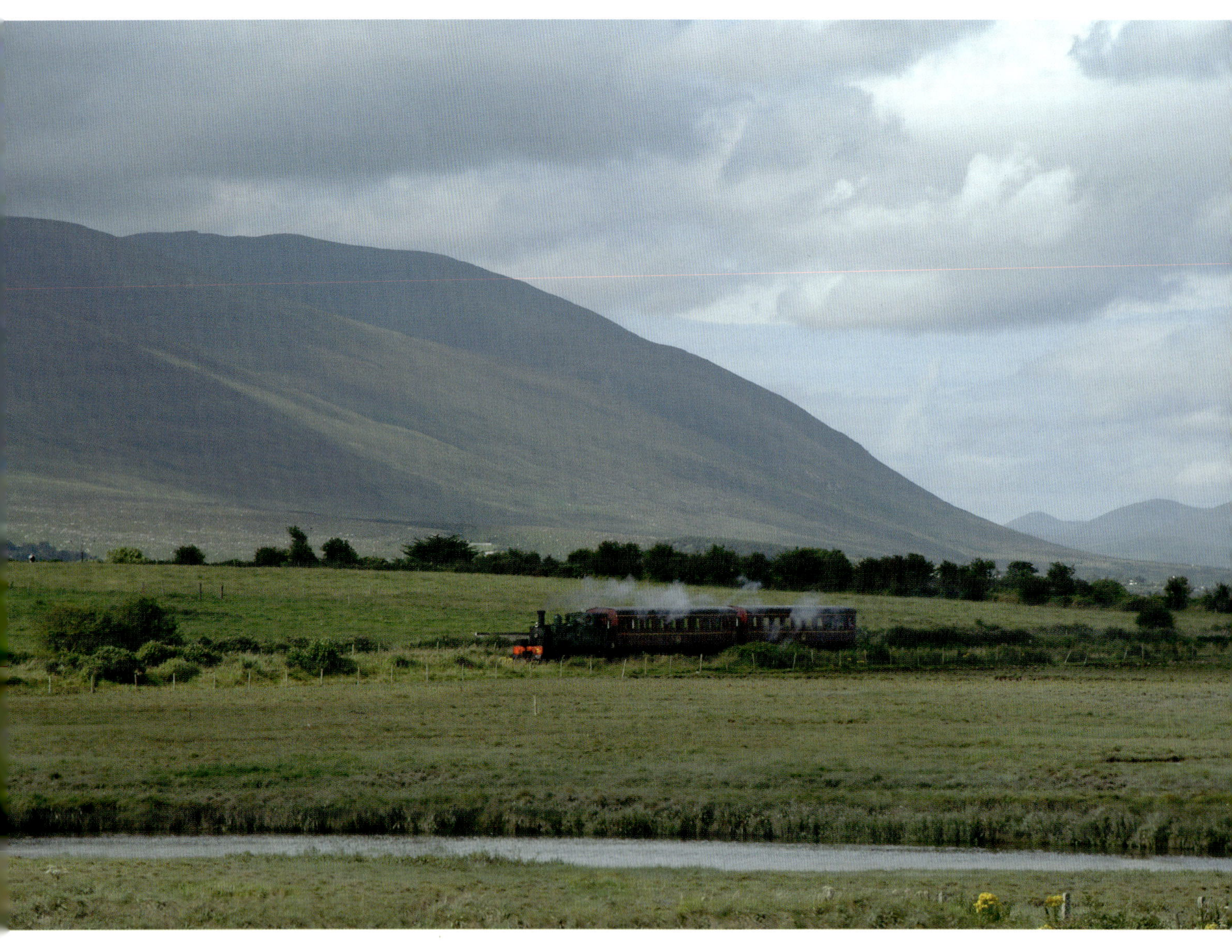

No 5T has just left Blennerville on 8 August 2004 and makes her way around the salt marsh of the River Lee. The Tralee & Dingle was notorious for its sharp curves and horrendously steep gradients which were the direct cause of at least one fatal accident in its early years. Here the beautiful Slieve Mish mountains give a taste of what was to come for westbound trains in the old days. No 5T survived the Cavan & Leitrim's closure thanks to Edgar T. Mead, a philanthropic US enthusiast who bought her for a museum in Vermont. When enthusiasts from Kerry mooted a plan to repatriate her in the 1980s, Mr Mead generously sold her for a nominal sum. She was restored to working order and a short section of the old line out of Tralee reopened in 1994. The carriages, from the Basque railways in Spain, carry the rich red paint scheme of the old Great Southern which operated the line from the 1920s. Sadly, she hasn't run since 2006 but moves are afoot to restore her.

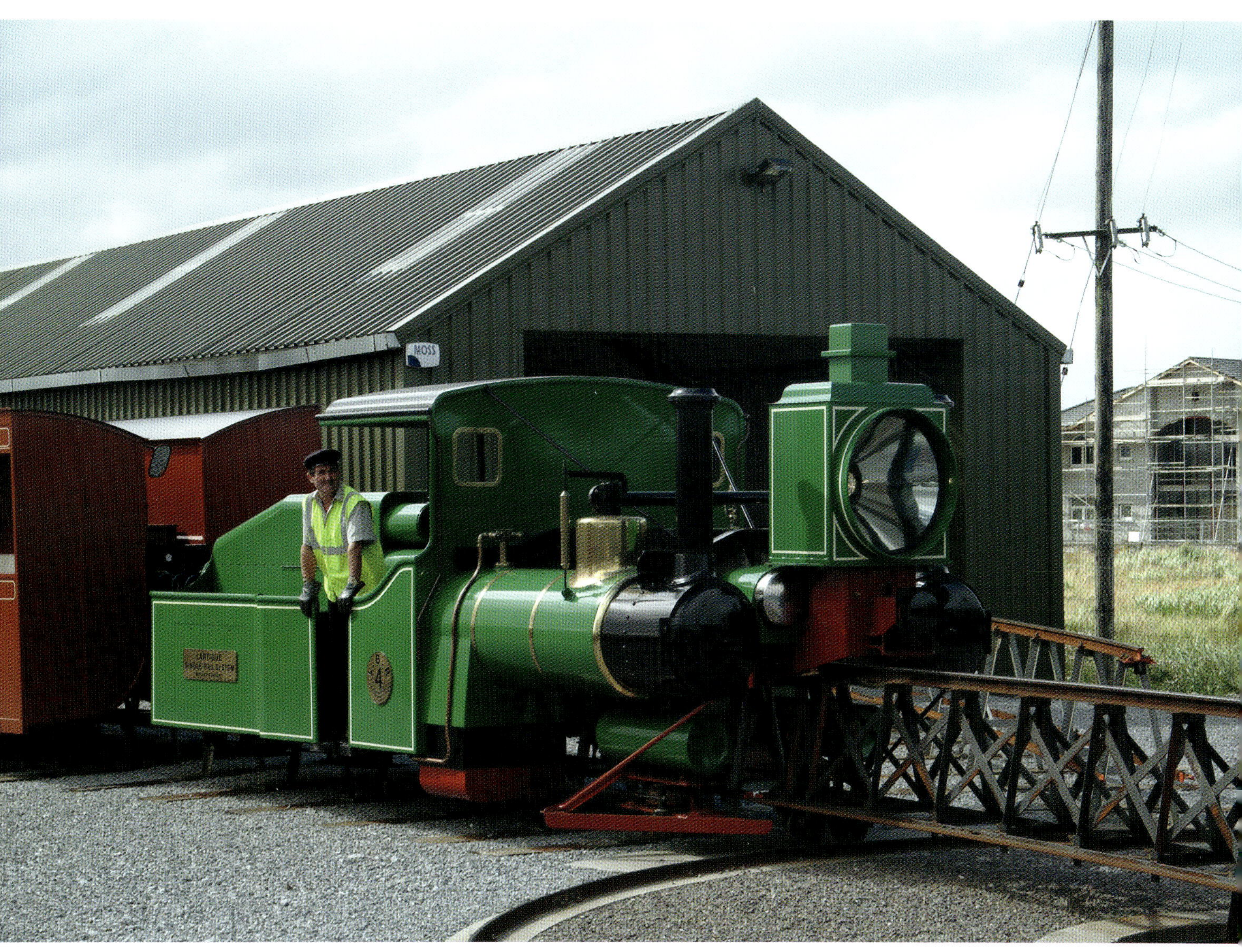

The three 0-3-0s on the Listowel and Ballybunion Railway, a Lartigue monorail opened in 1888, must have been amongst Hunslet's and the world's most unusual machines with their two parallel boilers while the coaches, with two body sections straddling the rail, were equally odd. Speed was not their most notable feature! The only subsequent Lartigue line was built in the 1890s between Feurs and Panissières in France. It was equipped with two 0-3-0T's built by Biétrix et Cie of St Etienne but wasn't allowed to open whereas the Irish line served the public until 1924. In 1992, the Listowel and Panissières councils agreed to conserve their unusual shared heritage and in 2003 a short replica line opened at Listowel. The train was built by Alan Keef's who have done so much to further the cause of narrow gauge railways in the British Isles and beyond. Here it has just completed its run on 8 August 2004. 0-3-0 No 4 (AK 62/2002) is diesel-powered but looks just like the originals. A non-working replica of a Biétrix loco is on show at Panissières.

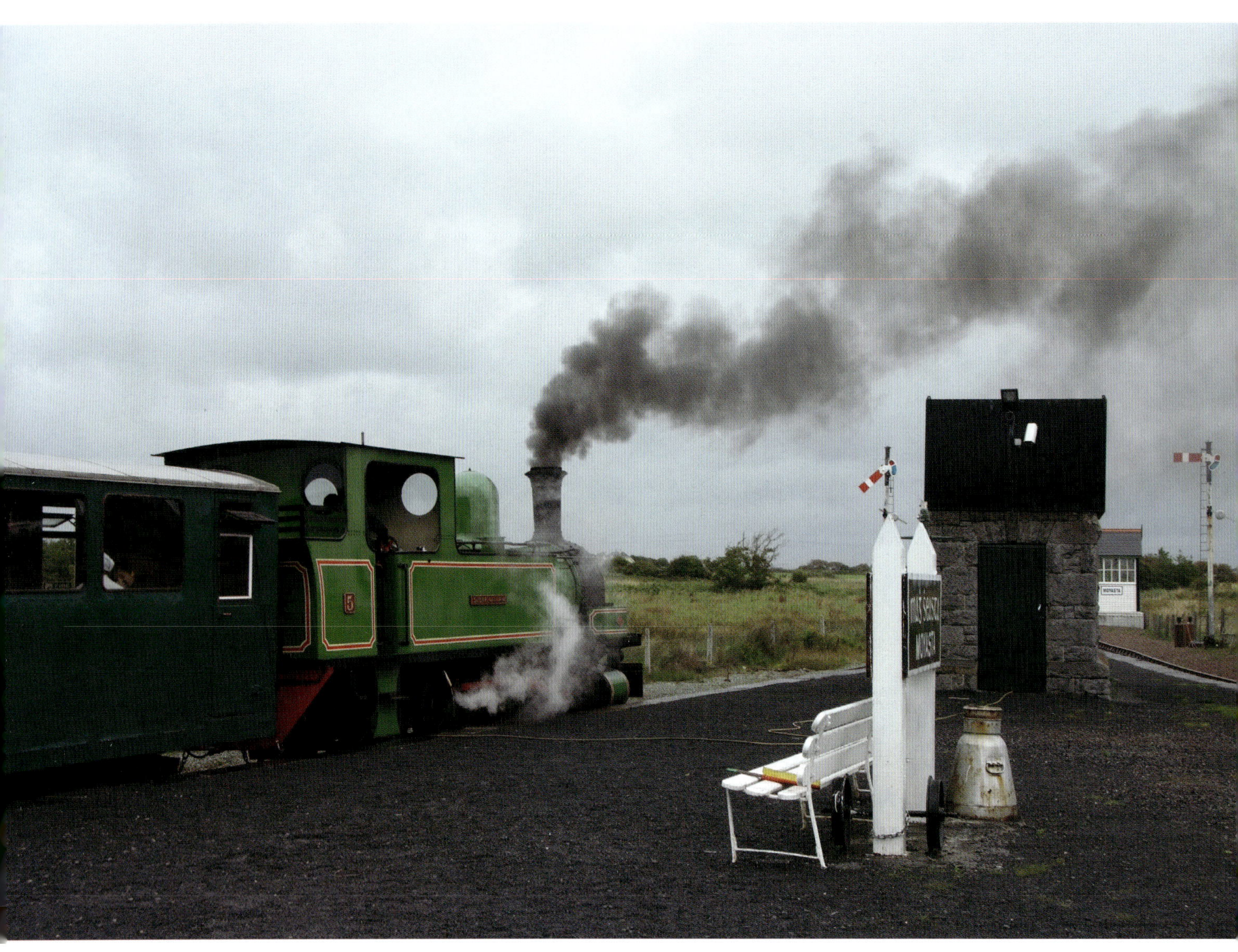

It's not far from Listowel to the Shannon car ferry. As with many things in this beautiful country the crossing is spectacular, both for the superb scenery and because the many dolphins who live in the estuary often treat the passengers as travelling companions. Once ashore in County Clare, you're close to Kilrush, one of the termini of the old 3ft gauge West Clare Railway which opened in stages between 1887 and 1892 and closed in 1960. Jackie Whelan, a local businessman, has reopened a short section at Moyasta Junction and, with the aid of EU and other grants, has had the old line's 0-6-2T No 5 *Slieve Callan* (Dübs 2890/1892) restored at Alan Keef's works near Ross-on-Wye. She returned to service in 2009 and here waits to leave Moyasta on 2 August 2010.

THE ISLE OF MAN

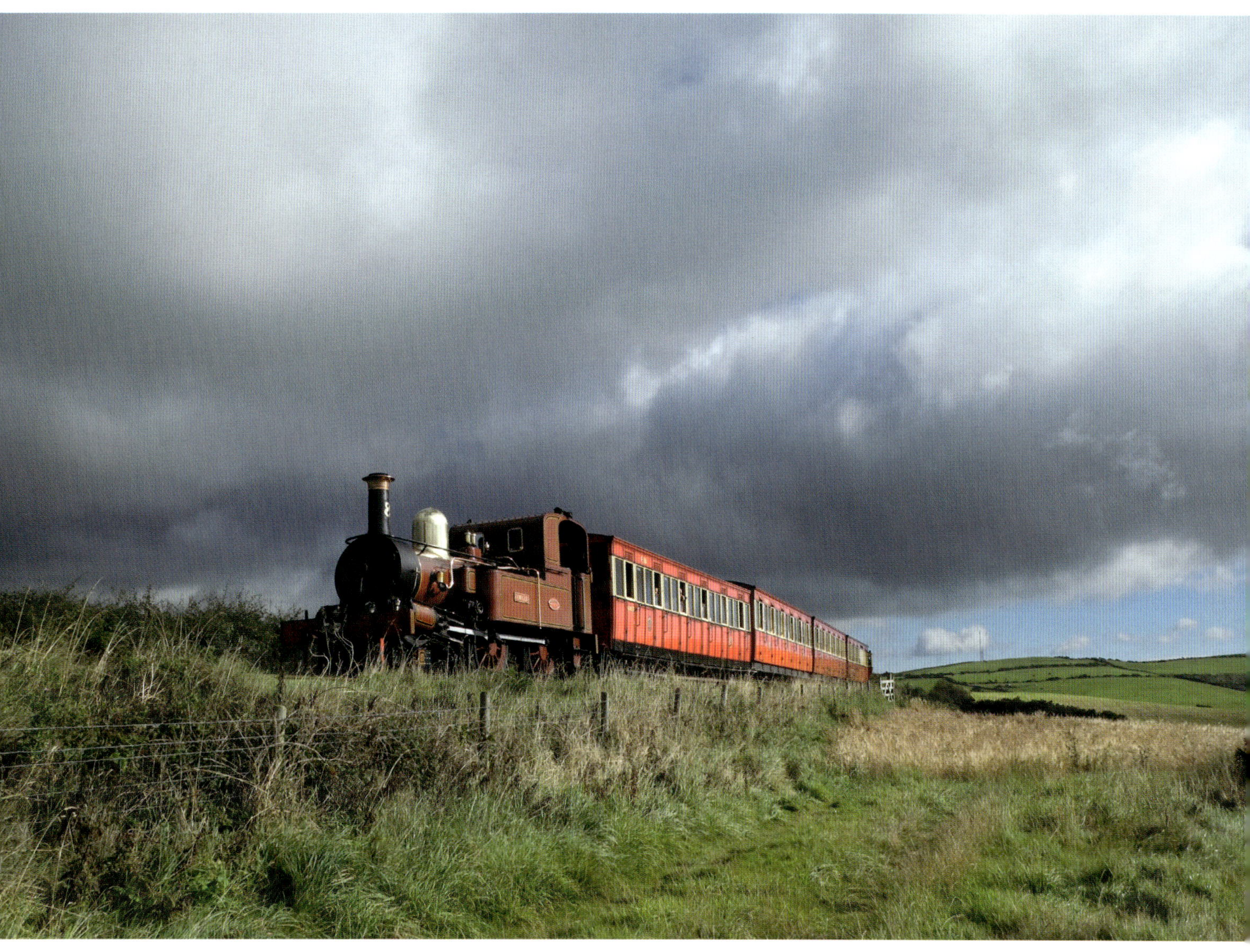

The 3ft gauge Isle of Man Railway's 2-4-0T No 8 *Fenella* (BP 3610/1894) passes Keristal on her way to Port Erin on the stormy morning of 4 September 2016. Locos Nos 1-9, built from 1873 when the first section opened, were generally similar as was No 14 *Thornhill*, built in 1880 for the Manx Northern Railway. Nos 10-13 were considerably larger and Nos 4-6 were later rebuilt to match them while the final loco, No 16 *Mannin* which arrived in 1926, was the biggest of all.

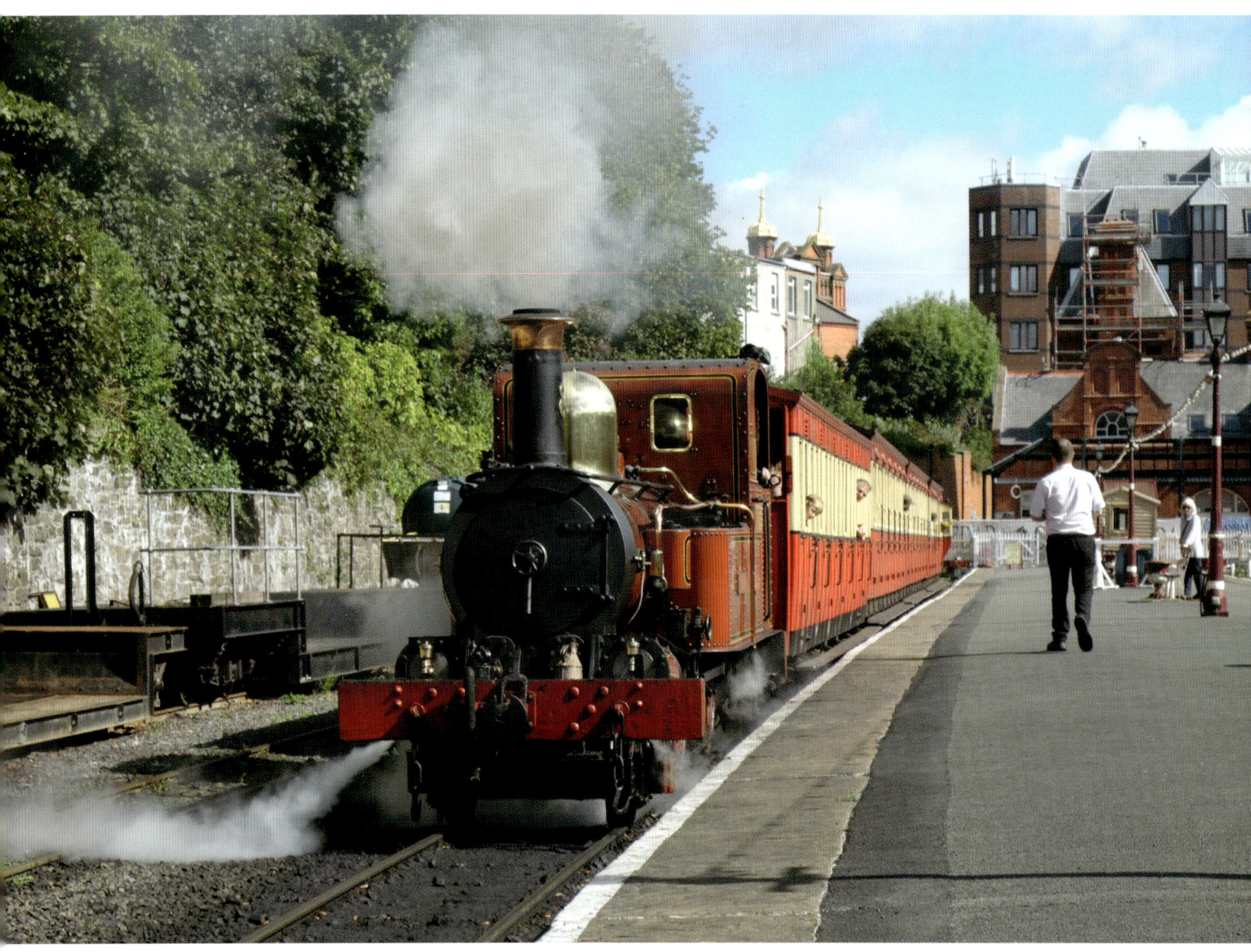

The stationmaster at Douglas walks back down the platform on the afternoon of 4 September 2016 as *Fenella* leaves Douglas station, possibly after giving her driver instructions about track repairs at Castletown following a derailment there. The golden cupolas sit on top of the station's splendid gateway from the town centre but sadly at platform level much of the old grandeur has gone. The earlier Manx locos were similar to the Norwegian class IV's, twenty-five of which were built between 1866 and 1883, and the Beyer Peacock works drawings for them which still exist are headed 'Norwegian Narrow Gauge Tank'. They were smaller versions of the standard gauge 4-4-0Ts the firm was building for London's Metropolitan Railway, one of which is now at the London Transport Museum, the four-wheeled bogie being replaced by the now familiar Bissell front truck.

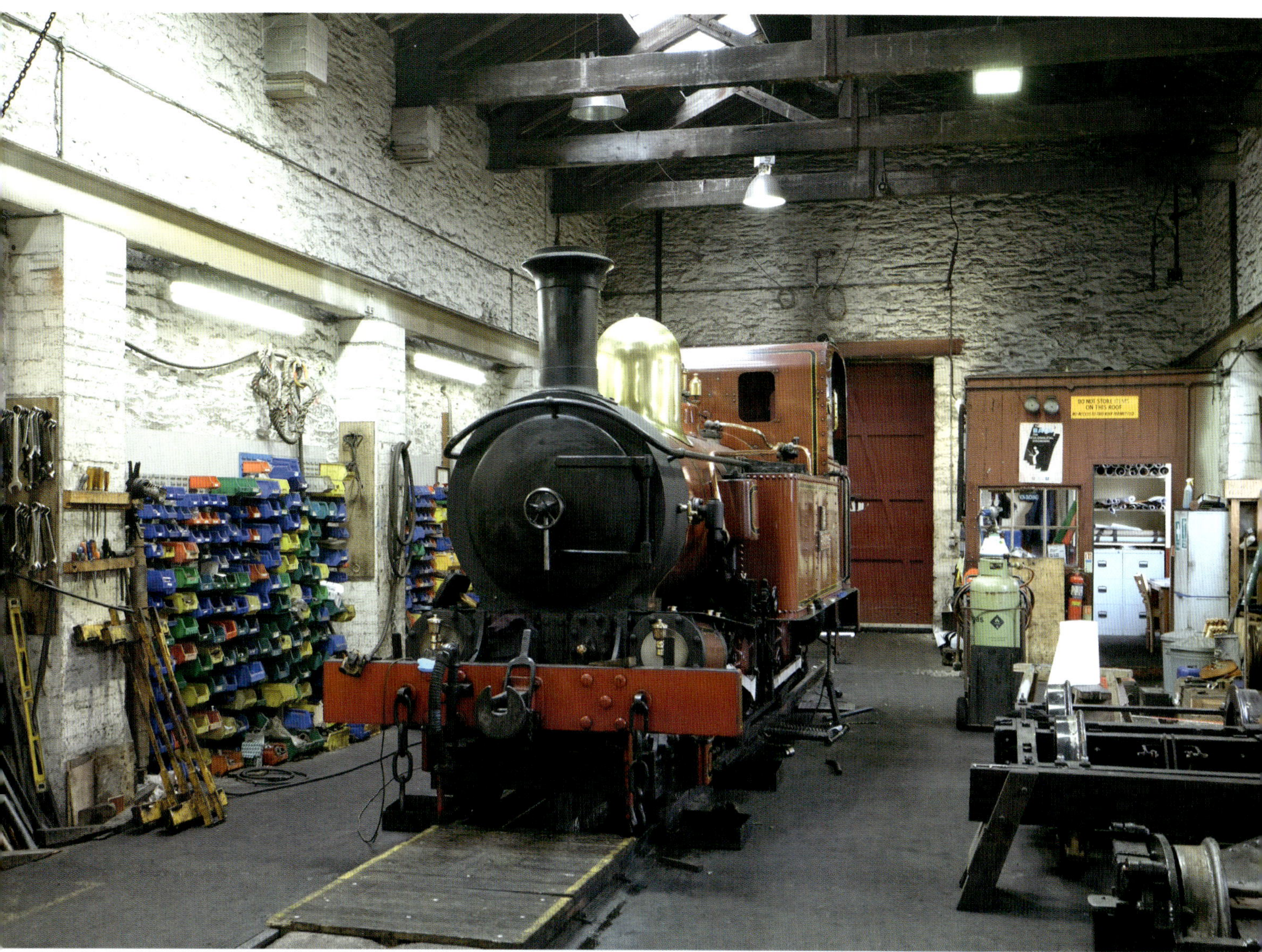

On 26 June 2014, 2-4-0T No 12 *Hutchinson* (BP 5126/1908), one of the medium-sized locos, stands in Douglas workshops, an amazing place full of fascinating old equipment. Another predecessor of the Manx locos was No 1 *Bolivar* of the Barranquilla Railway and Pier Co (BP 984/1870), the first loco to run in present-day Colombia. Altogether four class IV-style locos ran in Colombia and two on the Ballymena & Larne from 1877 and in the 1880s two more were built for a logging concern in Western Australia. In Norway there were also the ten generally similar class Vs built in 1881 and 1882 by Motala, one of which, No 10 *Hugin* (Motala 43/1881), was the last of NSB's 2-4-0T's when she was withdrawn in 1948. She now keeps *Alf* company at the Hamar museum. In the days before its Beyer Garratts were widely adopted the firm's chief engineer described the 2-4-0T's as one of its most successful designs.

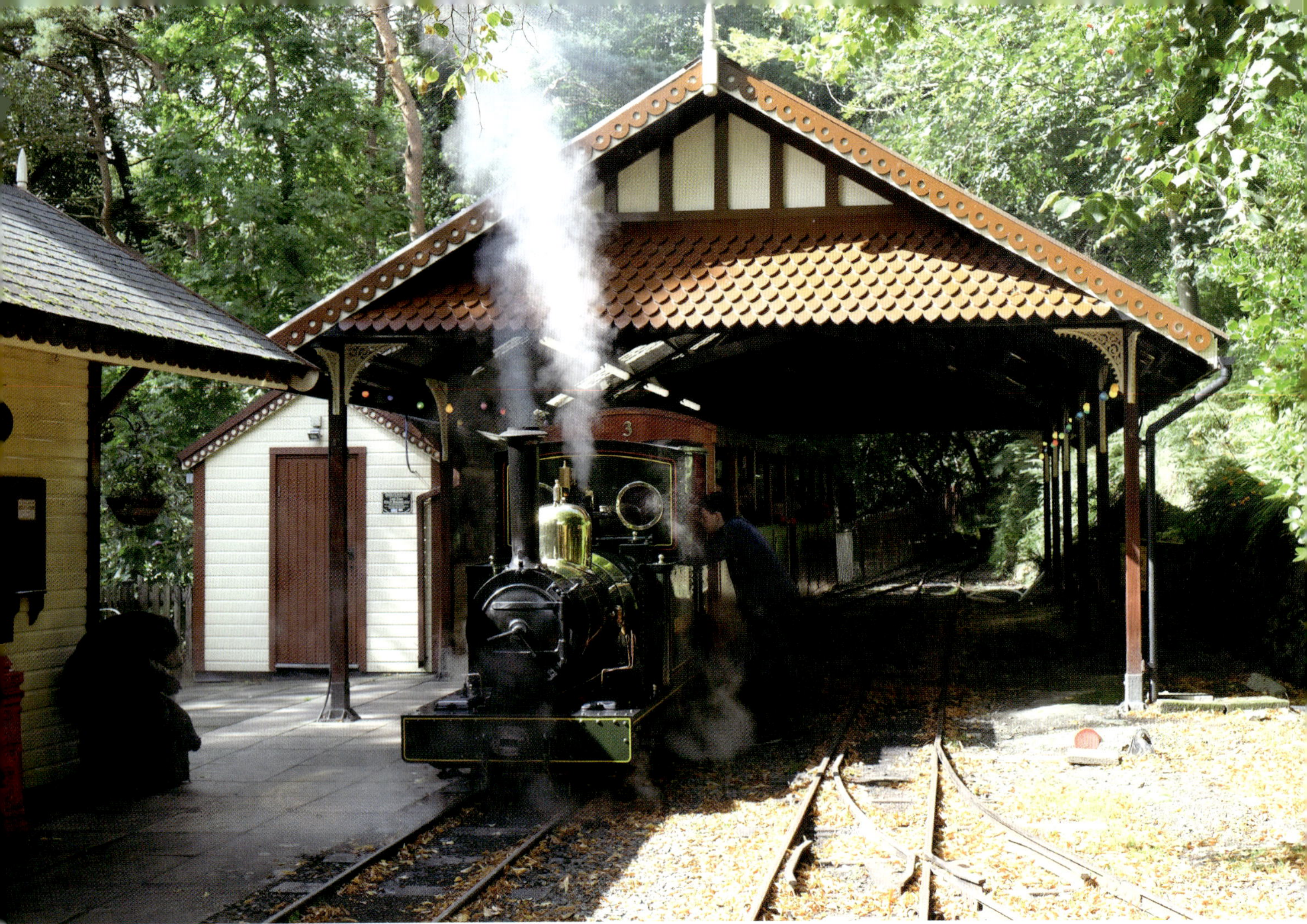

Above: The 2ft gauge Groudle Glen Railway is a major restoration success. Its 2-4-0T *Sea Lion* (Bagnall 1484/1896) stands with her train at Lhen Coan station with its beautifully recreated overall roof on 4 September 2016. The furry passenger with his luggage is in no hurry to board! The little line, on the Isle of Man's east coast, opened in 1896 as a tourist attraction. It closed in 1962.

Opposite above: When I first visited in 1968, the line was derelict almost beyond belief. *Sea Lion* had been used as a source of spares for a sister loco since the 1940s and any thought that she or the line itself would be restored seemed fanciful. However, this is just what the railway's volunteers have achieved. Here she emerges from the woods on 4 September 2016.

Opposite below: The Groudle line may be tiny but the 1ft 7ins gauge Laxey Mines Railway is even smaller. The mine there is notable for the Lady Isabella waterwheel, the largest in the world. A railway was built to take out the ore, worked by two tiny 0-4-0Ts built by Stephen Lewin, *Ant* and *Bee* (SL 684 and 685/1877). Lewin's locos were always quaint, but these were perhaps the oddest of all with their front-mounted water tanks which needed to be removed every time their boilers were cleaned. The railway was dismantled and the two locos scrapped in 1935. Now replicas have been built and run along a reconstructed section of the old line. *Bee* (GNS 21/2004) stands outside their shed at Laxey on 28 June 2014.

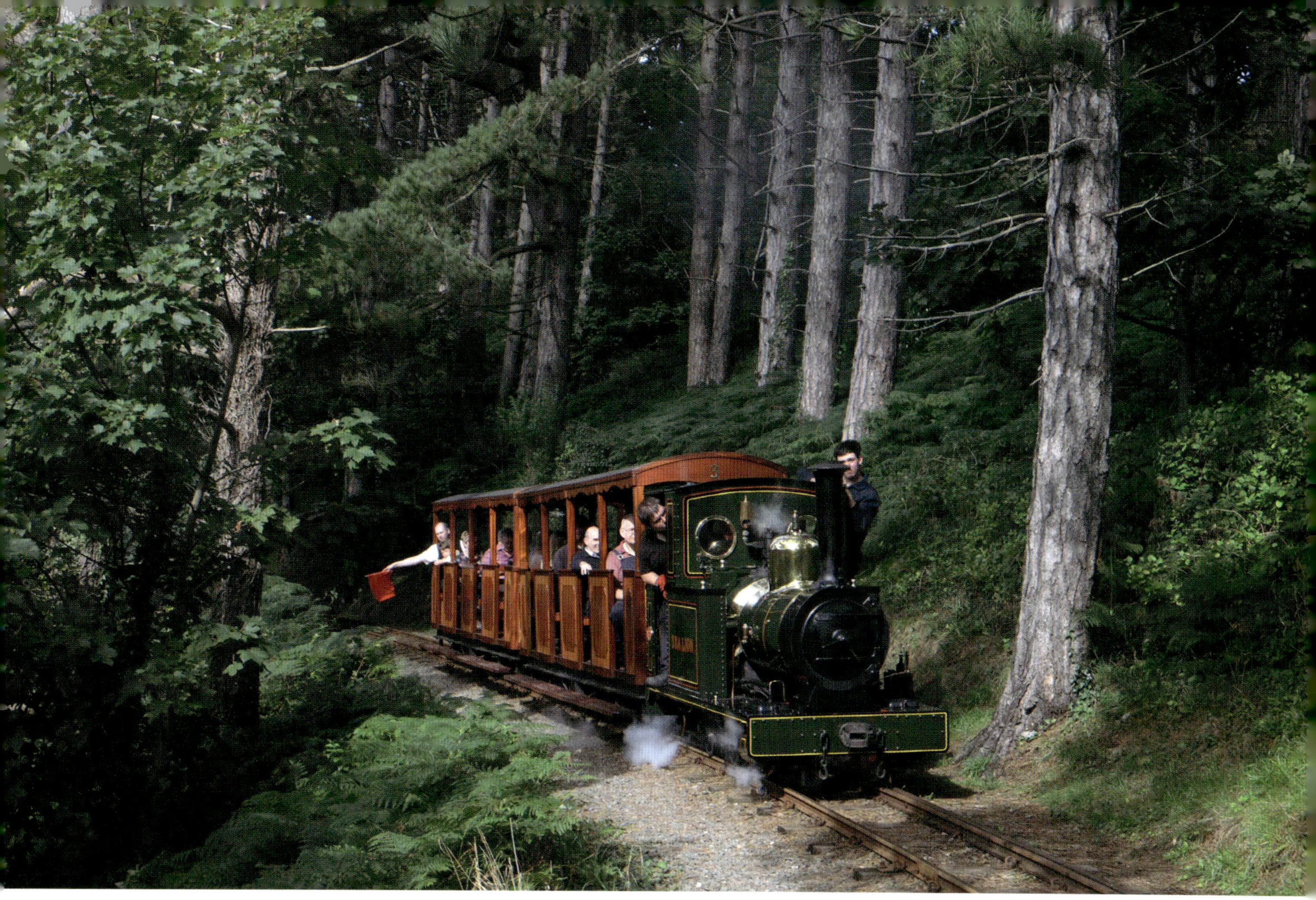

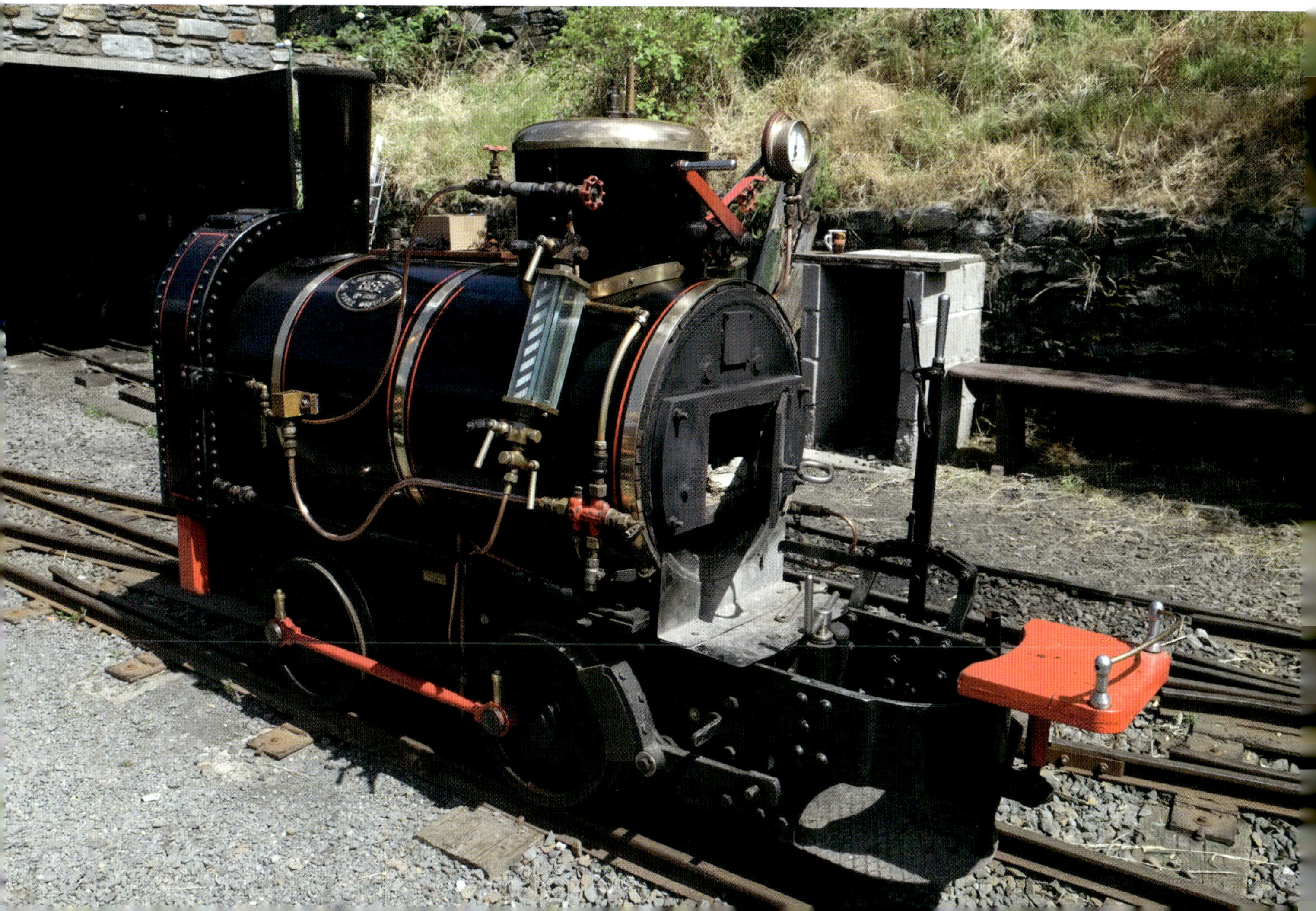

WALES

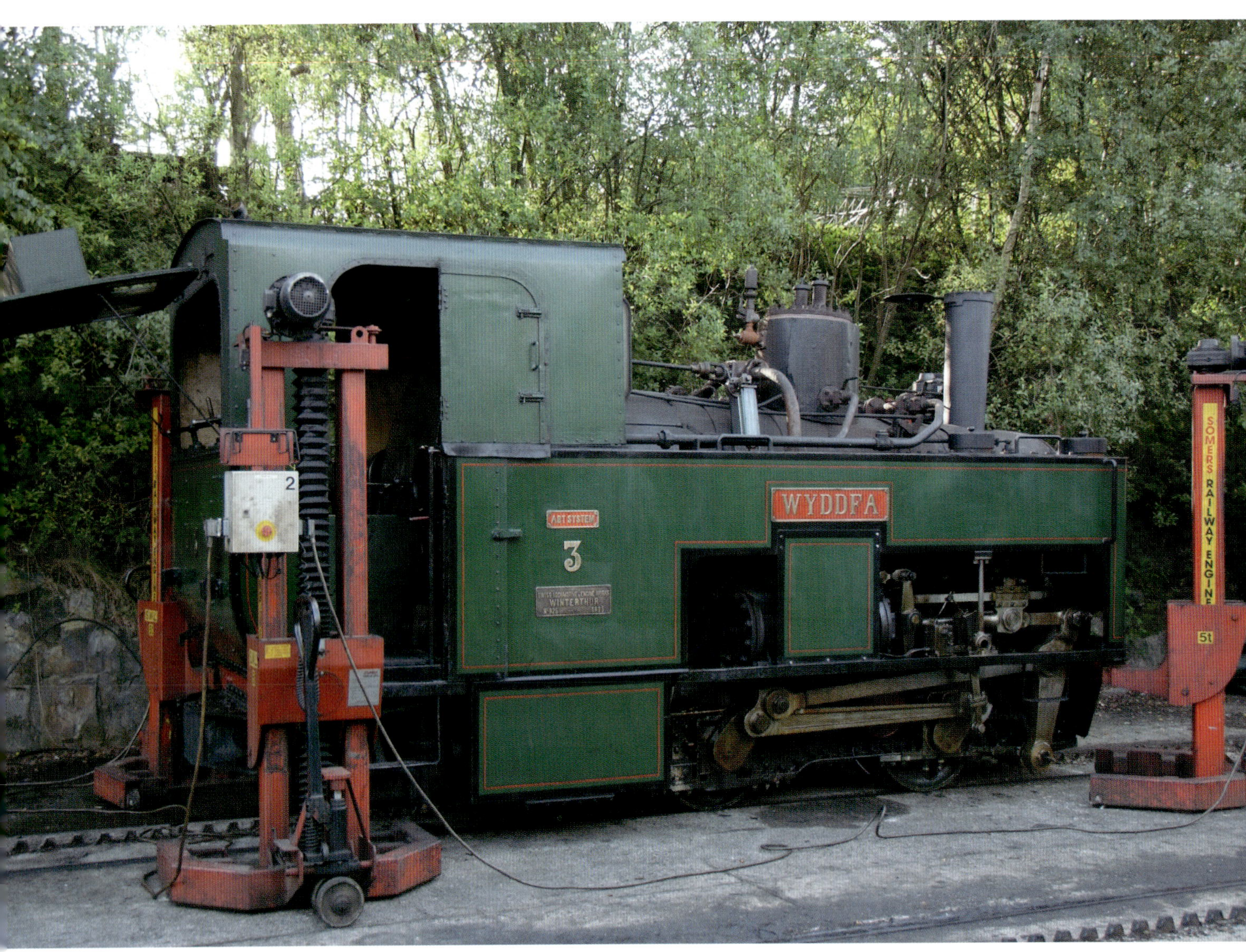

On 3 September 2010 0-4-2RT No 3 *Wyddfa* (SLM 925/1895) has been receiving attention outside Llanberis engine shed on the 800mm gauge Abt-rack Snowdon Mountain Railway. No's 2-5 are Abt-Brown type 2 machines, the only survivors anywhere. The Abt-Brown system involved mounting the cylinders high up above the ground between the driving axles, useful for keeping out dirt and grit, with the drive being transmitted via a front-mounted rocking beam.

0-4-2RT No 4 Snowdon (SLM 988/1896) is under repair inside Llanberis shed on 3 September 2010. The railway handles most loco overhauls though No 4 carries a Hunslet rebuild plate dated 1963.

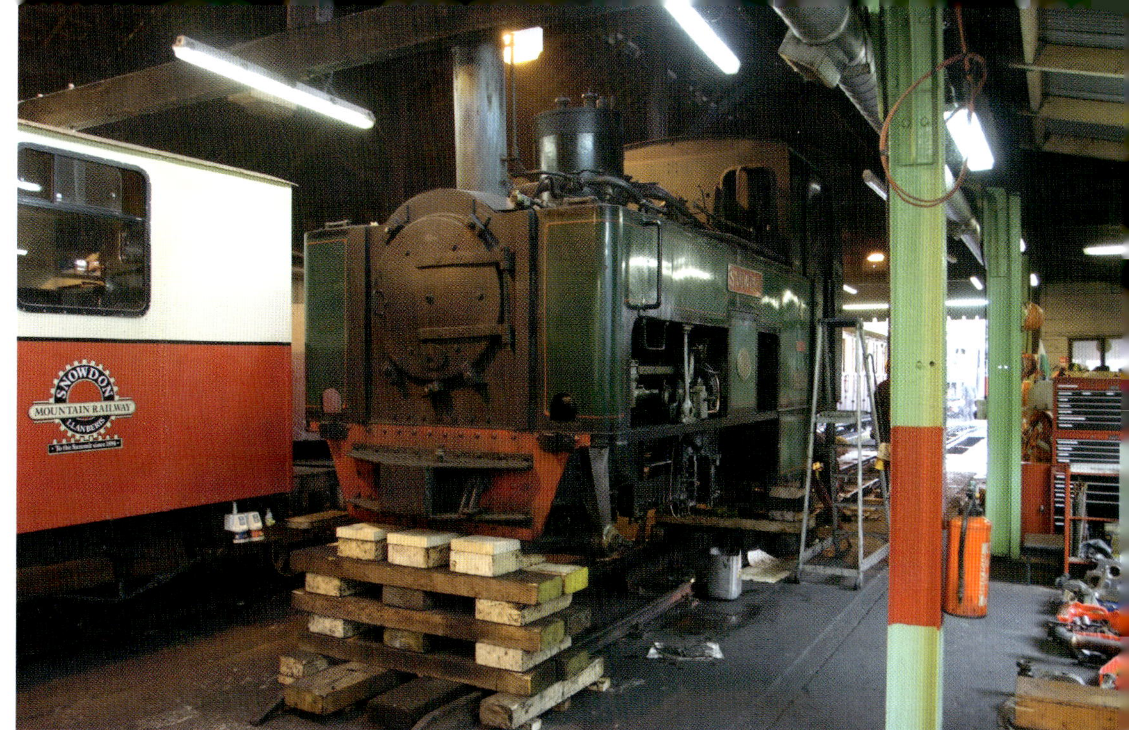

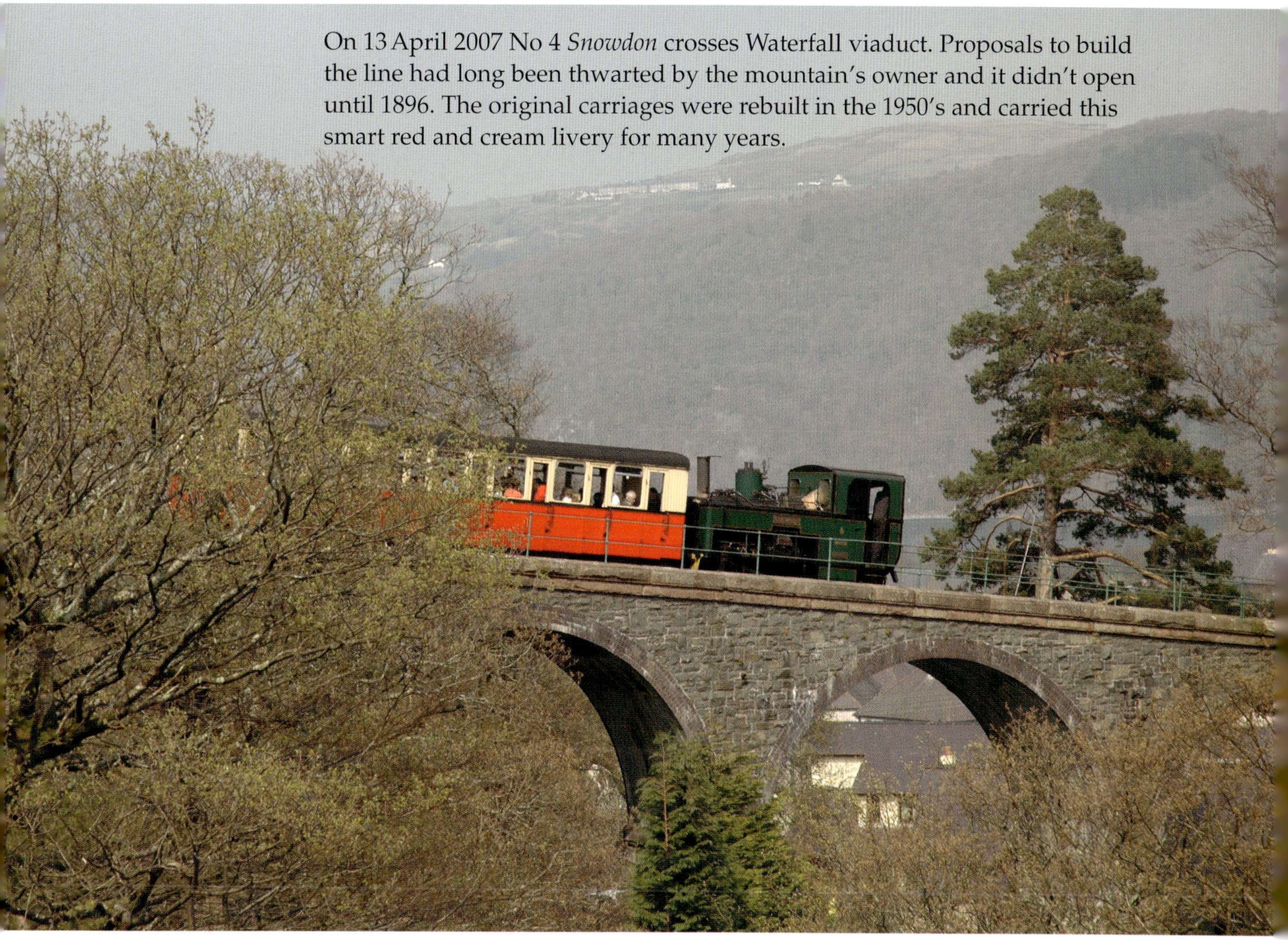

On 13 April 2007 No 4 *Snowdon* crosses Waterfall viaduct. Proposals to build the line had long been thwarted by the mountain's owner and it didn't open until 1896. The original carriages were rebuilt in the 1950's and carried this smart red and cream livery for many years.

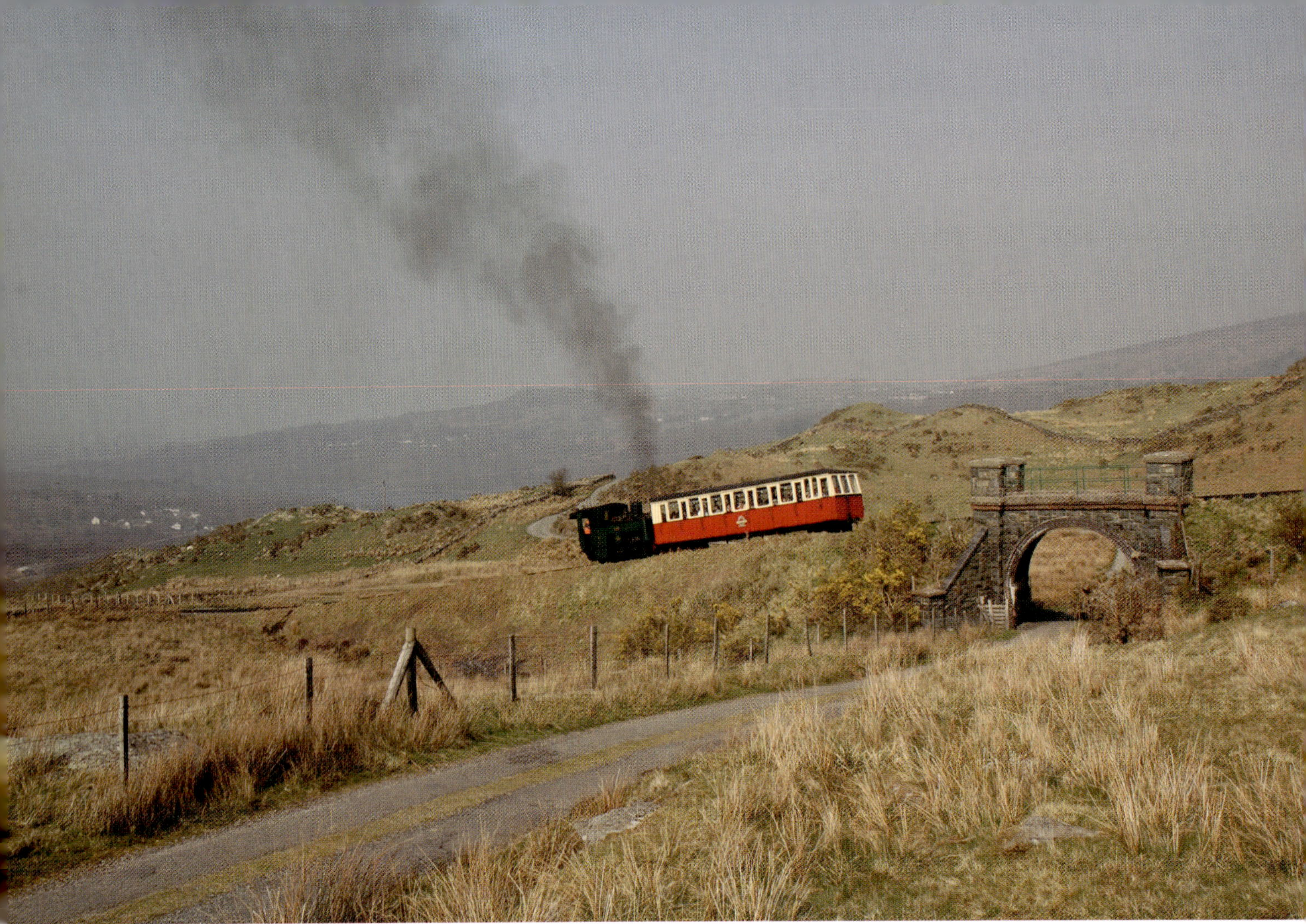

Above: A little later, 0-4-2RT No 2 *Enid* (SLM 924/1895) is about to cross the mountain road as she climbs away from Llanberis. The frequent changes of gradient are obvious here and were the subject of criticism by Roman Abt, the system's inventor, after a fatal accident on the line's opening day.

Opposite above: 0-4-2RT No 6 *Padarn* (SLM 2838/1922) approaches Waterfall viaduct on 3 September 2010. She's an Abt-Brown type 3, the final design, and is the world's last working example. Three were supplied to the railway in the 1920s.

Opposite below: Very early in the morning of 16 September 2016, three old Penrhyn quarry locos ventured out from its Coed-y-parc workshop, the first time this had happened for at least fifty years. The workshop is part of a complex built almost entirely of slate blocks, much of which is now an industrial estate. The building with its old travelling hoist remained intact and a few years ago was made available to a preservation venture. Here 0-4-0T *Marchlyn* (Avonside 2067/1933) and 0-4-0ST *Winifred* (Hunslet 364/1885) are prepared outside the workshop. They were among eleven locos which emigrated to North America in 1965 and 1966 from Penrhyn and from Dinorwic quarry at Llanberis. All have now returned to the UK.

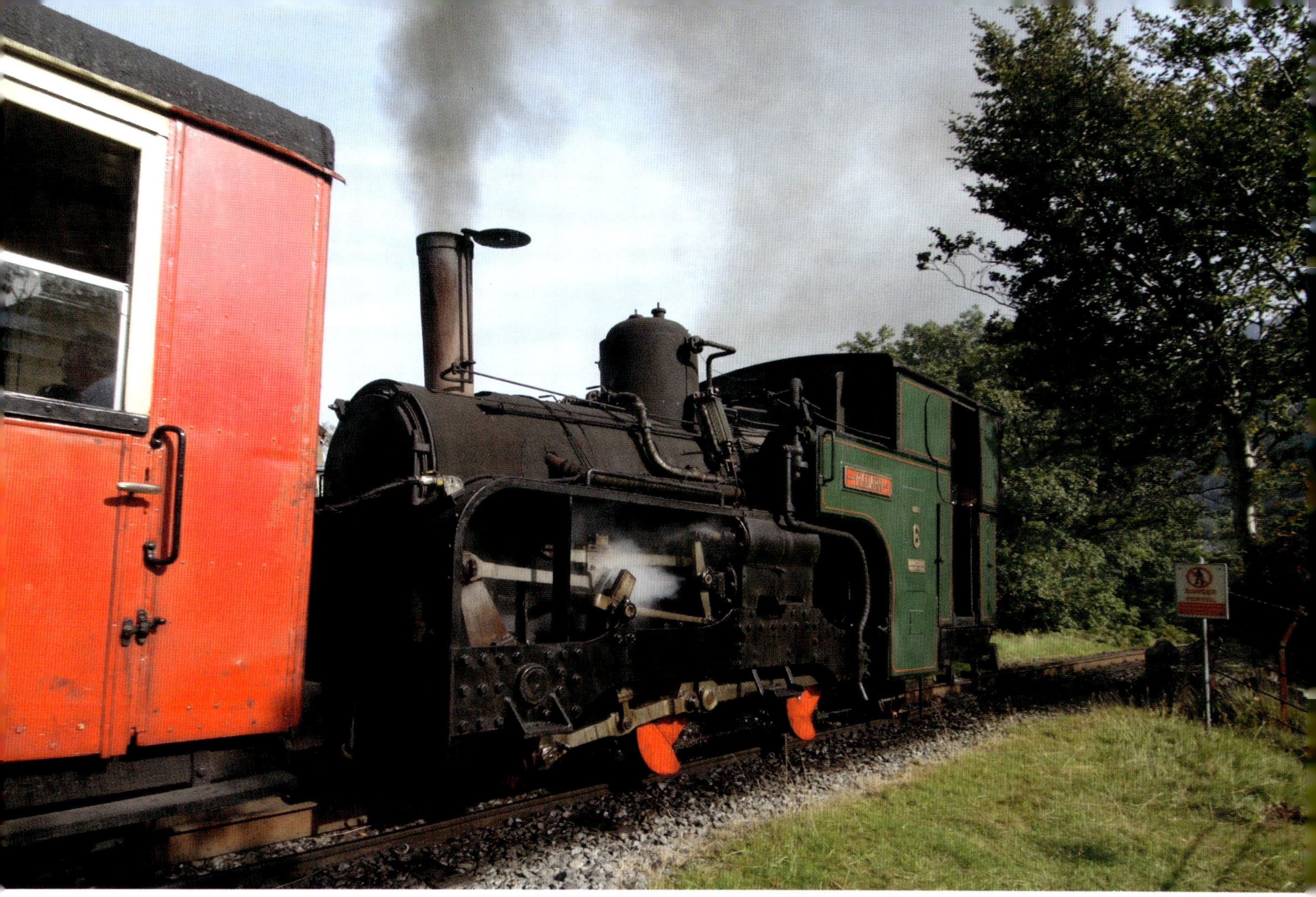

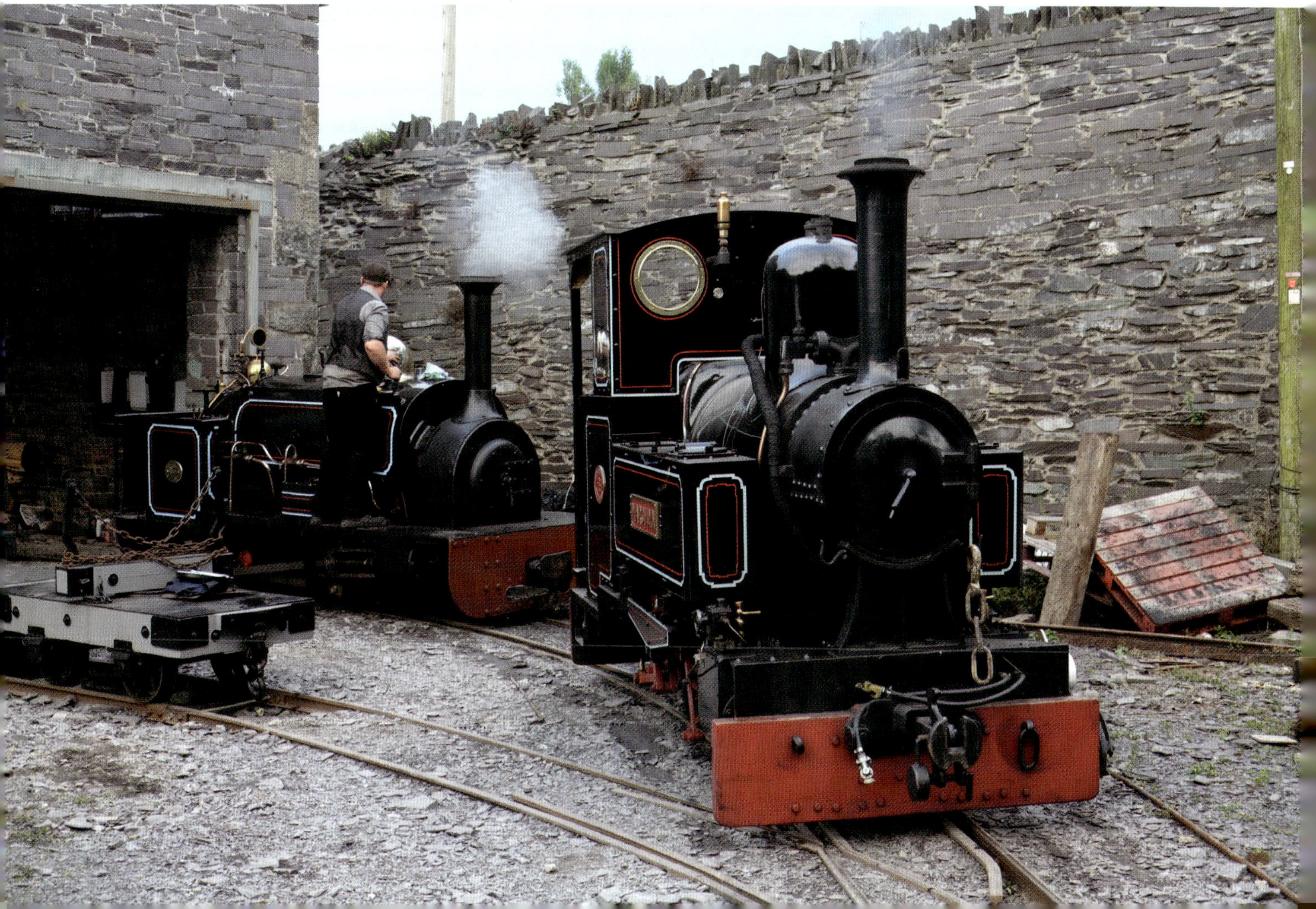

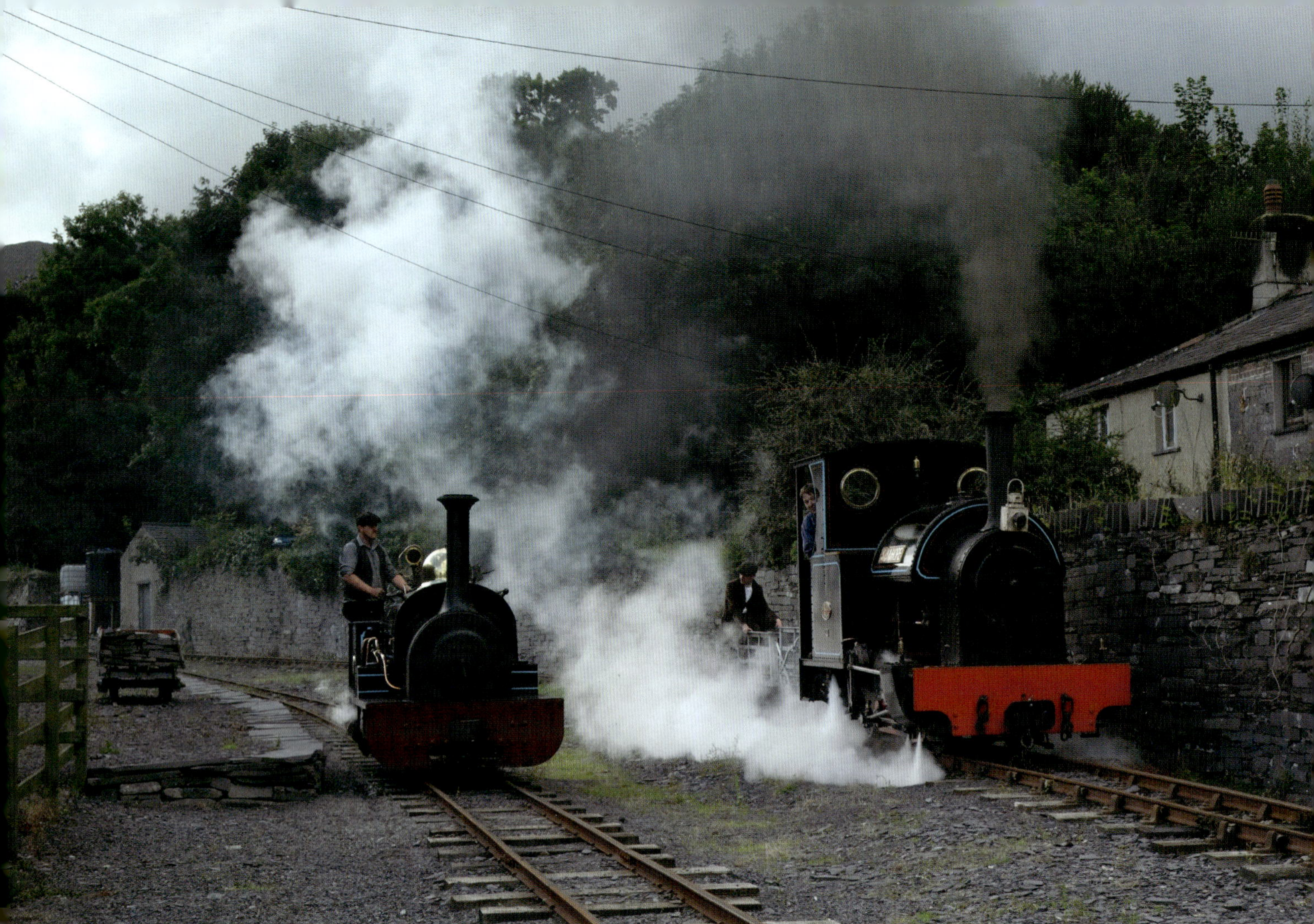

Above: Winifred and 0-4-2ST Tattoo class *Stanhope* (KS 2395/1917) pass a terrace of quarrymen's cottages at Coed-y-parc on 16 September 2016. A tramway to convey slate to the coast at Port Penrhyn from the huge quarry, on the north eastern side of Elidir Fawr near Bangor, began operations in about 1798. It was one of the earliest railways in Wales and may have been the first line of approximately 2ft gauge anywhere in the world. In 1879, it was replaced by the new 1ft 10¾ins gauge Penrhyn Quarry Railway which closed in 1963 and the last lines within the quarry soon followed. The Hunslets became almost synonymous with the Welsh slate quarries whereas *Stanhope* was the only loco of her kind at Penrhyn and is an unlikely survivor. She was withdrawn as long ago as 1947 and stripped of parts over many years; even her frame was cut in two. Alan Keef's completed her restoration in 1999. She heads a short train of typical Welsh slate wagons. The leading one comes from the Great Western which built fifty in 1899 and another fifty in 1903 for the Blaenau Ffestiniog quarry traffic.

Opposite: A little later *Winifred* heads north along the route of the old mainline. This short heritage operation had a rich history and was full of slate railway character, especially when Penrhyn locos were visiting. It promised much for the future but closed suddenly in July 2017 – a great loss. Most of its equipment has now left the site.

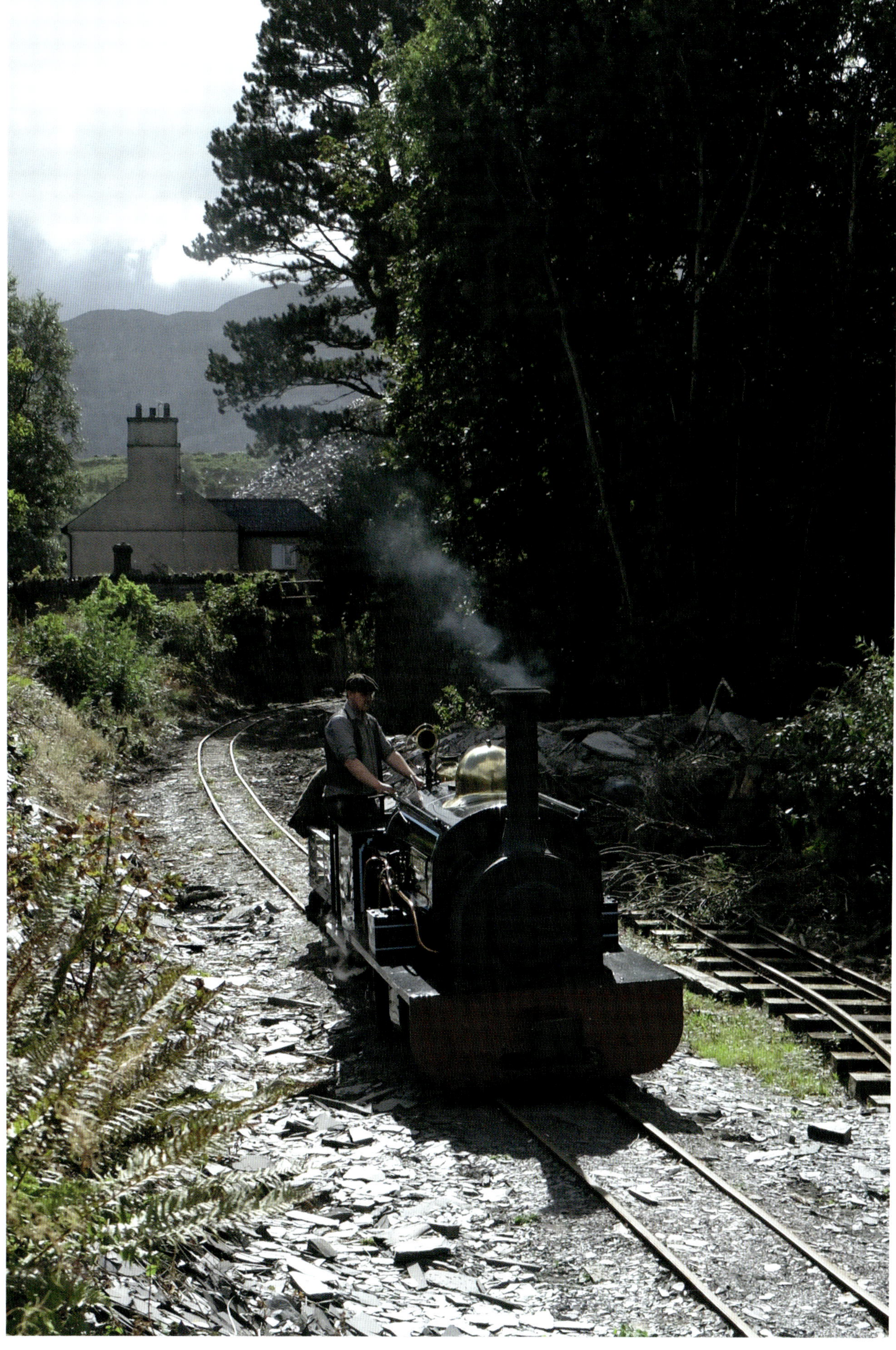

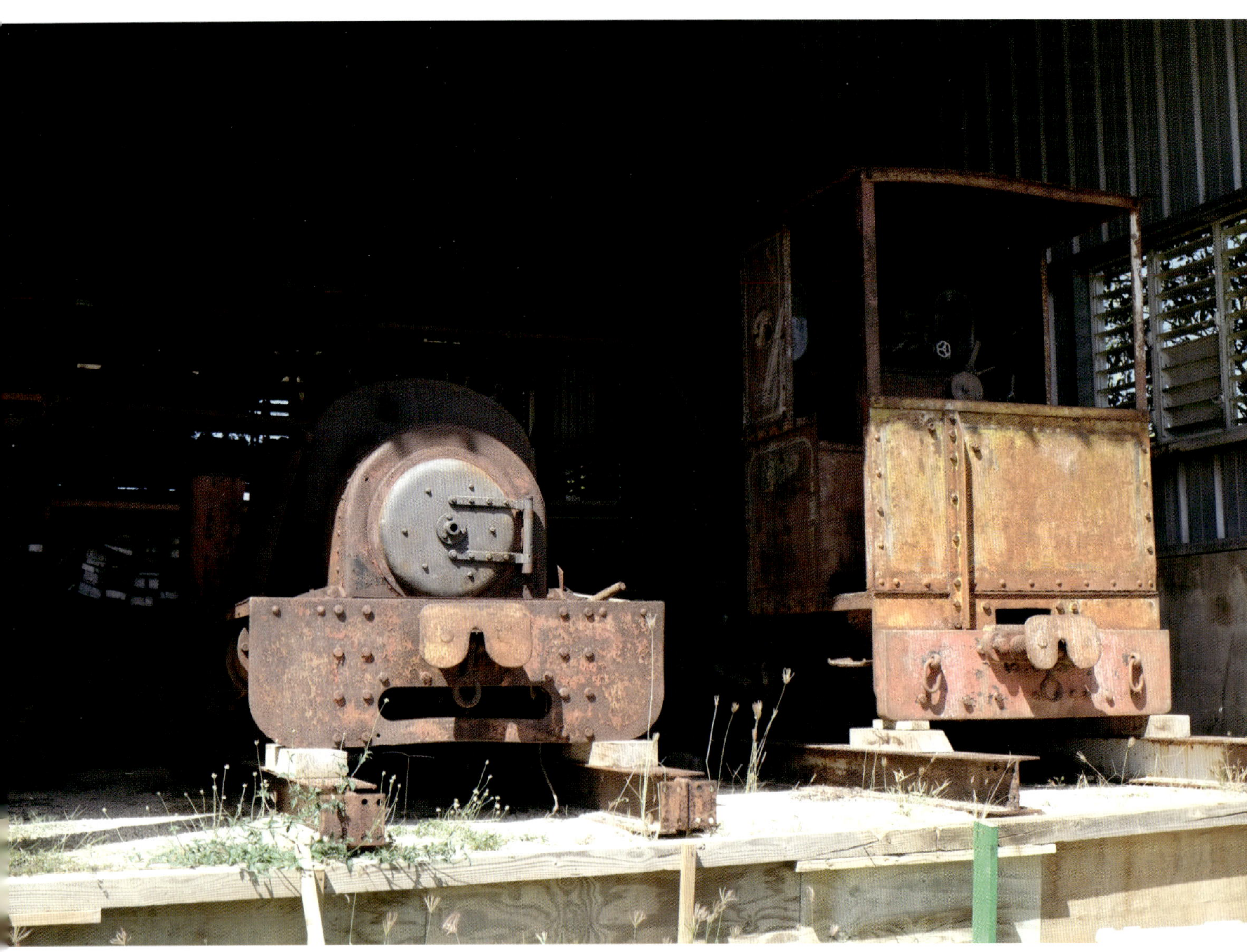

Of all the transatlantic émigrés these two Penrhyn locos, 0-4-0ST *Nesta* (Hunslet 704/1899) and E class 0-4-0T *Cegin* (Barclay 1991/1931) travelled the furthest, spending many years at the Hacienda La Esperanza near Manatí on the US island of Puerto Rico. It houses a museum of Caribbean slavery and was an appropriate home for them since the cost of developing Penrhyn quarry was met out of the fortune its owning family had made from Jamaican sugar plantations worked by hundreds of slaves in the 1600s and 1700s. Here the locos are in store at La Esperanza on 24 February 2013. The distinctive Penrhyn lining-out on *Cegin's* cab is still visible, despite her many years exposed to the sea air. Sadly, the museum couldn't afford to restore them and in 2016 they became the last of the US locos to return.

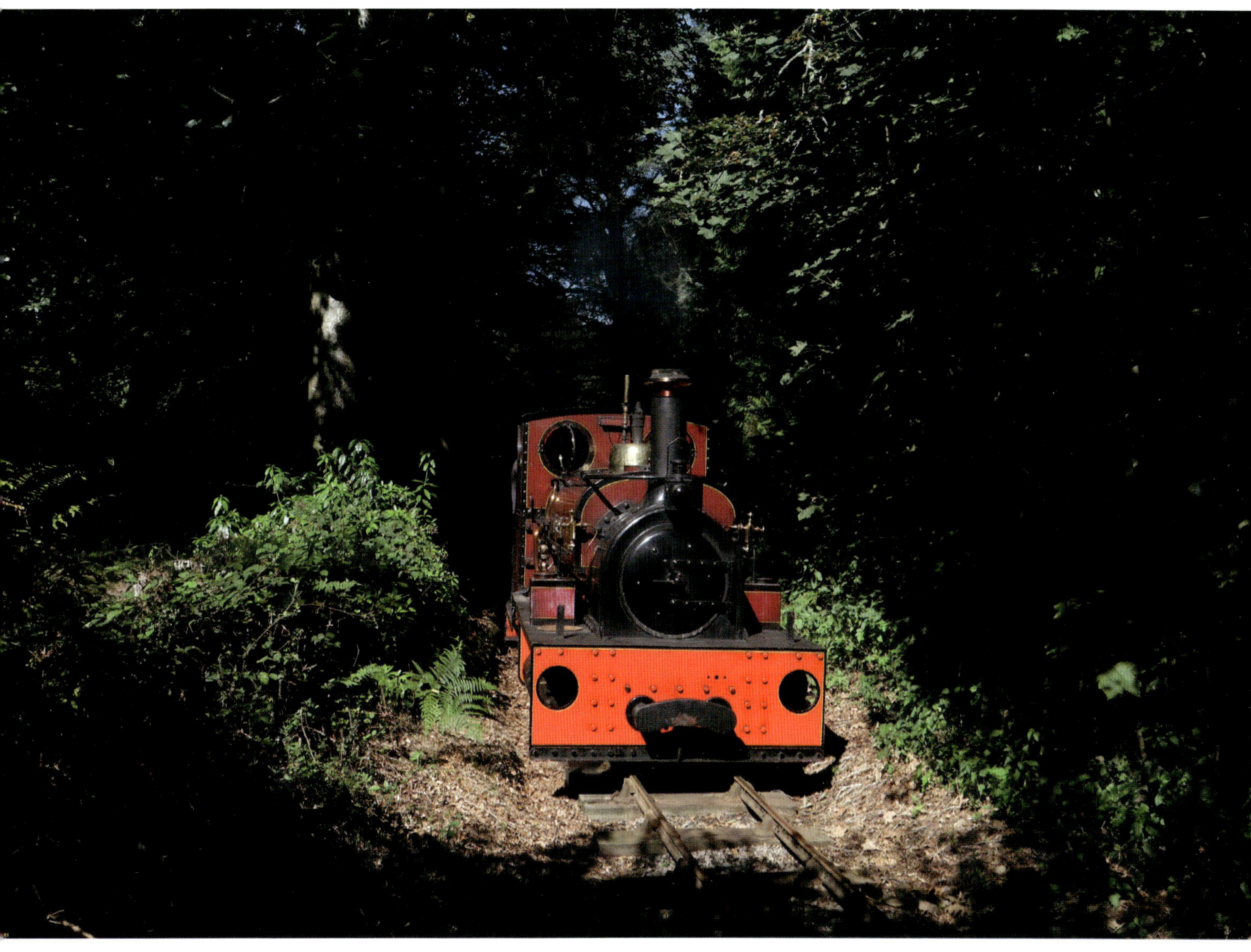

Dinorwic quarry, which lay on the opposite side of Elidir Fawr and ate away at the same slate vein, was home to another 1ft 10¾ins gauge system. After haulage to Gilfach Ddu, its wagons were loaded onto transporters on a 4ft gauge line which ran to Penscoins near the coast. They were then offloaded to run down a cable-worked incline to the port. The railway closed in the 1960s like the Penrhyn line and by the end of the decade so had the quarry. A reminder can be found at the Hollycombe Steam Museum in West Sussex. In 1968, its founder bought *Jerry M* (Hunslet 638/1895), one of two extra-large 0-4-0STs built for the Gilfach Ddu tramway, along with some of the distinctive chaired Dinorwic track which he laid out at his home. *Jerry M* looks the part on 26 August 2016 and perhaps the Hollycombe woods look a little like those at Gilfach Ddu!

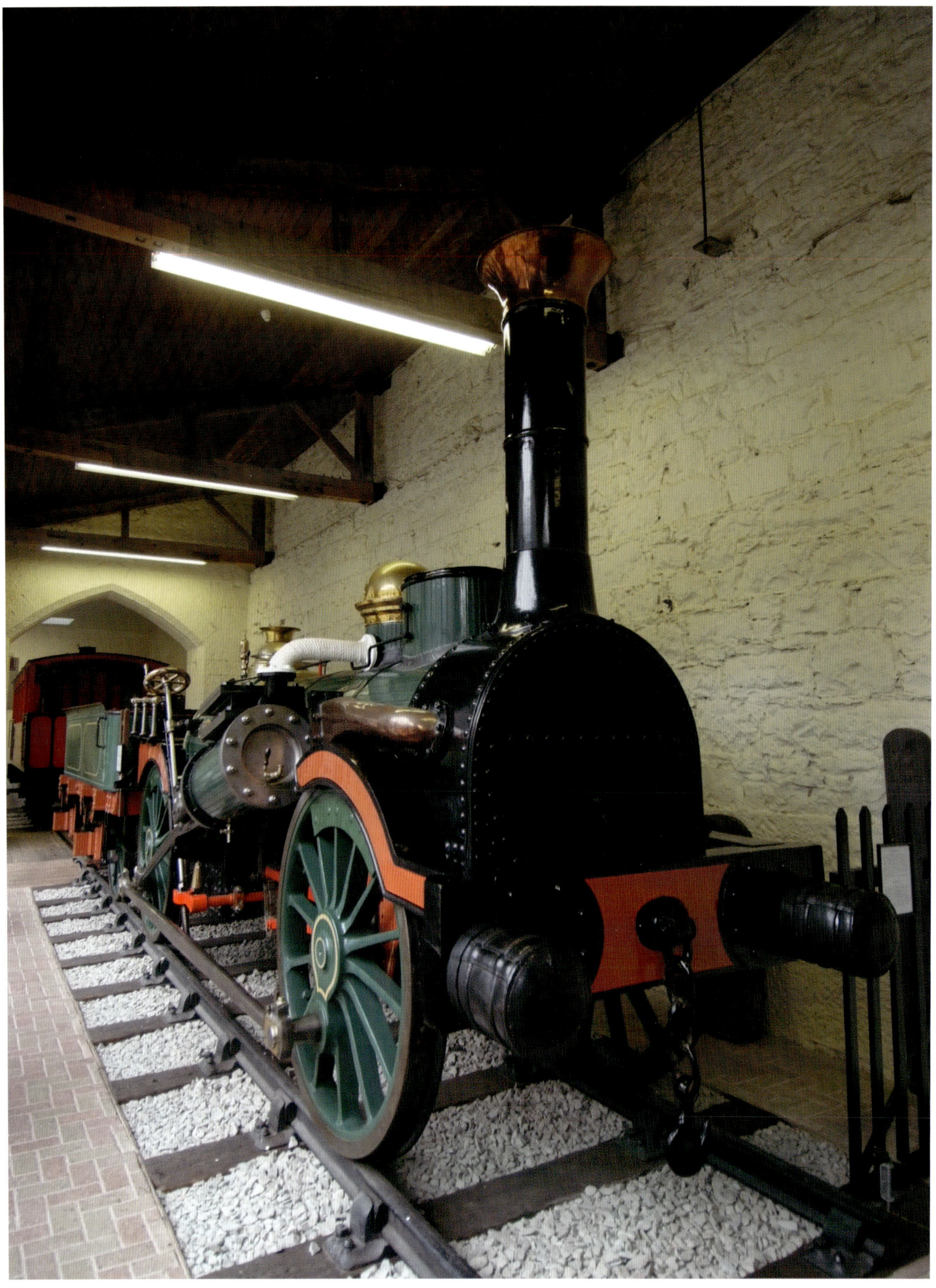

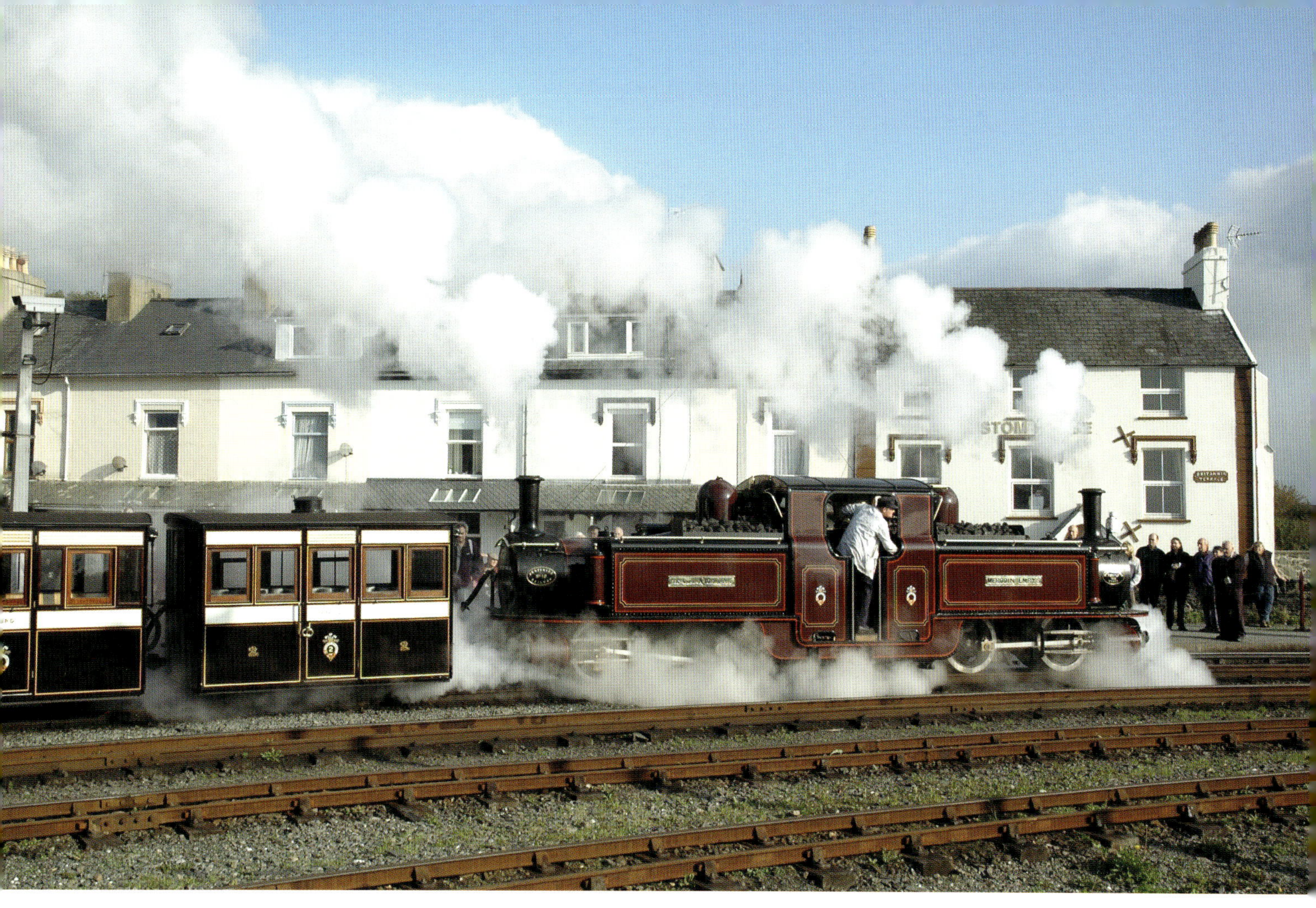

Above: The 600mm gauge Ffestiniog Railway was built in the early 1830s. Its constant gradient allowed gravity working over a distance of more than twelve miles, a brilliant achievement considering the difficult terrain. It wasn't the first narrow gauge steam railway when locos took over in 1863 but it had an enormous influence around the world and attracted even more attention when its first Double Fairlie arrived in 1869. Here, 0-4-4-0 No 10 *Merddin Emrys* leaves Porthmadog with a train of superbly restored 4-wheeled carriages on 14 October 2005. She dates from 1879 and was the first loco constructed at the railway's Boston Lodge shops. In preservation she has become both longer and taller but still has something of the traditional Ffestiniog Fairlie look.

Opposite: Fire Queen (Horlock, 1848) was one of two Crampton-type 0-4-0s which worked Dinorwic's 4ft gauge railway to Penscoins between 1848 and the 1880s. After withdrawal, her sister *Jenny Lind* was scrapped but *Fire Queen* was just tucked away in her shed at Gilfach Ddu works, reportedly because the quarry owner's daughter had a soft spot for her. For many years, cleaning the loco was a weekly ritual for the works apprentices. When Dinorwic closed she moved to a new museum at Penrhyn, was given a fresh coat of paint and has been on show ever since, unfortunately in conditions almost as cramped as her previous home. Is she the world's oldest surviving narrow gauge loco?! Here she is on 3 October 2014; behind her is the owner's private saloon, built in 1895. Other exhibits here include a Penrhyn Hunslet and two 3ft gauge locos. One is a survivor of at least sixty-nine 0-4-0VBT's built by de Winton at Caernarfon. The other is "Kettering Furnaces No 3" (BH 859/1885), one of its builders' distinctive 0-4-0ST's which, remarkably, included five constructed to Brunel's celebrated 7ft gauge, three for South Africa and two for the Azores where one still exists.

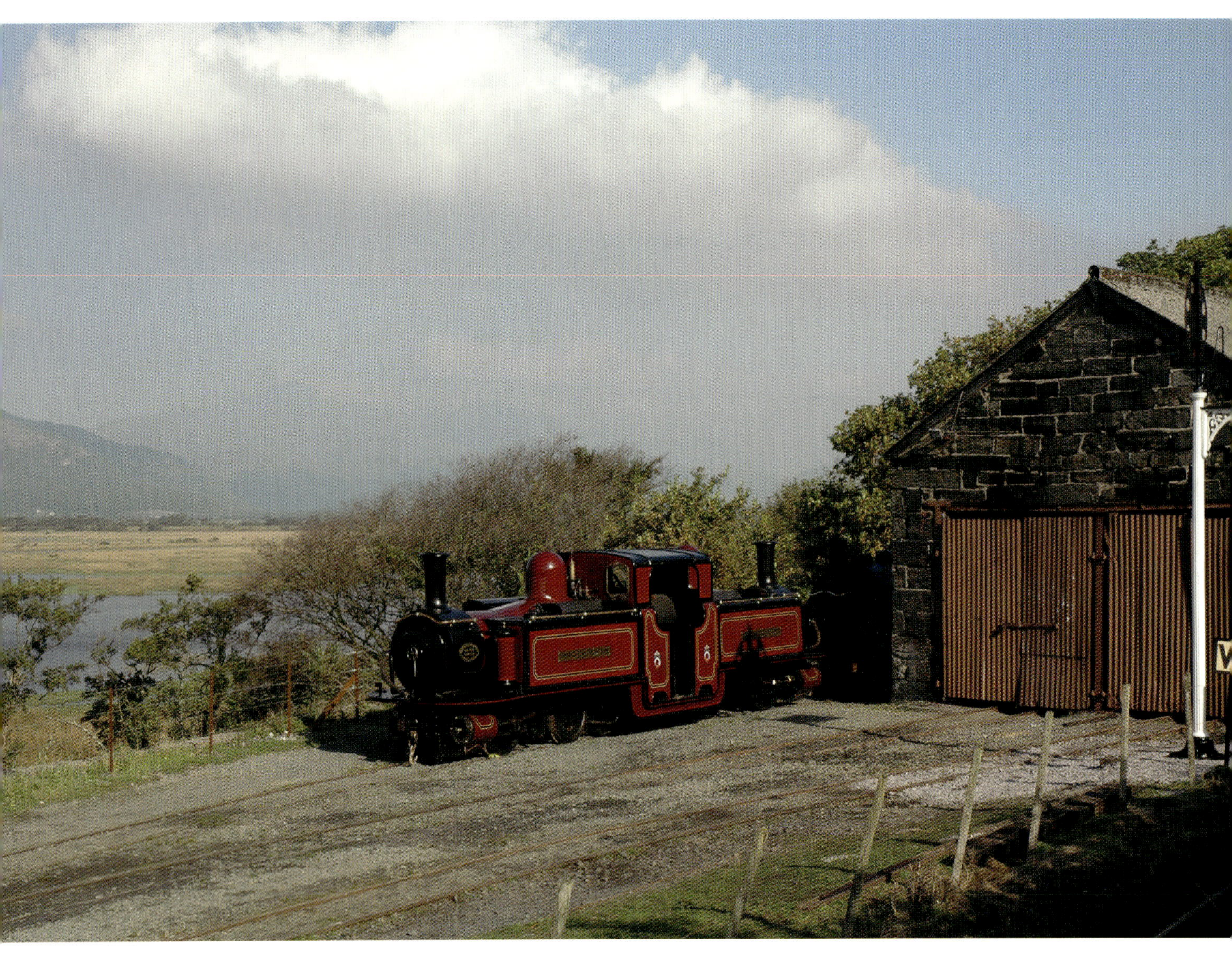

0-4-4-0 No 3 *Livingston Thompson* (Boston Lodge, 1885) has kept her old size and shape and looks much as she did after her last major rebuild in 1905. She hasn't run since 1971 and owes her survival to a group of Ffestiniog members who stopped her being stripped of parts for use in a replacement loco. She normally lives at the National Railway Museum at York but on 14 October 2005 stood outside the old Boston Lodge shed – which also then kept its original shape but has since been widened. Note the traditional Ffestiniog disc signal. Behind her is 0-4-0ST *Welsh Pony* (GE 234/1867), now being restored to working order after being out of use since 1942.

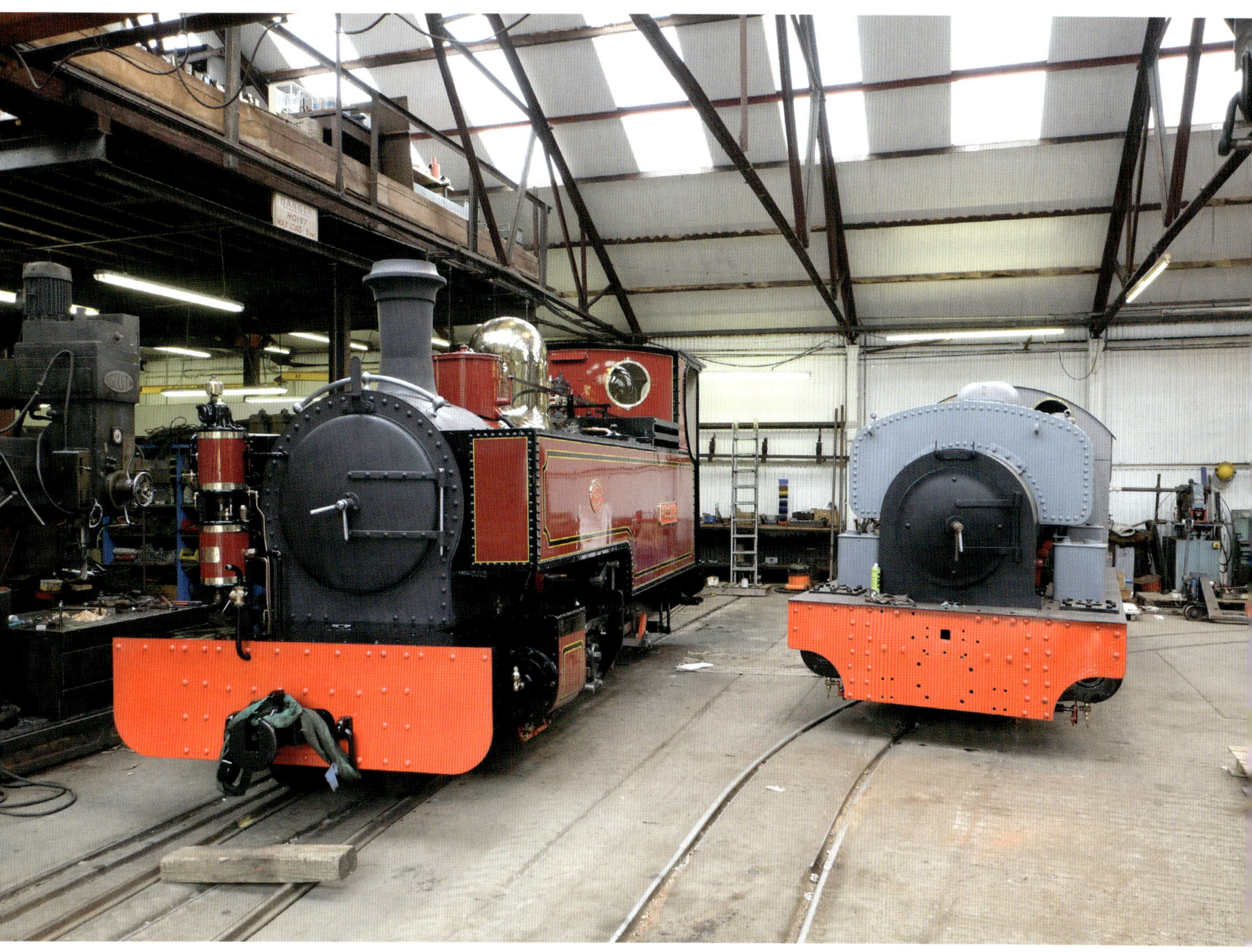

The old Welsh Highland Railway closed in 1937 but now the Ffestiniog has rebuilt it all, in fact more than there ever was in the old days as it also runs over the old standard gauge route into Caernarfon. This was originally part of the 3ft 6ins gauge Nantlle Railway, the southern end of which continued in service under British Railways as a horse-worked plateway until 1963. The reconstruction was an enormous achievement for a small organisation. 2-6-2T *Russell* (Hunslet 901/1906), the only surviving original loco, is now in the care of the Welsh Highland Heritage Railway at Porthmadog and it would be marvellous if she could run again over her old line. Here she stands in Alan Keef's workshops on 30 July 2014, magnificently restored to as-new condition and about to begin her journey home. Next to her is the 2ft gauge Harrogate Gasworks Railway's 0-6-2ST *Barber* (TG 441/1908) which now lives at the South Tynedale Railway.

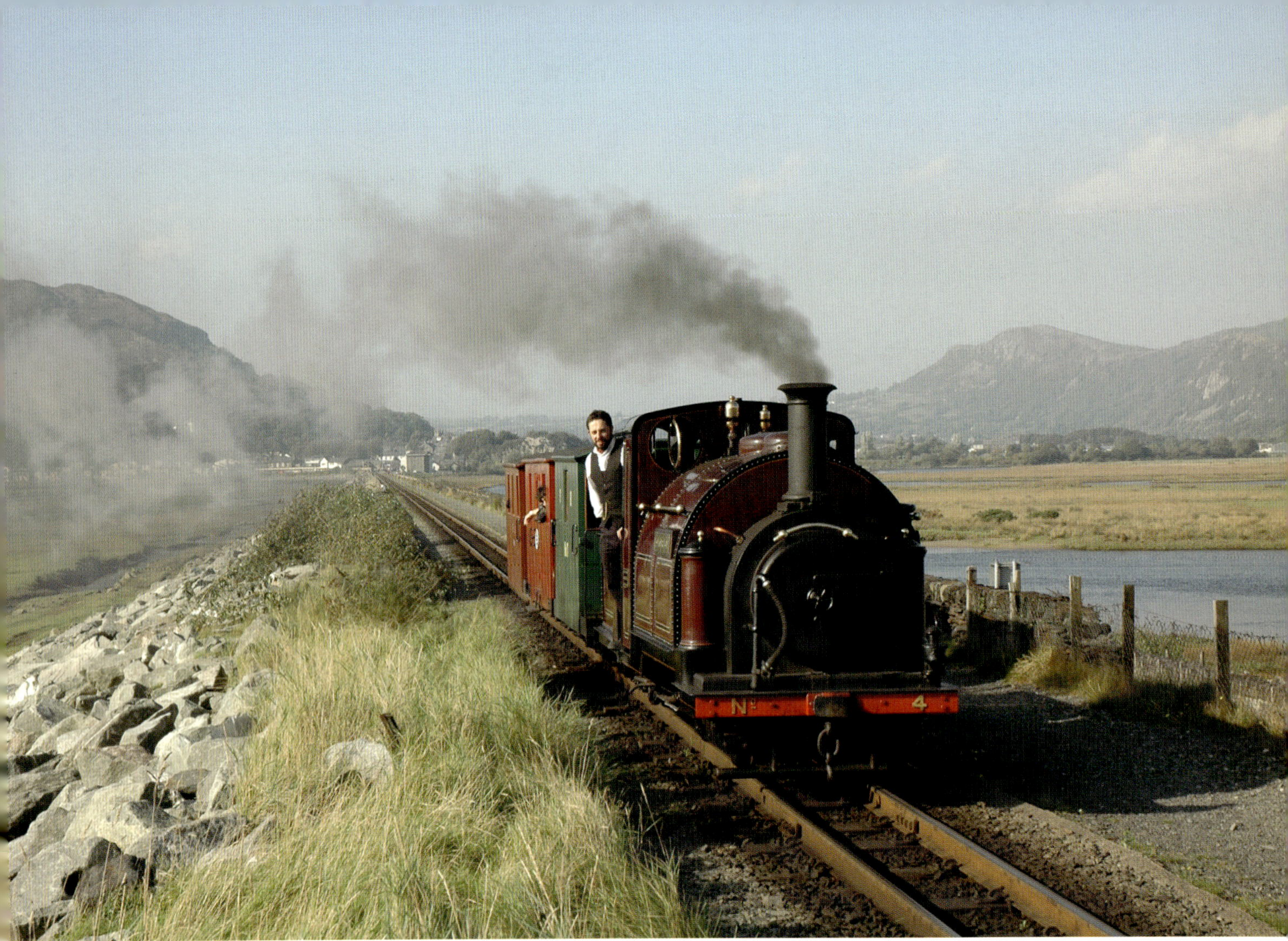

Above: On the Ffestiniog 0-4-0ST No 4 *Palmerston* (GE, 1864), one of the railway's four original locos, has run across the Cob on 14 October 2005 with a train of quarrymen's coaches and approaches Boston Lodge. Like *Livingston Thompson* she was rescued by Ffestiniog members who bought her in 1974. More recently the railway accepted her back and has painstakingly restored her to working order.

Opposite above: The enthusiast world owes a debt of gratitude to the 2ft 3ins gauge Talyllyn Railway for showing how preservation by enthusiasts could succeed. It was the world's first narrow gauge line designed for steam operation when built in the early 1860's. Here 0-4-2ST *Talyllyn* (FJ 42/1864) brings empty wagons up the Fathew valley near Quarry Siding on 30 March 2017.

Opposite below: Both the original locos and all five of the old carriages and brake van together with three wagons head up the valley above Tan-y-coed Uchaf on 31 March 2017. The Talyllyn was unusual in that all this stock was still on site when the preservation society took over in 1951. Recently the two locos have been magnificently restored to what is, at least conjecturally, their original livery.

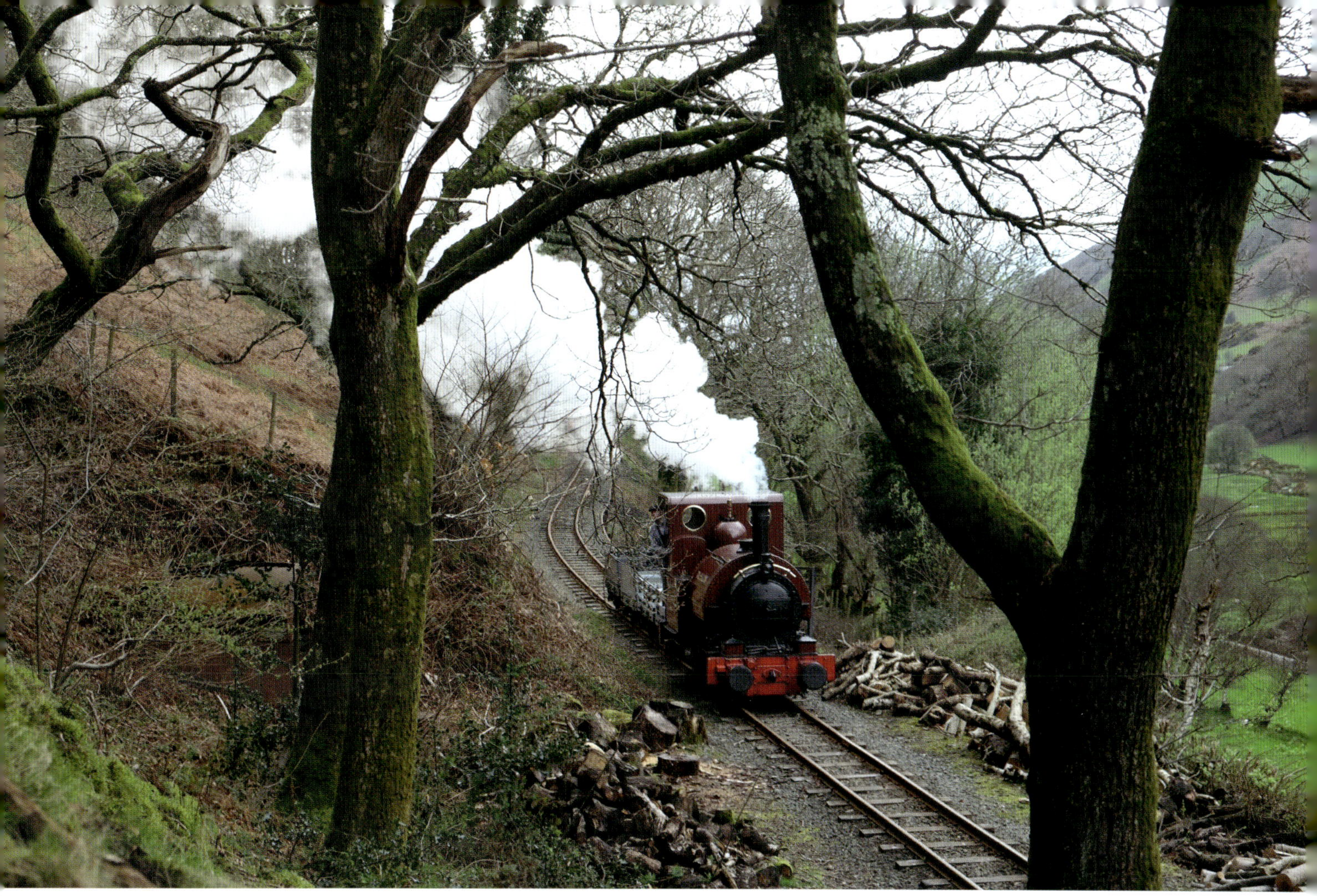

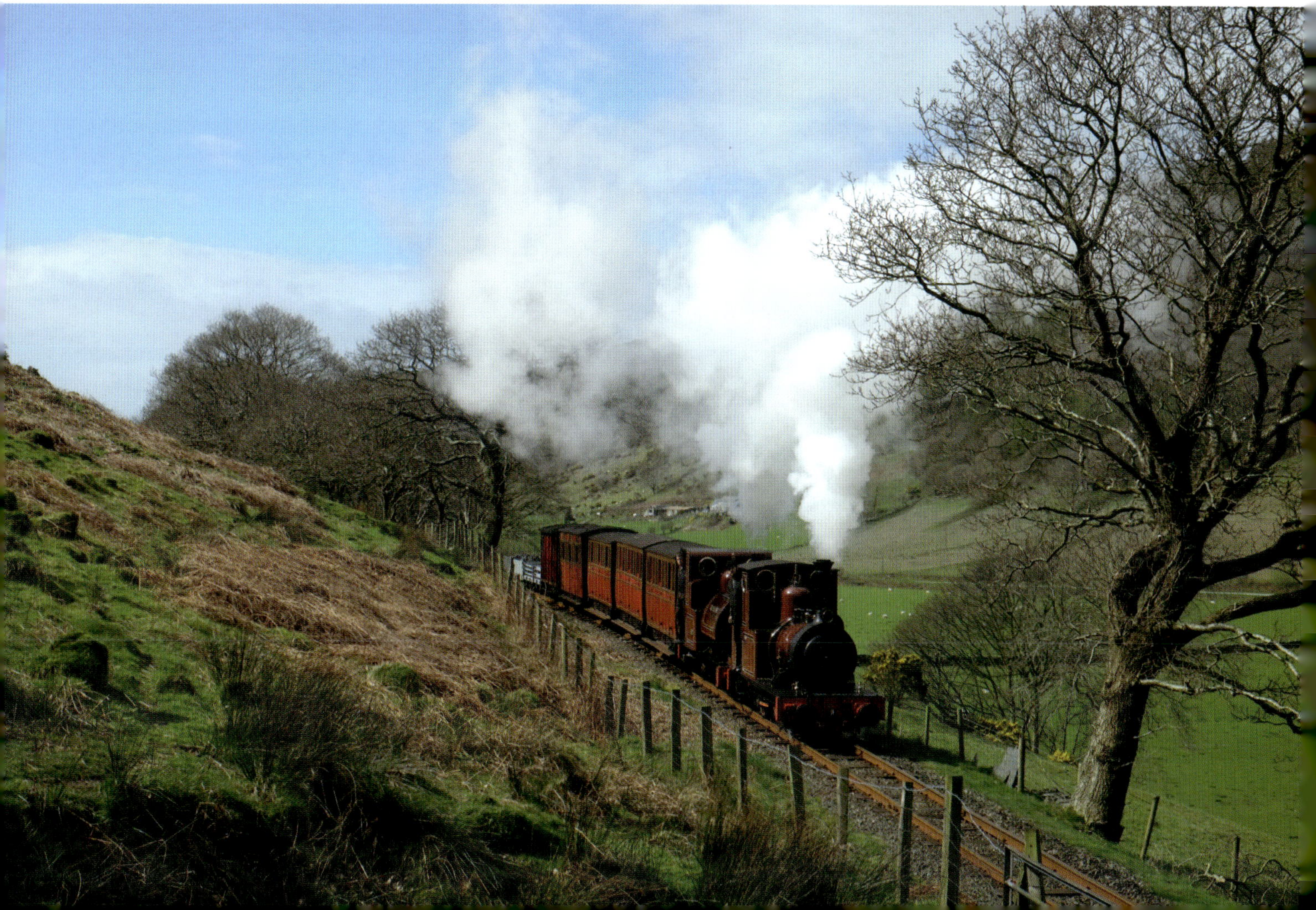

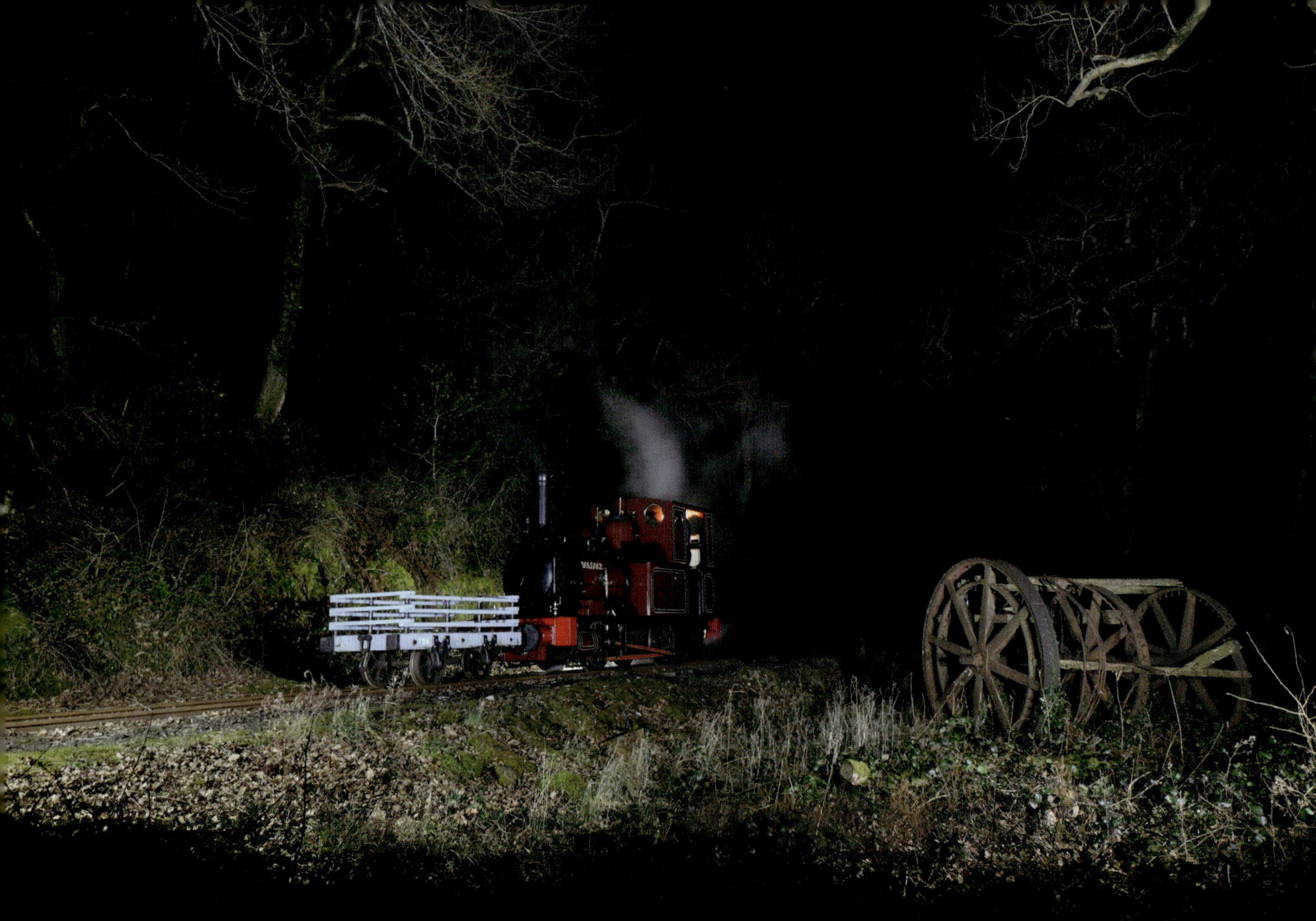

Above: 0-4-0WT *Dolgoch* (FJ 63/1866) and a slate wagon pause at the site of the Abergynolwyn incline winding house on 21 March 2016. The incline was used to transport goods to the village. Sadly, the winding house disappeared when the line beyond Abergynolwyn station was rebuilt to accommodate passenger trains. The drum is all that remains but happily the somewhat similar winding house at the head of the incline at Nant Gwernol is well looked-after.

Opposite above: On 10 November 2017 2-6-2T No 8 (Swindon, 1923) crosses the Afon Rheidol near Aberystwyth with a mixed train on the 600mm gauge Vale of Rheidol Railway. The line opened in 1902 and was bought by the Cambrian in 1913. Under the 1922 Grouping it became part of the GWR which lost no time building three new 2-6-2Ts. The cattle wagon is one of two also built in 1923; fourteen years later they were regauged and moved to the Welshpool & Llanfair. This one has recently been superbly restored to its original condition at Aberystwyth.

Opposite below: No 8 runs between Glanrafon and Capel Bangor on 10 November 2017. The valley is pastoral for much of its length. Local passenger and freight traffic on the railway soon dropped away after the Grouping and from 1 January 1931 it became a summer-only tourist operation and was energetically promoted as such. The returns can't have made much contribution to the GWR's profits but the line was hugely important to Aberystwyth's holiday trade. When the coaches were becoming tired in 1938, Swindon built these smart new ones featuring the large panoramic windows which had recently become standard on the GWR's mainline carriages.

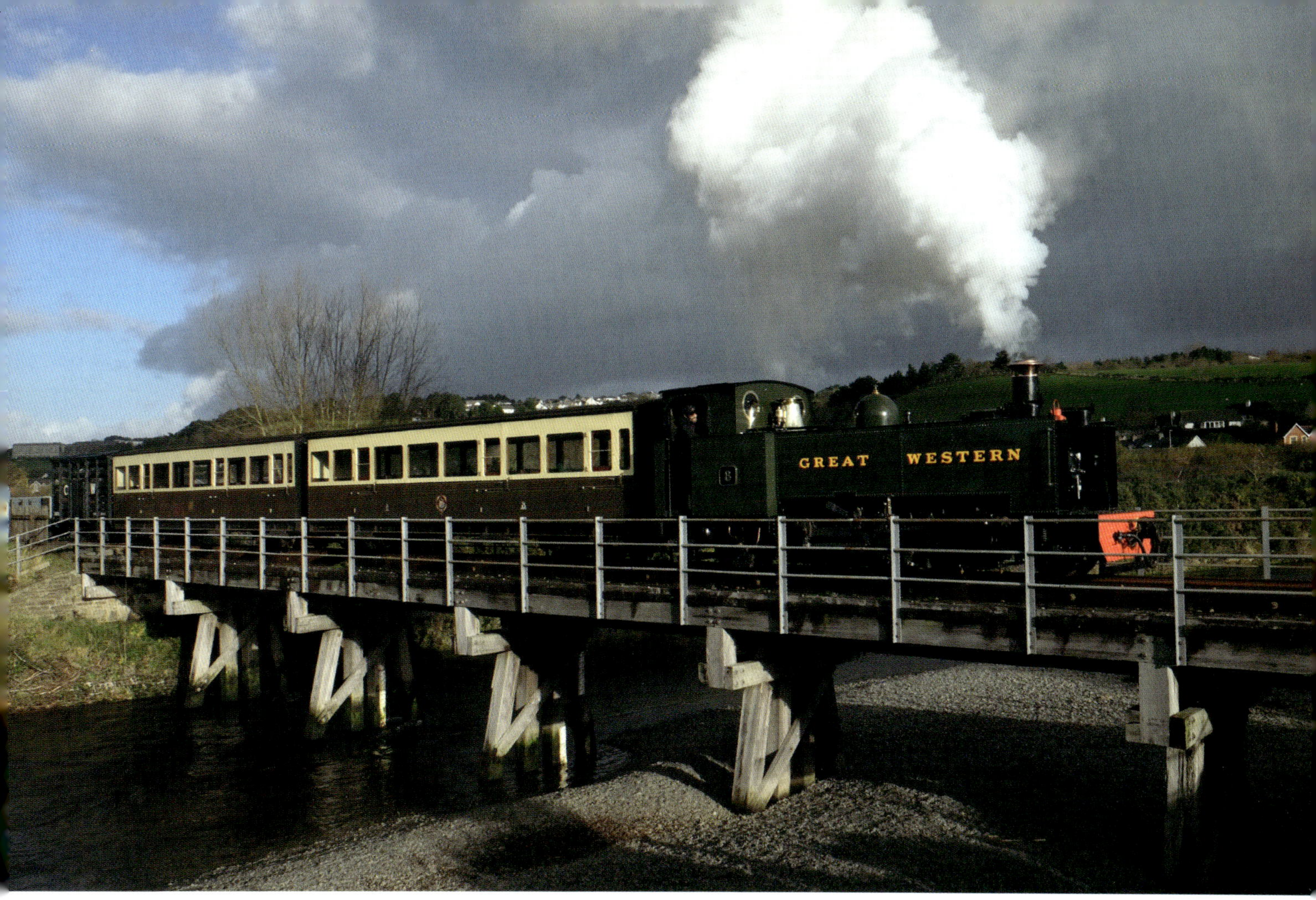

GREAT WESTERN

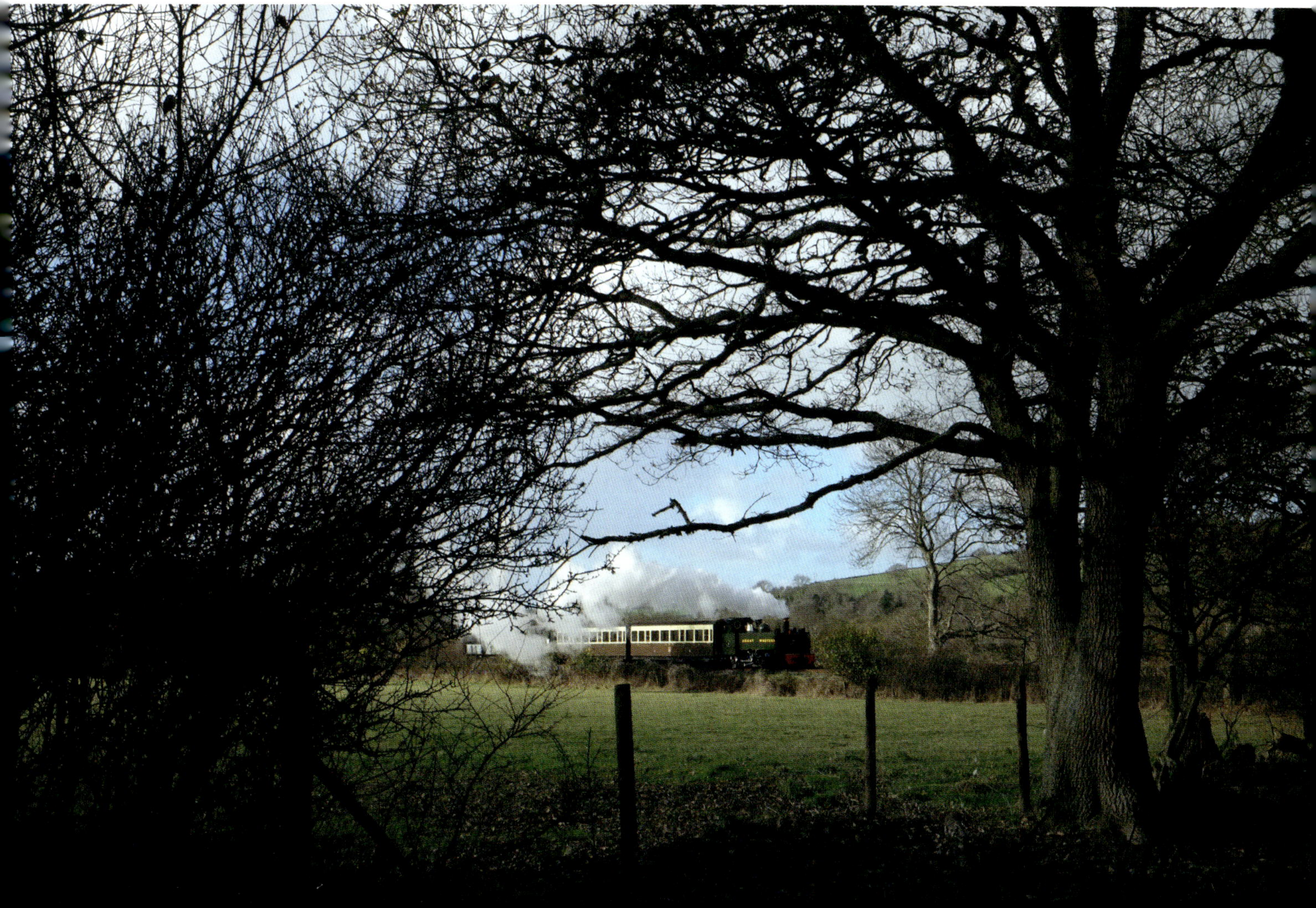

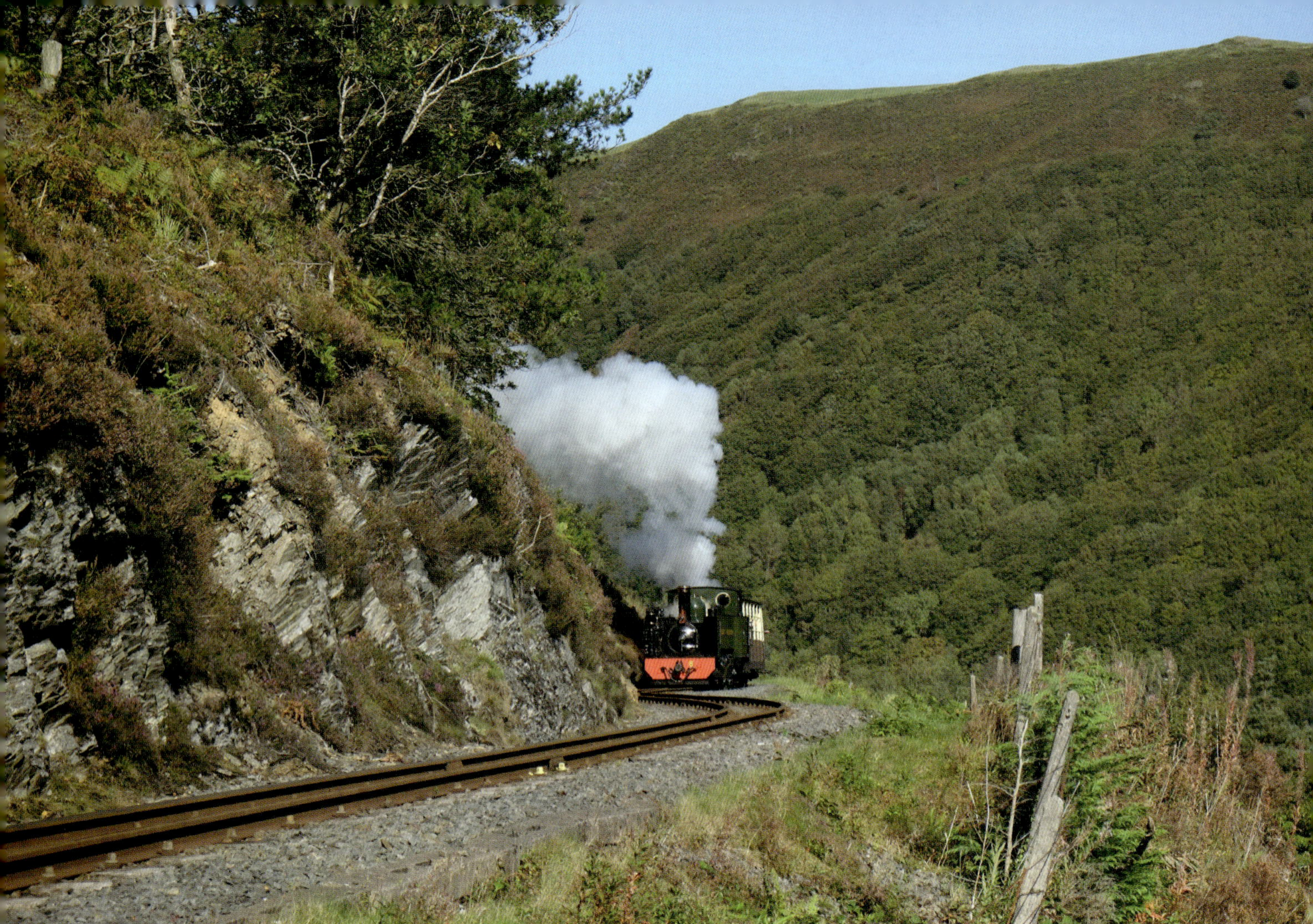

Above: British Rail sold the line in 1989 and it's now a fine heritage railway. On 27 September 2015, No 8 climbs through the spectacular gorge near Devil's Bridge. Her air brake pump, fitted in the 1990s, was still mounted on her front but has now been concealed to restore her original appearance.

Opposite above: 0-6-0T No 823 *Countess* (BP 3497/1902) has just arrived at Llanfair Caereinion on the 2ft 6ins gauge Welshpool & Llanfair in the early evening of 3 September 2011 as No 822 *The Earl* (BP 3496/1902) stands in the yard. The line opened in 1903, was worked by the Cambrian and at the Grouping also became a part of the GWR which soon upgraded the locos to Swindon standards with new boilers and GWR fittings. The smart copper chimney caps and curvy brass safety valve bonnets were hallmarks of true Great Western locos even if they were sometimes painted over. With their fat boilers and short wheelbase, the two locos were well suited to the steep and twisty line.

Opposite below: There wasn't much tourist traffic and passenger services ended completely on 7 February 1931. The GWR took a more benevolent attitude towards its rural railways and the communities they served than other mainline companies. Although it scrapped the three carriages, freight services continued for the remainder of its independent existence. The line was closed by British Railways in 1956 and the preservation society came into being shortly afterwards. In the 2000s, beautiful replica carriages have been meticulously built by the Ffestiniog at Boston Lodge. Here is brake third No 6338, the last of the three to be completed, at Llanfair Caereinion station on the evening of 3 September 2011.

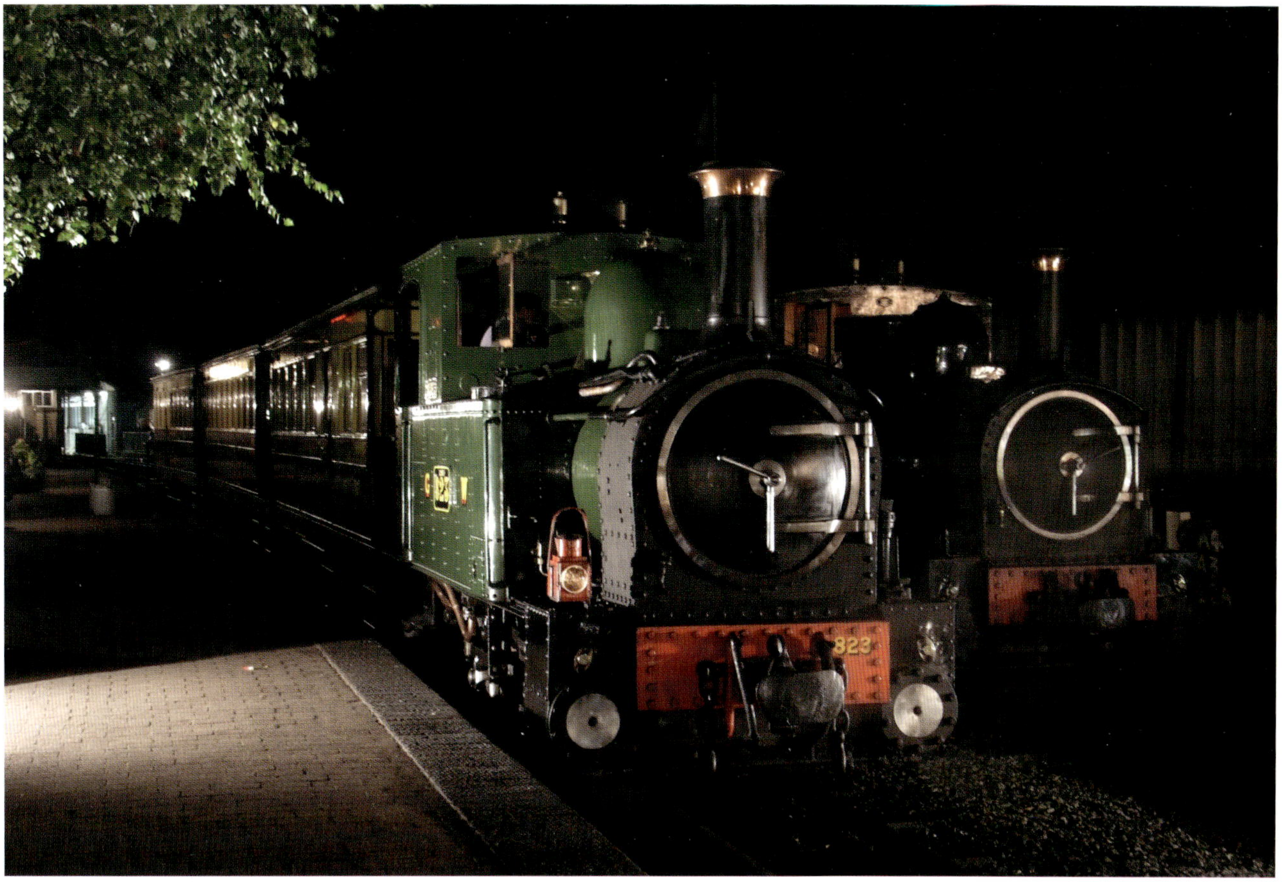

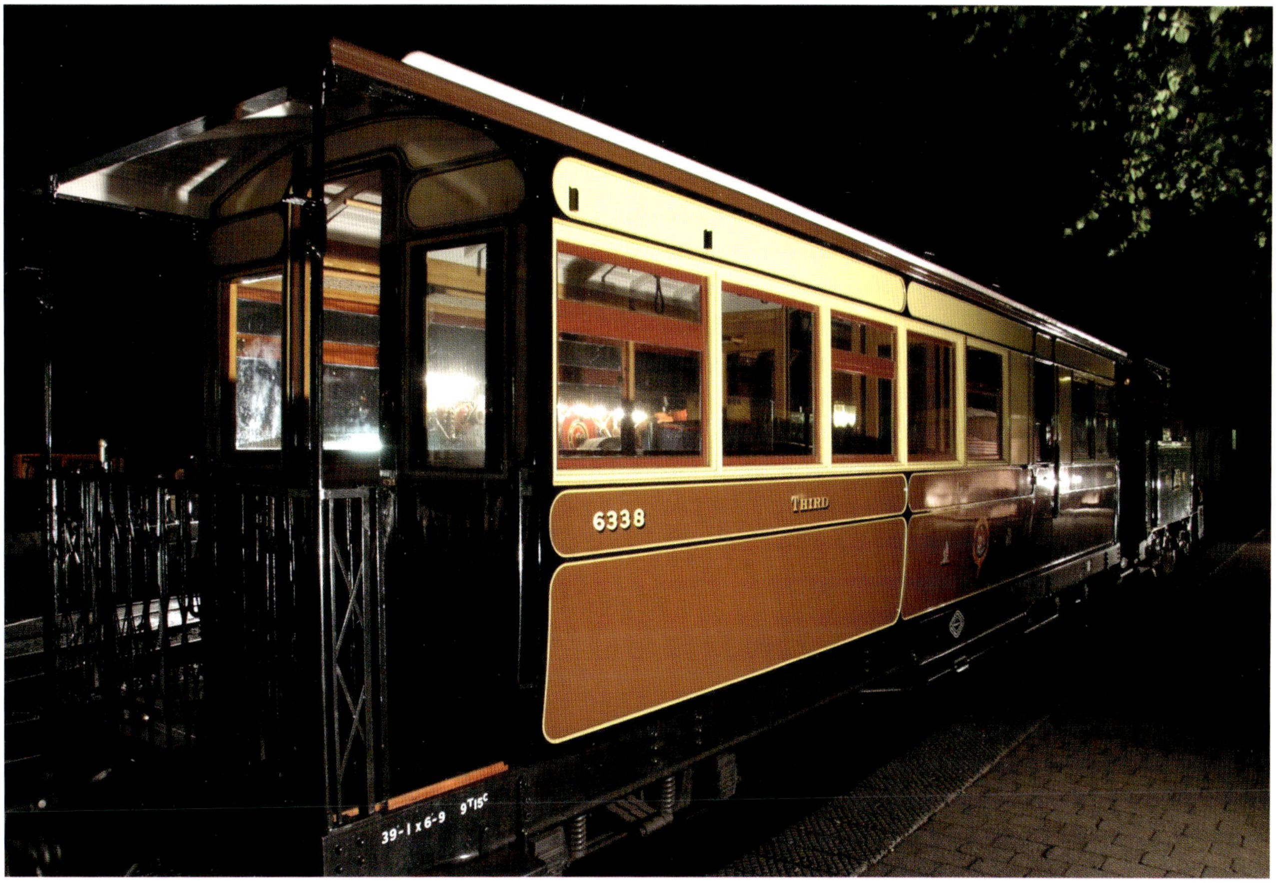

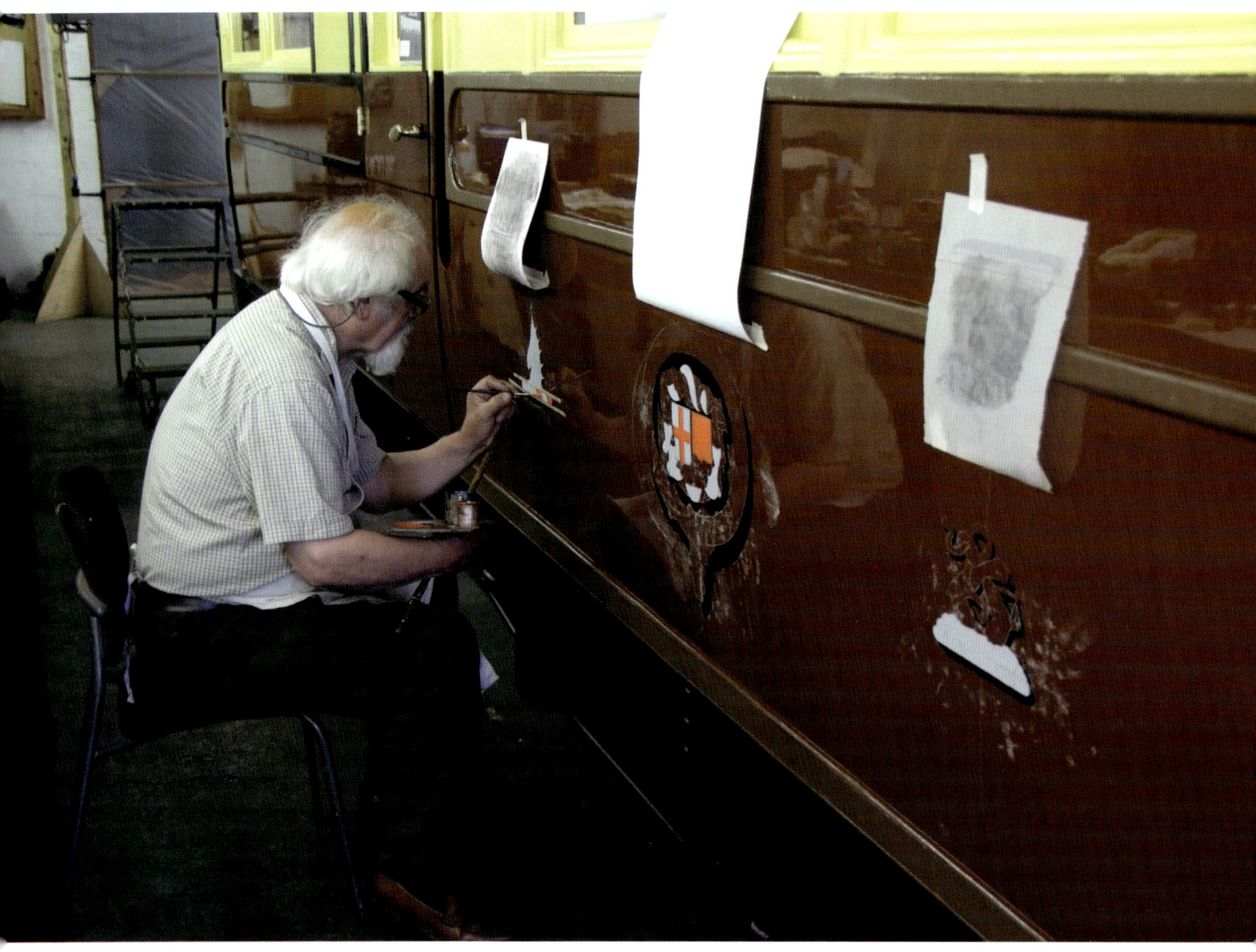

Above: Craftsmanship of a high order! This gentleman, Bob Timmins, is painting the GWR's regalia on No 6338 at Boston Lodge on 30 June 2010.

Opposite above: On 3 September 2010, the first day of operation of the complete train of three carriages, No 823 *Countess* has just crossed the River Banwy and approaches Heniarth. The GWR also fitted each loco with an elaborate part-concave and part-convex smokebox door surrounded by a smart steel ring, the design of which dated back to broad gauge days but went out of fashion around the turn of the century. The only later locos to carry these doors from new were the five little 1361 class 0-6-0STs built in 1910 but the GWR fitted them to a number of small locos it had taken over at the Grouping and before. Maybe Swindon had a stock left over from many years earlier and this was a good way to use them up!

Opposite below: A little later No 822, *The Earl*, painted BR black, approaches Heniarth with a goods train. Although the GWR didn't alter the coaches, it did upgrade the wagons and built new ones. The cattle wagon is the twin of the one at the Vale of Rheidol.

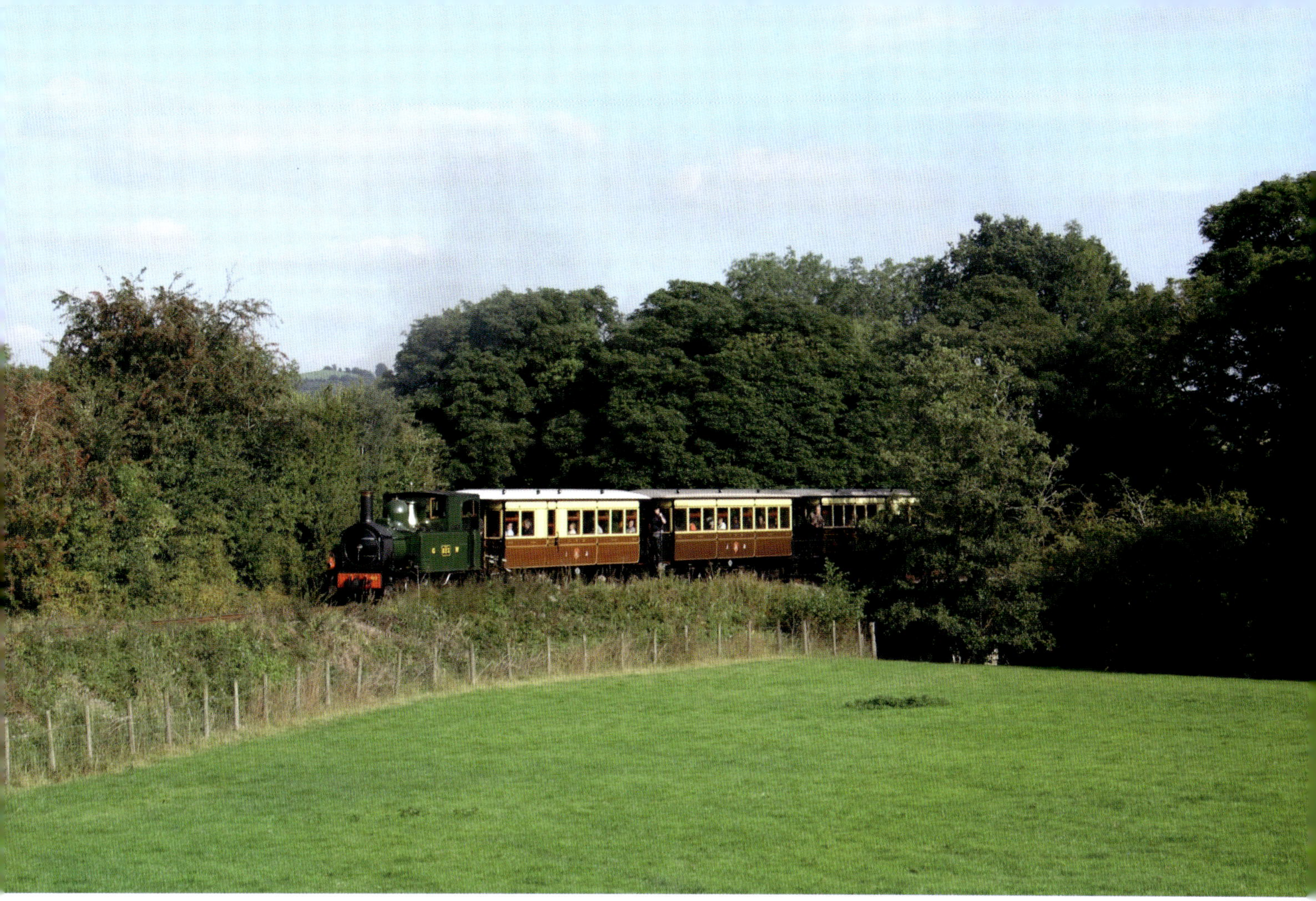

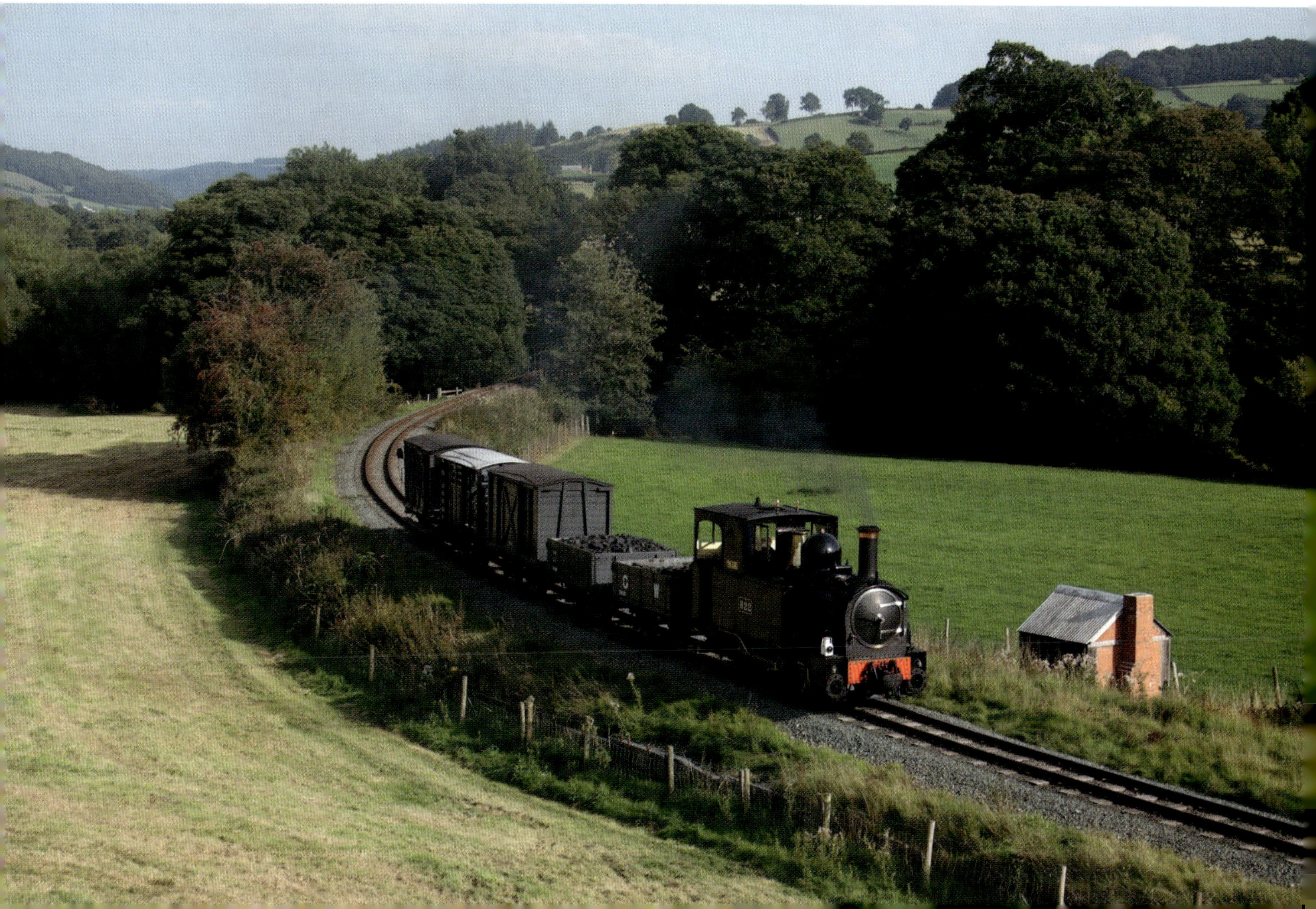

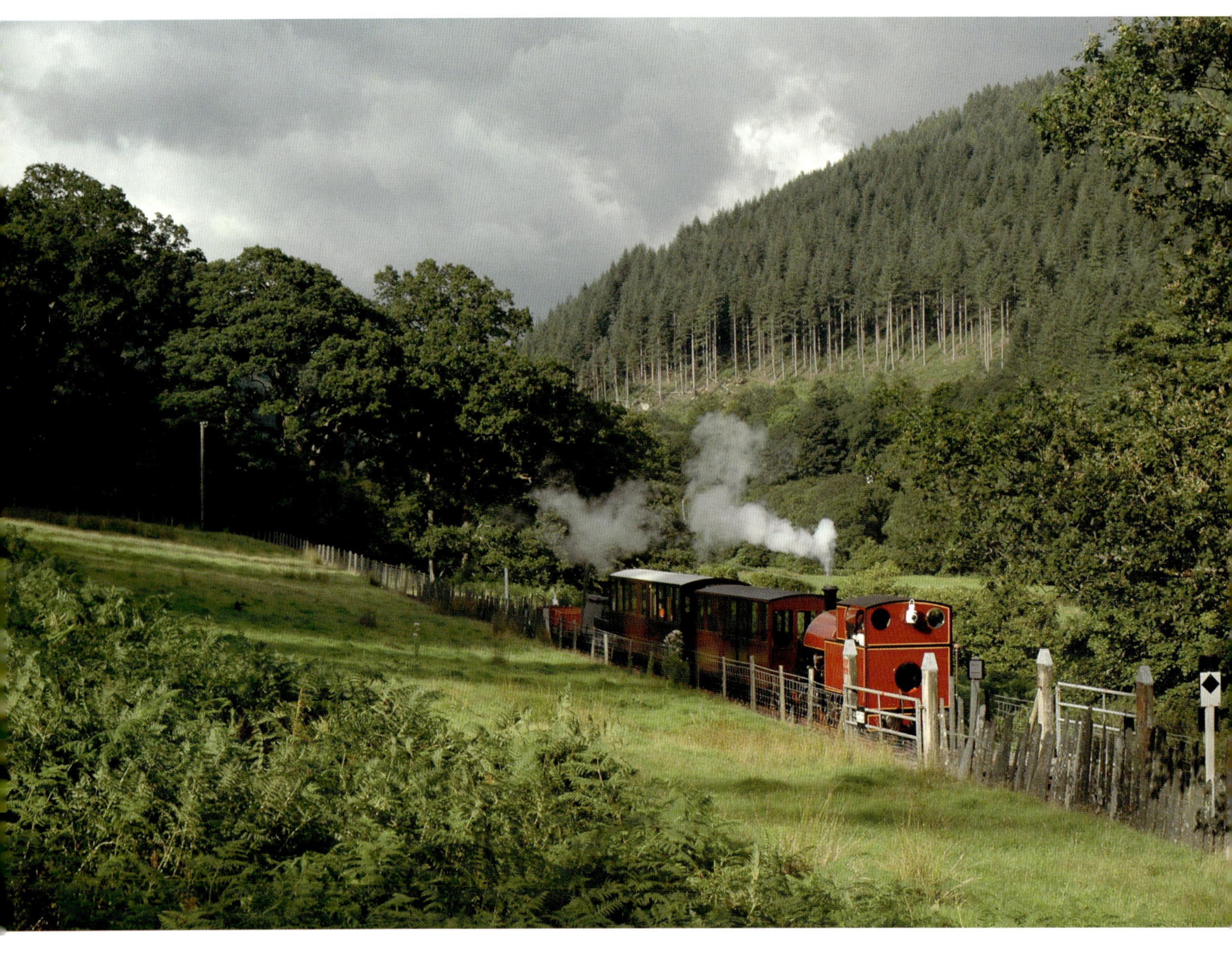

The 2ft 3ins gauge Corris Railway originated as a horse tramway in 1858. Twenty years later, three Hughes locos arrived and the old 4-wheeled tramcars were gradually rebuilt as bogie vehicles and supplemented by new ones. The GWR took over in 1929 as part of a much larger deal, mostly involving bus services. Passenger trains finished on 1 January 1931 which was clearly a bad year for the Great Western narrow gauge! Freight traffic was at a low ebb, too, but continued even though it can't possibly have been profitable. Flooding brought about closure soon after nationalisation in 1948. A very active preservation society has rebuilt a short section and has overseen construction of 0-4-2ST No 7 (Winson 17), a replica of the old Tattoo class No 4 (KS 4047/1921). Here the new loco approaches Maespoeth Junction with a mixed train on 20 August 2005, her very first day in service.

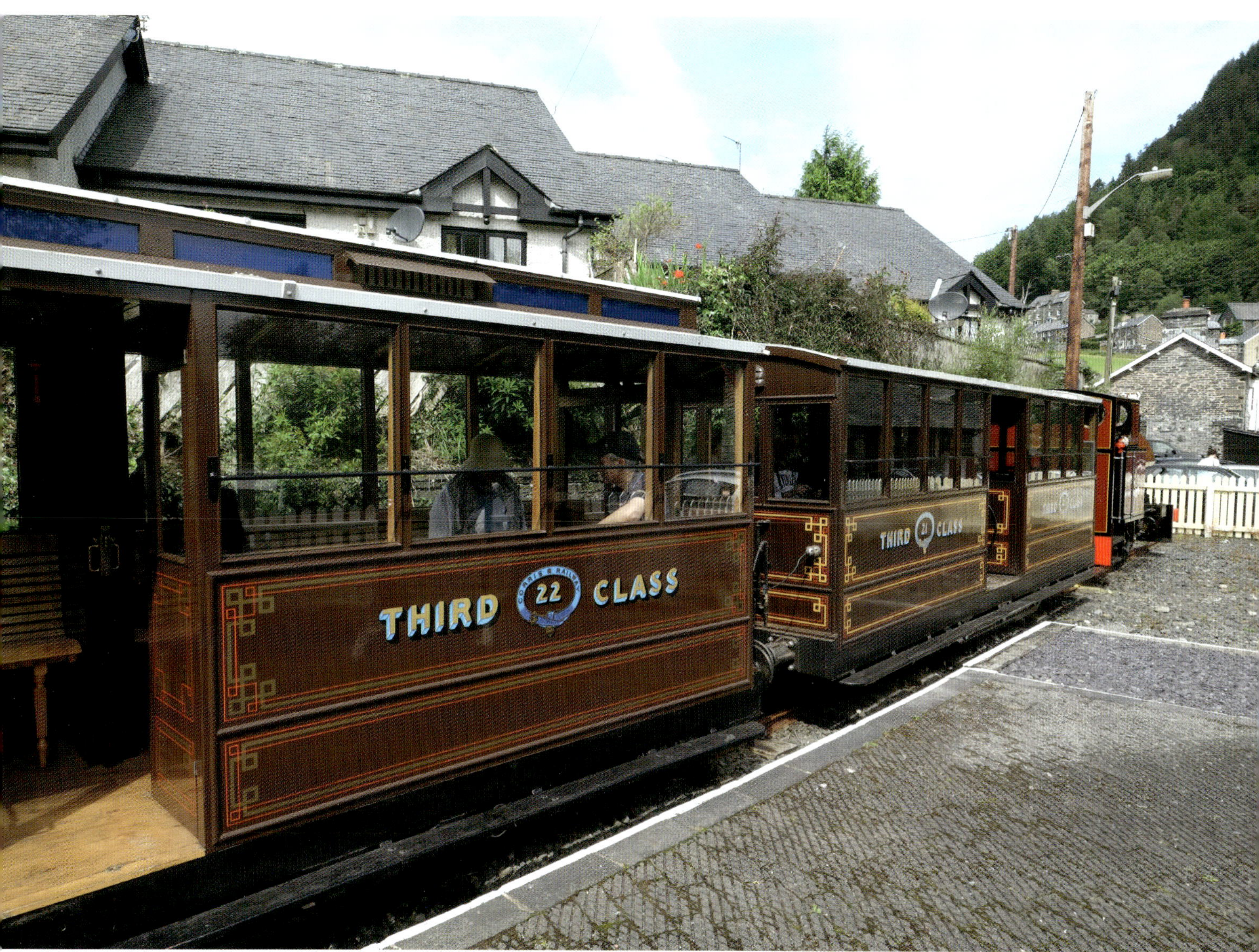

The GWR sold two of the carriages, parts of them surviving into preservation, and scrapped the rest. Despite visiting Swindon, the locos kept their old paint schemes and weren't given GWR numberplates or, apparently, any other fittings except for Swindon's distinctive fore-and-aft lampirons. Carriages Nos 22 and 23, which entered service in 2003 and 2016, are replicas of the old railway's two main types of bogie vehicle and stand at Corris with No 7 on 7 August 2017. They carry the elaborate lining used until the First World War. Construction of a replica Hughes loco, rather like the one at Hagfors, is well advanced at Alan Keef's works and the boiler, frames, cylinders and driving wheels are all now complete. Rebuilding of the old line south of Maespoeth is also under way.

ENGLAND

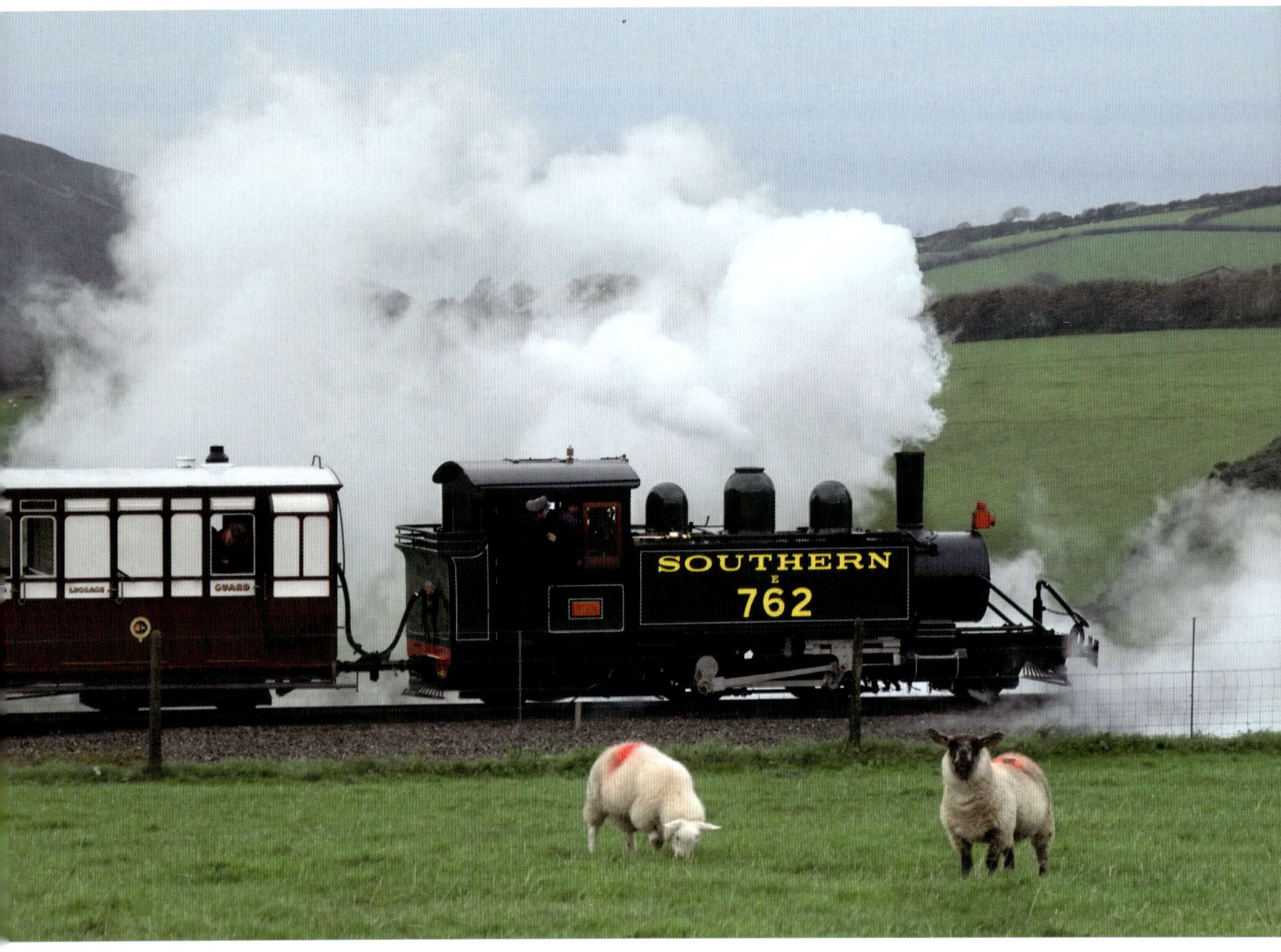

Another new loco though the sheep aren't impressed! 2-4-2T *Lyn* (Baldwin 15965/1898) on the 600mm gauge Lynton & Barnstaple Railway was built a few months after the line opened. She was needed in a hurry and as British builders couldn't supply in time Baldwin won the order. The railway became a part of the Southern at the Grouping and closed in 1935. If only it had gone to the GWR instead, not impossible as they ran into Barnstaple, maybe they would have kept it on and nurtured its tourist traffic as they did at Aberystwyth. Most of the stock, including *Lyn*, was promptly scrapped. Now Alan Keef's have built this superb replica (AK 92/2017) for the ambitious preservation society which is rebuilding the line. Here she heads for Woody Bay during her second weekend of operation on 14 October 2017. The Welsh coast is on the horizon. Sometimes you just can't keep Wales out of a narrow gauge photo!

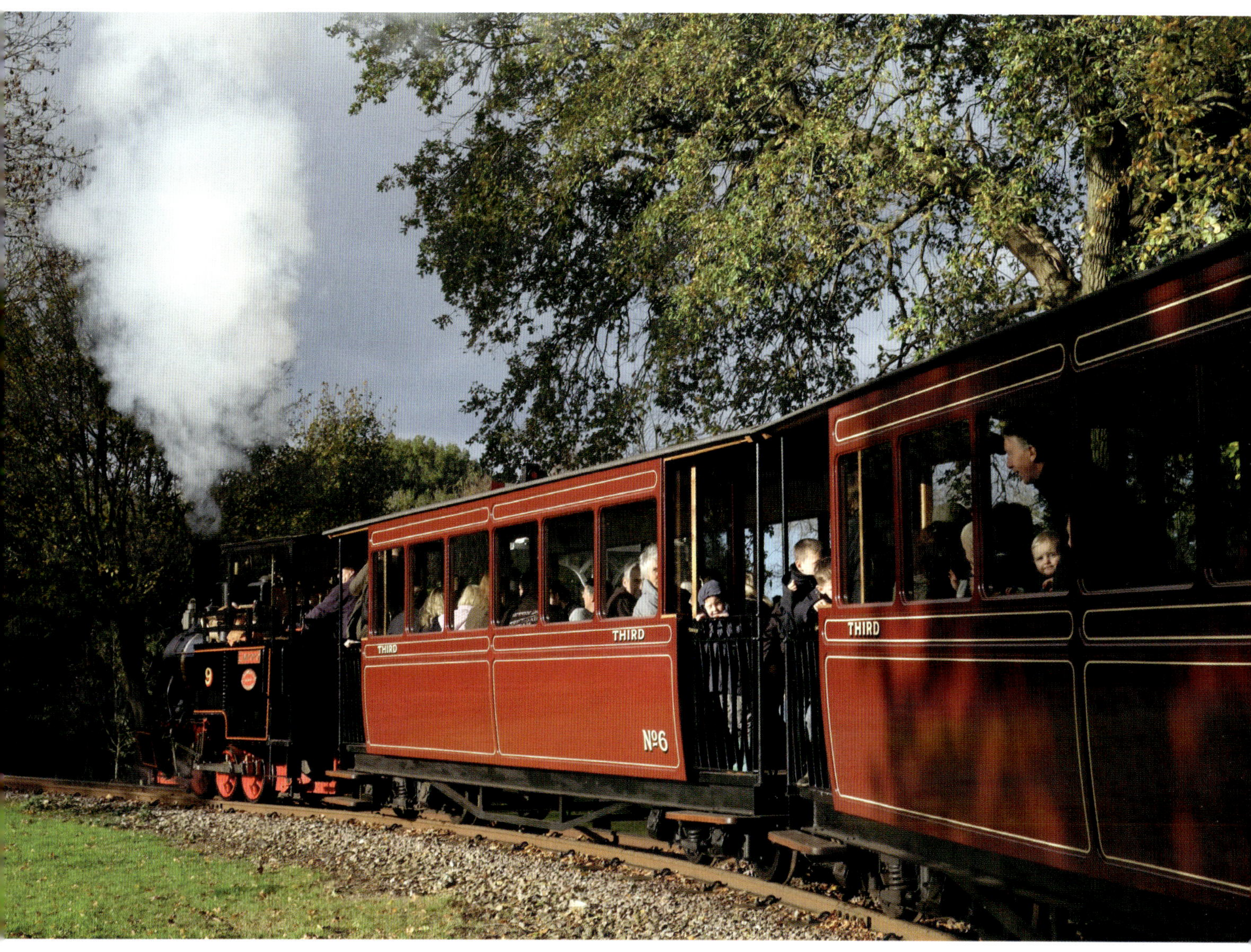

Privately-owned pleasure railways have been features of the English narrow gauge scene for more than one hundred years. One of the finest is the 2ft gauge Bredgar & Wormshill in mid-Kent, a family-friendly line which has welcomed visitors since the 1970s. These two superb carriages, typical of many which once ran on the minor railways of Britain and Ireland, were built almost entirely by the line's small group of volunteers. On 30 October 2017 they're being hauled by 0-6-0T No 9 (Fowler 18800/1930) which worked in Mozambique, firstly for Wigglesworth & Co Ltd who ran sisal plantations, and later at the Sena Sugar Estates.

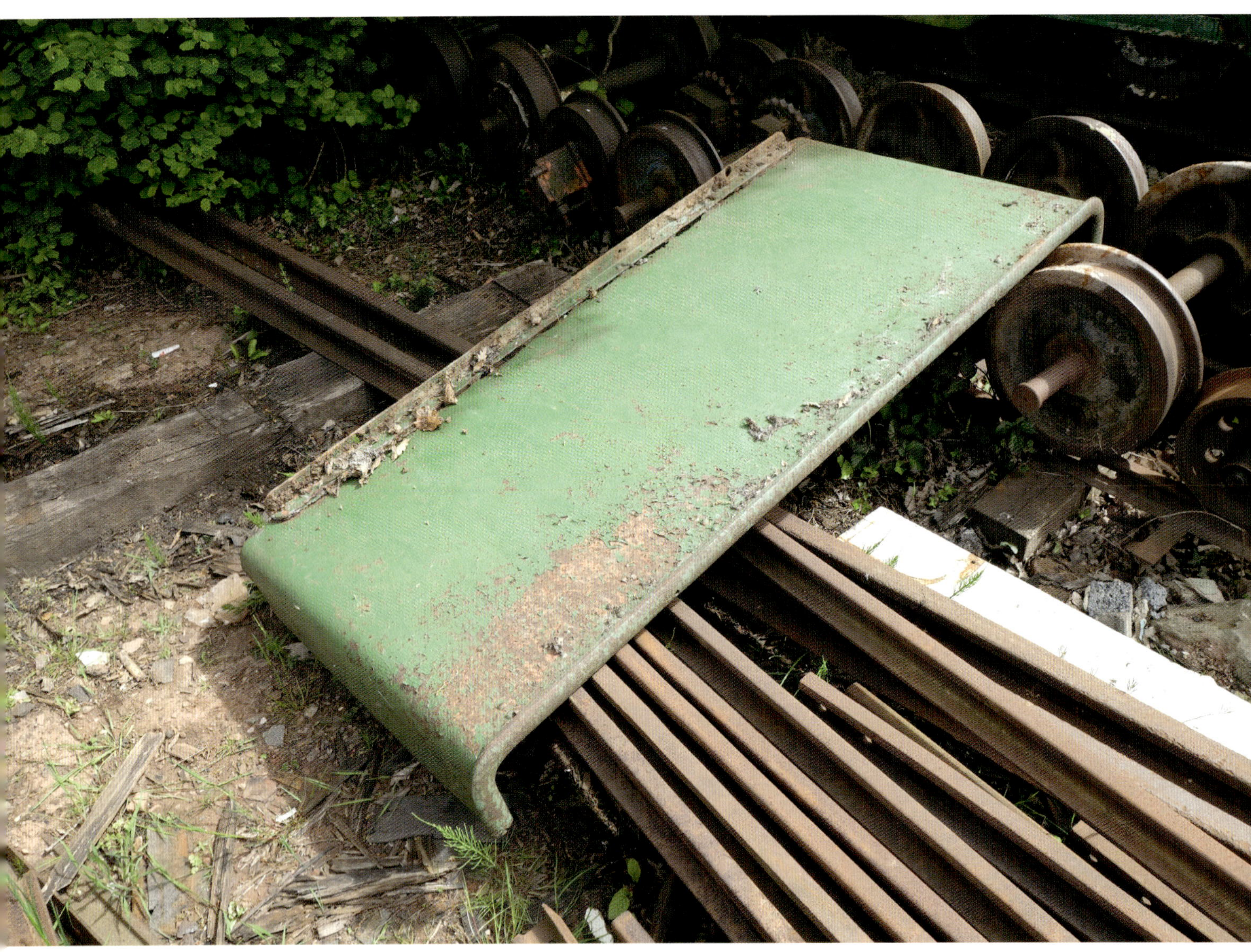

Preservation brings all sorts of surprises! In 1868 Stephen Lewin built *Tiny*, one of his idiosyncratic 0-4-0T's, for a 3ft 9ins gauge tramway serving ball clay pits near Corfe Castle in Purbeck. In 1948, new working practices called for smaller wagons which could be manhandled by one person and the tramway was regauged to 600mm, the first loco being none other than *Russell*, late of the Welsh Highland. Poor *Tiny* was scrapped – but her cab backsheet found a new use holding up a stack of ballast. Fast forward to 1972 and the 600mm gauge line closed. Alan Keef's bought some stock – and gave the backsheet a new home at their yard. Forty years later *Tiny's* ghost must have been surprised when *Russell* arrived for a reunion! Here's this last little relic on 22 May 2015, the beading nearest the camera marking its upper edge.

THE NETHERLANDS

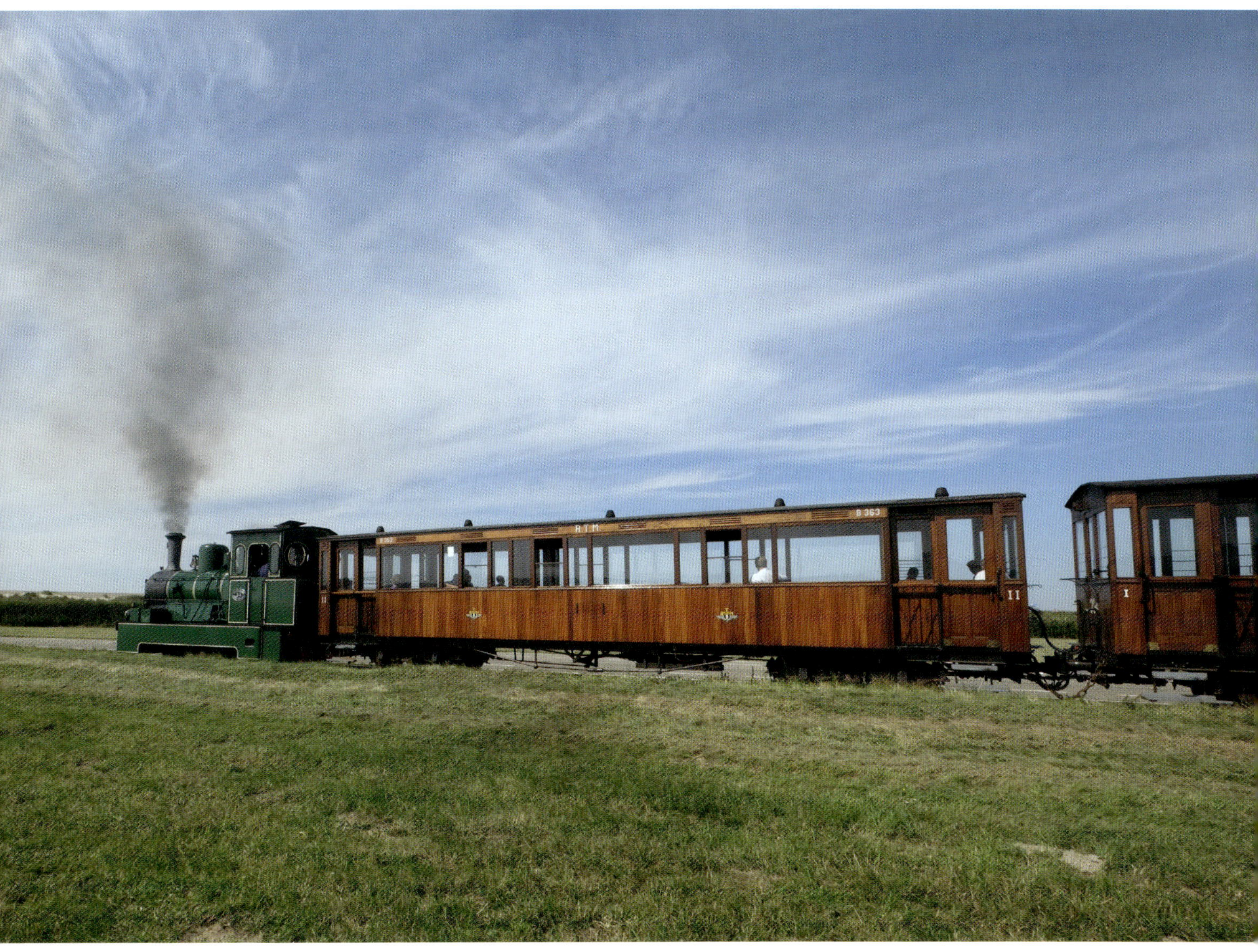

This 3ft 6ins gauge 0-6-0Tm No 54 (OK 8065/1915) and her train of splendid wooden carriages, seen here on 18 August 2016, came from the RTM, Rotterdam's first tramway company which started business in 1878, initially operating a horse-drawn tram service through the city's streets. Between 1898 and 1909 it built a network connecting the city's Rosestraat station with the districts to its south and west and the islands along the coast. Closures began in the 1950s and the last tram ran in 1967. A preservation society rescued much of the equipment and now runs it on a new line along the coast at Ouddorp, the terminus of one of the old routes. The leading carriage No B363 was built by HSP in 1903.

GERMANY

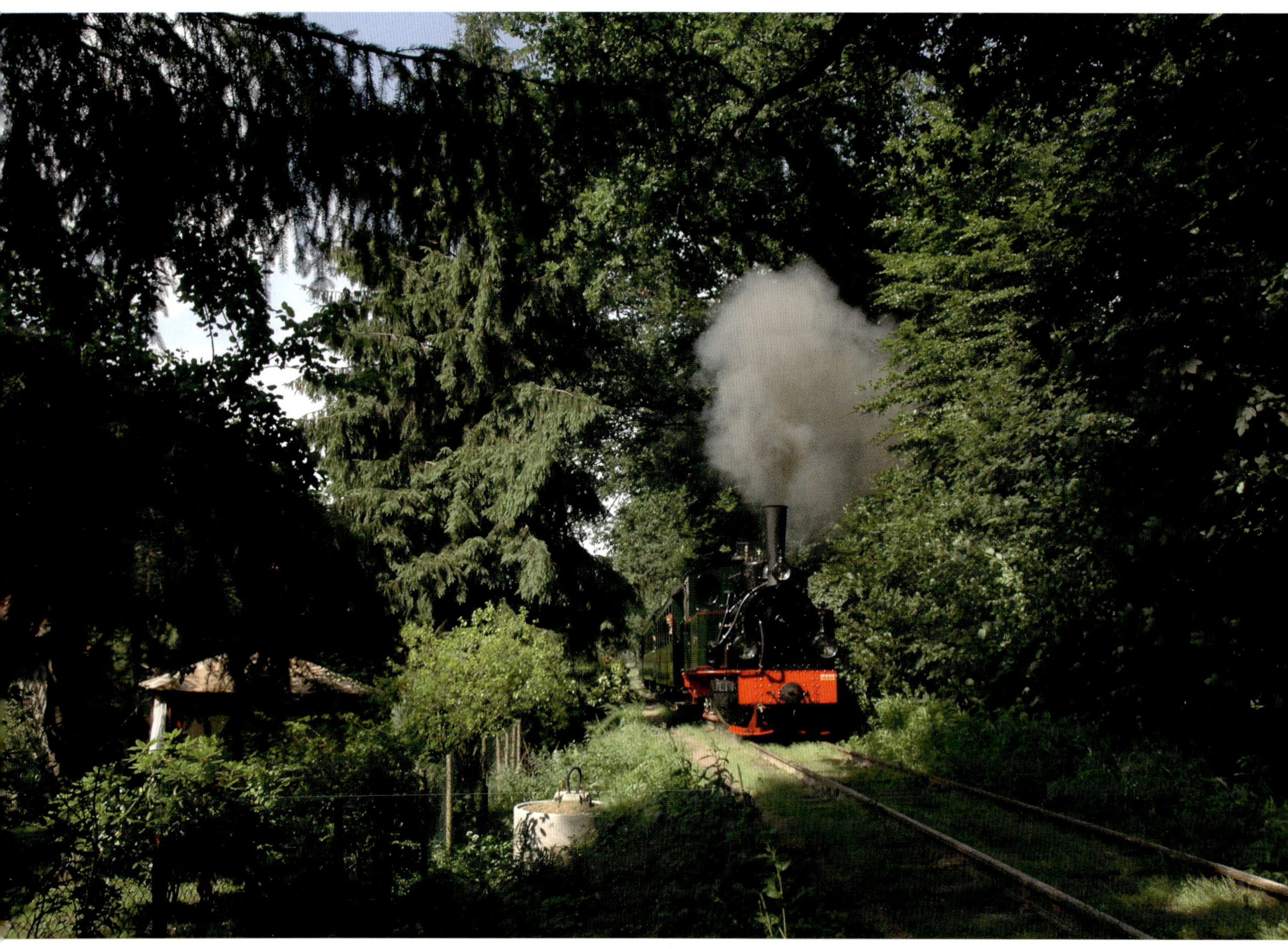

On 6 June 1900, a metre gauge network opened between Hoya and Syke in Lower Saxony, worked by five Hanomag 0-6-0Ts. Named after towns along the route, they were distinctive machines with solid disc wheels and outside Stephenson-link motion. A sixth one followed in 1912. The system has always been privately owned. Its mainline was converted to standard gauge between 1963 and 1965 but a branch between Bruchhausen-Vilsen and Asendorf, which had become freight-only in the 1950s, wasn't altered. Enthusiasts began to run weekend trains over it in 1966 using *Bruchhausen* and later *Hoya*, the last two steam locos, and took it over outright in 1971 when the freight service ended. It was Germany's first heritage railway. Here No 31 *Hoya* (Hanomag 3341/1899) runs through the trees near Vilsen Ort on 16 June 2007.

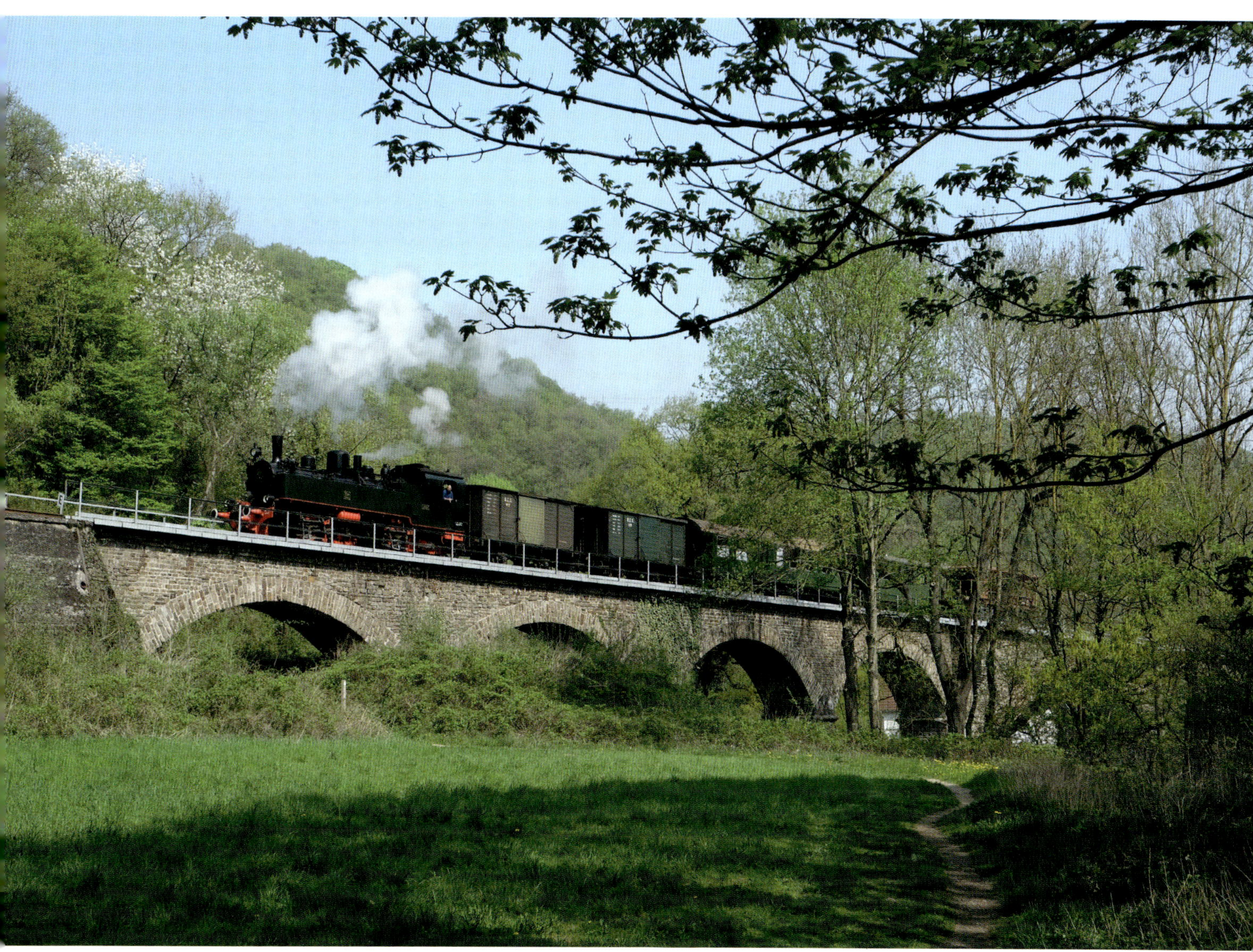

The metre gauge Brohltalbahn opened in 1901 and runs through the wooded Brohl valley to the west of the Rhine and up into the Eifel hills. It includes a section on a gradient of 1 in 20 which was rack-worked for many years, near the top of which is a quarry whose stone is still sent out by rail. On 21 April 2018 0-4-4-0 Mallet tank No 11 (Humboldt 348/1906), the line's only surviving steam loco, crosses the Tönissteiner viaduct on its way up the valley.

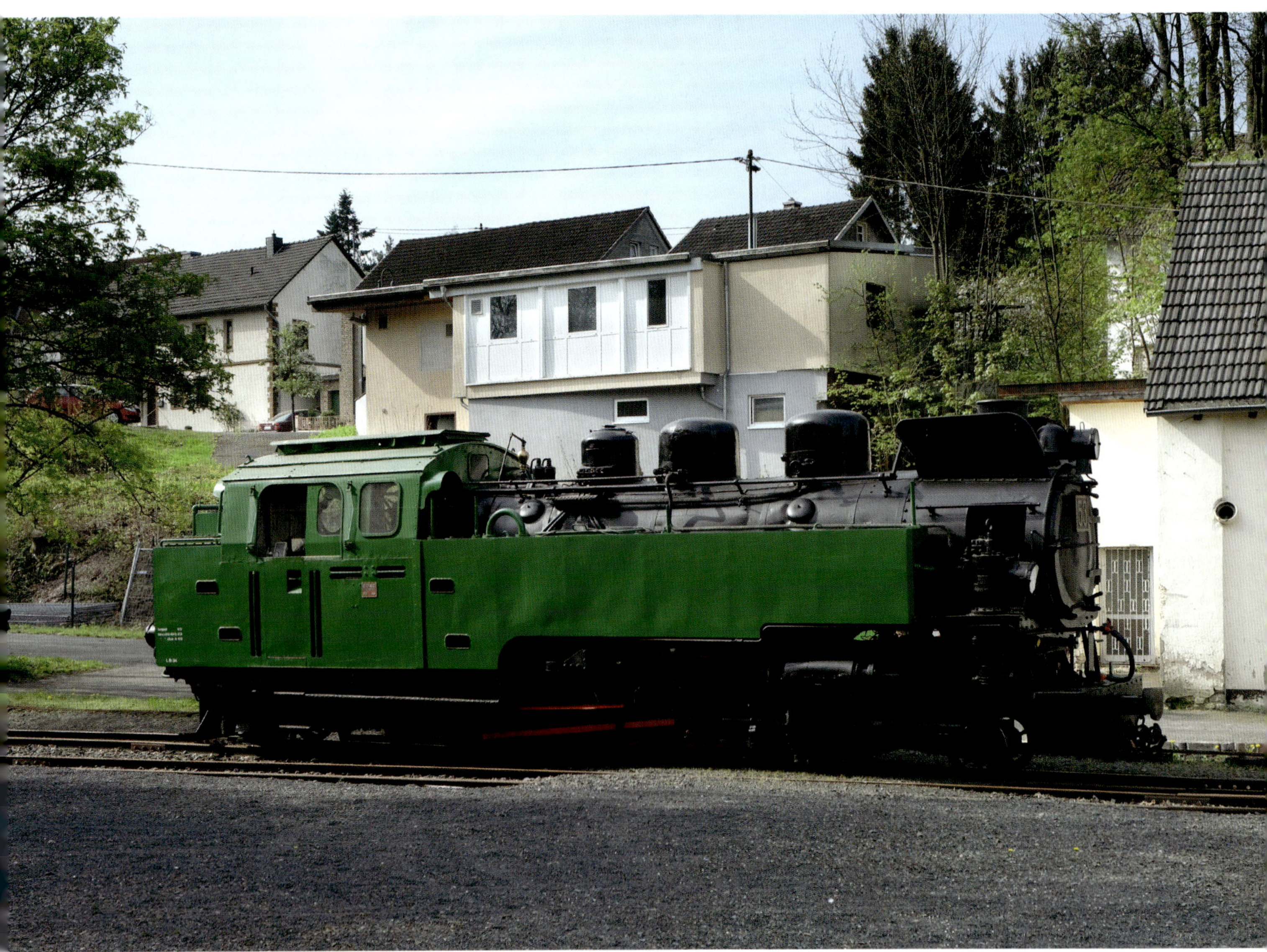

Above: The first narrow gauge line within Germany's present borders was the 785mm gauge Bröltalbahn, only a short distance to the east of the Brohltalbahn. It opened in 1862 and in 1921 changed its name to the Rhein Sieg Eisenbahn to avoid confusion with its younger neighbour. The line's last section closed in 1967. Its attractive 2-8-2T No 53 (Jung 10175/1944) is the only surviving steam loco. On 22nd April 2018 she stands outside the railway's old loco shed at Asbach which now houses an excellent small museum.

Opposite: The railway between Putbus and Binz opened in 1895 and was the first of several 750mm gauge lines on the Baltic island of Rügen. They were taken over by the regional government in 1940 and became part of Deutsche Reichsbahn in 1949. 2-8-0T no 99 4801 (Henschel 24367/1938) runs through the woods near Jagdschloss on 18 October 2006. She's one of two similar locos built for the Kreisbahn Jerichow 1 which were transferred to Rügen after it closed in 1965.

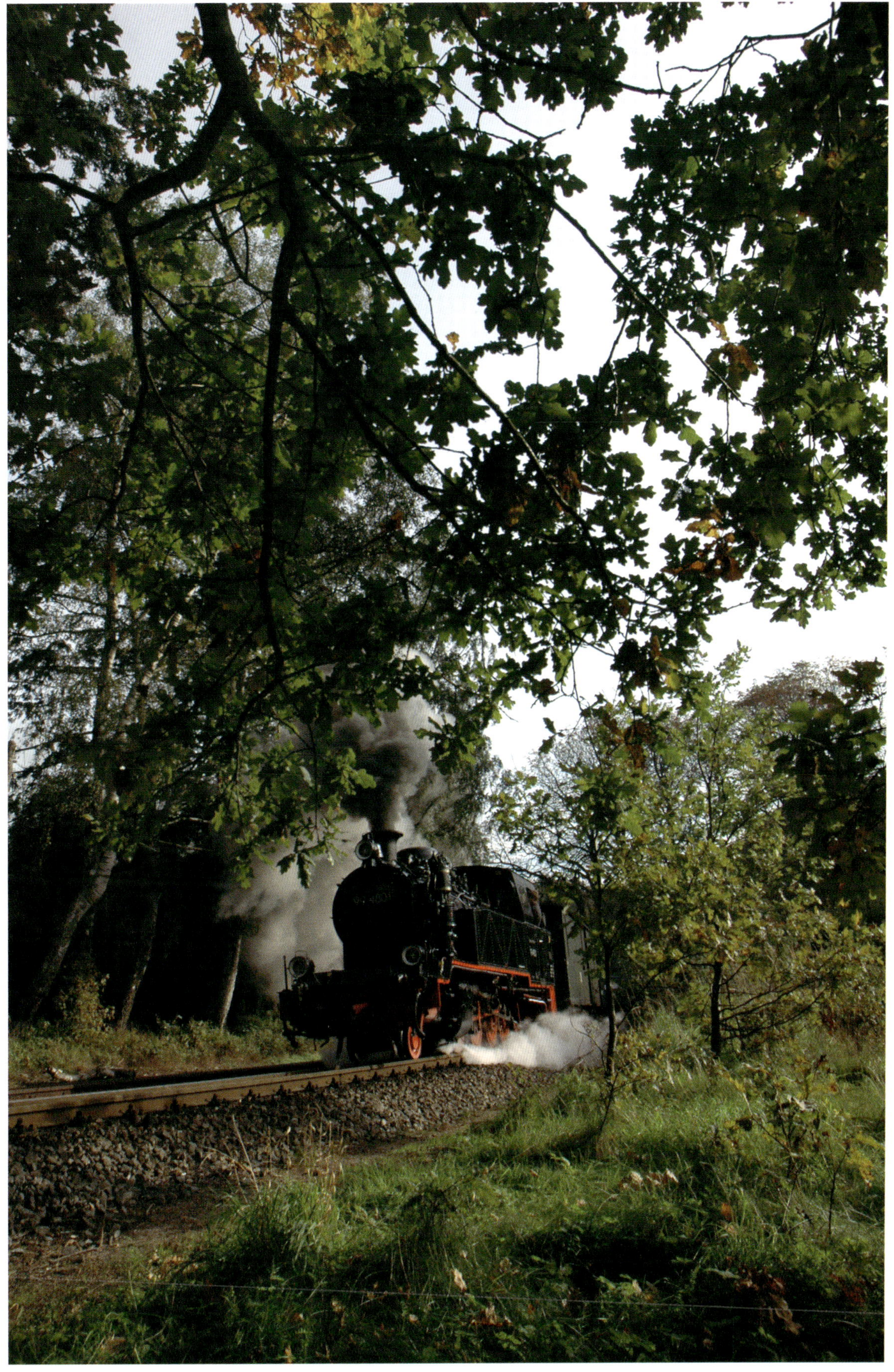

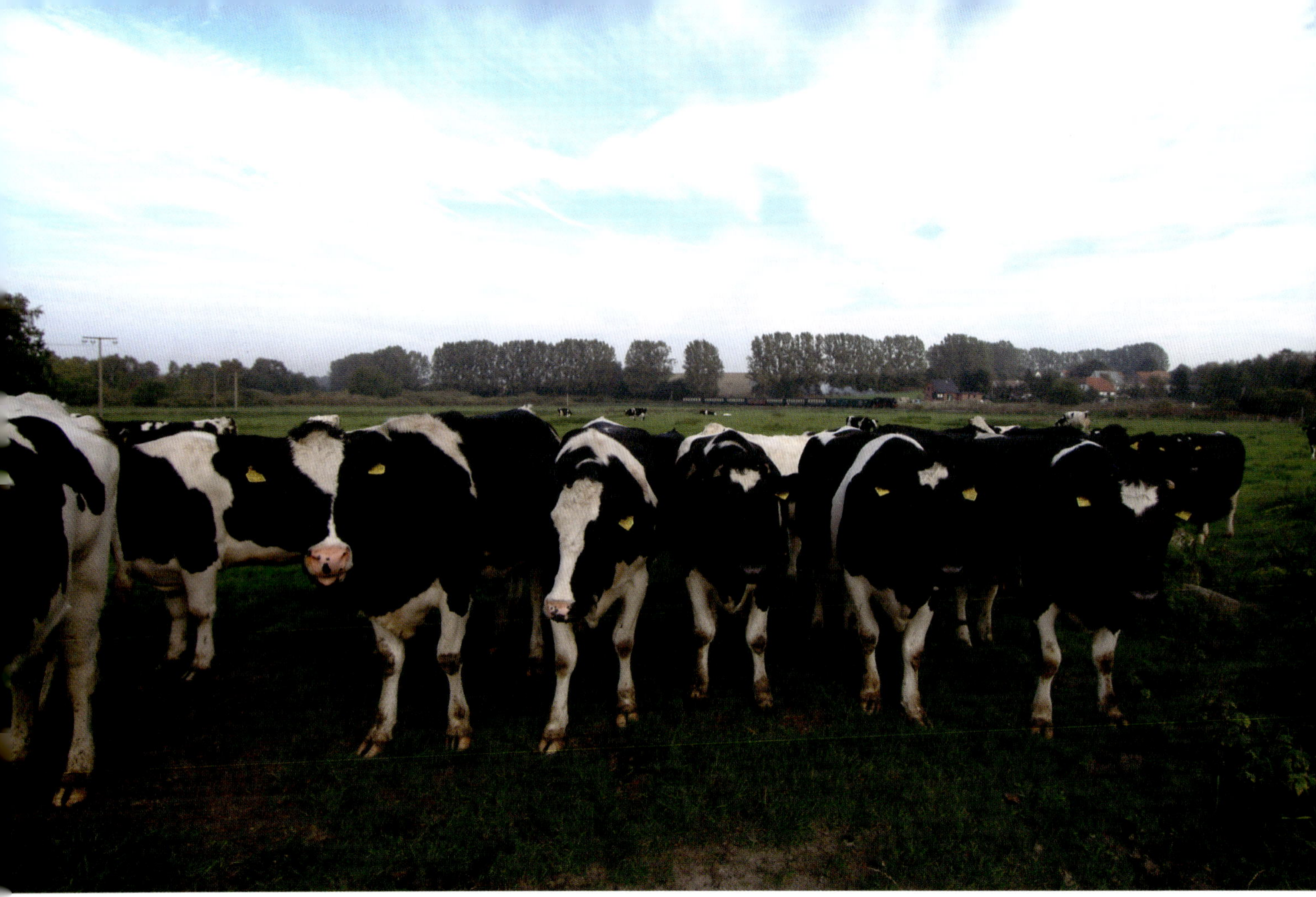

Above: No-one's coming into our field! A scene near Putbus on 18th October 2006 as 2-10-2T no 99 782 (LKM 32021/1953) heads towards Göhren. She's one of twenty four 99.77-79 class locos built between 1952 and 1957 to replace those of the generally similar 99.73-76 or VIIK class machines which had run in Saxony from the 1920's until going to the Soviet Union as reparations after the Second World War. Four of the 99.77-79's moved to Rügen in the 1980's.

Opposite above: Putbus loco yard on 18 October 2006 with No 99 4801 and 0-8-0T No 99 4632-8 (VS 3851/1925), one of two locos surviving there from the system's independent days. Most of the Rügen lines closed between 1967 and 1970, leaving only the original route from Putbus to Binz and its later extension to Göhren. Today it's one of those marvellous old East German lines which run steam locos in everyday service.

Opposite below: The much-loved 900mm gauge Mollibahn started life as a tramway in 1886, running through the streets of Bad Doberan and alongside the road to Heiligendamm on the Baltic coast. In 1890, it was taken over by the regional government and became a part of DR when it took over Germany's state-owned lines in 1920. It soon outgrew its tramway origins and a succession of larger machines took the place of its little 0-4-0Tm's. In 1932, three 2-8-2Ts arrived, much bigger than anything it had previously seen and with their 50kph maximum speed they're still amongst Germany's fastest narrow gauge locos. A fourth one was built in 2009. The trains still run through the streets. It's 7.13am and not yet fully light on 3 November 2017 and the bakery is the only shop open as No 99 2324-4 (Meiningen 203/2009) makes her way along Mollistraße – what else could this street be called?!

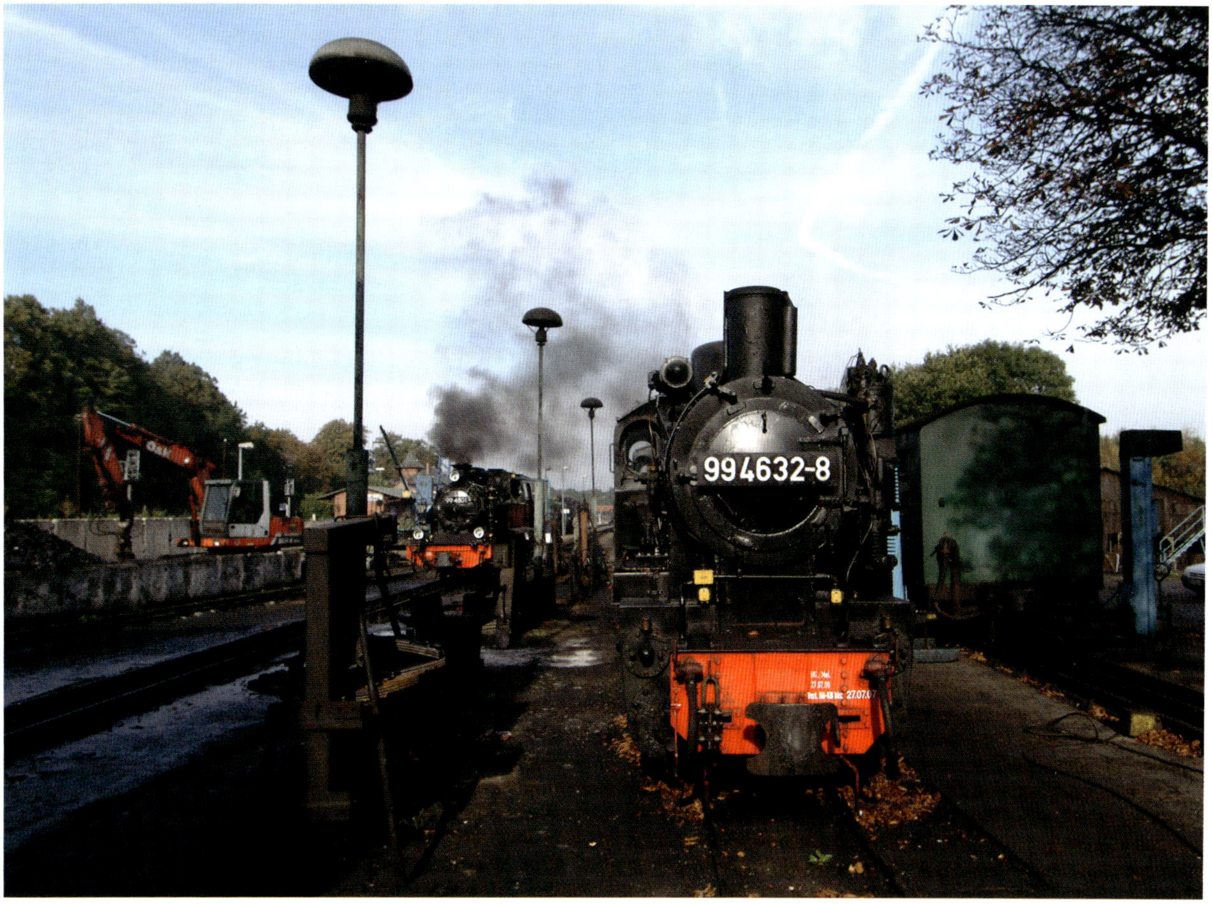

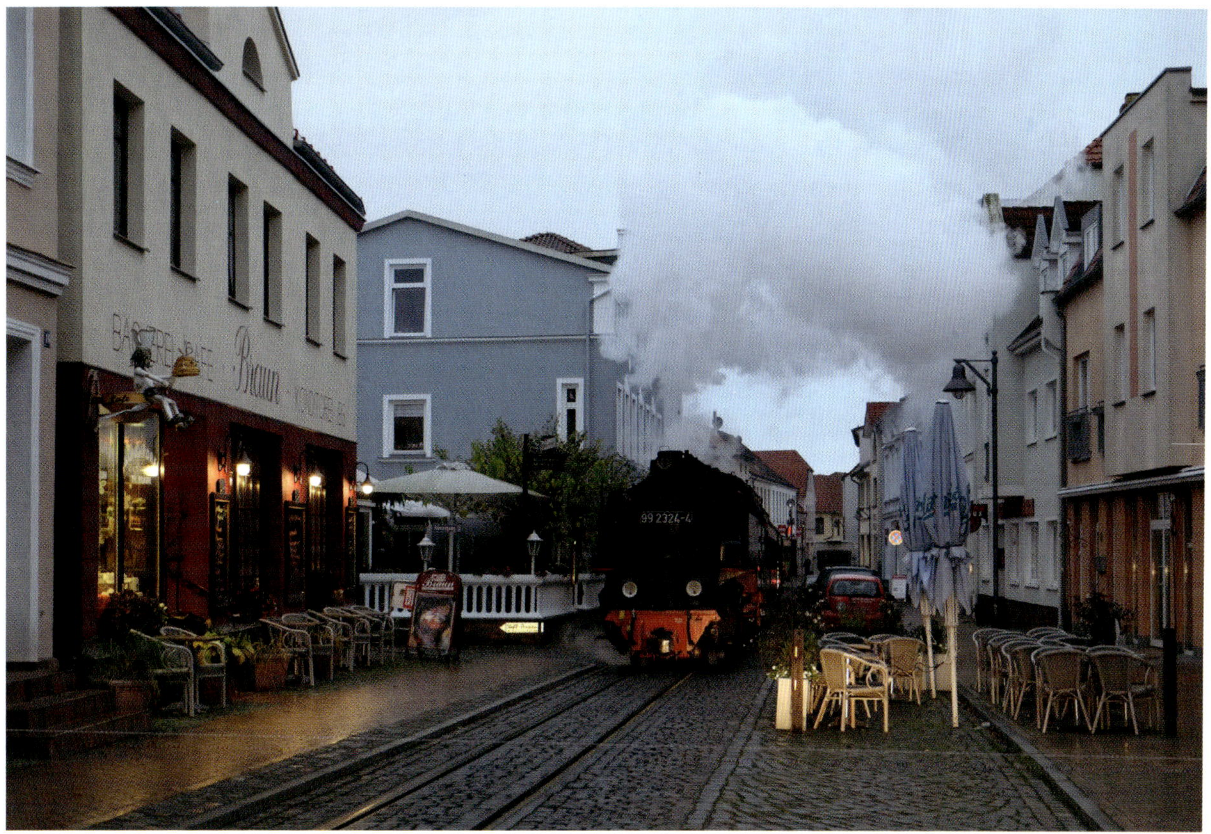
Braun
99 2324-4

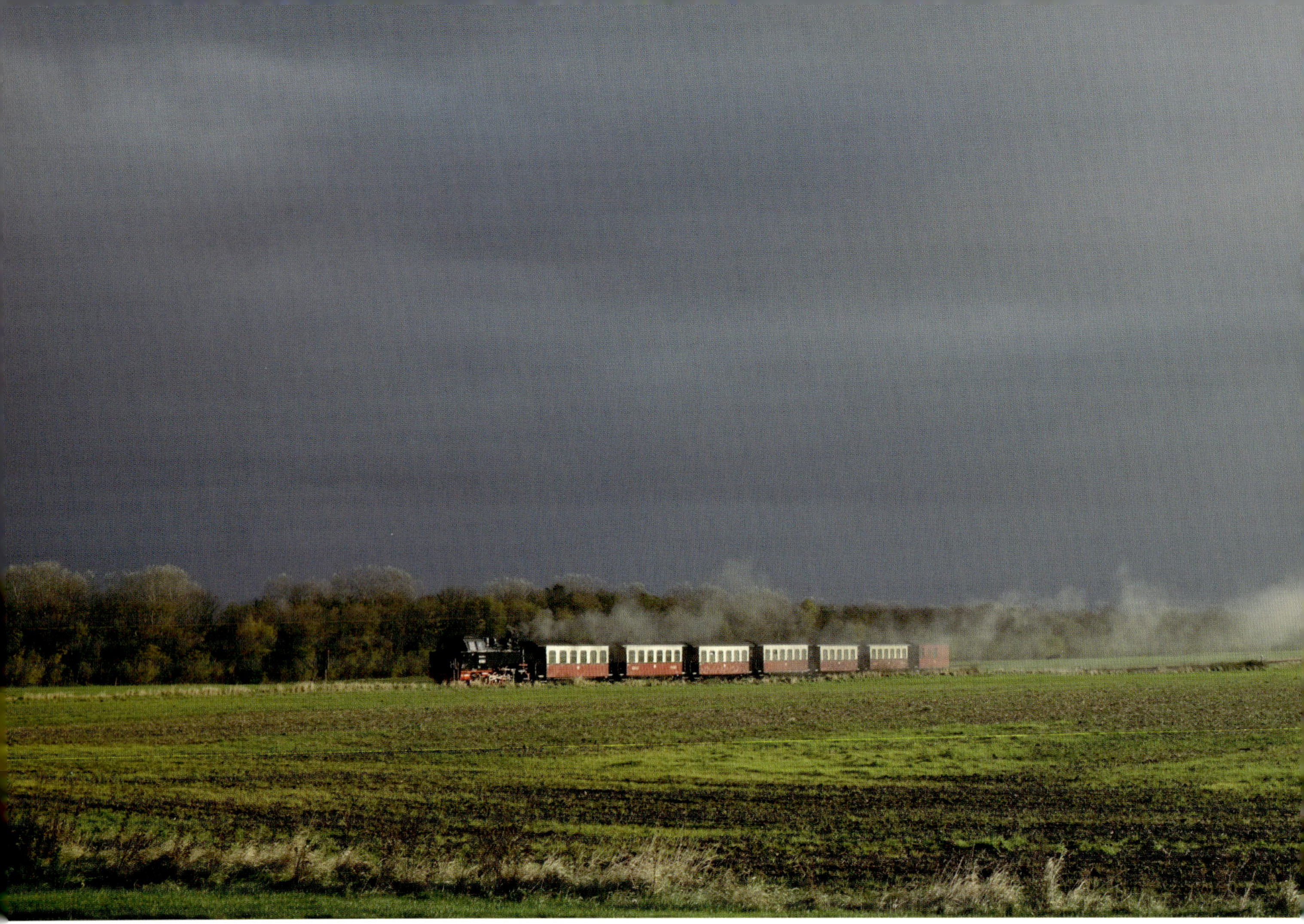

Above: Little more than one hour later, there's a storm out over the Baltic as No 99 2324-4 heads west from Heiligendamm over an extension to Kuhlungsborn West built in 1910. The sea lies just beyond the trees but seldom comes into view. Like all the surviving East German narrow gauge railways, it has been handed over to a private operator. This one's called the Mecklenburgische Bäderbahn Molli, so conferring official status on the name by which the line has long been known!

Opposite above: The 750mm gauge Prignitzer Kleinbahn north west of Berlin opened in 1897 and closed between 1969 and 1971. Since 2002, a preservation society has rebuilt 9kms of the old route southeast from Mesendorf. On 2 November 2017, Saxon-type IVK 0-4-4-0 Meyer tank No 99 568 (Hartmann 3450/1910) runs through the rolling countryside near Brünkendorf.

Opposite below: On 7 March 2016, 2-10-2T no. 99 7247-2 (LKM 134028/1957) stands with a short train at Alexisbad station south of Gernrode on the metre gauge Harzquer Schmalspurbahn, now the most extensive steam-worked narrow gauge system anywhere in Europe. Its oldest section, between Gernrode and Magdesprung, was built by the Gernrode-Harzgerode Eisenbahn, opening in 1887, and it reached Hasselfelde five years later. Next was what became the Nordhausen-Wernigerode Eisenbahn, whose line between the two towns in its name opened between 1897 and 1899 along with a branch from Drei Annen Hohne to Brocken. Finally, the Hasselfelde line was extended in 1905 to join the NWE at Eisfelder Talmühle. Seventeen of these 2-10-2T's were built in the 1950s and handle most steam services.

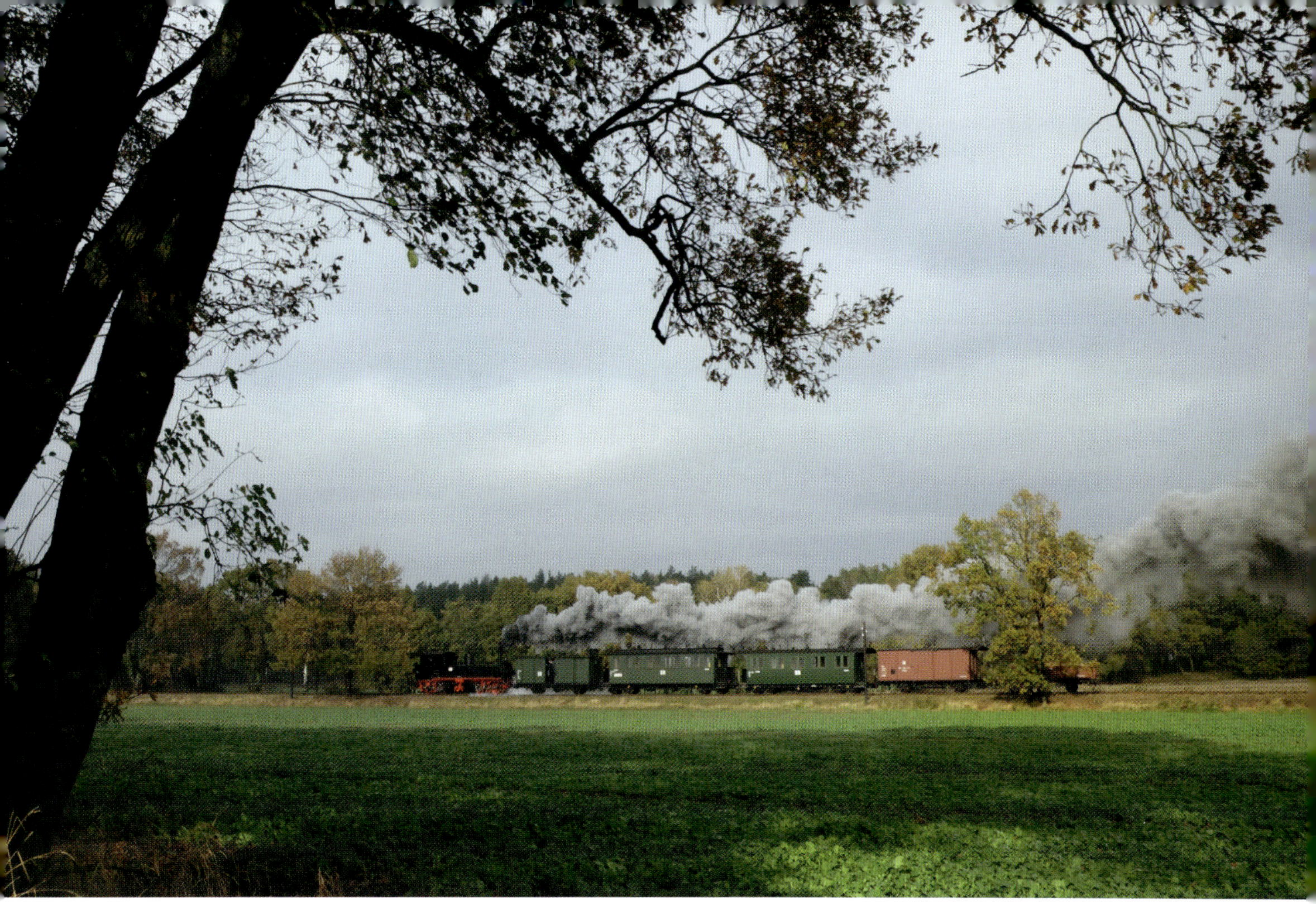

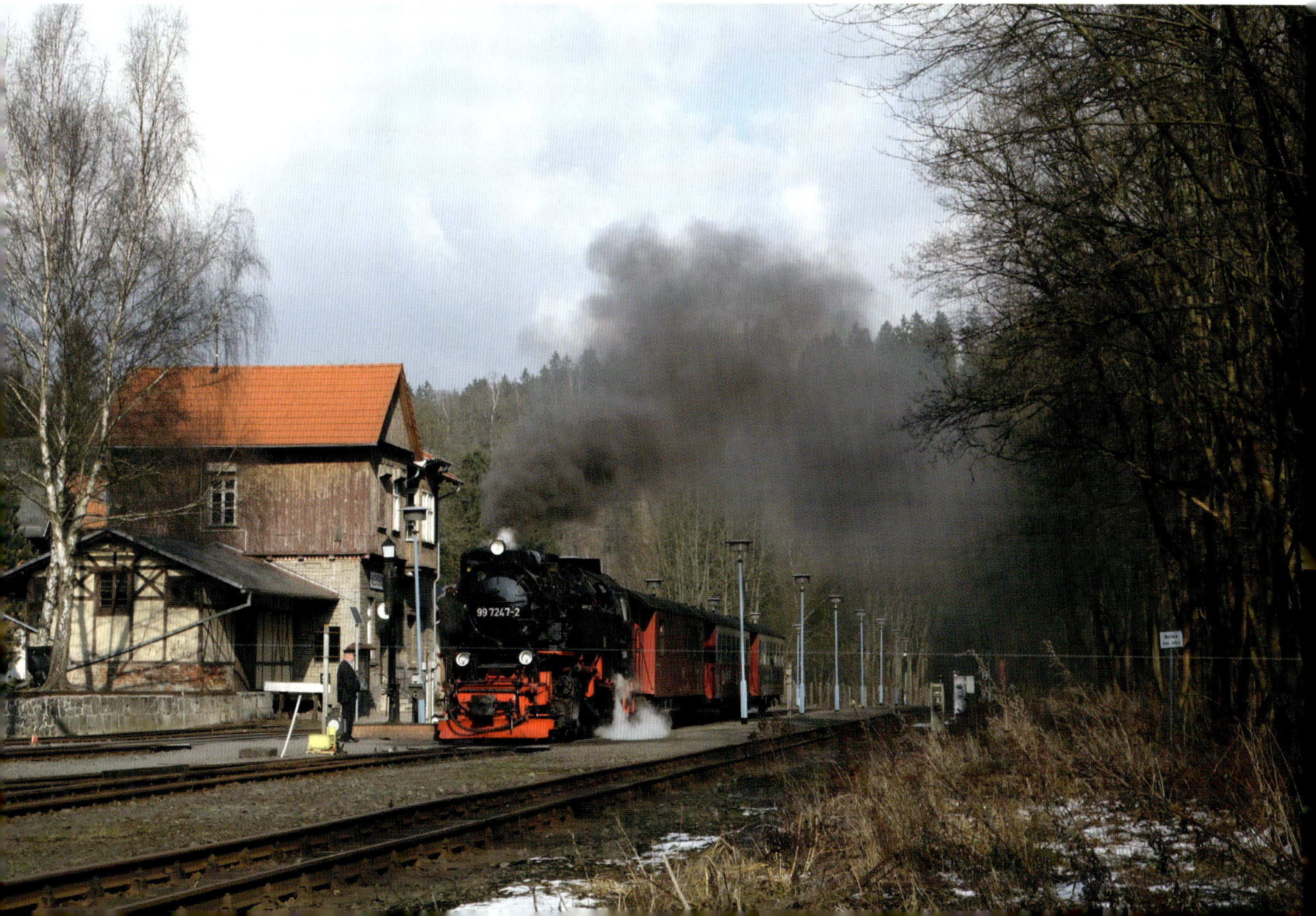

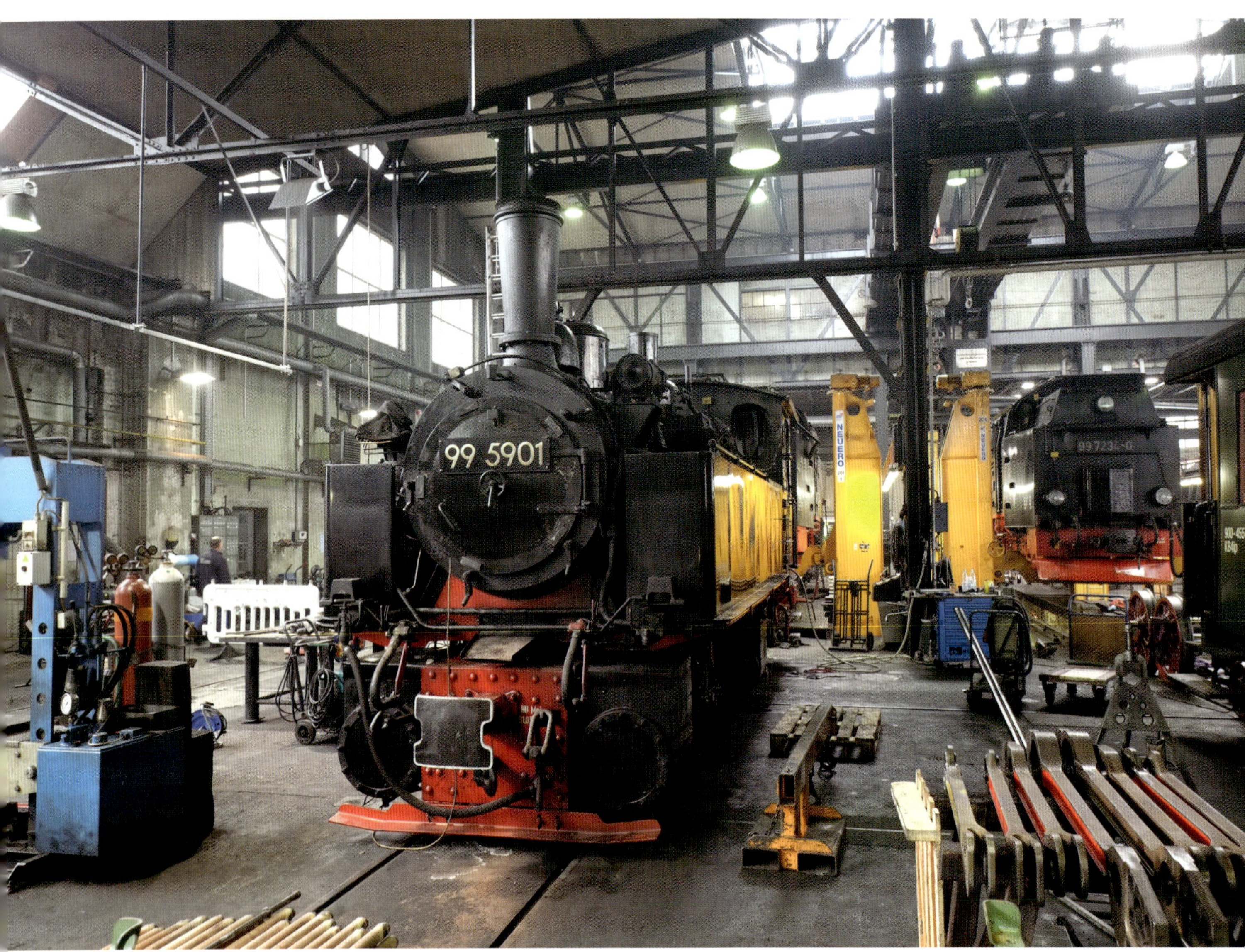

Above: No 99 5901 (Jung 258/1897) stands in the HSB's shops at Westerntor on 8 March 2016. She's one of three survivors from a group of twelve 0-4-4-0 Mallet tanks built as the NWE's first locos between 1897 and 1901. Behind her 2-10-2T's no's 99 7235-7 and 99 7234-0 are receiving repairs.

Opposite: On 20 April 2011, 99.77–79 class 2-10-2T No 99 1771-7 (LKM 32010/1952) runs through the Rabenau gorge on the 750mm gauge Weißeritztalbahn near Dresden which opened from 1882. The line suffered major flood damage in the early 2000s and only reopened throughout in 2017. It was once home to Saxon Nos 18 and 19, 0-4-4-0 Double Fairlies which were built by Hawthorn Leslie in 1885 and withdrawn in 1903 and 1909.

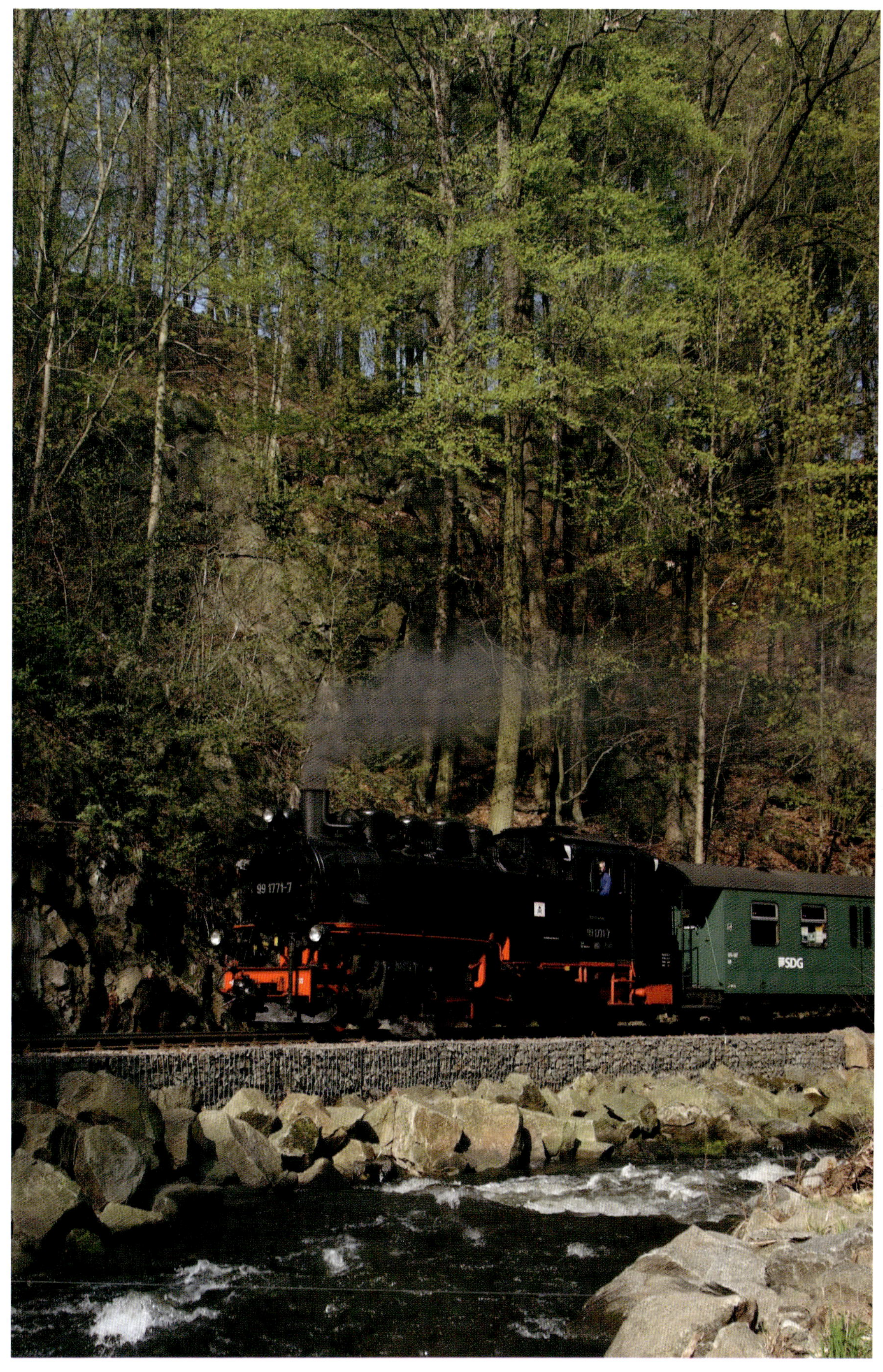
99 1771-7
SDG

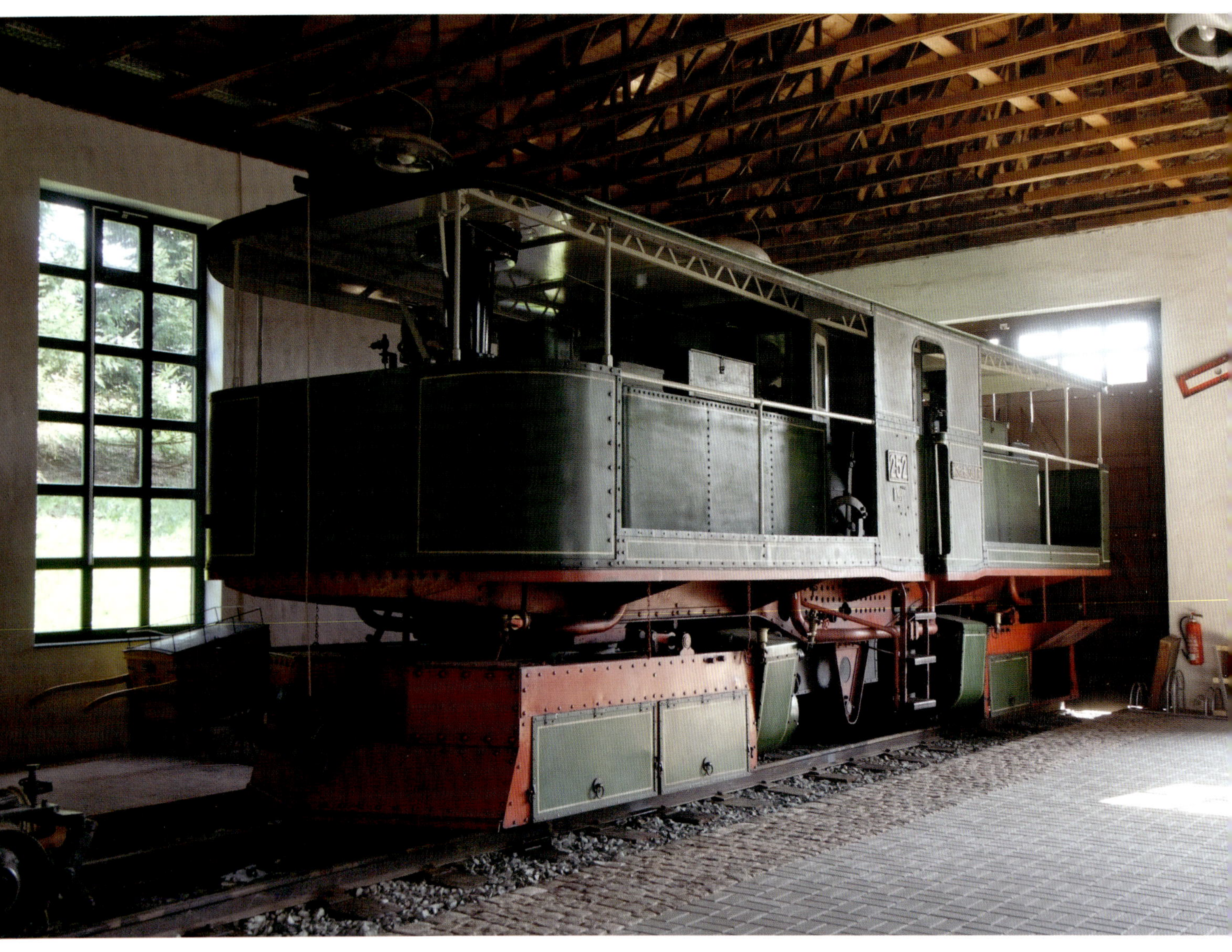

Above: The Saxon State Railways' metre gauge Reichenbach-Oberheinsdorf line, built in 1902, is one that didn't survive. Because it ran alongside the road, its three 0-4-4-0 Double Fairlies, the only other ones in Saxony, were built with controls at both ends. One was sunk en route to Greece during the Second World War and the others were withdrawn in 1962, the railway's final year. In 1971, DR restored No 99 162 (Hartmann 2648/1902) to her original condition as Saxon No 352 and on 19 April 2011 she shows off her elegant lines in the excellent replica engine shed built for her at Oberheinsdorf in 1999.

Opposite: On the 600mm gauge Waldeisenbahn Muskau 0-8-0T No 99 3312-8 (Borsig 8472/1912), built for the railway and originally named *Diana*, runs beside a lake near Weißwasser on 22 October 2006. Although mostly an industrial line carrying timber, sand and coal it was a common carrier and as such was incorporated into DR on 1 January 1951. It closed in 1978 and a part is now run by a preservation society.

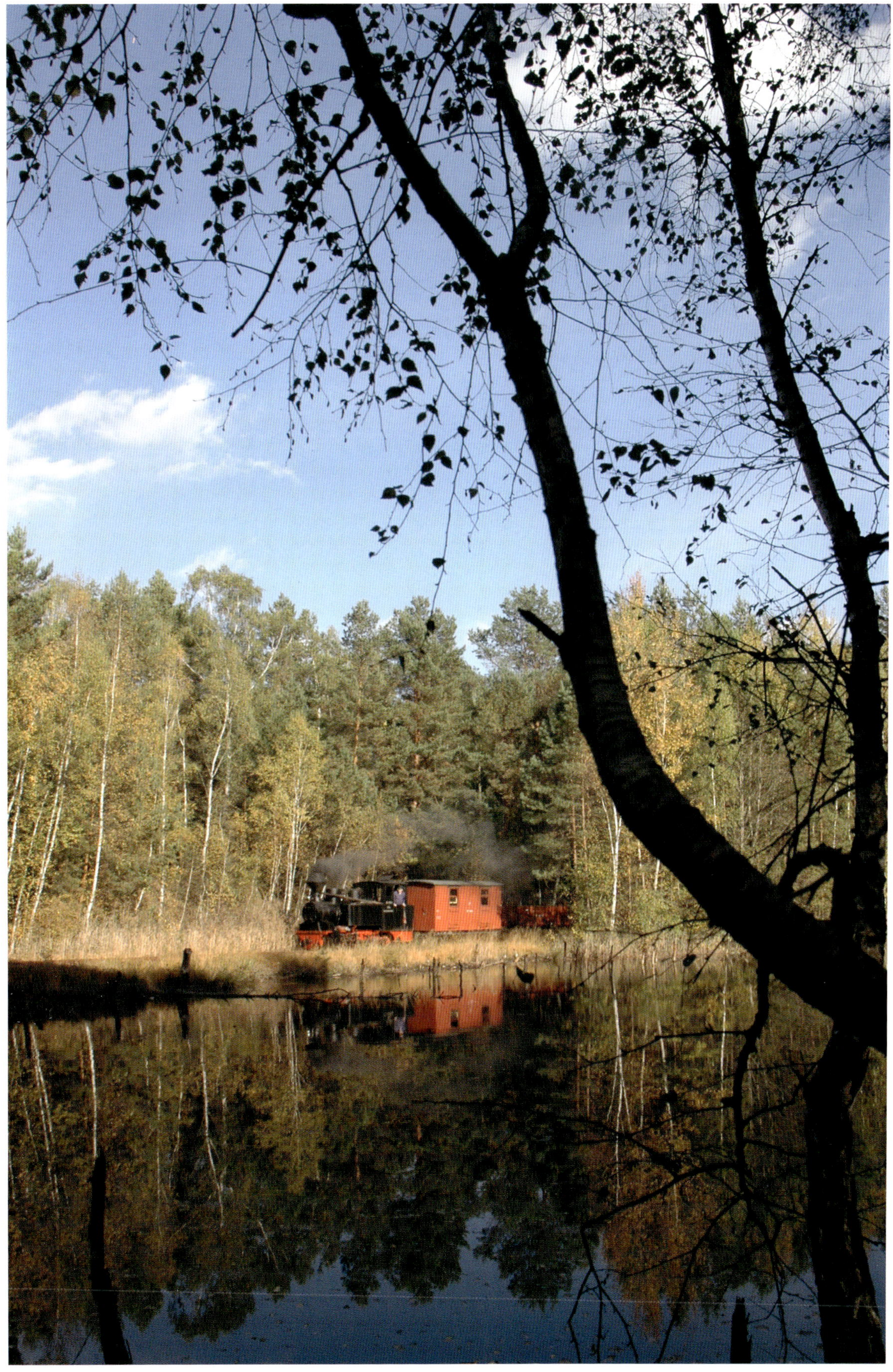

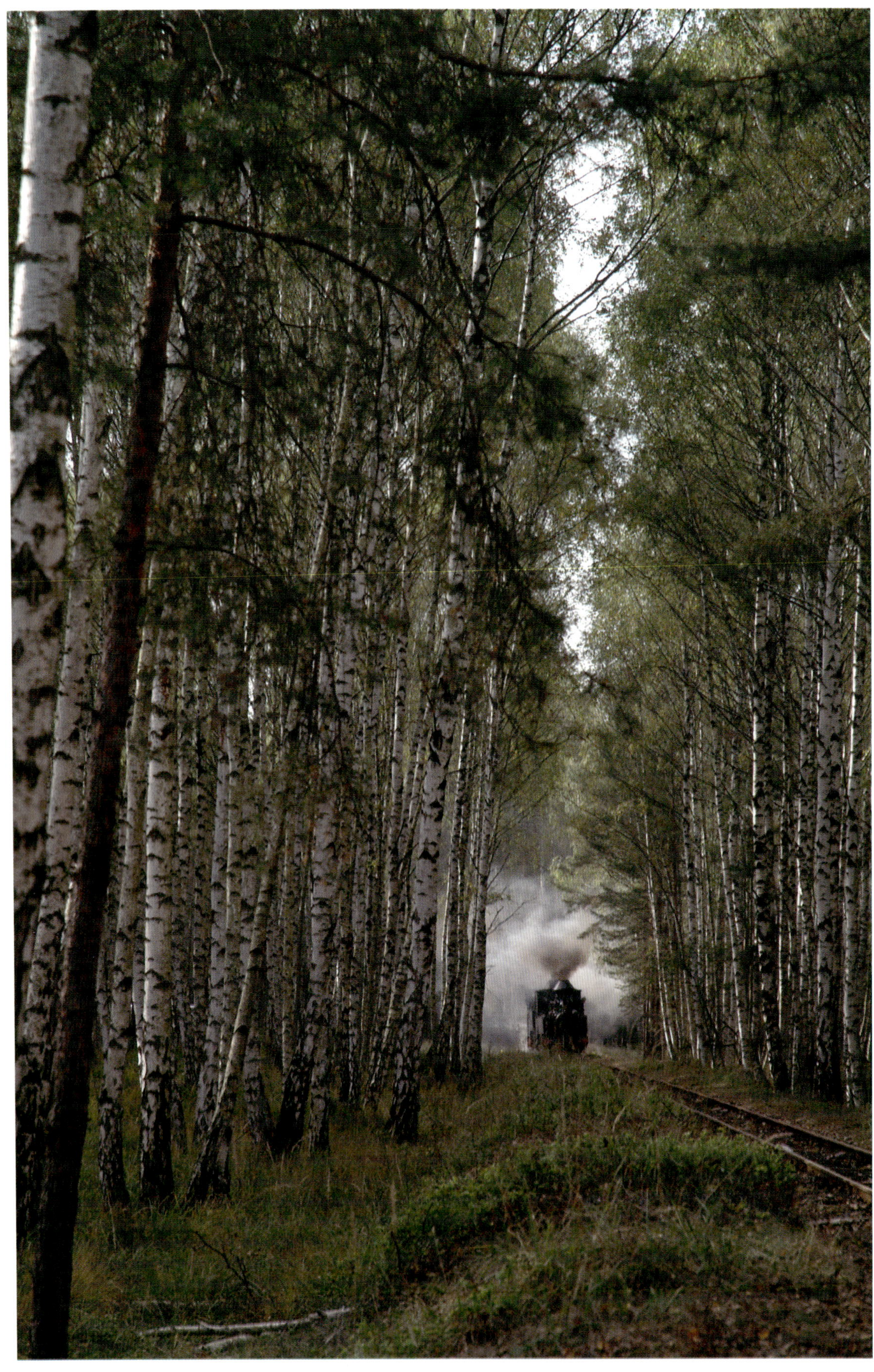

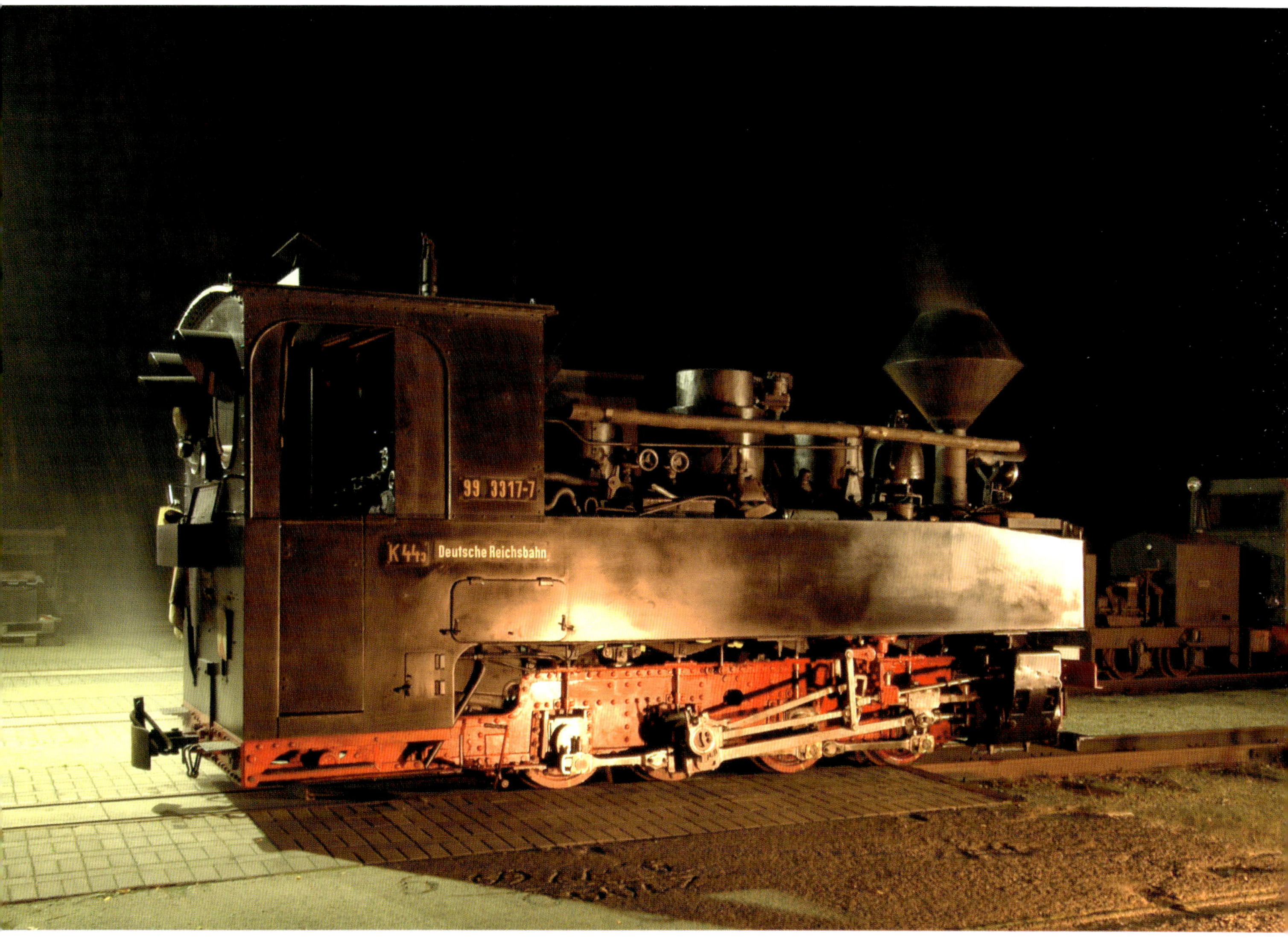

Above: No 99 3317-7 stands outside the preserved railway's Weißwasser shed on the evening of 21 October 2006. She moved to Germany during the Second World War and in about 1948 was acquired by the Frieden lignite mine at Weißwasser which was served by the Waldeisenbahn Muskau. She was taken into DR stock in 1952 and worked out of the old Weißwasser shed until 1977.

Opposite: Several Brigadelok 0-8-0T's ran on the line from the 1920's although No 99 3317-7 (Borsig 10306/1918) didn't arrive until 1952. She was in the part of Lithuania which Poland took over in 1919 and worked for PKP, the Polish state railway, as their No 4241. When the Poles were ejected in 1939 she became Lithuanian No K 4-448. She and *Diana* are dwarfed by the woods on 21 October 2006.

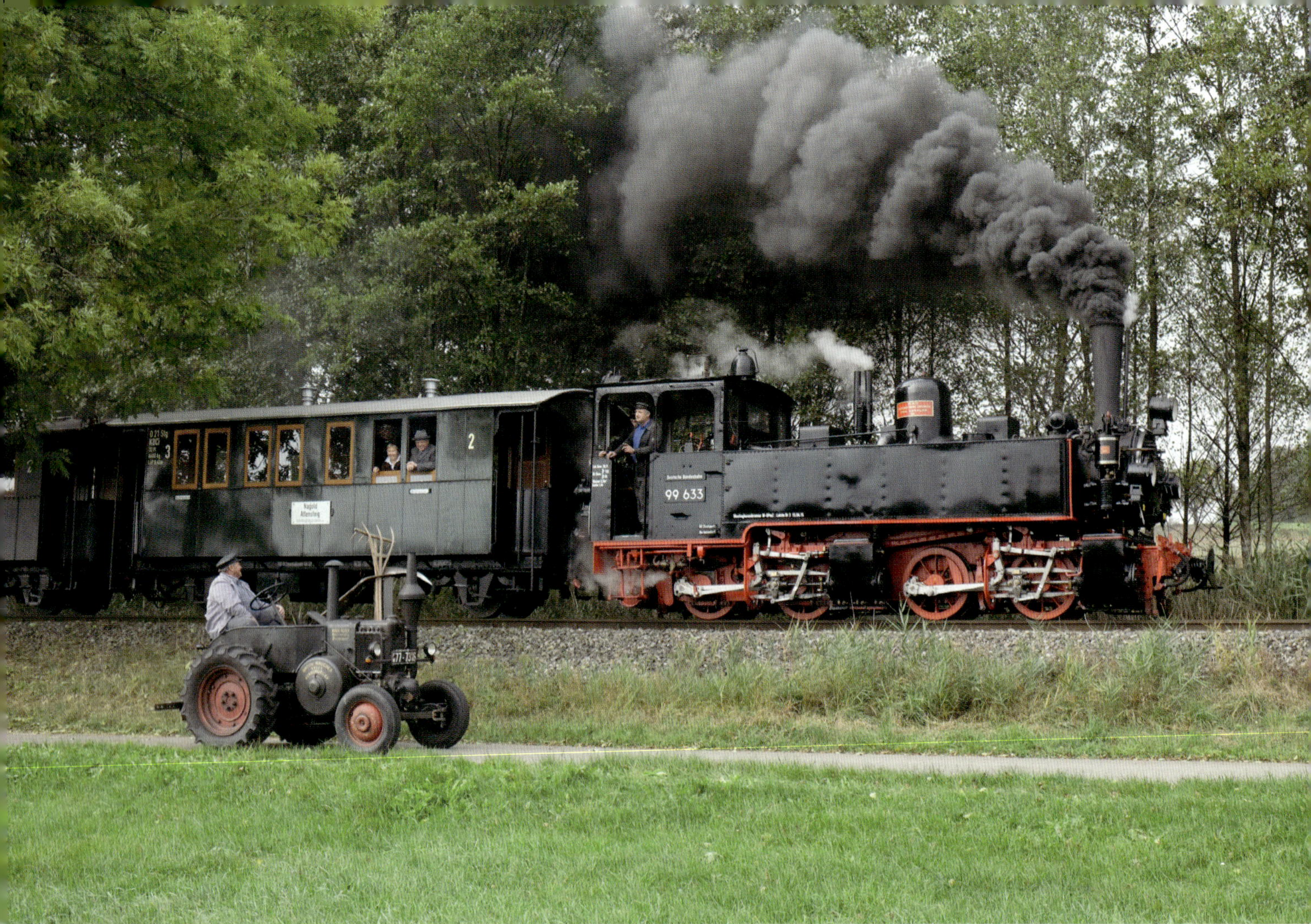

Above: The Öchslebahn, opened in 1899, was one of the Württemberg state railway's four 750mm gauge lines. It became a part of DR in 1920 and Deutsche Bundesbahn in 1949. No 43, later DR and DB No 99 633 (Esslingen 3072/1899), one of three 0-4-4-0 Mallet tanks built for the opening, was based there almost continuously until 1940 and returned occasionally until withdrawn on 18 March 1969. Now she's back after extensive overhaul and here heads a train of vintage Württemberg stock near Ochsenhausen on 9 October 2015.

Opposite above: A silhouette of the Württemberg train on 9 October 2015. The line closed on 31 March 1983 but most of it soon reopened as a heritage railway.

Opposite below: The metre gauge Chiemseebahn's train passes a pond at Prien on 31 July 2013. The railway runs for a little over 2kms between Prien and Stock in Bavaria and opened in 1887, equipped with this 0-4-0Tm (KM 1813/1887), five open and two closed third class coaches, a brake compo and a first class saloon. Most remarkably it has used the same stock ever since, the only significant addition being a small second-hand diesel obtained as a backup in 1985.

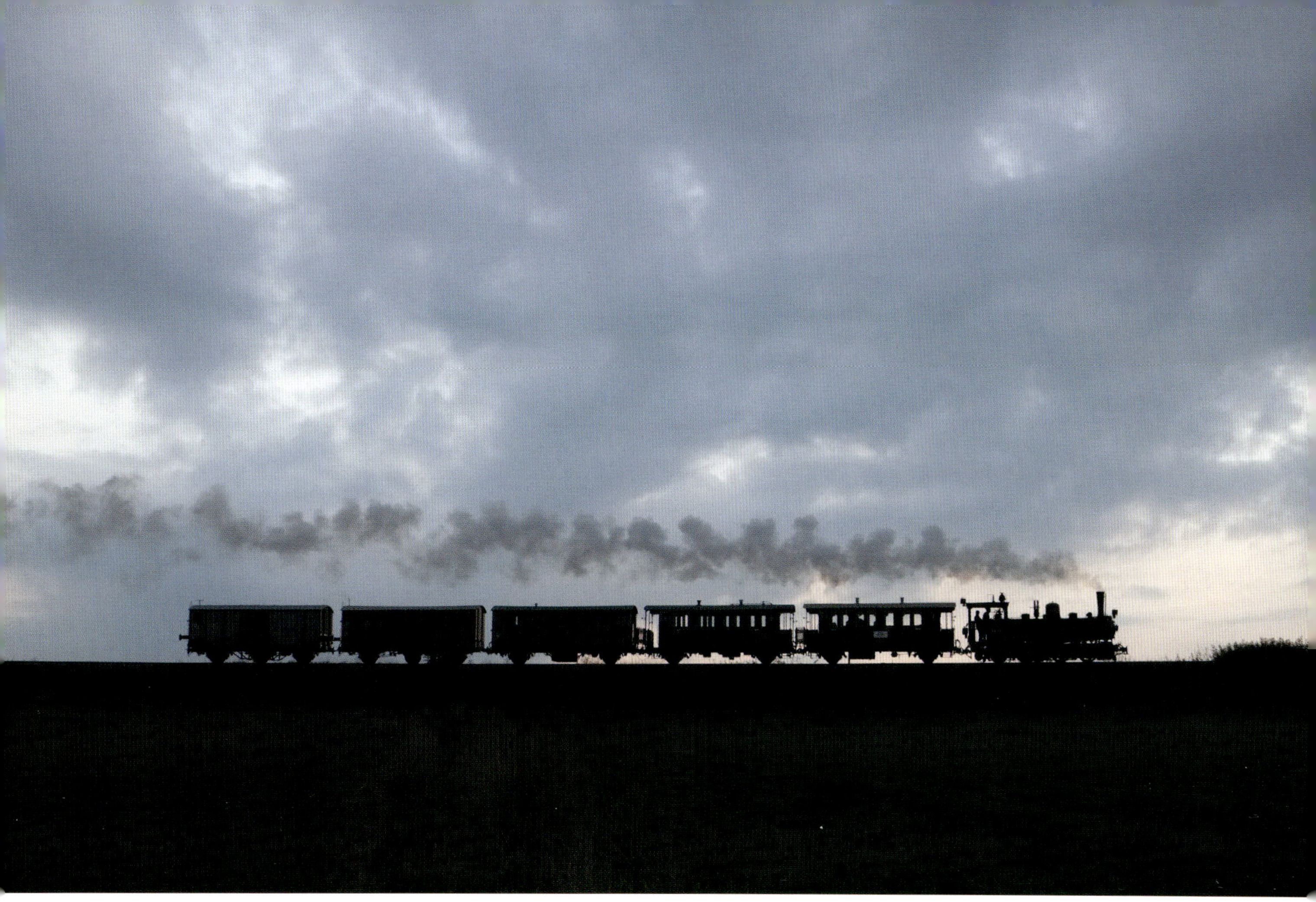

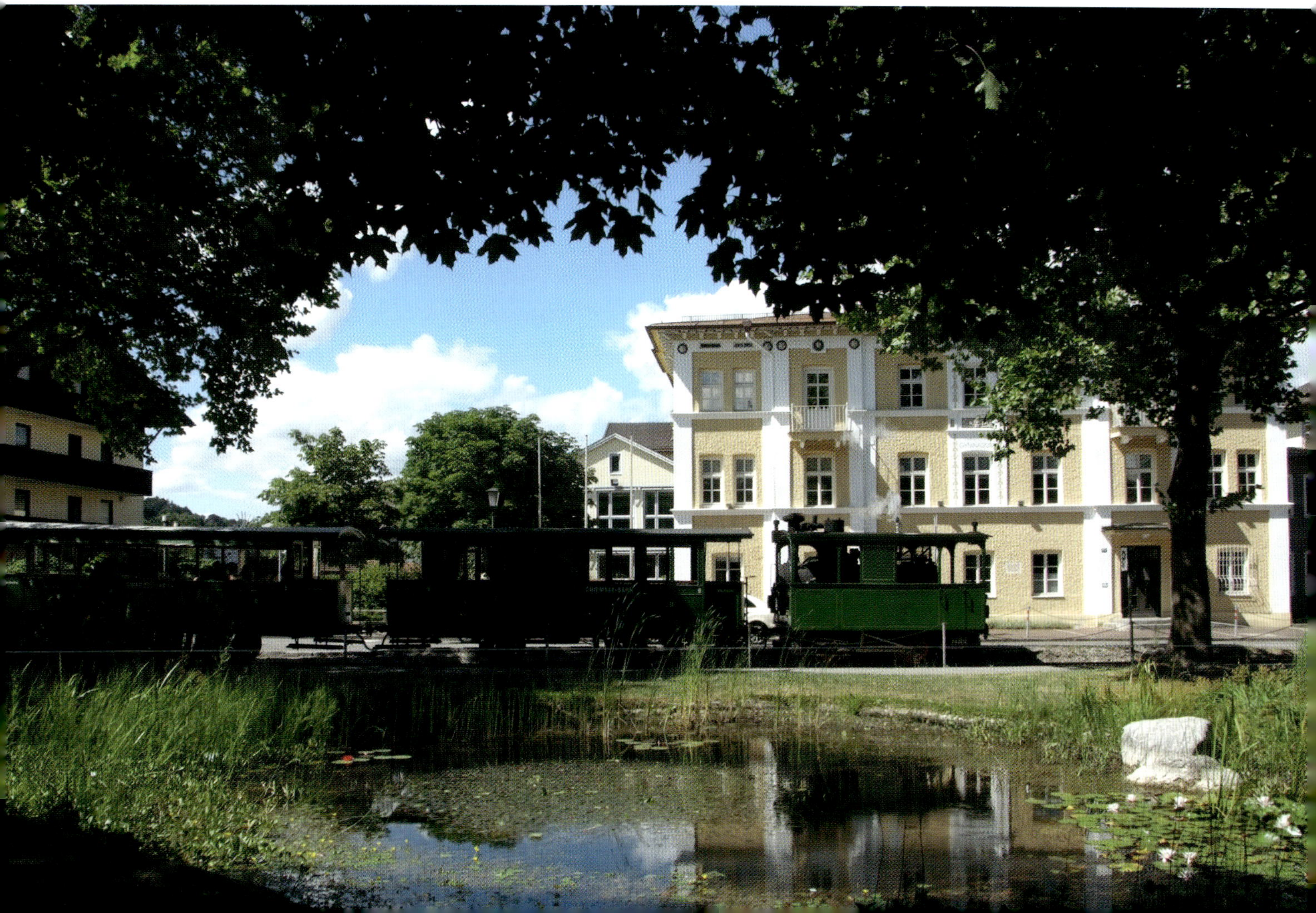

POLAND

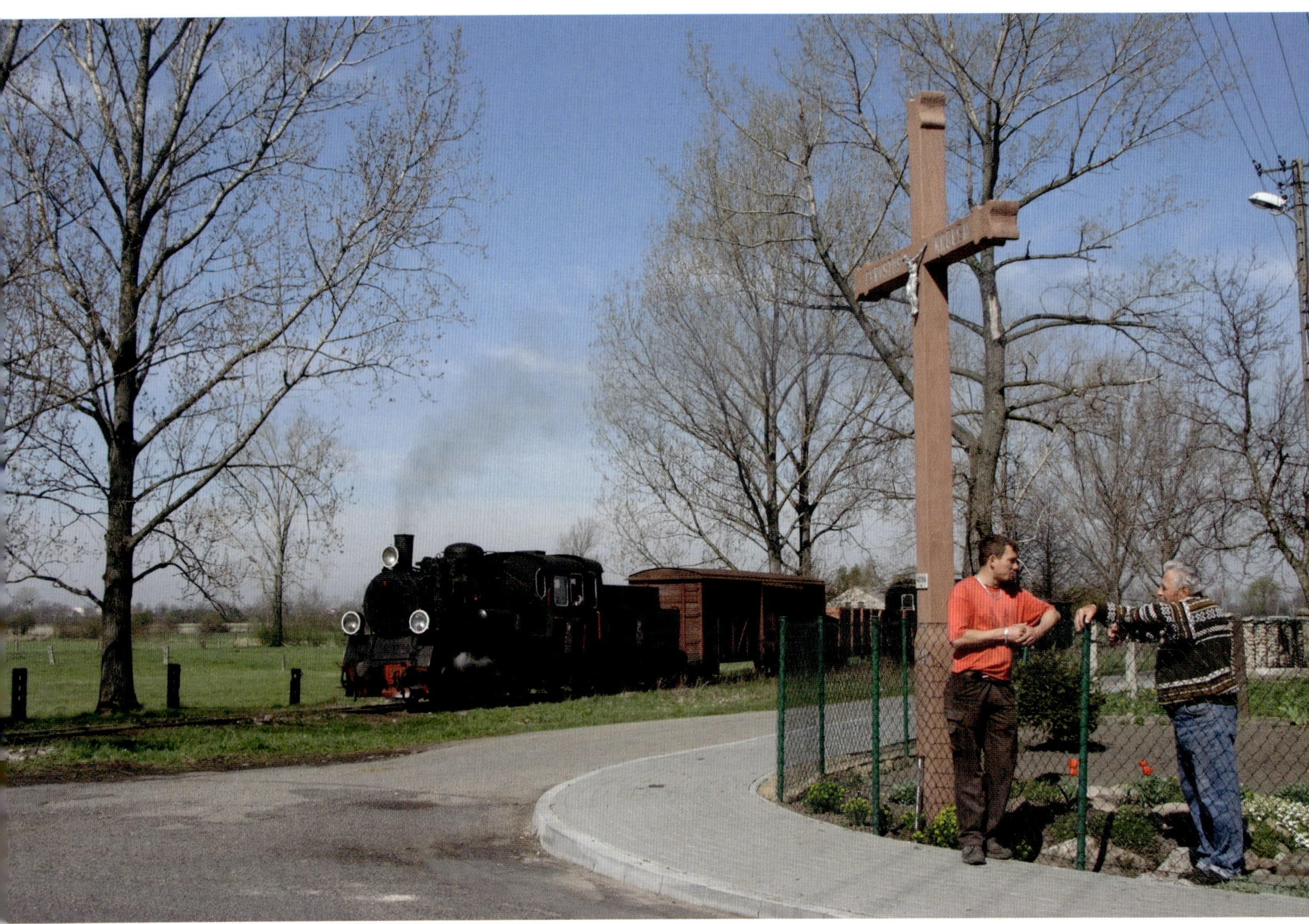

0-8-0 No Px48-1919 (Chrzanów 4507/1955) pauses at Miroszka on the Gnieźno-Anastazewo railway on 26 April 2012. Poland lost its independence in the late eighteenth century and for many years was partitioned between Germany, Russia and Austria. They had differing ideas about railways, often using them to tie their portions of the country into their own economies rather than to serve local needs. There were also incompatible policies over things like gauges and it's hardly surprising that the new Polish state created after the First World War inherited a highly disparate group of lines. The Gnieźno railway, built from 1883, lay in the old German part and was built to 900mm gauge. It was converted to 600mm in 1895 and reached Anastazewo in 1911. It was converted again in the early 1950s, this time to 750mm to enable it to be worked by the Px48 class 0-8-0s which were being mass-produced for the PKP. The local authority now runs it as a tourist line.

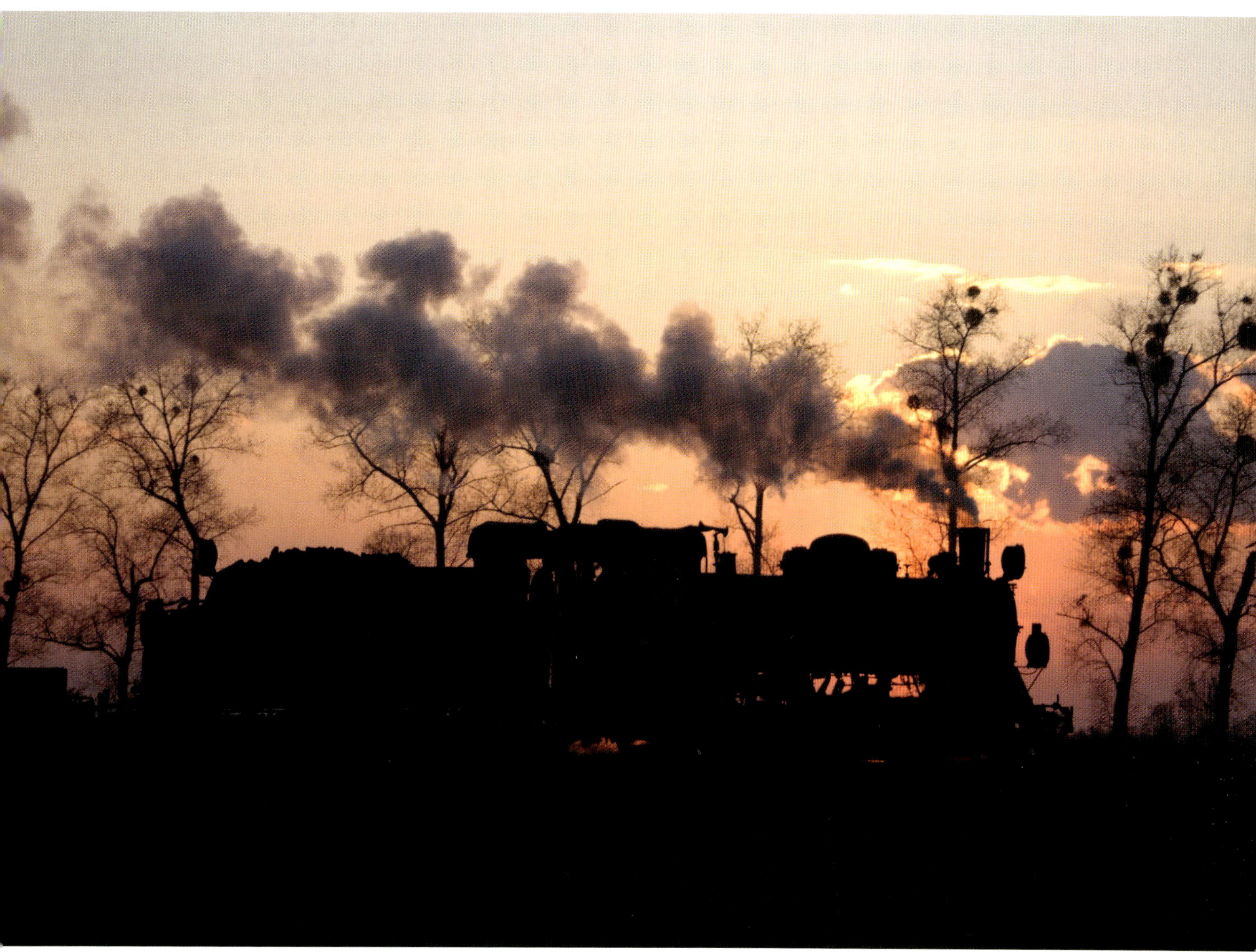

No Px48-1756 (Chrzanów 2253/1951) at sunset on 25 April 2012 on the Środa-Zaniemyśl railway, opened in 1909. It's the small remaining part of what was originally the Schrodaer Kreisbahn, an extensive metre gauge system in the German part of Poland built from 1902 which was also converted to 750mm in the early 1950s so that the Px48s could run on it. Steam working here lasted almost until the end of the twentieth century. The line closed to regular traffic in 2001 and the local authority reopened it as a tourist railway two years later.

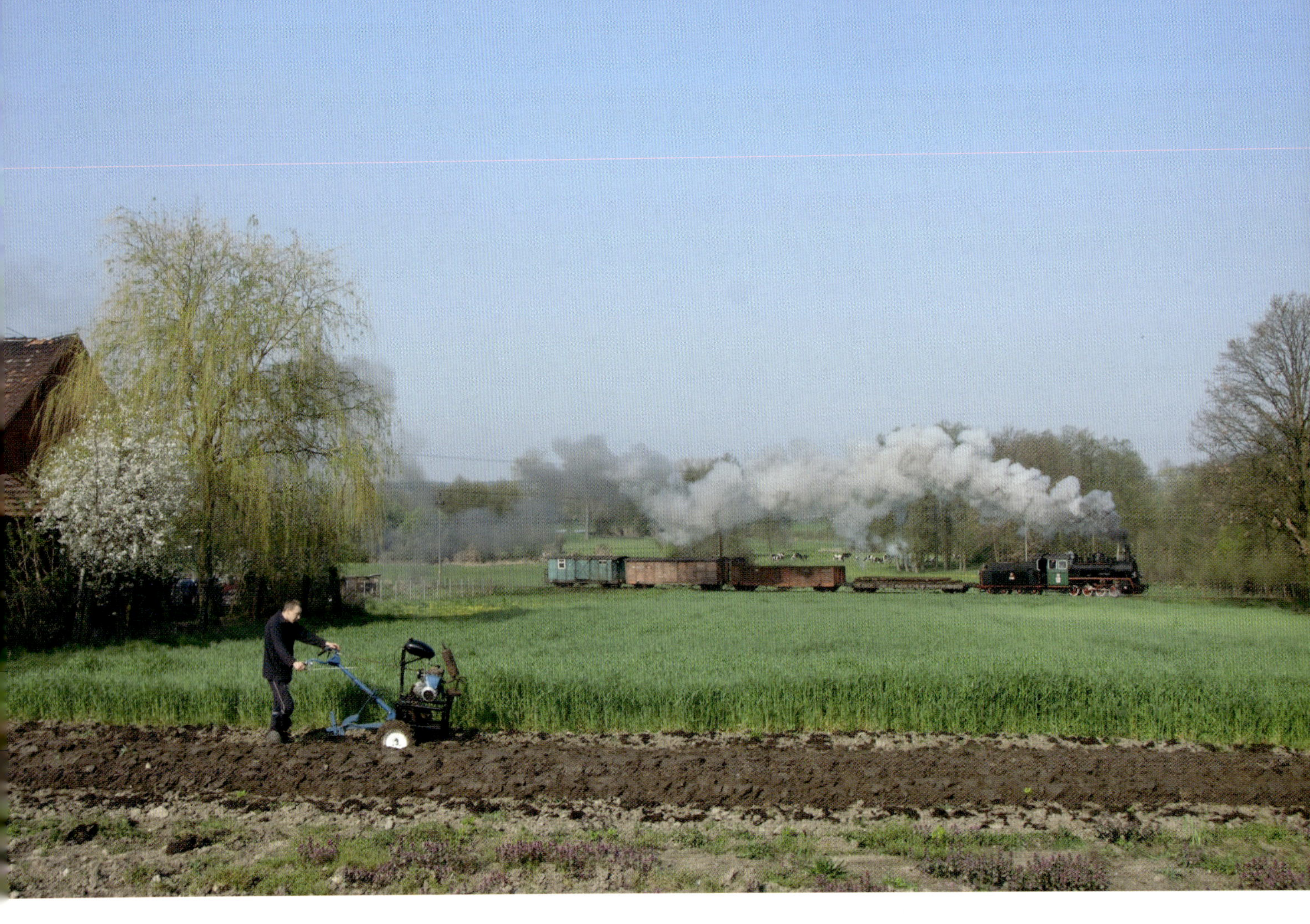

Above: No Px48-1919, visiting from Gniezno, approaches the mainline junction at Stare Bojanowo on the Smiegel railway on 26 April 2008. Another line on old German territory, it was opened in 1900 as the metre gauge Schmiegeler Kreisbahn and again was converted to 750mm in the 1950s. Poland's narrow gauge railways emerged from the Second World War in very poor shape; many locos had been destroyed, damaged beyond repair or removed and much of the track needed wholesale reconstruction. The plan behind the conversion was to retain sufficient lines of each gauge which could be worked by the surviving locos of that gauge and to rebuild all the other lines to 750mm for operation by the Px48s, the idea being that the economies of scale arising from the locos' mass-production would more than offset the cost of the work.

Opposite above: Later the same day, No Px48-1919 and her train of transporters carrying standard gauge wagons have passed under the mainline at Stare Bojanowo station and are attracting admirers as they climb up towards the exchange sidings on its eastern side.

Opposite below: 0-8-0 No Px48-1752 (Chrzanów 2247/1951) makes her way through the woods near Ełk, up in the top right-hand corner of Poland, on 23 July 2012. The Ełk railway started out life in 1913 as the metre gauge Lycker Kleinbahn in a part of the country which remained in German hands until 1945. It's now a popular holiday district. The line was converted to 750mm in 1951 and closed in 2001, after which Ełk town council took over to promote tourist services.

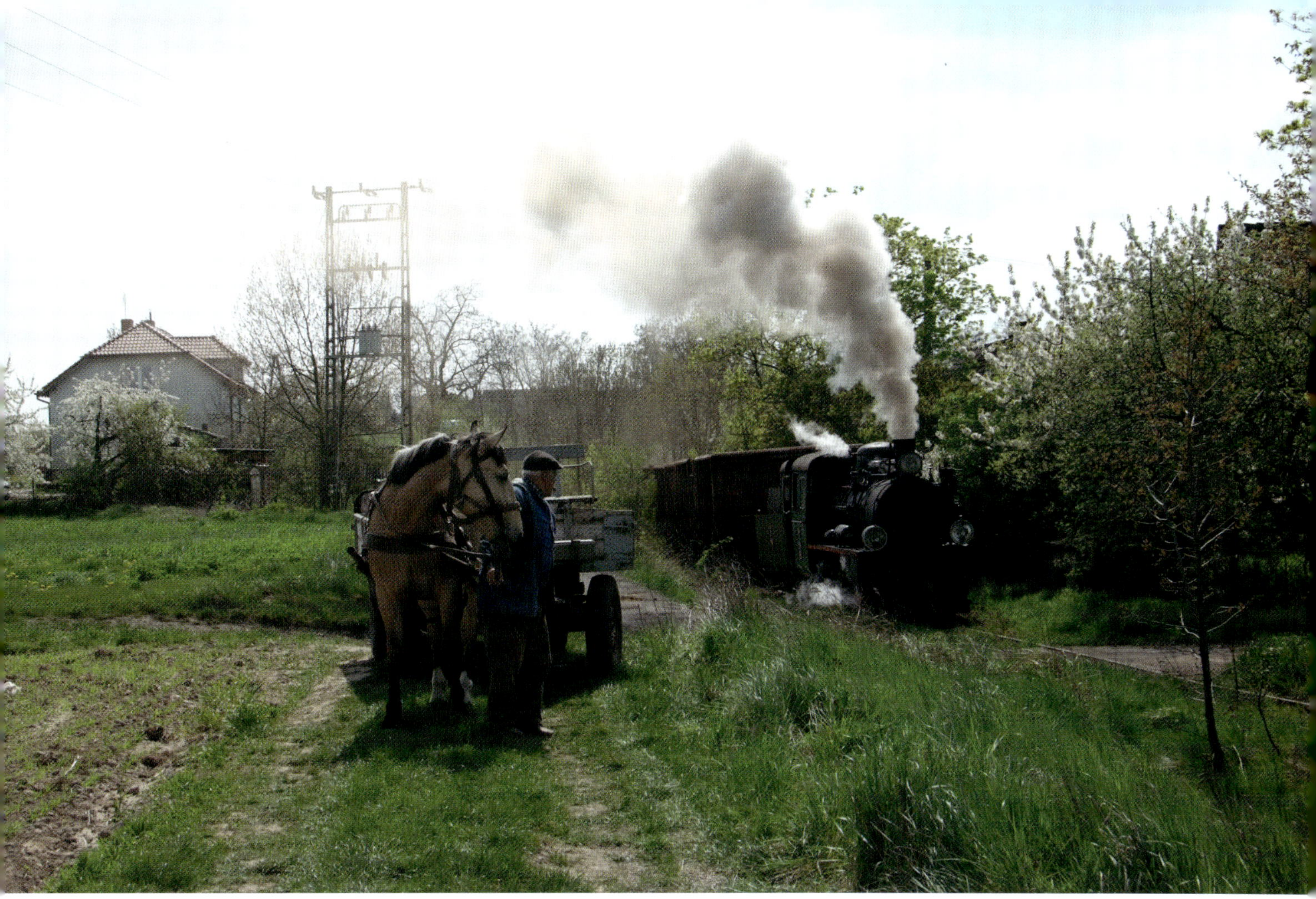

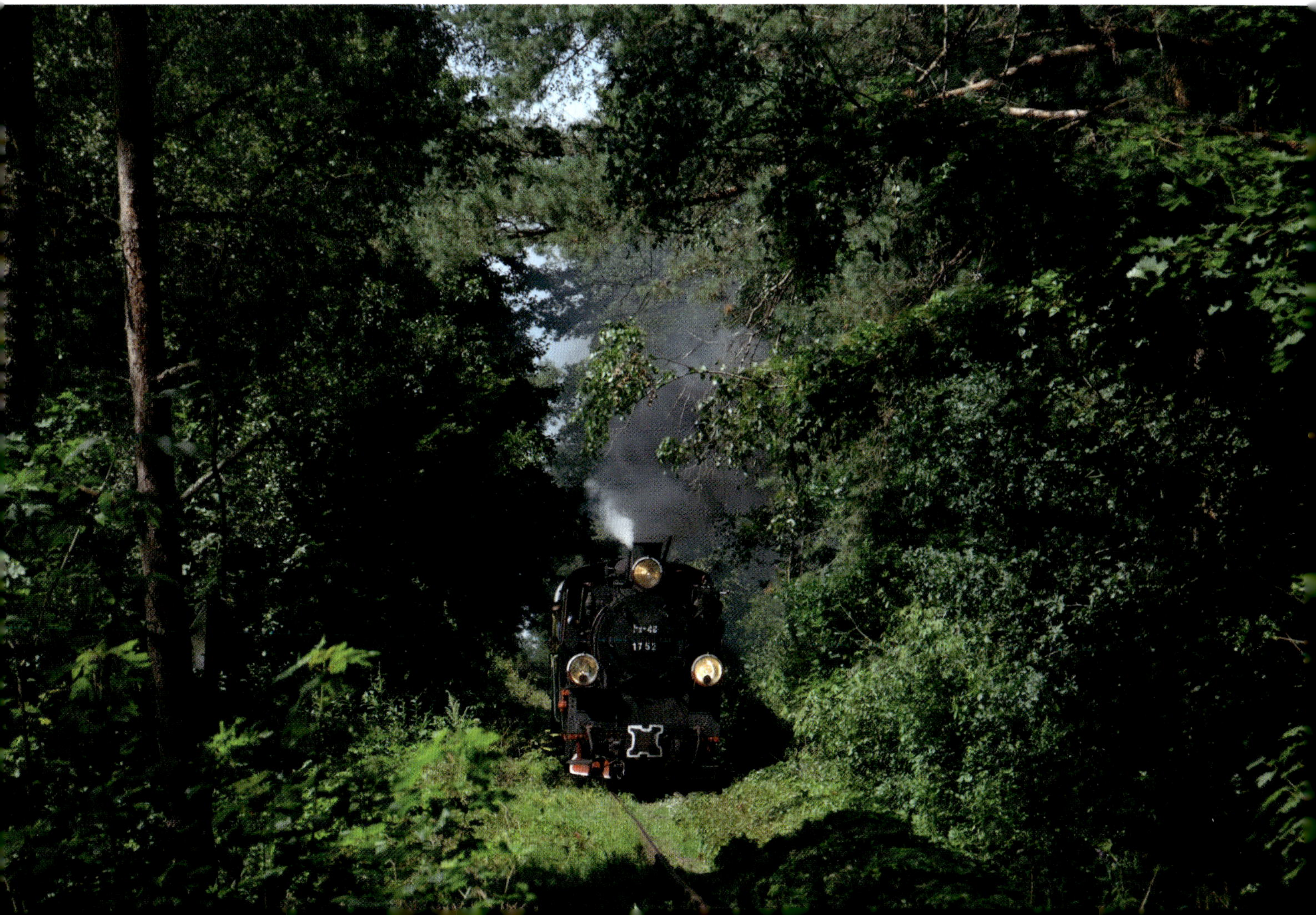

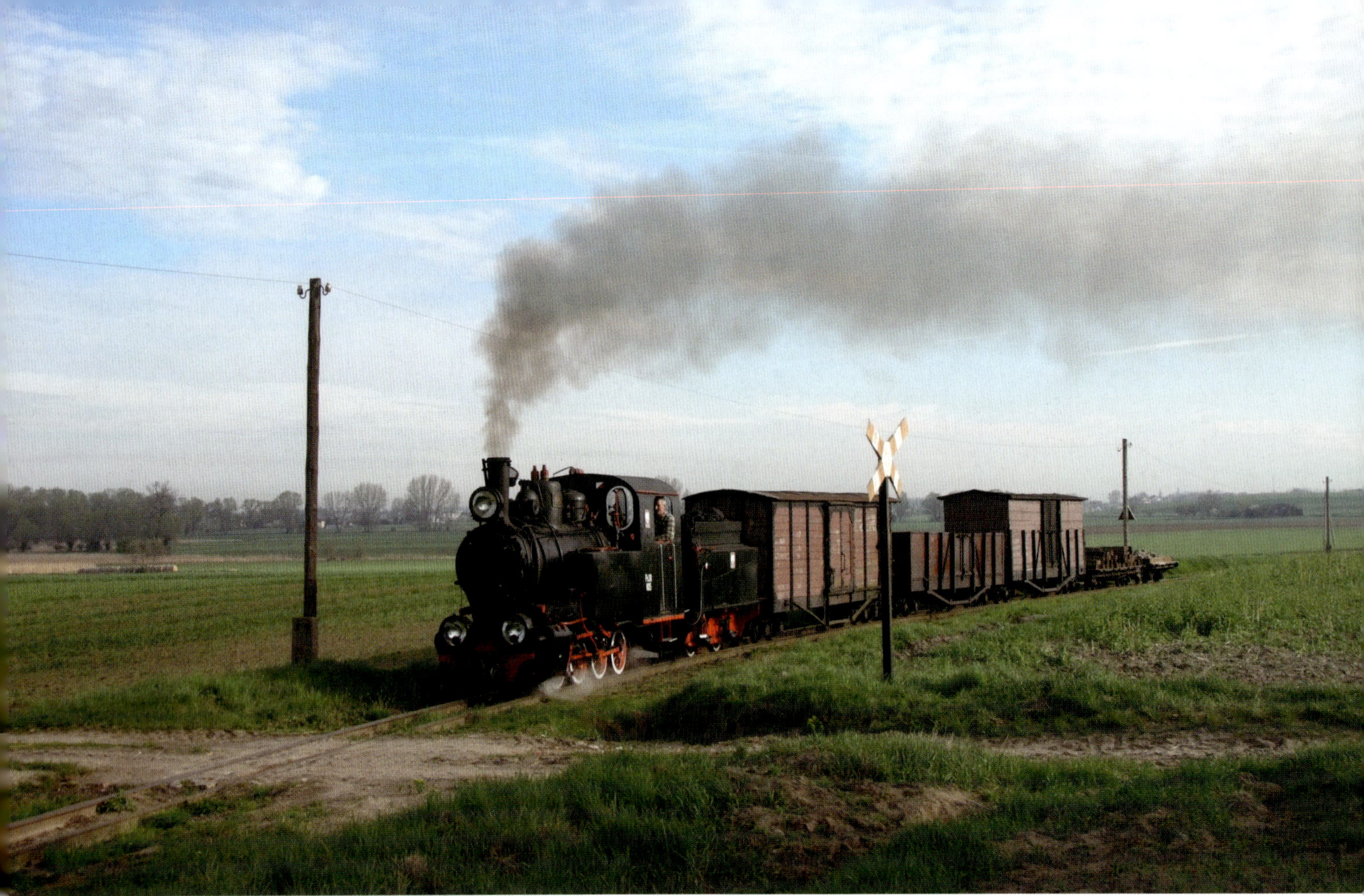

Above: On 27 April 2012 0-8-0T No Px38-805 (Chrzanów 727/1938) heads away from Żnin on a line which has always been 600mm gauge. The first section of the old Kleinbahn des Kreises Znin, between Żnin and Gonsawa or Gerlingen (now Gąsawa) in the German part of Poland, opened on 1 July 1894. It developed into a sizeable system which closed to passengers in 1962. Freight services were cut back after 1963 and ended in 1995 when just about the only remaining traffic was sugar beet bound for a large factory at Żnin. Things looked up for the first section between Żnin and Gąsawa when the PKP set up its 600mm gauge railway museum at Wenecja, midway along it, in 1972 and over the years no fewer than seventeen steam locos have found a home there. Tourist trains started between Żnin and Gąsawa in 1976 and the line is now privately operated.

Opposite above: Las-type 0-6-0T No Ty-1884 (Chrzanów 4967/1956) leaves Smolnik with an empty train on the Bieszczady or Cisna forestry railway in south eastern Poland's Carpathian Mountains on the frosty morning of 29 April 2010. The district was part of the Austrian empire until 1918 and the line started out as a typical Austrian-style 760mm gauge railway running from the mainline at Nowy Lupkow to Cisna and on to a terminus at Moczarne.

Opposite below: No Ty-1884 crosses the Osława river near Smolnik on 29 April 2010. The railway experienced its fair share of turmoil during the two world wars, being partly dismantled by the retreating Austrian army in the first one and again by the Poles when the Germans and the Russians invaded in 1939. More than 141,000 people from the district, mostly of Ukrainian origin, were forcibly resettled in former German territory in western Poland in 1947 and others were deported to the Soviet Union. Few potential passengers were left and when the line was converted to 750mm in the early 1950s it became freight-only, mostly serving the timber industry, until passenger services restarted in 1963.

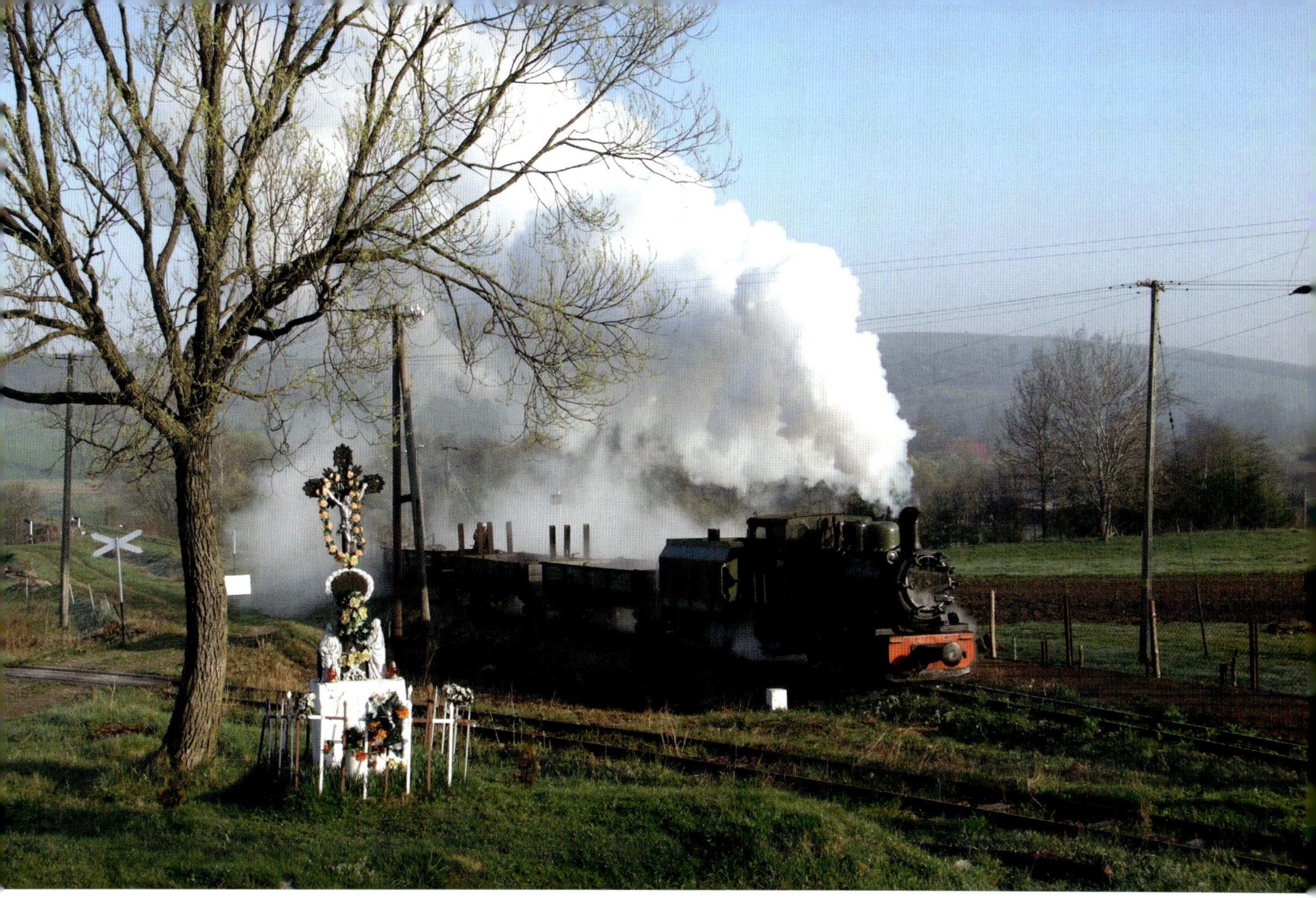

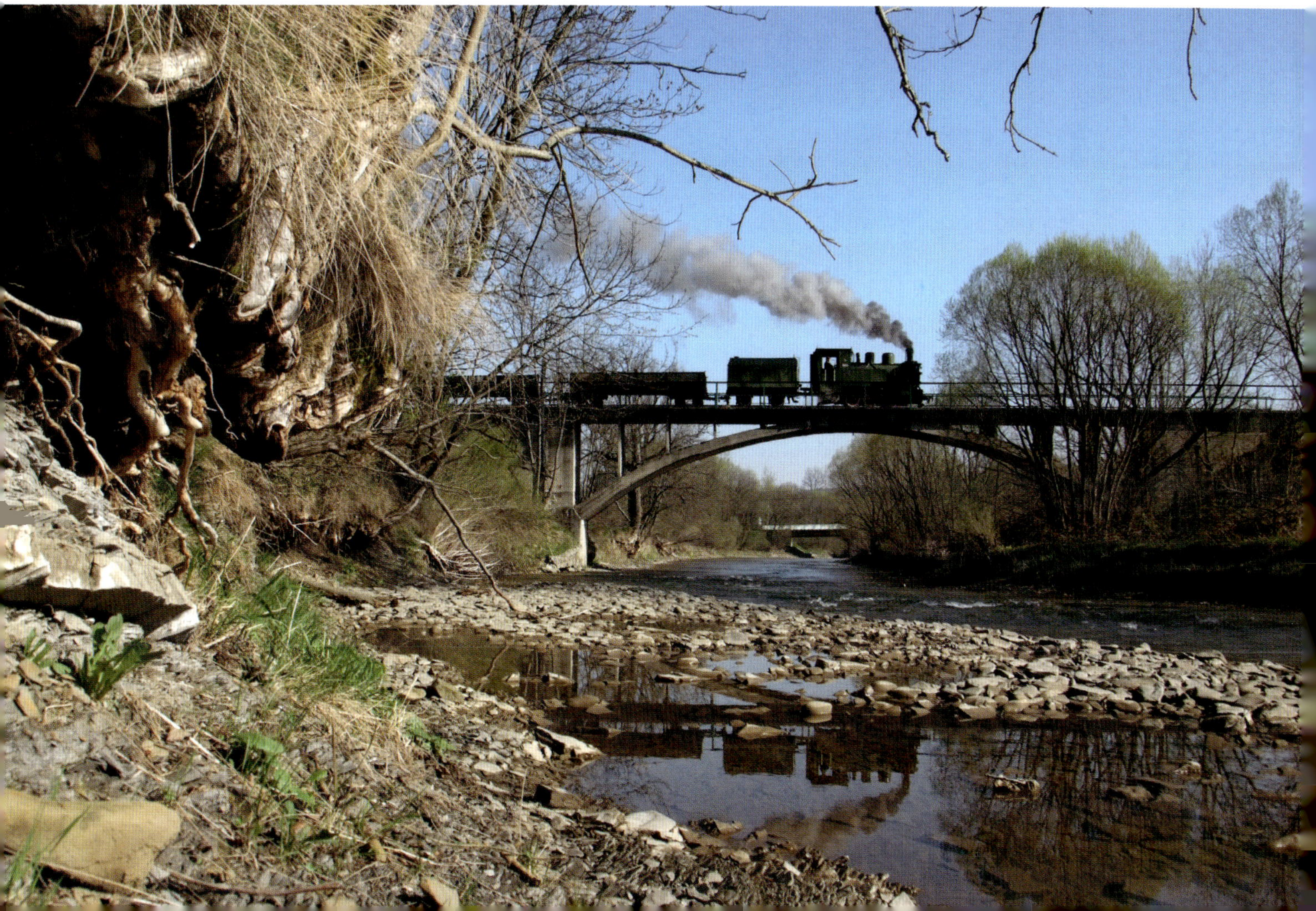

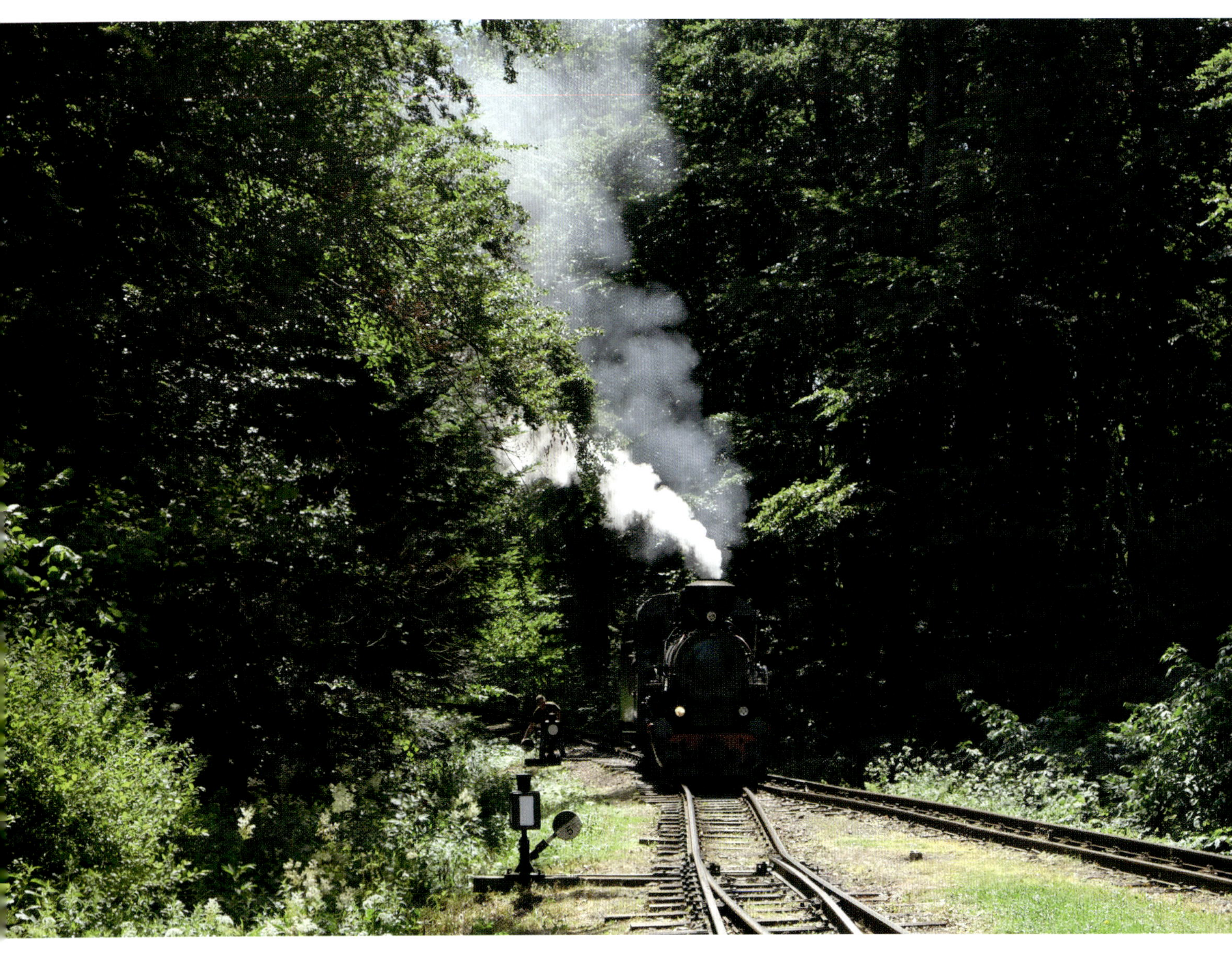

PT-4 type 0-8-0 No Kp-4-3772 (Chrzanów 3772/1957) runs around her train at Balnica, at the summit of the line, on 7 July 2016. After the gauge conversion the railway was worked for a short period by the little 12-tonne Las 0-6-0Ts but they proved to be too small and were replaced by several of the Polish-built PT-4's which didn't go to the Soviet Union, much heavier machines at 28 tonnes, as well as a couple of the 42-tonne Px48's. It closed in 1993 and a tourist service started a few years later. It's now an established feature in an increasingly popular holiday district. These two Bieszczady locos spent their working lives at the Kruszwica sugar factory in central Poland.

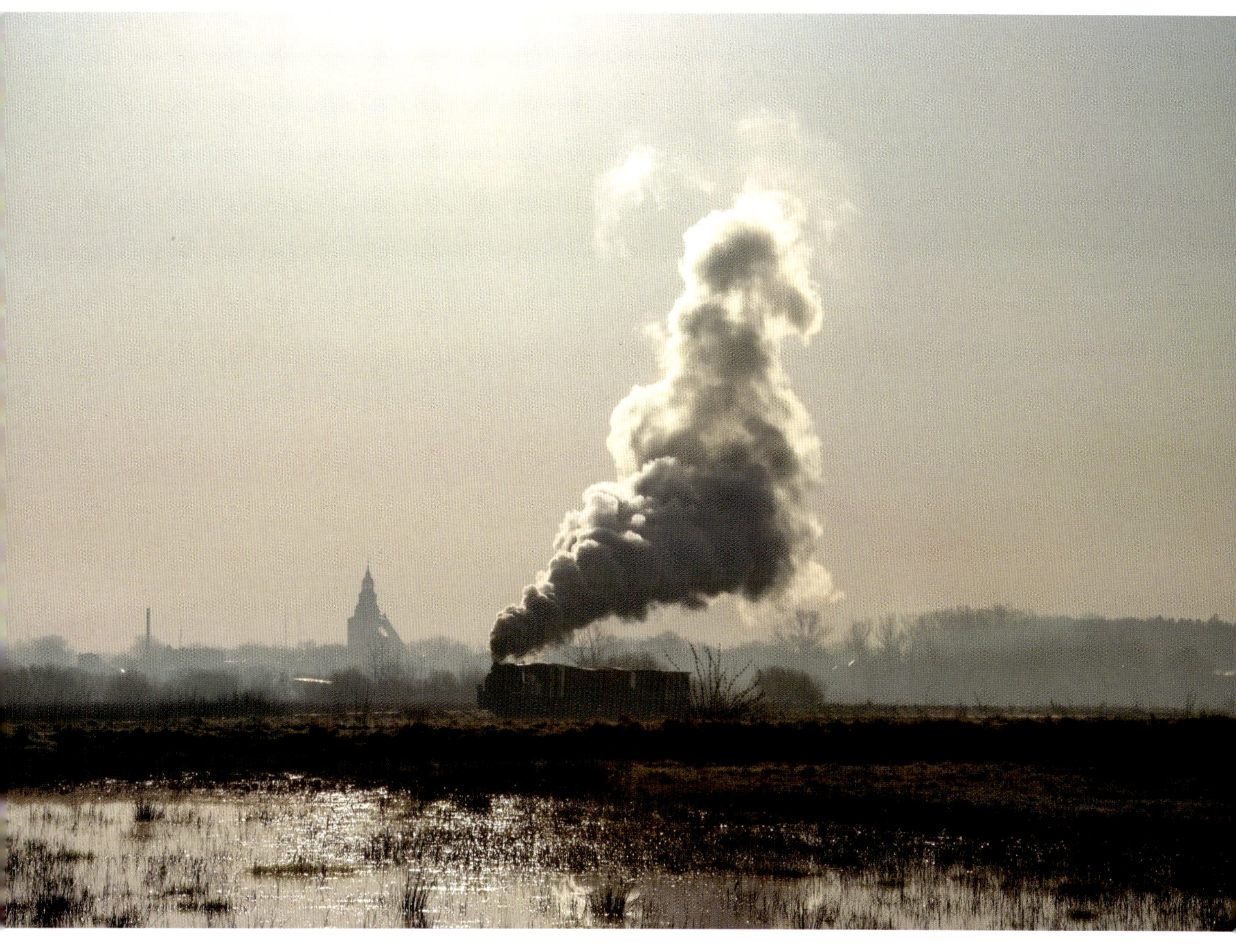

0-8-0 No Px48-3916 (Chrzanów 2022/1950), on long-term loan from Warszaw Railway Museum, crosses the floodplain near Gryfice soon after dawn on 24 April 2008. This metre gauge railway in the top left hand corner of Poland started out in 1896 as the first part of the Greifenberger Kleinbahnen, a 750mm gauge line from Gryfice (then called Greifenberg) to Niechorze (Horst Seebad). Extensions and branches rapidly followed and in 1899 a neighbouring metre gauge system expanded to join it. The break of gauge was overcome the following year by widening the Gryfice lines. The district was very much a part of Germany until 1945 and although its German population was expelled in many ways it still feels more German than Polish.

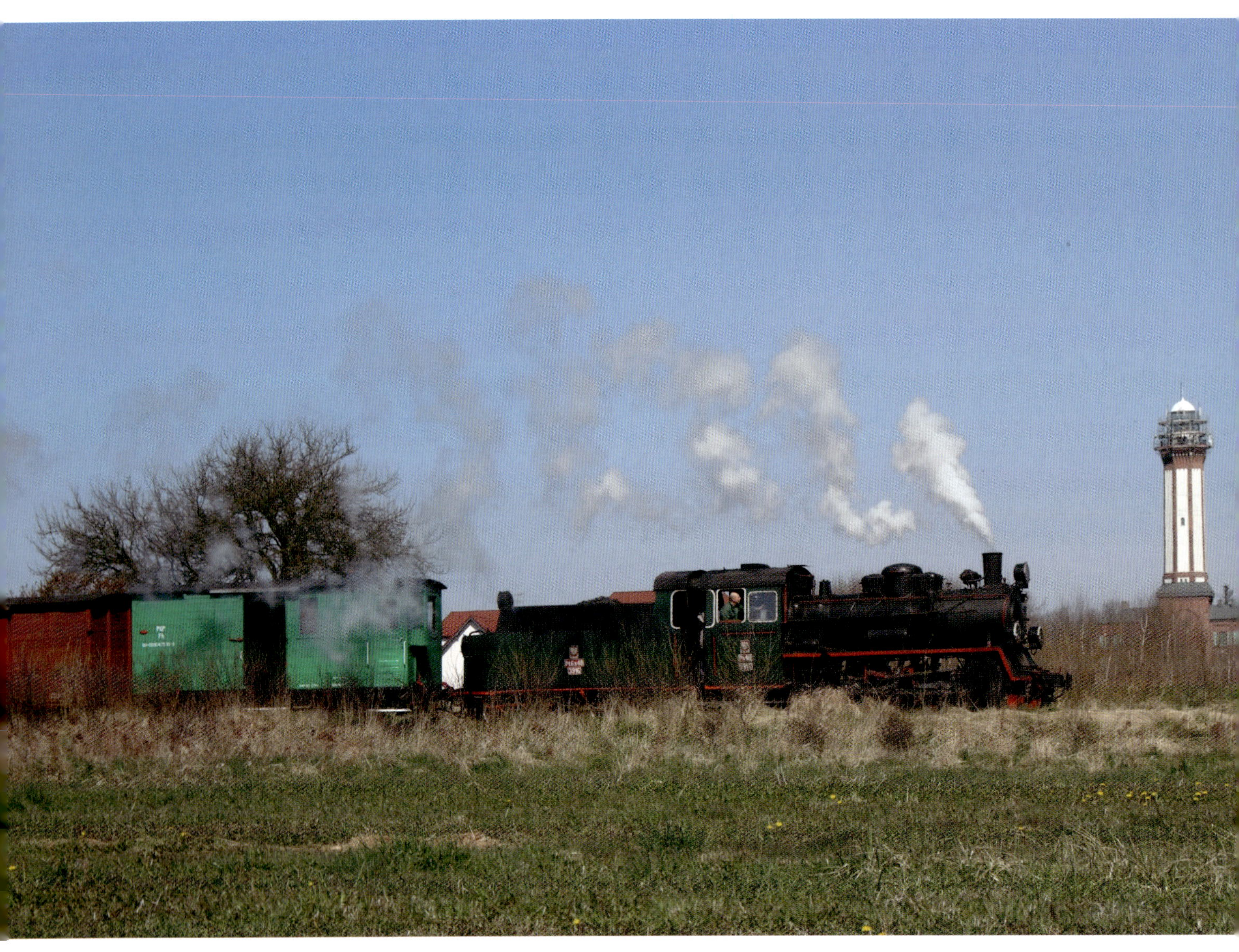

No Px48-3916 passes Niechorze later that day. Like the Rügen and Molli lines, the railway runs close to the Baltic coast but seldom, if ever, within sight of the sea, though Niechorze's historic lighthouse shows that it's not far away! This network of metre gauge lines was the largest within Poland's current borders. Most of it closed in the 1990s and only tourist trains have run since 2001. By the 1960s, there was a shortage of metre gauge locos and seventeen Px48's were converted from 750mm between 1969 and 1974. In its 750mm days this loco's number was Px48-1722.

FRANCE

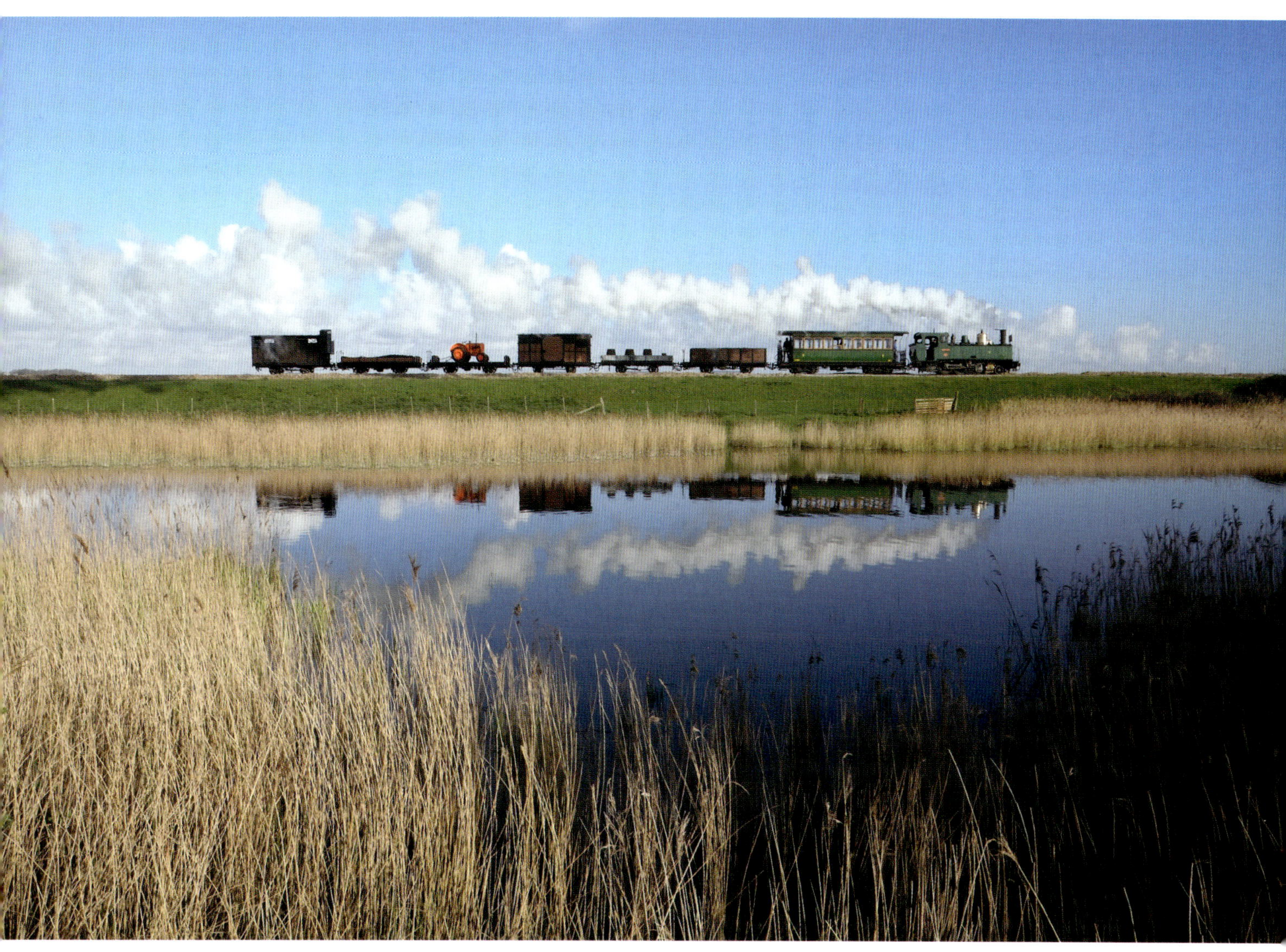

2-6-0T No 15 (HSP 1316/1920) heads a short mixed train on the CF de la Baie de Somme between Noyelles and St Valery on 17 April 2016. This has been a popular holiday district ever since 1858 when the CF du Nord opened its St Valery branch from Noyelles on the Paris-Calais mainline. The branch changed radically in the 1880s when Noyelles became the junction of three metre gauge railways. One ran inland and another to Le Crotoy on the north side of the bay. The third involved conversion of the Nord branch to mixed gauge and extending the metre gauge to the coast at Cayeux. The inland line went many years ago, but the two coastal ones remained busy until closure in 1969 and 1972 and were soon rescued by preservationists. None of the original steam locos have survived but No 15 is similar, if not identical, to locos built to make good losses during the First World War.

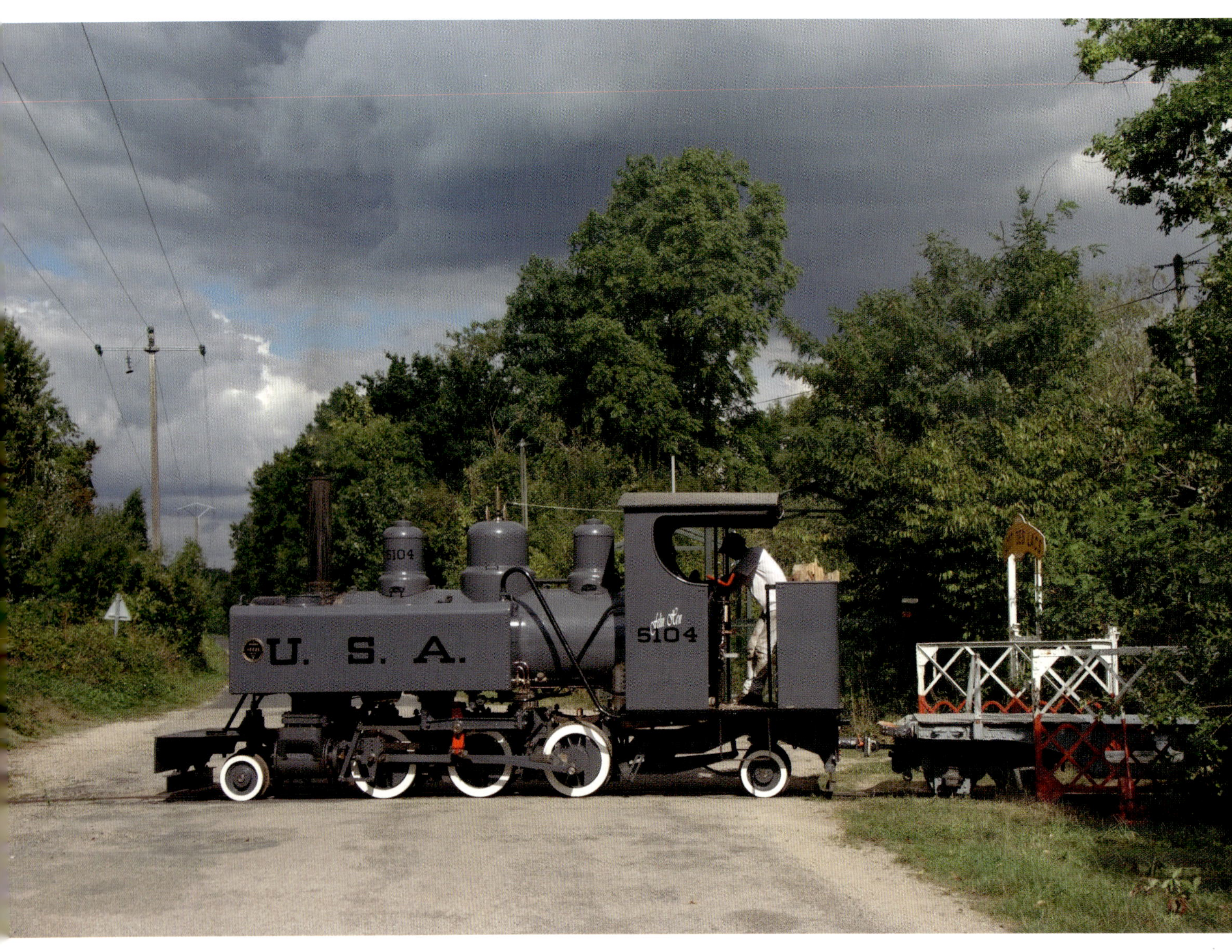

Felin Hen (Baldwin 46828/1918) is the only survivor of 250 600mm gauge 2-6-2Ts built for the US military during the First World War but she didn't reach Europe until 1919. Between then and 1924, she was one of four which served the US Navy at Calais helping to rebuild France's shattered infrastructure, after which three moved to the Penrhyn Quarry Railway. *Felin Hen*, named after a village on the Penrhyn line, started work late in 1925 but the locos weren't liked and less than two years later she went into store in Port Penrhyn shed. In 1940, the others were scrapped but *Felin Hen* moved to Fairymead sugar factory in Queensland, was rebuilt in 1956 as a 0-6-2T with different-shaped tanks and ran until 1965. She was bought in 2002 by Patrick Mourot who runs the Tacot des Lacs, an old sand quarry line near Fontainebleau now carrying tourists and has been restored to her original appearance. Here, Patrick drives her across the Chemin de Montcourt aux Chapelottes on 10 September 2013. Although she's back in her pre-Penrhyn condition, look closely and you'll see that the *Felin Hen* name hasn't quite disappeared!

SWITZERLAND

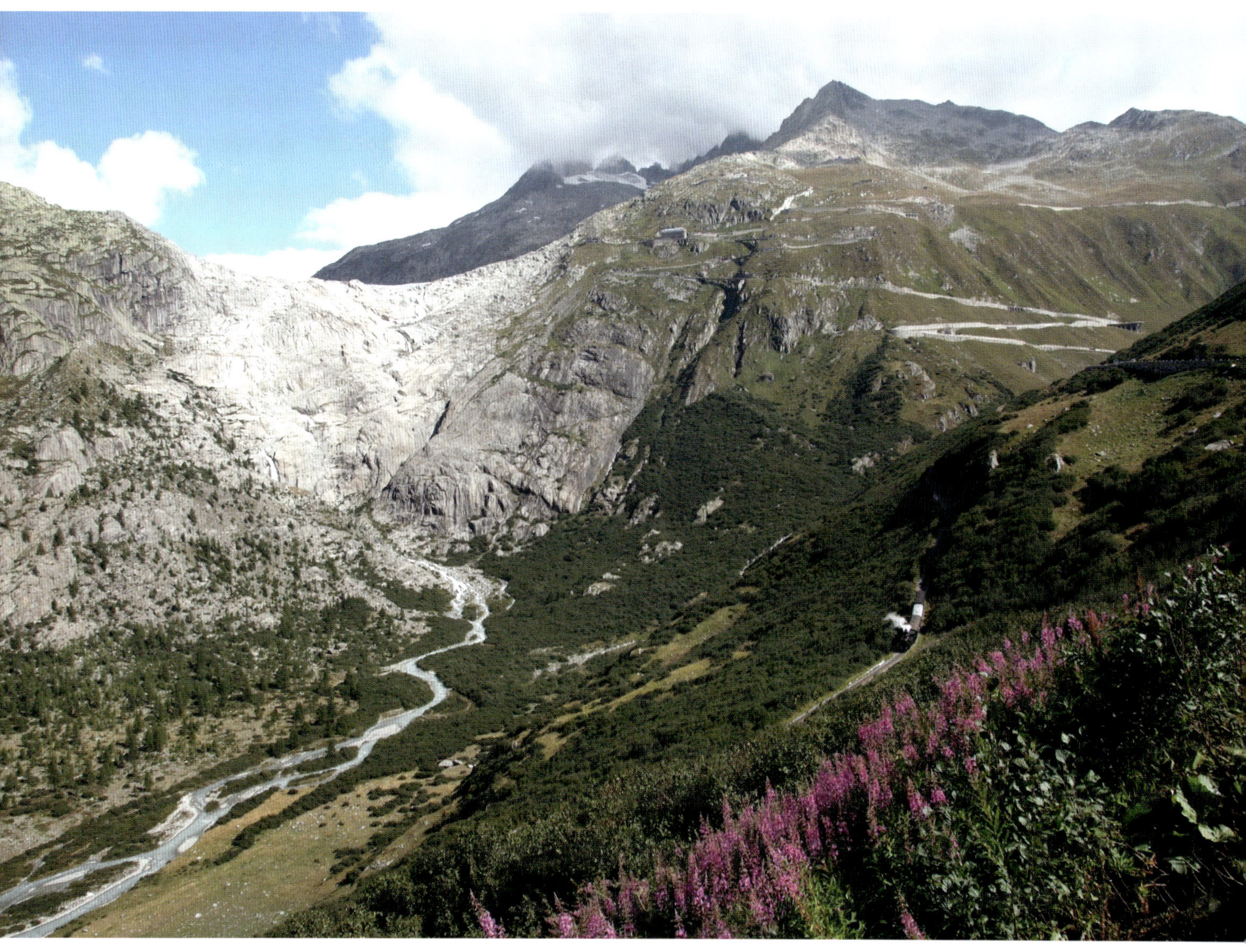

The metre gauge Furka-Oberalp Bahn's 2-6-0T No 4 (SLM 2318/1913) is dwarfed by the spectacular Rhone glacier on 11 September 2009 as she descends from Furka summit towards Gletsch on this Abt-rack and adhesion railway. It took many years to complete this most difficult section between the Rhine and Rhone valleys and it didn't open until 1926. It was always unsatisfactory as it couldn't be kept open in winter and was replaced by a base tunnel in 1982. The old line has gradually been rebuilt by volunteers.

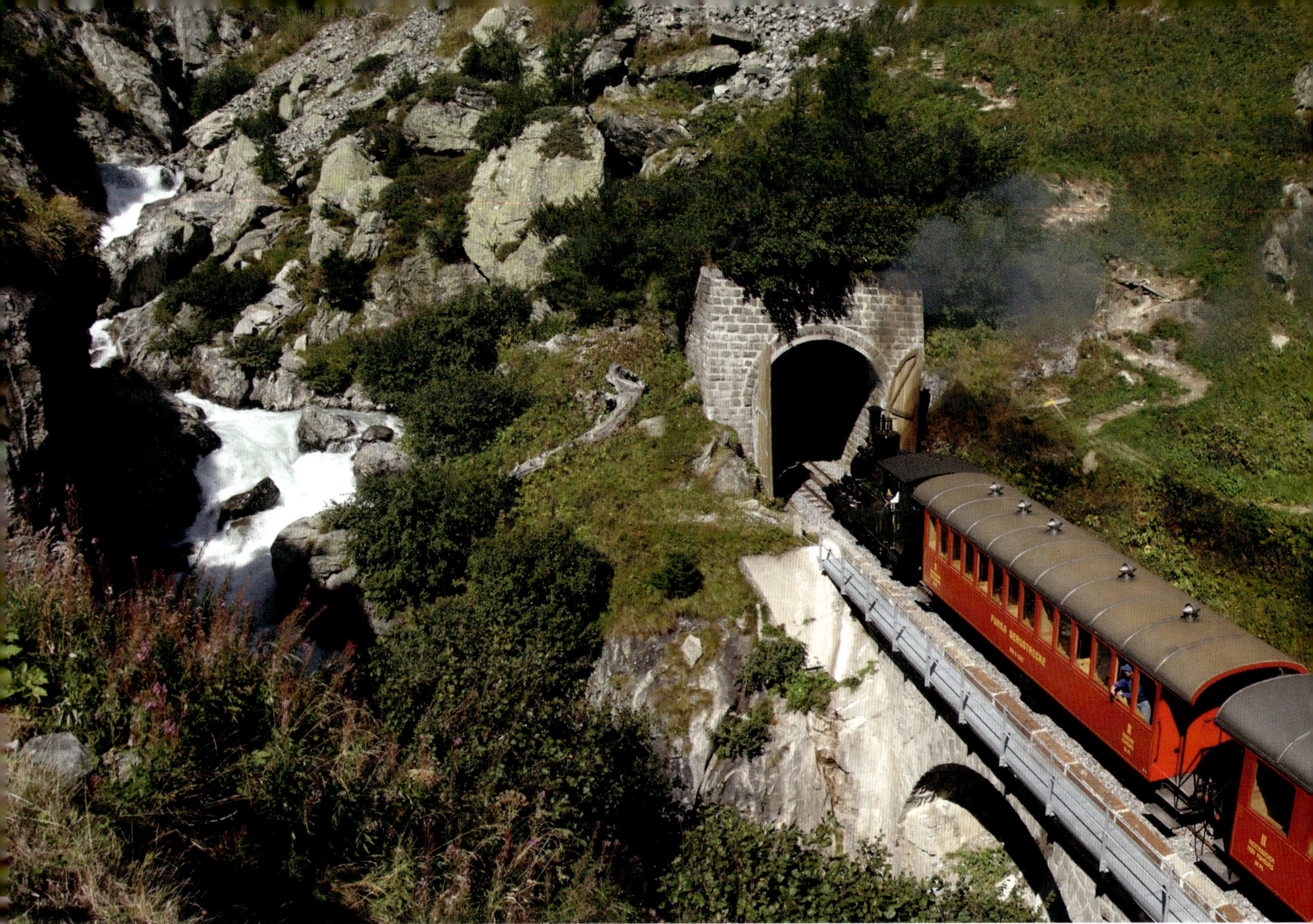

Above: Later that afternoon the Brig Visp Zermatt Bahn's 0-4-2RT No 6 *Weisshorn* (SLM 1410/1902) enters a spiral tunnel south of Gletsch. The line here was still being rebuilt and this was a publicity photo special. The BVZ made an end-on junction with the FO at Brig and worked it for many years.

Opposite above: Near Scuol-Tarasp on the Engadine line, 2-8-0 No 108 (SLM 1710/1906) crosses one of the Rhätische Bahn's many fine bridges on 19 February 2008. The metre gauge RhB is far from being a preserved railway and it's barely a steam one either. However, it retains two of these 2-8-0s from its pre-electrification days and some years ago bought back its first loco, 2-6-0T no. 1 *Rhätia*, and restored her to working order. It has also restored this train of steam-era carriages, several historic electric locos and some 1930s Pullman cars. It's thus no mean player in the preservation field.

Opposite below: There's also Xrot No 9213 (SLM 2149/1910), the Bernina line's 0-6-6-0 Meyer snowblower. She's still kept in reserve at Pontresina for use when the snow is really heavy and makes occasional enthusiast outings. It's before sunrise as the crew tests her rotor at Pontresina shed before one such trip on 1 March 2009. Most of the RhB's rolling stock, both heritage and modern, is kept in pristine external condition. Not so No 9213, which wore the scars of her labours in the district's extreme weather and made no pretence of being a pampered pet.

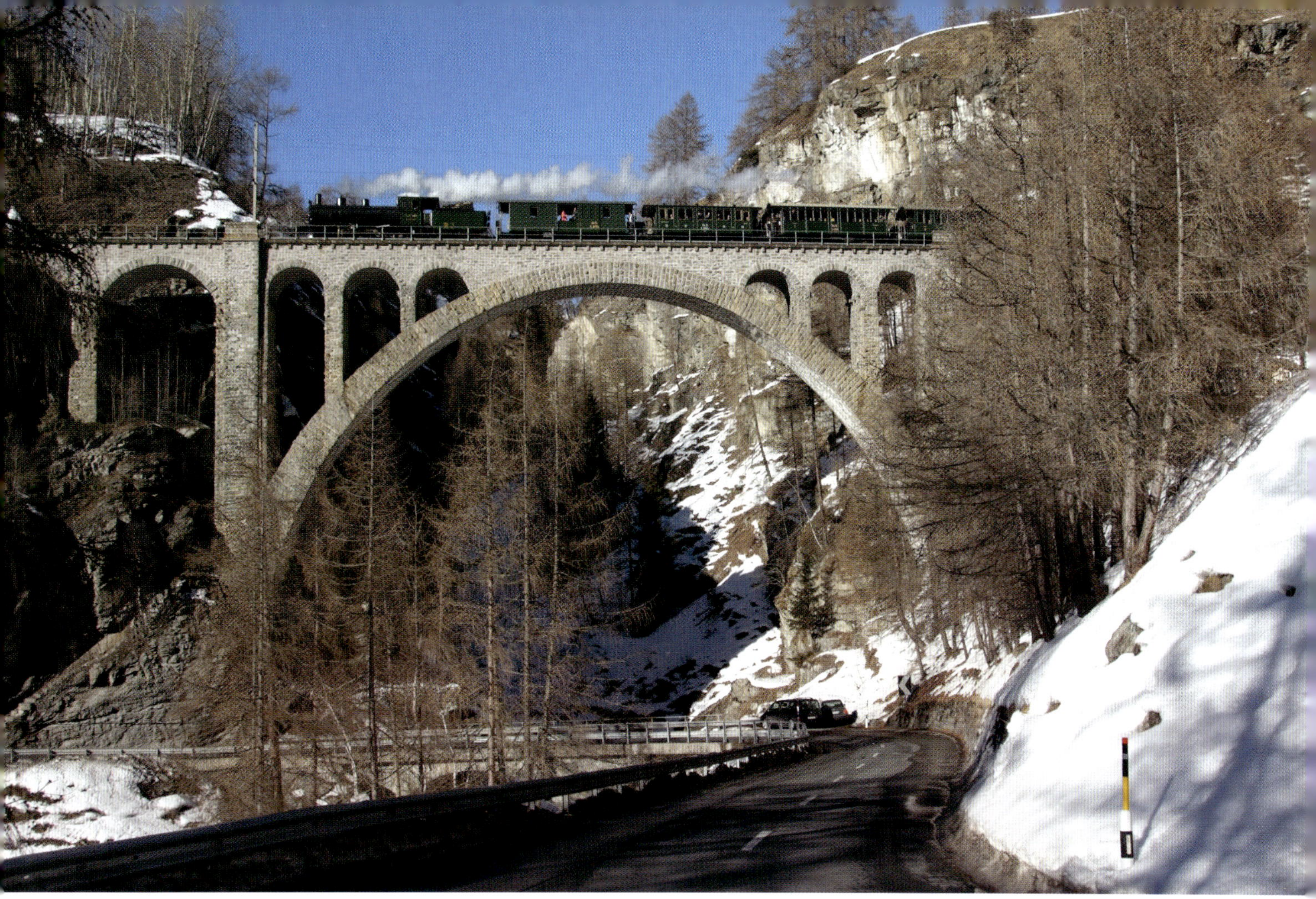

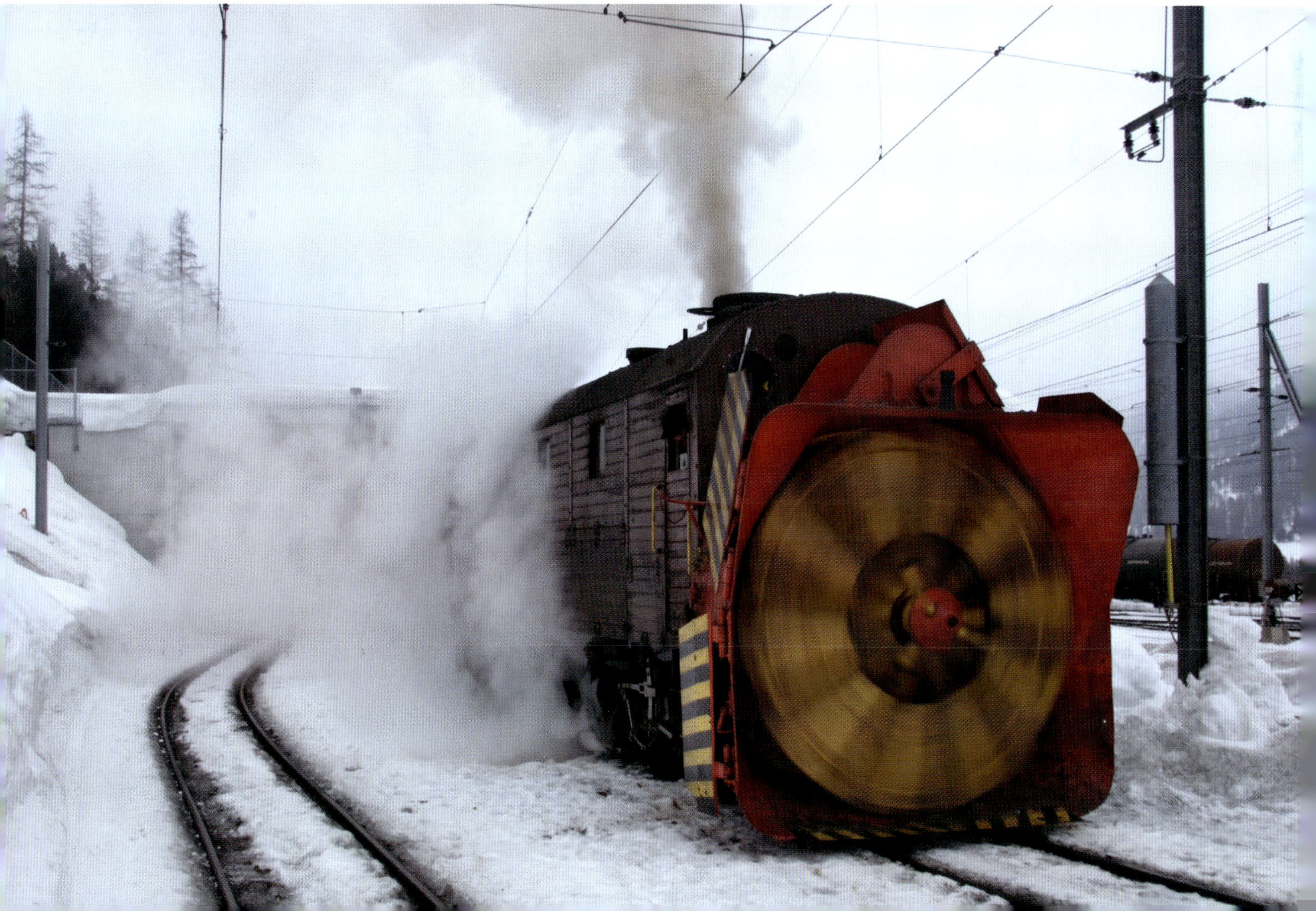

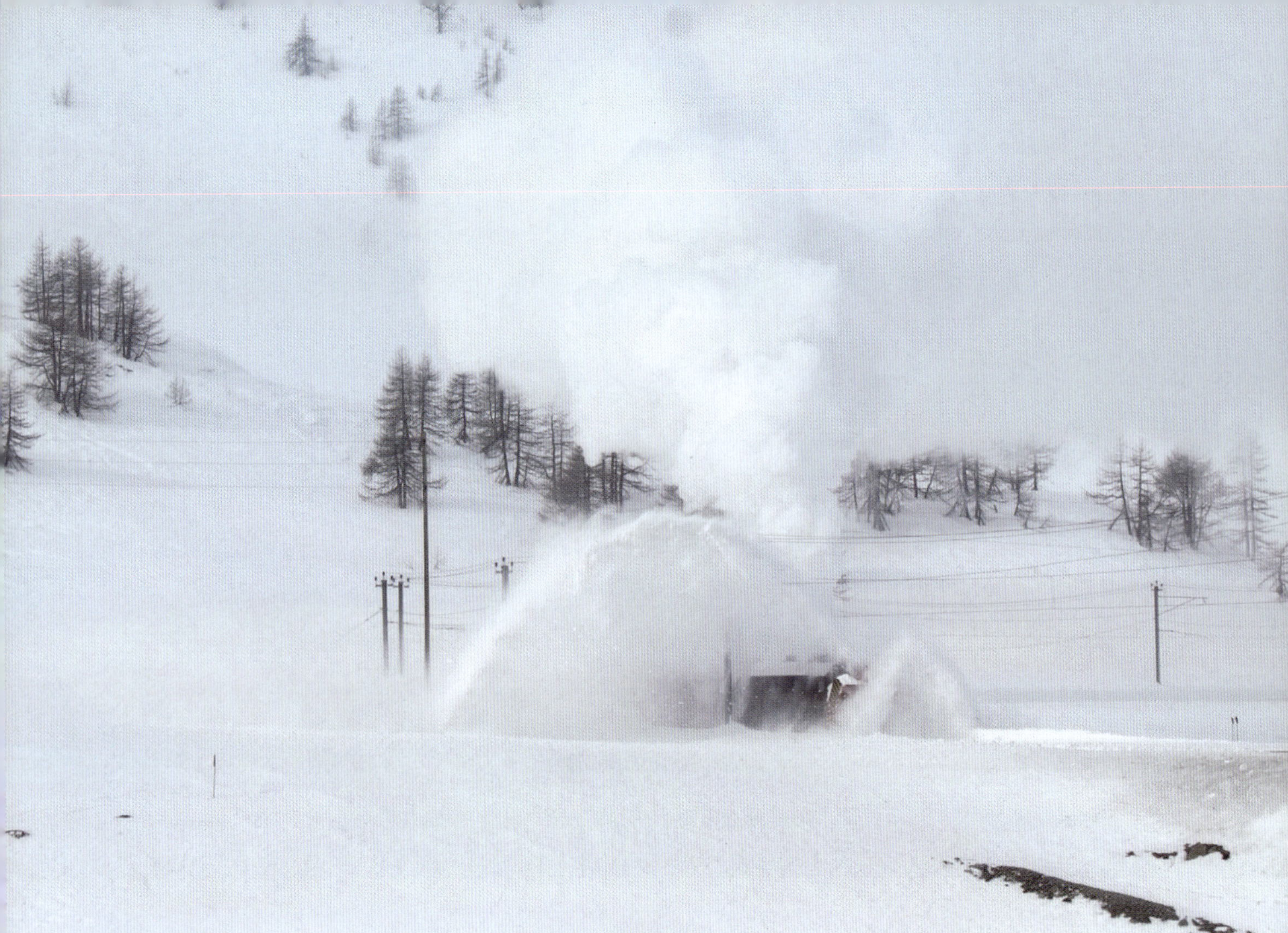

Above: Later that morning little of No 9213 is visible as she does what she's intended to do near Bernina summit!

Opposite above: A Swiss tragedy! The Waldenburgerbahn runs through the Frenke valley near Basel and is Switzerland's only public 750mm gauge railway. It opened in 1880 and was electrified in 1953. 0-6-0T No 5 *G. Thommen* (SLM 1440/1902) was put back into working order in 1980 for its centenary celebrations and the railway held several volunteer-run steam days each summer between then and 2014. They became hugely popular but sadly the trains stopped running and now the line has been taken over by the Basel tramway authority which plans to convert it to metre gauge. Back in happier times on 16 May 2010 No 5 runs beside the River Frenke.

Opposite below: The metre gauge CF Lausanne-Echallens-Bercher's 0-6-0T No 8 (SLM 2095/1910) heads through open, wheat-growing country typical of central Vaud as she approaches Bercher with some of the railway's old carriages in the hazy morning sunshine on 31 October 2010. The line was Switzerland's first narrow gauge railway and opened in stages from 1873 using rail and stock displaced from the short-lived 1,100mm gauge Mont Cenis Fell railway, constructed by British interests to speed up transport to India as a temporary measure while the Mont Cenis tunnel between France and Italy was being built. One of the Mont Cenis carriages was preserved at Echallens until 2016. Today the LEB is one of the country's four metre gauge railways still operating at least one of its old steam locos and the only one with a distinctly branch line character.

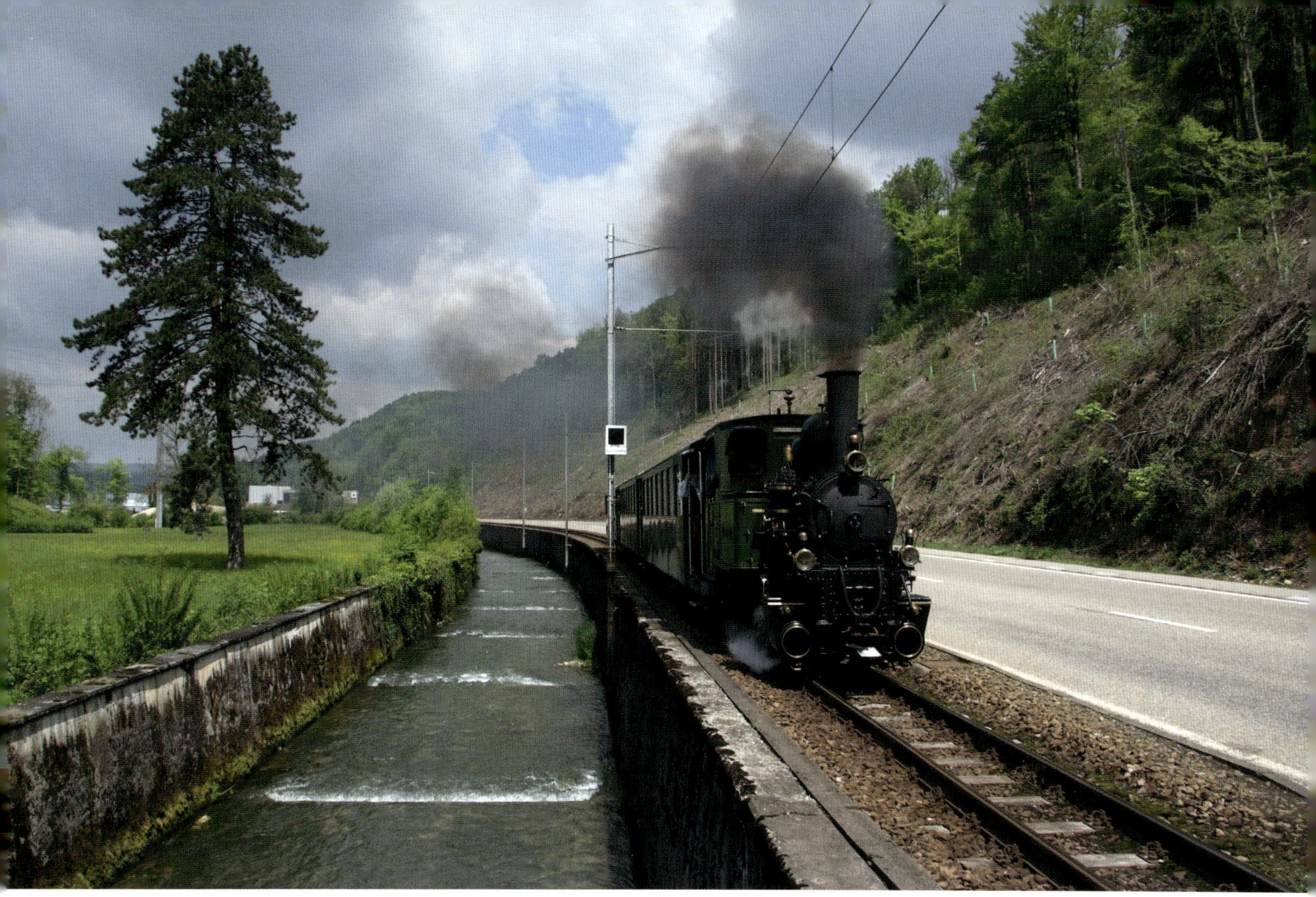

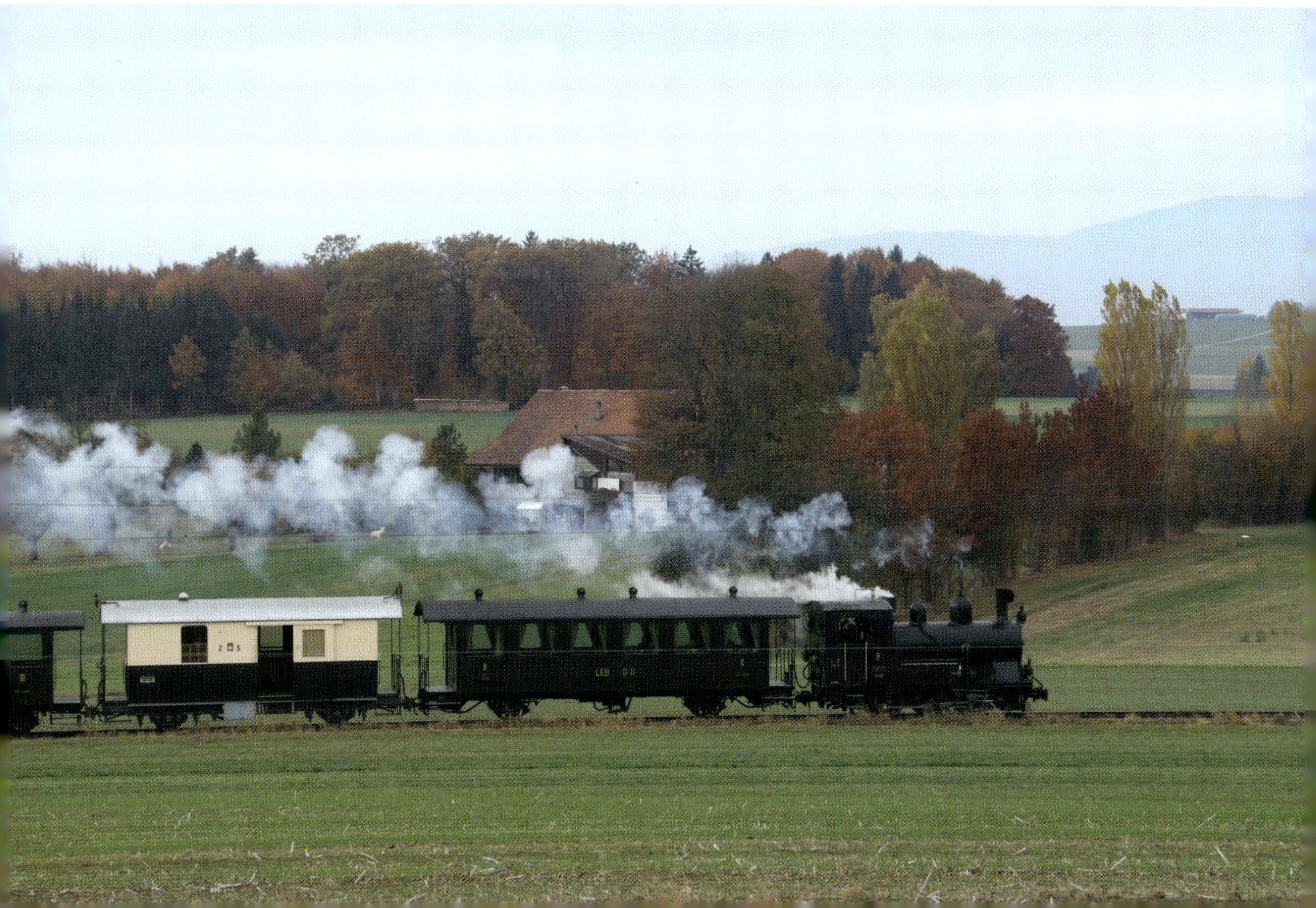

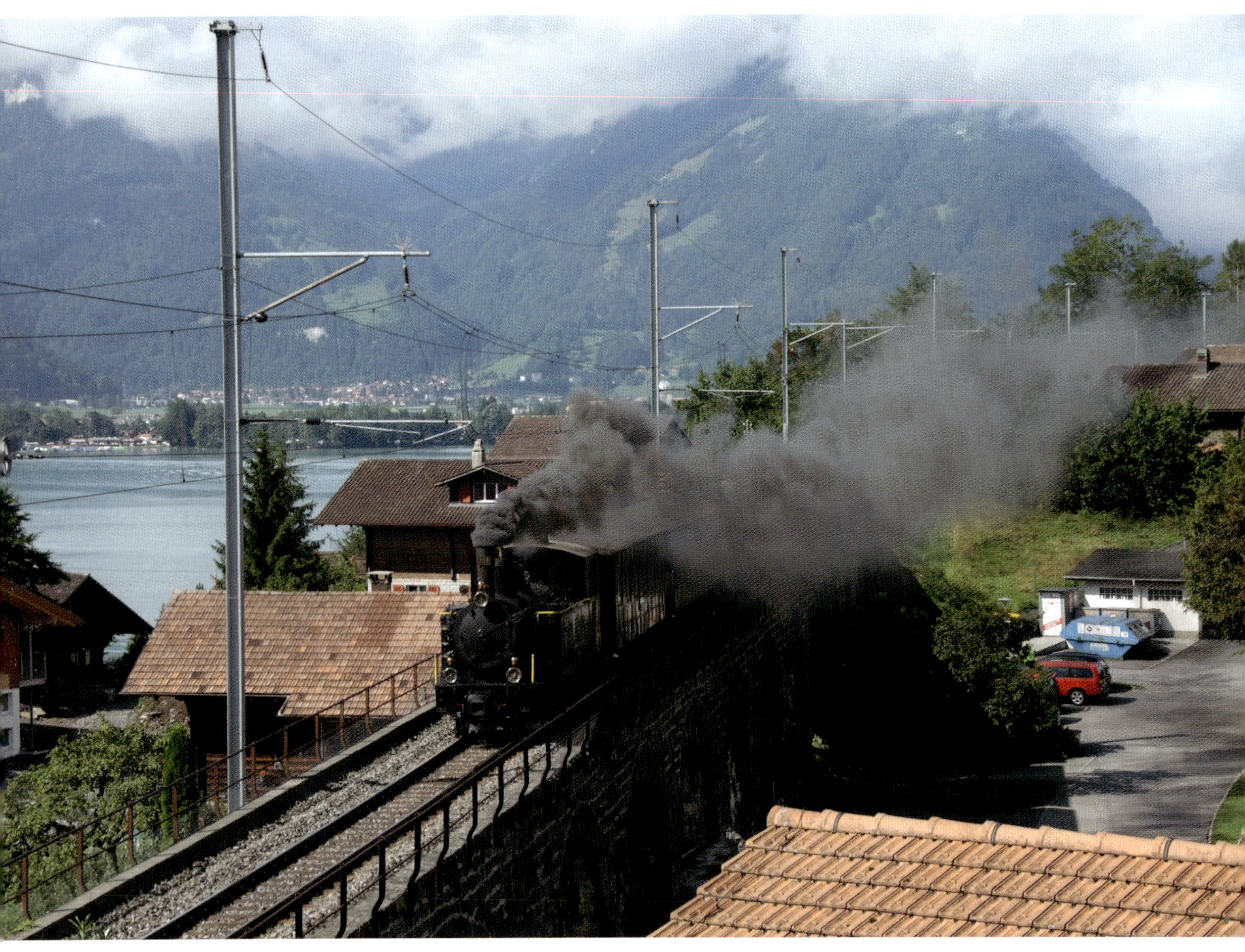

Above: The Brünigbahn's 2-6-0T No 208 (SLM 2403/1913) runs alongside Lake Brienz at Ringgenberg on 18 July 2010. This busy metre gauge mainline between Interlaken and Luzern opened from 1888 and was electrified in 1941 and 1942. Thanks to much voluntary effort some of its old steam locos and carriages still occasionally operate.

Opposite: After a reversal at Meiringen, there's a Riggenbach-rack section up to the summit at Brünig-Hasliberg followed by three more as the line drops down to Giswil. 0-6-0RT No 1067 (SLM 2083/1910) had just engaged the rack at the start of the climb from Meiringen.

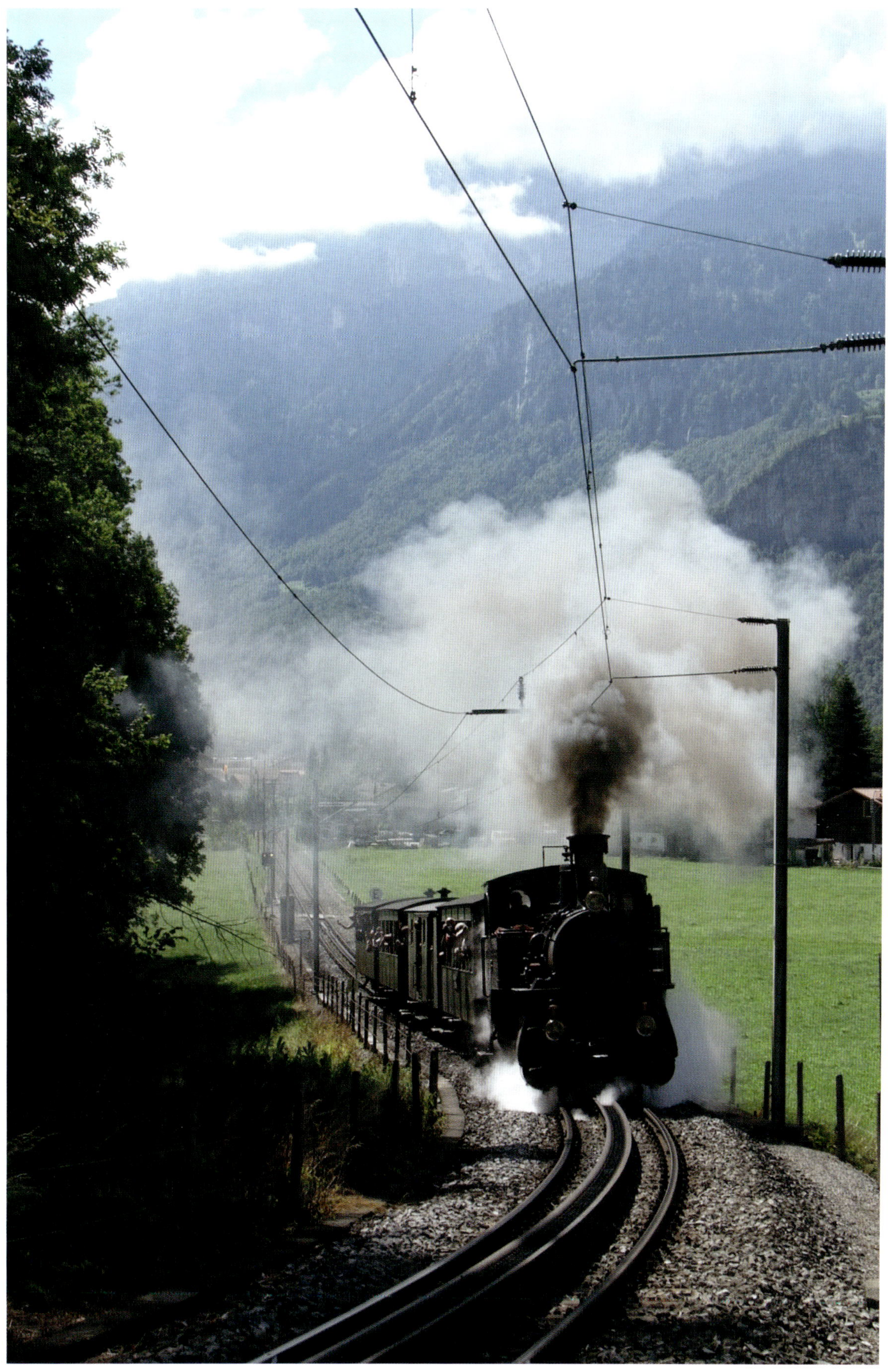

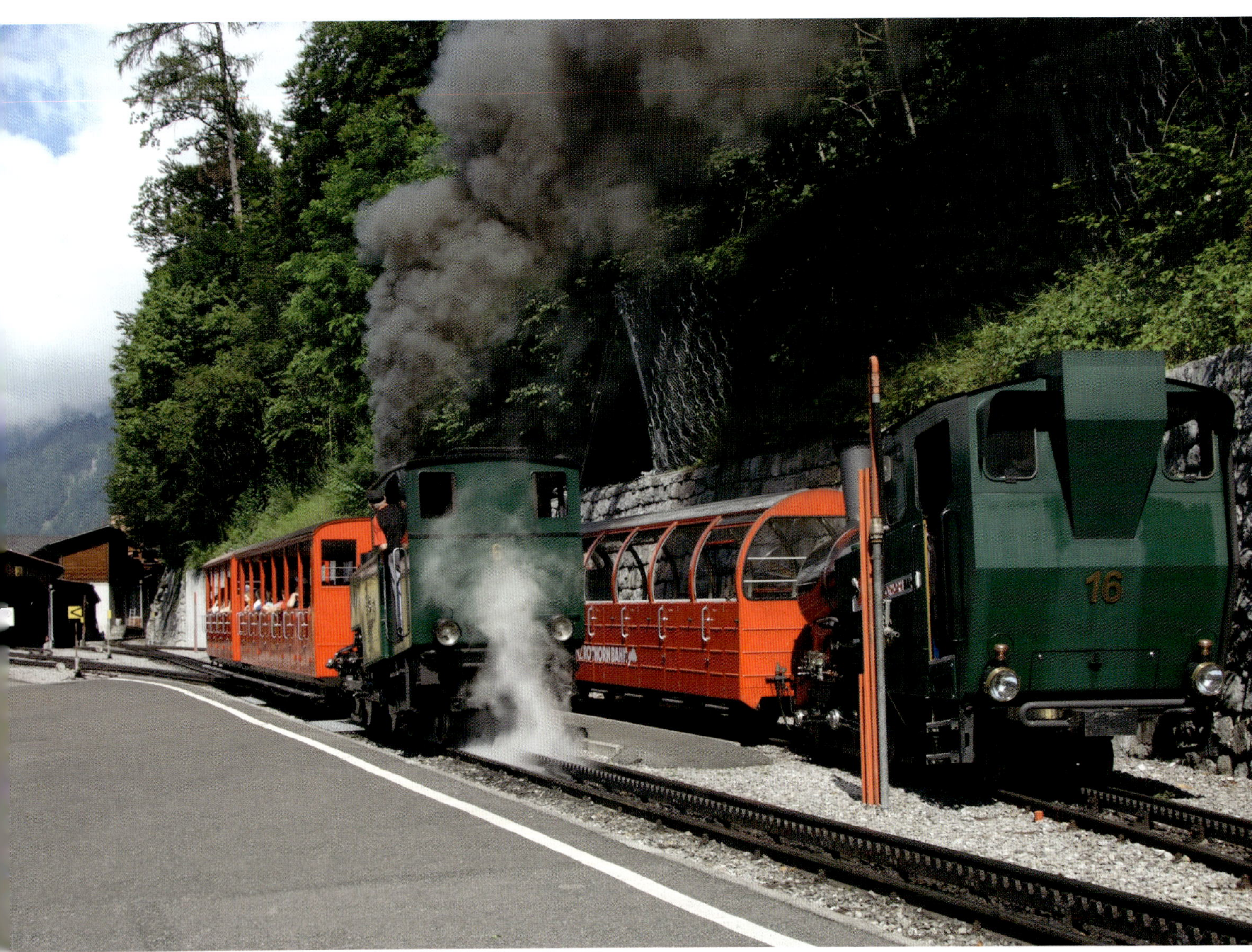

Above: At Brienz, the line connects with the 800mm gauge Brienz Rothorn Bahn. 0-4-2RT No 6 (SLM 3567/1933), the first of two locos which incorporated gears in place of the rocking beams used in the old Abt-Brown designs, sets off on 18 July 2010 as 0-4-2RT No 16 (SLM 5457/1992), one of four modern hi-tech machines developed from them, waits with its train. This Abt-rack railway opened on 17 June 1892 but attracted fewer passengers than expected and soon ran into financial difficulty. Things got even worse with the opening in 1893 of the Schynige Platte Bahn on the other side of Lake Brienz which enjoys superb views over the high Alps and the Jungfraubahn, which reached their peaks, in 1898. It closed during the First World War and didn't reopen until 13 June 1931. It couldn't afford to electrify and this has proved a great blessing as it's now one of Switzerland's most popular mountain lines, such is the appeal of steam in a country of electric railways.

Opposite: After a bright sunny morning on the Schynige Platte Bahn the weather was closing in and Abt-Brown type 1 0-4-2RT No 5 (SLM 1881/1894) took a closed coach for her afternoon run on 17 July 2010. My wife and I watched this spectacle from the balcony of the Hotel Alpenrose at Wilderswil as the sun made a final brief appearance.

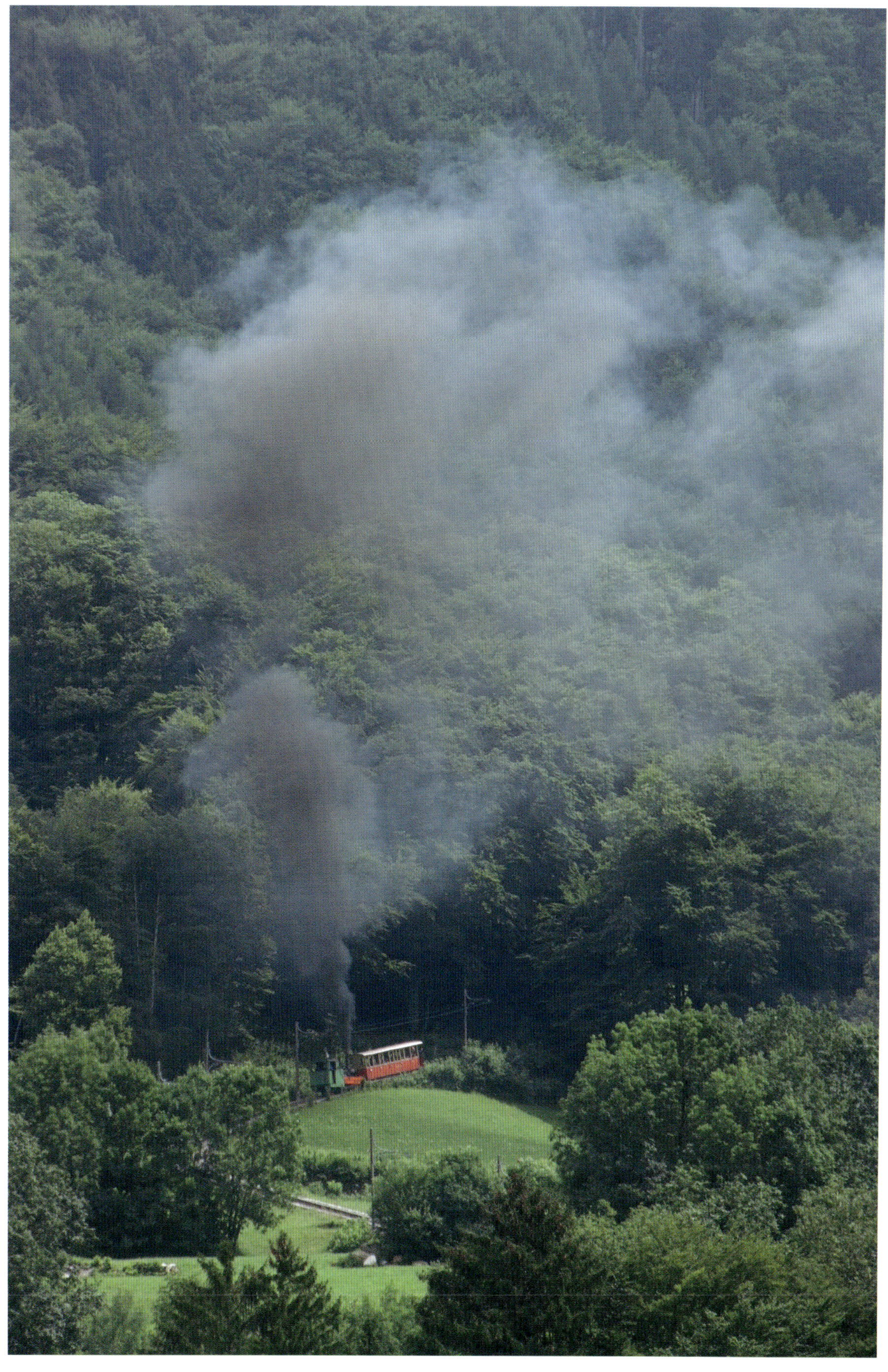

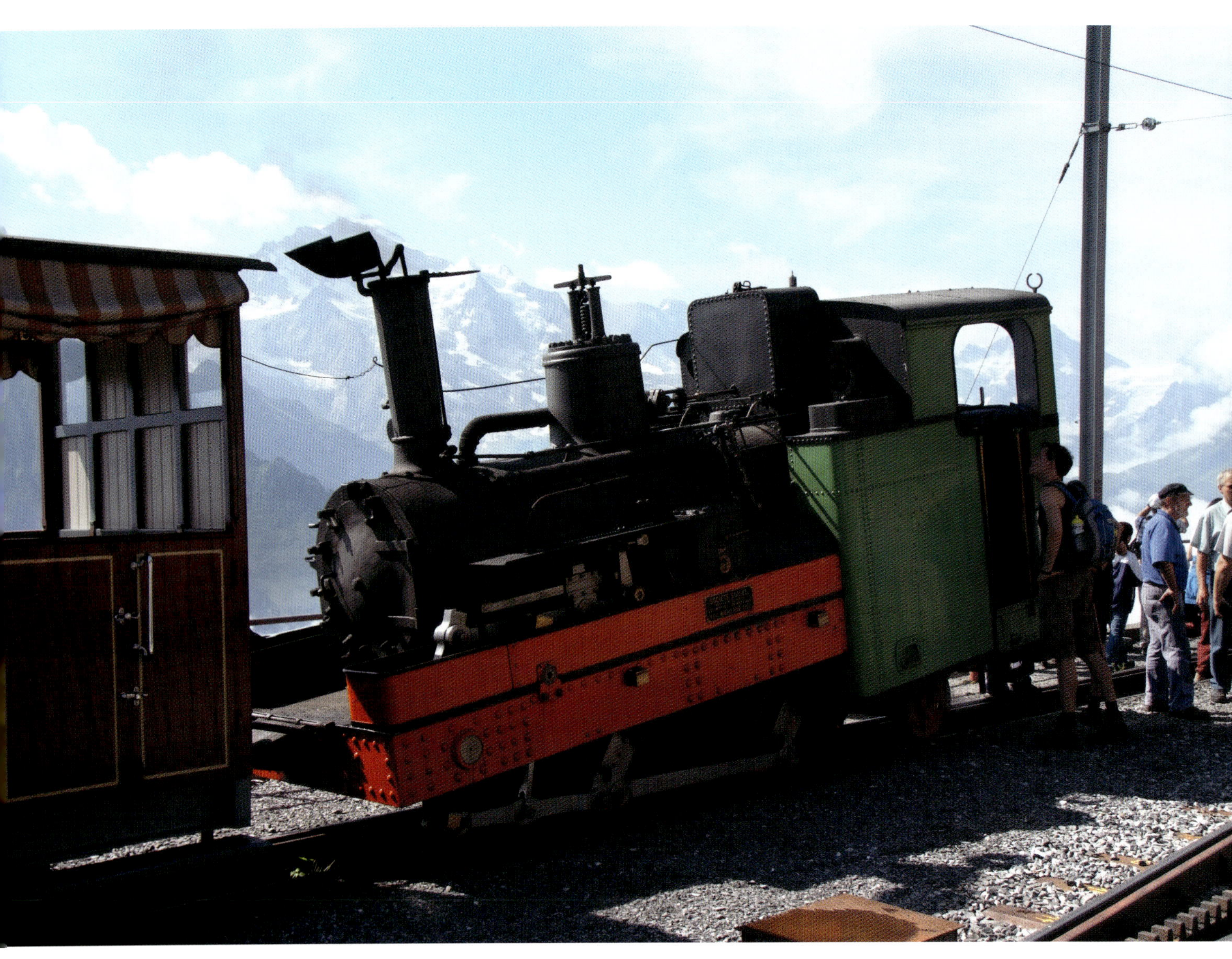

Earlier in the day No 5 takes a rest at the summit with the high Alps as a backdrop, attached to an open coach dating from the railway's earliest years. The 800mm gauge Riggenbach-rack line was electrified as long ago as 1914 but this old loco is still in use, working occasional steam specials and also permanent way trains at the beginning and end of the season when parts of the overhead catenary are put up and taken down.

AUSTRIA

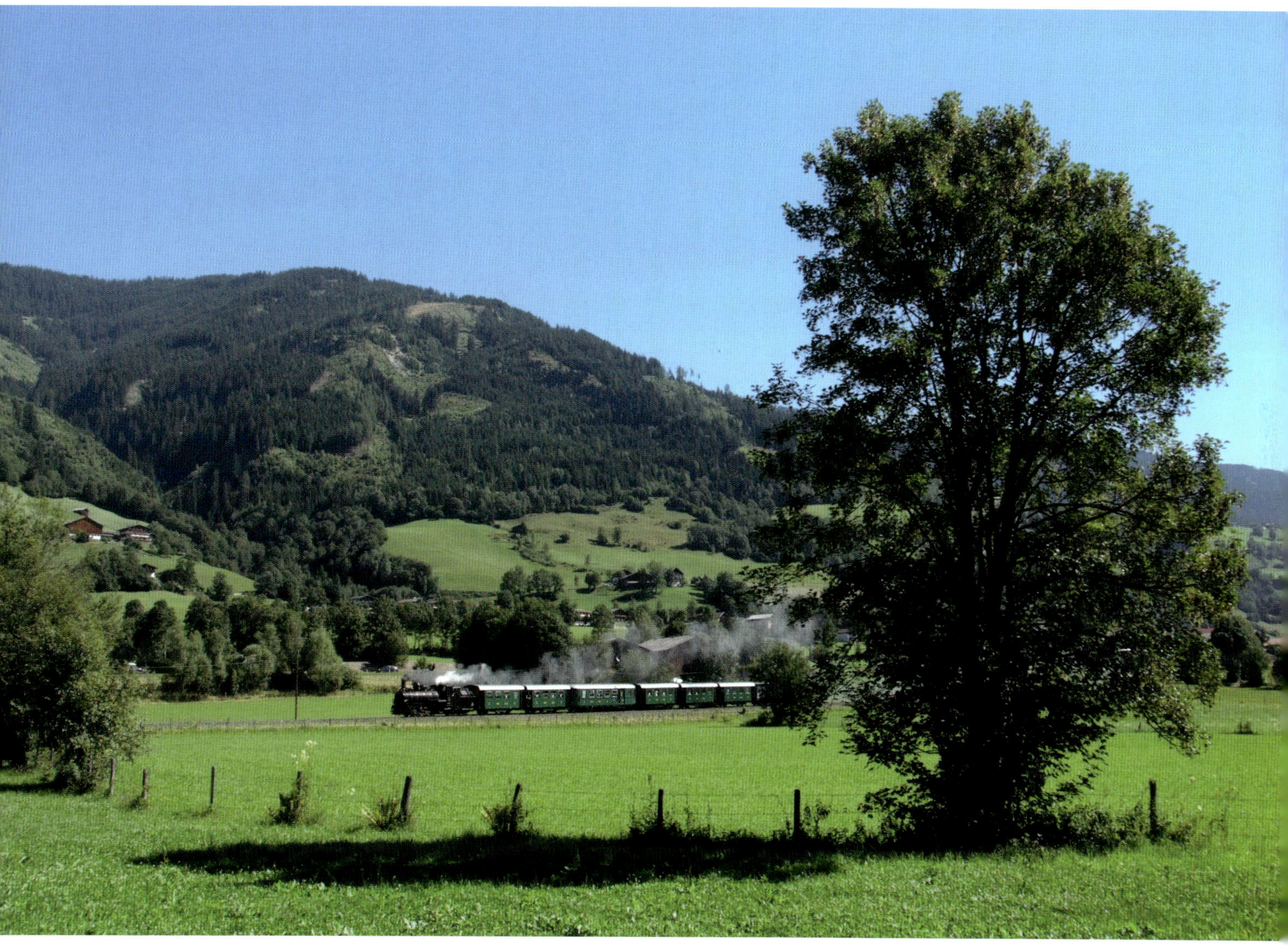

The 760mm gauge Pinzgaubahn between Zell am See and Krimml opened in 1898, became a part of the state railway in 1906 and was taken over by the Salzburgerland regional government in 2008. There's now a busy passenger service and under the guidance of Gunther Mackinger, its enthusiastic manager, summer steam trains have been reintroduced. This Engerth 0-8+4, formerly No 399.03 (KL 5433/1906) of the Österreichische Bundesbahnen, as the Austrian state railway is now called, runs along the valley near Mittersill on 1 August 2013. She's one of a class which saw occasional service on the line before diesels took over.

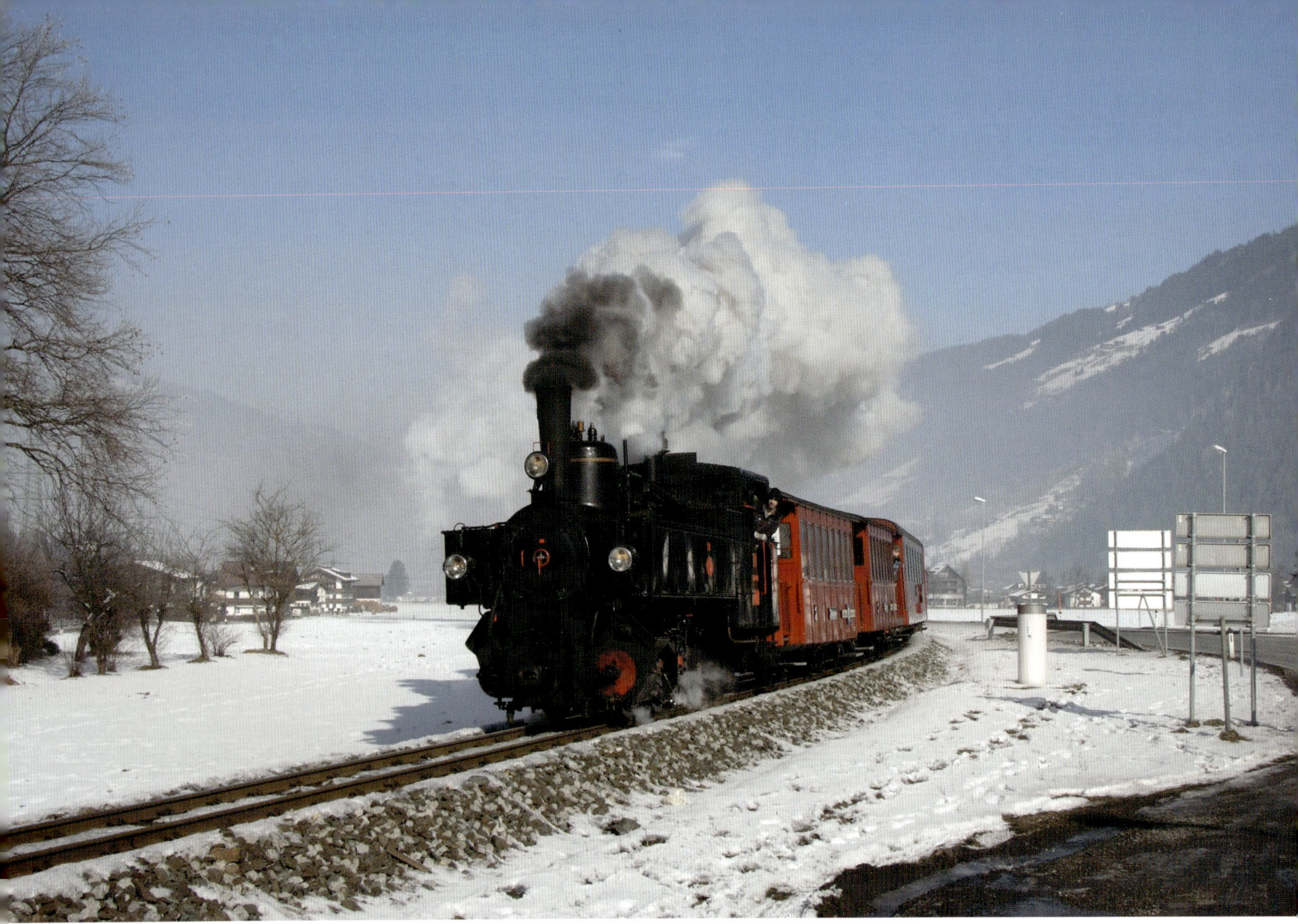

Above: It's only a short journey over the Gerlos Pass from Krimml to the Zillertal, whose 760mm gauge railway has always run steam trains, nowadays fitting them in between its frequent everyday services. It has examples of the three main types of Austrian 0-6-2Ts, Nos 1 and 2, the original U class locos, No 3, an enlarged Uv 2-cylinder compound version and No 5, one of the much bigger Uh superheated machines. No 3 *Tirol* (KL 4790/1902) approaches Mayrhofen at the end of her journey from Jenbach on 3 February 2011.

Opposite above: The Zillertalbahn's well equipped workshops at Jenbach handle steam repair work for many railways. On 2 October 2012 the Steirmarkische Landesbahnen's 0-10-0T No 101 (KL 1419/1926) is receiving a heavy overhaul. She normally lives at Weiz in Styria. Note the mechanism for the Klien-Lindner articulation system on the nearest wheelset, something normally hidden away between the loco's frames.

Opposite below: Jenbach is also the start point of the metre gauge Achenseebahn. Here, 0-4-0RT No 3 (Floridsdorf 703/1889) waits outside Jenbach shed on 31 July 2013. The line dates from 1889 and is Austria's oldest surviving rack railway. It climbs steeply up the mountainside on the Riggenbach rack and continues as an adhesion railway to the Achensee, Austria's largest lake.

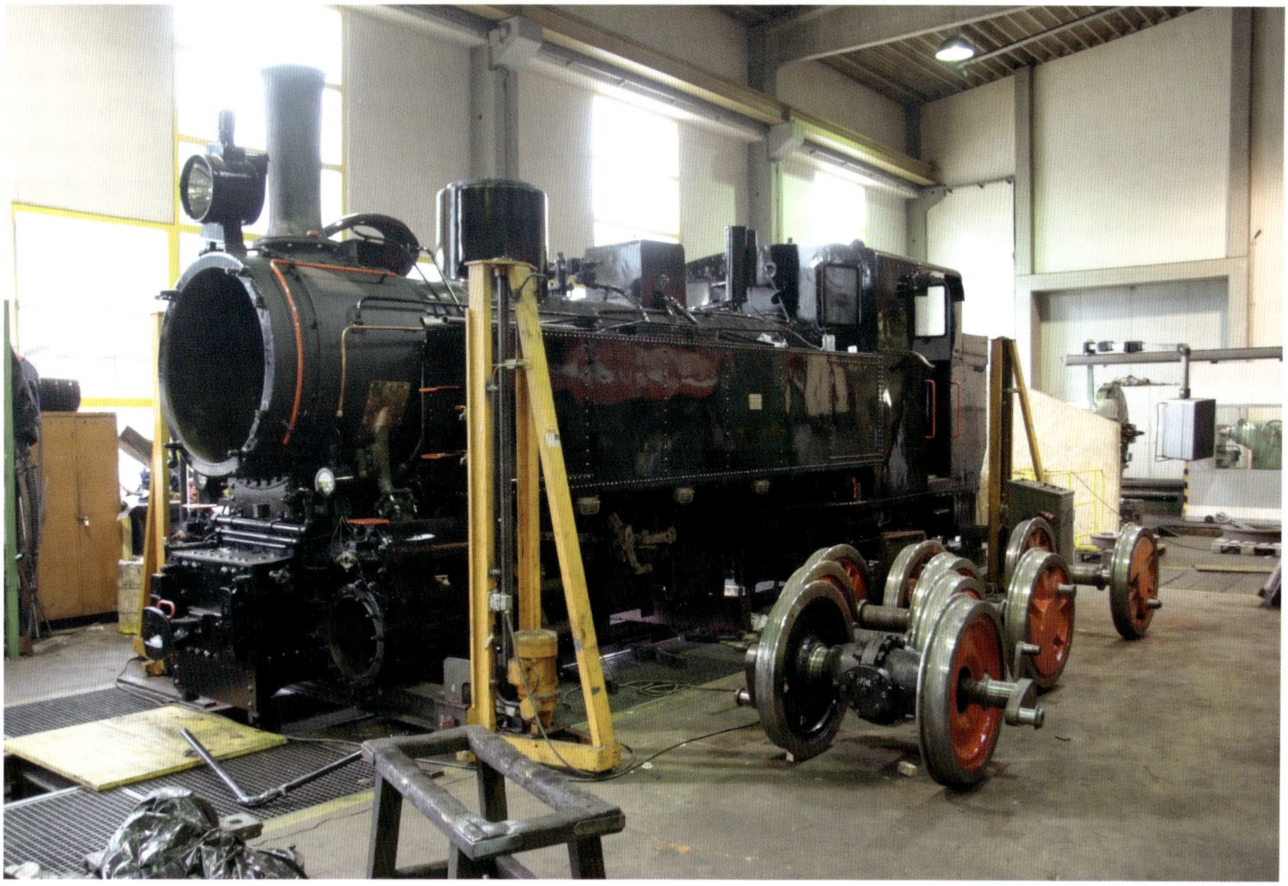

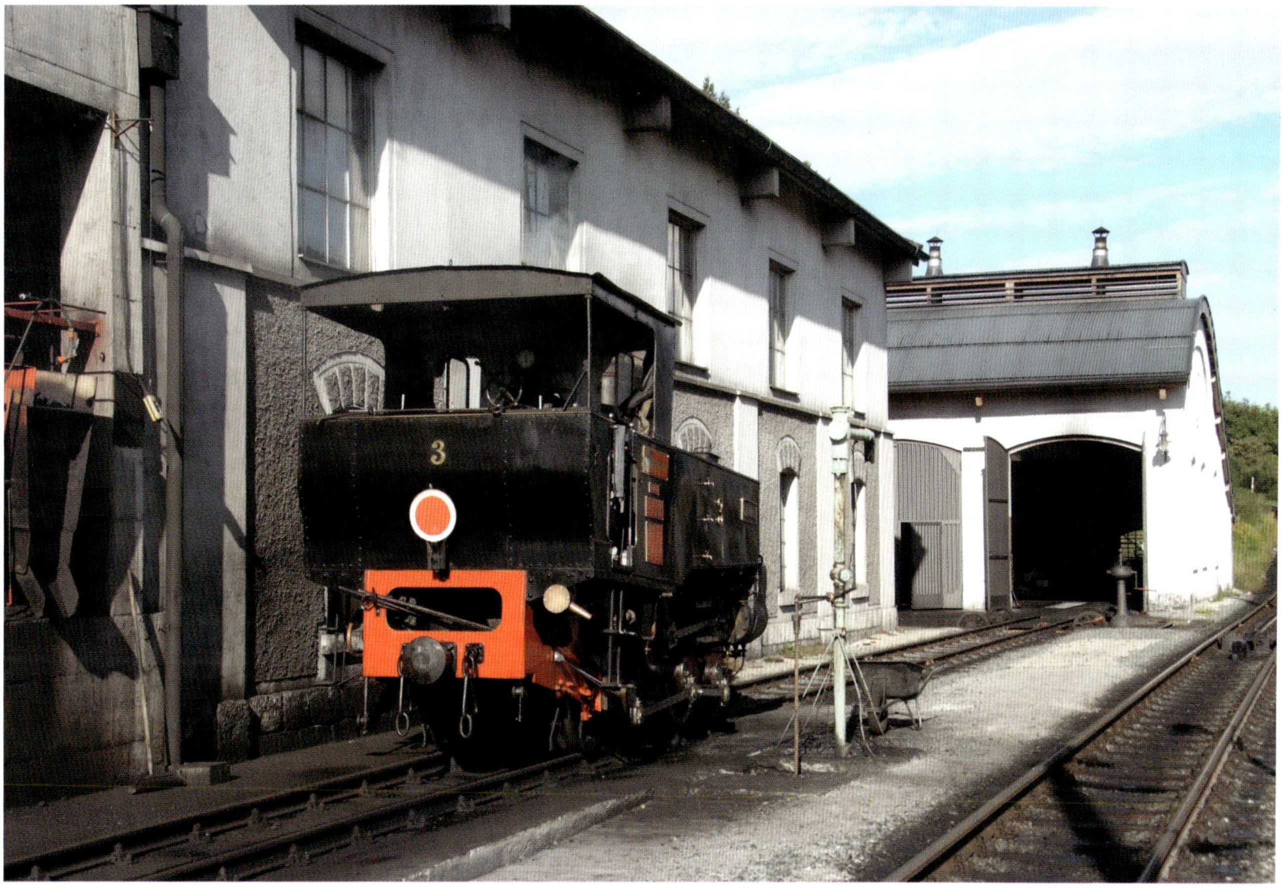

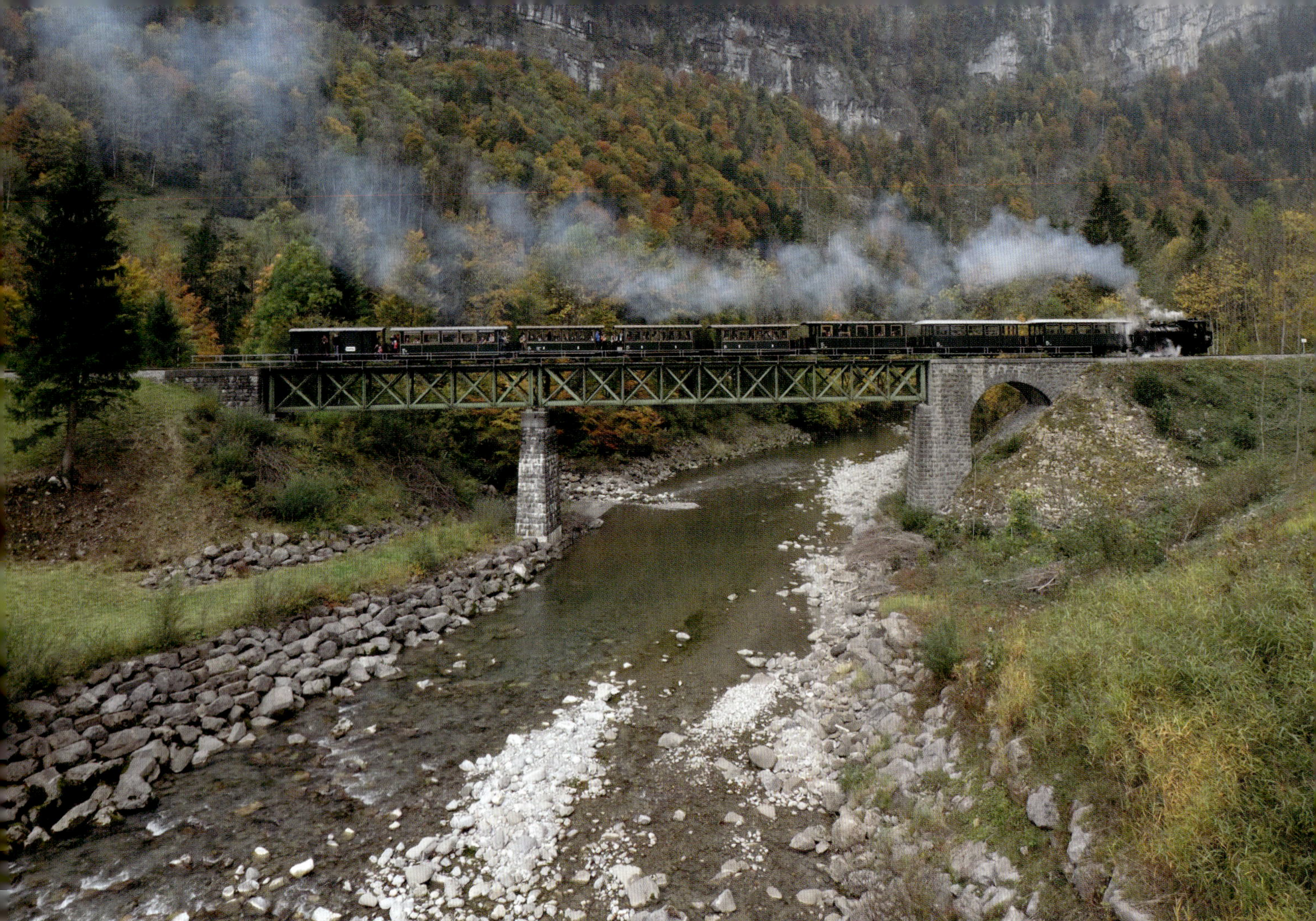

Above: The 760mm gauge Bregenzerwaldbahn ran for 35kms between the shore of Lake Constance at Bregenz and Bezau, up in the hills to the east. It opened in 1902 and was always state-run until it closed eighty years later. A short section at Bezau was reopened by enthusiasts in 1987 and on 10 October 2015, ÖBB Uh class 0-6-2T No 498.08 (Floridsdorf 3038/1931), the very last steam loco built for Austria's 760mm lines, takes her train across the Sporenegg bridge, always a highlight of travel on the old line.

Opposite above: An anniversary special! The Steyrtalbahn was Austria's earliest 760mm gauge railway and 0-6-2T No 2 *Sierning* (KL 1994/1888) hauled the first train between Garsten and Grunburg on 19 August 1889. Exactly 125 years later to the day, she sets off from Steyr Lokalbahnhof. The railway was nationalised in 1931 and closed by ÖBB in stages until 1982. Enthusiasts reopened the Steyr-Grunburg section three years later.

Opposite below: On 2 August 2013, 0-4-2RT No Z14 (SLM 5688/1996) climbs the last few metres to the summit station on the metre gauge Abt-rack Schafbergbahn as No Z13 (SLM 5687/1996) waits to depart. The line was built by the old Salzkammergut Lokalbahn and opened in 1893. It became a part of DR after the Nazi annexation of Austria in 1938 and duly passed to ÖBB. They still own the track but in 2006 operation was handed over to the Salzburgerland government. All the line's old Abt-Brown type 1 0-4-2RT's survive but nowadays four Swiss-built hi-tech locos like the ones at Brienz work most trains. The station is a little short of the mountaintop and this cable-worked incline connects it with the summit hotel for the transport of supplies and guests' luggage.

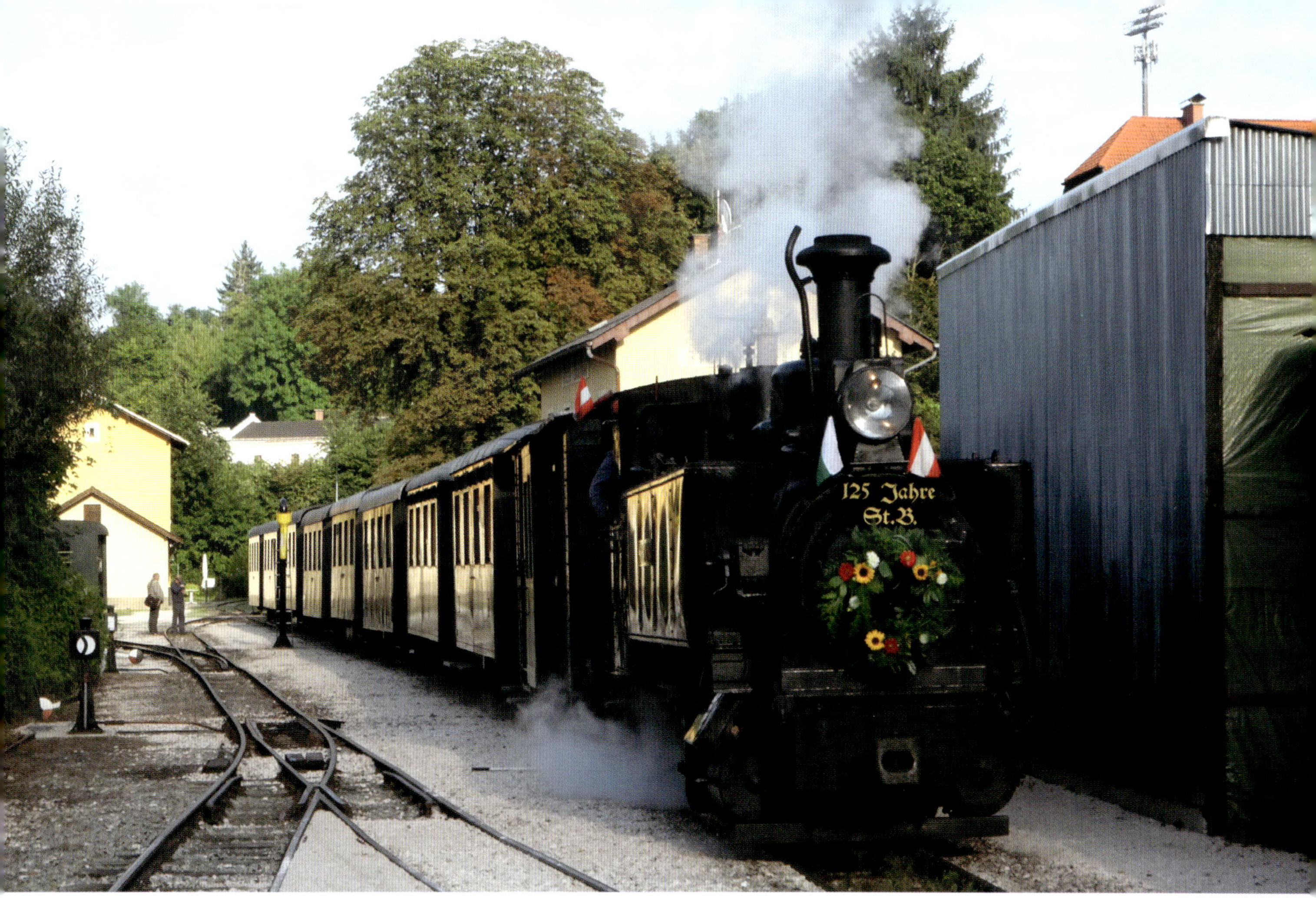

125 Jahre
St.B.

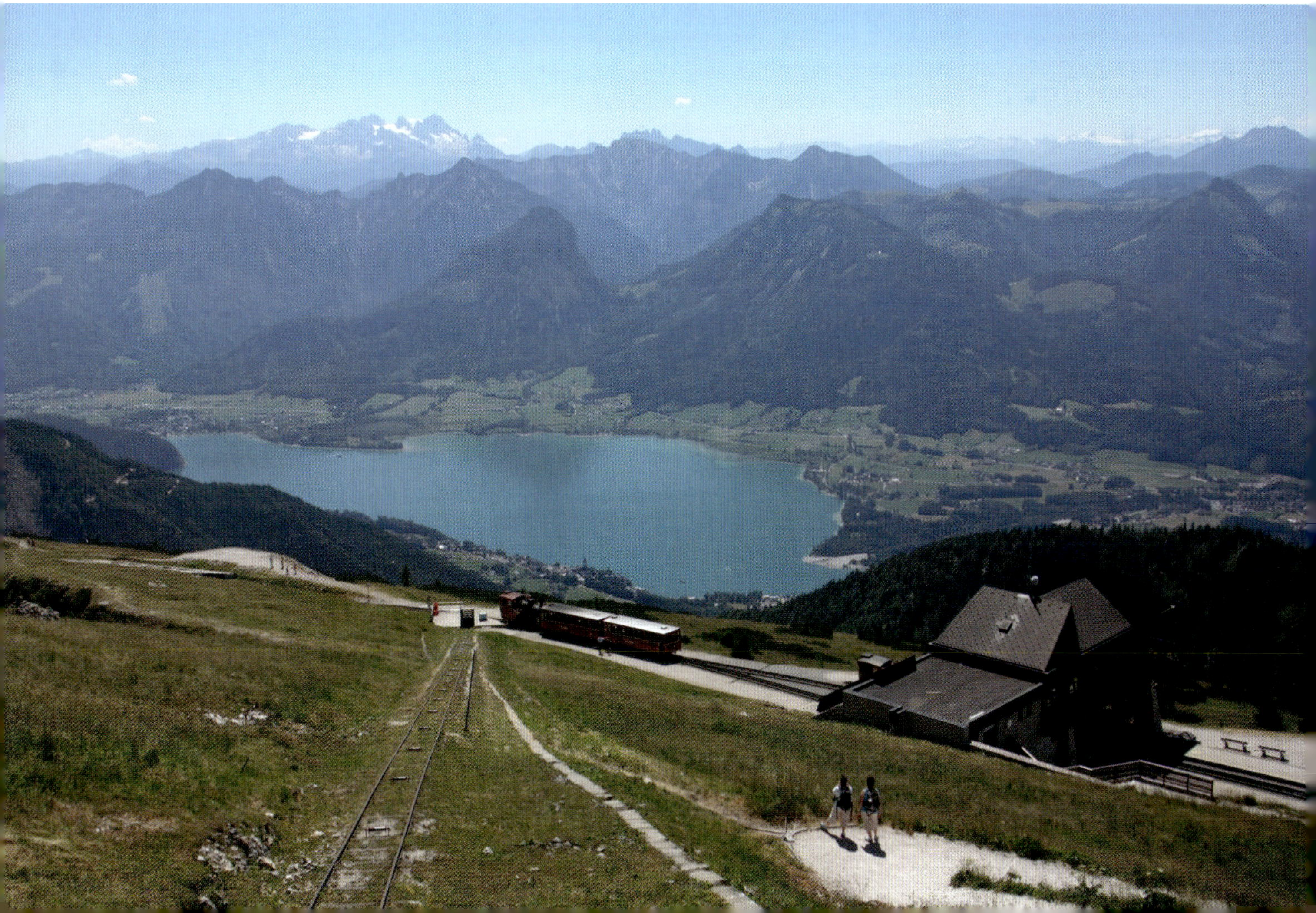

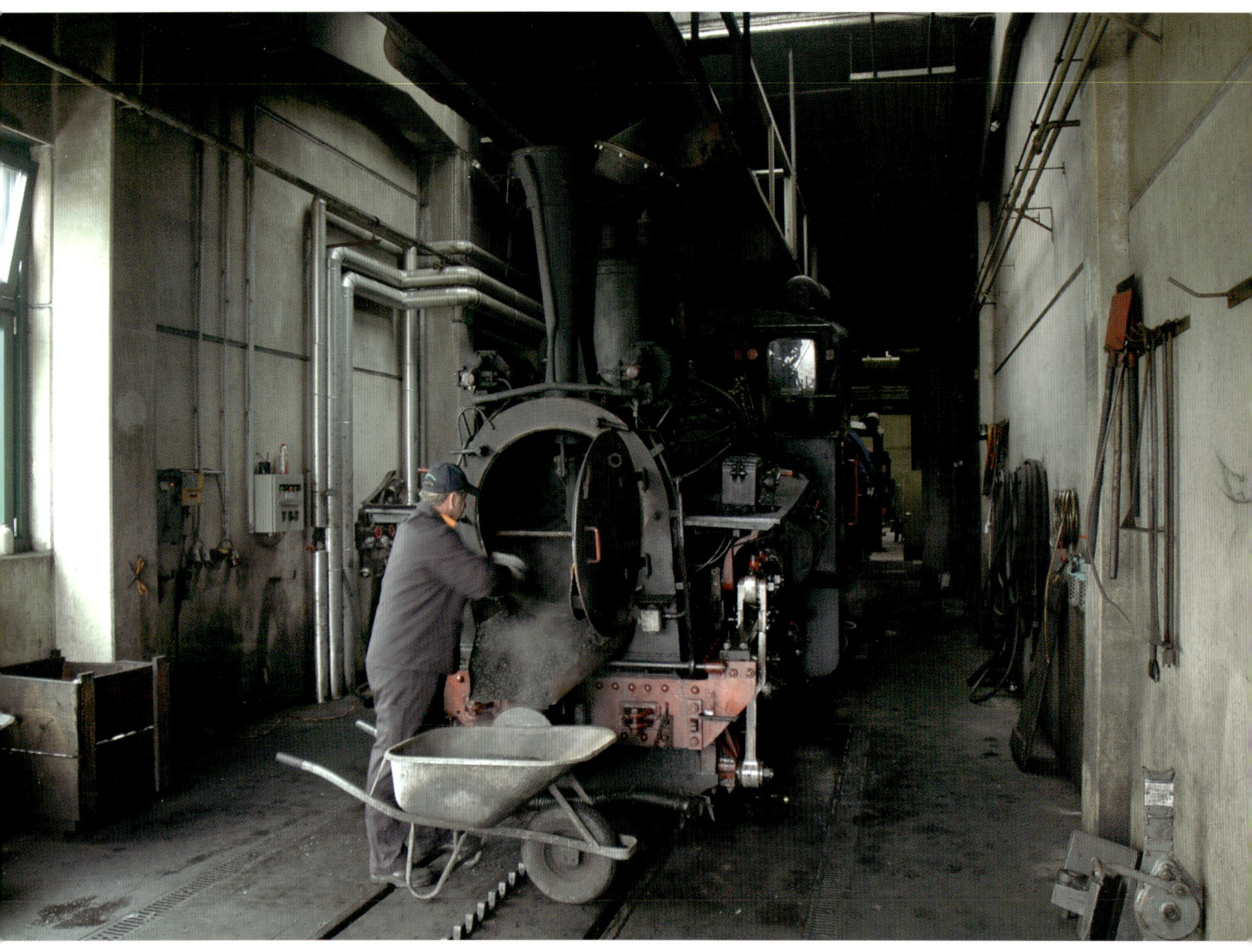

The Schneebergbahn, another metre gauge Abt-rack railway, opened in 1897 and also retains most of its historic locos. Today it's run jointly by the regional authority and ÖBB and only occasionally operates steam trains. There's no disguising the dirty working conditions, inseparable from conventional steam locos, as the driver cleans out 0-4-2RT No 999.03 (KL 3402/1897) at Puchberg shed on 5 August 2006. Behind her are sister locos Nos 999.05 (KL 4215/1900) and 999.02 (KL 3401/1897).

CZECH REPUBLIC

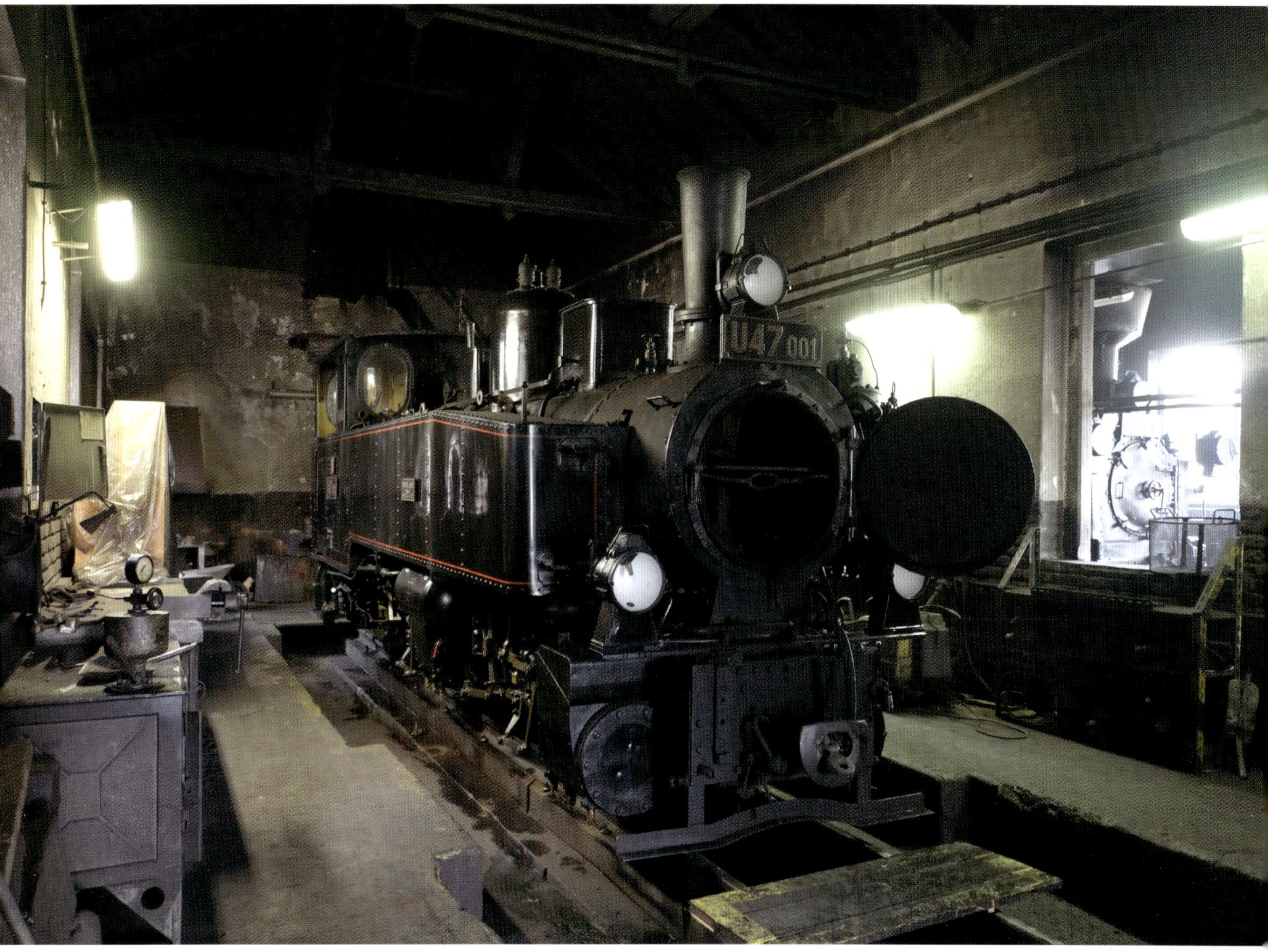

Henschel and Hohenzollern built ten 0-4-4-0 Mallet tanks for Serbia's 760mm gauge lines between 1907 and 1911. Four of them found their way north during the First World War and became the U47 class of ČSD, Czechoslovakia's state railway. They stayed there for the rest of their days. On 18 August 2014, No U47.001 (Henschel 7930/1907) receives attention at Jindřichův Hradec shed on the Jindřichohradecké Místní Dráhy or JHMD, a former ČSD line which still provides everyday services. She was on loan from the Czech Republic's national technical museum and returned to their store at Chomutov in December 2017. No U37.002 (KL 3814/1898), one of eleven Austrian U class 0-6-2T's taken over by ČSD, stands on the right.

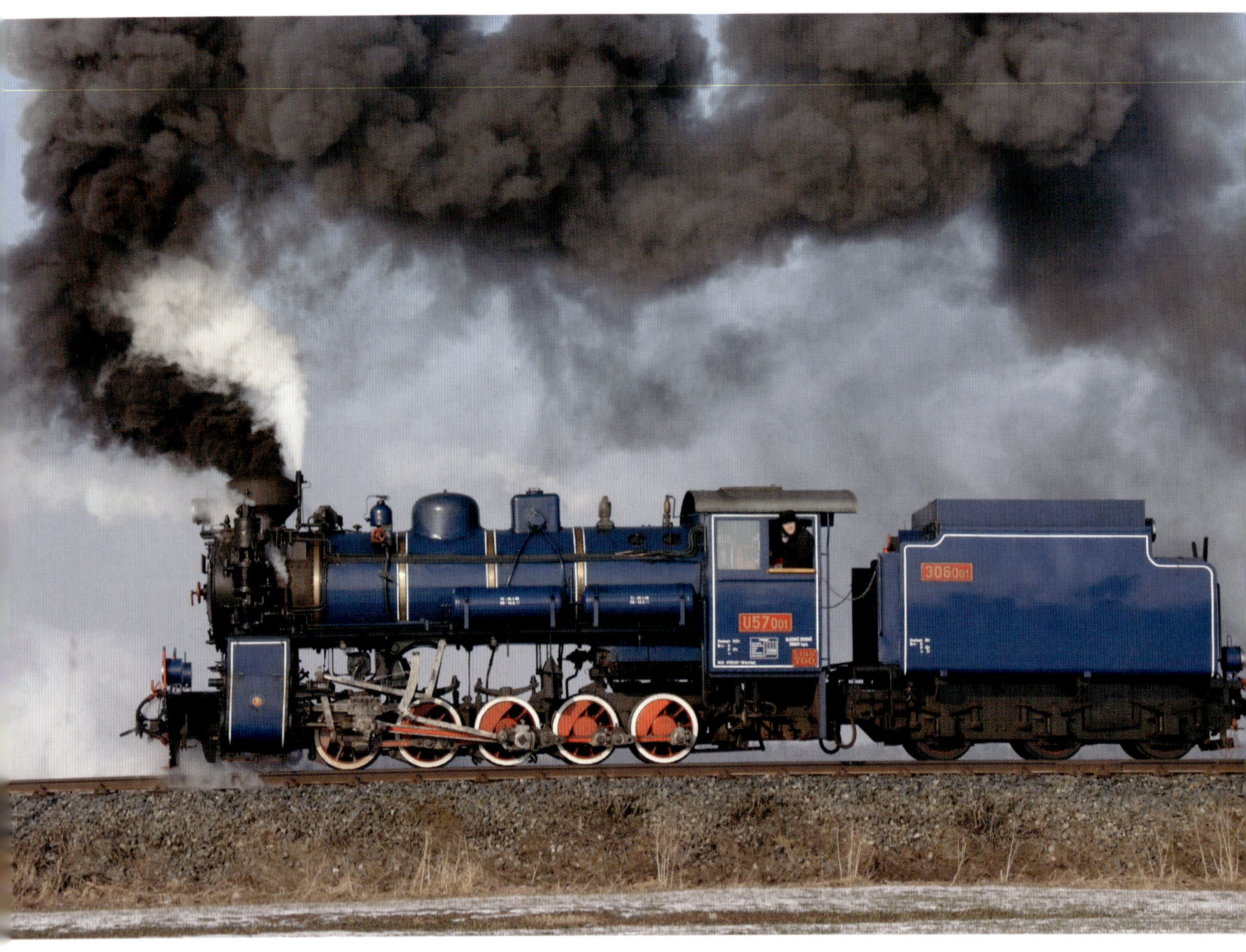

This 760mm gauge 0-10-0 (Skoda 1932/1949) is one of a class of six built for JZ, the Yugoslav state railway, as No 1932 for service on the Steinbeisbahn in western Bosnia. Enthusiasts now operate her on the Třemešná ve Slezsku-Osoblaha branch, the last surviving state-run narrow gauge railway in the Czech Republic. It's easy to see the resemblance these locos bear to the stylish machines which the Czechoslovaks built for their mainlines in the 1940s and early 1950s and if new narrow gauge steam locos had been needed then perhaps this is how they would have looked. They only painted their most important steam locos blue, but what else is No U57.001, as she's known under the Czech numbering system, if she's not one of her country's best machines!

SLOVAKIA

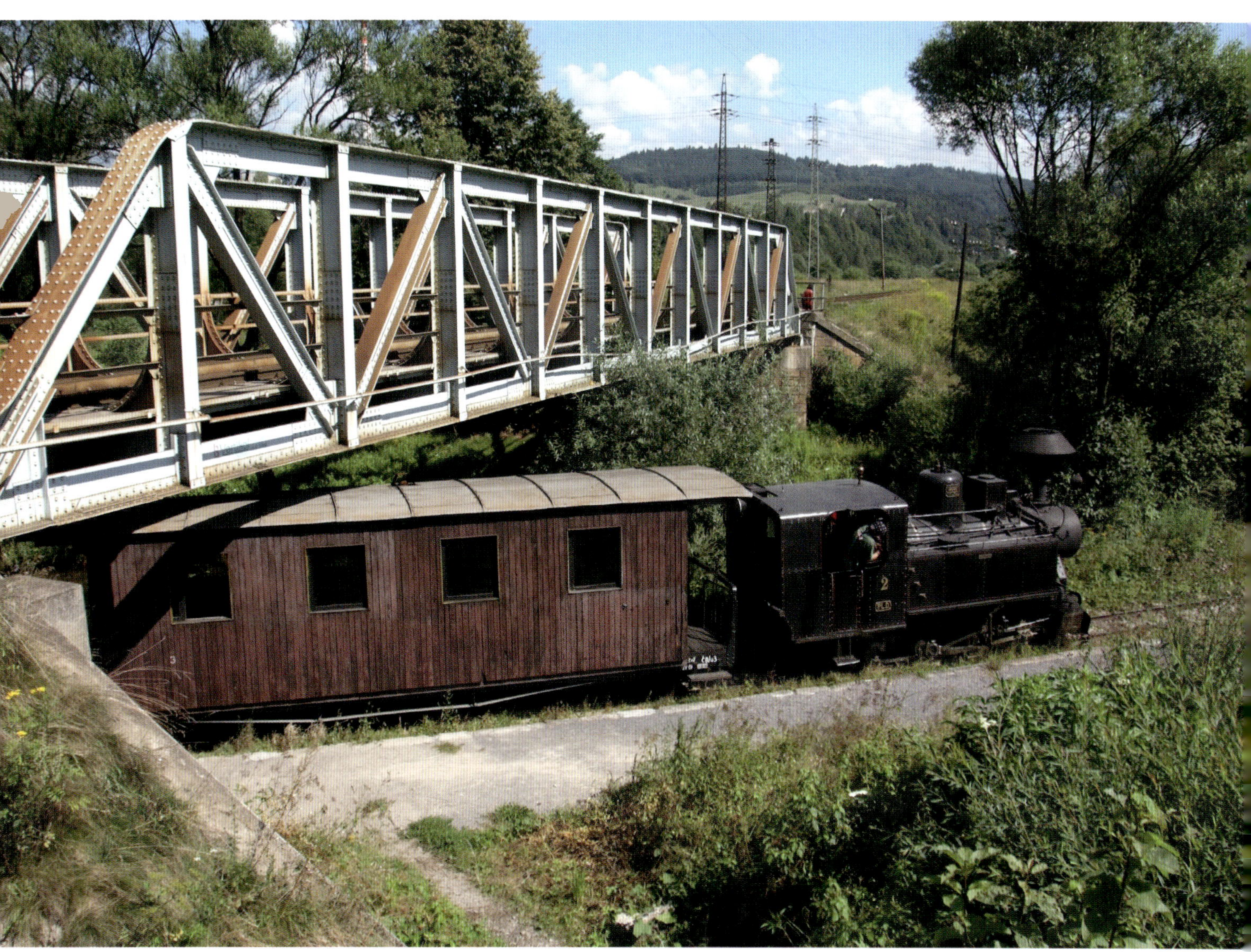

The Považská Lesná Zeleznica was one of Slovakia's major 760mm gauge forestry railways. Its No 2 or U45.903 (Budapest 4280/1916) is a Hungarian 490 class 0-8-0T, 142 of which were built between 1905 and 1950. She now works tourist trains on the nearby Čiernohronská Železnica, another old forestry line. On 12 August 2010 she passes under the mainline at Chvatimech.

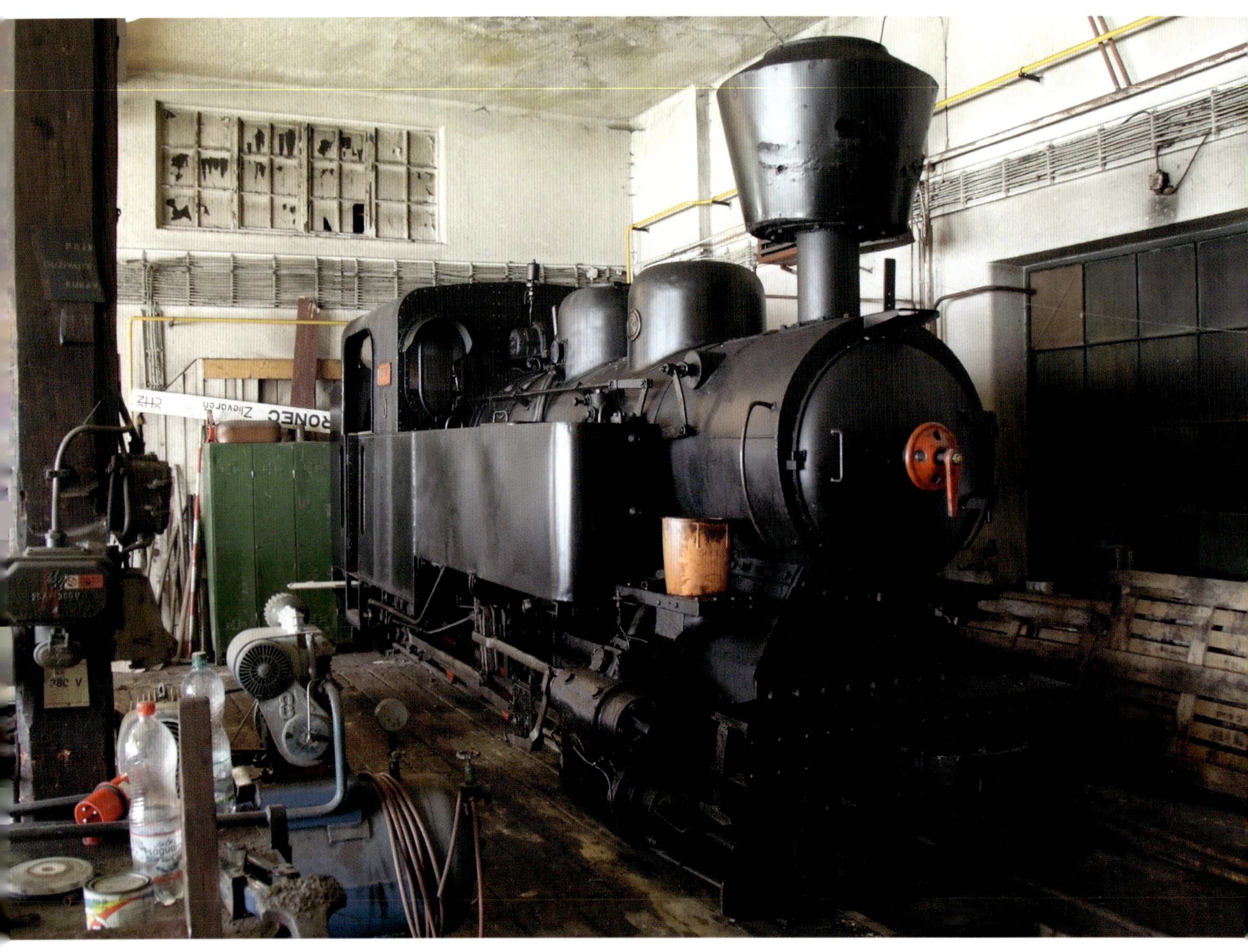

Six smart C 760/90d class 0-6-0Ts were built by ČKD for the Slovakian forestry railways in 1948 and at various times five worked on the ČŽ. Three are still there and in this photo, No 5 or U35.902 (ČKD 2611/1948) awaits overhaul in the workshop at Hronec on 11 August 2010. She returned to service late in 2017. Another ten were built as 750mm gauge locos for the Soviet Union where at least one worked on a forestry railway at Svalyava in the Ukrainian part of the Carpathians and another at Klasson peatery near Moscow. They all disappeared long ago.

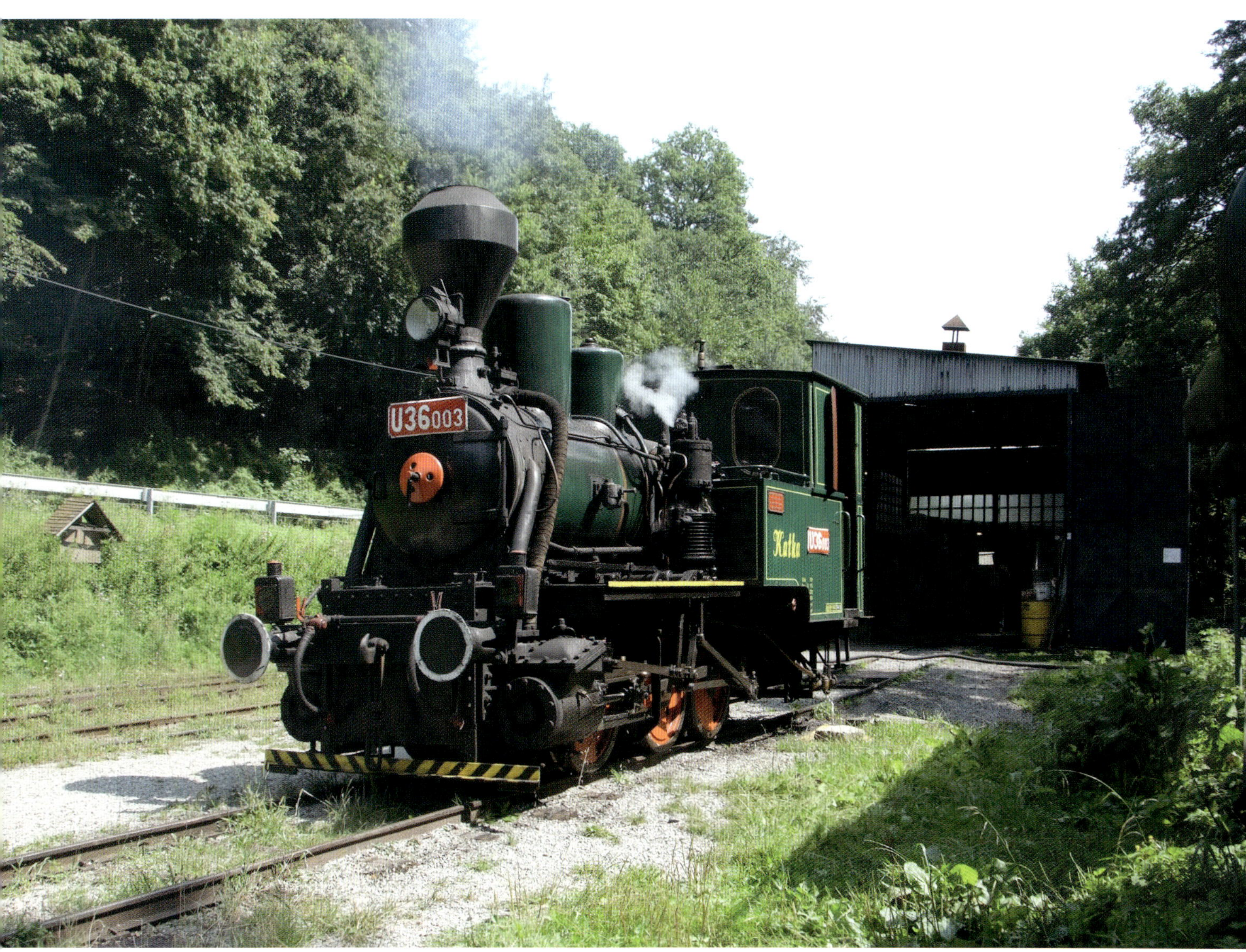

ČSD metre gauge 0-6-0T No U36.003 (Hagans 174/1884) raises steam at the Kosice Children's Railway on 13 August 2010. The line was built in 1955 and 1956 and runs for more than 4kms through the beautiful, steep-sided Cermel valley. Like the children's railways in Russia, its main purpose is educational though now there's also an emphasis on fostering tourism in what is a somewhat neglected part of Slovakia. The loco was one of four similar machines. She worked until 1965, mostly on a railway between Gelnica and Smolnicka Huta, and then spent another nine years as a stationary boiler at Spišská Nová Ves. She began a second life at Kosice in 1991 and soon became known as *Katka*. In the spring the annual 'Waking up Katka' festival, when she comes back to life after her sleep through the winter, is a popular local event.

ROMANIA

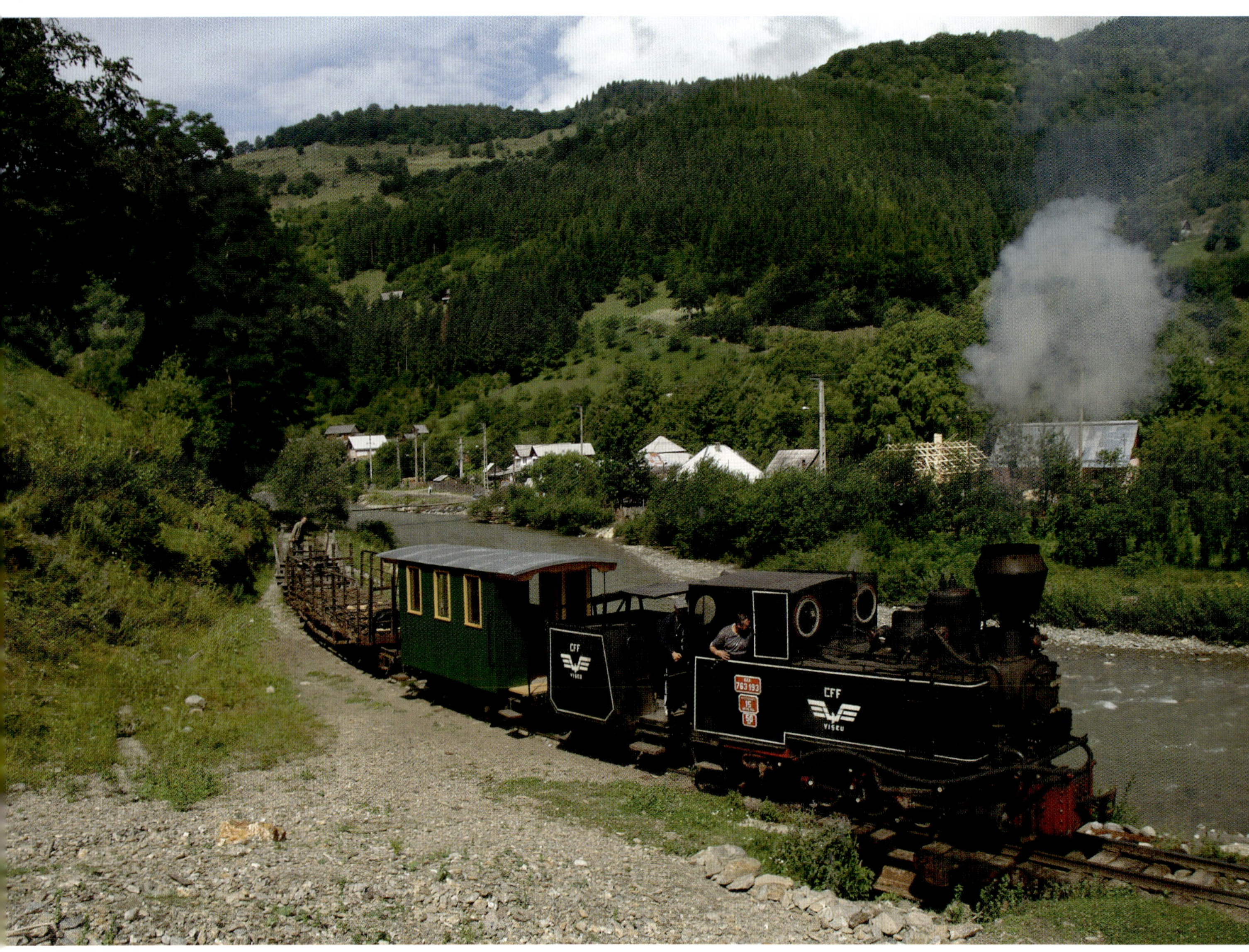

0-6-0T No 763.193 (KL 1919/1921) heads up the Waser valley a short distance out from Viseu de Sus in the Romanian part of the Carpathians on 8 August 2006. Forestry has been an important activity in the region for centuries. Many 760mm gauge logging railways were built but only this one still serves its original purpose. Construction began in 1932 and the first section opened the following year. It has survived mainly because the cost of building even a crude road through this difficult country would be prohibitive. In the early 2000s, Swiss enthusiasts started a support group to promote tourist services and brought in interesting locos displaced elsewhere. No 763.193 worked on forestry railways at Falcau between 1962 and 1974 and Moldovita from 1975 until moving to Viseu in 2004.

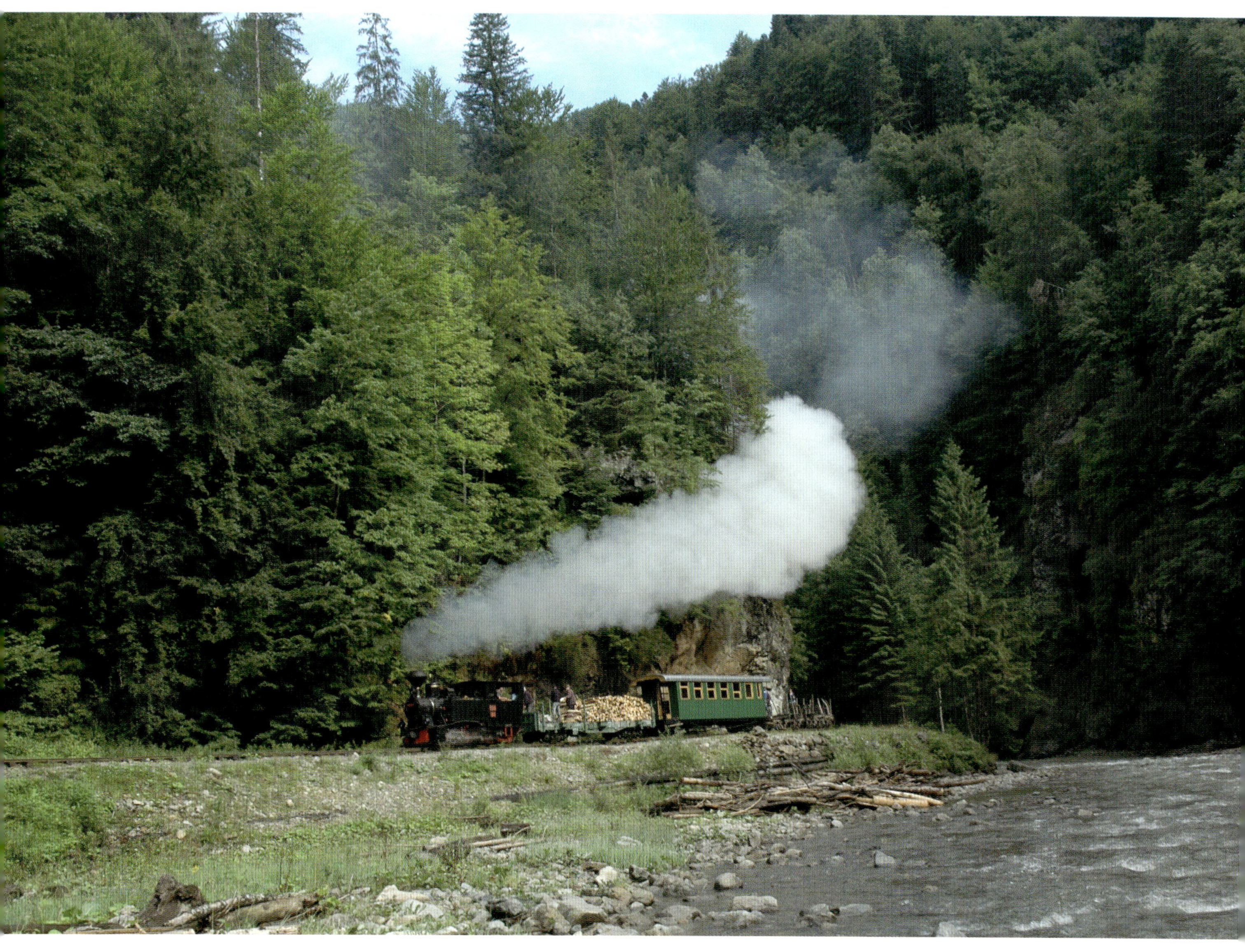

0-8-0T No 764.211 (OK 3980/1910) heads an empty train near Valea Scradei in the early morning of 7 August 2006. She worked on forestry railways at Margina between 1962 and 1970 and Berzasca between 1971 and 1993 and then spent time at a museum in Bucharest before the Swiss group brought her to Viseu. Horses and carts still bring timber to the railway's loading points, sometimes using the riverbeds as thoroughfares when the water isn't in flood. And flood it most certainly can. Traffic was severely disrupted by heavy rain in 2002 but this was nothing compared with the wholesale destruction caused by a catastrophic inundation in July 2008.

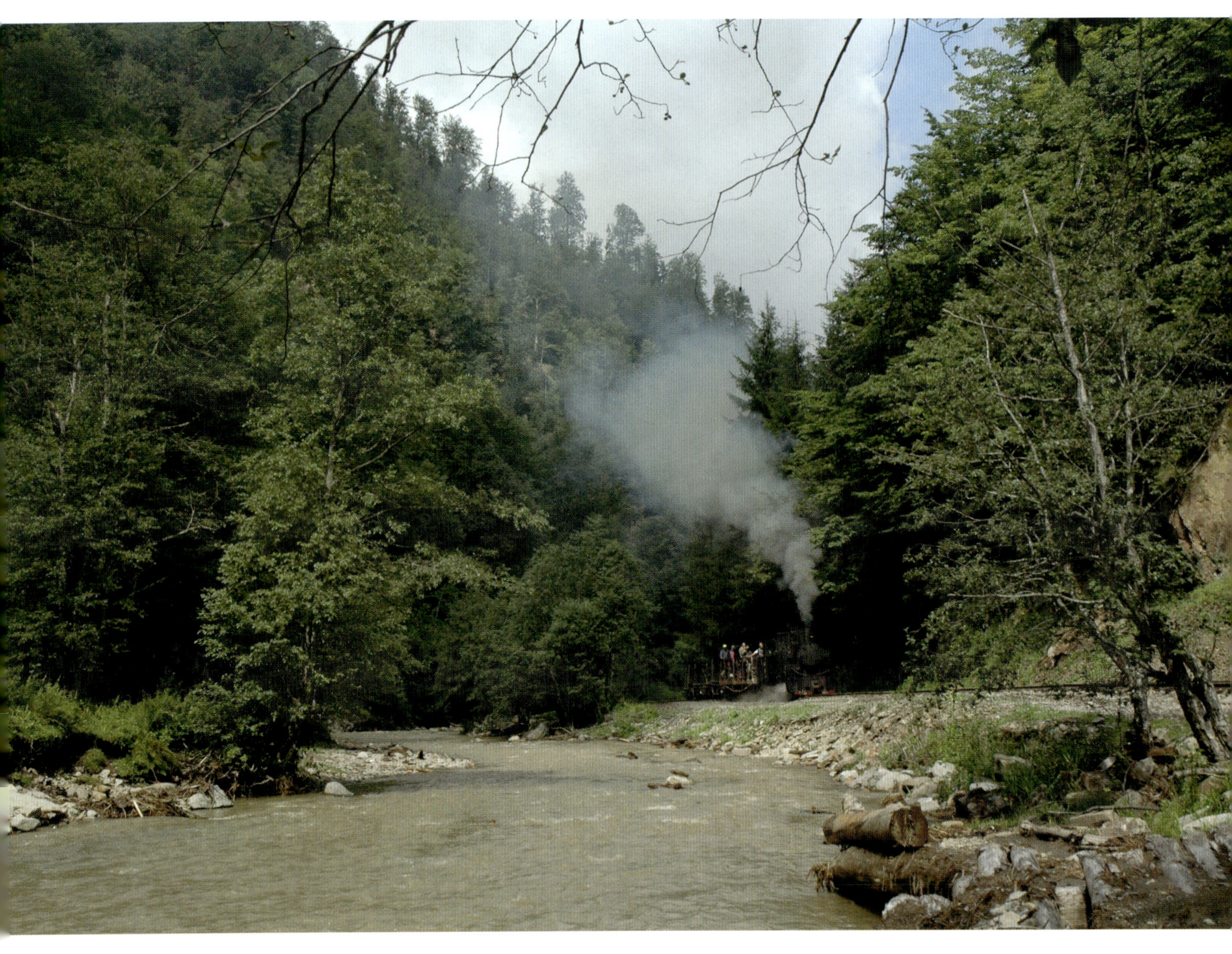

When I visited, some of the forestry trains were still steam-hauled. On 9 August 2006, 0-8-0T No 764.469 (Reșița 2253/1956) heads empty wagons near Ihoat on the Novat valley branch, a line which has yet to be rebuilt after the 2008 floods. She has worked on the railway since 1962 and is one of this Romanian builder's many 0-8-0T's which became almost synonymous with the country's logging railways.

BULGARIA

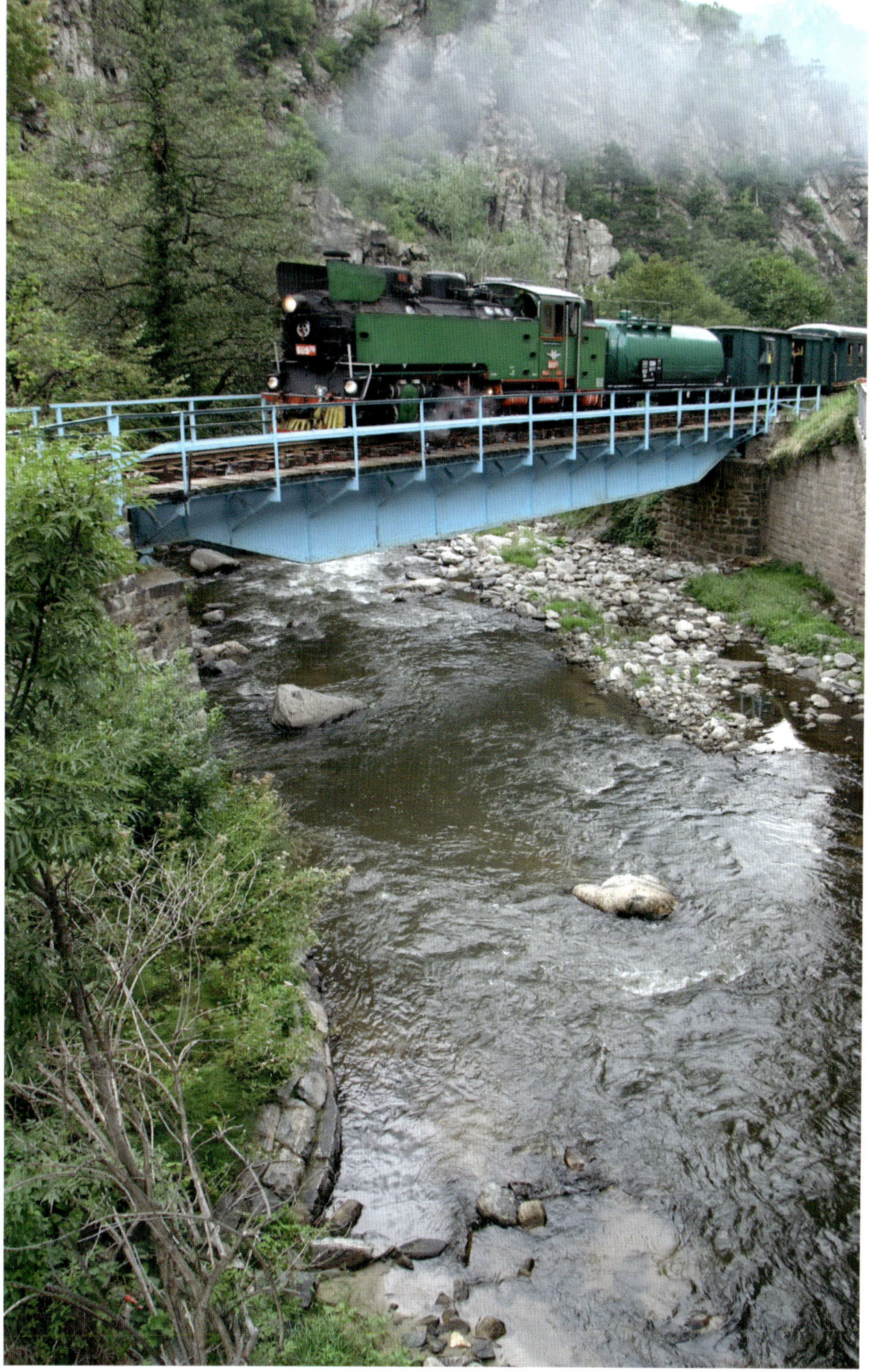

On 5 September 2007 2-10-2T No 609^{76} (Chrzanów 1929/1949) heads an enthusiasts' special towards Velingrad on the 760mm gauge branch through the Rhodope mountains between Septemvri and Dobrinište, 124kms away to the south west. Built in the early 1920s, it is now the only narrow gauge line run by BDŽ, Bulgaria's state railway, and still provides everyday transport for the people of this remote district as well as serving its growing tourist trade. Schwartzkopff built five of these locos, similar to the Saxon 99.73-76 class, in 1940 and Chrzanów ten more in 1949. No 609^{76} was withdrawn in 1977 and was restored to working order in the early 2000's. Examples of the country's earlier 760mm types can also be found at Septemvri shed but haven't worked for many years.

SPAIN

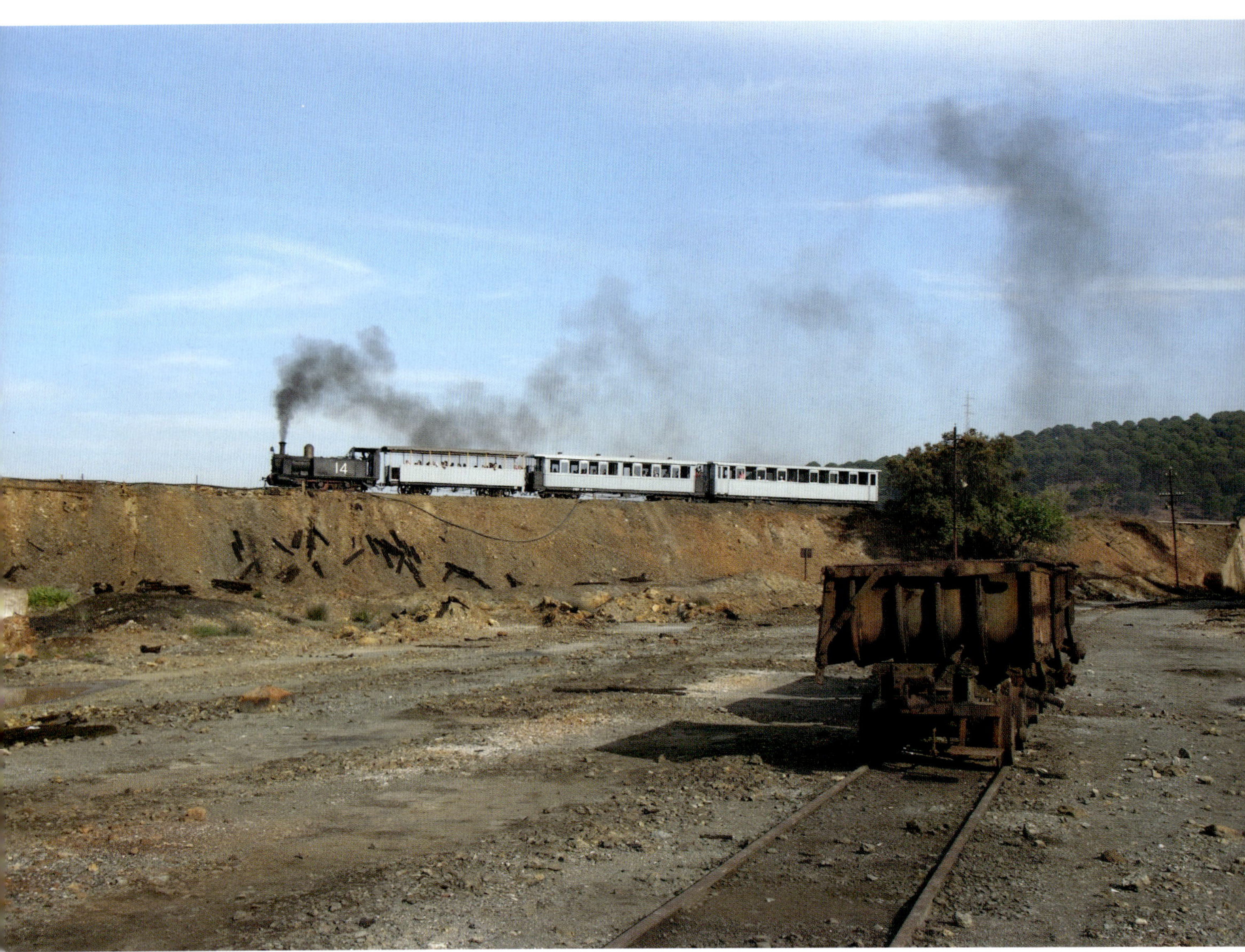

The copper mines at Rio Tinto in Andalucía were worked by the ancient Romans who left some impressive remains. A British company reopened them in the early 1870s and built a 3ft 6ins gauge railway to the port town of Huelva, about 80kms away. The mines were worked on a huge scale and more than 120 locos were in stock when operations were at their peak. Most of this is just a memory but part of the railway now runs for tourists. C class 0-6-0T No 14 (BP 1439/1875), the oldest working loco in Spain, passes one of the many remnants of the old mining lines on 5 April 2009.

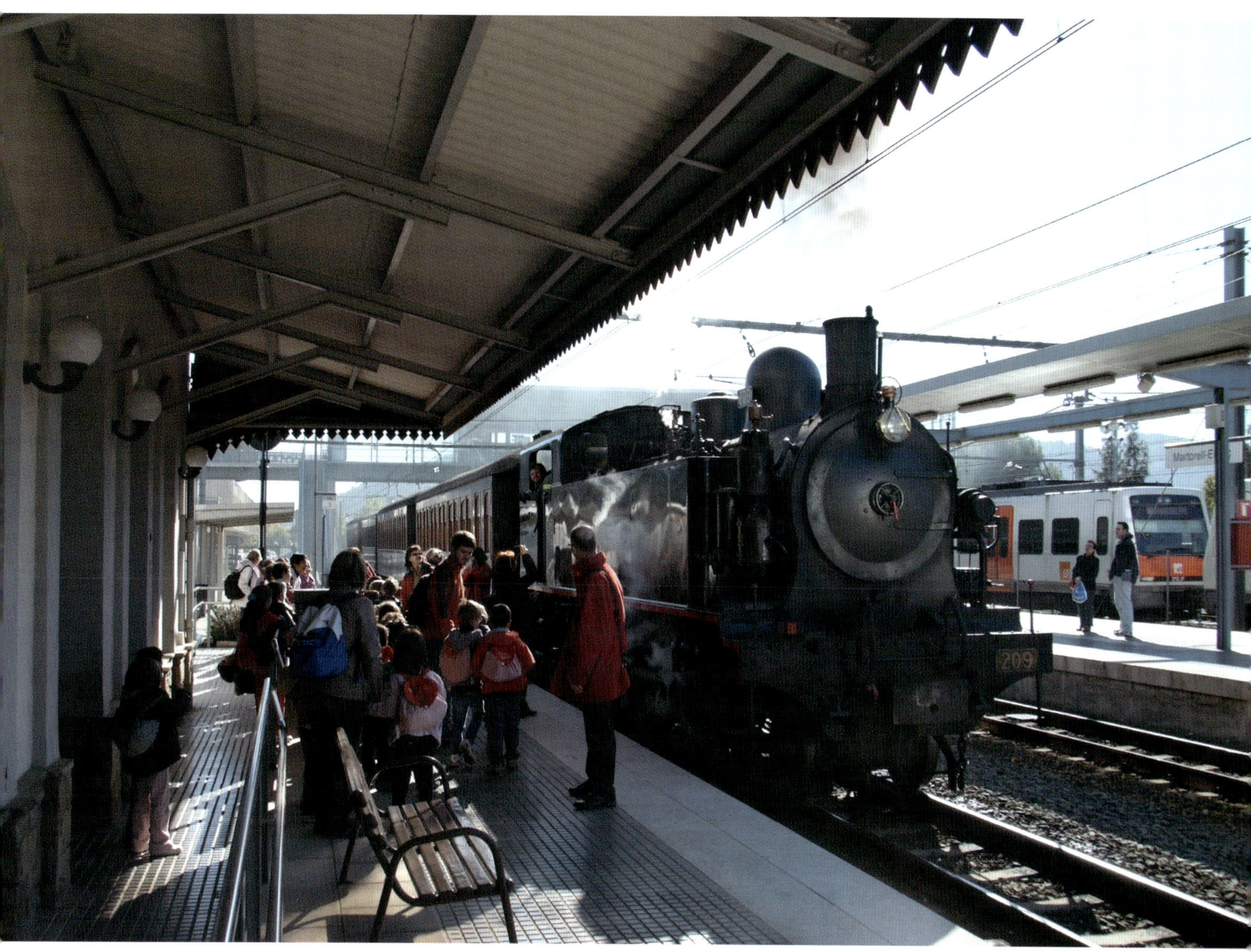

CGFC 2-6-2T No 209 (Energie 513/1948) draws into the heritage platform at the busy Martorell Enllaç station to collect a school group on 11 November 2010. Taking this photo directly into the sun was tricky but a train passing at the next platform momentarily reflected the sunshine onto the loco. The long metre gauge railway from Barcelona up into the foothills of the Pyrenees has a complex history and opened in stages between 1885 and 1926. The FGC, the devolved Catalan administration's railway authority, has a most refreshing approach to conservation and operated this historic train for many years.

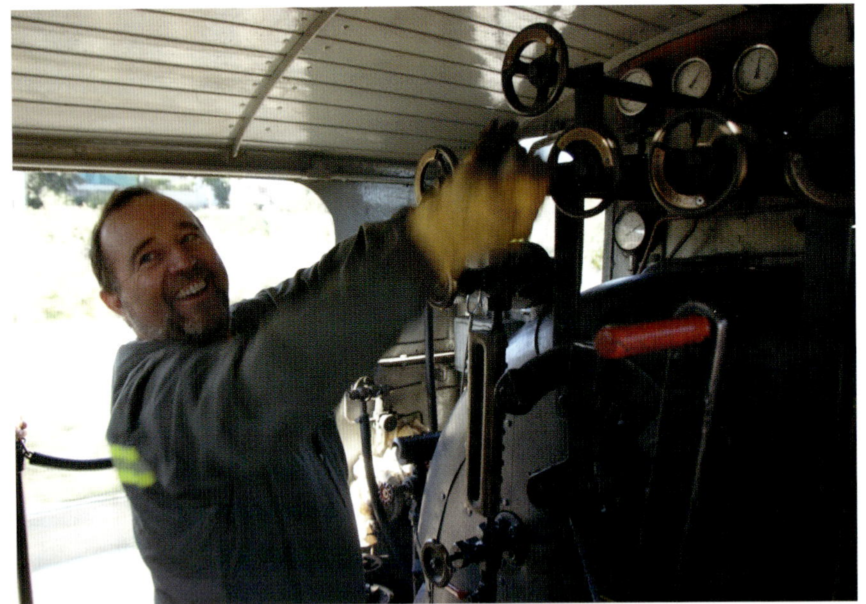

No 209 spent her working life at a colliery at Berga and a dispute about ownership meant she lasted long enough for her heritage value to become appreciated. Her cheerful driver welcomed me onto the footplate for the ride to Monistrol de Montserrat on 11 November 2010. I'd long wanted to visit the mountain-top monastery at Montserrat and never thought that my first sight of it would be from the cab of a steam loco! Sadly, budget constraints have caused the end of this operation and we can but hope that it will restart one day.

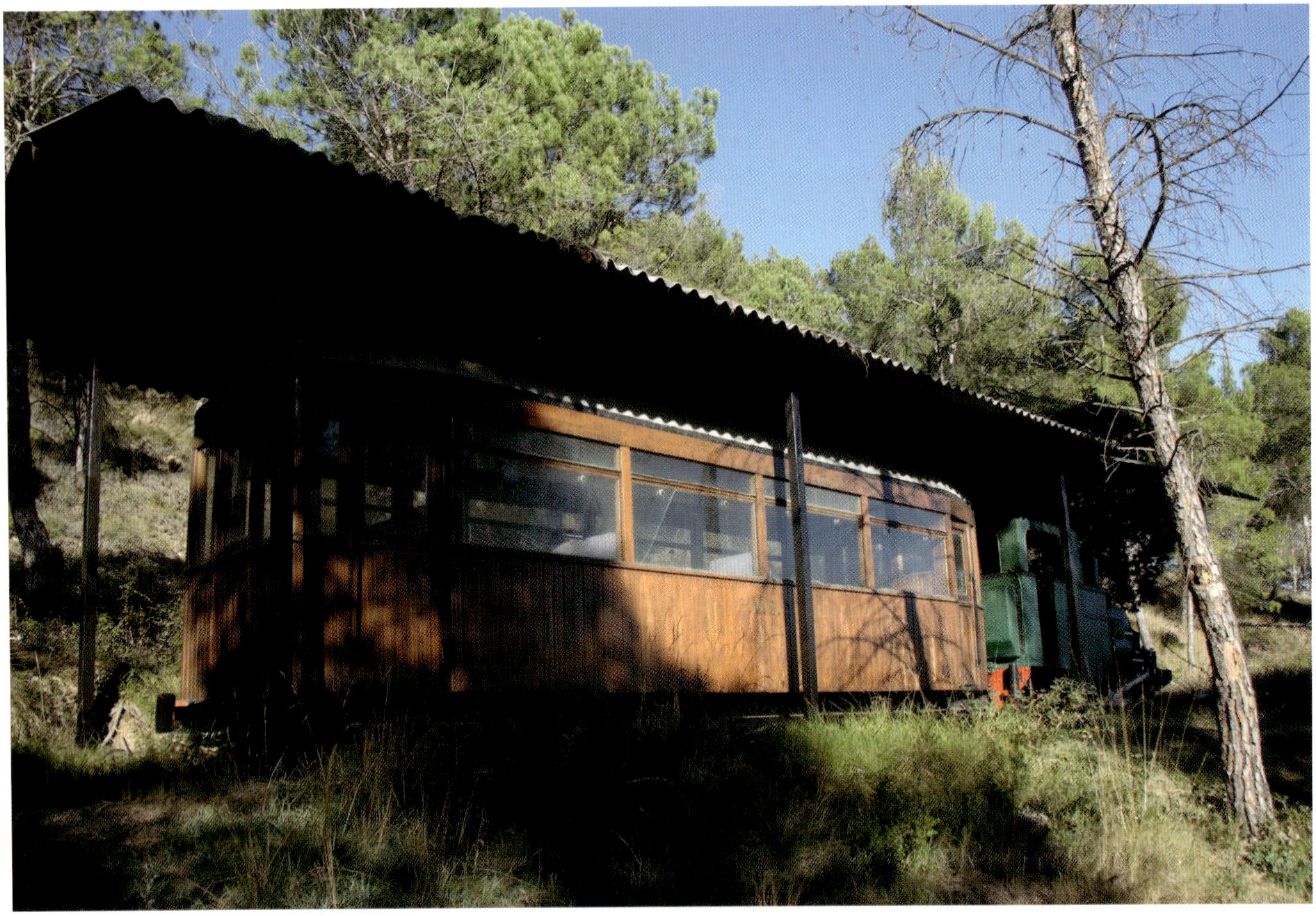

The old metre gauge Montserrat Abt-rack railway closed in 1957 but in 1982 a well-wisher found room for 0-4-2RT No 2 *Monistrol* (Cail 2353/1892) and her saloon coach in the garden of his home near Balsareny where I visited them on the sunny afternoon of 11 November 2010. After he died, his family presented them to the FGC who have rebuilt the line and they're now on show at Monistrol Vila station.

ITALY

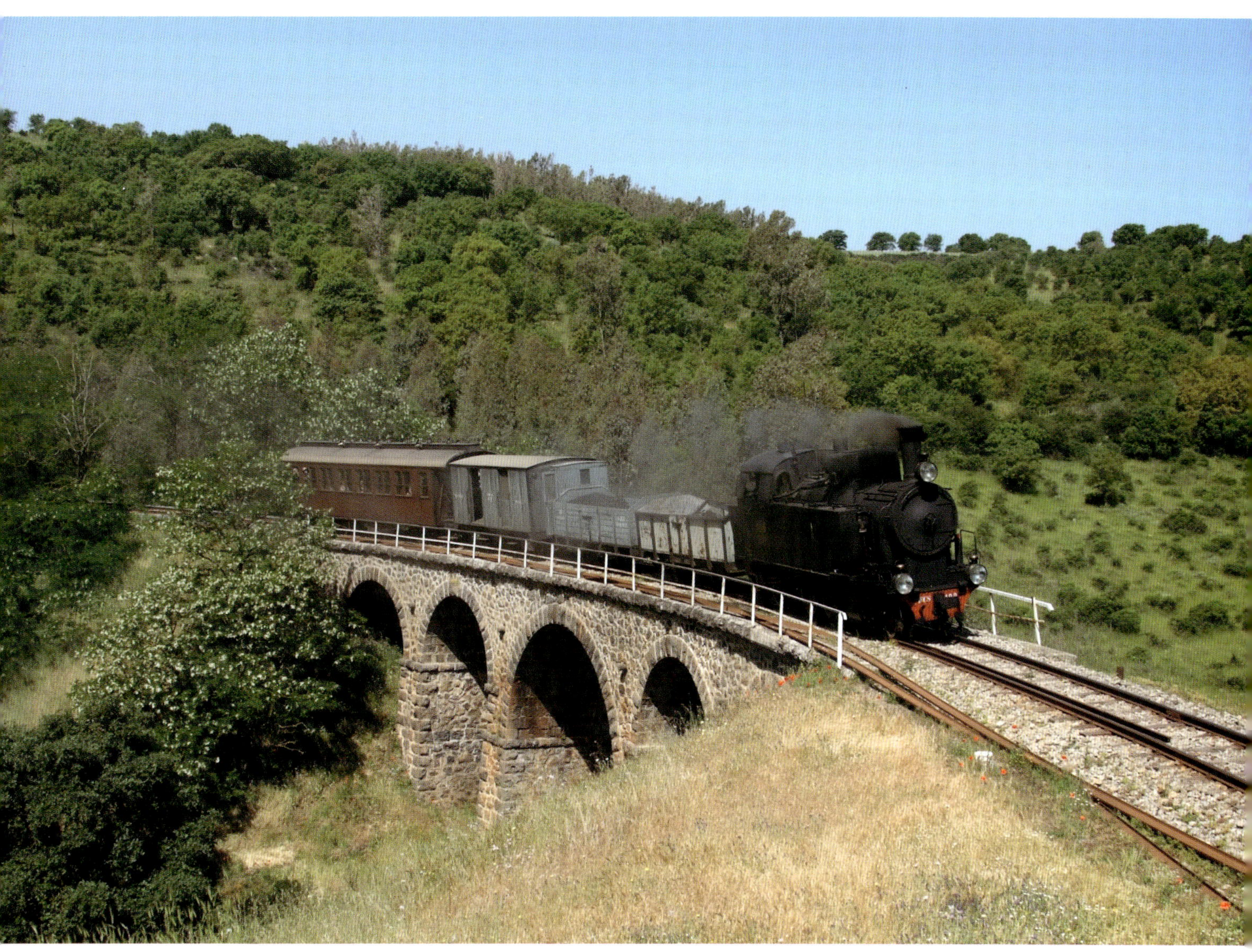

2-6-2T No 400 (RE 133/1931) runs through the beautiful Sardinian countryside on her way to Arbatax on 20 May 2009. The 950mm gauge was popular throughout Italy and its colonies. It's said to have originated with a horse-worked railway in the south west of Sardinia which was intended to be metre gauge but measured its gauge between the mid-point of the rails instead of their inside edges. This method broke down when heavier, wider rails were introduced and 950mm, measured conventionally, became the accepted gauge. The lines north of Cagliari, Sardinia's capital, were opened in stages from 1889. Parts are still in everyday use while the remoter stretches have been kept on for tourist trains.

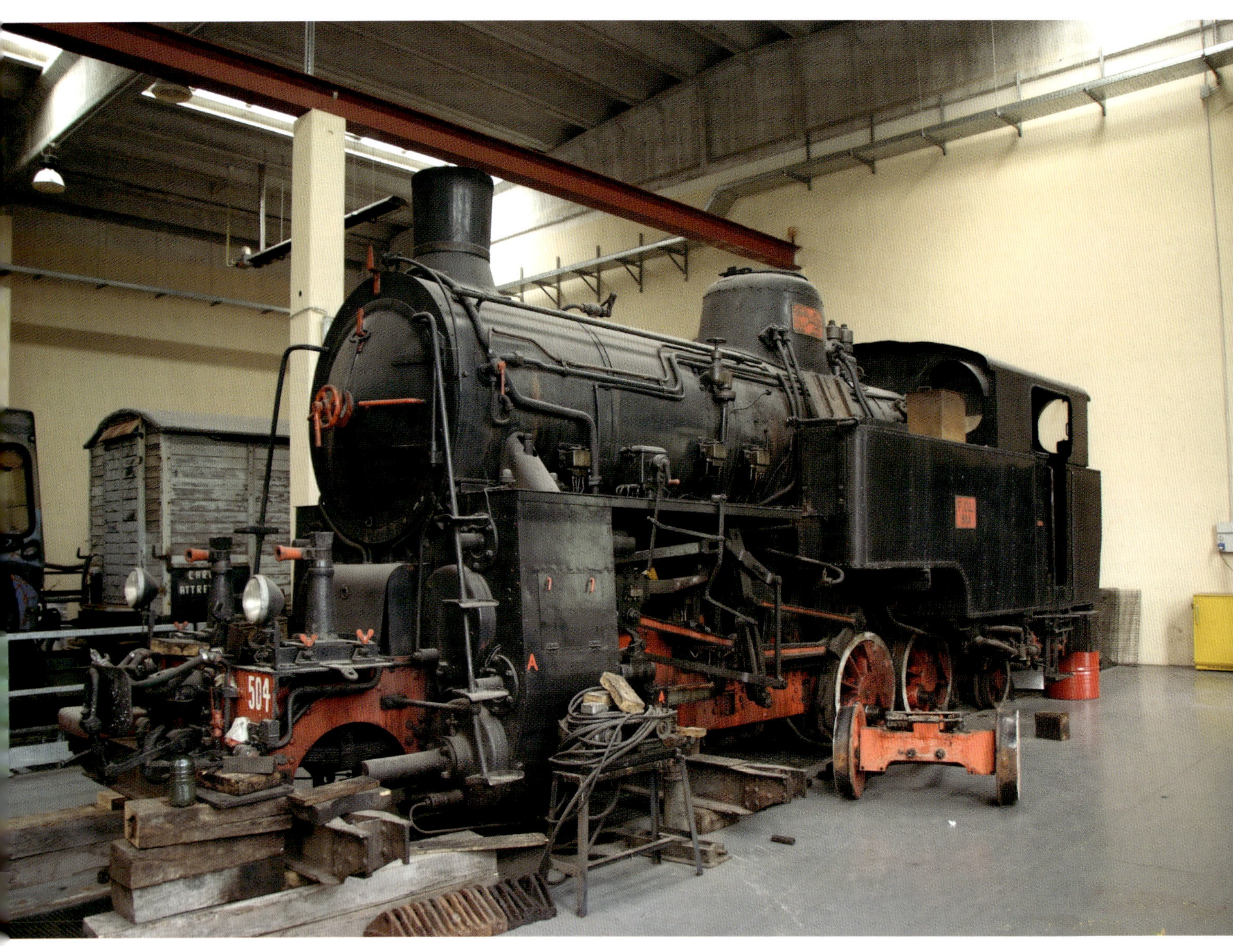

The Ferrovie Mediterraneo Calabro-Lucane's 950mm gauge system in southern Italy was built from 1915. At its greatest extent, it consisted of nine unconnected railways and included Abt-rack sections at Catanzaro and Castrovillari. 2-6-2RT No 504 (CEMSA 967/1932) was one of six locos built with design input from SLM and is the system's only steam loco which has never officially been withdrawn from service. She was receiving front end attention at Cosenza depot on 13 September 2008.

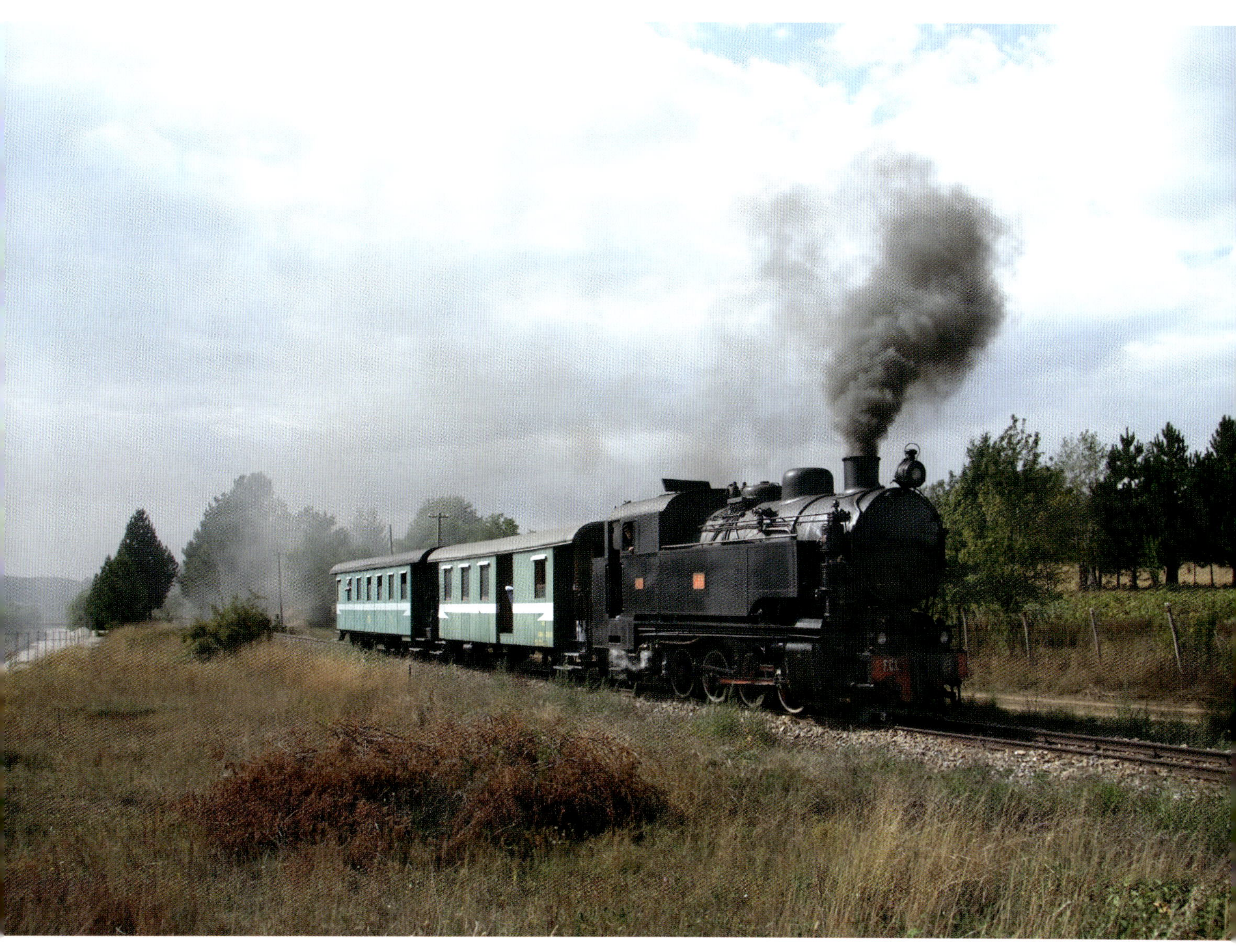

Later that day, 0-8-0T No 353 (Borsig 11940/1926) climbs away from Camigliatello Silano bound for San Giovanni in Fiore on a section near Cosenza built as recently as the 1950s to promote development of this remote region. She's big and chunky, very much a hill-climbing machine, and was one of three of these 350 class locos fitted with Walschaerts gear. Eight more with Caprotti gear came later from Breda and Ansaldo.

BOSNIA

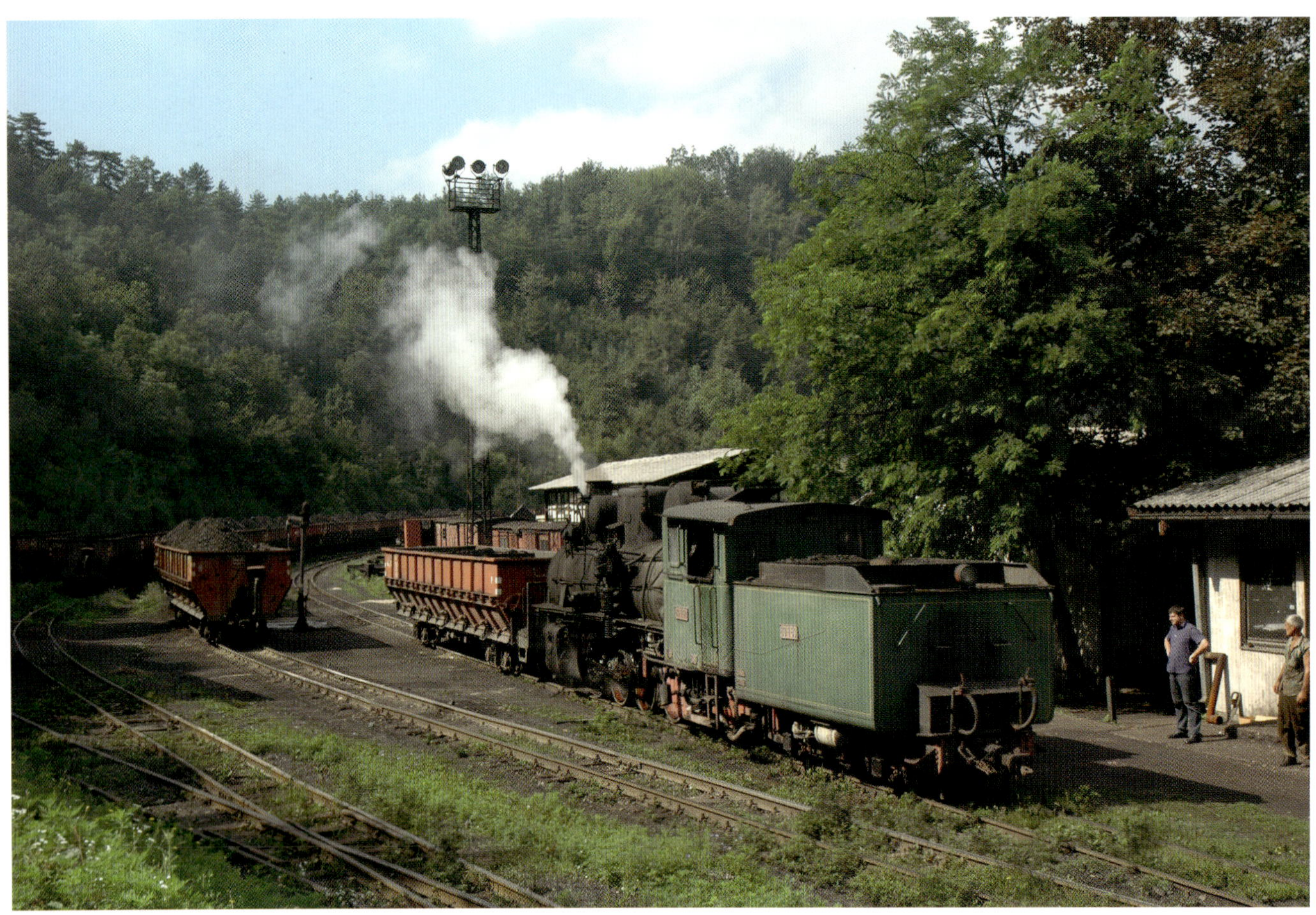

Above: Former JZ 760mm gauge 0-8-2 No 83-159 (Đuro Đaković 54/1948) shunts at Oskova, near Banovići in northern Bosnia, on the sunny morning of 22 July 2005. The railway at Banovići was built to serve collieries developed around the town from the mid-1940's. It acquired six of these locos to work its mainline after diesels replaced them on the extensive JZ narrow gauge system in Bosnia in the early 1970's.

Opposite above: This gentleman has the unenviable job of releasing the hopper doors as these coal wagons are drawn slowly through the unloading point at Oskova by 0-6-0T No 25-33 (ČKD 2533/1949) on 10 November 2005. The ten locos of this class were much enlarged and more powerful versions of the C 760/90d 0-6-0T's built for the Slovakian forestry railways the previous year. According to some reports, another fifteen were built for North Korea, possibly in 1957.

Opposite below: The Hungarian 490 class 0-8-0T design was updated in 1940 and No 55-99 (Budapest 5844/1949) was one of probably twelve supplied to Banovići. She spent many years on a plinth but on 9 November 2005 returned to the workshops for restoration to working order. Here her motion is being stripped down the following morning.

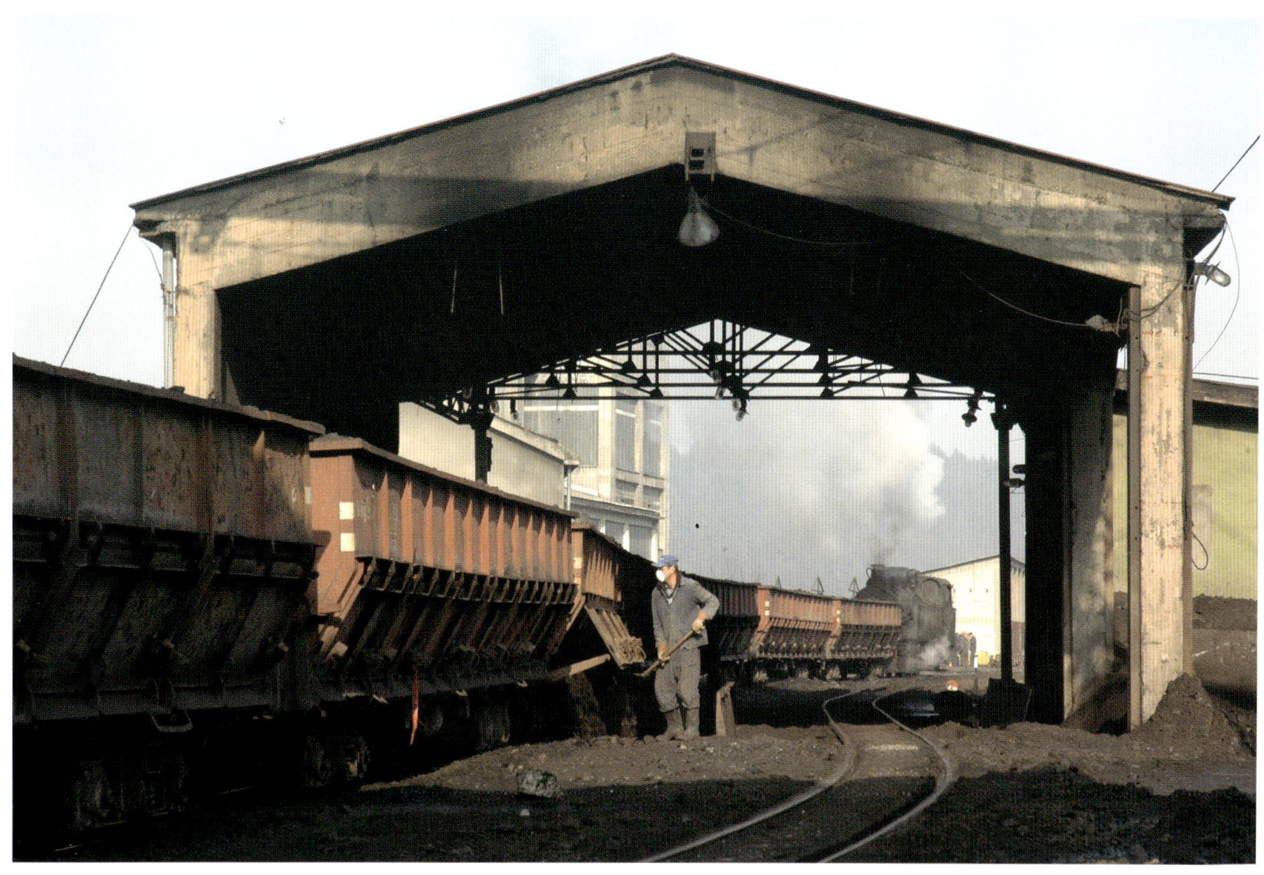

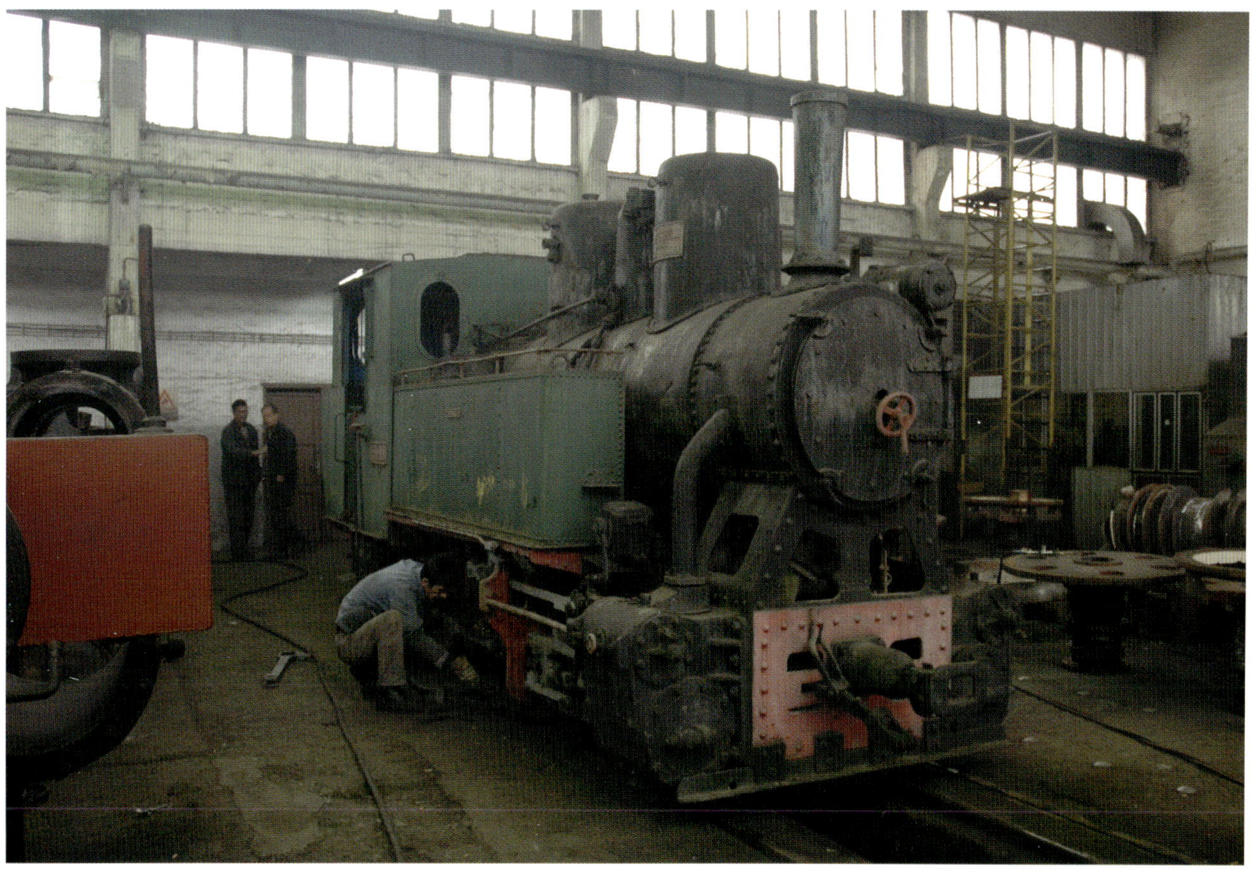

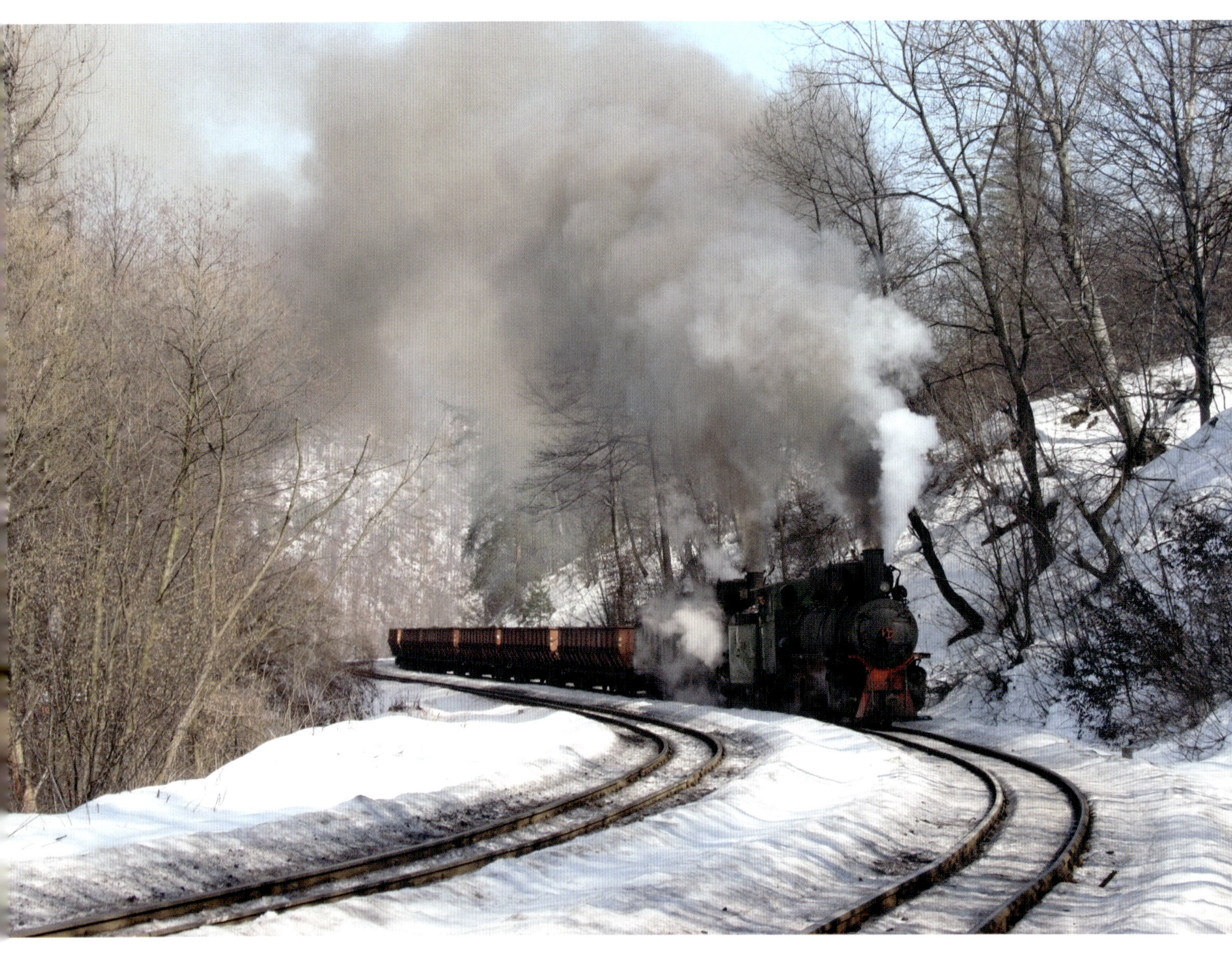

The last JZ narrow gauge line in Bosnia closed in 1978. Three of its diesels, then only seven years old, followed the 83s to Banovići and relegated them to shunting work at Oskova. Almost forty years later two of the 83s are still in stock. On the snowy morning of 25 February 2012 no's 83-159 and 83-158 (Đuro Đaković 53/1948) relive their early Banovići years as they head along the double-track mainline. They're painted in the smartly lined-out green paint scheme used throughout Yugoslavia for industrial locos.

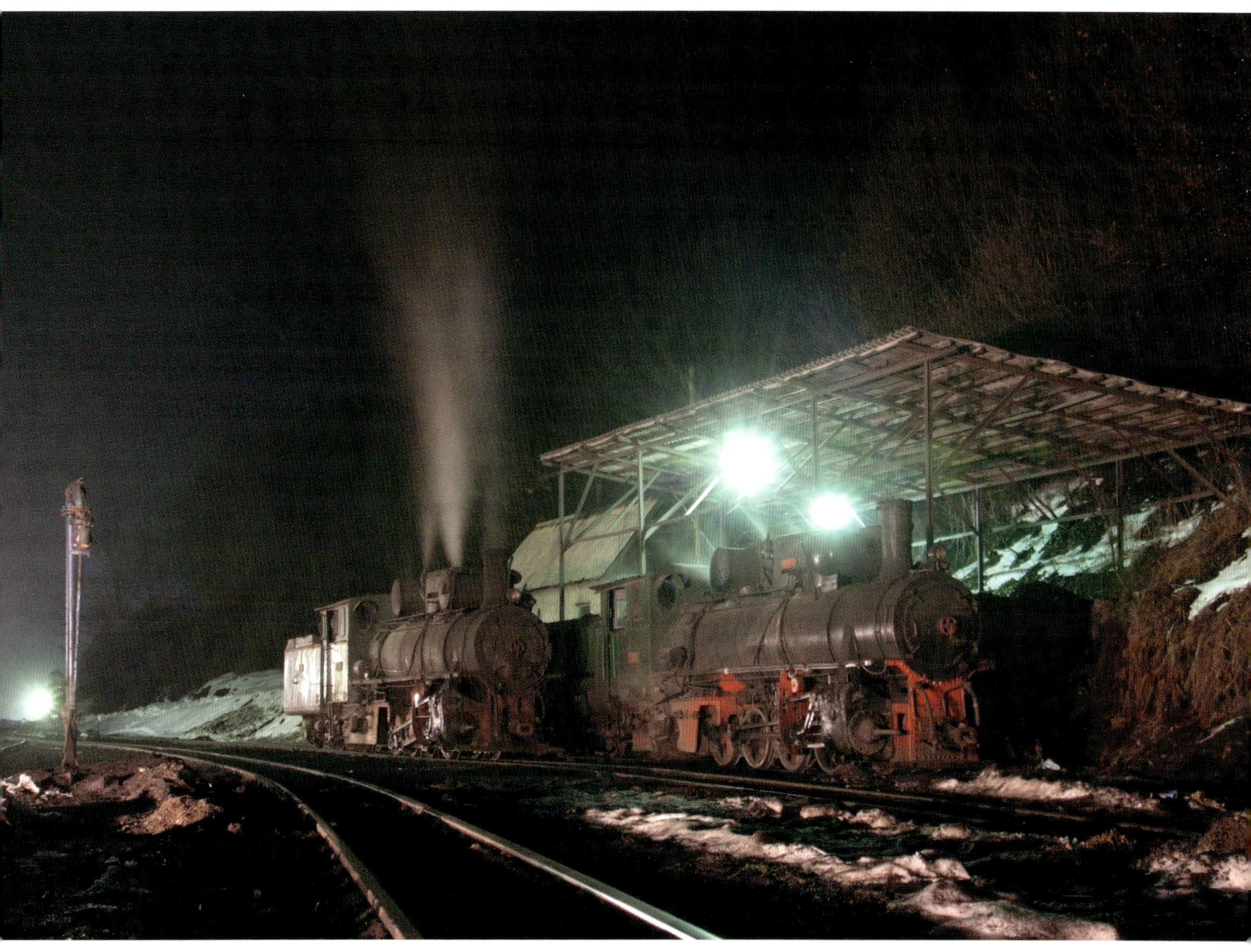

The two 83s pose at Oskova on the evening of 25 February 2012. For many years, one loco would be in service while the other was being overhauled and seeing both in steam together was a rare treat. The first of the 83s was built by the Austrians as far back as 1903 when Bosnia was an Austrian colony and no fewer than 185 had been constructed by the time production ceased in 1949.

SERBIA

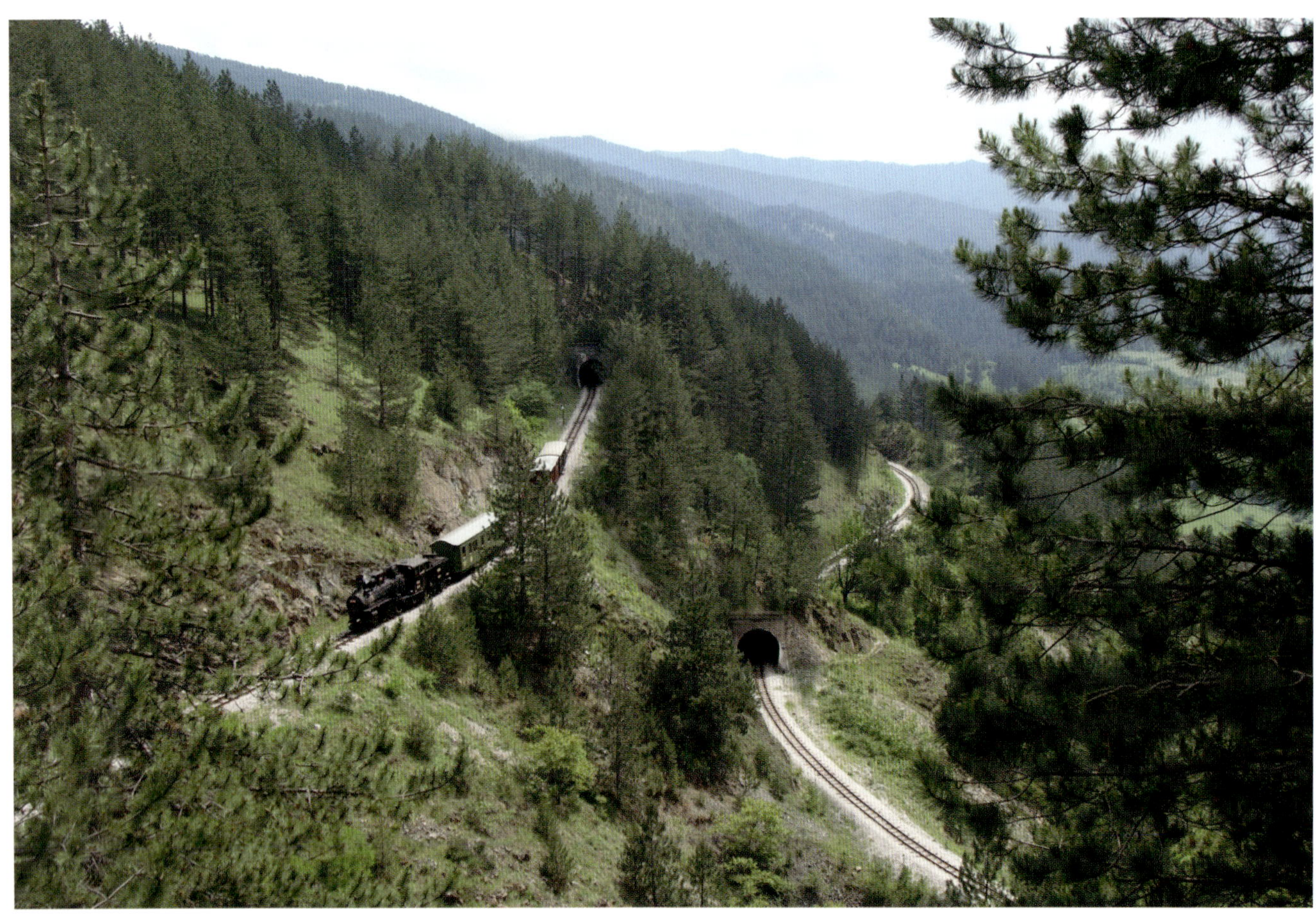

Above: When Yugoslavia was formed in 1919, there was an urgent need to join up the 760mm gauge railways of Bosnia and Serbia to provide a through route between Belgrade and Sarajevo. This involved building a convoluted line up the mountainside at Mokra Gora in south western Serbia, completed in 1925 and a source of considerable pride for the young nation. This didn't prevent its closure in 1974, a victim of the country's drive to rid itself of its narrow gauge railways, but it has since been rebuilt as a tourist line. No 83-173 (Đuro Đaković 129/1949), makes her way up this spectacular railway on 9 June 2008, seen from another part of the route further up the hillside.

Opposite above: The lignite deposits at Kostolac were first mined in about 1885 and the coal was taken away along a 600mm gauge railway to the nearby River Danube for shipping. After they invaded in 1941, the Germans expanded production and built a network to the 900mm gauge they often preferred for industrial railways. The United Nations sponsored the urgent construction of ten 0-8-0s in 1945 to replace locos removed by the Germans when they withdrew and as European builders had full order books they were supplied by Davenport in Iowa. No 13 and her train are dwarfed by the two dragline diggers at Klenovnik pit on 7 November 2005.

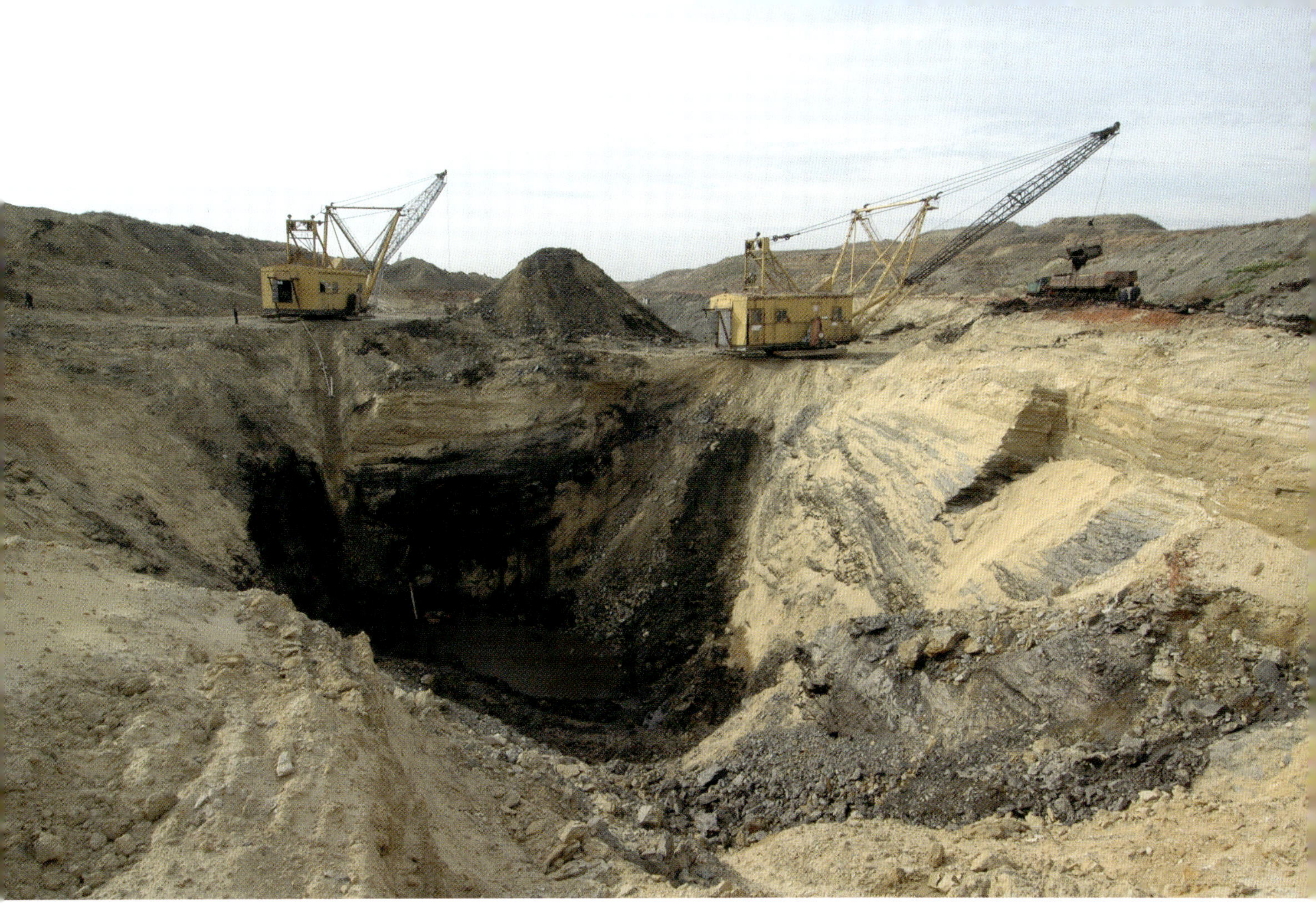

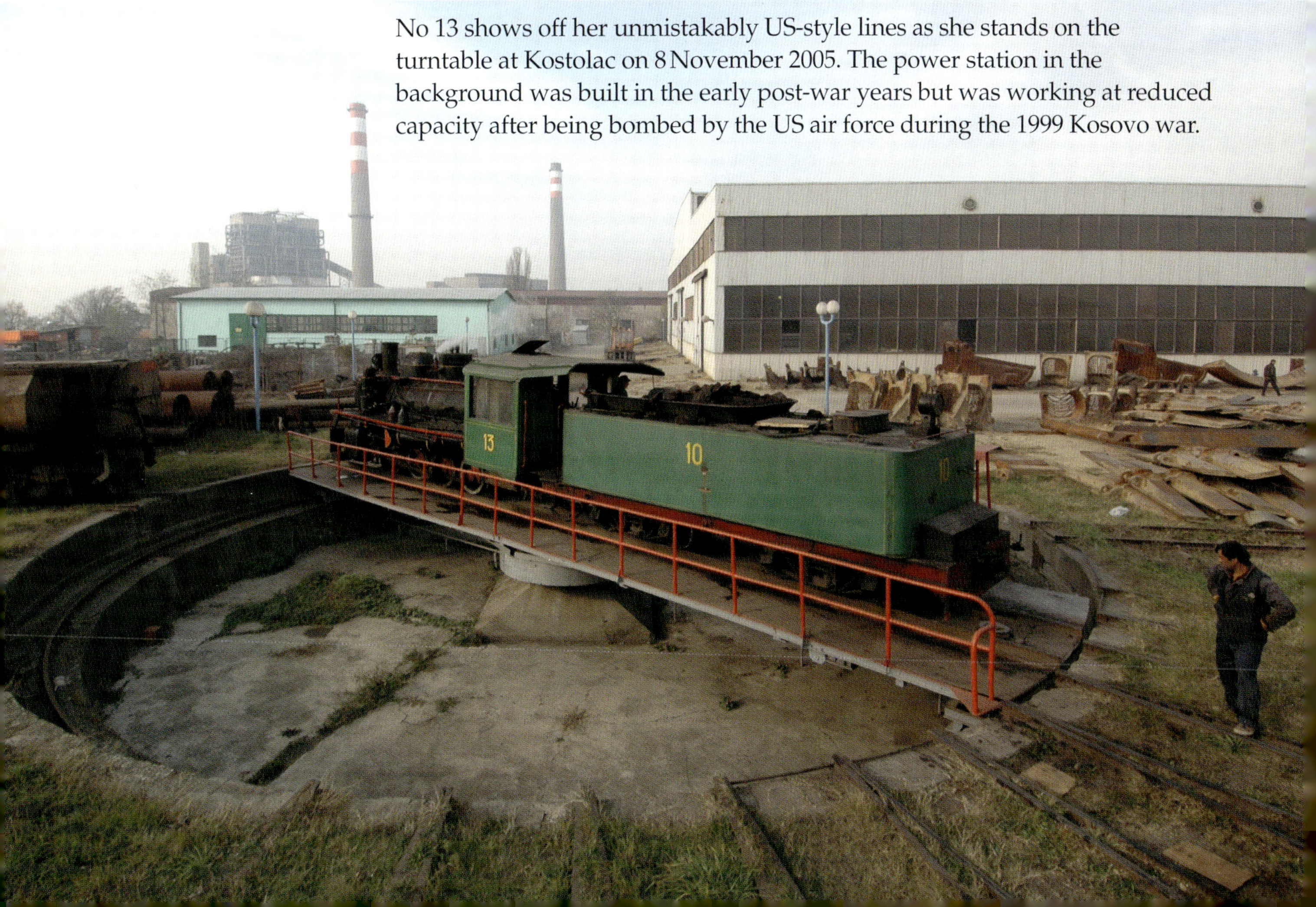

No 13 shows off her unmistakably US-style lines as she stands on the turntable at Kostolac on 8 November 2005. The power station in the background was built in the early post-war years but was working at reduced capacity after being bombed by the US air force during the 1999 Kosovo war.

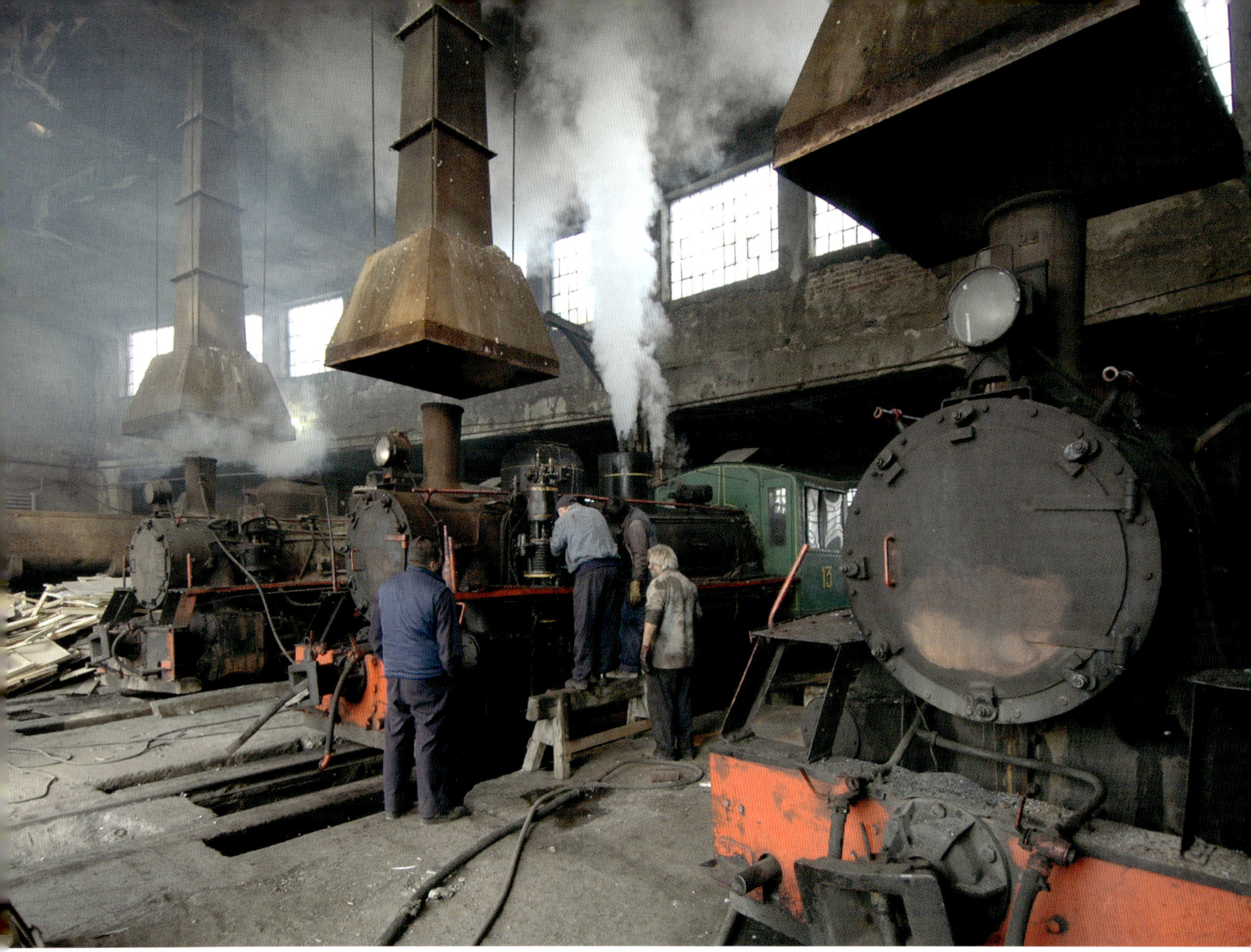

Above: The magnificent eighteen-road roundhouse at Kostolac was built in about 1950. No 13 has come in for out-of-course attention on 8 November 2005 and is flanked by Nos 12 and 14. The works numbers of these three locos were 2881-3 but it's not known which one was which.

Opposite above: 0-4-4-0 Péchot-Bourdon *Kostolac* (Baldwin 41983/1915) stands at Pozega narrow gauge museum in Serbia on 8 June 2008. She was one of two which the Germans moved to the 600mm gauge railway at Kostolac in 1941. The Péchot-Bourdon was essentially a Double Fairlie but only had one centrally mounted dome. The French army adopted the type for its field railways as early as 1888 and by 1914, fifty-two had been built. On 1 February 1915 280 were ordered from Baldwin, mostly for the Western Front, and another fourteen came from North British. Several served the Germans after 1940, possibly moved from the Maginot line where many had been based. They weren't the first Péchot-Bourdons in Serbia as two of the Baldwins worked on the Sukovo-Rakita colliery line for a few years until they were scrapped in 1934. *Kostolac* is one of only two survivors.

Opposite below: No 13 shunts her train through the unloading point at the power station on 7 November 2005. In 1975, the line to the largest pit at Ćirikovac was electrified but trains serving Klenovnik, worked only in the winter, continued to rely on the 0-8-0's until it closed in 2009.

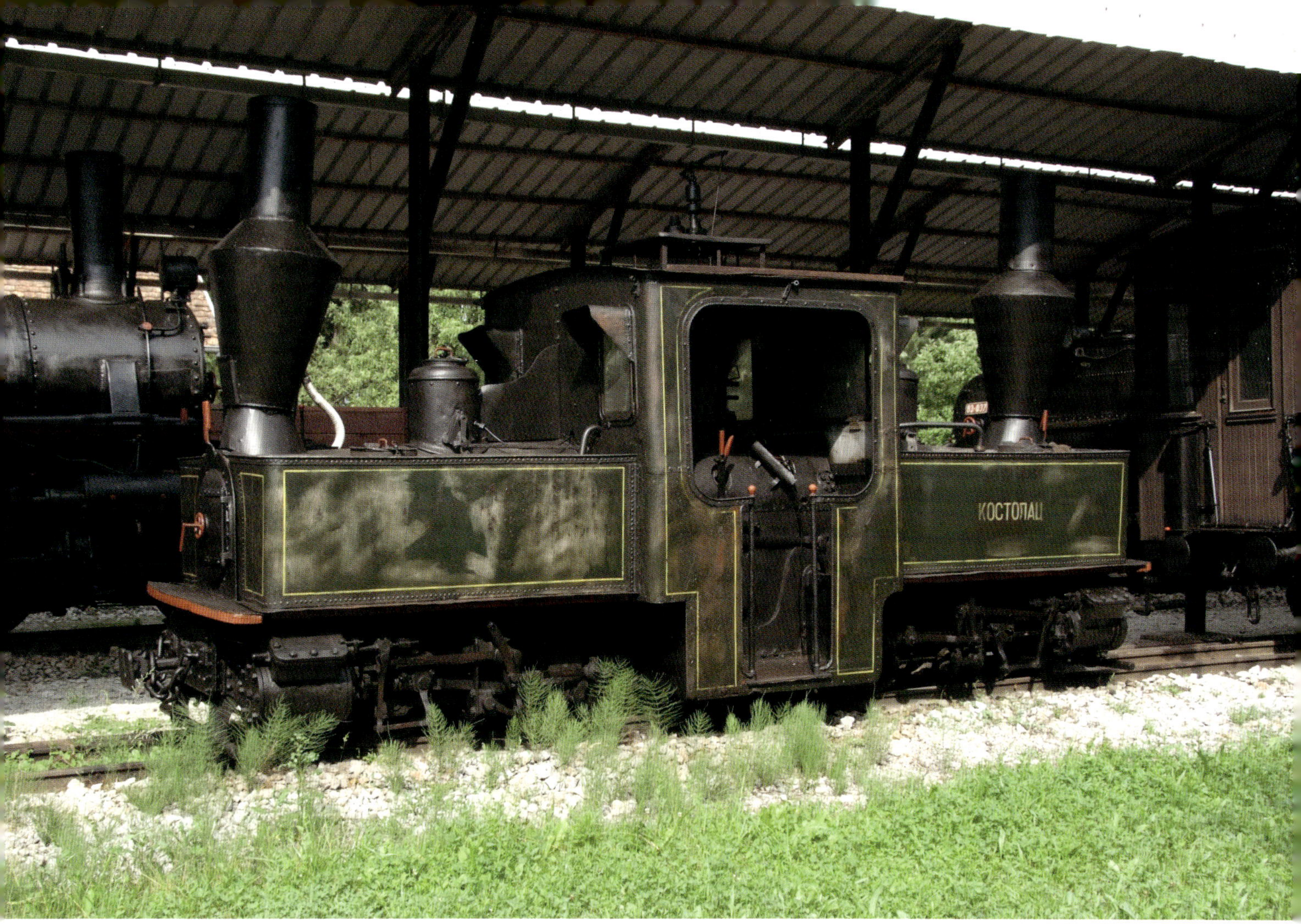

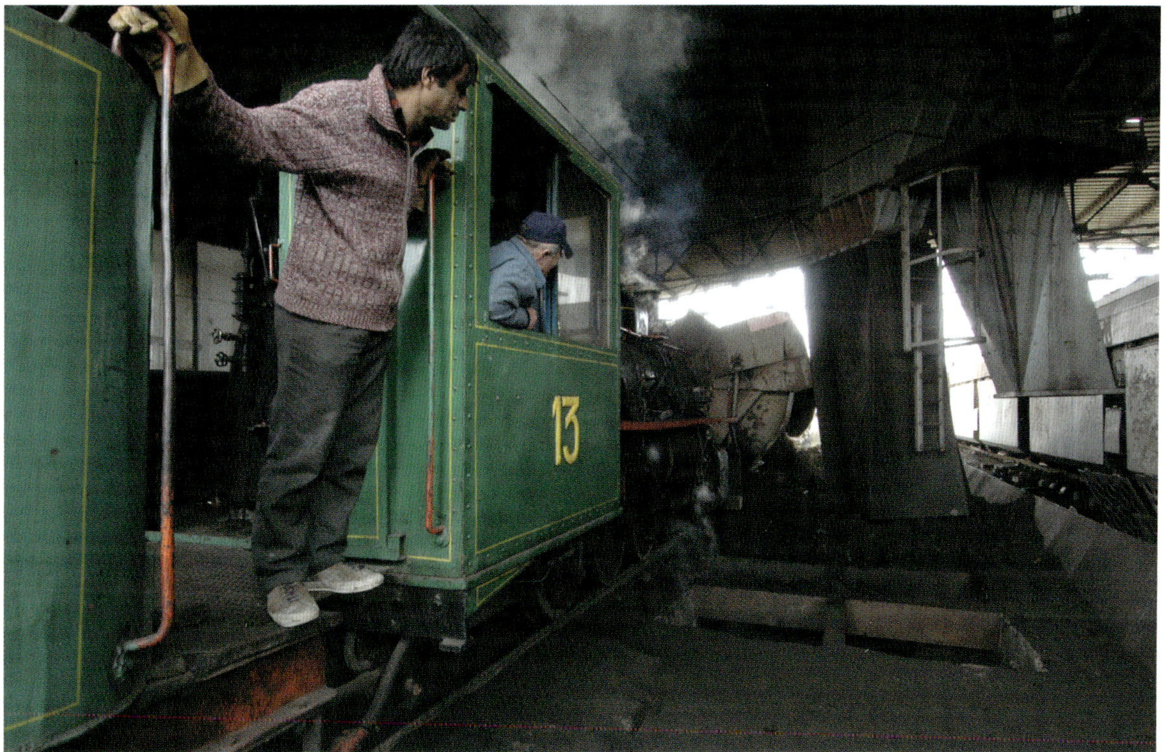
13

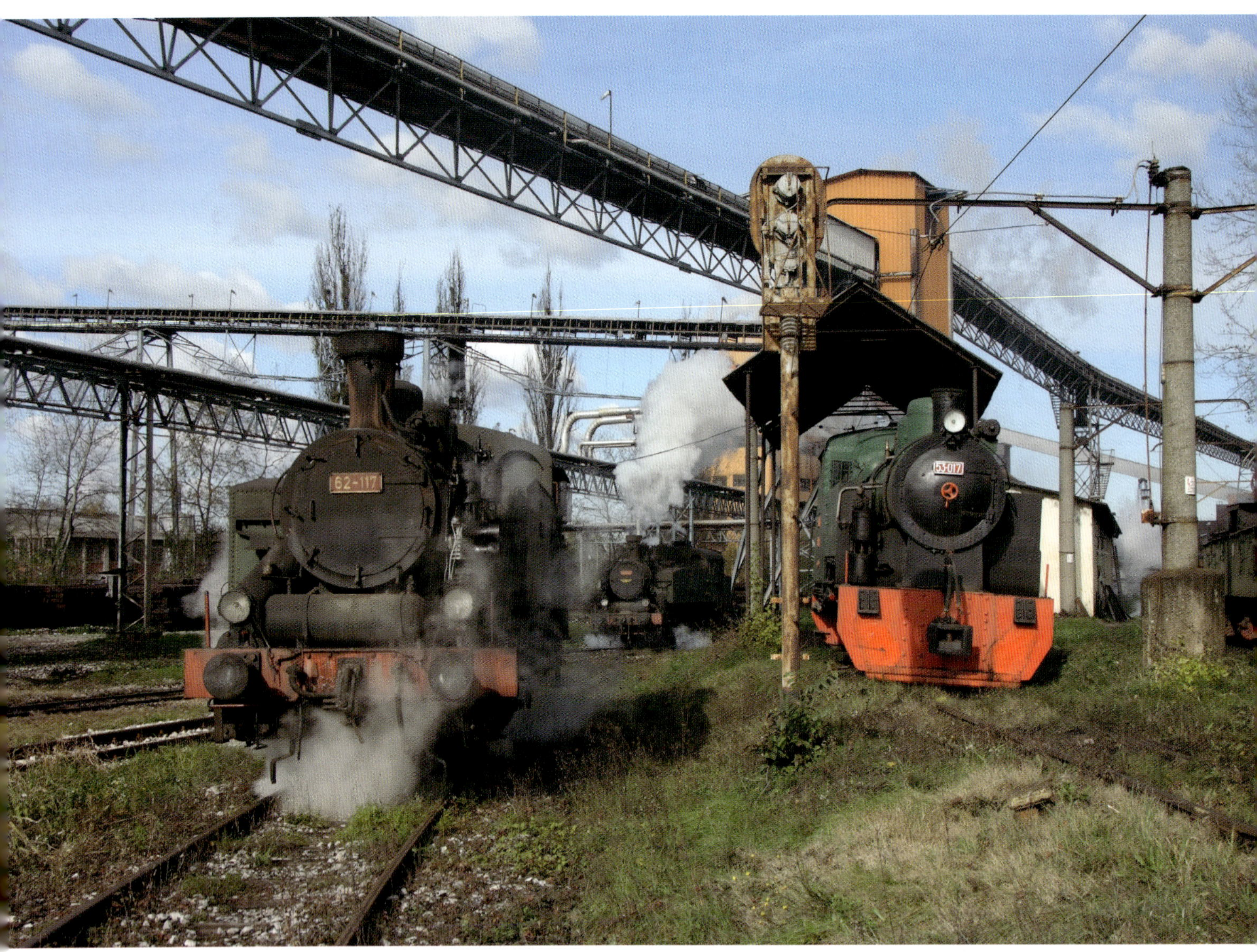

Above: Present-day Serbia's other principal coalfield in the Kolubara valley underwent rapid expansion from the late 1940s and 900mm gauge railways were built to serve it. Twenty Decauville 0-6-0Ts, part of a batch of thirty supplied to Yugoslavia and the firm's last-ever steam locos, worked there from new and a few stayed on after electrification. 0-6-0T No 53-017 (Decauville 5317/1953) stands at Vreoci washery on 10 November 2007 as standard gauge 0-6-0Ts Nos 62-117 (Đuro Đaković 622/1955) and 62-635 (Đuro Đaković 635/1957) pass on the left. On the far right is 900mm gauge Bo-Bo electric No 15 (LEW 12476/1971).

Opposite above: No 53-017 and Bo-Bo electric No 17 (LEW 16431/1978) shunt a short train at Vreoci on 19 April 2009 as Bo-Bo electric No 17E2-2 (Skoda, 1983) arrives with empties from Veliki Crljeni power station which is separately run and has its own allocation of locos. It acquired two of these Czech-built machines in the mid-1990s from Sokolov colliery in the Czech Republic.

Opposite below: 0-6-0T No 53-018 (Decauville 5318/1953) and Bo-Bo No 7 (BB 5355/1942), Serbia's oldest electric loco, stand at Rudovci shed at the eastern end of the system on 10 November 2007.

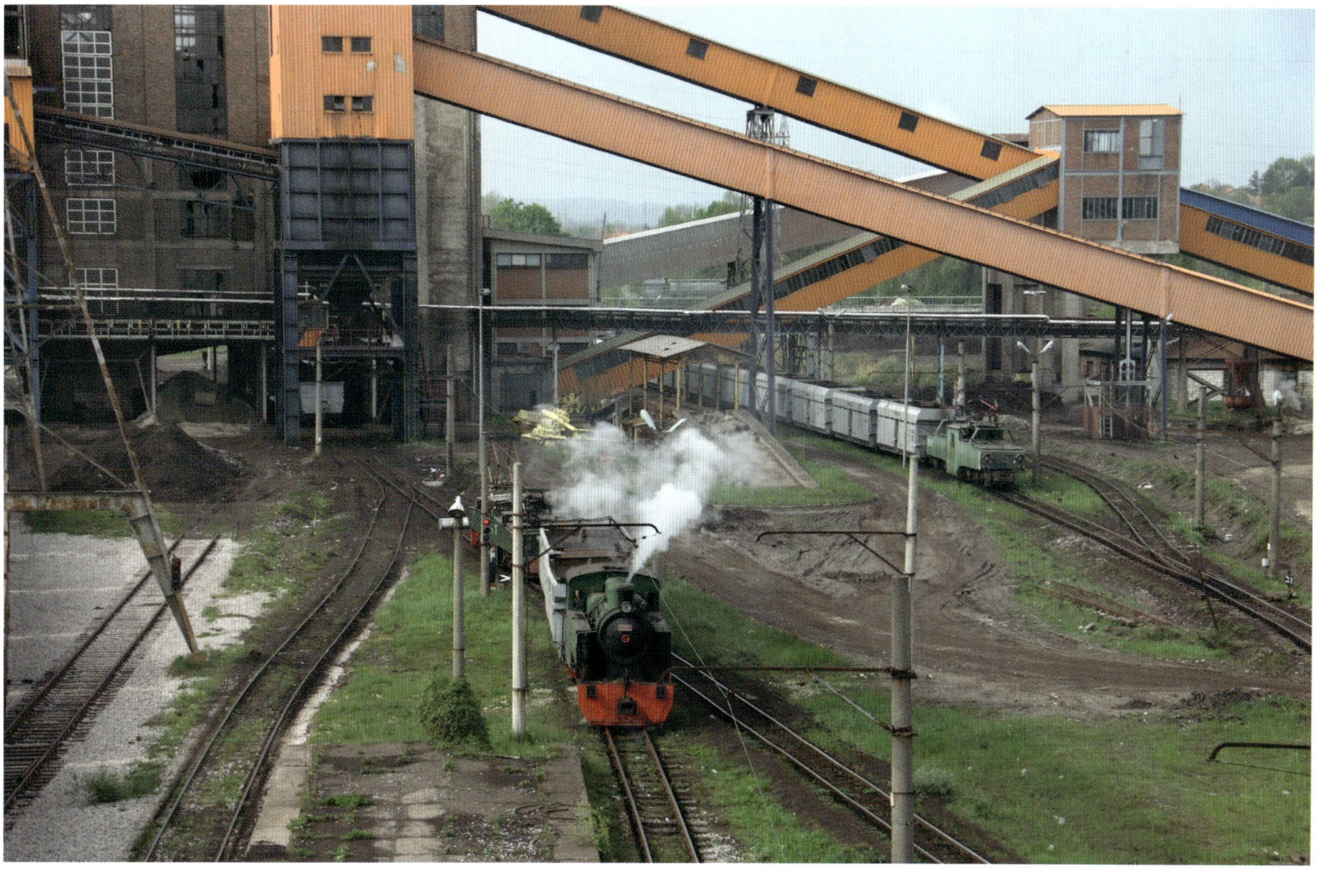

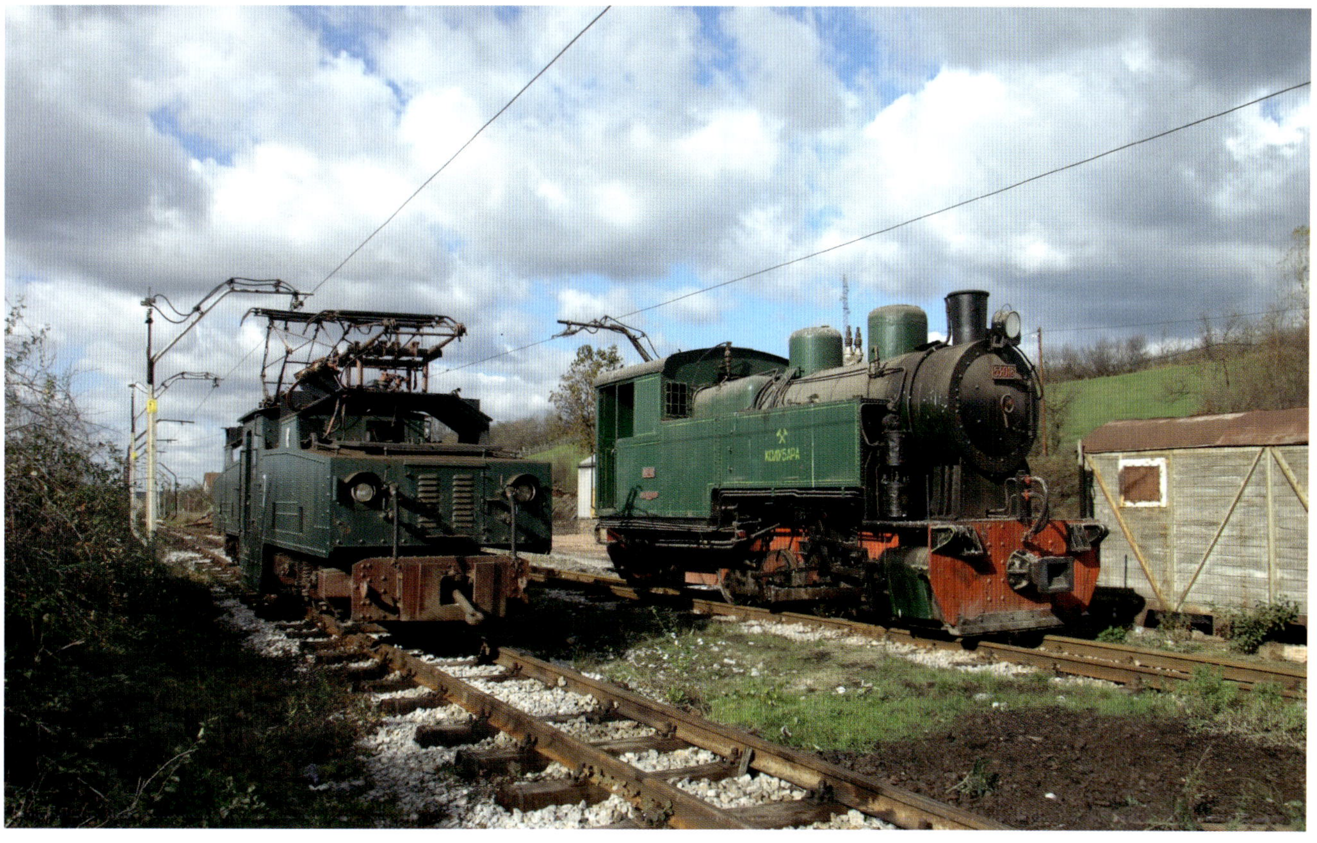

GREECE

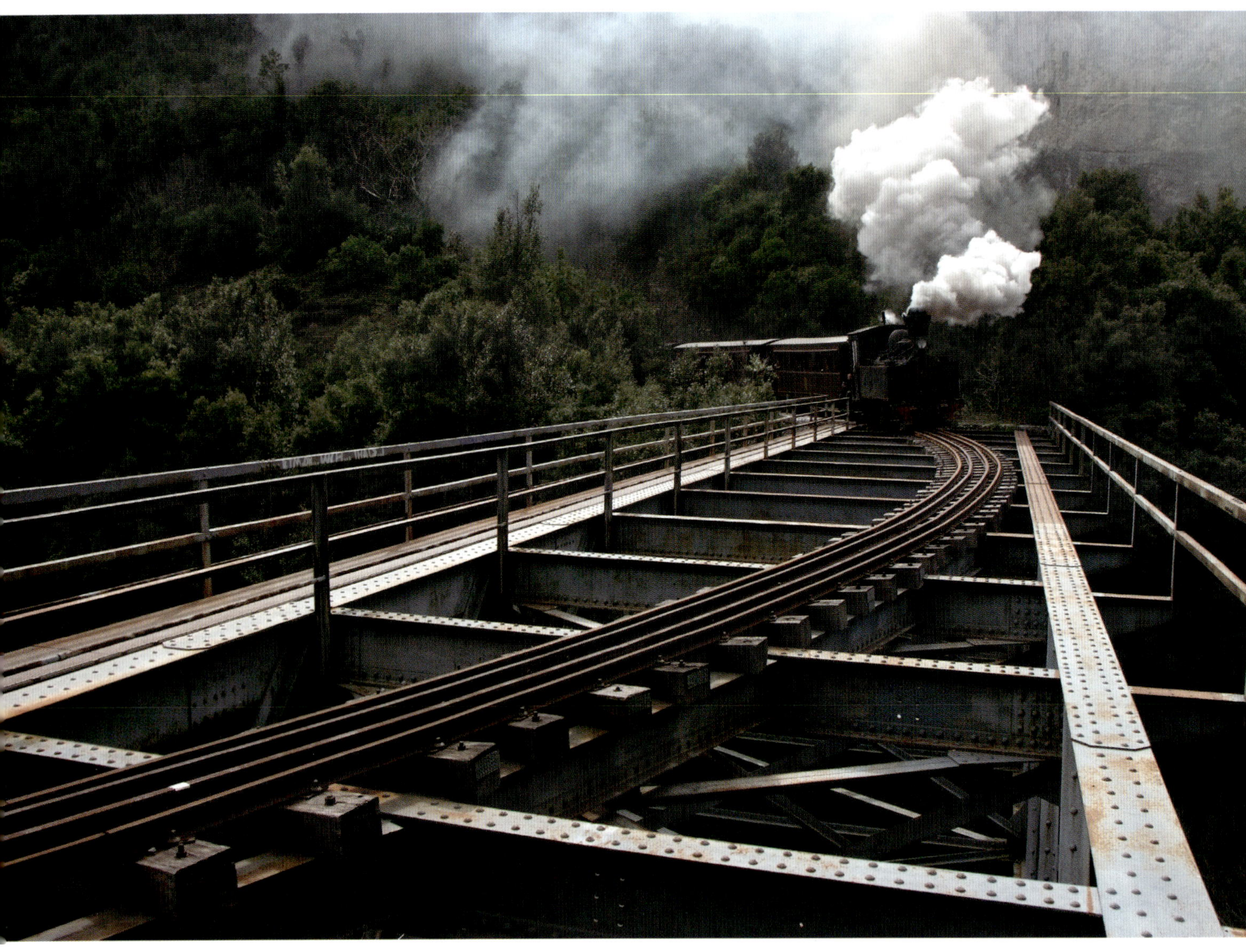

The 600mm gauge Mount Pelion Railway was built between 1892 and 1903 as an extension of the metre gauge Thessaly Railways' system eastwards from Volos. It closed in 1971 but part now operates as a tourist railway. On 6 March 2010, 2-6-0T No 101 *Miliai* (Tubize 1339/1903), the last working steam loco, crosses the long single-span girder bridge over a deep ravine shortly before the terminus at Miliai, 28kms from Volos. Sadly, this turned out to be her last journey to date as she suffered a major tube failure at Miliai and is now in store.

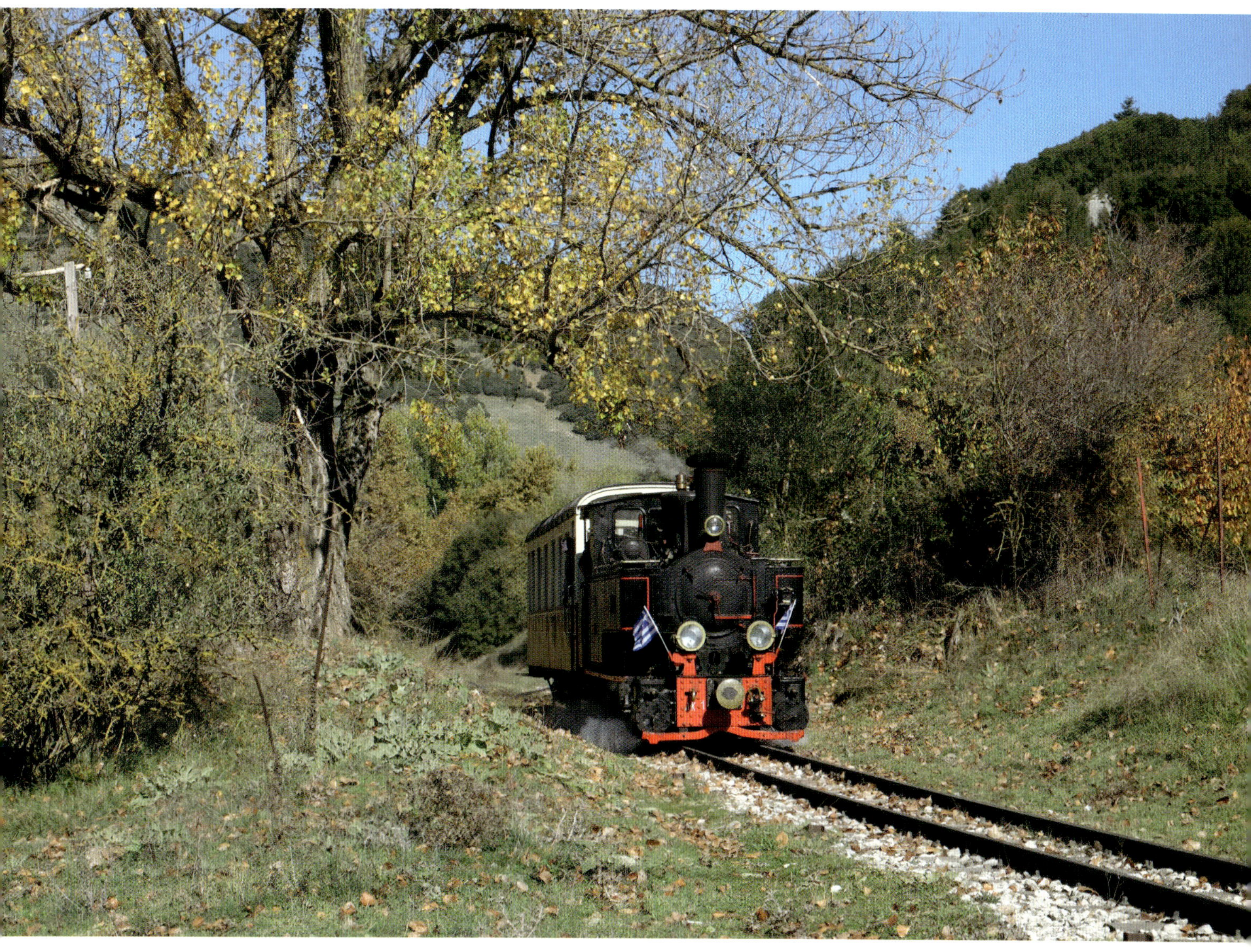

The 750mm gauge Diakofto-Kalavryta Abt-rack and adhesion railway in the Peloponnese opened in 1896. Regular trains have been diesel-worked since 1967 but all six steam locos have survived. The oldest one, 0-6-2RT No Dk 8.001 (Cail 2343/1891), was put back into working order for the line's 120th anniversary celebrations held on 5 November 2016 and on the previous day approaches Kalavryta on a trial run.

CYPRUS

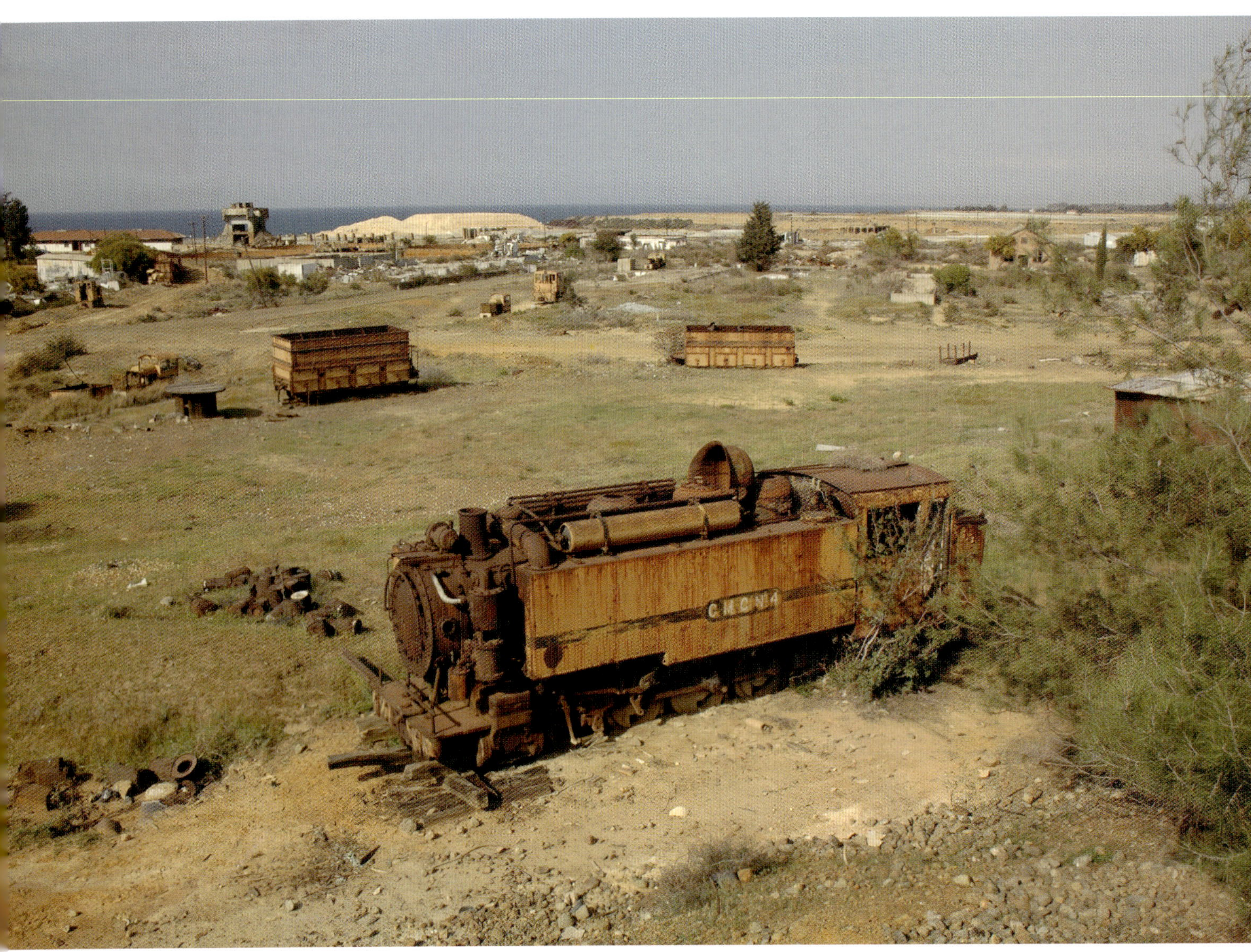

The US-run Cyprus Mines Corporation's 2ft 6ins gauge 0-8-2T No 4 (Baldwin 60344/1927) still looks dignified in the old mine yard at Xeros in Northern Cyprus on 30 March 2006, despite the surrounding dereliction, and no fewer than seven petrol or diesel locos are spread around in the background. She hadn't run for more than forty years. At the top left hand corner can just be seen the train, still full of ore, which was abandoned when it arrived on the day Turkey invaded Cyprus in 1974 and the CMC shut up shop, leaving the poisonous mining residues to leach into the sea ever since. Everywhere was eerily quiet but the silence gave way to a gentle tolling of bells as a herd of goats made its way into the yard and started to pick at the meagre shrubs around No 4.

ERITREA

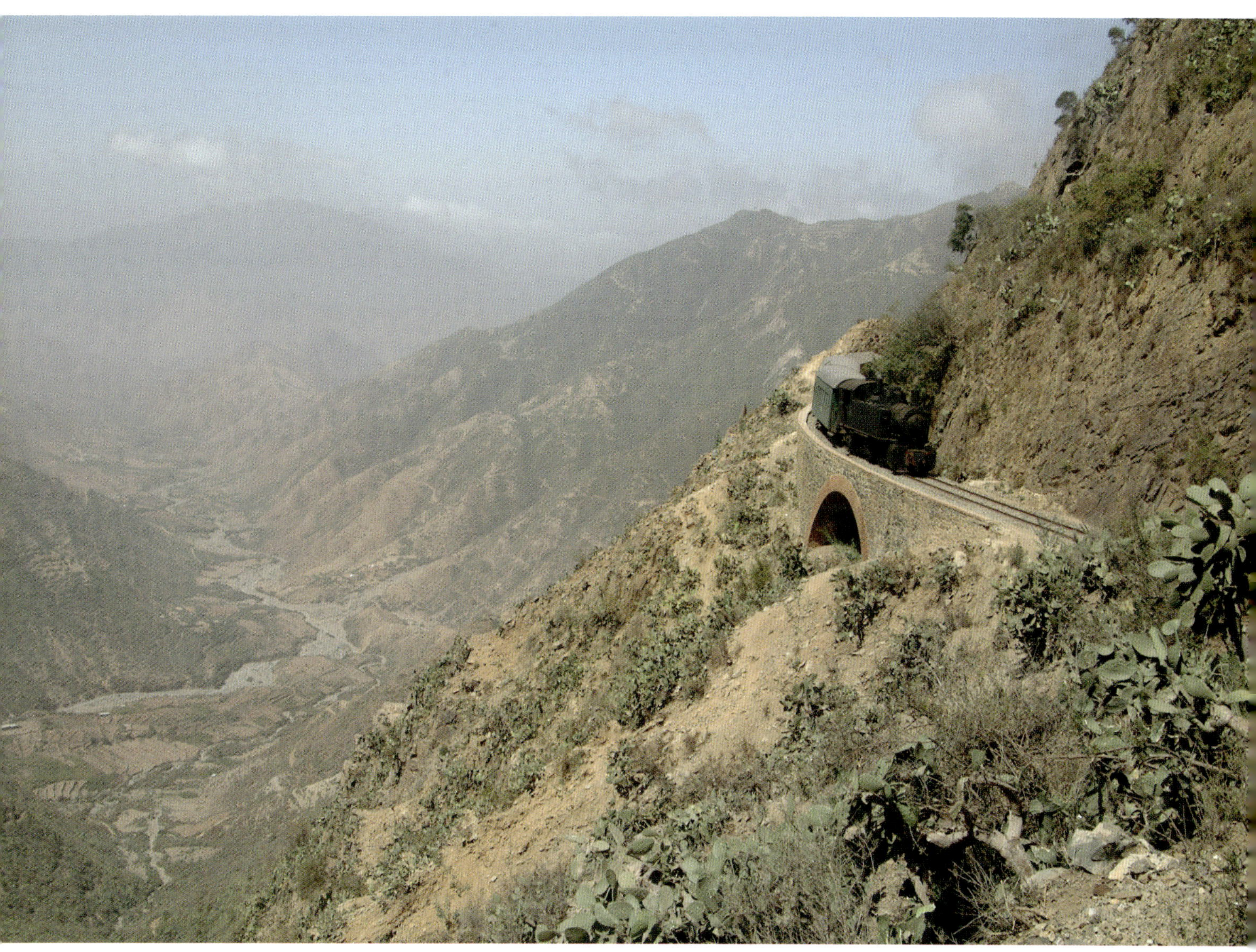

Construction of the 950mm gauge Eritrean railway by the Italian colonial government began on the coast in 1887. It was completed as far as Asmara in 1911 and was later extended. 0-4-4-0 Mallet tank No 442.54 (Ansaldo 1364/1938) passes the Porta del Diavolo with its view down towards the Great Rift Valley on 6 March 2005. These eight big Mallets were the last steam locos to be built for the railway.

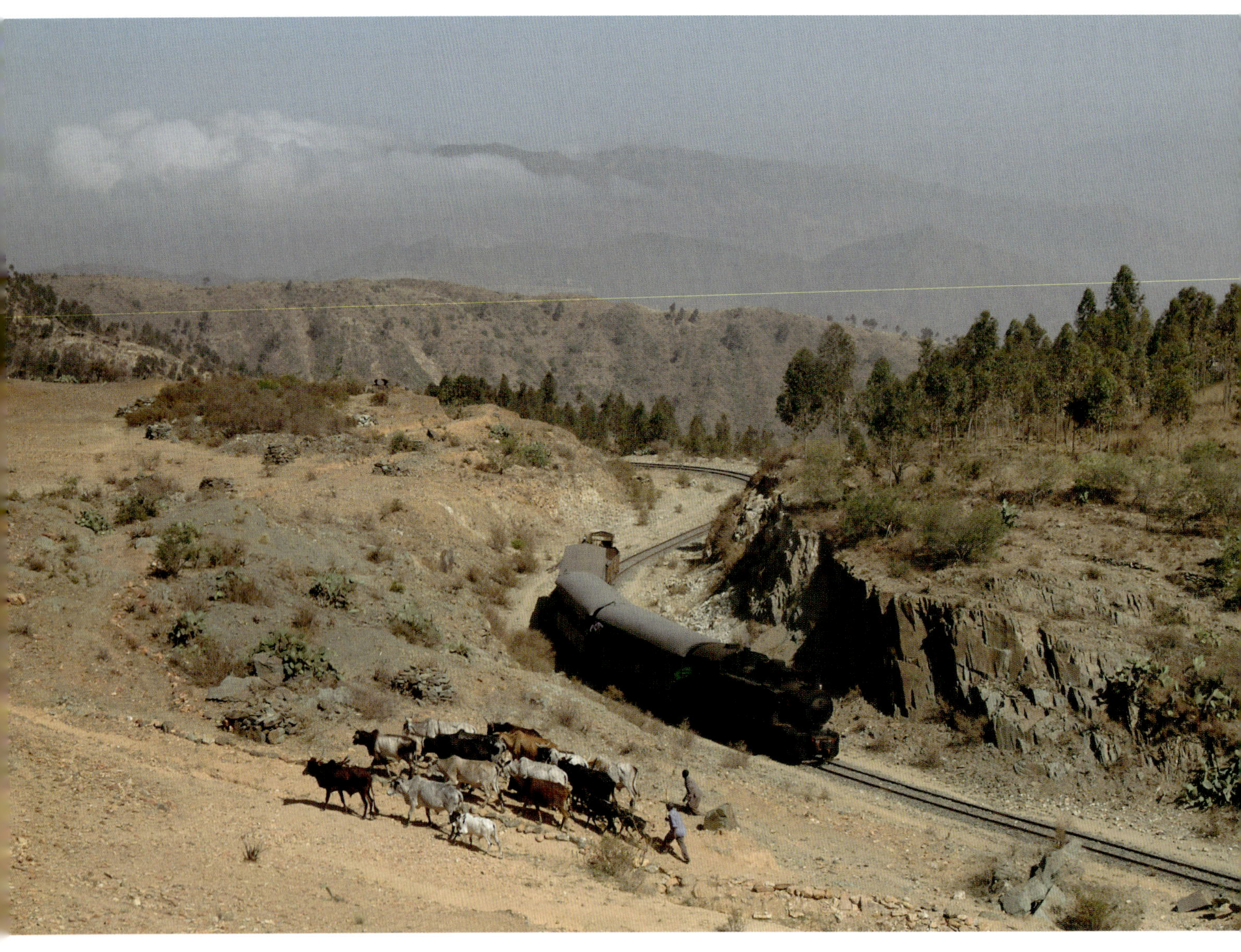

A little later No 442.54 waits as cattle cross the line near Asmara. It closed in 1976 during the country's war of liberation from the Ethiopians who subsequently scrapped four of the 442s and several smaller locos. The railway's rehabilitation was written off as hopeless by international consultants, but the Eritreans completed it as far as Asmara in 2003 without outside help, a most impressive achievement.

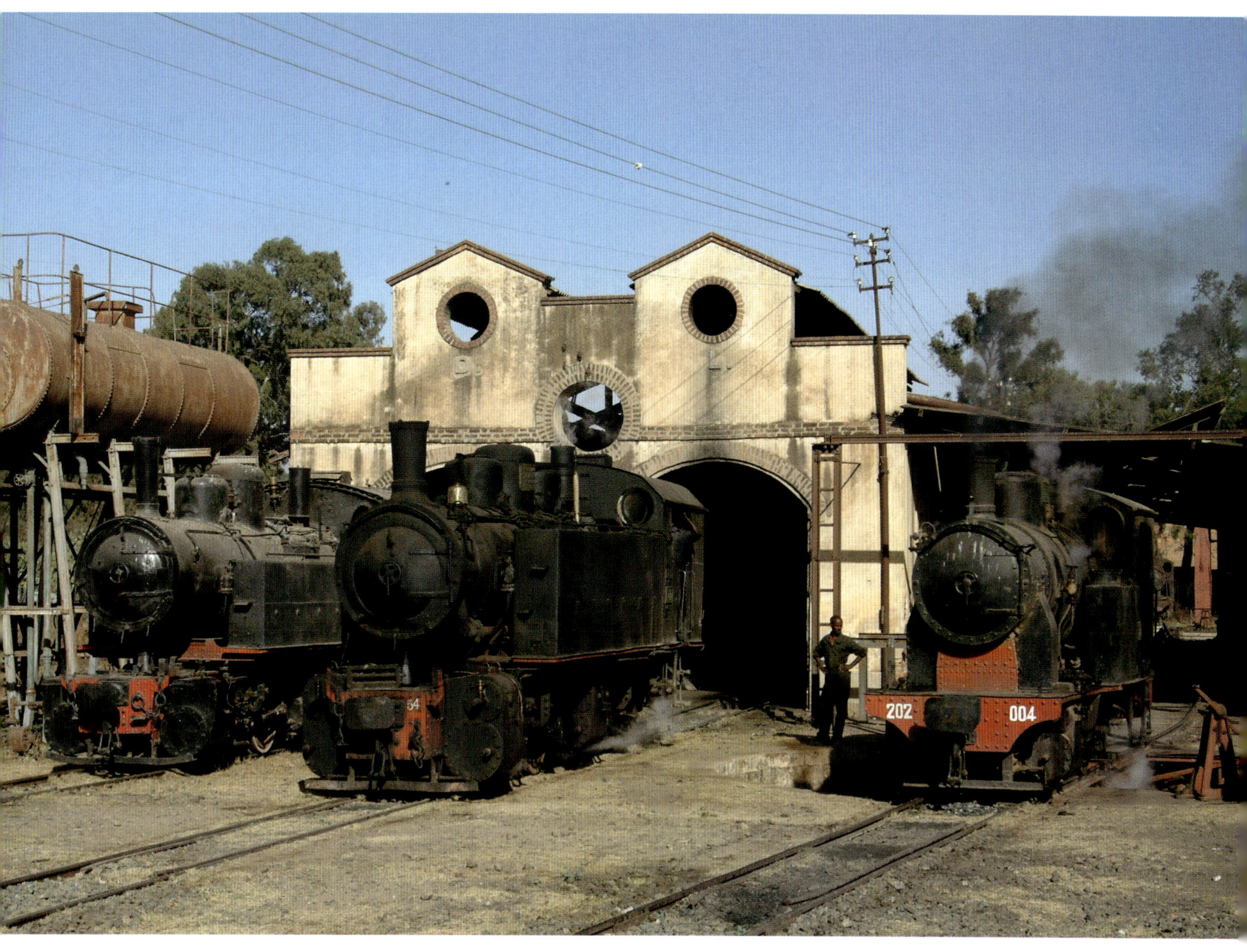

The three surviving steam loco types on parade at Asmara shed on 5 March 2005. On the left is 0-4-4-0 Mallet tank No 440.008 (Ansaldo 1162/1915). No 442.54 is in the middle and 0-4-0T No 202.004 (Breda 2272/1929) is moving into position on the right. The first three 440s were built by Maffei for Eritrea in 1907. Thirteen followed from Ansaldo between 1911 and 1914 and twelve more were built in 1914 and 1915 for service on FS, Italy's state railway. No 440.008 went new to Assoro in eastern Sicily but by 1925 was working on construction of the Appenine tunnel on the new Direttissima line between Florence and Bologna. In 1936 all the Italian 440s were sent to join their sisters already in Eritrea.

KENYA

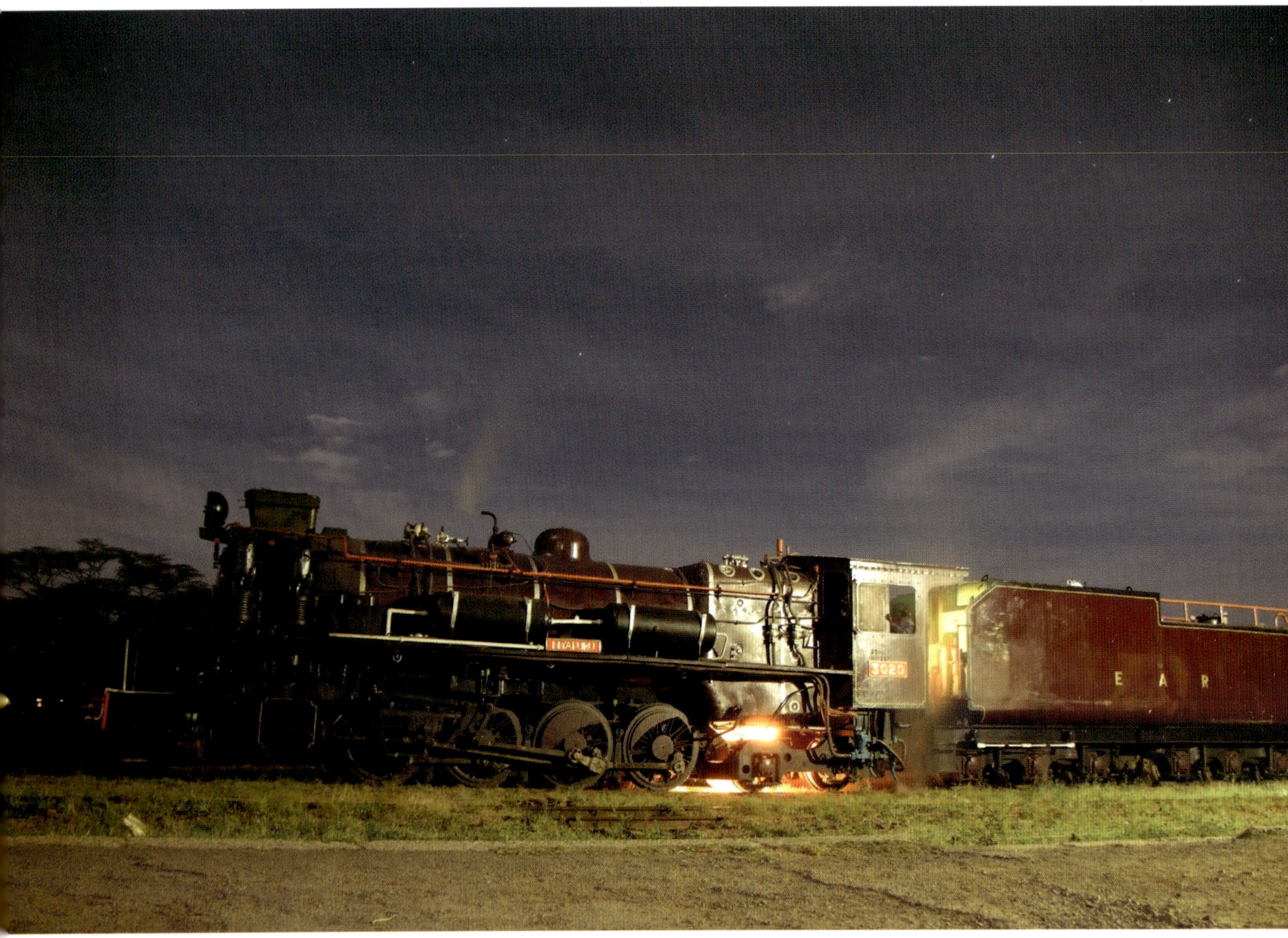

Above: It's before dawn on the starry morning of 19 May 2011 as the metre gauge East African Railways' 2-8-4 No 3020 *Nyaturu* (NB 27466/1955) raises steam at Naivasha. The twenty-six 30 class locos with their enormous tenders were built for the waterless stretches of line in Tanzania but No 3020 ended up in Kenya.

Opposite above: On 19 May 2011 No 3020 climbs out of the Great Rift Valley with Mount Longonot as a backdrop.

Opposite below: The magnificent 4-8-2+2-8-4 Garratt No 5918 *Mount Gelai* (BP 7649/1955), shunts at Nairobi station on 20 May 2011. The thirty-four 59s were the world's largest metre gauge locos. Behind her is a restaurant car, furnished in Art Deco style, which normally lives in Nairobi's railway museum. By good fortune, the other coaches in this photo also still carried the old EAR crimson and cream paint scheme.

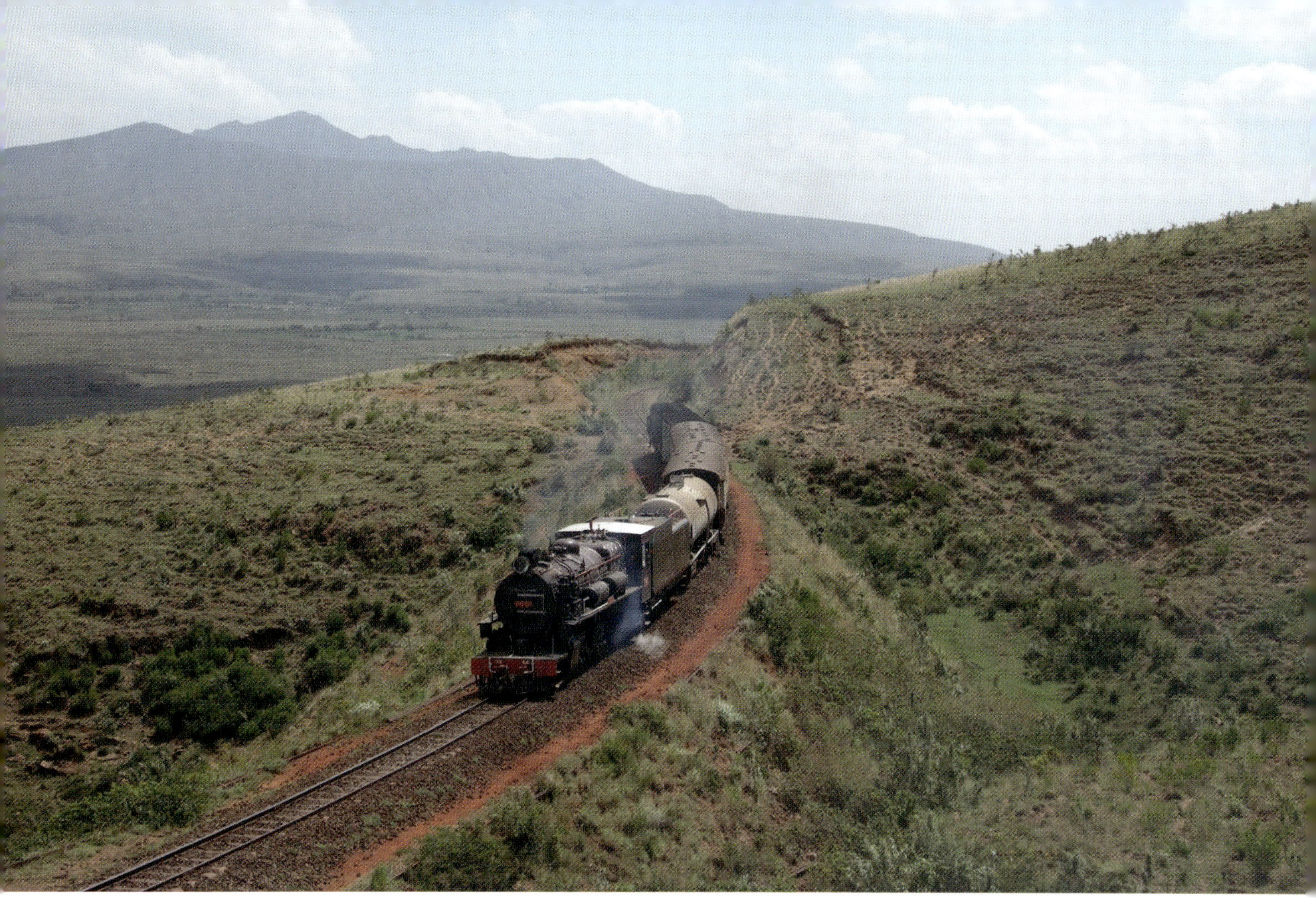

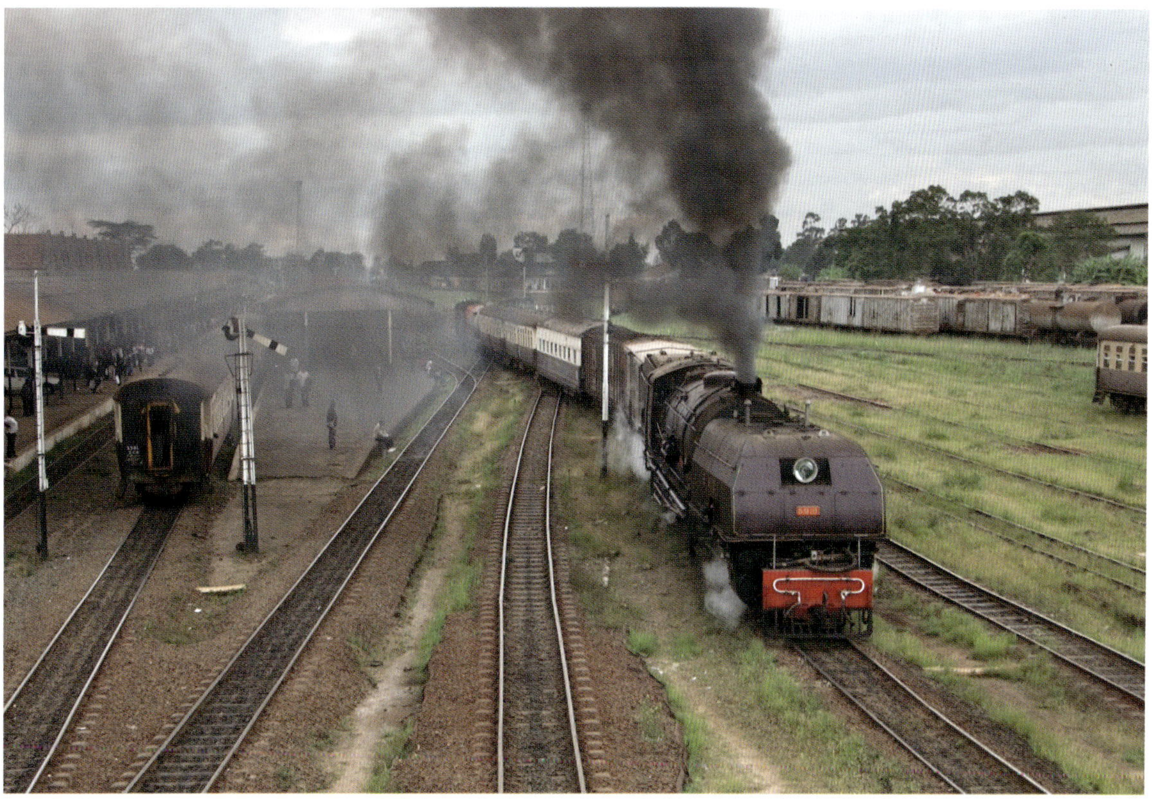

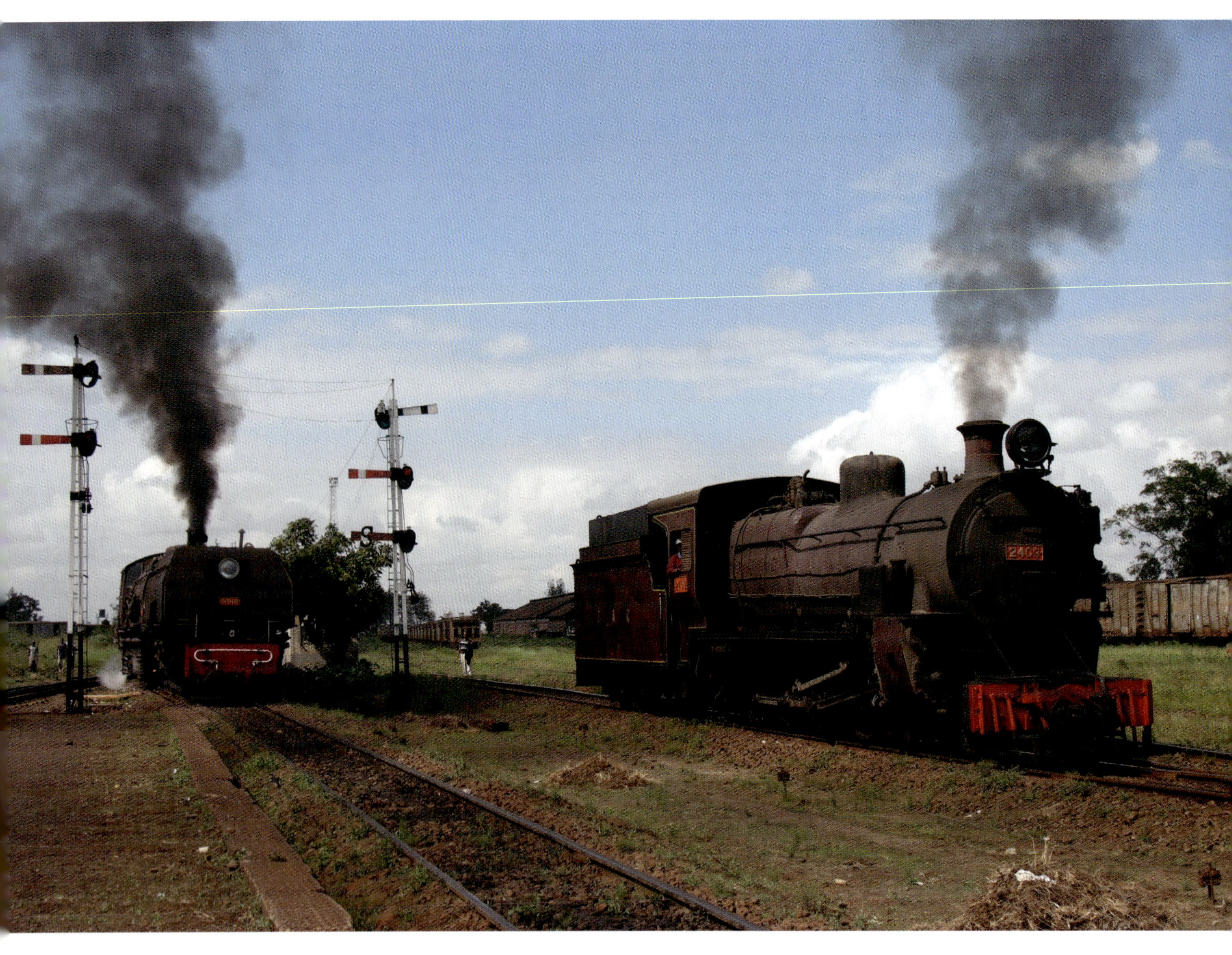

4-8-0 No 2409 (VF 3581/1922), from an earlier generation of EAR locos which shared many features with their cousins in India, stands at the eastern end of Nairobi station with No 5918 on 21 May 2011.

MAURITIUS

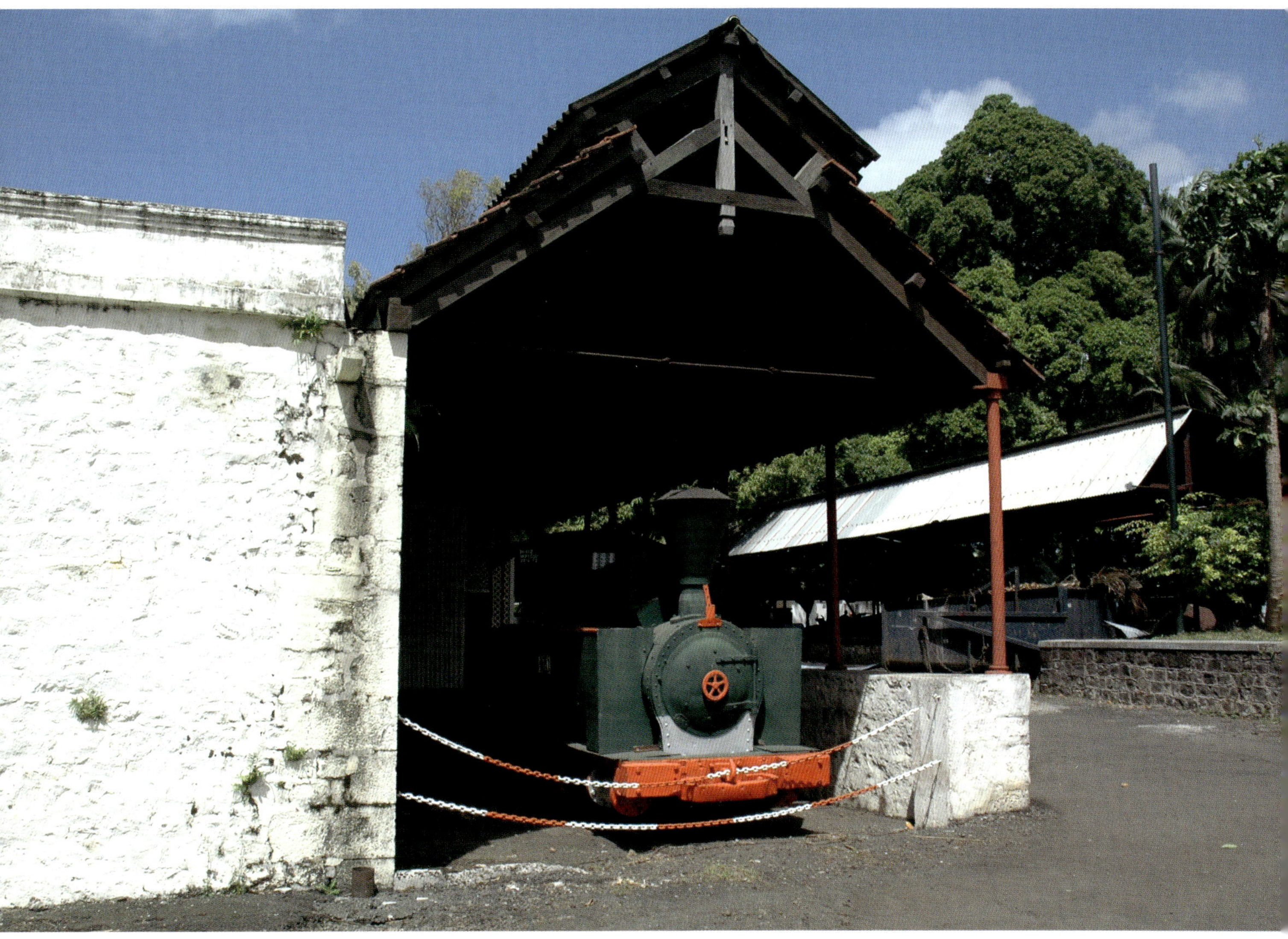

Beau Champ sugar factory in eastern Mauritius is one of the world's most advanced producers and the source of many of the speciality sugars sold in the UK. It once operated an extensive 3ft gauge system and was home to six 0-4-2s built between 1883 and 1891 by Fletcher Jennings & Co and their successors at Lowca, Cumberland. They were later rebuilt with side tanks. Two are preserved at the factory and a third, bought by Marine & Tar Products Ltd for use as a stationary boiler, is now displayed at their premises at Port Louis. 0-4-2T No 190 *Harriette* (FJ 190/1883) sits in her old shed at Beau Champ on 2 September 2005, looking for all the world as if she's awaiting her next trip, though her last inspection date in 1975 suggests she's been waiting for a long time! FJ built six similar locos from 1879 for two other sugar estates on the island with different gauges.

SOUTH AFRICA

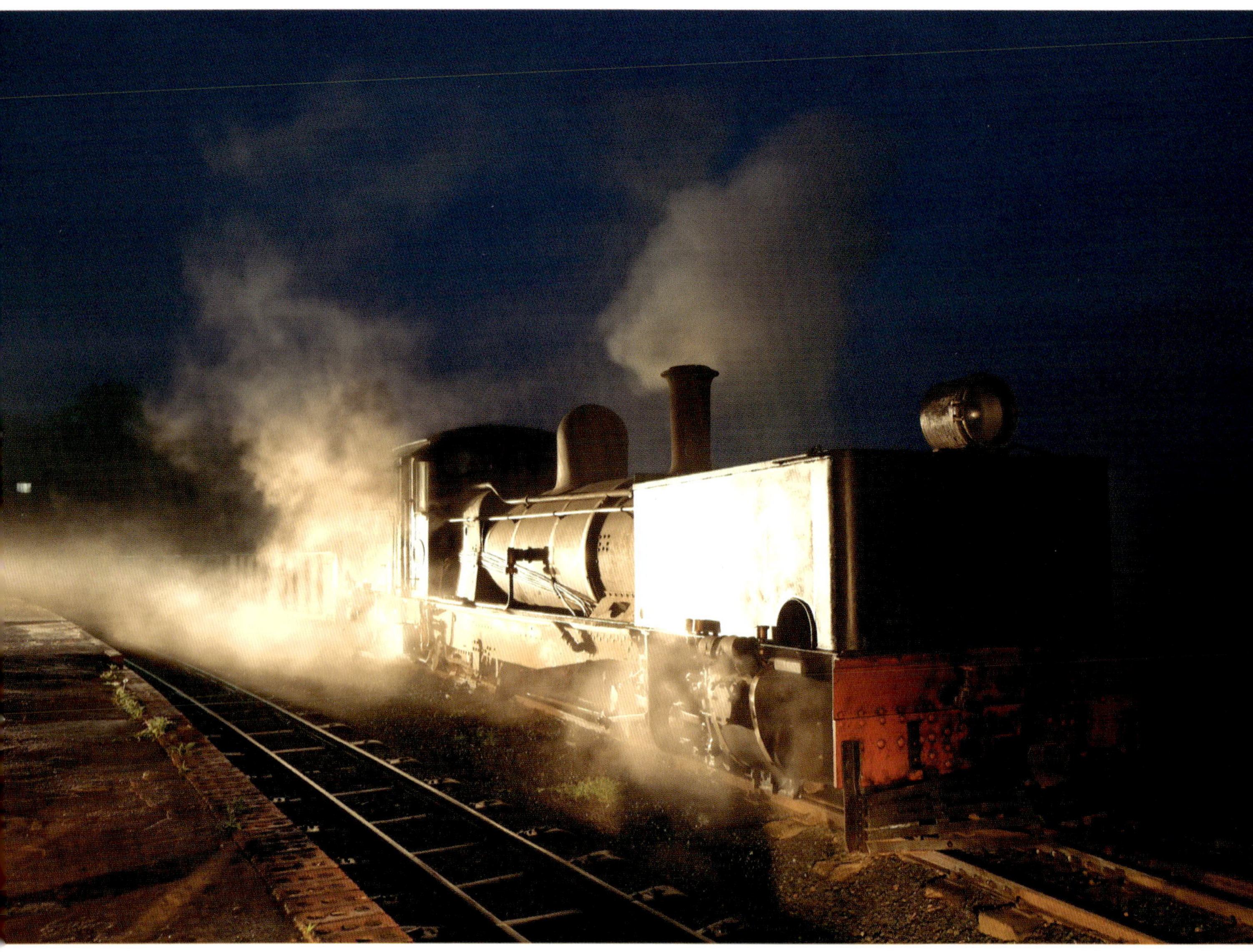

In the early evening of 29 November 2014, NGG11 class 2-6-0+0-6-2 Garratt No 55 (BP 6200/1925) stands at Allwoodburn station on a 2ft gauge branch line in KwaZulu Natal from Ixopo down into the Umzimkulu valley which is now preserved as the Paton's Country Railway. The NGG11s were South African Railways' first 2ft gauge Garratts.

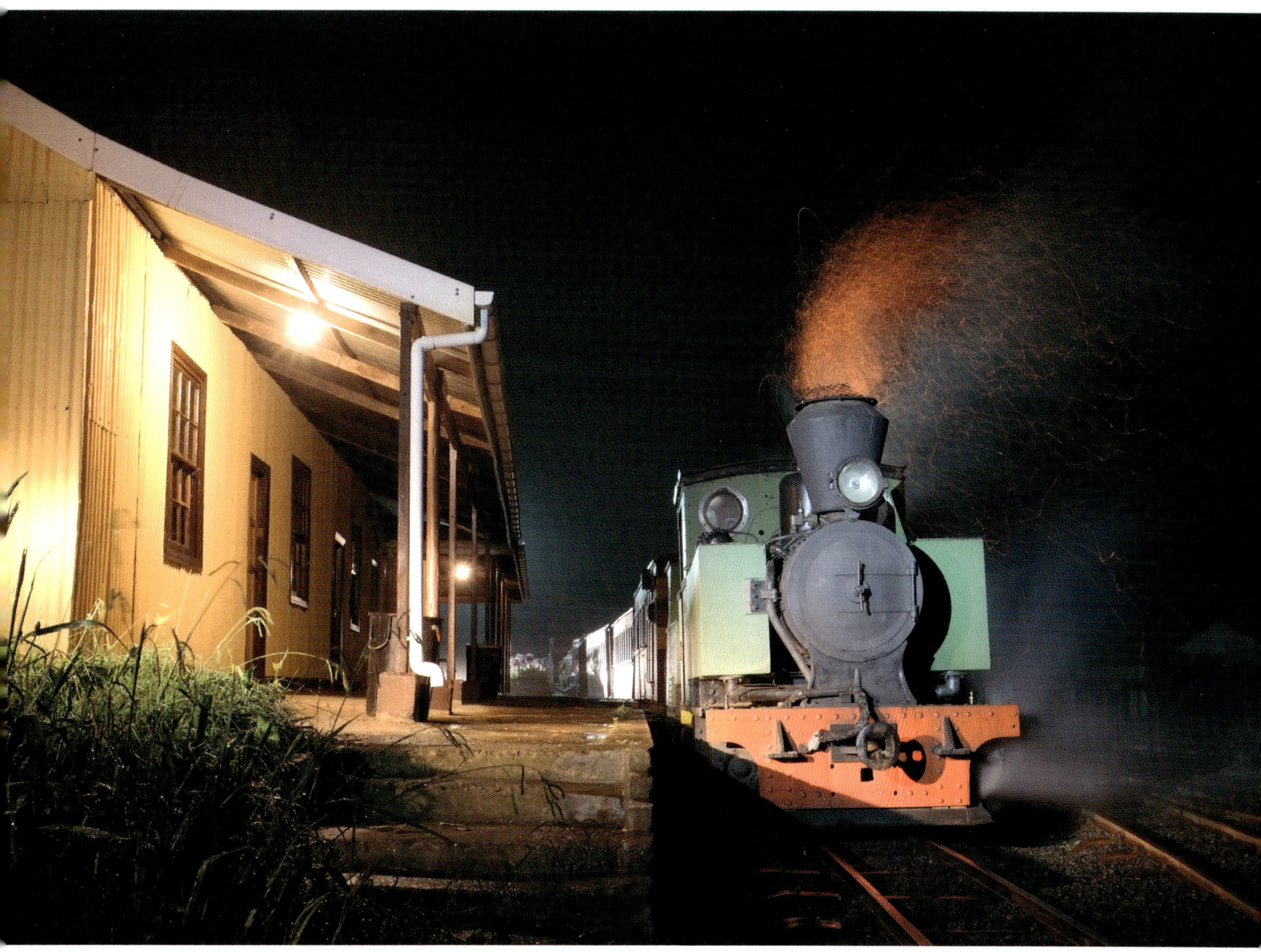

A little later, Umtwalume Valley Estates' 0-4-2T No 2 (Avonside 2065/1933) puts on a fireworks show at Allwoodburn and behind her is another 0-4-2T (Avonside 2038/1929) which worked for many years at Darnall sugar factory. The Paton's locos now burn offcuts from local eucalyptus plantations, giving a whole new meaning to the station's name! At Ixopo, the branch once joined the 2ft gauge Umzinto-Donnybrook railway, much of the track of which was lifted for reuse on the first section of the Welsh Highland near Caernarfon. Fortunately for the Paton's line, it wasn't wholly successful there. Later sections used new rail and the branch was mostly left intact.

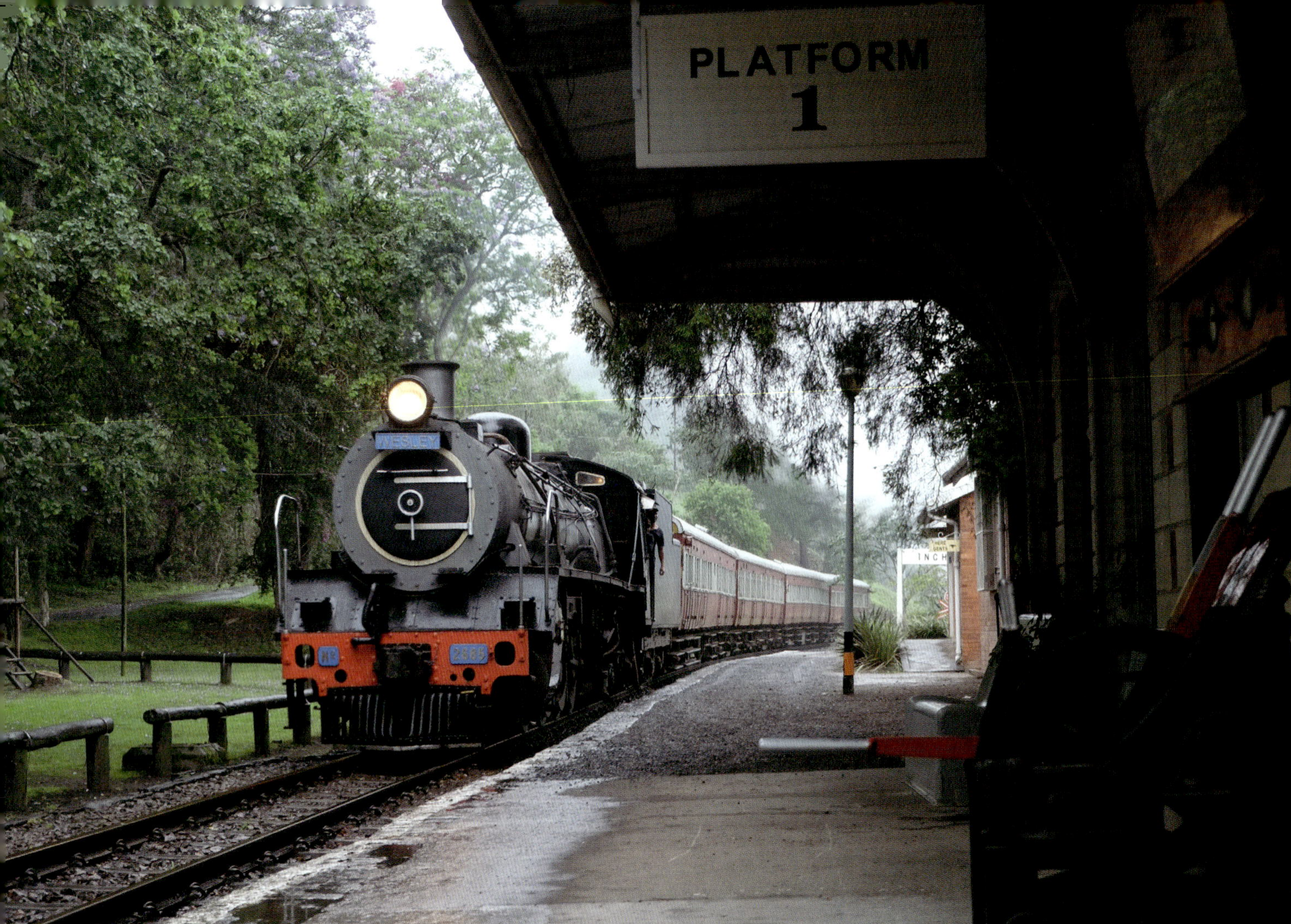

Above: On the very wet afternoon of 30 November 2014, 19D class 4-8-2 No 2685 (Borsig 14736/1938) arrives at Inchanga on the Umgeni Steam Railway. It's part of the old 3ft 6ins gauge mainline through the hills inland from Durban which has been replaced by a newer, less twisty route.

Opposite above: That evening, GMA/M 4-8-2+2-8-4 Garratt No 4074 (Henschel 28703/1954) was in steam at Creighton engine shed, a preservation site associated with the Paton's line. Here she passes 19D No 2669 (Krupp 1852/1938).

Opposite below: Sappi Saiccor's mill at Umkomaas on the Indian Ocean coast of KwaZulu Natal is the world's largest producer of chemical cellulose or dissolvable wood pulp. Production started in December 1955. It's the start of the afternoon shift at its railway on 1 December 2014 and driver Bheki Shezi climbs on board 19D No 3 (RSH 7280/1947), ex-SAR No 2767, as 19D No 2 (Škoda 928/1938), ex-SAR 2633, rests in the shed.

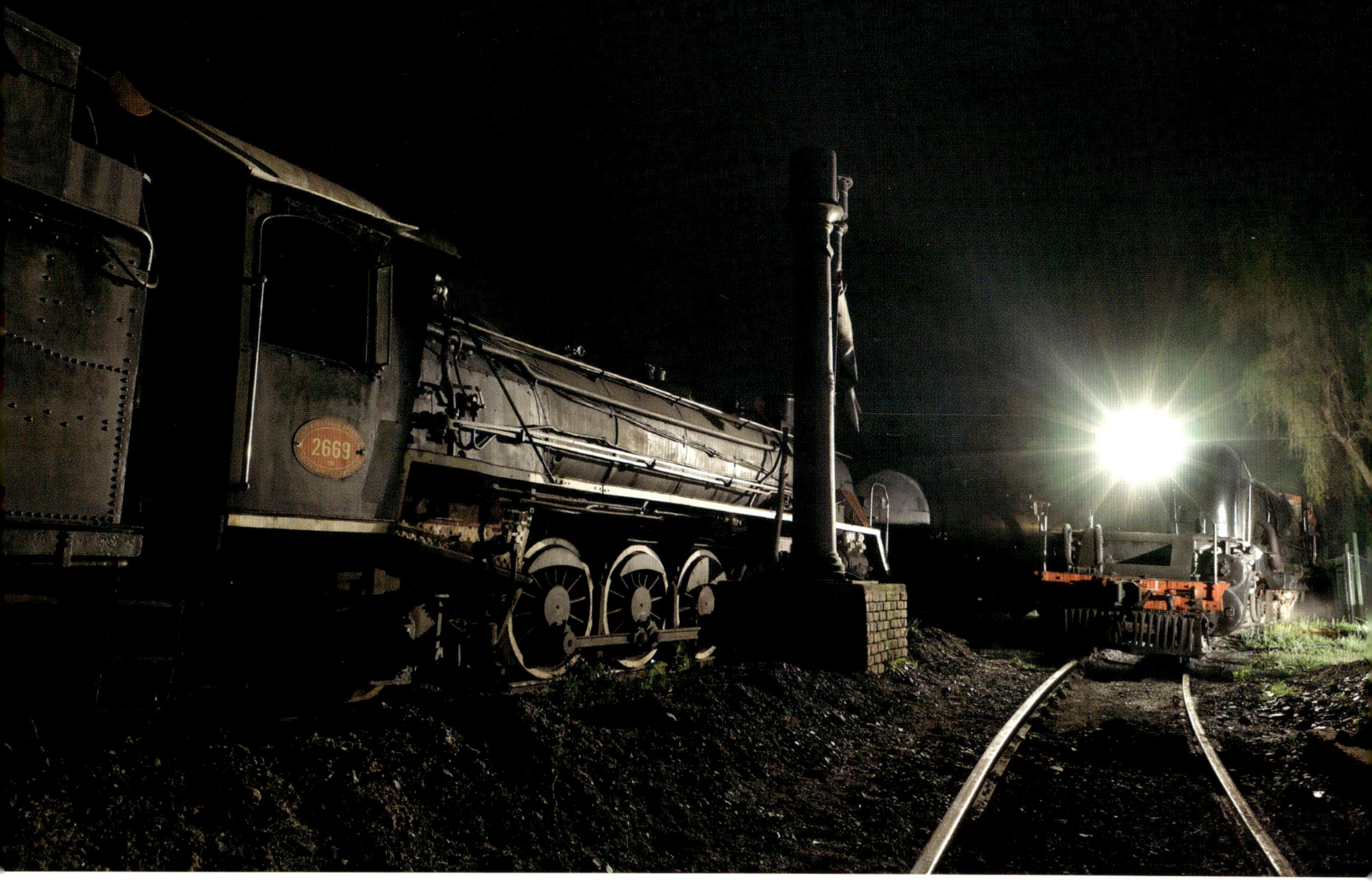

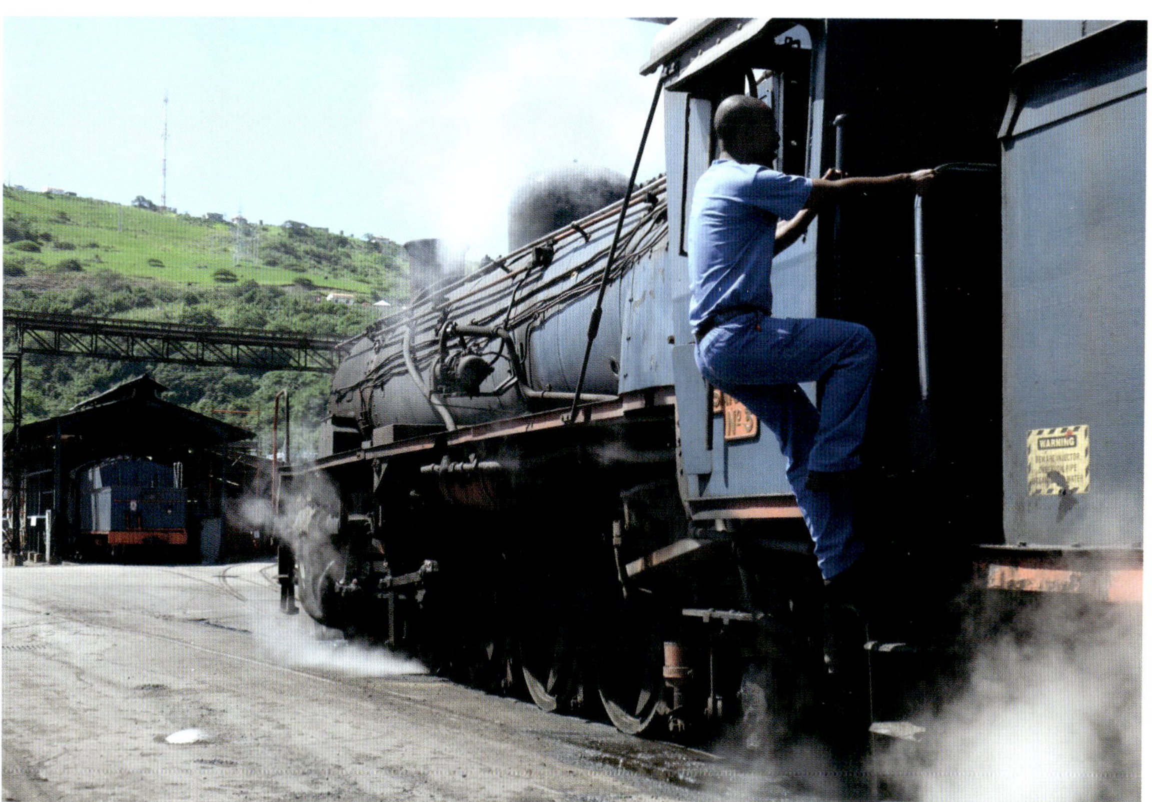
WARNING

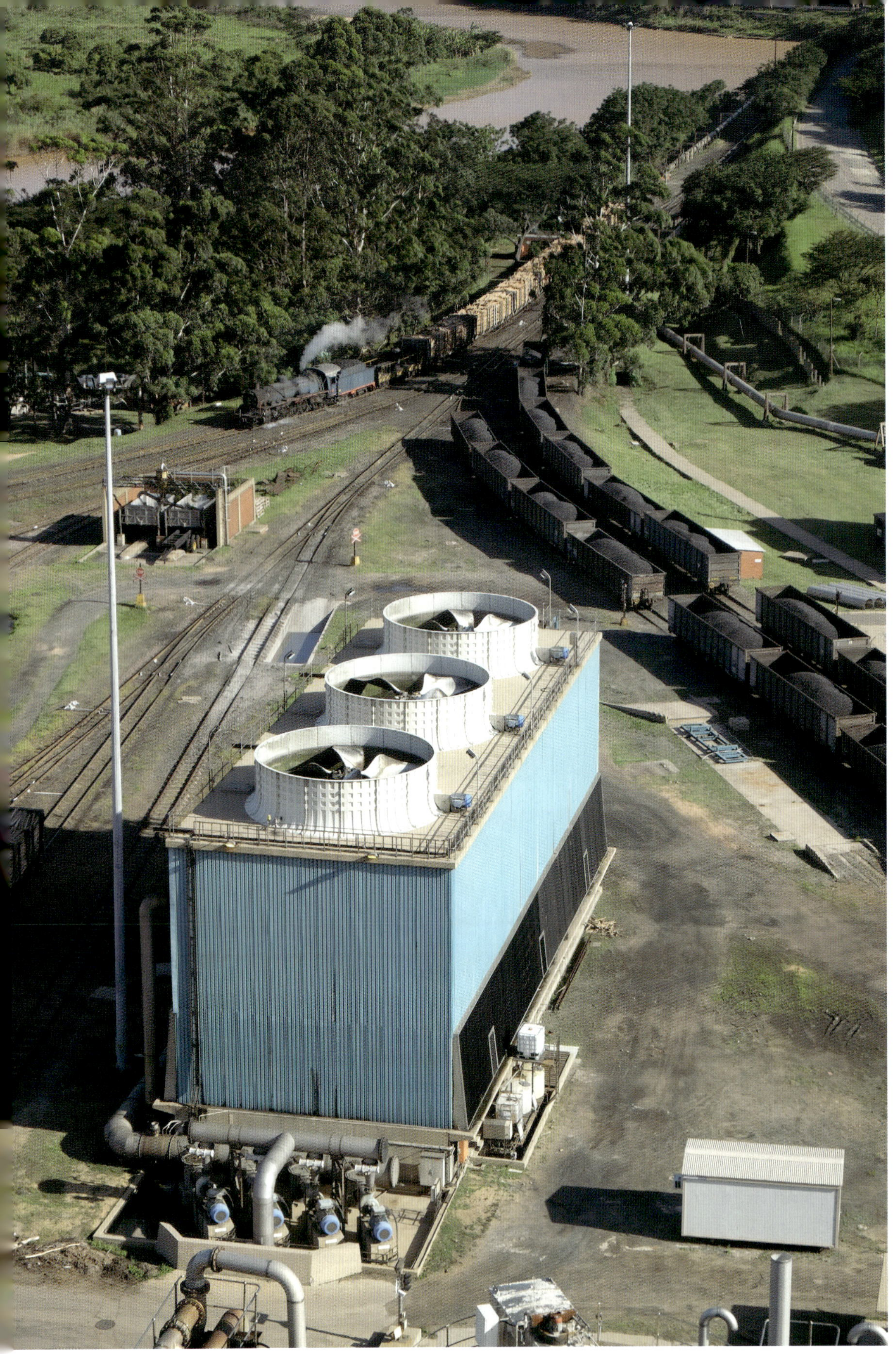

A view from the highest point at the Sappi plant as No 3 arrives on 1 December 2014. Until 2015, trainloads of the eucalyptus wood which forms its raw material and coal for its furnaces were hauled over its branch from the SAR mainline by one of its 19D's.

SYRIA

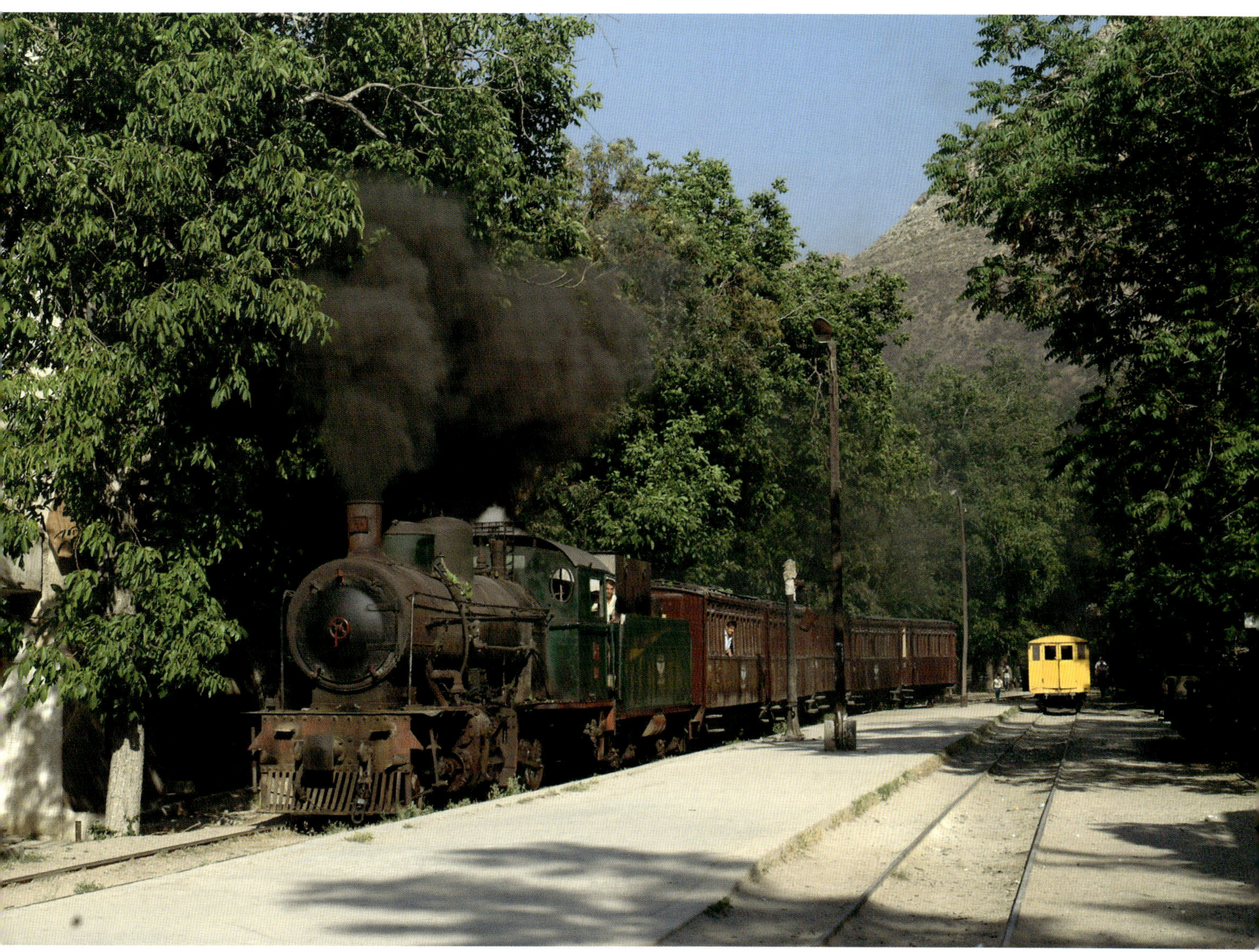

Hedjaz Railway 2-8-0 No 90 (Hartmann 3039/1906) arrives at Ain Al-Fijeh station in the outskirts of Damascus on the line to Beirut on 25 May 2005. This heavily engineered 1050mm gauge railway crossed two mountain ranges using Abt-rack sections. It opened in 1894 but by 2005 this was the westernmost point still in use.

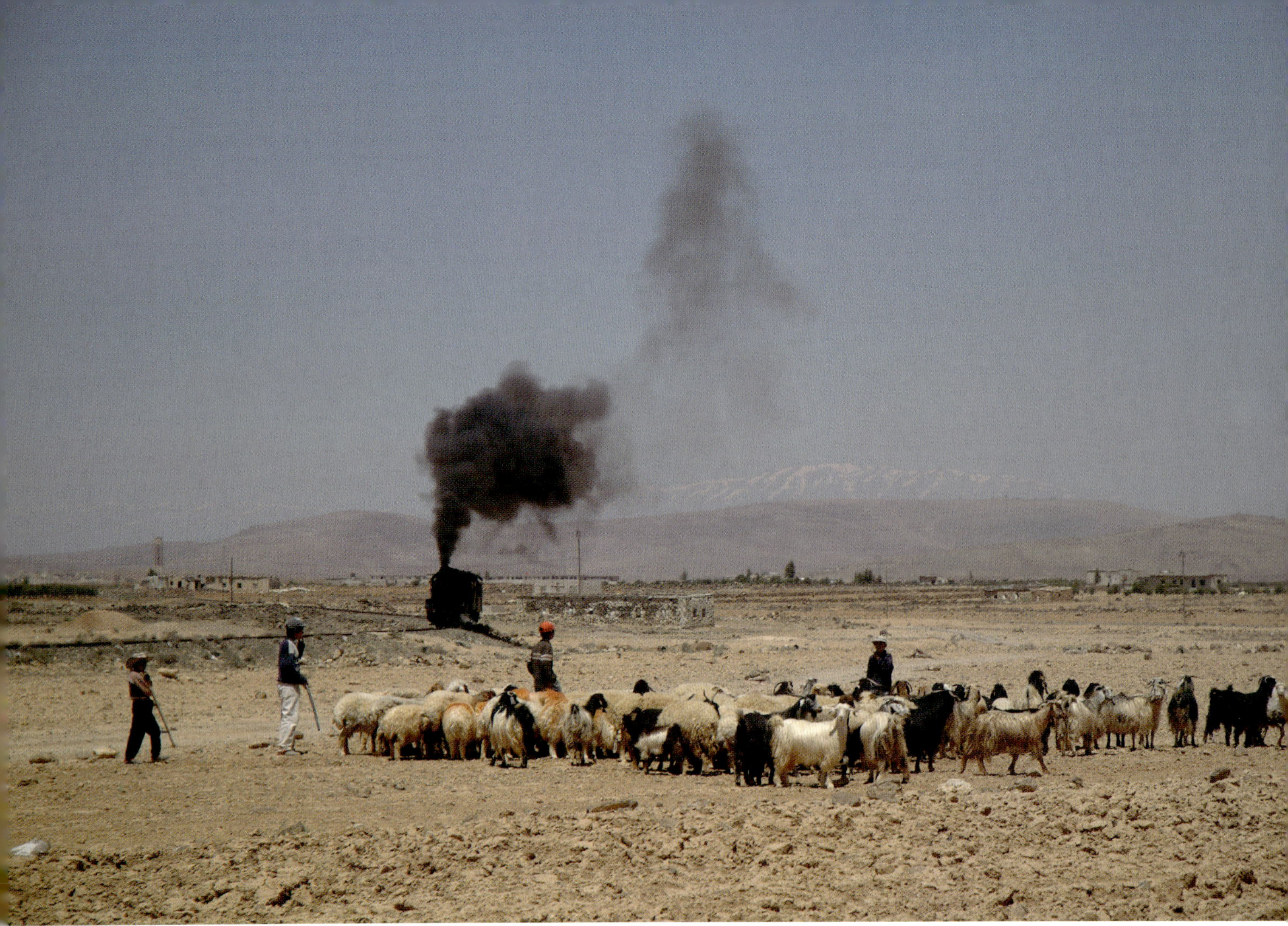

Above: At Damascus, the Beirut line joined the Hedjaz Railway, promoted by the Ottoman government to connect the city with the Muslim holy places in present-day Saudi Arabia. On 26 May 2005, 2-8-2 No 260 (Hartmann 4029/1918) runs through the arid country near Jubb As Safa. In the background there's still snow on Mount Hermon, close to where the borders of Syria, Lebanon and Israel meet.

Opposite above: Further south, the country is more fertile. No 260 crosses a dried-up stream to the north of Dera'a with more than its fair share of boulders on 26 May 2005.

Opposite below: 0-4-4-2 Mallet tank No 962 (Hartmann 3001/1906) was built for the Beirut railway. On 27 May 2005, she crosses Yarmuk bridge No 15 on the lengthy branch from the Hedjaz mainline at Dera'a which once dropped down below sea level to cross the River Jordan and ended at Haifa on the Mediterranean coast.

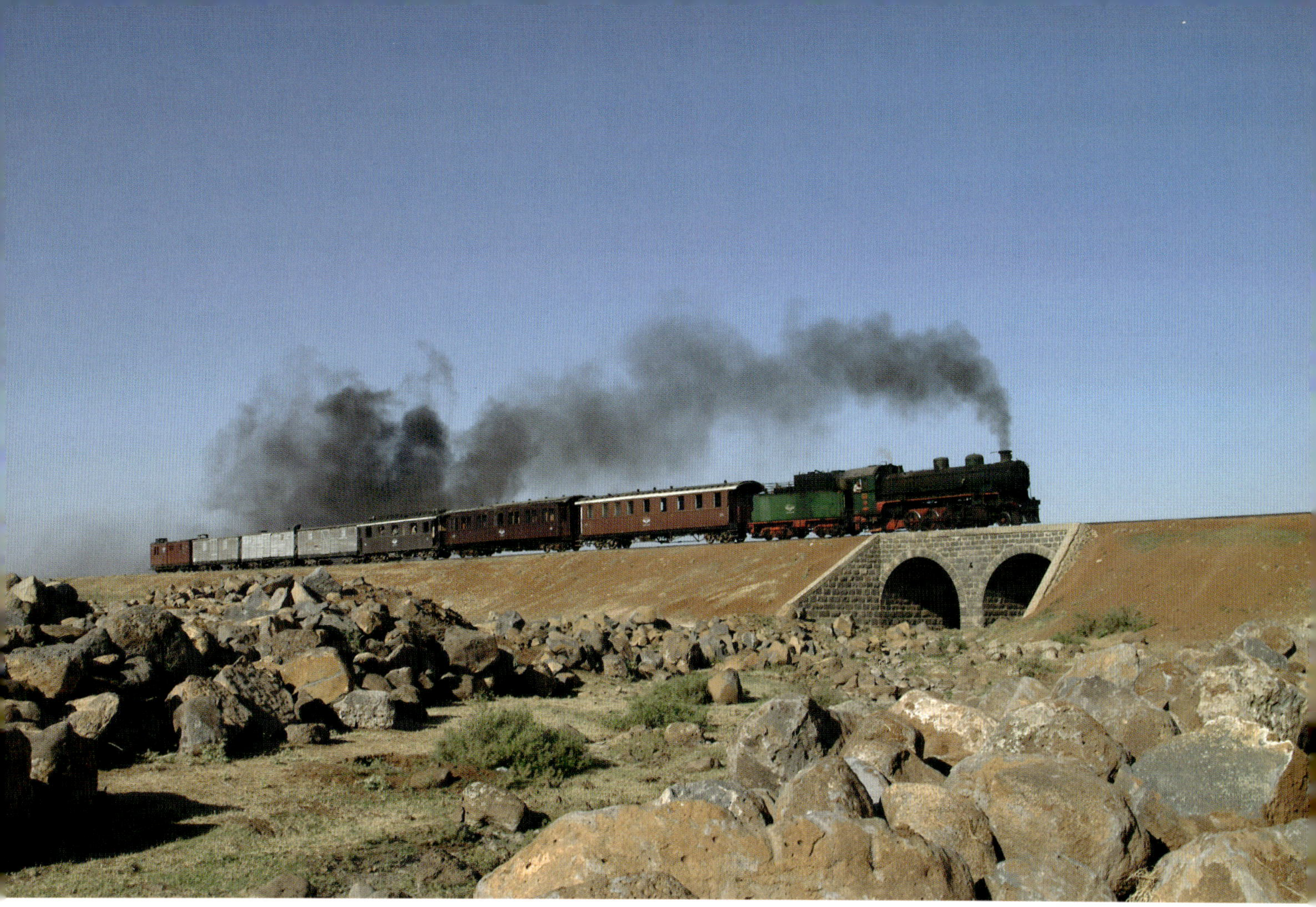

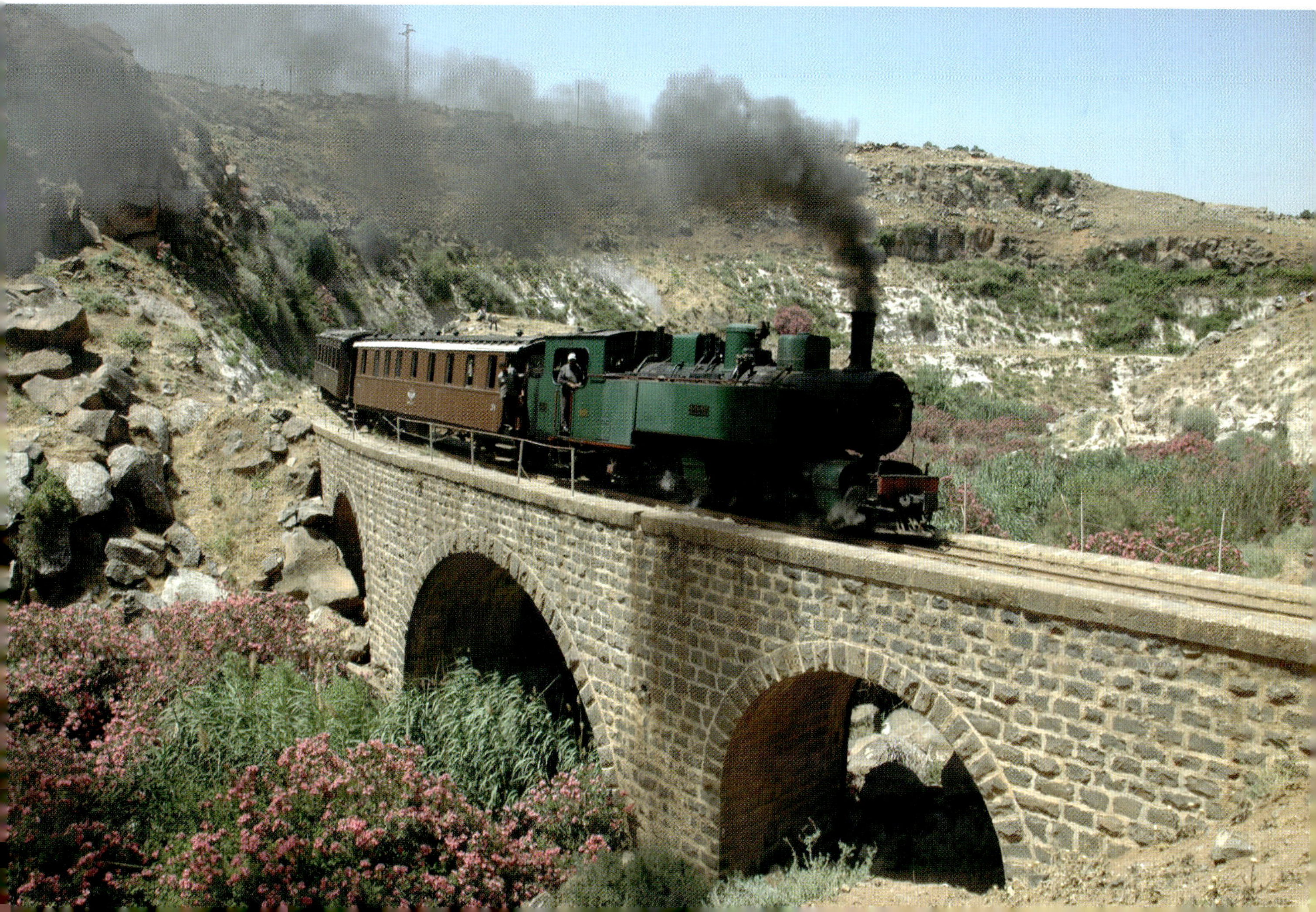

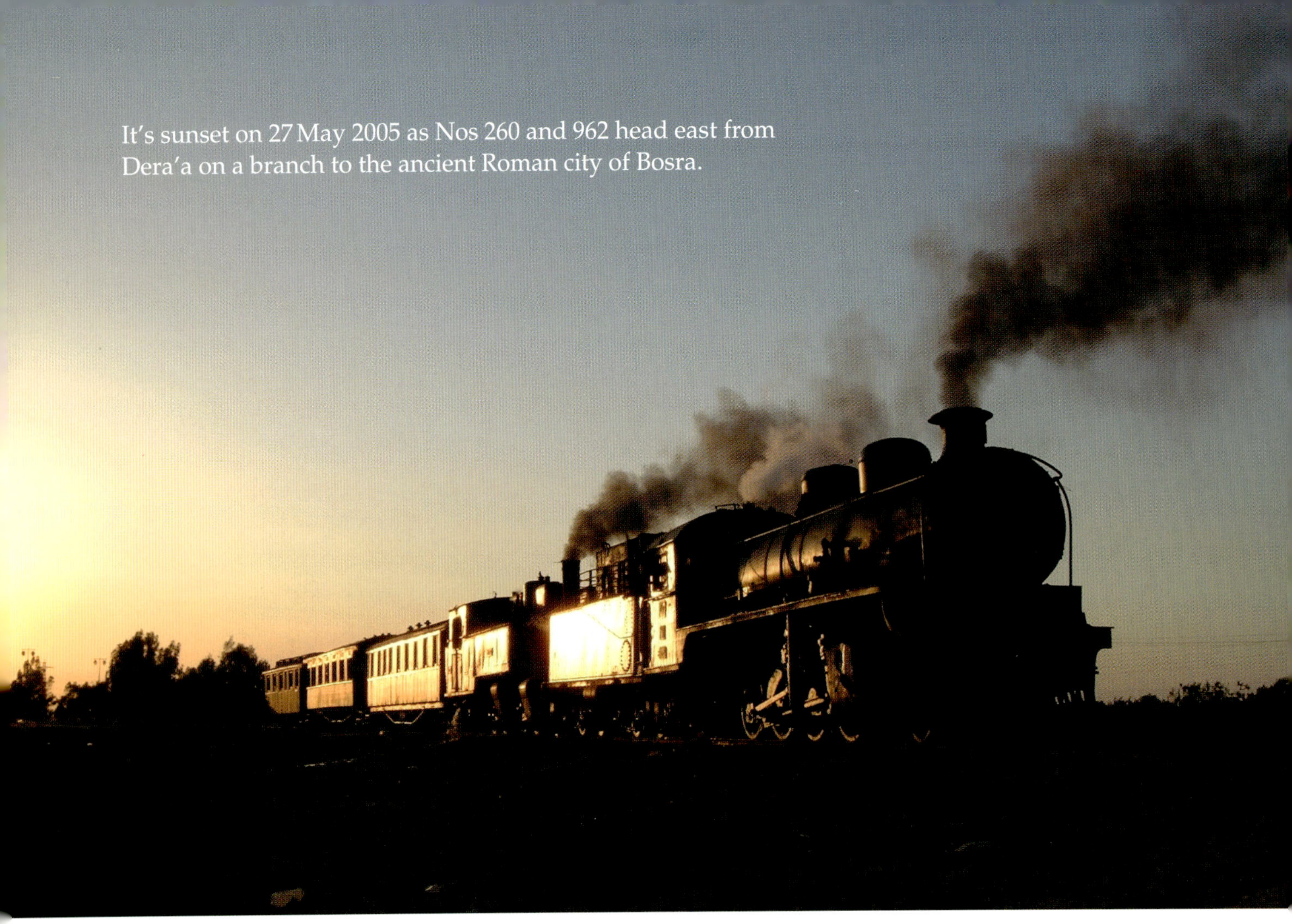

It's sunset on 27 May 2005 as Nos 260 and 962 head east from Dera'a on a branch to the ancient Roman city of Bosra.

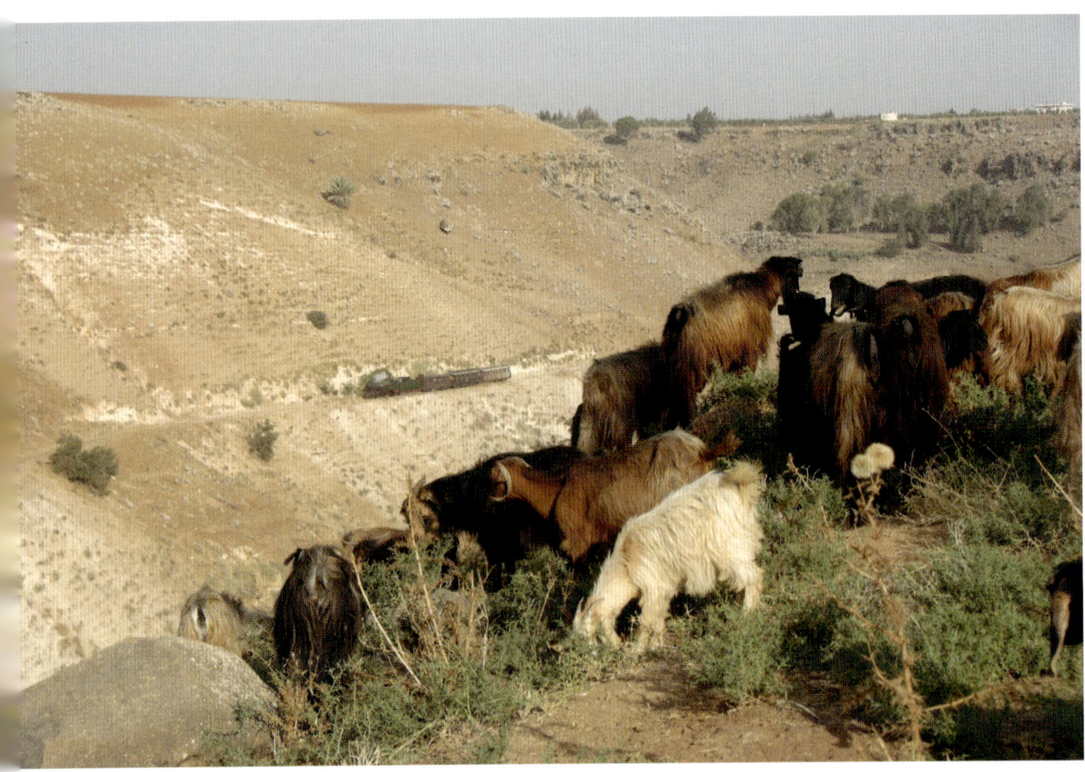

Goats graze beside the line in the Yarmuk gorge as 2-8-0 No 160 (Borsig 9009/1914), built for the Peloponnese railway but diverted during the First World War, climbs up its opposite side on 19 October 2007. Unhappy Syria still had several working steam locos when its dreadful civil war began in 2011.

JORDAN

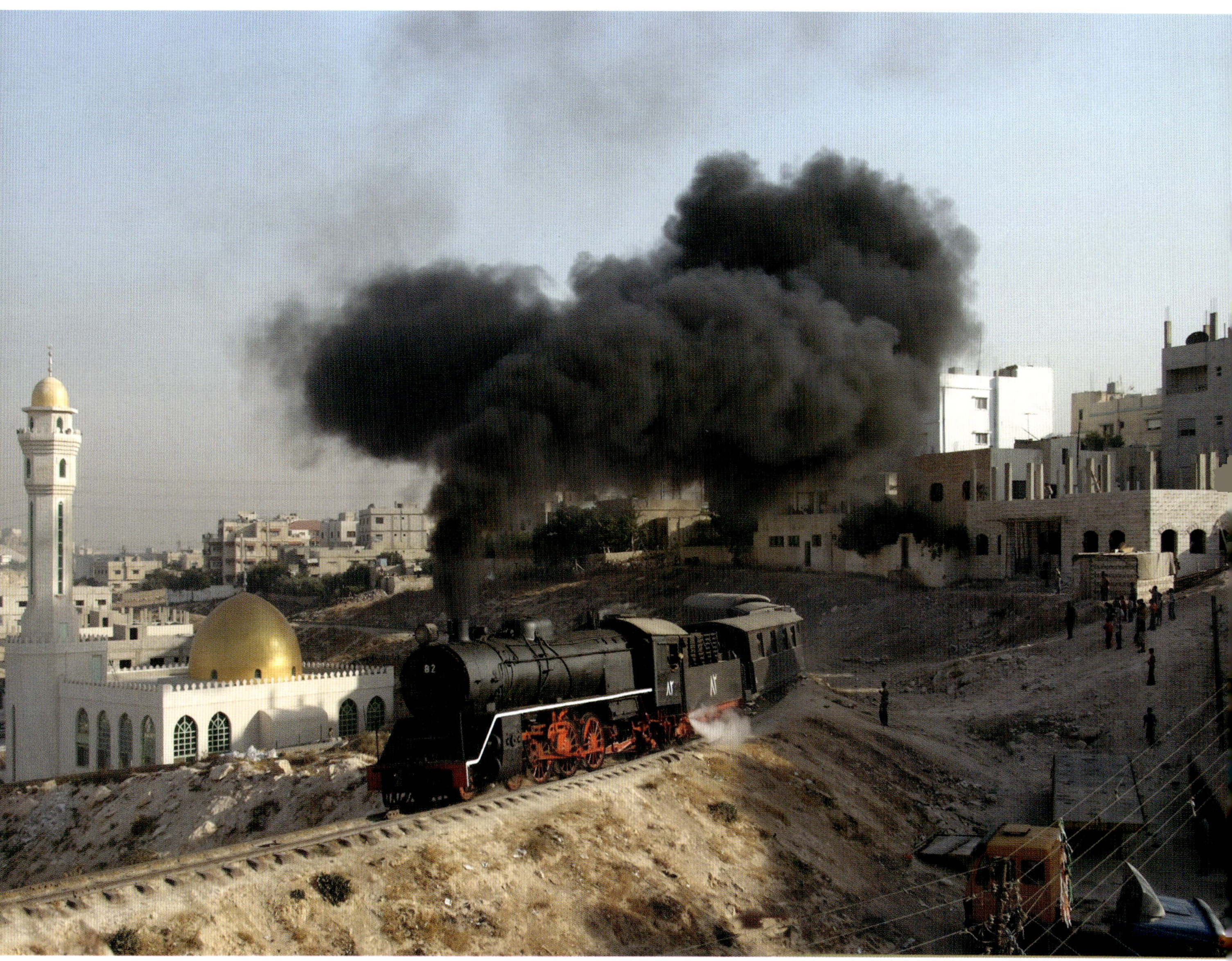

The Jordanians bought new steam locos for their section of the Hedjaz Railway in the 1950s. Pacific No 82 (Nippon 1610/1953) climbs through the southern suburbs of Amman on 20 October 2007.

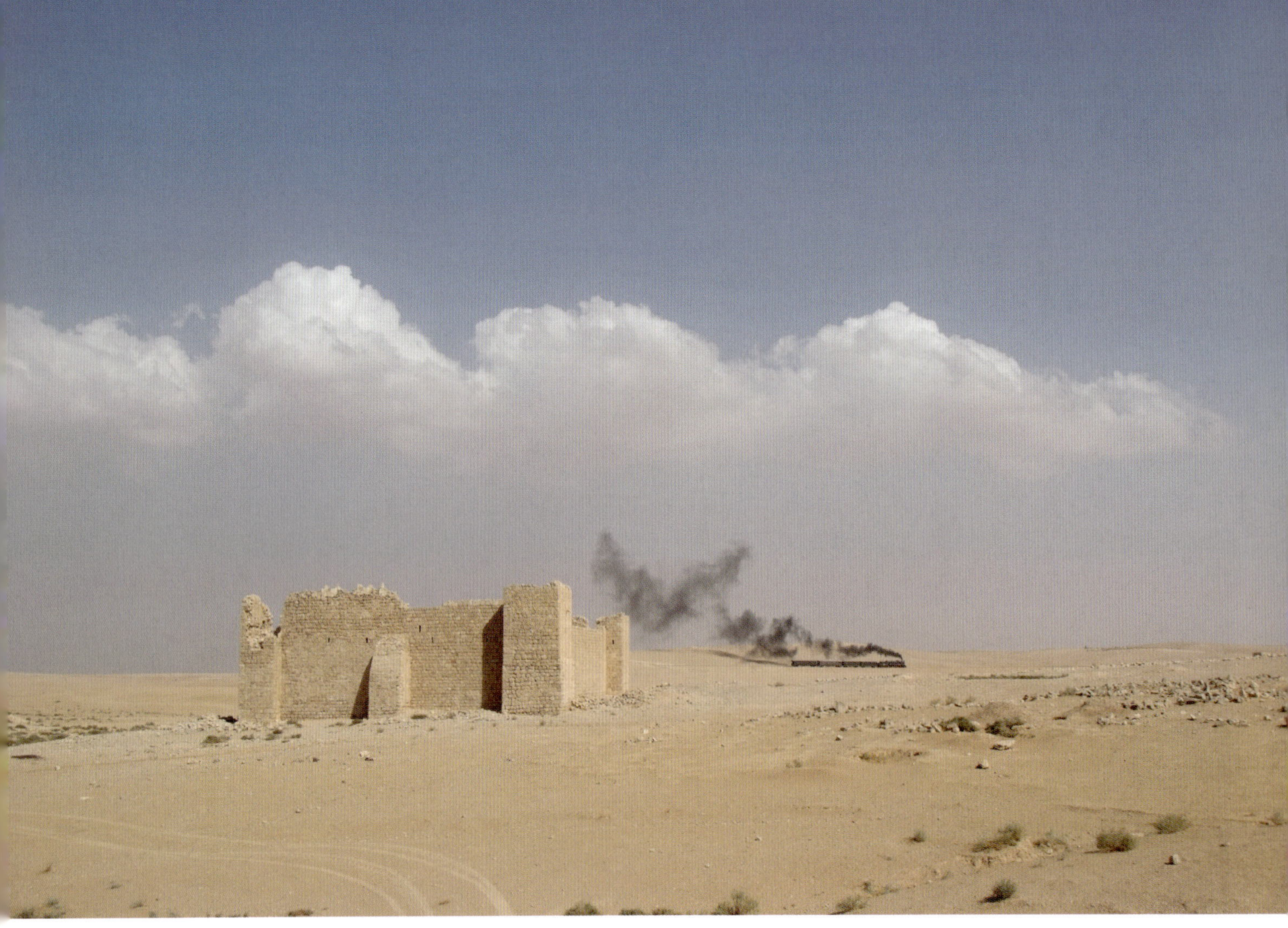

Above: No 82 and her train look lost out in the desert as they pass a ruined Ottoman fort on 20 October 2007. She was one of five Pacifics supplied in 1957 which were originally built as metre gauge locos for the Thai railways but never delivered.

Opposite above: 2-8-2 No 51 (Jung 12081/1955) runs through Al Zarqa in the northern outskirts of Amman in the late afternoon of 19 October 2007.

Opposite below: 2-8-2 No 71 (HSP 2144/1955) south of Amman on 21 October 2007. She was one of a batch from the Belgian builder consisting of three 2-8-2s and three 2-6-2Ts. There were also three RSH-built Indian standard YD class 2-8-2s. Many of the 1950s locos still exist in and around the city.

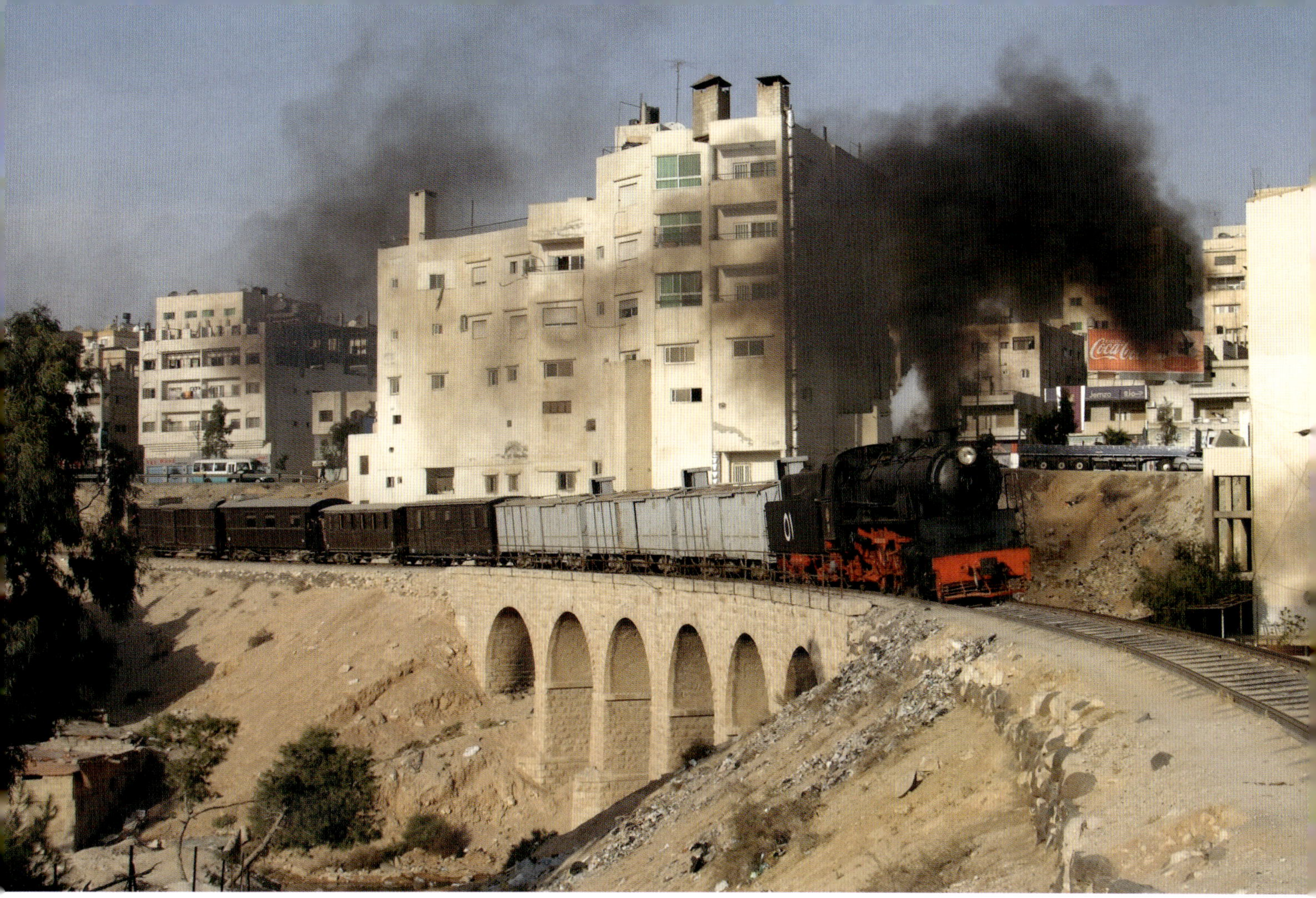

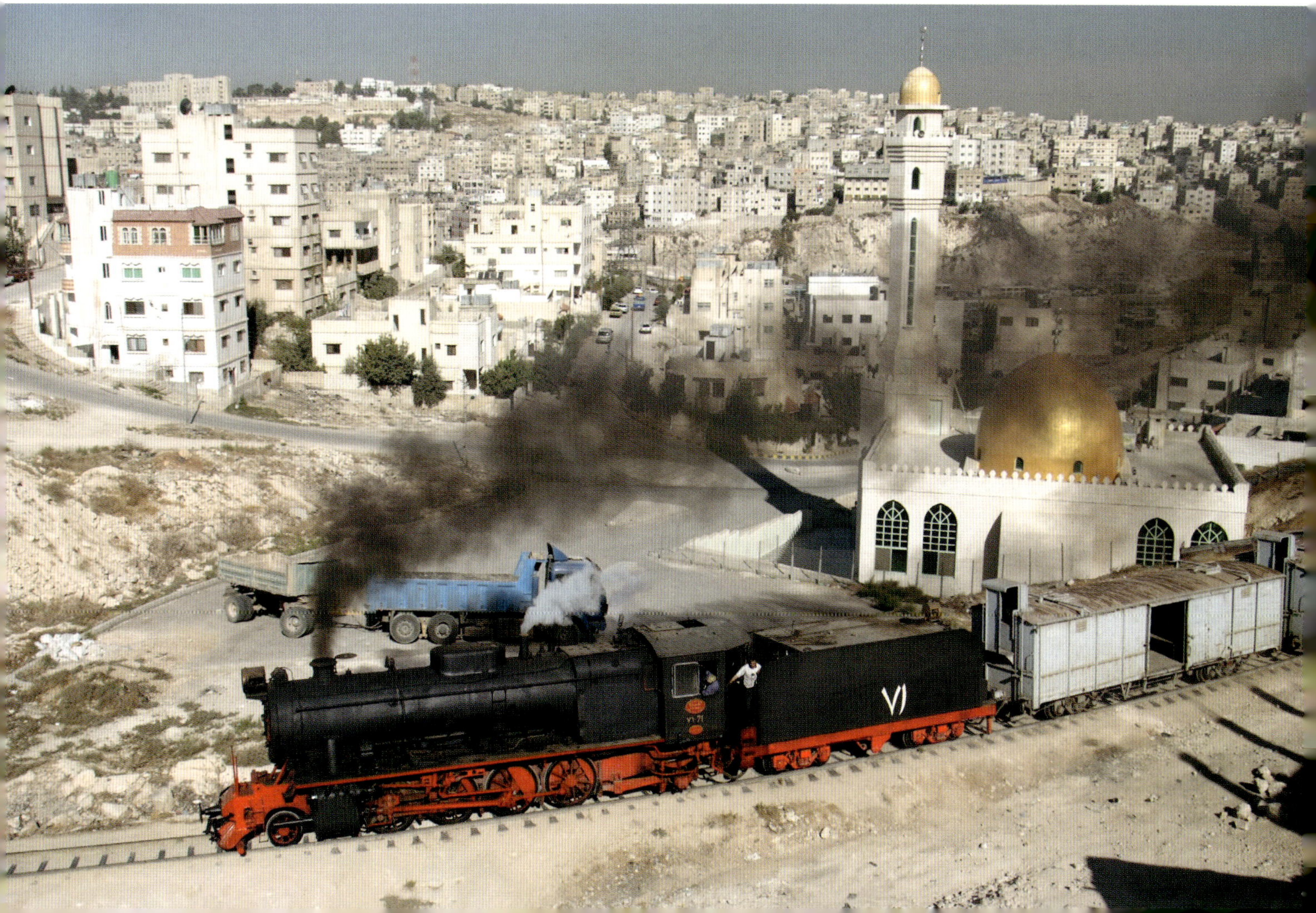

PAKISTAN

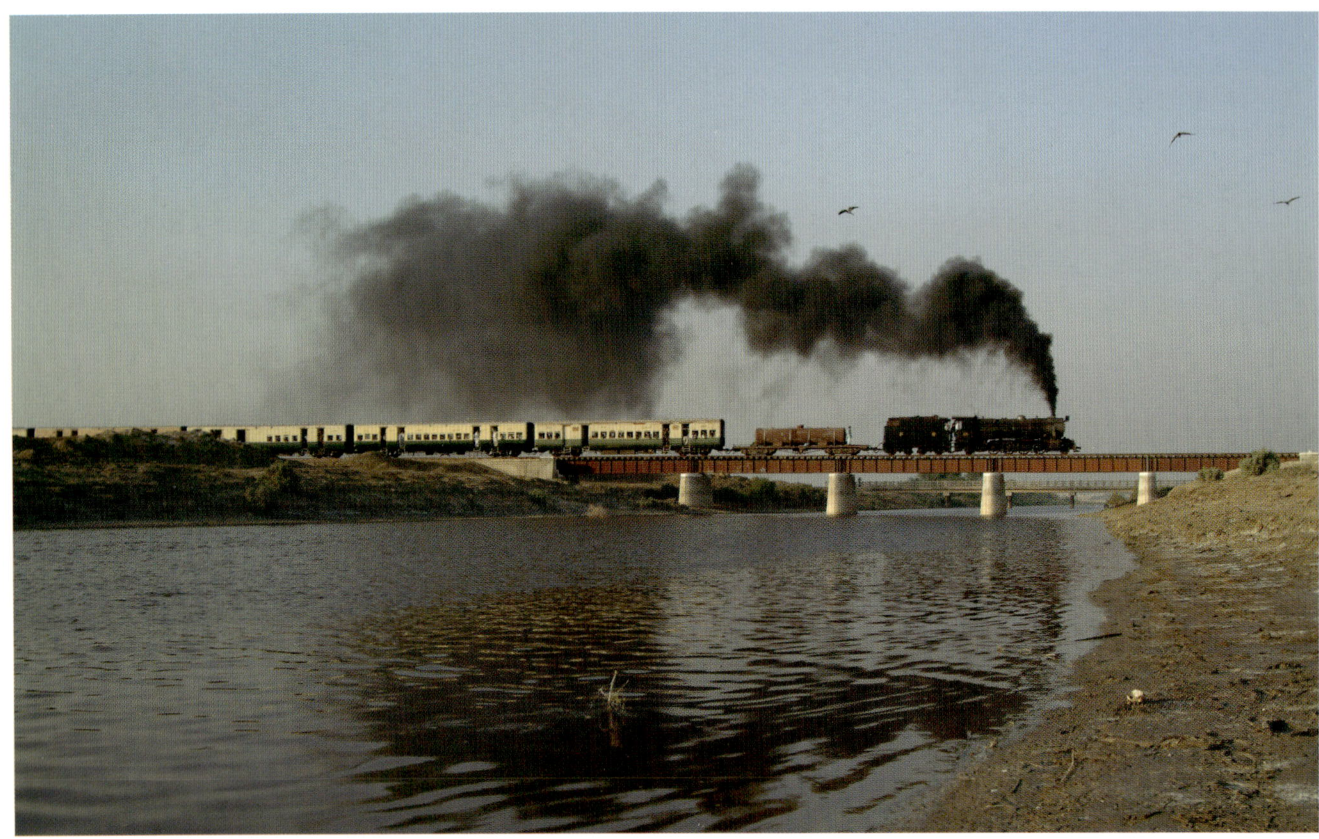

Above: On 29 November 2004 YD 2-8-2 No 519 (VF 4402/1929) crosses the Gihori irrigation canal east of Jamrao with the 15.00hrs train to Khokhrapar on the metre gauge Mirpur Khas network in southern Pakistan. In pre-independence days it formed part of the Jodhpur Railway, based in present-day India. For many years this line across the Thar desert continued in use mainly to serve the numerous army camps along Pakistan's sensitive eastern border.

Opposite above: YD 2-8-2s Nos 518 (VF 4401/1929) and 524 (Ajmer/1932) at Mirpur Khas shed on the evening of 1 December 2004. Nos 518 and 519 were built for the Assam-Bengal Railway as their no's 218 and 219. The Bombay, Baroda and Central India Railway built No 524 at their Ajmer works but she was immediately transferred to the Assam-Bengal as their number 264. All the YD's at Mirpur Khas worked in the old East Pakistan, now Bangladesh, until moving west in 1954.

Opposite below: SP class 4-6-0 No 138 (KS 4120/1921), built to a classic Edwardian design, heads the Mirpur Khas to Nawabshah branch train at sunrise on 1 December 2004. This service only operated twice a month. There were no non-enthusiast passengers and the friendly operating staff made many run-pasts for us. The mainline to Khokhrapar was converted to broad gauge and reconnected to the Indian system in 2005 and its two branches were closed.

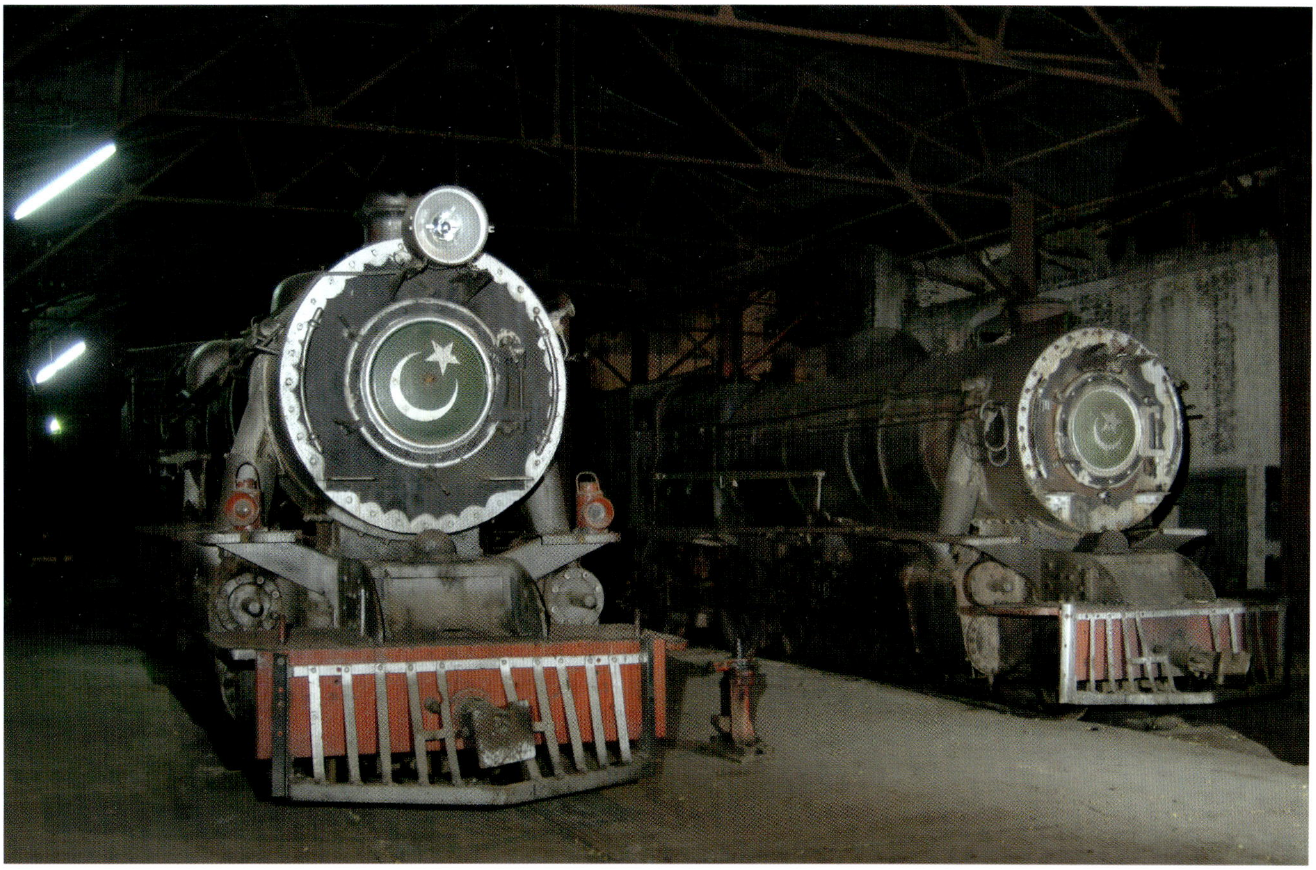

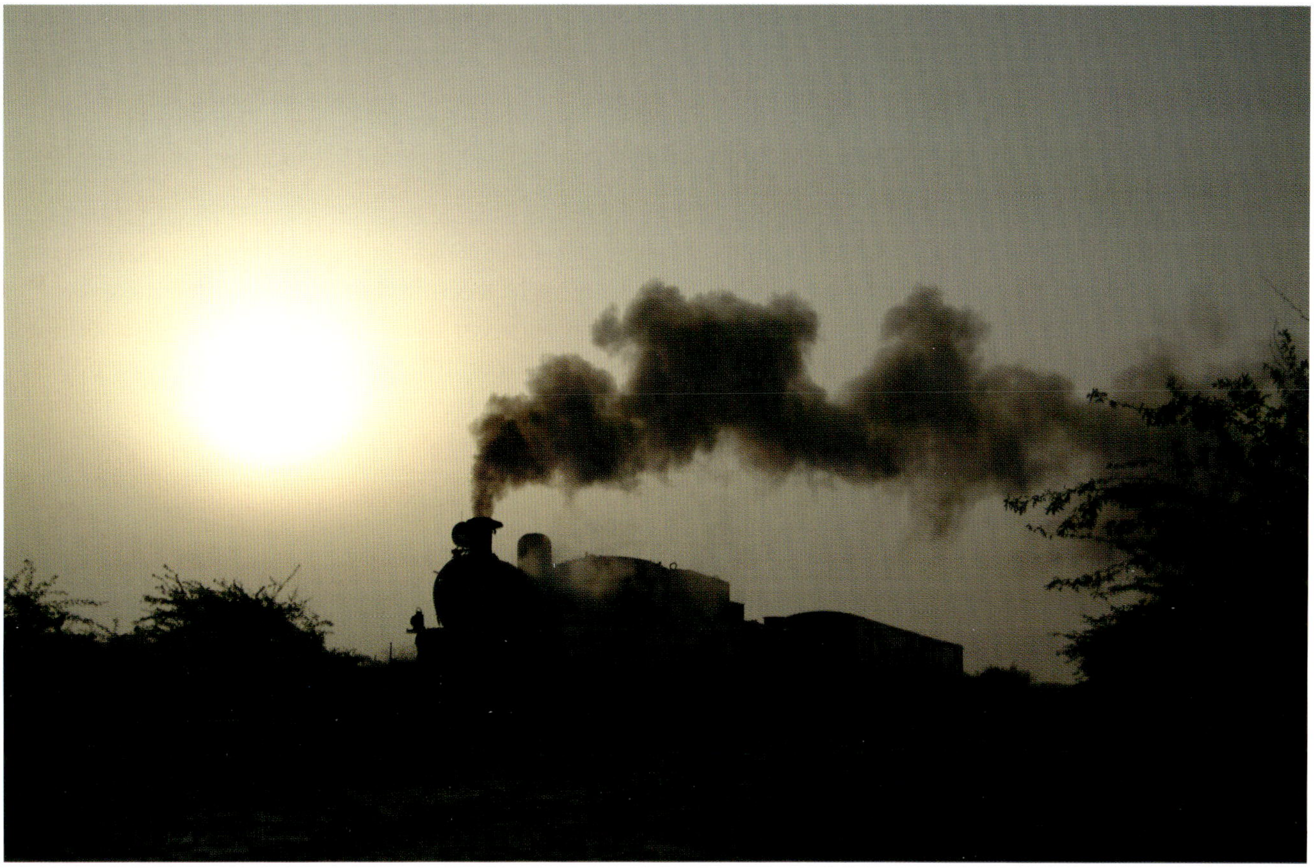

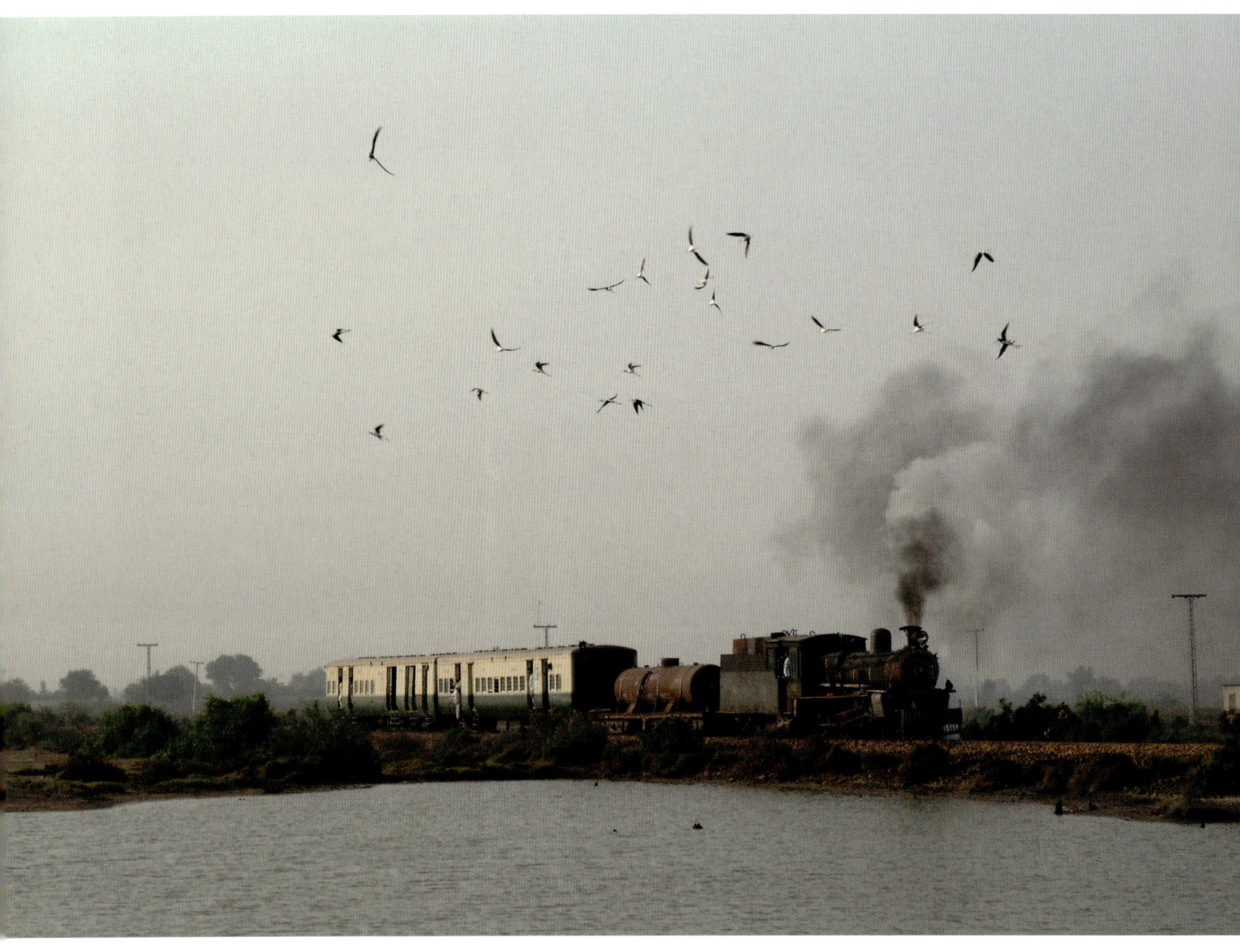

No 138 scatters the birds as she approaches Khadro station on 1 December 2004. The Jodhpur Railway continued to work the lines around Mirpur Khas for almost one year after partition, in the aftermath of which its staff moved enormous numbers of refugees to safety in both directions across the new border in very difficult conditions and the appalling communal violence elsewhere was mostly avoided. The Pakistanis took over on 31 July 1948. The JR handed over four SPs, three of which were still in service in 2004. They ran under the same numbers for all their long lifetimes. As I write this all these 2-8-2s and 4-6-0s are still at Mirpur Khas shed.

INDIA

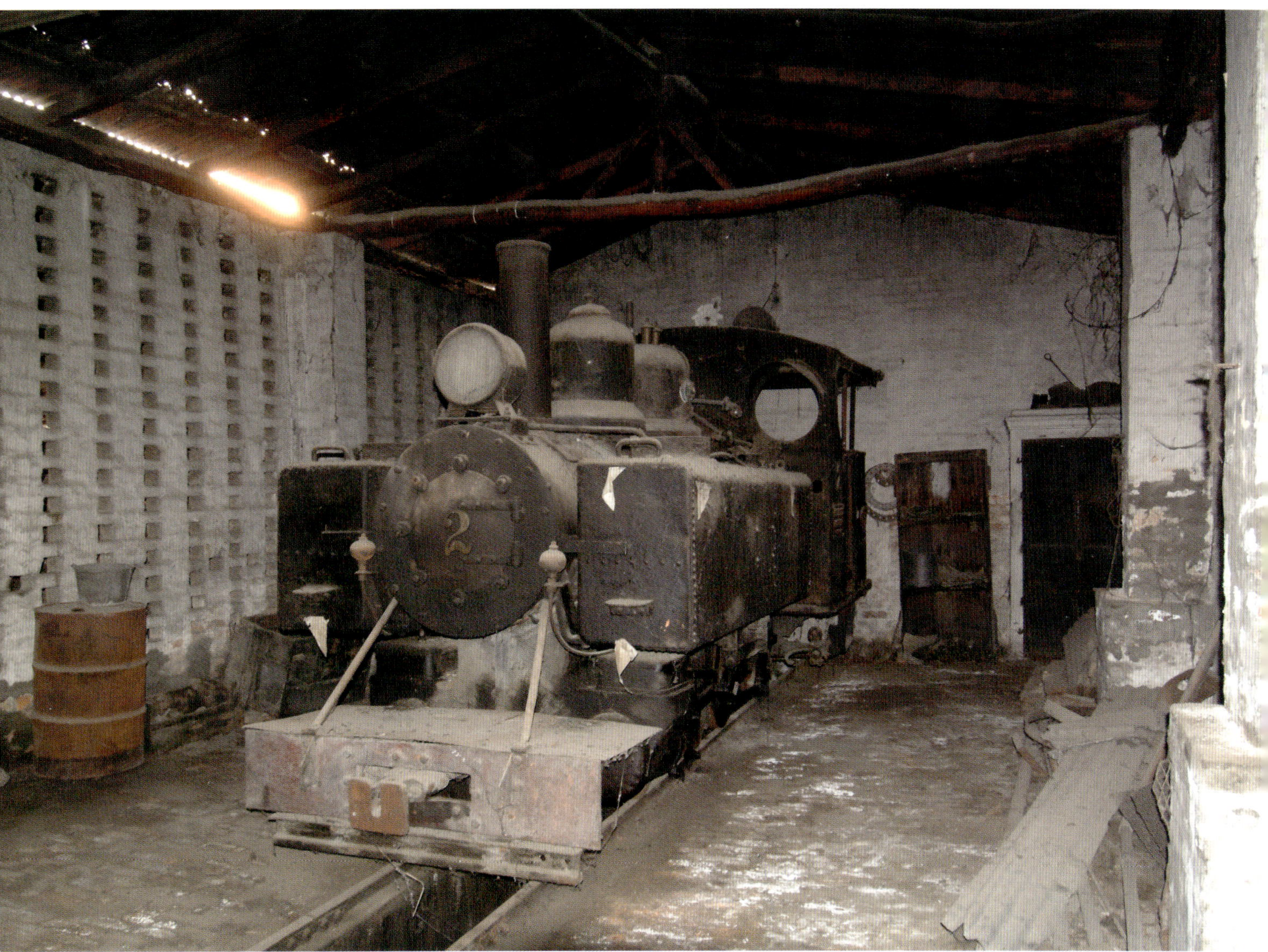

Motipur sugar factory opened in 1933 and acquired some fascinating locos. It was compulsorily acquired by the Bihar state government in 1985 and closed twelve years later. Because of recurring litigation, the locos are still there and on 16 March 2004 No 2 (Baldwin 45231/1917) sits at the back of the 2ft gauge shed. She's one of 495 class 10-12-D 4-6-0Ts which Baldwin built for the British army during the First World War, fifty of which ended up in India. Most were extensively altered over the years but No 2 was still in her original condition – a remarkable survivor. There was virtually no light in the shed and photography presented an interesting challenge!

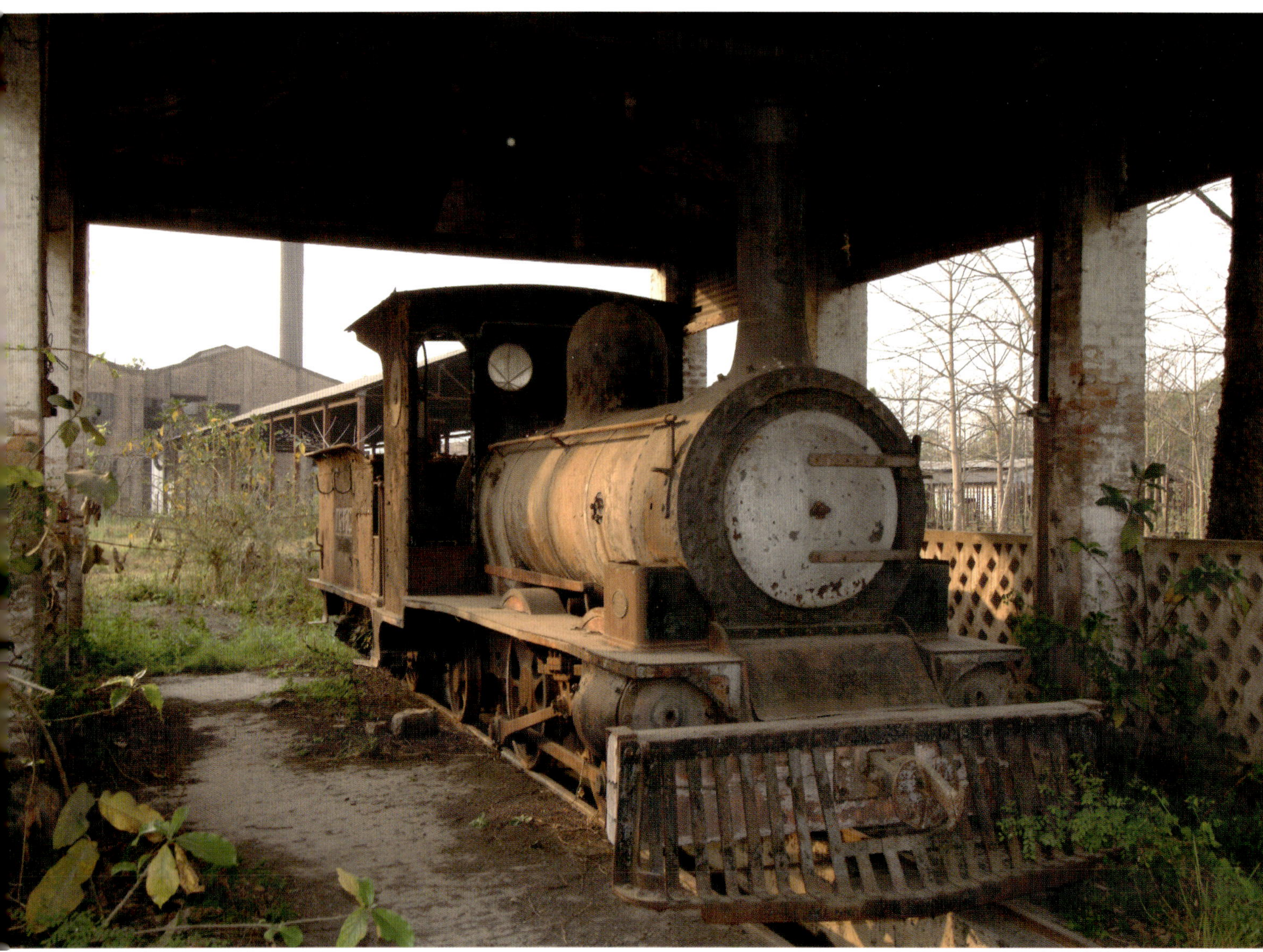

Above: The identity of Motipur 0-4-2 No 3, formerly BB&CIR No 917, is an enigma. She's the only Indian State Railways metre gauge E class loco to survive in anything like her original condition and was sold to Motipur in 1933. There are no surviving records saying who built her. Her works plates are no help at all as one came from Vulcan Foundry in 1876 and the other from Neilson in 1875! Here she stands in her open-sided shed on 16 March 2004. The Es were built in considerable numbers from 1874, just two years after the country's first metre gauge line opened. They worked throughout much of India and Burma from where some moved on to help build Malaya's railways. In 1886 Sharp Stewart built two for the Welsh railway in Patagonia.

Opposite: The 2ft gauge Darjeeling Himalayan Railway, built in 1880 and 1881 to serve India's first hill station, is for the most part a heavily graded and twisty roadside tramway and in the hills only leaves the road when the gradient is too steep and Z reverses or loops were built. Here B class 0-4-0ST No 805 (NB 23300/1925) approaches a Z reverse near Agony Point with a test train on 18 March 2004. I was part of a small group driving up to Darjeeling for a four-day stay. This train should have been a bonus but word went out overnight from headquarters at Guwahati grounding all steam locos and so it was the only working we saw.

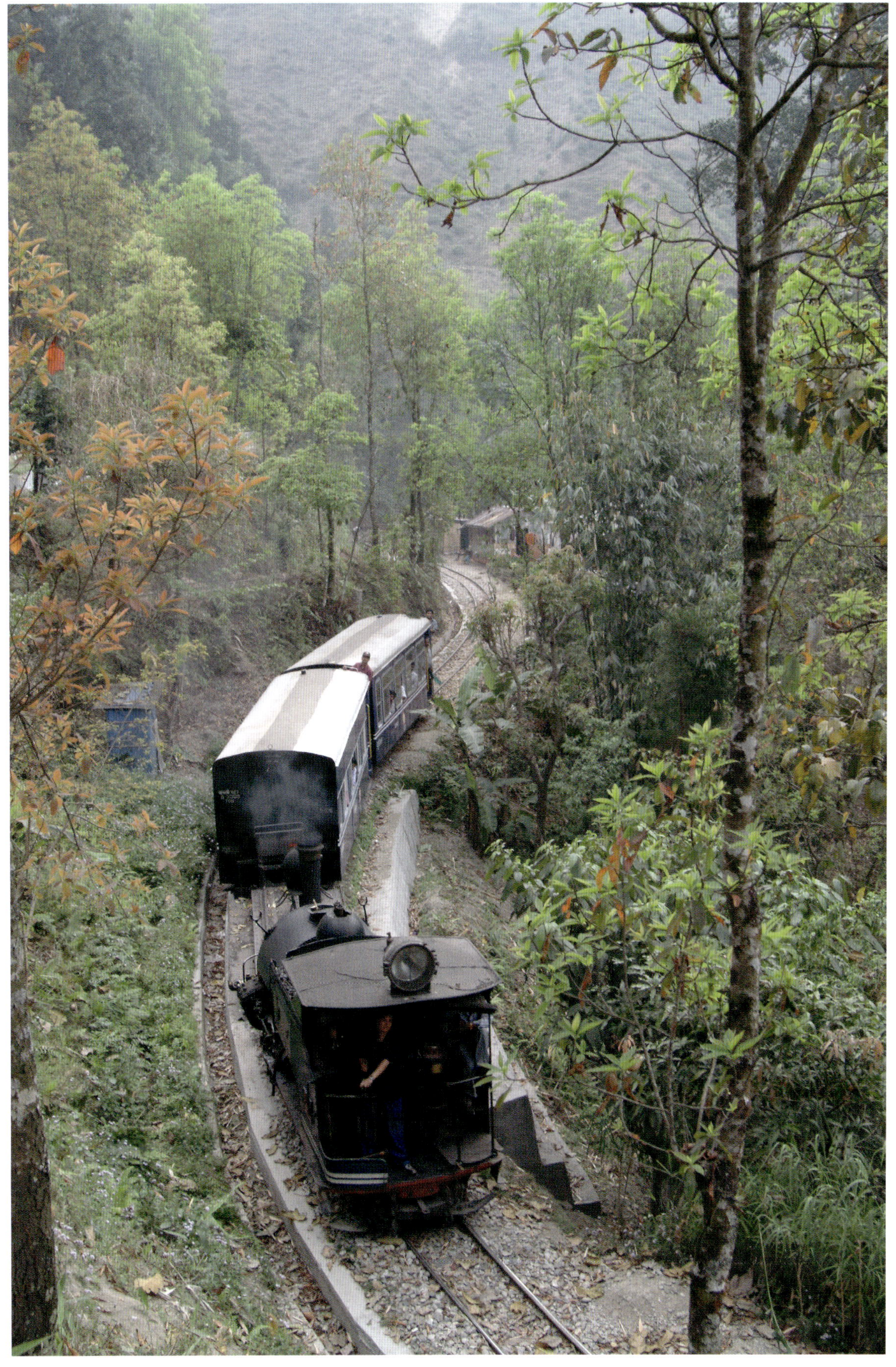

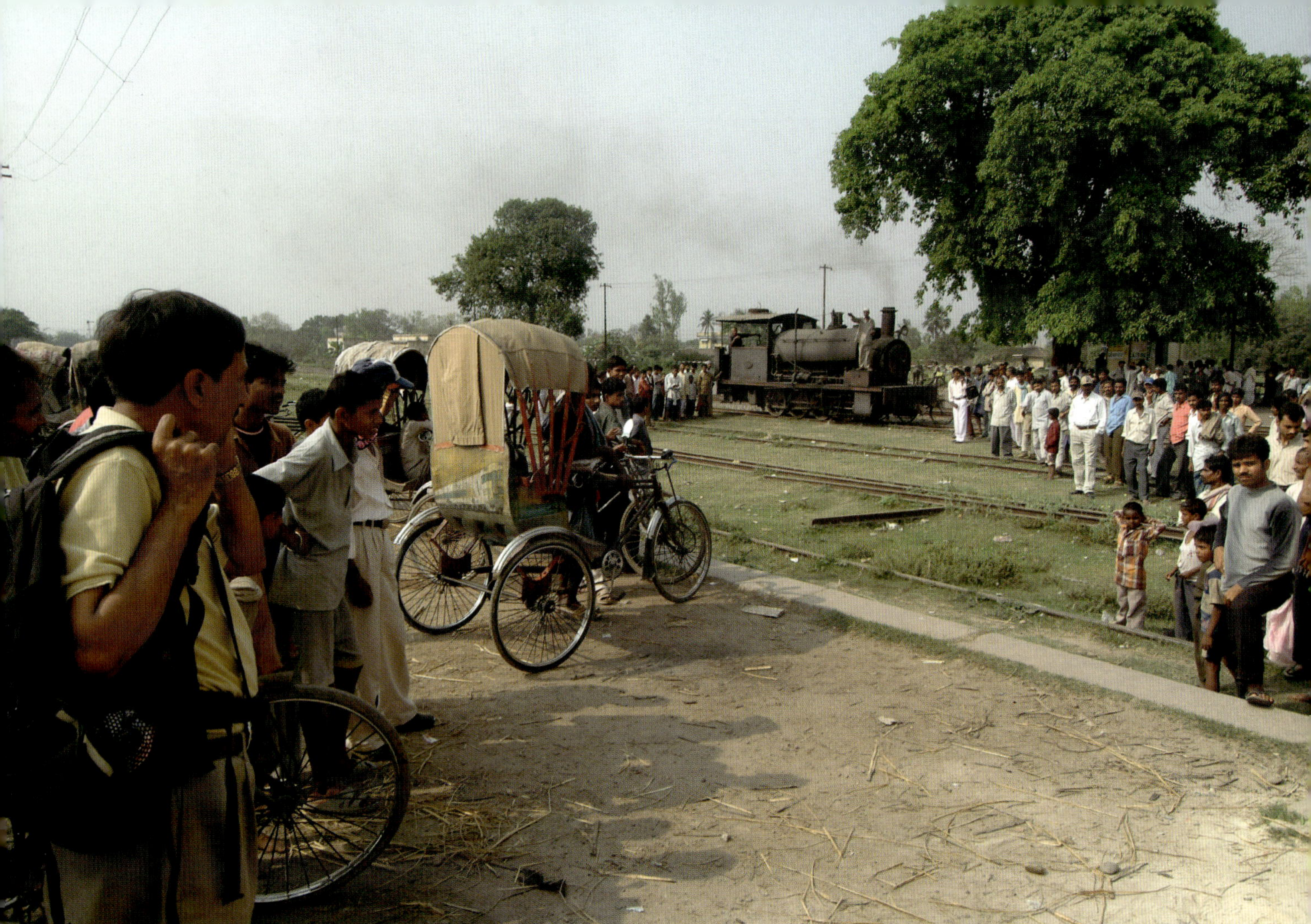

Above: The privately-owned Riga sugar factory is the only one still working in Bihar. It was served by a metre gauge branch about 2kms long from Riga station worked for many years by 0-8-0ST *Lilian* (HC 1644/1930) which came second hand from an oil company at Digboi, near Tinsukia in eastern Assam. Here she has attracted a large crowd at the station on 17 March 2004.

Opposite above: Ashok Sharma, our ever-helpful guide, took us to the headquarters to complain about the grounding of Darjeeling's steam locos as we passed through Guwahati on 25 March 2004 even though security meant it was supposed to be off-limits. It turned out that the general manager was about to visit Darjeeling and wanted to make sure there was enough coal for his train. By way of compensation, his assistant let us photograph DHR C class Pacific No 808 (NB 20642/1914), an unexpected treat as photography was usually forbidden. She and a sister worked a DHR line over the plains to Kishanganj until it was converted to metre gauge after partition to provide a route on Indian territory to Assam.

Opposite below: We were also taken to Guwahati shed, another place normally off-limits, and shown 4-8-2+2-8-4 GX class No 32086 (BP 7144/1945), the only surviving metre gauge Garratt in India. Twenty of these locos were supplied to the War Department to work over the hilly lines in Assam close to the front with the Japanese army but the tide of war was turning. Two went new to East Africa and nine others ended up there after a sojourn in Burma. They all became the EARs 5500 class and No 5505 is at the Nairobi museum. No 32086 is now the centrepiece of a small museum at Tinsukia.

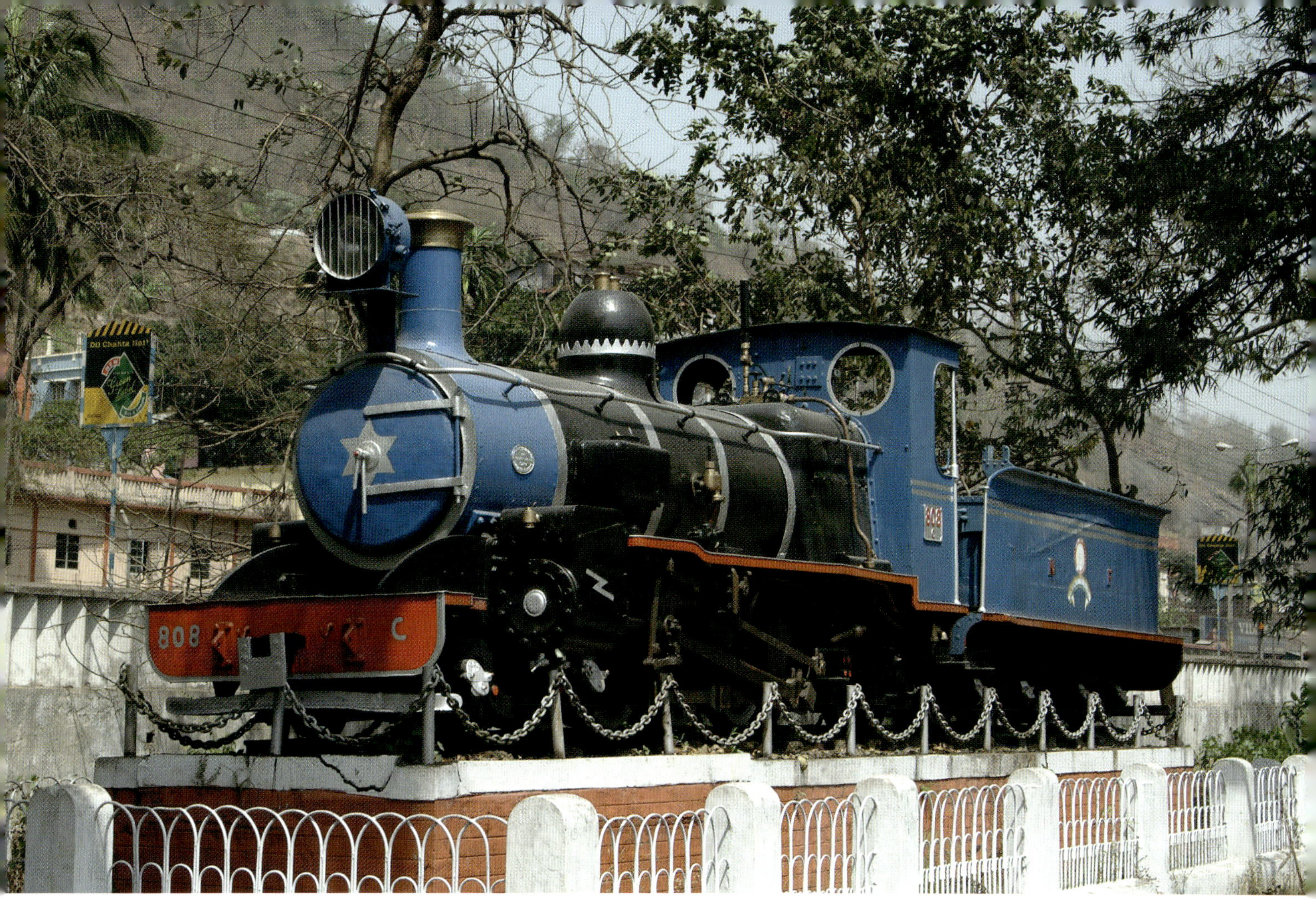

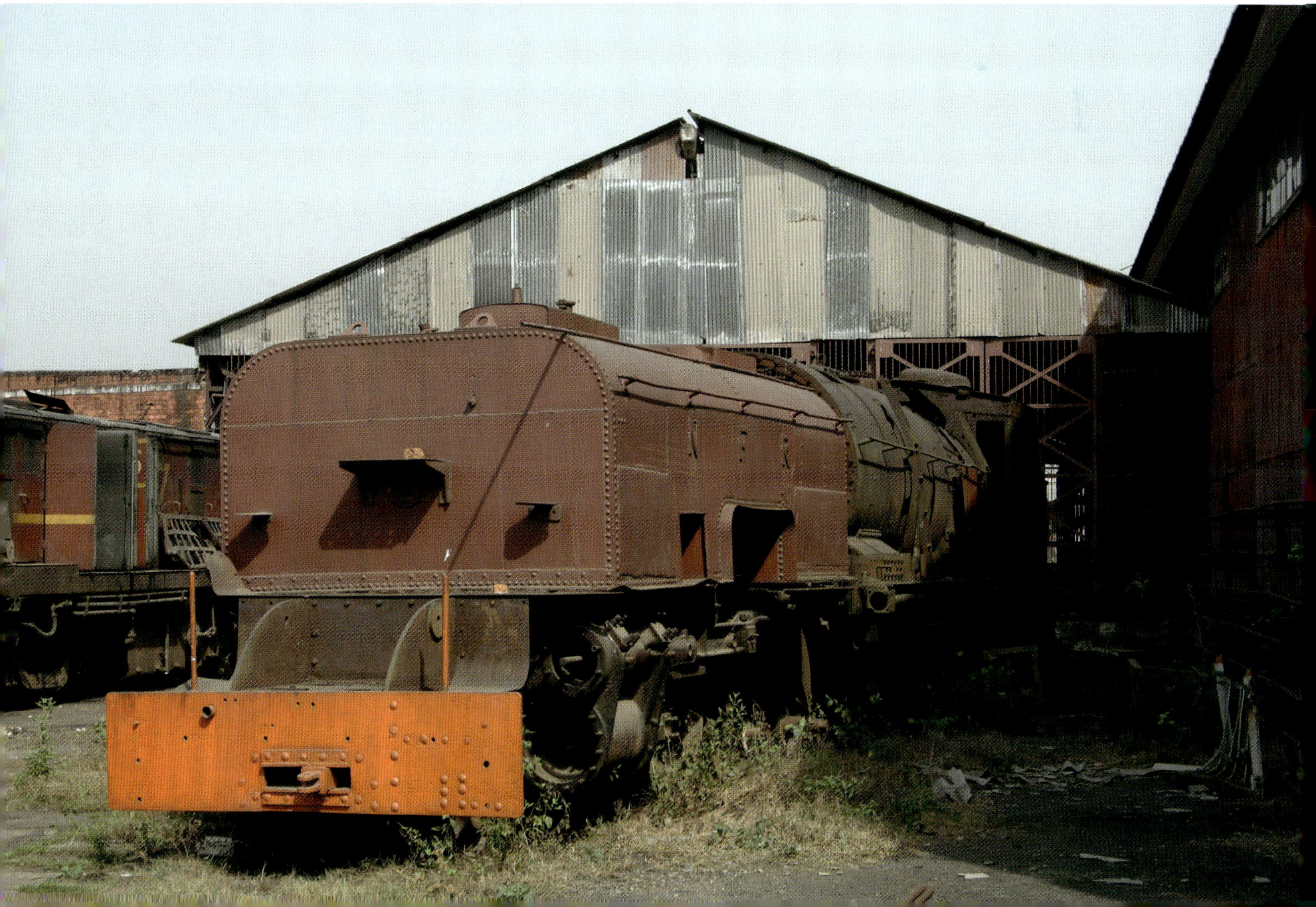

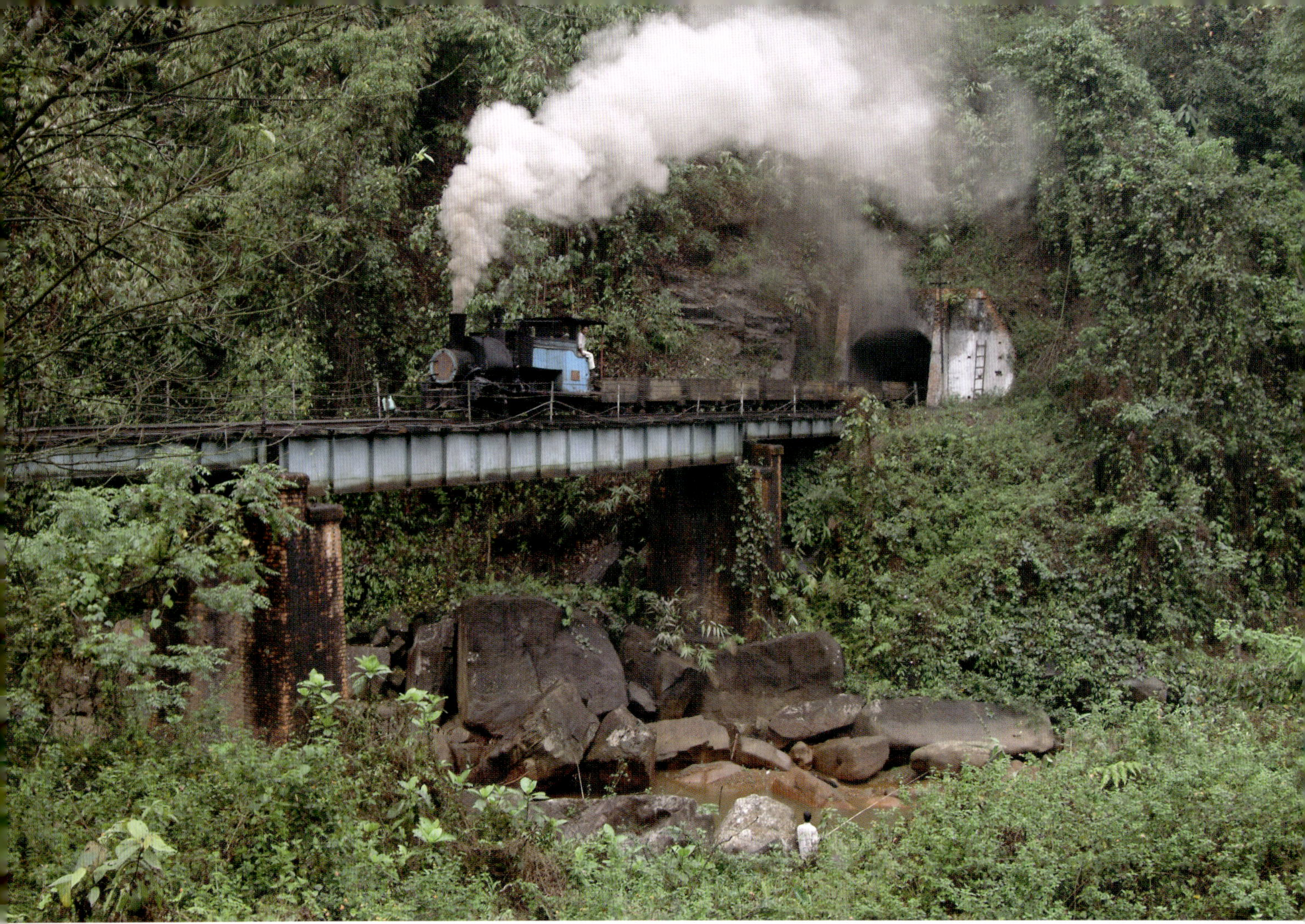

Above: The origins of mining at the Makum coalfield, in the far east of Assam, go back to discovery of a seam of high quality coal in 1876 and exploitation began in 1882. Tipong, the remotest colliery, opened in 1924. It lies near the head of the steep-sided Tipong Pani valley through which a 2ft gauge railway was built to take away the coal. 0-4-0ST No 789 (NB 20638/1914) crosses the river on 23 March 2004. She's one of four ex-Darjeeling B class locos bought in 1968 and has been heavily rebuilt with an array of weird and wonderful plumbing and other equipment.

Opposite above: Until the Darjeeling locos arrived the railway was worked by a series of small Bagnall machines. 0-4-0ST *David* (Bagnall 2134/1924) is the last working survivor and here sits out in the rain on the evening of 23 March 2004. The valley opens out at Tipong village and the 2ft gauge line used to meet a long metre gauge siding from Lekhapani station, once the start point of the Stilwell Road which provided a lifeline to south western China during the Second World War. The loading dock at the village was the most easterly point on Indian Railways until the siding closed in 1998 and lorries took over.

Opposite below: *David* was kept on to work a branch leading to a small mine and a cable-worked incline up to an opencast pit as the Darjeeling locos were too heavy for this bridge. *David* hauls a short train of loaded tubs on 24 March 2004.

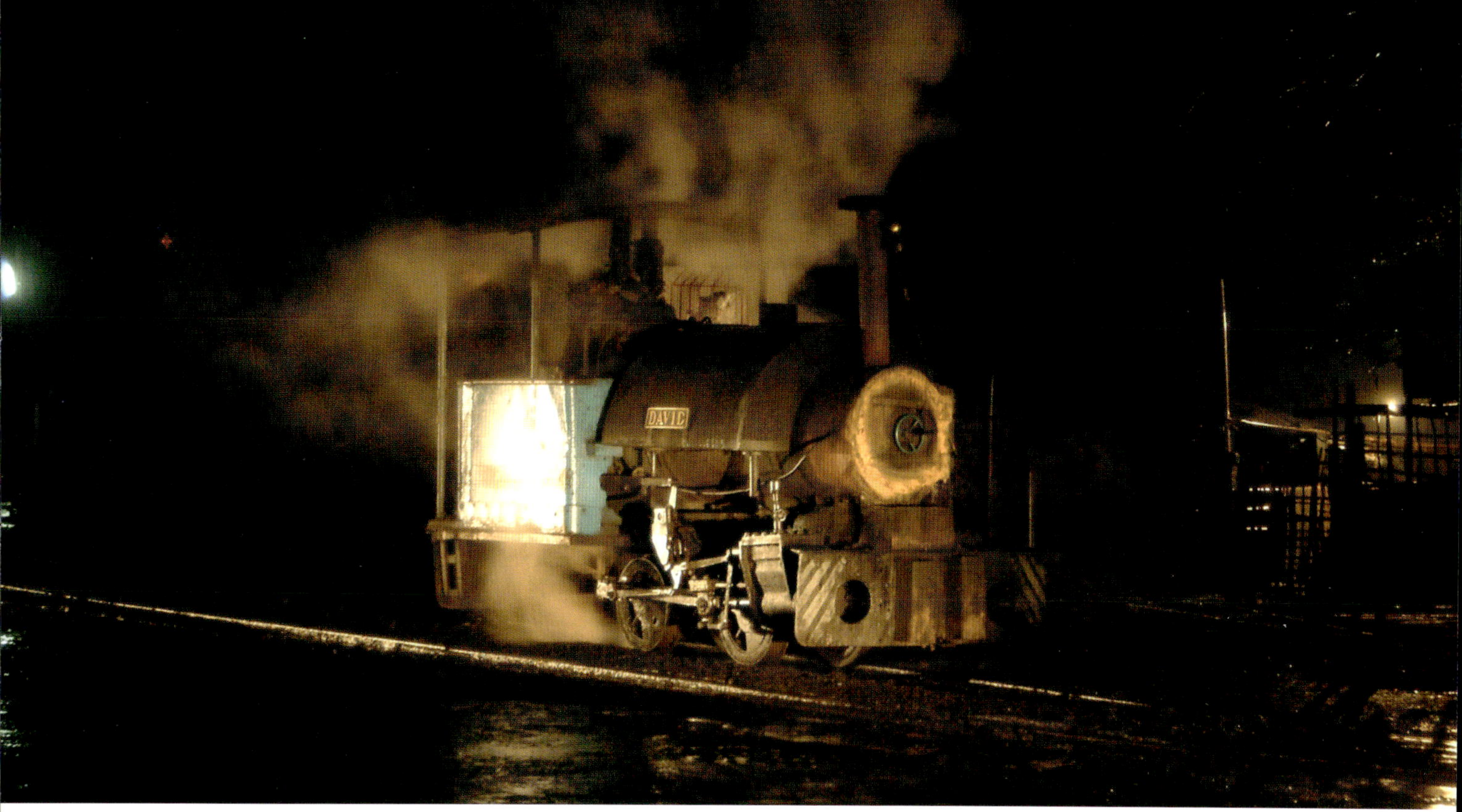

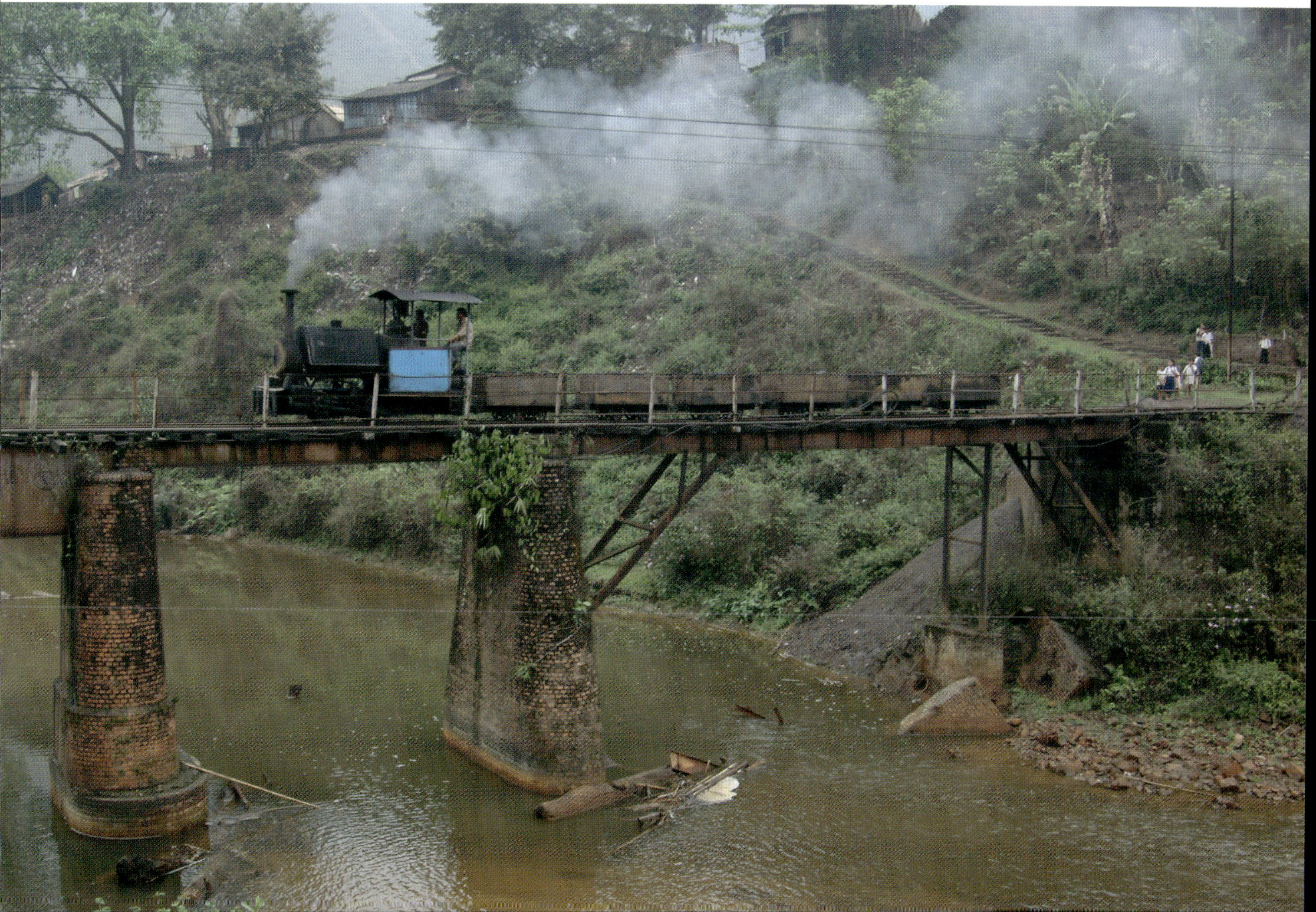

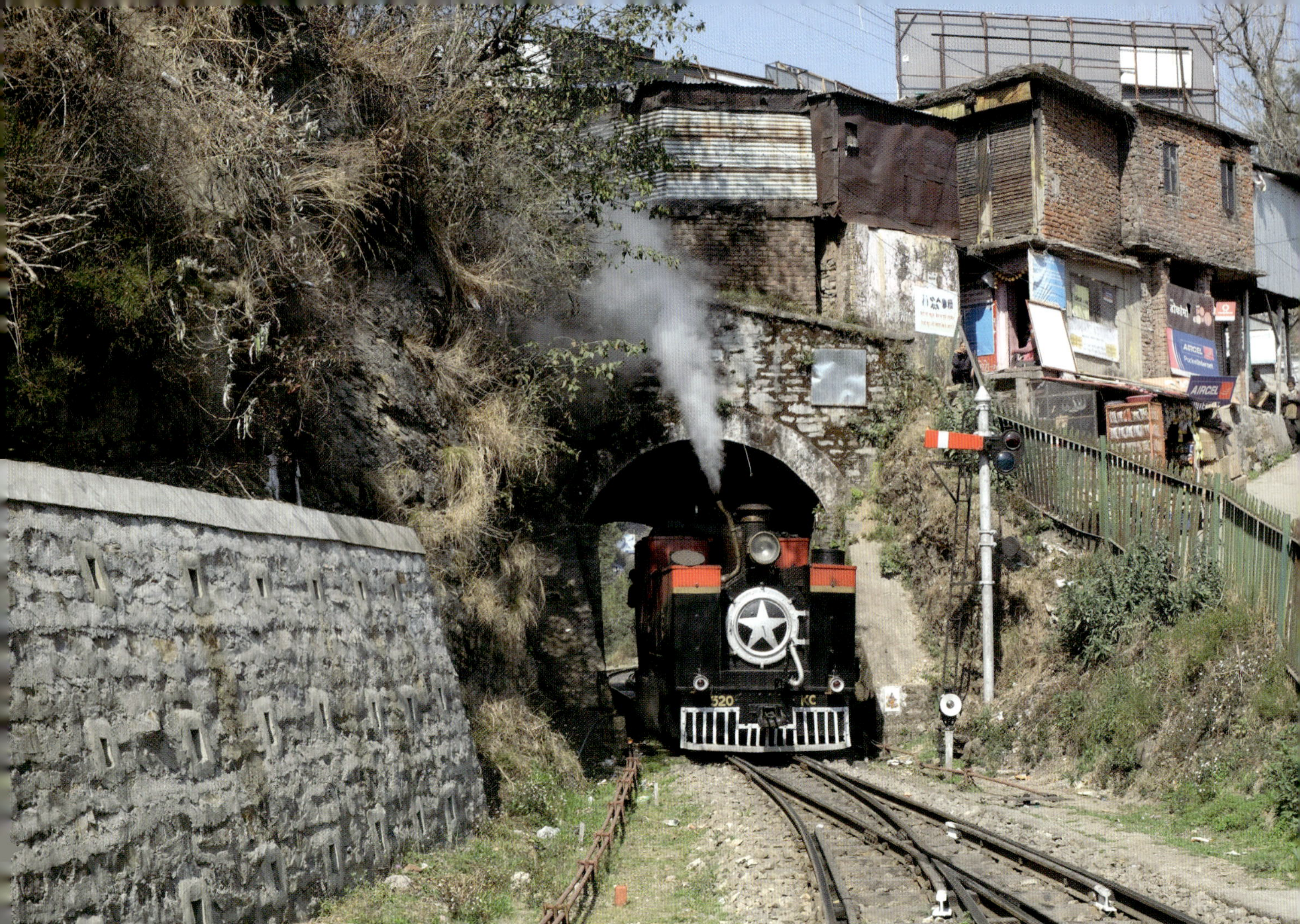

Above: The heavily engineered 2ft 6ins gauge Kalka-Shimla railway serves another of India's hill stations but, unlike the Darjeeling line, is anything but a slow roadside tramway. The gradient is gentle enough for lengthy trains and the use of loops and switchbacks was avoided, thanks largely to the construction of over 100 tunnels and 800 bridges. Diesels took over many years ago but KC class 2-6-2T No 520 (NB 16819/1905) later returned to Shimla and works occasional specials. Here she emerges from one of those many tunnels as she runs around her train at Taradevi on 26 February 2016.

Opposite above: No 520 sets off from Summerhill for Shimla on 26 February 2016. There's not much of her to see as she hides behind those enormous side tanks! This was supposed to be an empty stock working but the railway's helpful staff let our small group ride on it and made run-pasts en route.

Opposite below: On 29 March 2004, redundant sleepers are loaded aboard a permanent way special at Kaderi Road on the metre gauge line to Ooty, a hill station in the south of India, hauled by X class 0-8-2RT No 37386 (SLM 2735/1920). The railway's Abt-rack section from Kallar to Coonoor didn't open until 1899, eight years after construction began. It continued as an adhesion line to Ooty, reached in 1908.

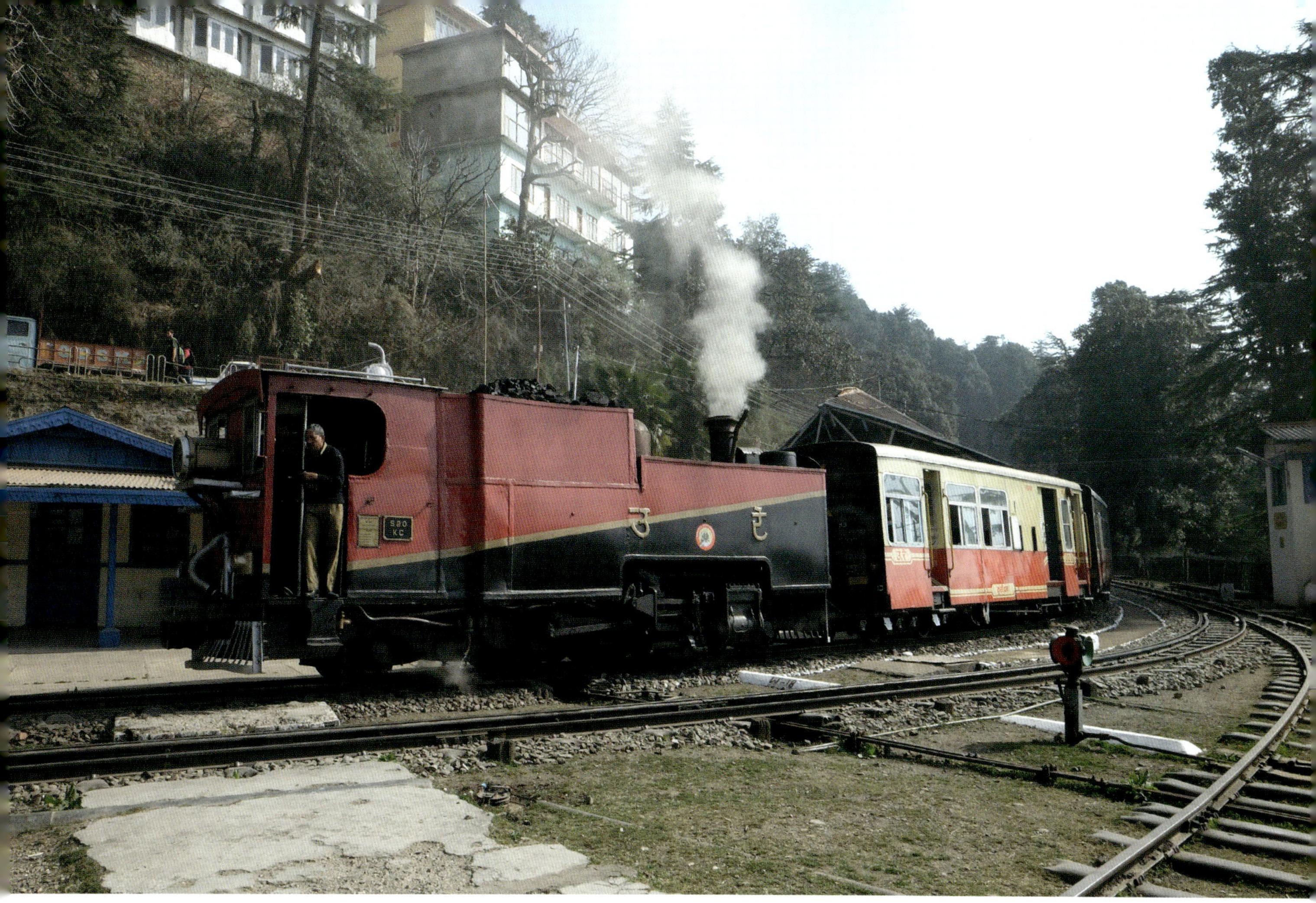

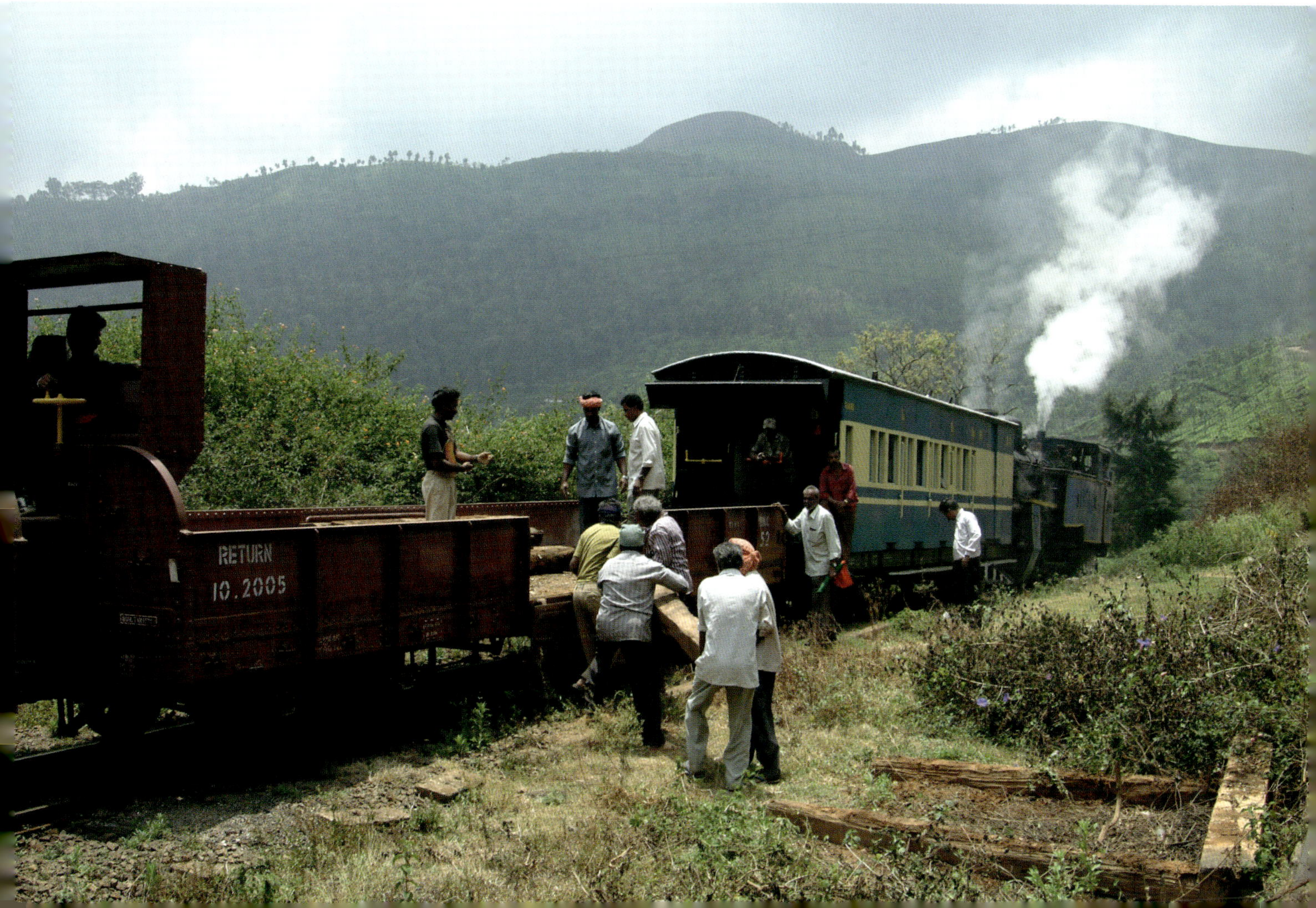

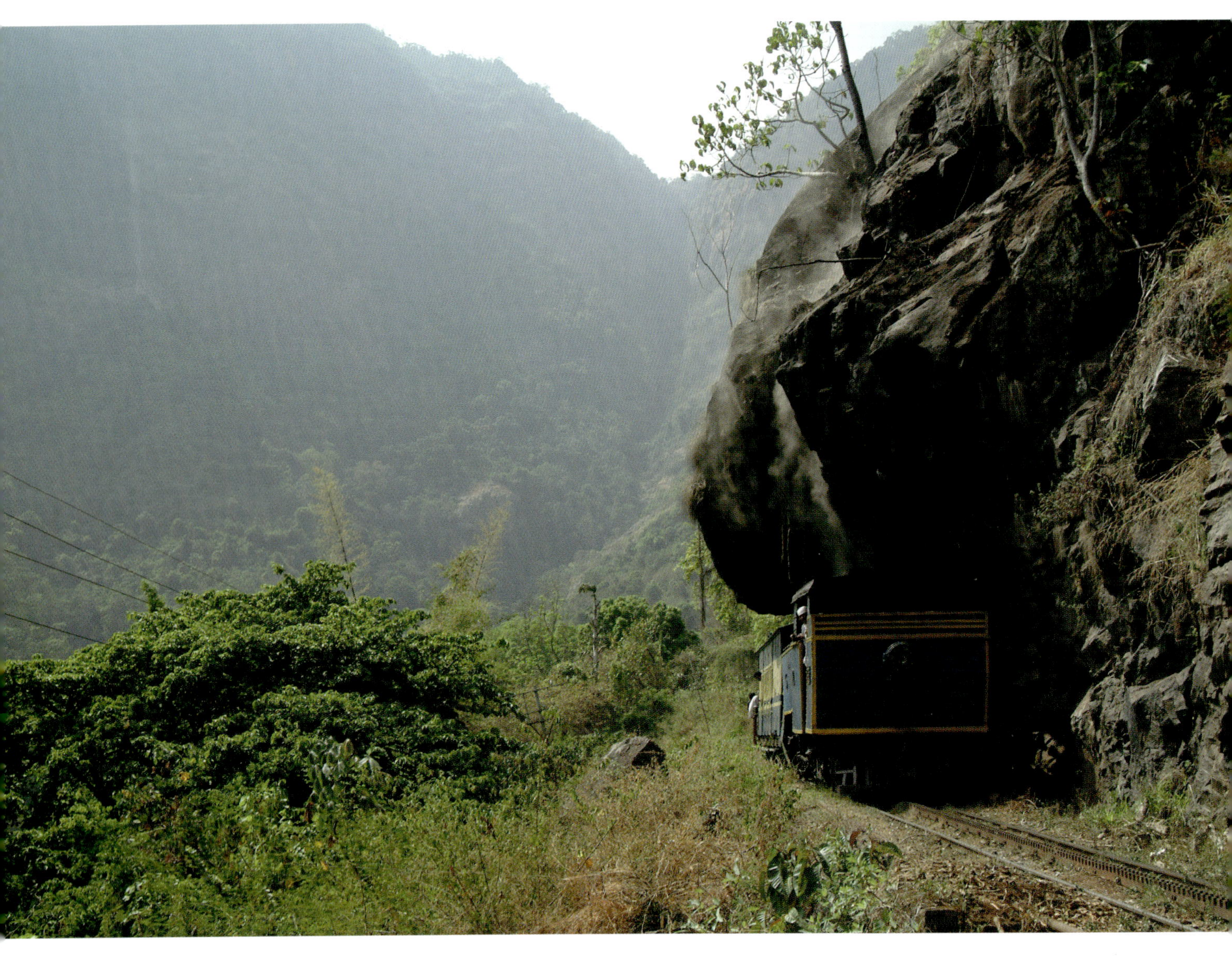

The difficult terrain can be appreciated in this photo of No 37386 and her special at the so-called half tunnel, in reality a granite rock which overhangs the line, on 29 March 2004. We were very lucky to be allowed to ride on the train for the cost of first class tickets, not much more than £1 each, and were treated to footplate rides and run-pasts. Indian hospitality at its very best!

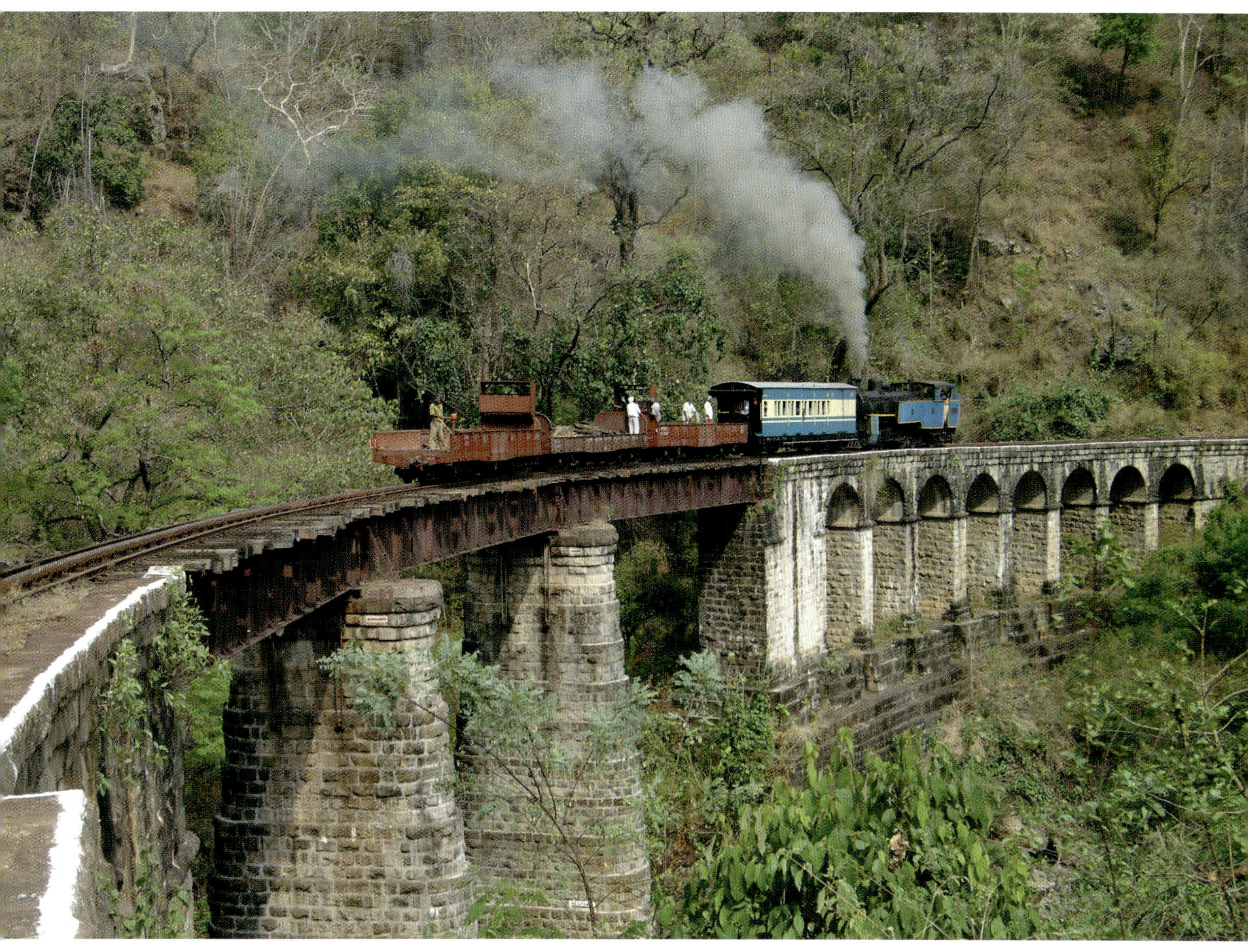

A little before sunset, No 37386's special crosses Bhawani bridge near Kallar, much the largest engineering feature on the line. Since my visit, four new oil-fired locos have been built at Golden Rock workshops, based on the Swiss design though looking rather different, and now work most regular trains.

BURMA

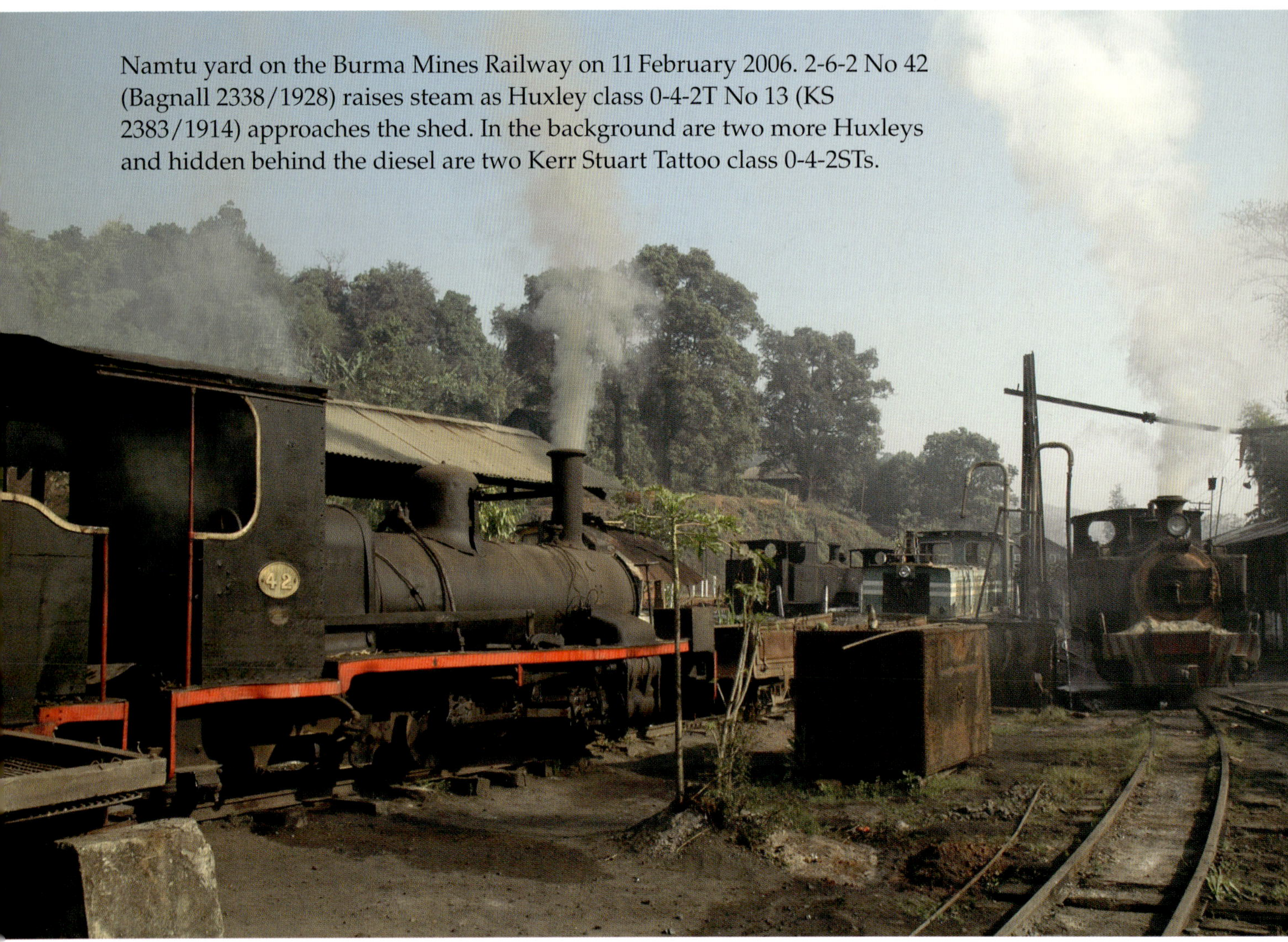

Namtu yard on the Burma Mines Railway on 11 February 2006. 2-6-2 No 42 (Bagnall 2338/1928) raises steam as Huxley class 0-4-2T No 13 (KS 2383/1914) approaches the shed. In the background are two more Huxleys and hidden behind the diesel are two Kerr Stuart Tattoo class 0-4-2STs.

Opposite above: No 13 heads a short train between Lopah and Wallah Gorge on 11 February 2006. The 2ft gauge line, about 80kms long, connected with the metre gauge Burma Railways' Lashio branch at Namyao, in Shan state in eastern Burma. It was built in 1907 to serve mines at Bawdwin, in the hills beyond Wallah Gorge.

Opposite below: No 13 shunts her train at the huge old staithes at Wallah Gorge on 11 February 2006 overlooked by a small pagoda, a typically Burmese sight. This section between Namtu and Tiger Camp, near Wallah Gorge, is the only one still in use but traffic is currently confined to home-made lorry-railcars making unofficial passenger trips and occasional trains taking supplies to the mines.

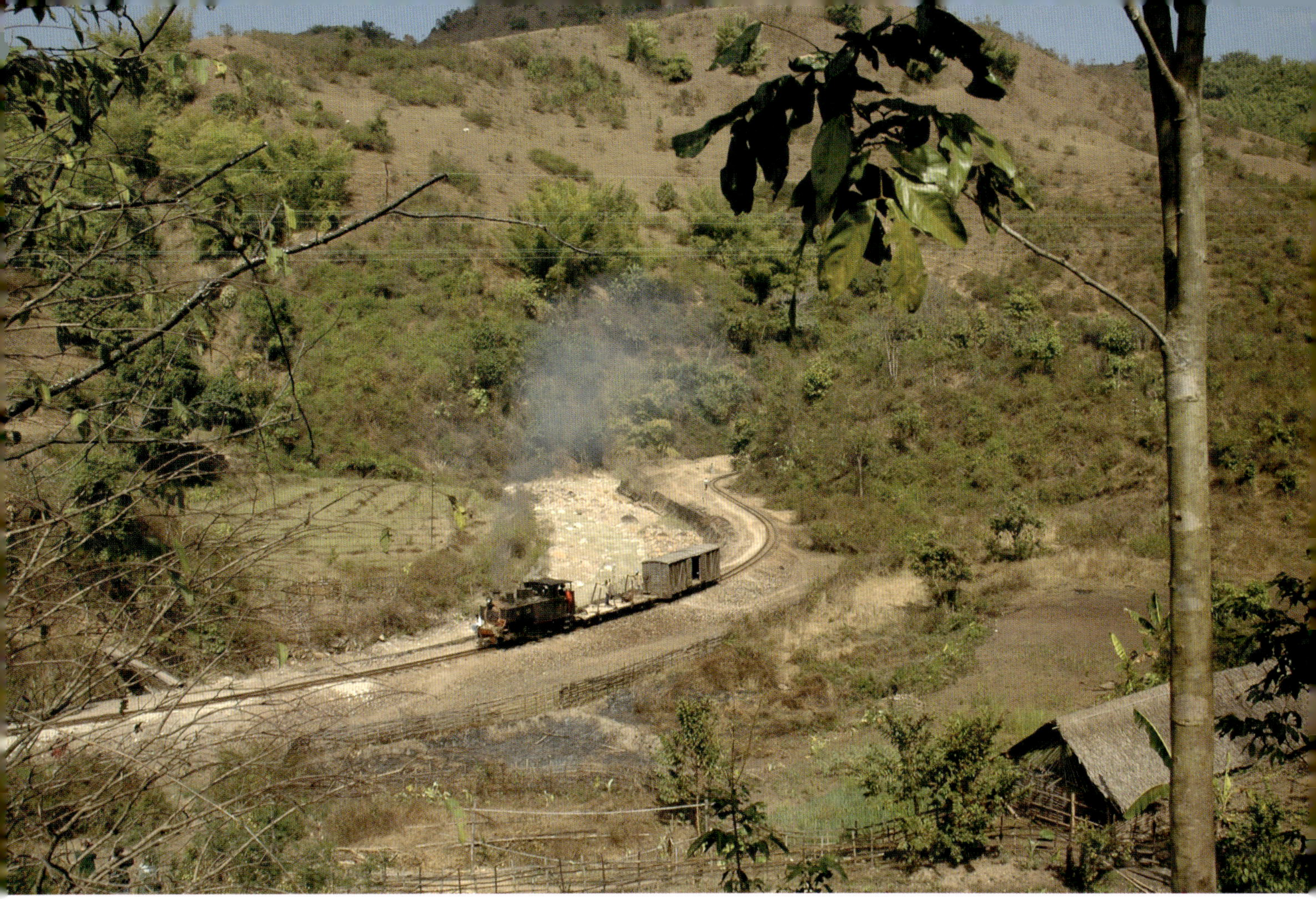

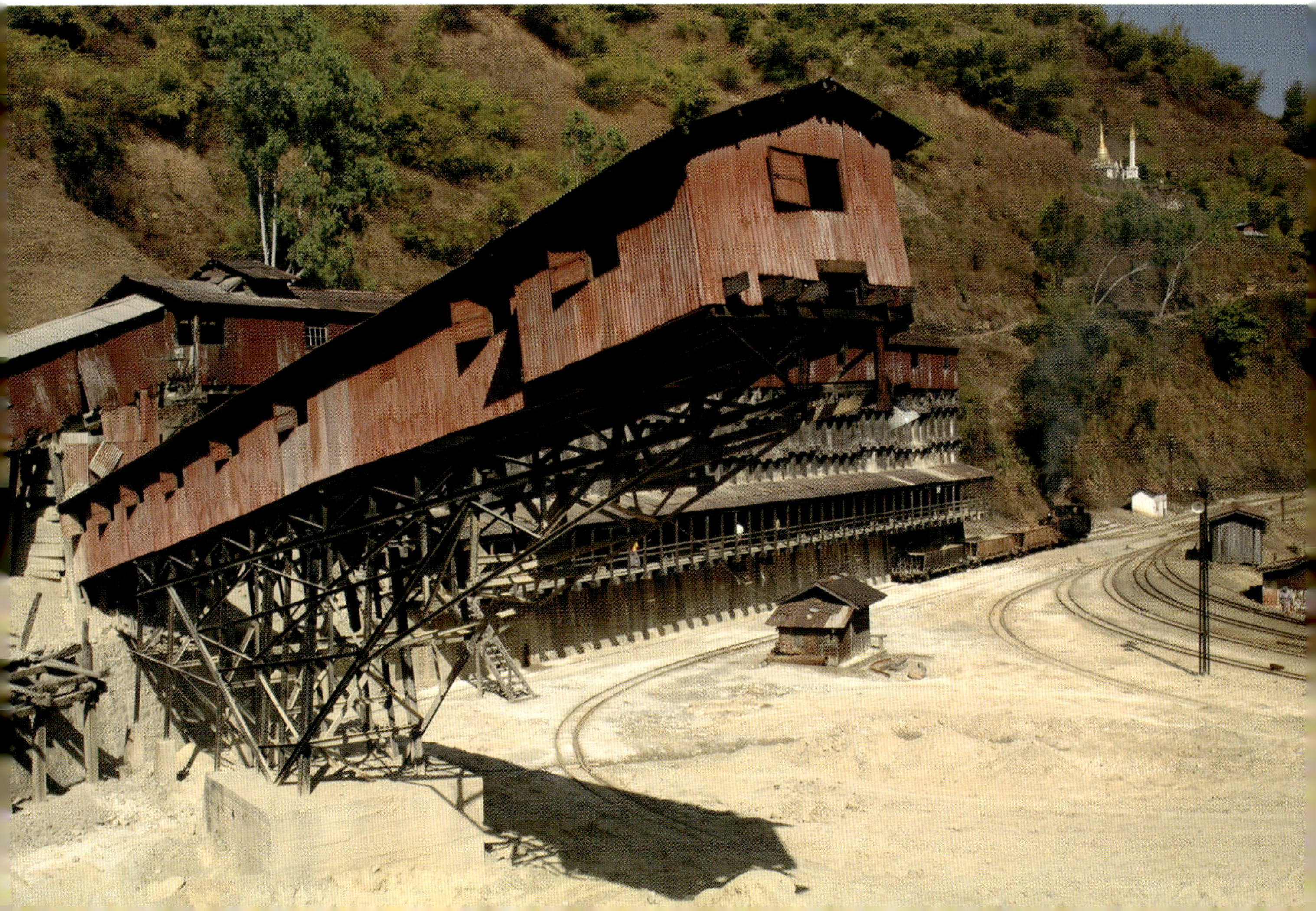

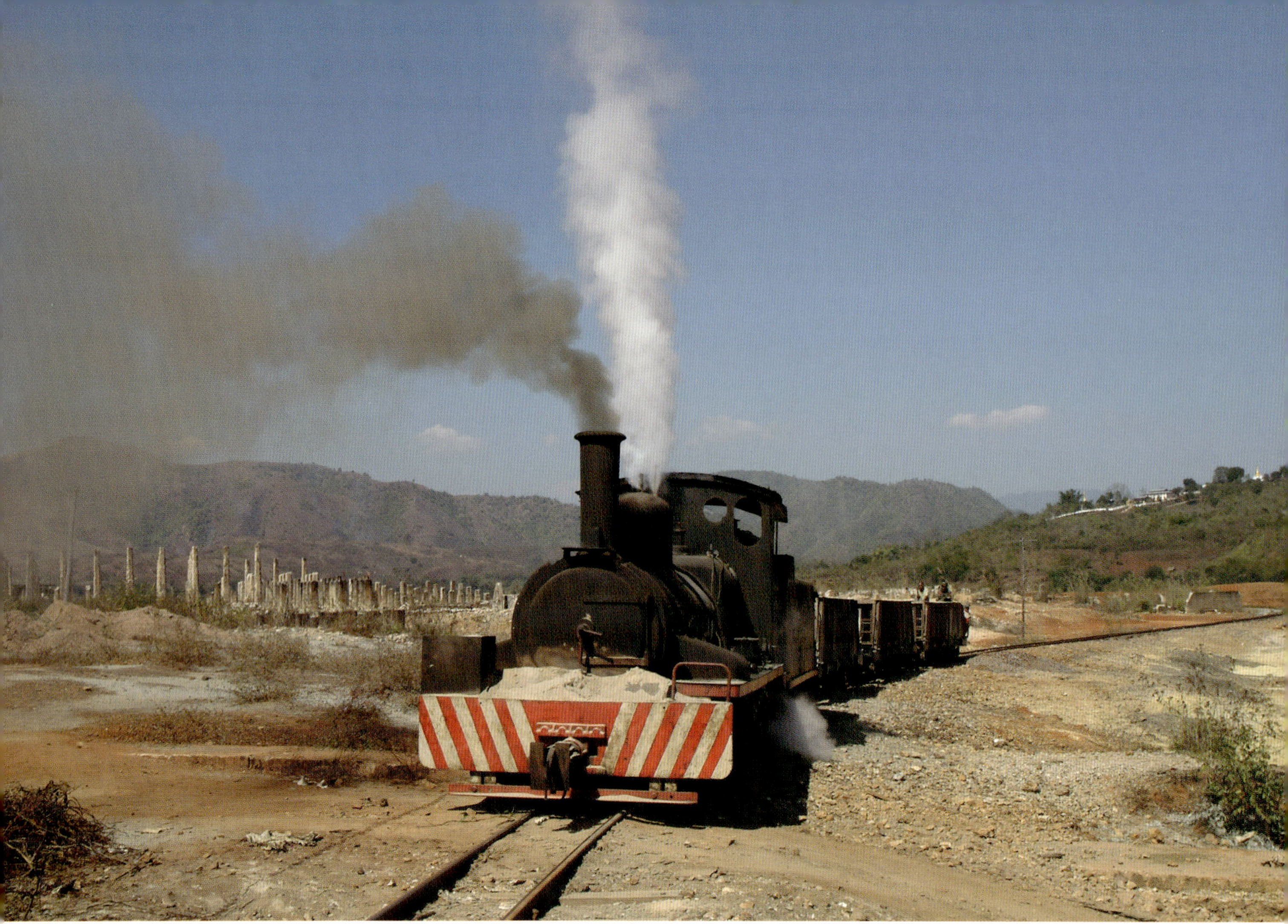

Above: On 12 February 2006, No 42 passes an old smelter southeast of Namtu which was destroyed during the Second World War.

Opposite above: Two ladies return from a shopping trip as the driver and fireman of Burma Railways' YD 2-8-2 No 972 (VF 5736/1949) take a break with their friends at the eastern end of Bago yard on the afternoon of 13 February 2006. Regular steam operation on the metre gauge Burma Railways ended in 2008.

Opposite below: YC Pacific No 629 (VF 5606/1948) sits in the sunshine at Bago shed on 13 February 2006. Ten of these large Pacifics arrived in 1947 and 1948. Like the YD's they were an Indian standard type though only a few ever ran in India proper.

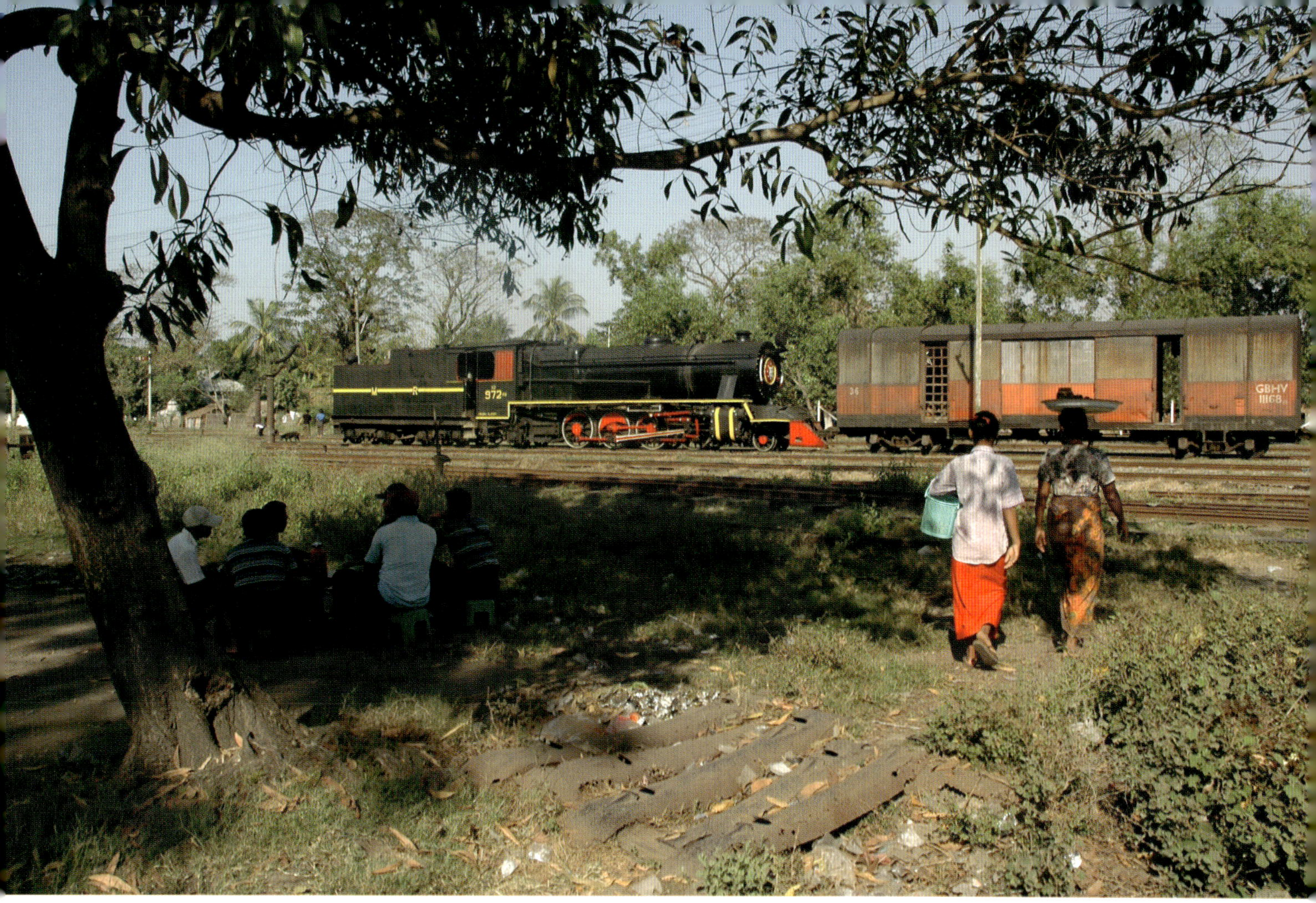

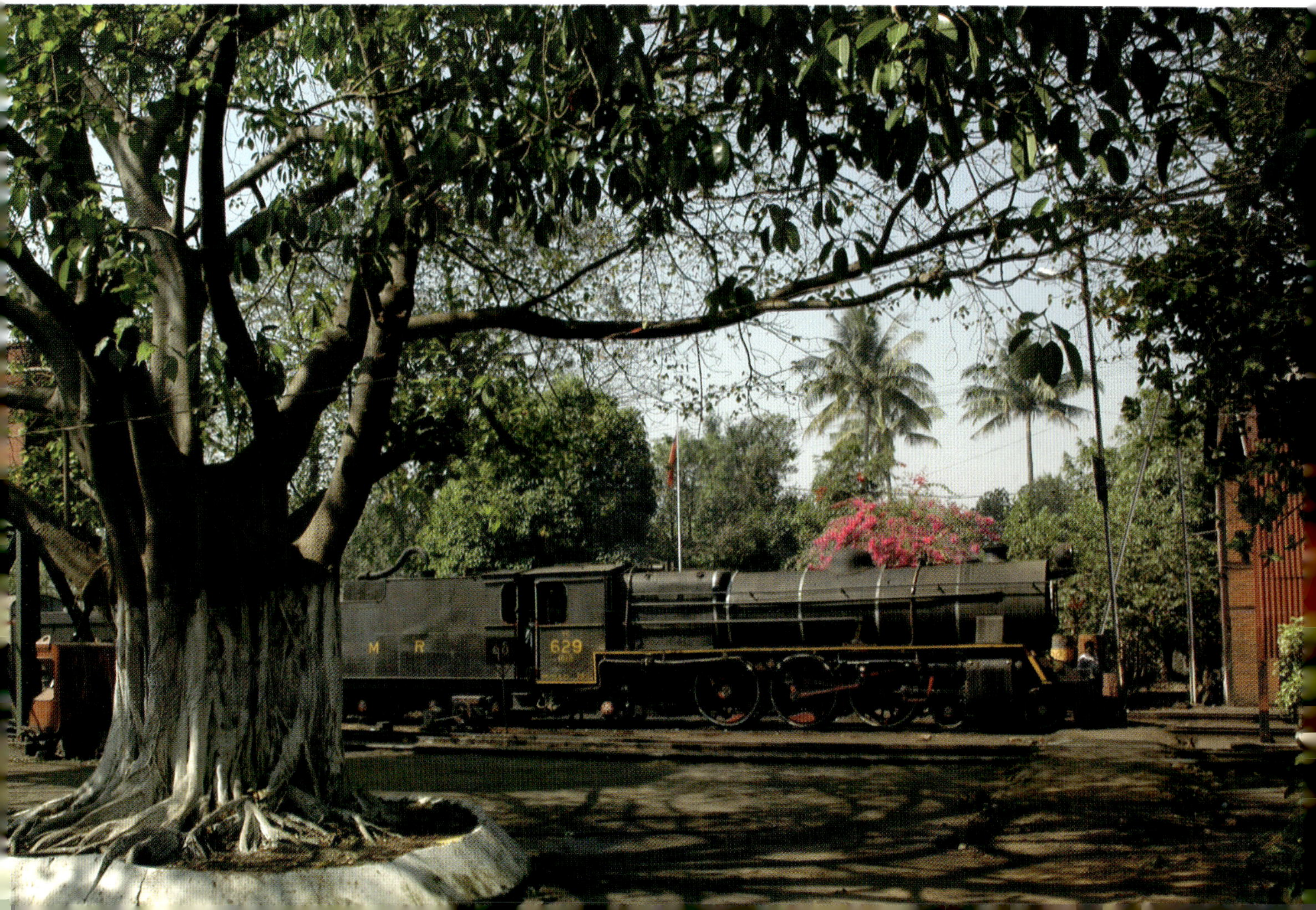

SRI LANKA

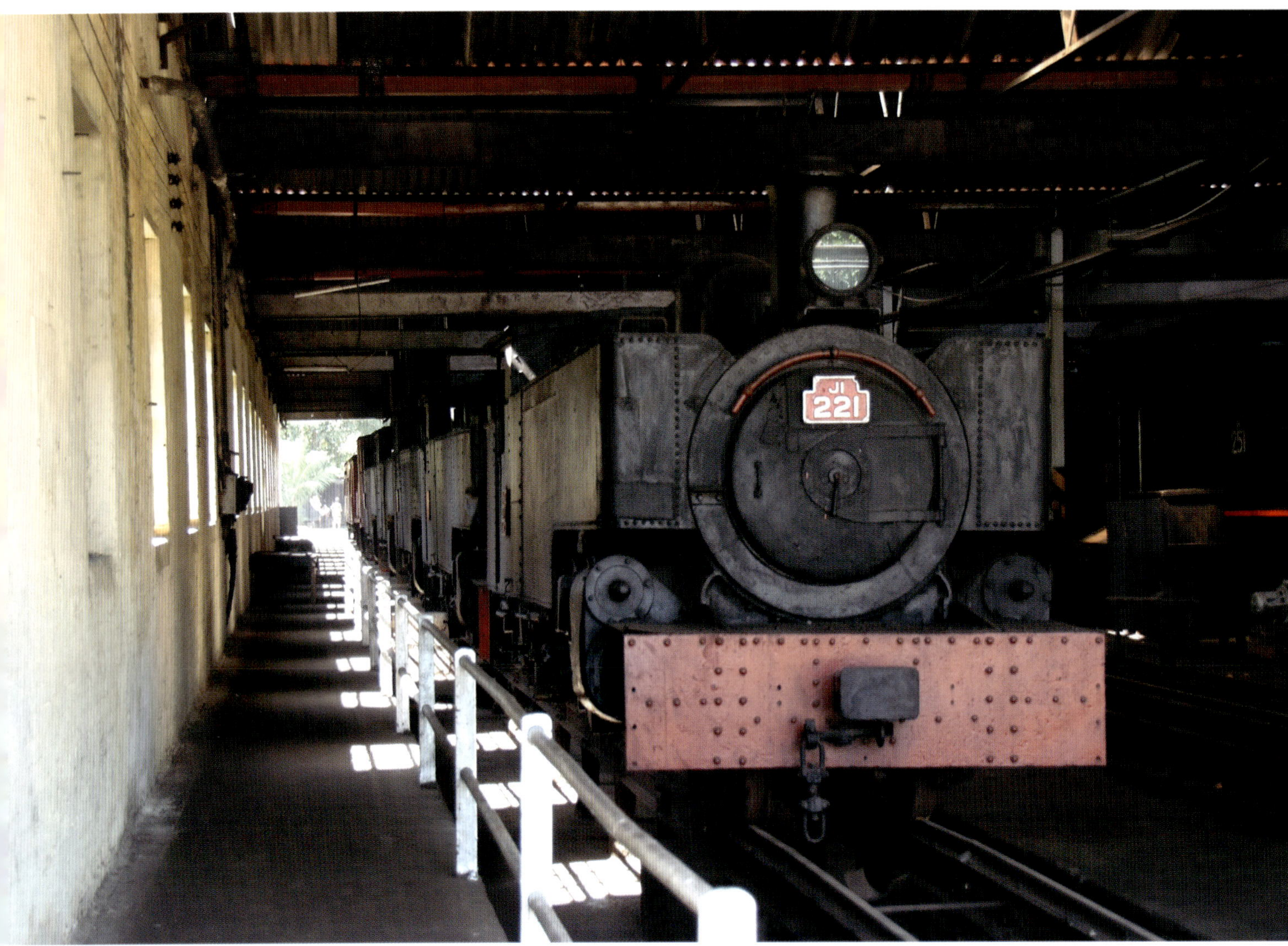

When I visited on 29 January 2010 Lalith Fonseka, the hospitable shedmaster at Dematagoda in the outskirts of Colombo, had recently overseen the centenary celebrations at his shed. It contained eight broad gauge roads and two 2ft 6ins gauge ones where stock from the old Kelani Valley line was stored. This included eight J1 and J2 class 4-6-4Ts and two Sentinel steam railcars while elsewhere in the shed were several broad gauge steam locos, a steam crane and historic carriages and wagons. Mr Fonseka understood their heritage value and made strenuous efforts to safeguard them, not an easy task when he had to cope with an autocratic government during the country's long civil war. J1 No 221 (Hunslet 1497/1925) is at the head of a line of five 4-6-4T's alongside broad gauge B1a class 4-6-0 No 251 *Sir Thomas Maitland* (BP 6469/1928).

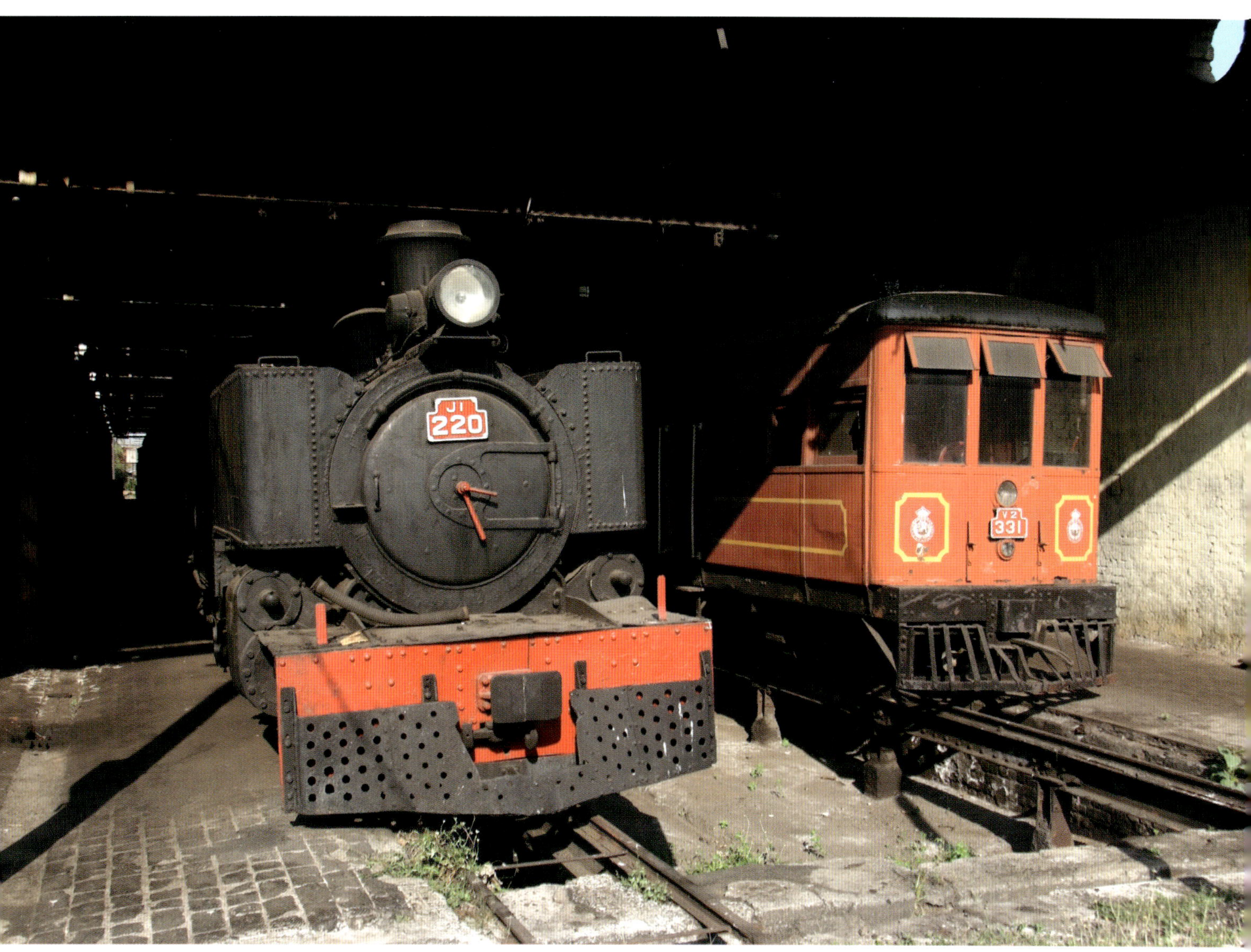

At the other end of the shed, J1 No 220 (Hunslet 1478/1924) and V2 steam railcar No 331 (Sentinel 7303/1928), both in working order, bask in the late afternoon sunshine. Alas, soon after Mr Fonseka retired the narrow gauge stock was dumped outside and the tracks within the shed removed. The country's railway museum is supposed to be acquiring one of the Sentinels but now they've lost much of their steel plating. More recently, No 331 has been moved to an open-sided shelter but even so its wooden framework won't last long exposed to the tropical climate.

THAILAND

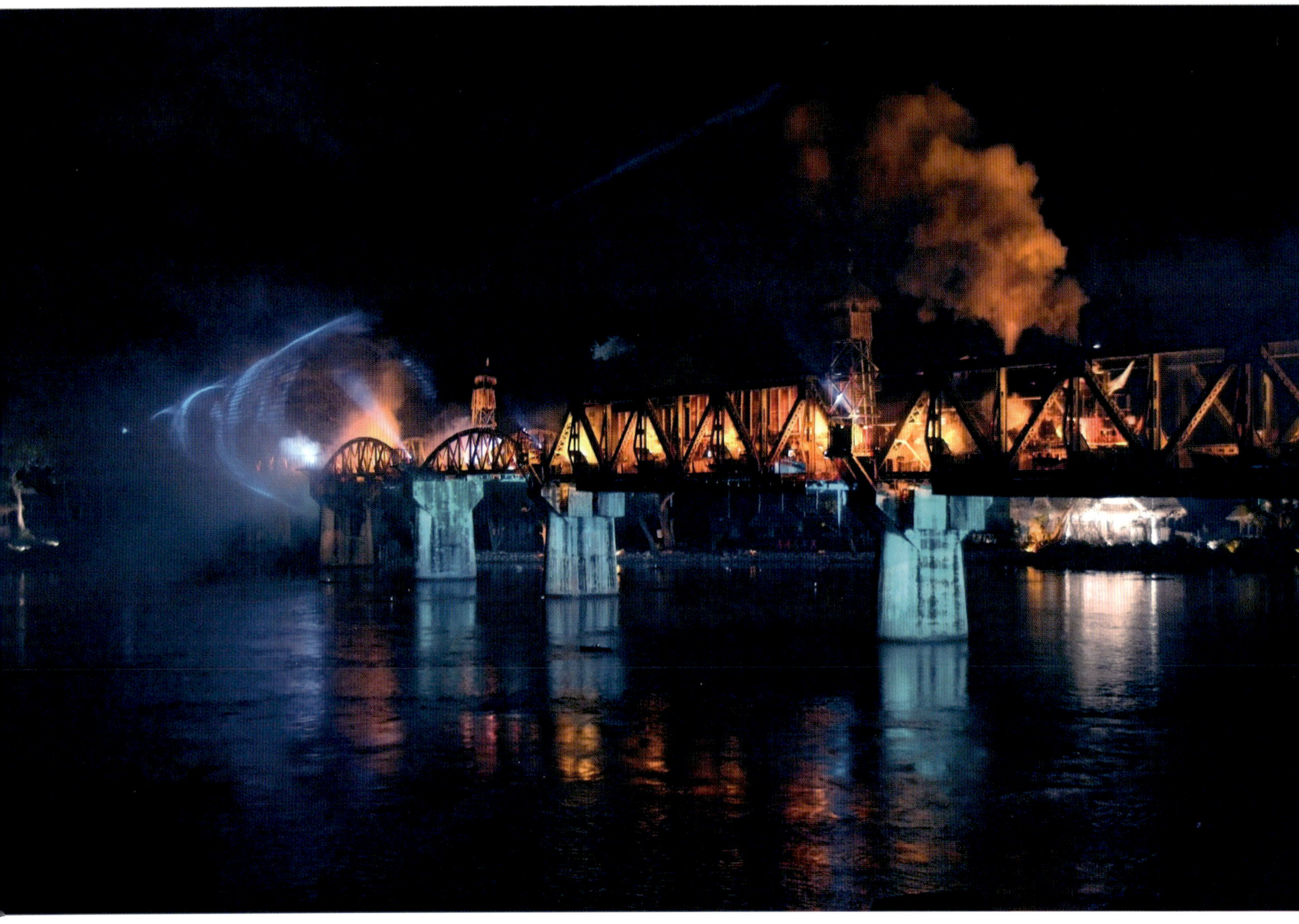

Above: 2-6-0 no 713 (Hitachi 628/1935), formerly Japanese No C56 15, stars in a festival at the River Kwai bridge at Kanchanaburi on 3rd December 2007.

Opposite above: For many years, the Thai railways have run a steam special on 5 December to mark the former king's birthday and this continues after his death. Forty Pacifics were built in Japan between 1941 and 1950 and here Nos 824 (Nippon (1524/1949) and 850 (Nippon 1547/1950) set off from Bangkok station with its fine arched roof on 5 December 2009, bound for Ayutthaya, the country's capital until 1767 when it was destroyed by an invading Burmese army.

Opposite below: The two Pacifics approach Bang Pa-In about two hours later. The birds overhead provide a reminder that much of Thailand is a wildlife paradise, even on its intensively-farmed central plain.

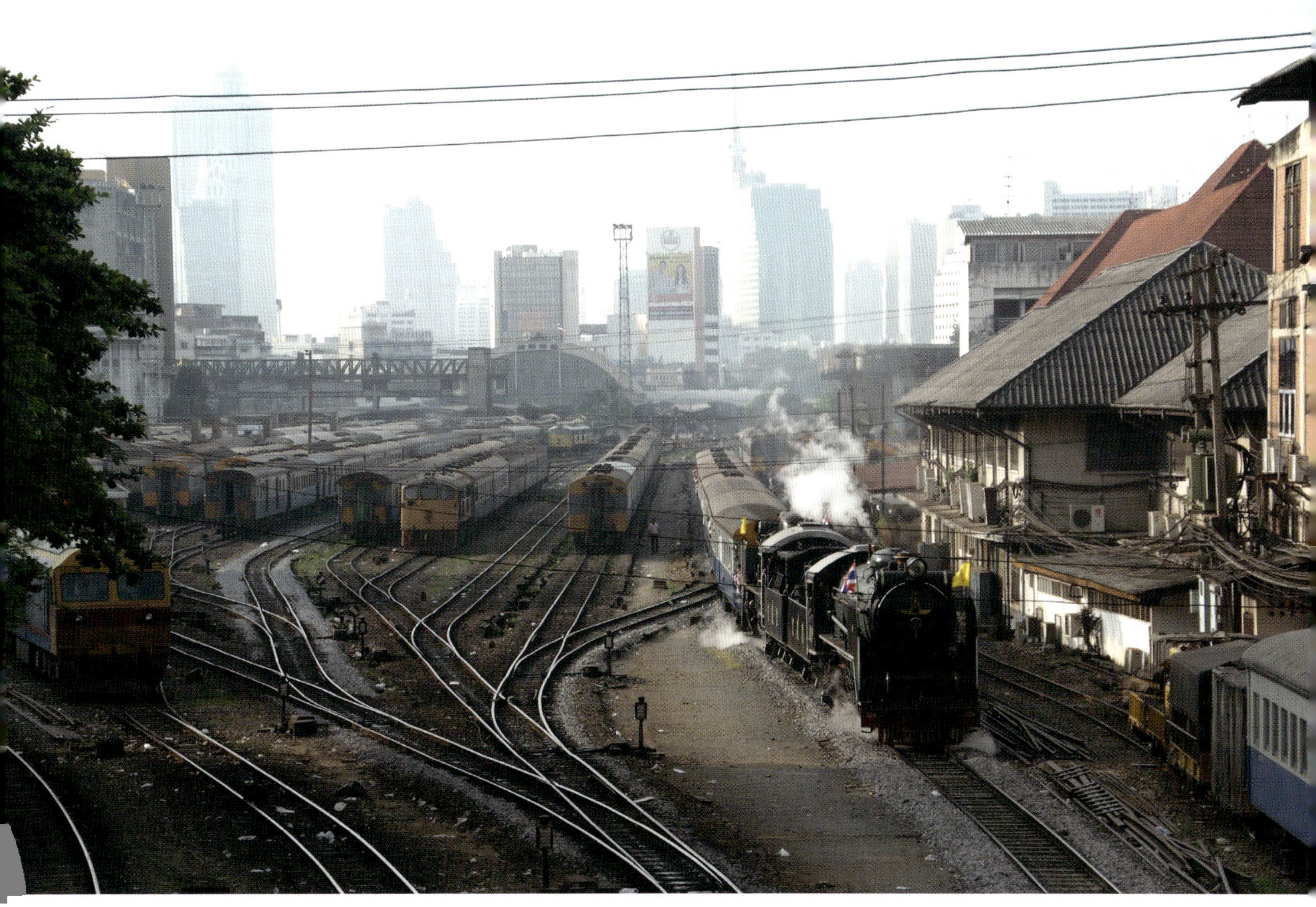

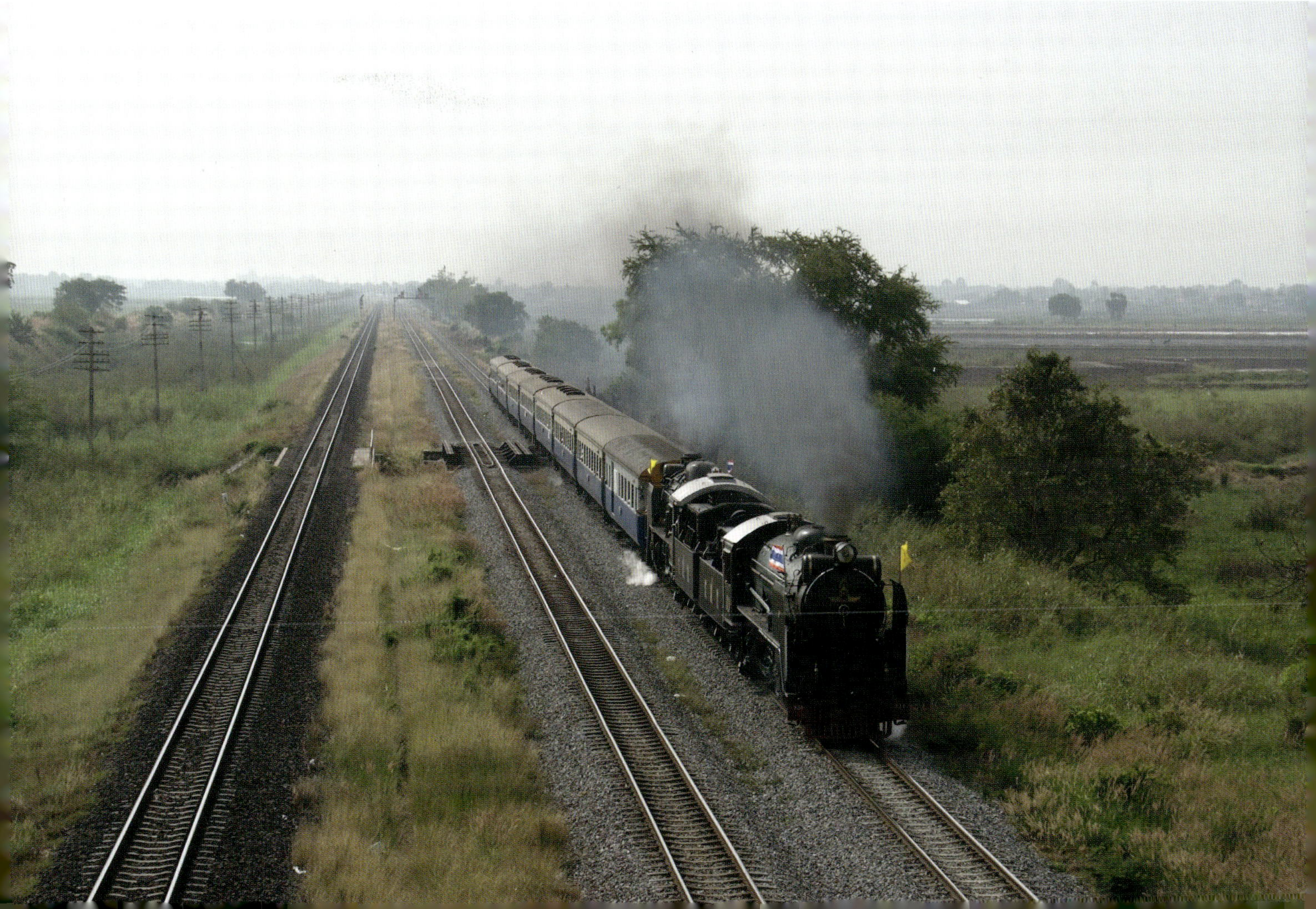

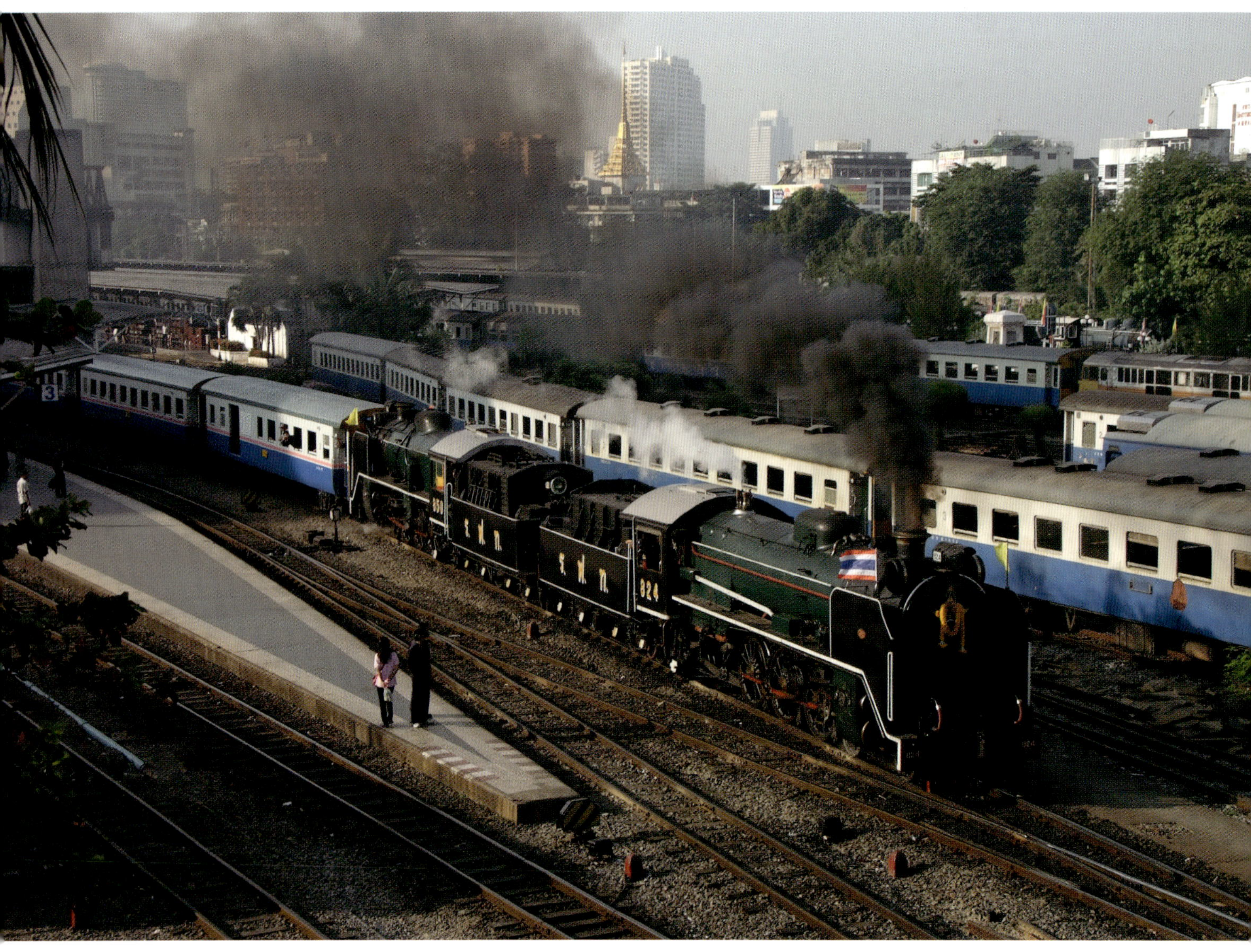

Exactly one year later the pair are in action again leaving Bangkok. The country's endlessly fascinating capital fully deserves its Thai name which means City of Angels. The Ayutthaya line was the first part of Thailand's mainline system when it opened on 26th March 1896, the anniversary of which is also usually celebrated with a steam run. To the right 2-6-0 No 714 (Hitachi 629/1935), formerly Japanese No C56 16, forms the centrepiece of a small shrine. Ninety C56 class locos were converted by the Japanese from their 3ft 6ins to metre gauge for use on the notorious Thailand-Burma railway during the Second World War. This involved setting the tyres back, shaving 2mm off the flanges, fitting springs under instead of over the wheels and cutting bites out of the outer firebox wrapper, all of which suggests that they weren't designed with gauge conversion in mind as is sometimes reported. Several worked in Thailand until 1975.

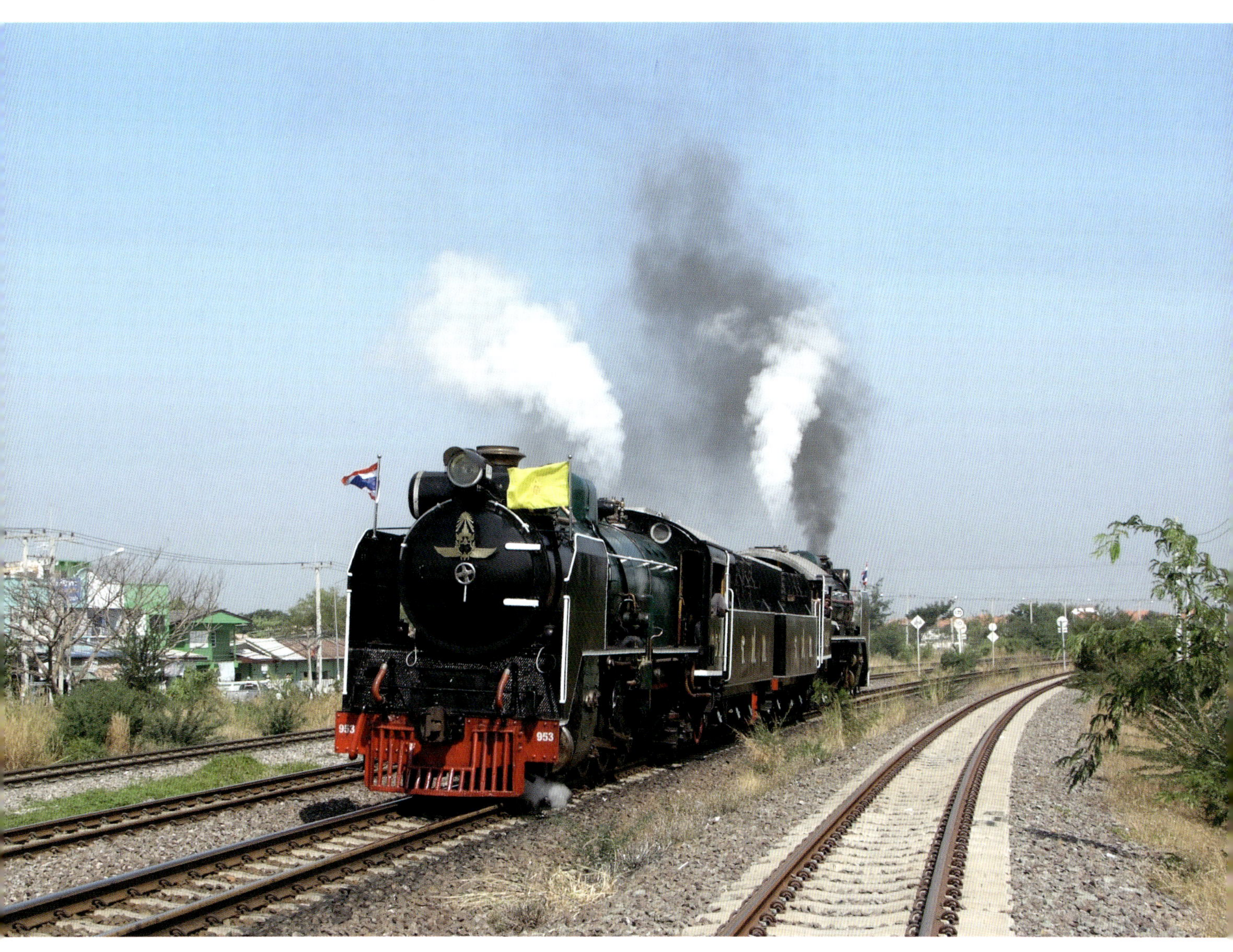

Nos 953 (Hitachi 2051/1950), one of ninety-eight Japanese-built 2-8-2s, and 850 at Ayutthaya on 5 December 2007. No 953 no longer runs but the two Pacifics were reboilered in 2012 and should operate for many years to come. The Pacifics and 2-8-2s built from the late 1940s were supplied under a barter arrangement in exchange for rice which was in desperately short supply in post-war Japan.

CAMBODIA

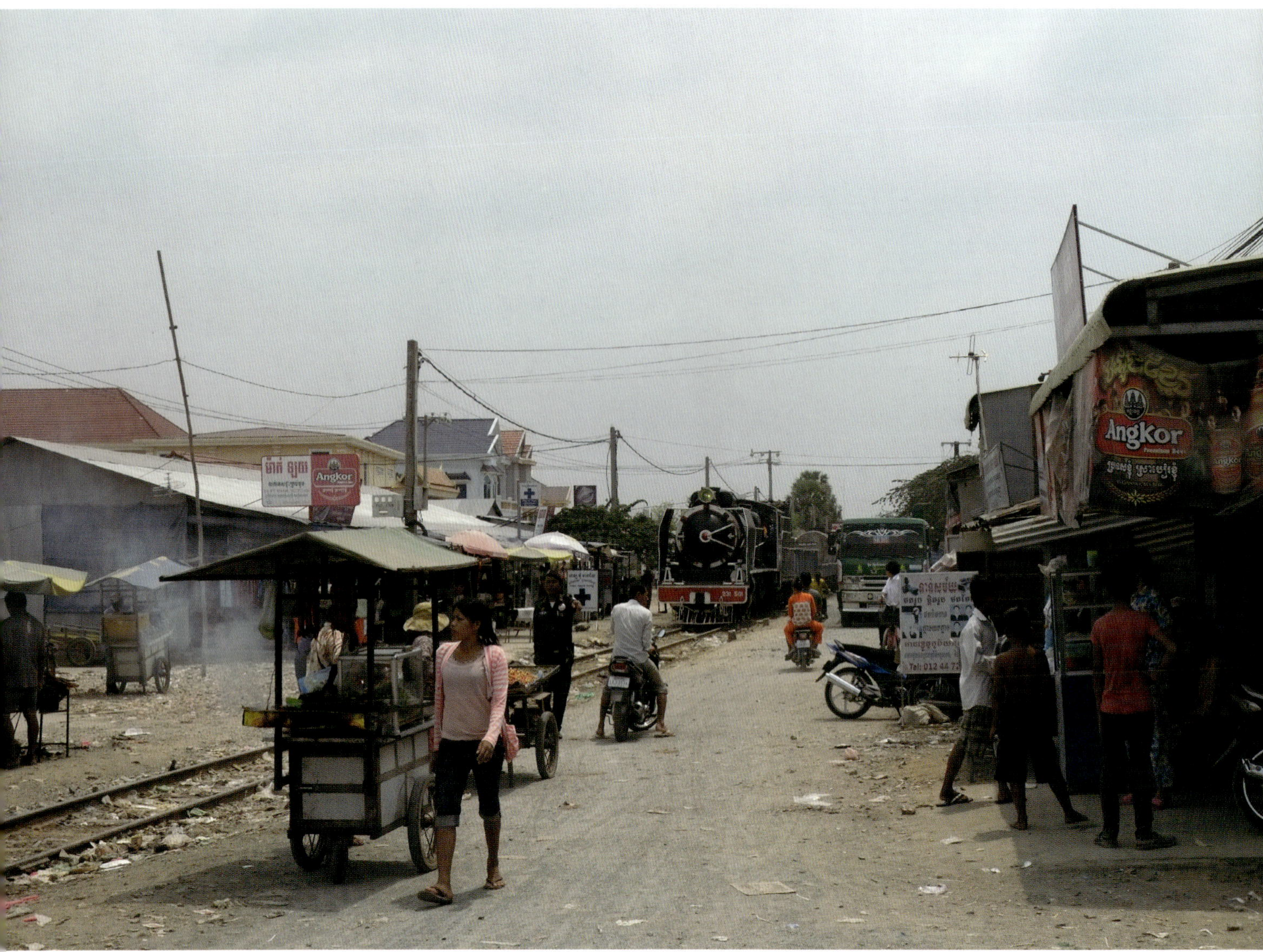

The first part of the metre gauge Cambodian system between Phnom Penh and the Thai border was built in 1932 and 1933 and a second line to Sihanoukville opened in 1954. Pacific No 231-501 runs through a market in the outskirts of Phnom Penh on 26 March 2014. The railway became very run down after the notorious Pol Pot regime gained power in 1975 and by the early 2000s was virtually defunct. Rehabilitation began in 2009 and happily No 231-501 was soon restored to working order. These locos, called Super Pacifics by the French colonial authorities, were amongst the many fine French-built machines to have served the railways of Cambodia and Vietnam.

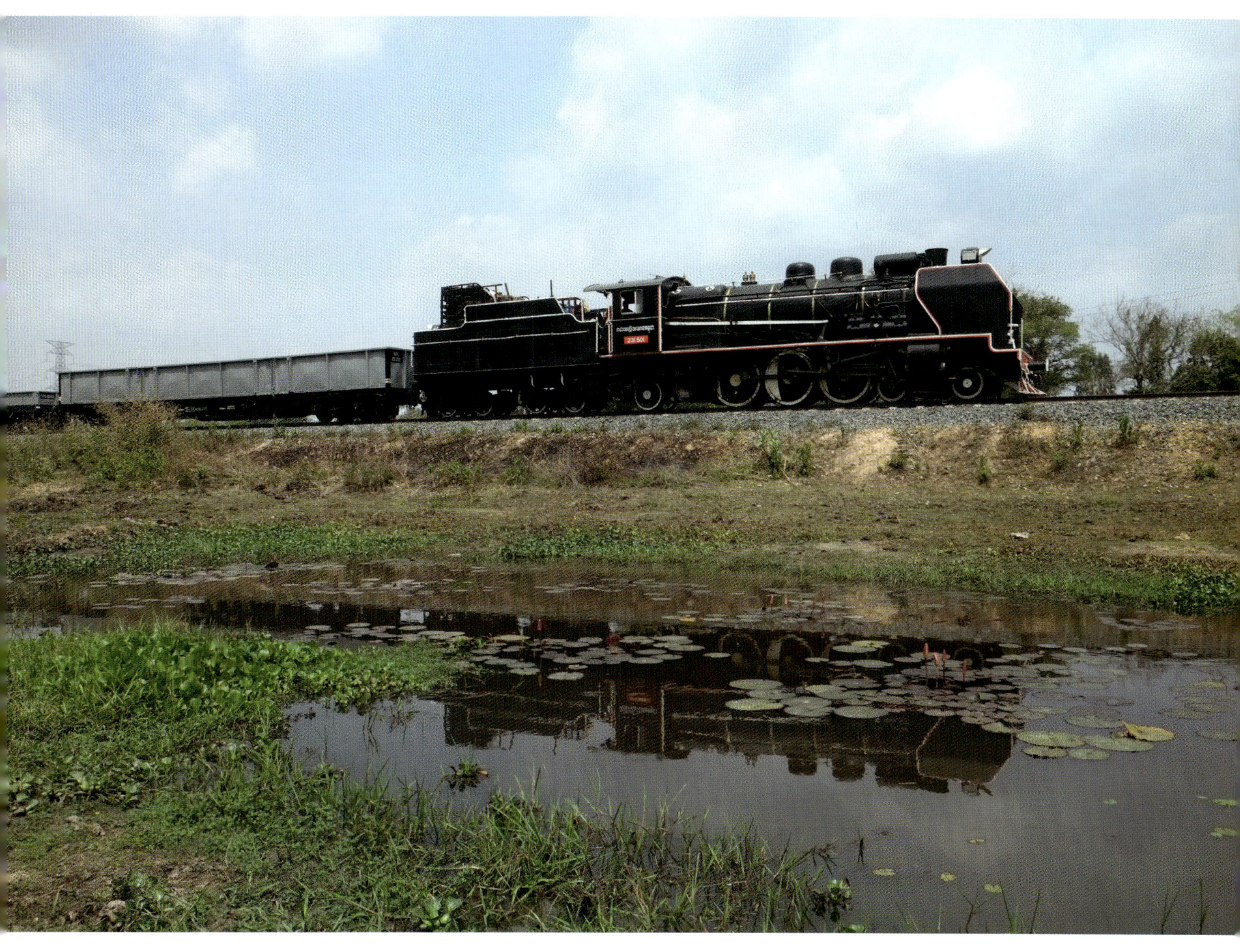

On the same day, No 231-501 stands at Takeo Ra loop on the Sihanoukville line. André Chapelon, the eminent French engineer, helped to design the Super Pacifics. They displayed many of his trademark features such as the Kylchap exhaust system though they didn't employ his much-loved compounding system. Maybe there wasn't room for its large low-pressure cylinders between the frames. The locos were developed from ten Pacifics delivered to Vietnam in 1933 which in turn were updated versions of eight built for the Tunisian railways between 1914 and 1928. SACM delivered fifty-one Super Pacifics from 1939 of which ten, built probably in 1948, went to Cambodia. The nine still there are the only survivors.

VIETNAM

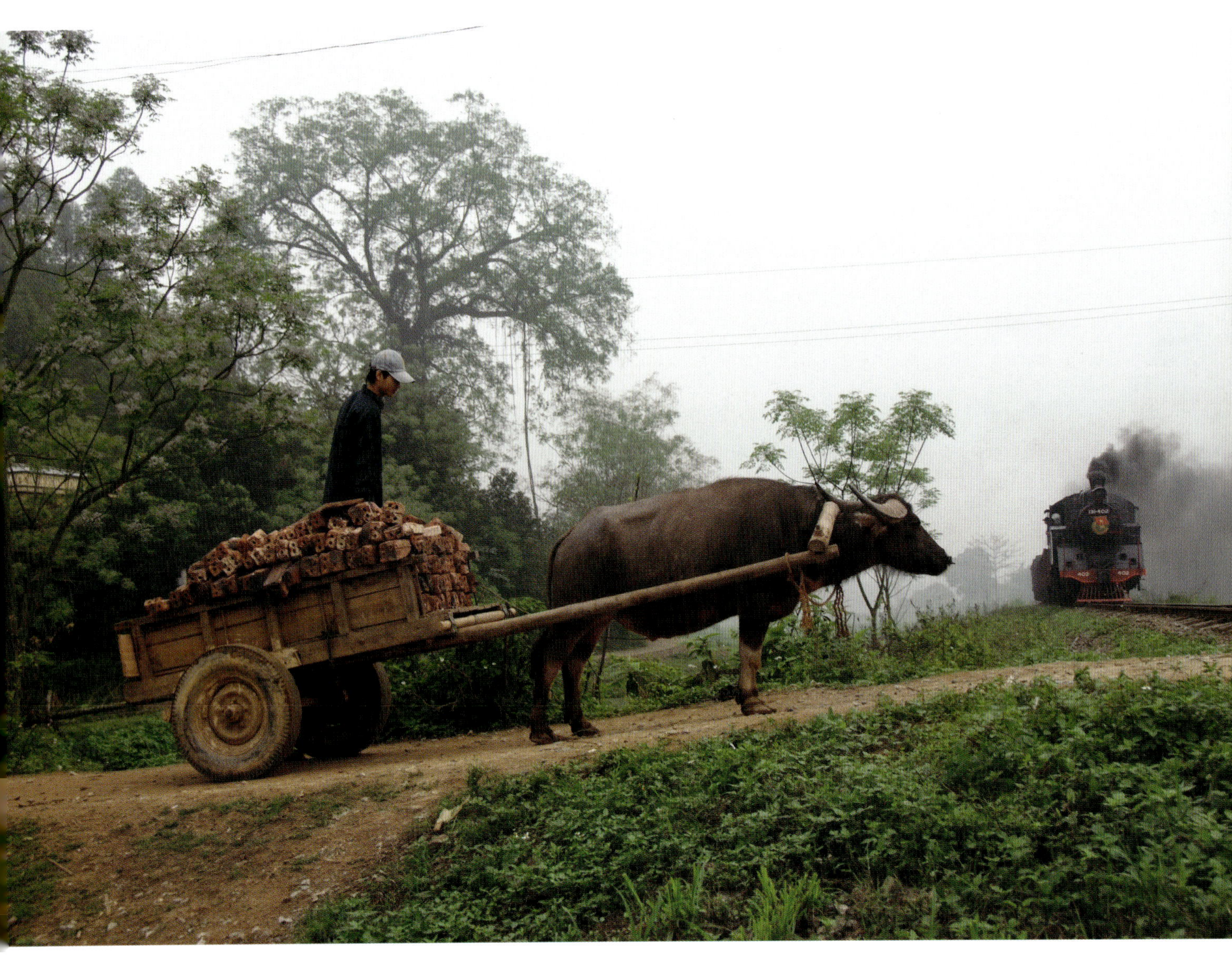

Construction of Vietnam's metre gauge system began in the late 1890s. This Japanese C12 class 2-6-2T, Vietnamese No 131-402, is one of sixty converted to run on metre gauge railways in China during the Second World War. At least forty-four, probably all the survivors, moved to North Vietnam when the last Chinese line was widened in the 1950s. She heads a short train near Yen Bai on 29 March 2008 and still carries the headboard awarded to her crew by President Ho Chi Minh in 1967 for efficient operation. Alas, she was no longer capable of being steamed and was being pushed by a diesel. Her original Japanese identity isn't known.

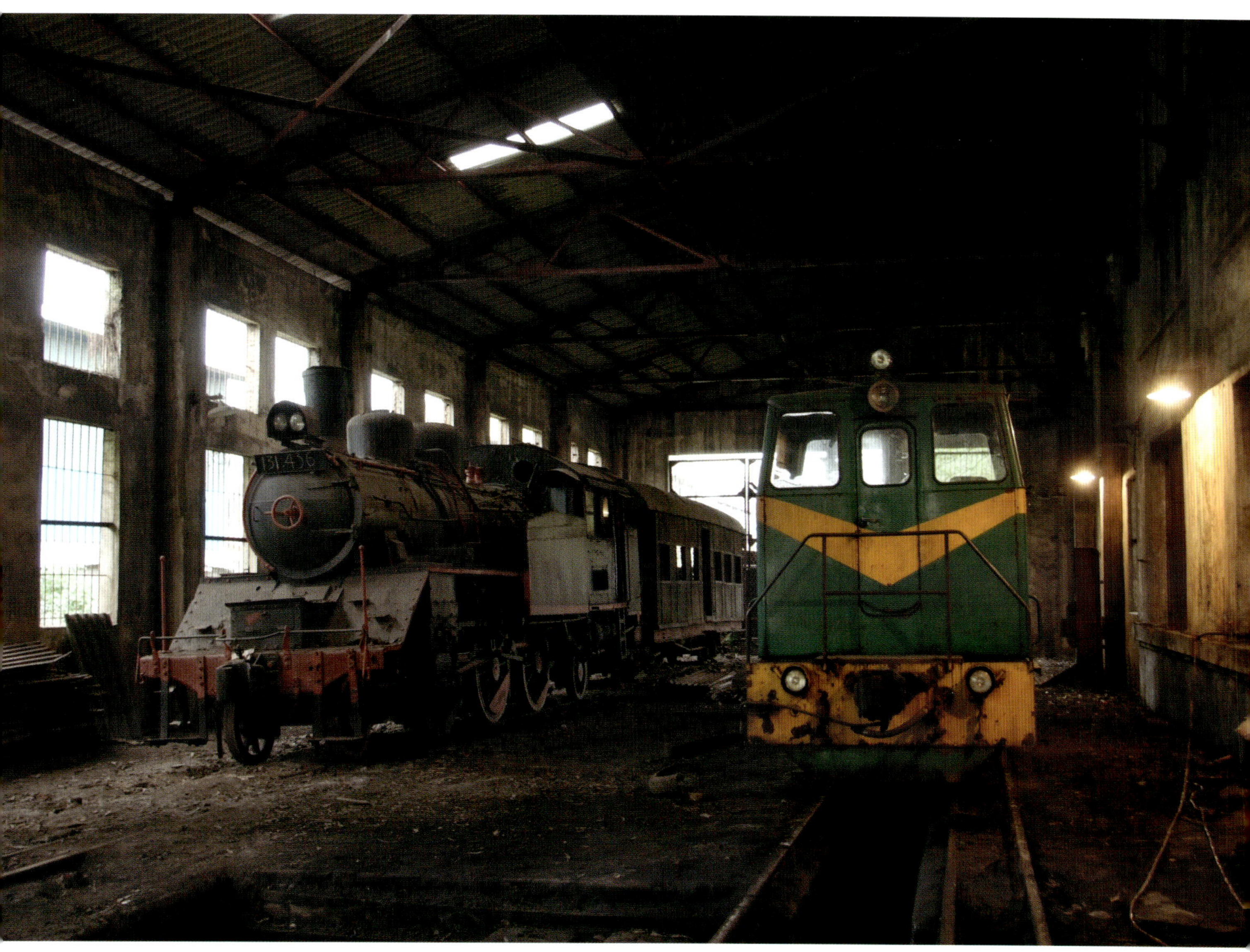

Vietnam's last working metre gauge steam loco was 2-6-2T No 131-436, believed to have been Japanese No C12 106 (Kawasaki 1610/1935). She worked out her days at the large steelworks at Thai Nguyen and on 31 March 2008 shares her shed with one of the Soviet-built Tu-7 diesels which had replaced her. The staff told me that she was still in good shape though her boiler certificate had expired five years earlier.

THE PHILIPPINES

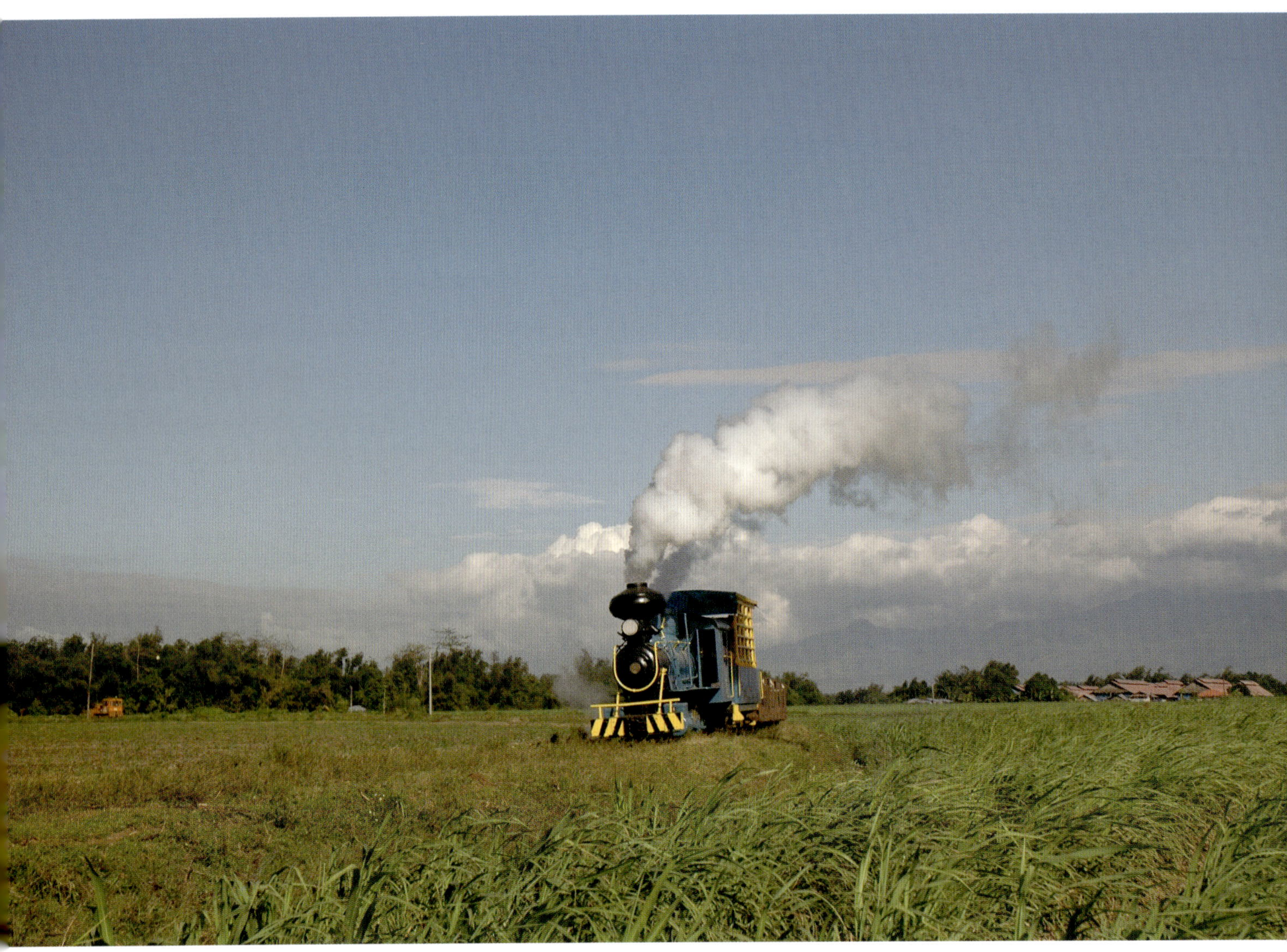

Filipinos call Negros 'sugar island'. Construction of central mechanised mills in the 1920s saw cane being brought in from far away and railways were soon built to transport it. The Hawaiian-Philippine factory, a thoroughly up-to-date establishment, is now one of the world's few producers of muscovado sugar, a distinction it shares with Beau Champ in Mauritius. 0-6-0 No 7 (Baldwin 60677/1928), newly painted in Hawaiian-Philippine's traditional blue and yellow paint scheme, heads a train through the cane fields near Sagay City in the late afternoon of 6 February 2007.

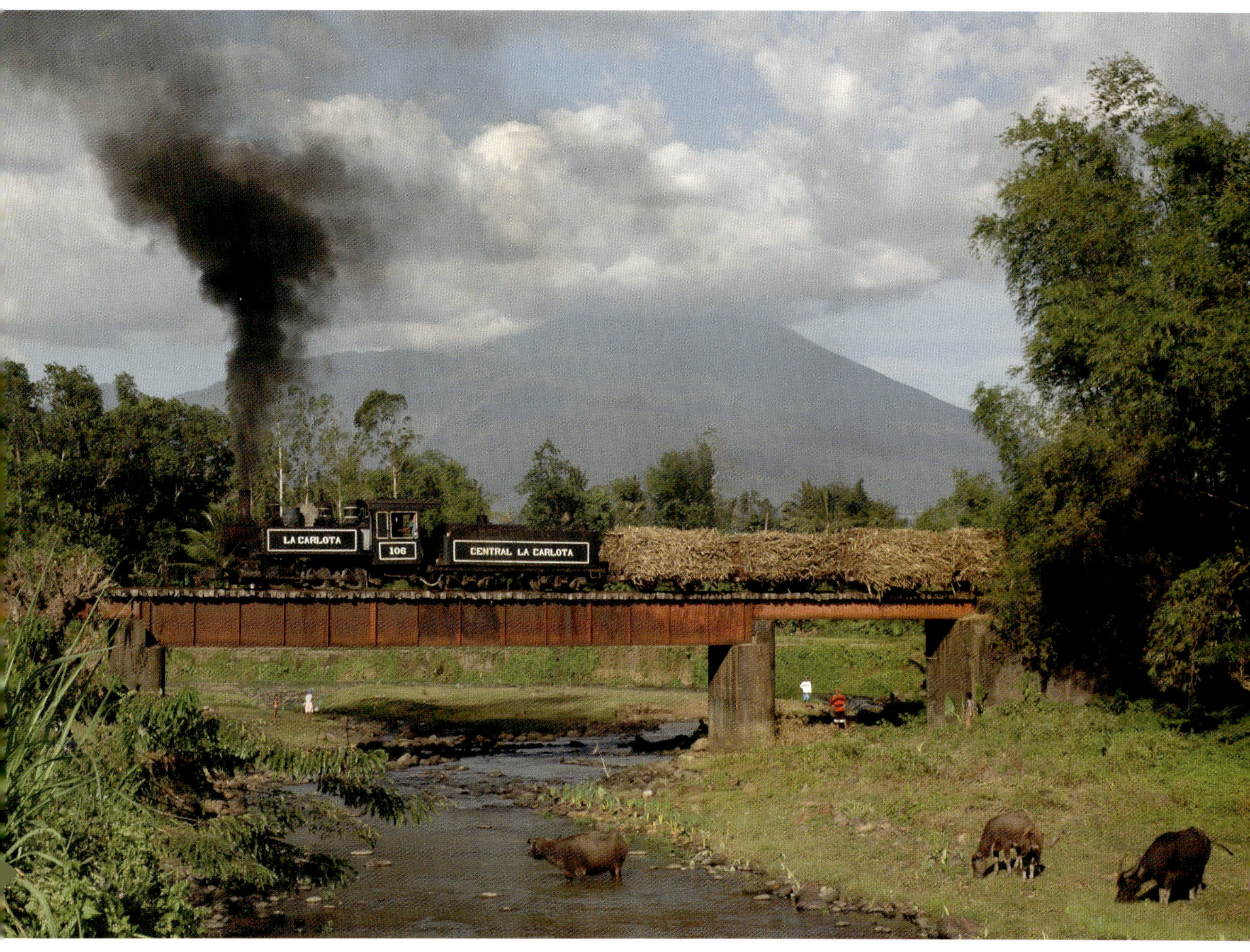

On 7 February 2007, the La Carlota factory's 0-6-0T+T No 103 (Baldwin 53181/1920) works a loaded train on the Velez Malaga line in central Negros with Mount Kanlaon, an active volcano and the island's highest mountain, as a backdrop. Both railways used the 3ft gauge much favoured in the US which administered the Philippines between 1896 and 1945. This was the last season for La Carlota's railways but the Hawaiian-Philippine system is still very much in use.

MALAYSIA

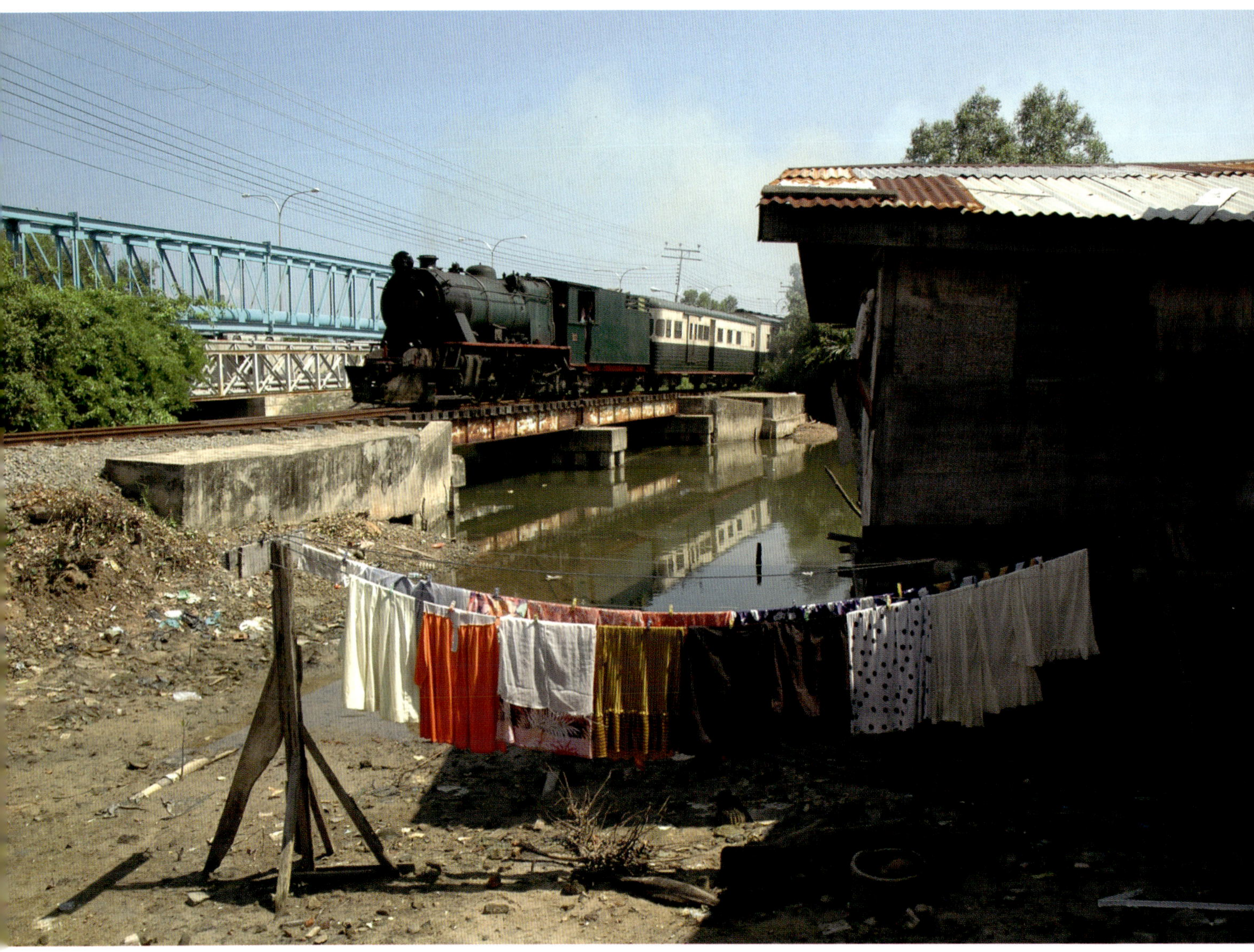

The metre gauge North Borneo Railway's 2-6-2 No 6-016 (VF 6276/1955) runs through the outskirts of Kota Kinabalu on 10 May 2006. The line's construction began in 1896 and this section opened in 1902. The three 2-6-2s were their builders' last steam locos and were in many respects scaled-down versions of the YD 2-8-2s which they built for Burma a few years earlier.

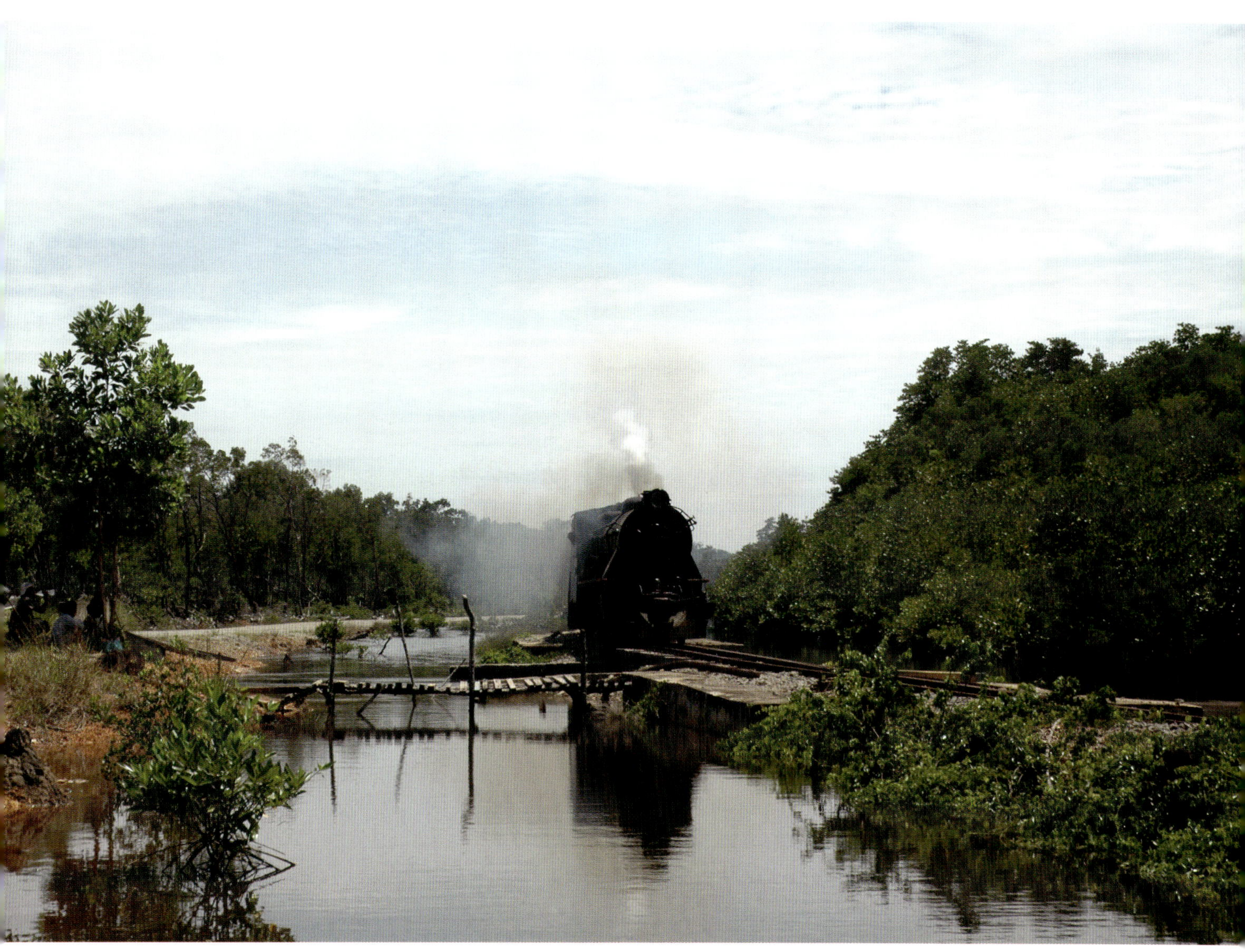

The fishermen by these mangroves between Pengalat and Kawang look up briefly to watch No 6-016 pass on 17 May 2006. During the steam era the locos were fired with mangrove wood cut in this neighbourhood. Diesels took over in the 1970s but two of the 2-6-2s were overhauled in the late 1990s for a tourist service between Tanjung Aru station at Kota Kinabalu and Papar. Five 1970s carriages were refurbished to run with them along with an old Wickham-built diesel railcar adapted to form a kitchen car.

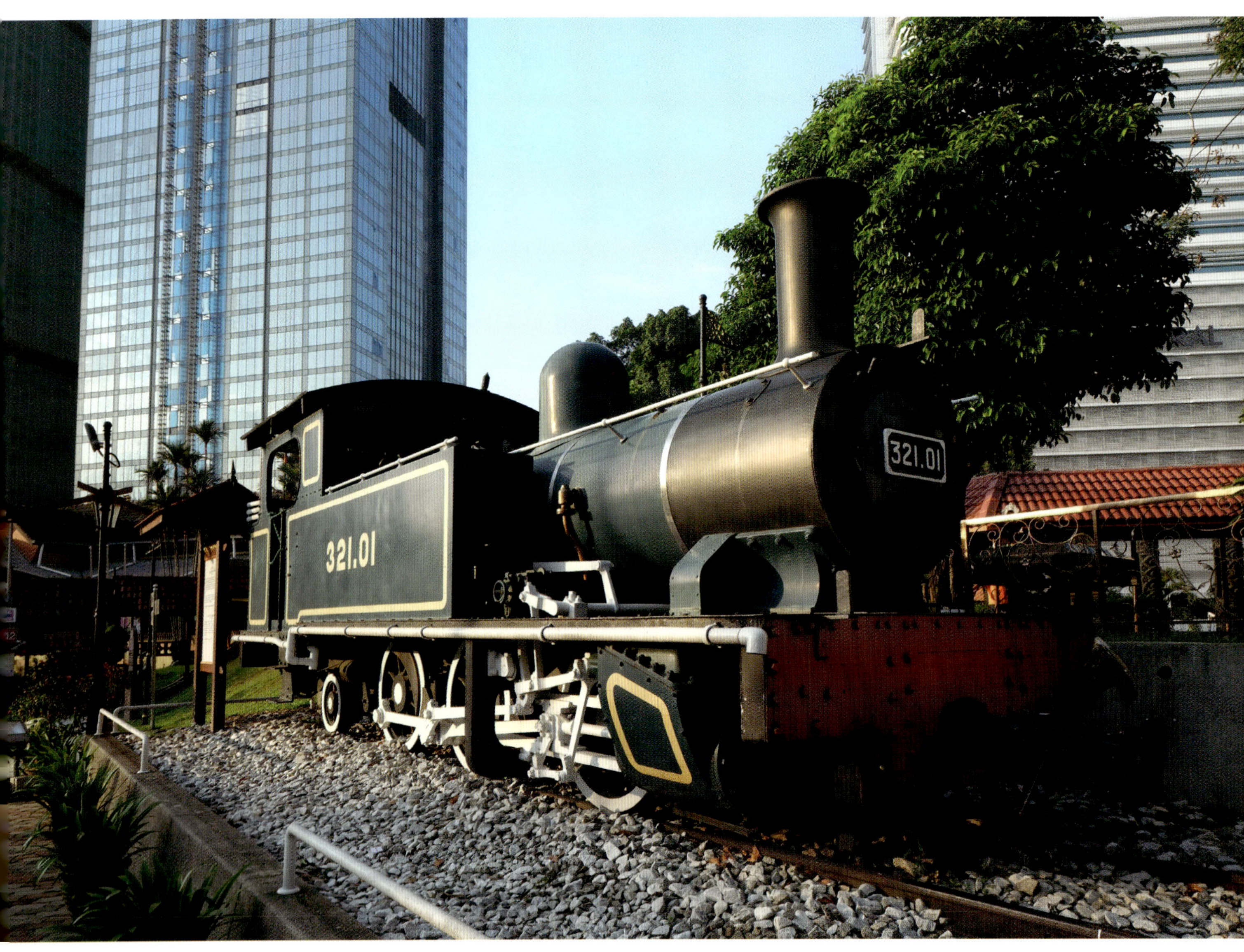

Steam working on the metre gauge Federated Malay States Railway ended in 1971. Only a few locos were saved and much the smartest are two at the Muzium Negara in Kuala Lumpur. It's close to the site of the city's old roundhouse now occupied by the modern KL Sentral station – not to be confused with the fine colonial-era one a little to the north still known simply as Kuala Lumpur. Here's 0-6-2T No 321.01 (Bagnall 2323/1927) just after sunrise on 28 July 2015. She was one of five similar locos used mostly for shunting at Port Swettenham and Singapore docks. They were the first British-built ones in Malaya with steel fireboxes. No 321.01 was sold to the Pan-Malaya Cement Company in about 1966 and they donated her for preservation.

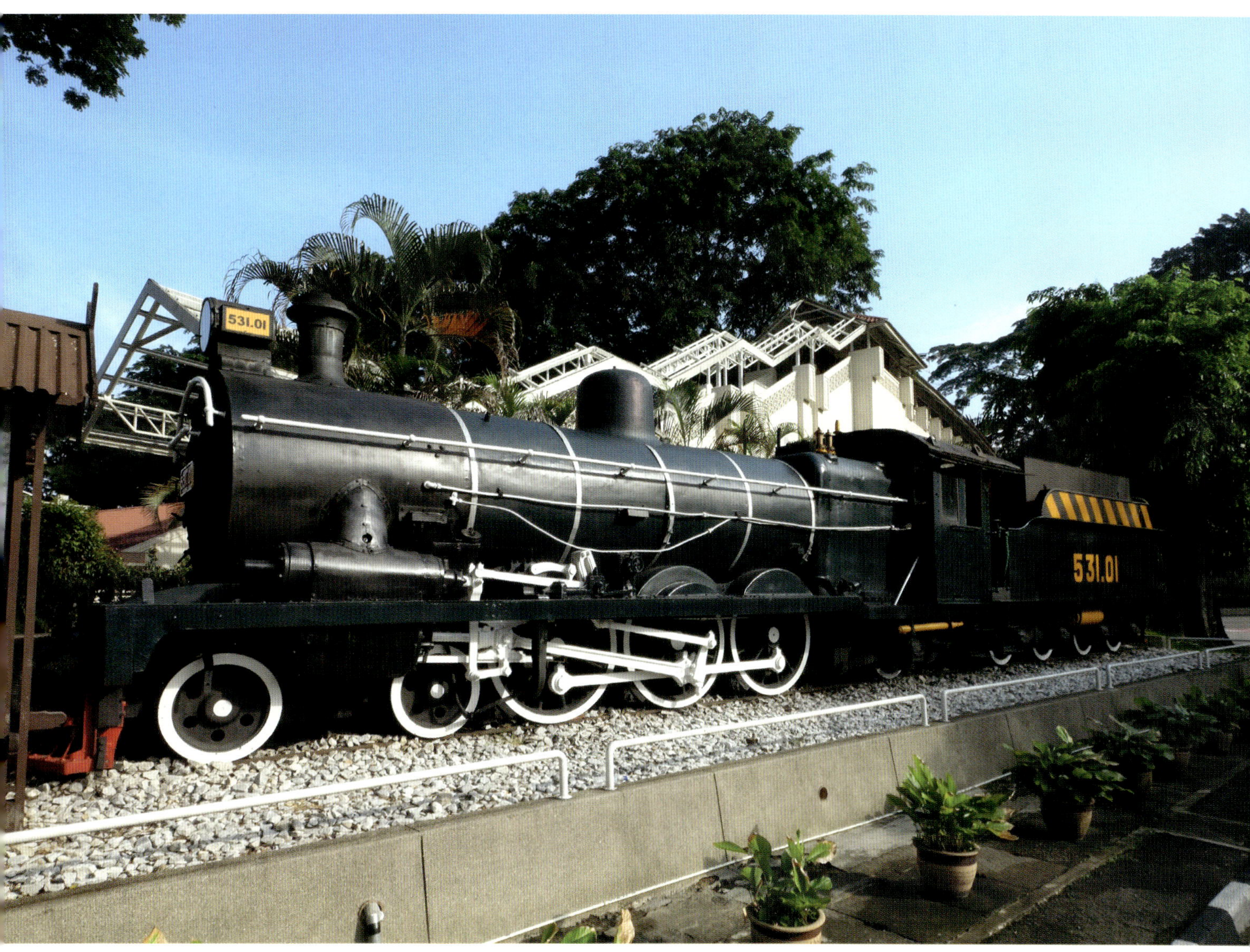

For many years, a large proportion of FMSR's locos were Pacifics. The first was built as early as 1907 and the railway eventually used them for most of its trains, both freight and passenger. L class No 531.01 (Kitson 5300/1921) is the other loco at the museum. Both of them carry the dark green used by FMSR for some of its locos in the 1960's. I saw a Kuala Lumpur to Singapore express in 1975 composed of carriages smartly painted in brown and cream. The locos' Swindon-style lampirons make it even easier to guess where some of those in charge must have received their training!

CHINA

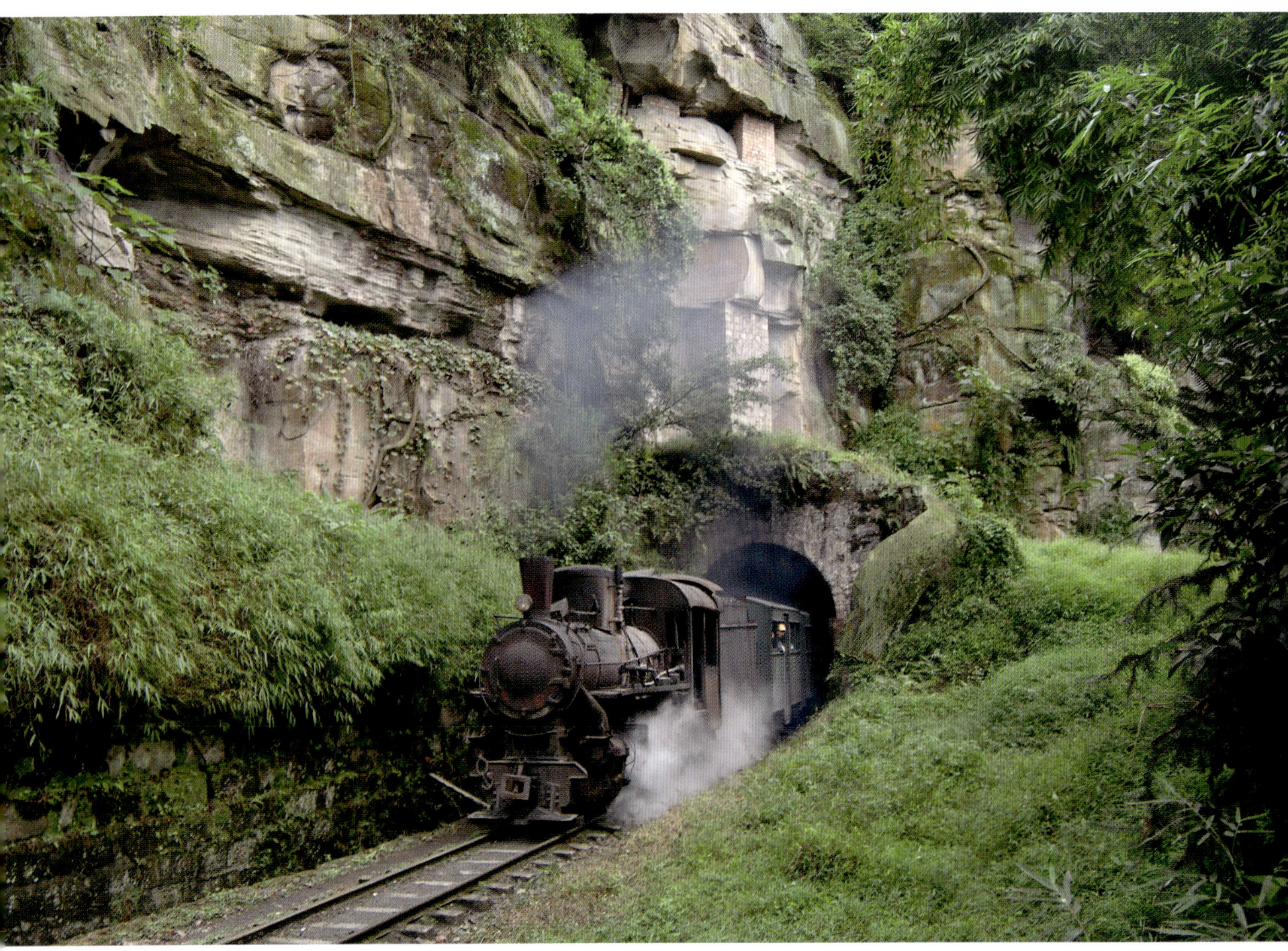

China once possessed numerous narrow gauge lines, most of the recent survivors being 2ft 6ins. Some were run by the state railway and offered full public passenger and freight services as did others operated by local concerns. More were purely industrial, ranging from forestry railways in the north to colliery and mineral lines throughout the country. Numerous new ones were built just before or during Chairman Mao's Great Leap Forward in the late 1950s, the first drive to industrialise the country, and they probably included all four of the lines I visited in 2004. The scenic Jiayang colliery railway, based at Shibanxi in Sichuan province, is known to have been built as a 600mm gauge line in 1959 and converted to 2ft 6ins one year later. On 5 October 2004 C2 class 0-8-0 No 14 leaves Nao Ying Zui Tunnel about 2kms north of Mifengyan. She may well have been built at Shibanxi works.

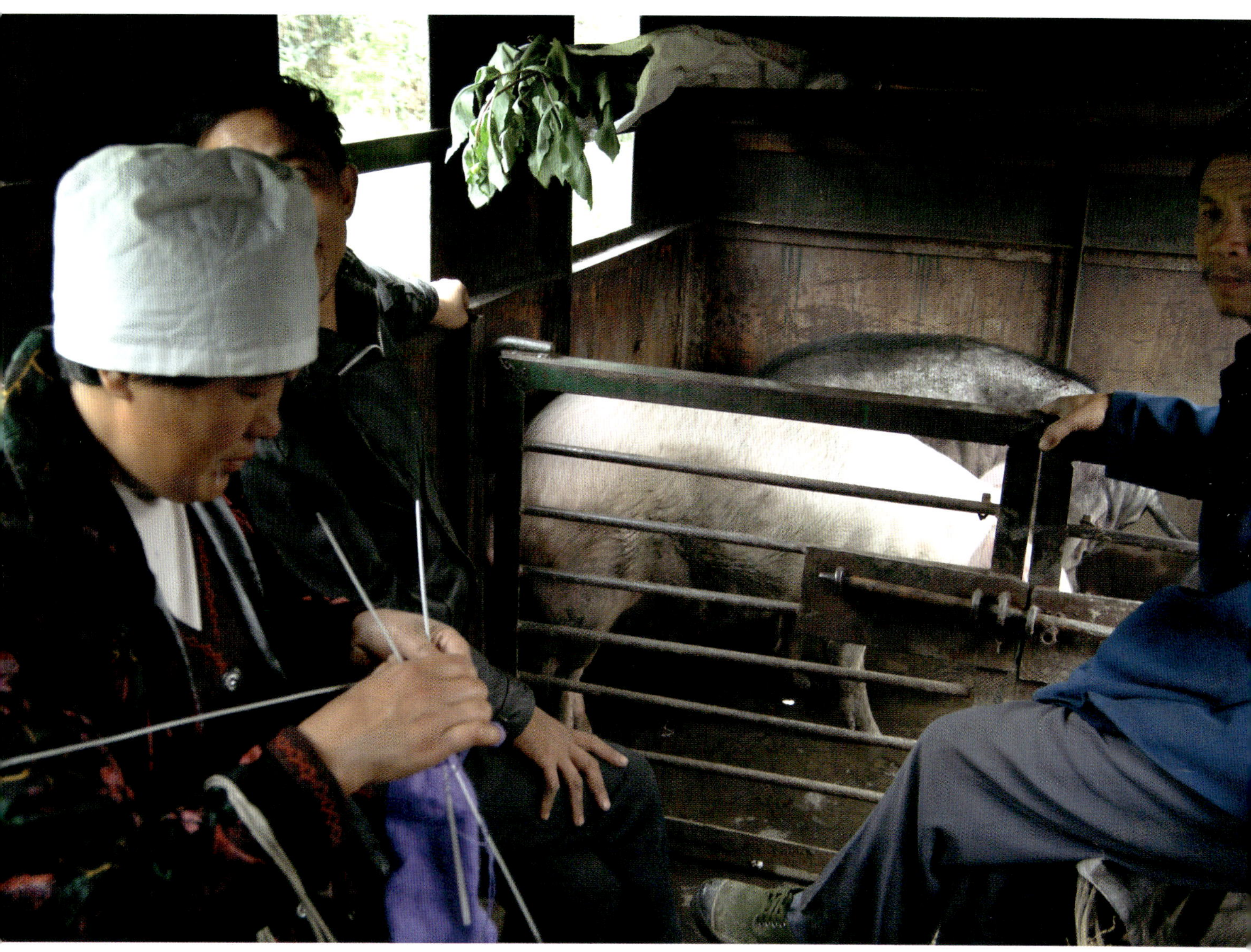

Humans aren't the only travellers in the Shibanxi line's carriages! On the same day these two pigs were most reluctant passengers. Maybe they knew they'd only been issued with single tickets and that this wasn't good news! There were once several 2ft 6ins gauge steam classes in China but by 2004 only the C2s, based on the Soviet PT-4 design, were left. The earliest were probably three supplied by Chrzanów and a few by MÁVAG, both in 1952. More, possibly ninety-six, followed from Chrzanów in 1959. After 1958 Shijiazhuang is reported to have built 575 until 1984 and Harbin 221 until 1988. A few more may have been built at other factories. Added to the Soviet and eastern European locos there were about 5,500 altogether, not counting the wood-gas machines! The PT-4/C2 story isn't yet complete as Shibanxi works is believed still to be building new ones. The line now has a flourishing tourist business while still providing transport for local residents – and their pigs!

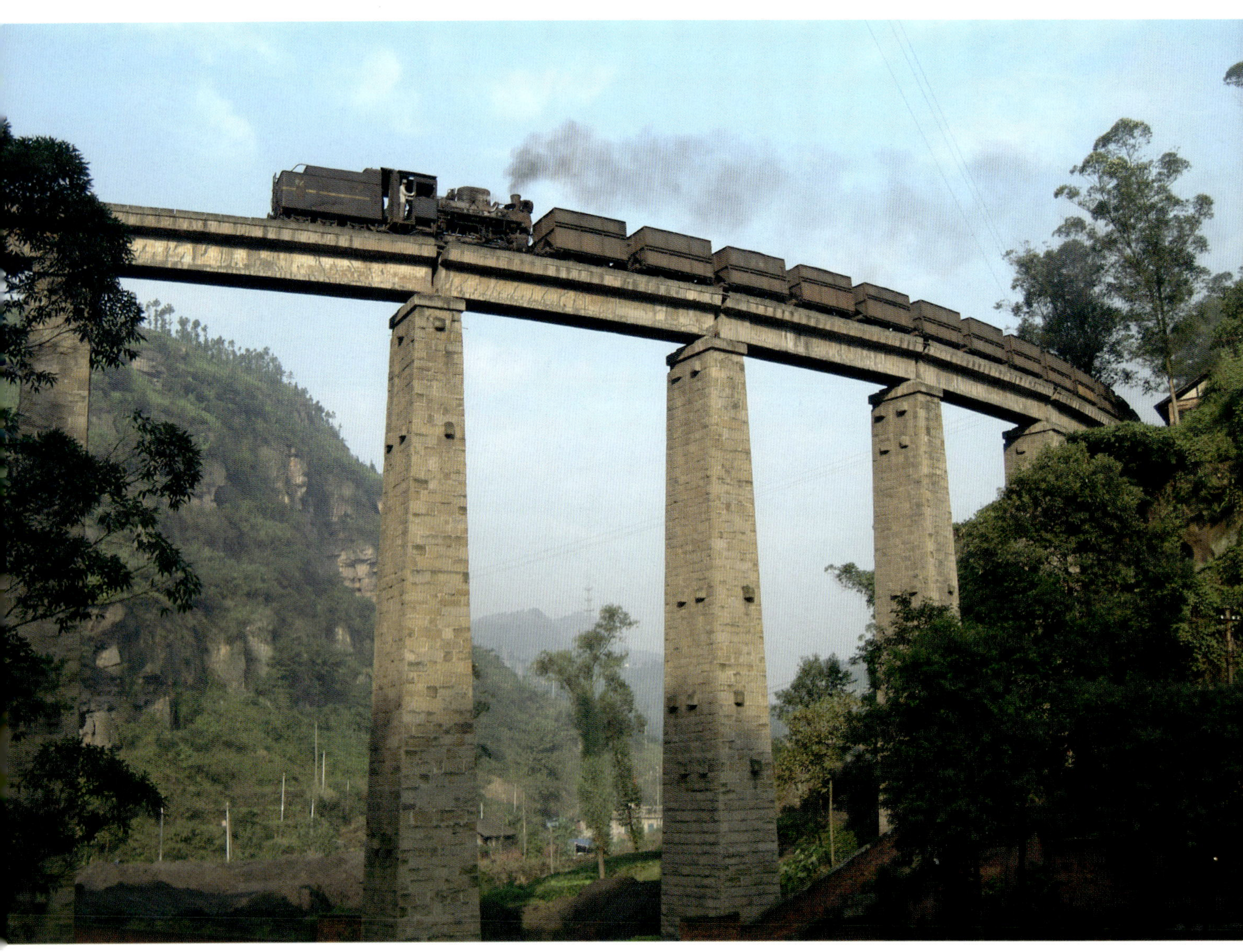

It took more than six hours on a rainy night to drive from Shibanxi to Huangjinggou, a coalmining village up in the hills whose short railway was an especial delight. Its main engineering feature was this splendid viaduct at Badong which C2 No 31 (Shijiazhuang X1982-09/1982) crosses on 7 October 2004. The coal trains consisted of small tub wagons and just outside the colliery gate ran through a market where the traders had to move their stalls in a hurry whenever they appeared. After its passenger service ended in 1988 only one train, or occasionally two, ran per day. The first usually left the colliery before sunrise and the second, when it ran, about two hours later. I was lucky as it was a fine sunny day and there were two trains. The line closed in 2007 and was immediately demolished.

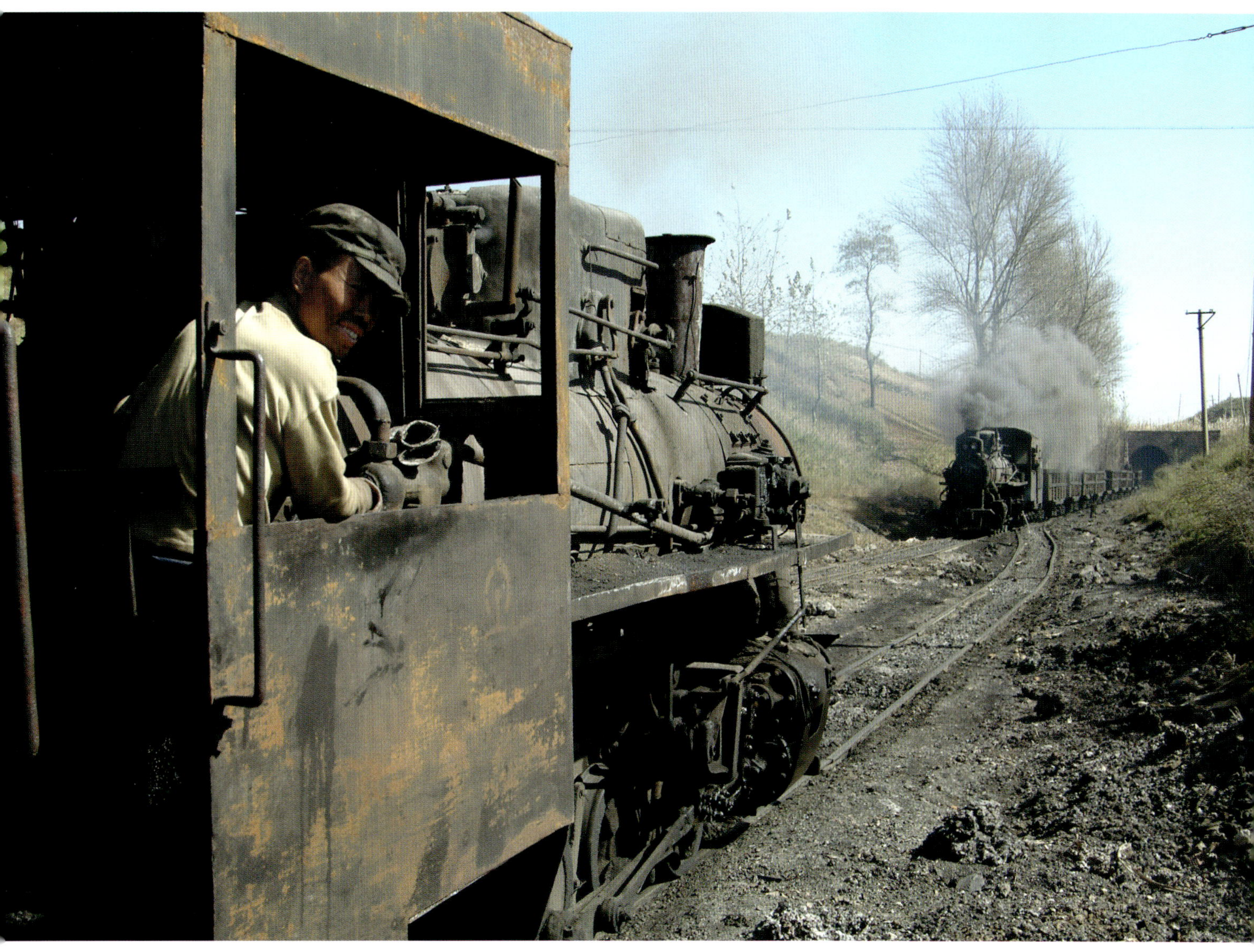

New discoveries amongst the world's narrow gauge steam railways have been very few in the twenty-first century but Japanese railfan Toshiaki Tsujimoto and his Mongolian guide Sen Chokt found a real gem when they made the first ever enthusiast visit to the Yinghao colliery railway in May 2004. It ran through the hills of Henan for about 9kms from Yinghao on the busy mainline between Zhengzhou and Xian. C2 No 3 with her cheerful driver is shunting at Xiangyang as a train of empties hauled by No 4 approaches on 11 October 2004. They were probably both built by Shijiazhuang. The local cuisine includes a green beer made from cucumbers – I tried it and let's just say that maybe it's an acquired taste! As ever in rural China, the people were overwhelmingly hospitable and friendly. Regular services finished in 2007 and the track had become unusable a couple of years later. At least five of the locos have moved to a new tourist operation on what was once a local line between Chaoyanggou and Qixian.

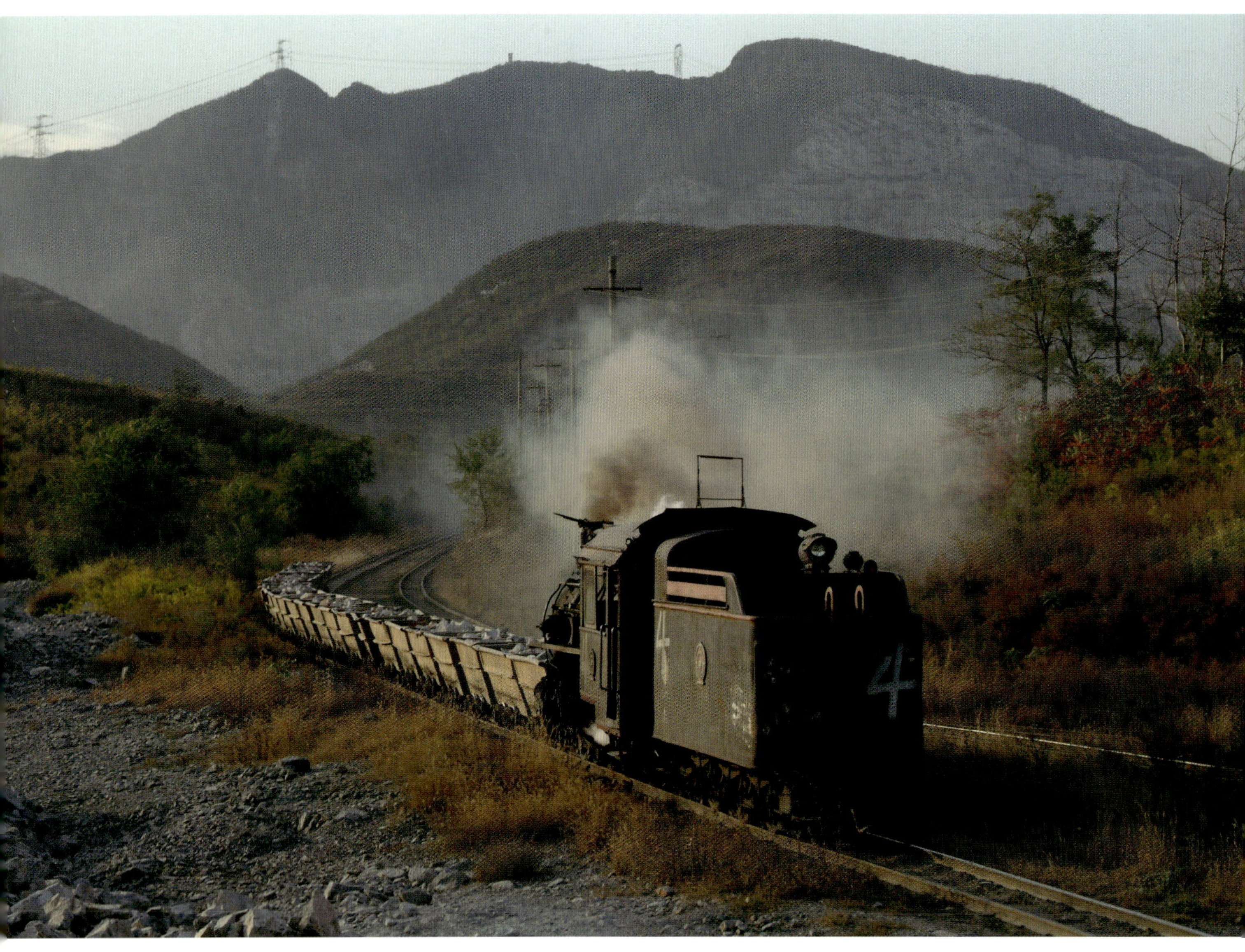

There couldn't have been more of a contrast between these rural lines and the Dahuichang quarry railway in the sprawling outskirts of Beijing from where the huge high-rise buildings downtown were clearly visible when the city's notorious smog wasn't too thick. A double track line ran between a limestone quarry, high above the line, and a cement factory about 2kms away. The stone was loaded through a chute inside a hill into wagons standing in a tunnel below. Operations involved two train sets and locos with up to eight runs per hour. Just before sunset, No 4 (Harbin 221/1988) approaches the factory on 11 October 2004. She was probably the last narrow gauge steam loco to be built for commercial service anywhere in the world. The line closed in late July 2005, though two of its four C2s were still there over ten years later. In 2006, No 4 moved to the Ffestiniog where she's being converted to 600mm gauge.

TAIWAN

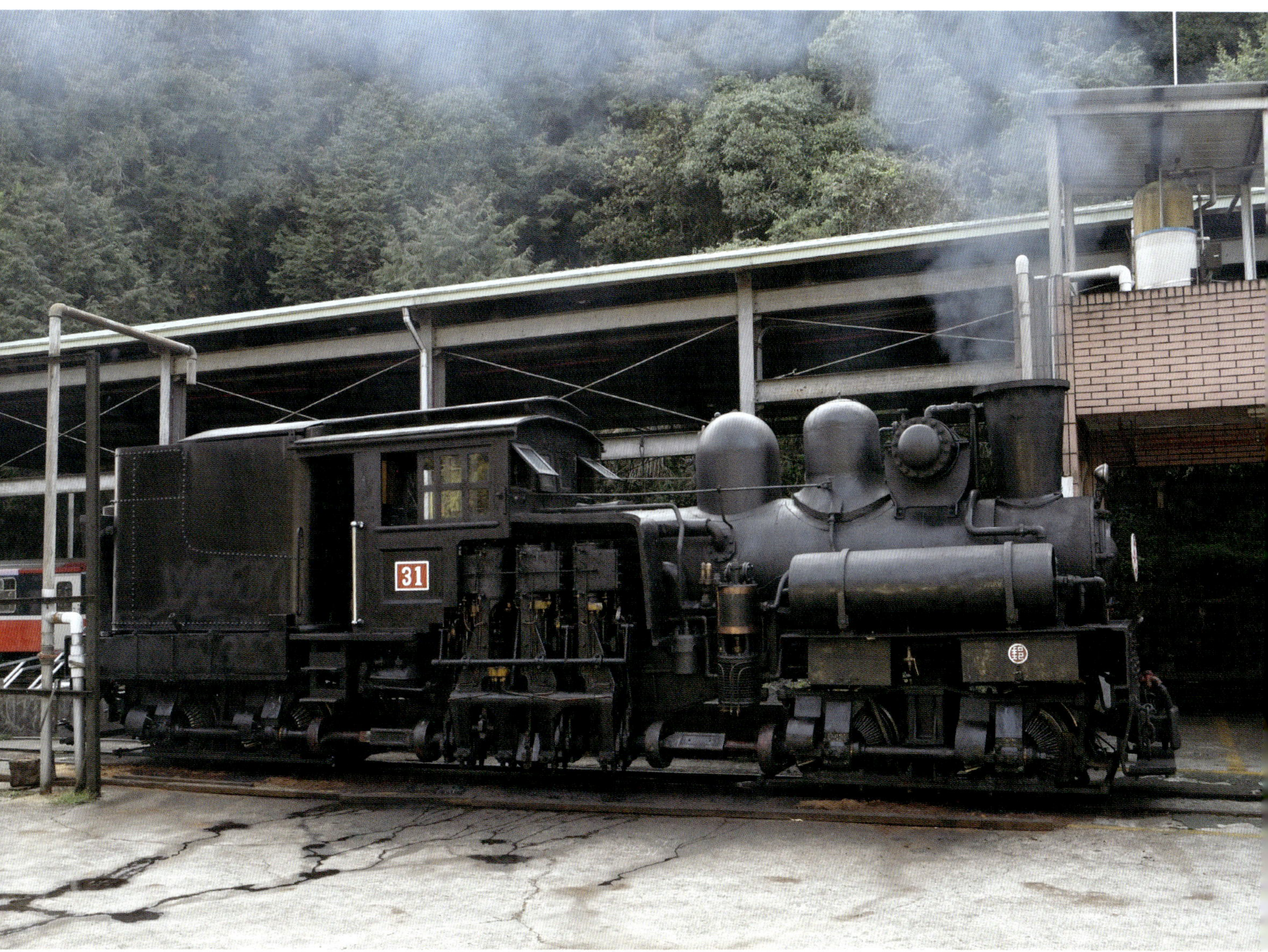

The 2ft 6ins gauge Alishan Forest Railway climbs up from the humid plain around Chiayi in western Taiwan through remarkable scenery for 80kms with tunnels, viaducts, zig-zags and a triple spiral. For the whole of the steam era it was worked by a series of twenty Shays, the remarkable geared locos mostly used on hilly, twisty logging railways in the US. Six type A two-cylinder 18-ton machines were built between 1910 and 1913 and twelve type B 28-ton ones between 1912 and 1917. Here, type B No 31 (Lima 2947/1917) brews up at Alishan engine shed early in the morning of 18 March 2015.

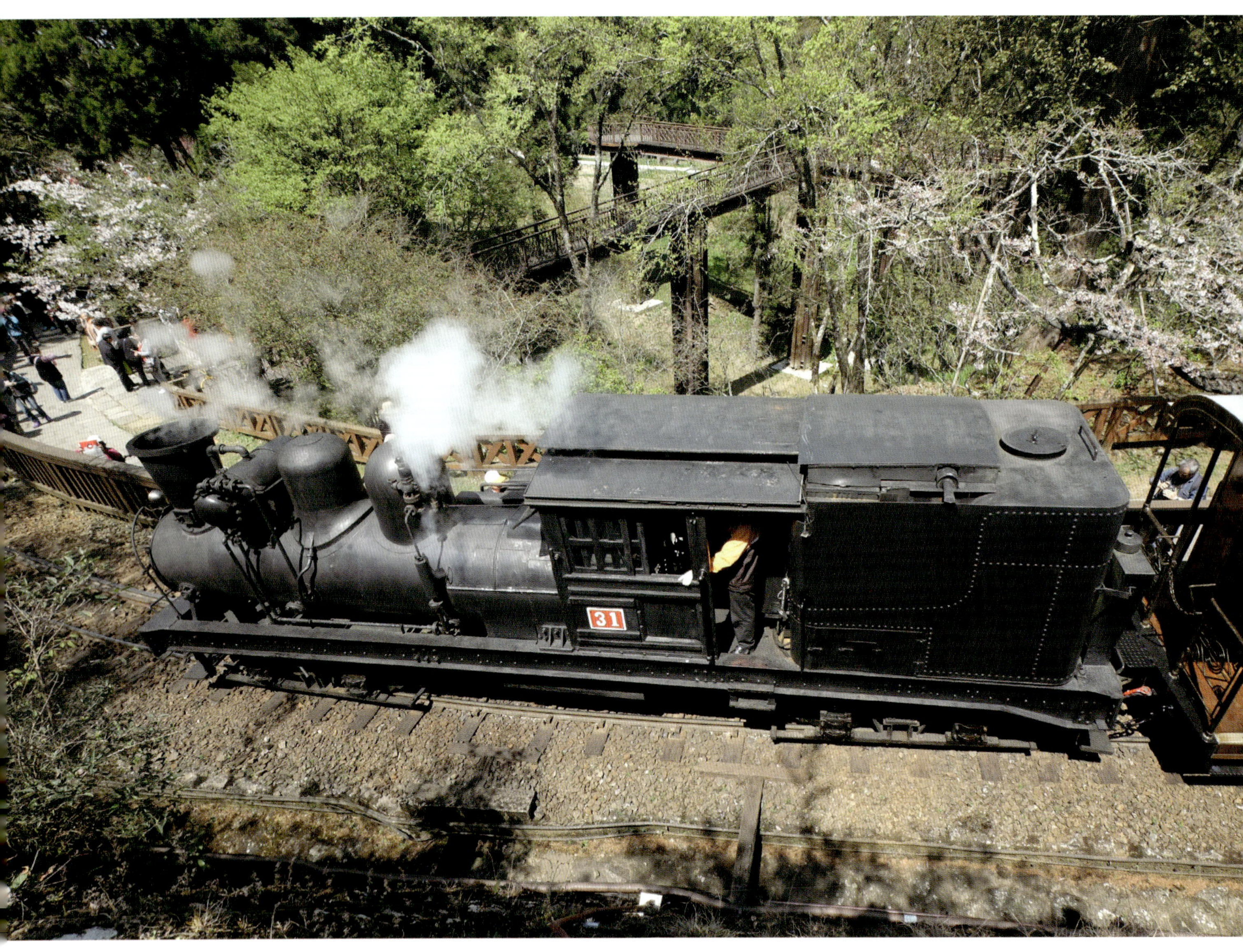

Later that morning, No 31 heads through a park with flowering cherry trees near Chaoping. The loco only makes public trips at Christmas and on a few days in Spring each year when the blossom is at its best – something of great importance to the Taiwanese and a legacy of the years between 1896 and 1945 when the island was run by Japan. The railway was built between 1907 and 1912 to open up the forests of ancient cedar and cypress trees around Alishan to commercial logging.

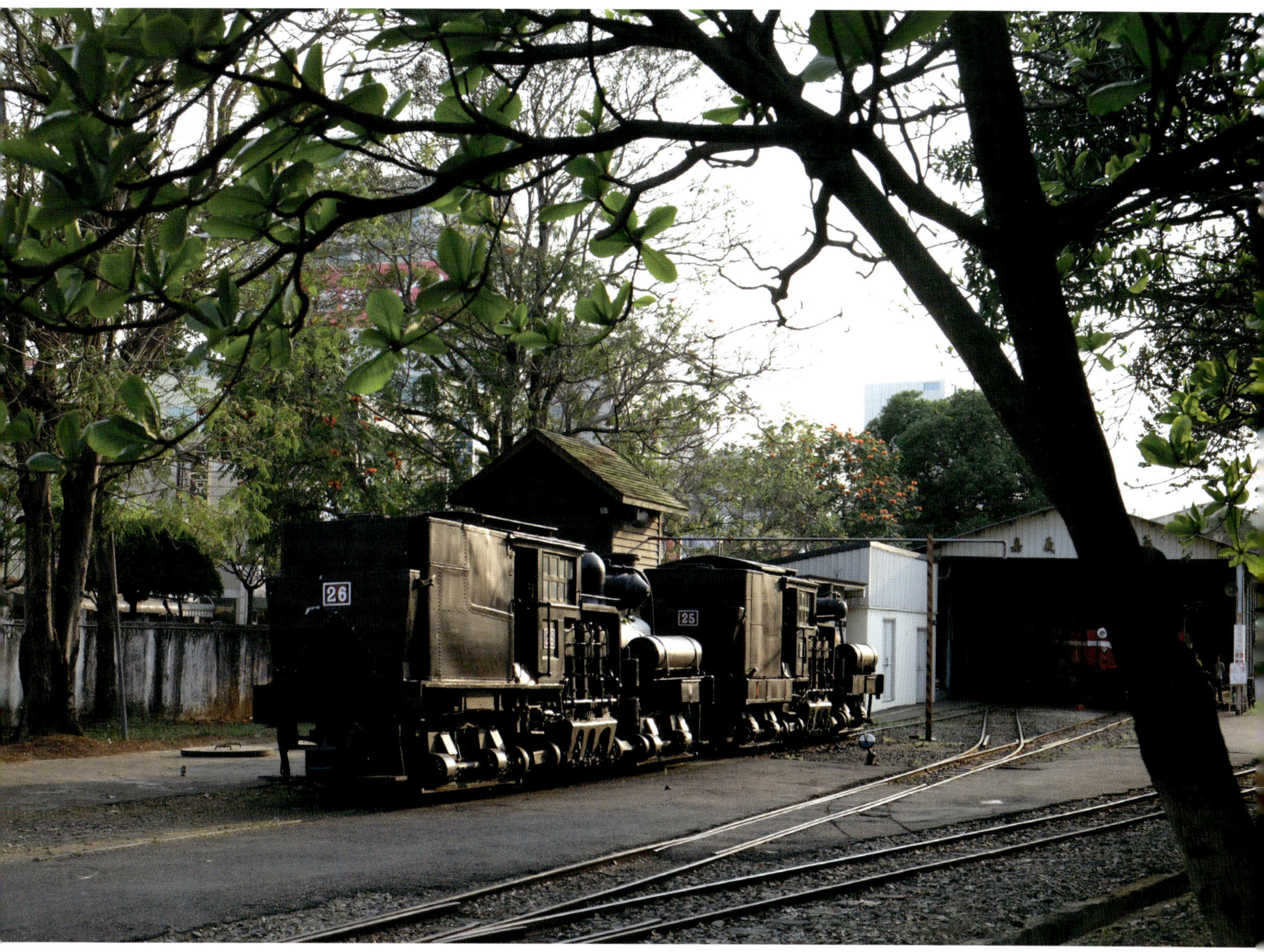

At Beimen shed in Chiayi type B Nos 26 (Lima 2789/1914) and 25 (Lima 2788/1914), the other two working Shays, bask in the sunshine late that afternoon. In recent years, the only public steam train at this end of the line has run on Christmas Day. By the time replacement of the Shays got under way in the 1960s and 1970s, public affection for them was so great that only four, all the victims of accidents, were ever scrapped. Ten are still on the railway.

JAPAN

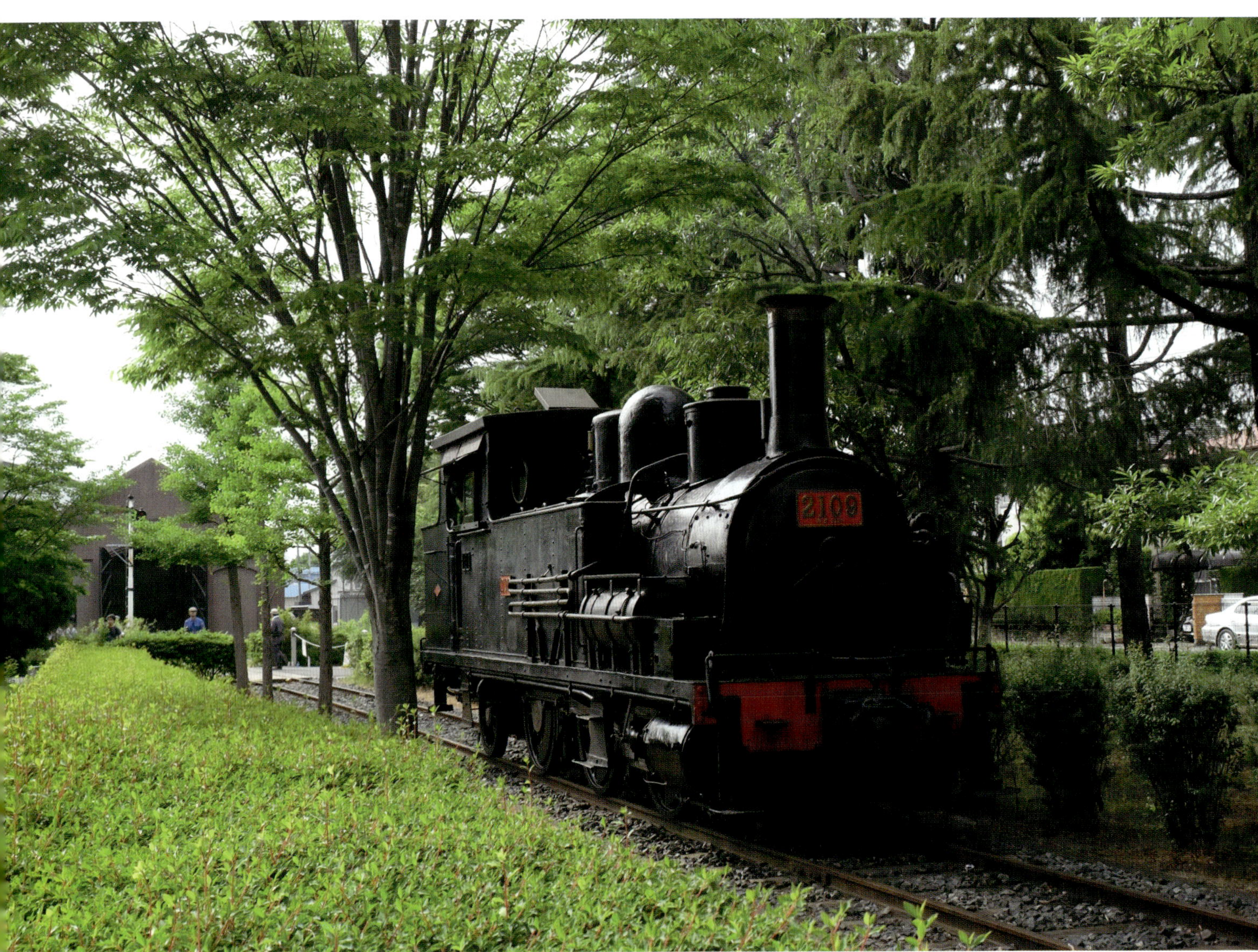

Railways came late to Japan due to its isolation from the outside world for about two centuries until 1868. Its first line opened in 1872 and grew into one of the world's busiest 3ft 6ins gauge networks. The early imported locos included many from the UK. 0-6-2T No 2109 (Dübs 2774/1891) was built for the Nippon Railway which until nationalisation in 1907 ran the mainline between Tokyo and Aomori on Honshu's north coast. She was rescued for preservation in 1970 by the Oigawa Railway, largely thanks to Mr Akira Shirai who became its chief engineer in 1969. The Oigawa later introduced regular heritage trains but she was too slow for these and eventually moved to the National Institute of Technology at Miyashiro where she runs every few weeks in summer. On 21 May 2016, she makes her way along their short track.

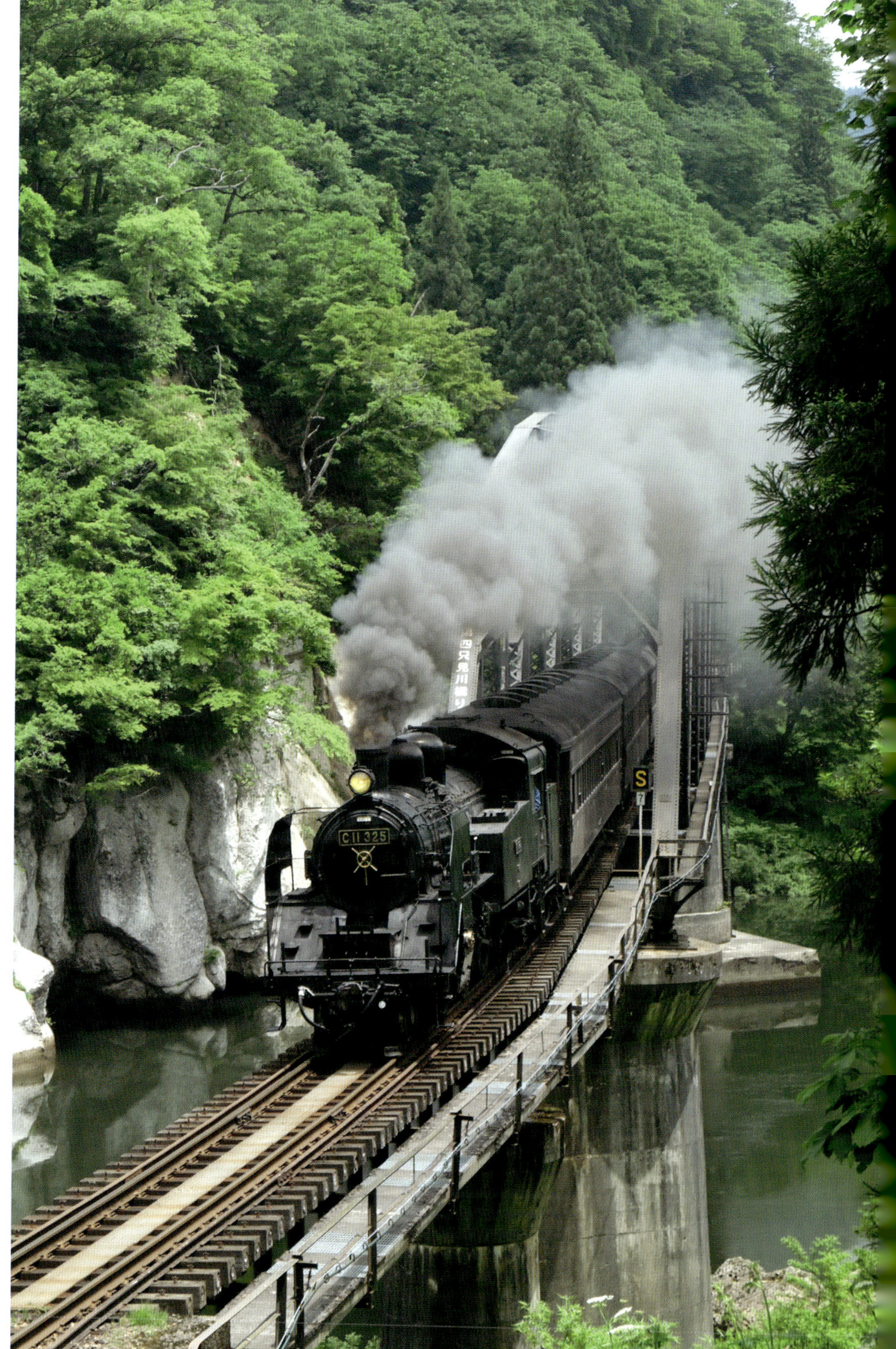

On 26 May 2016 2-6-4T No C11 325 (Nippon 1407/1946) crosses bridge No 4 on the Tadami line between Aizu-Miyashita and Aizu-Kawaguchi in central Honshu, a section built as recently as 1956. After 1914 the state railway went in for just a few loco types which were constructed in large numbers. 399 C11s were produced between 1932 and 1947.

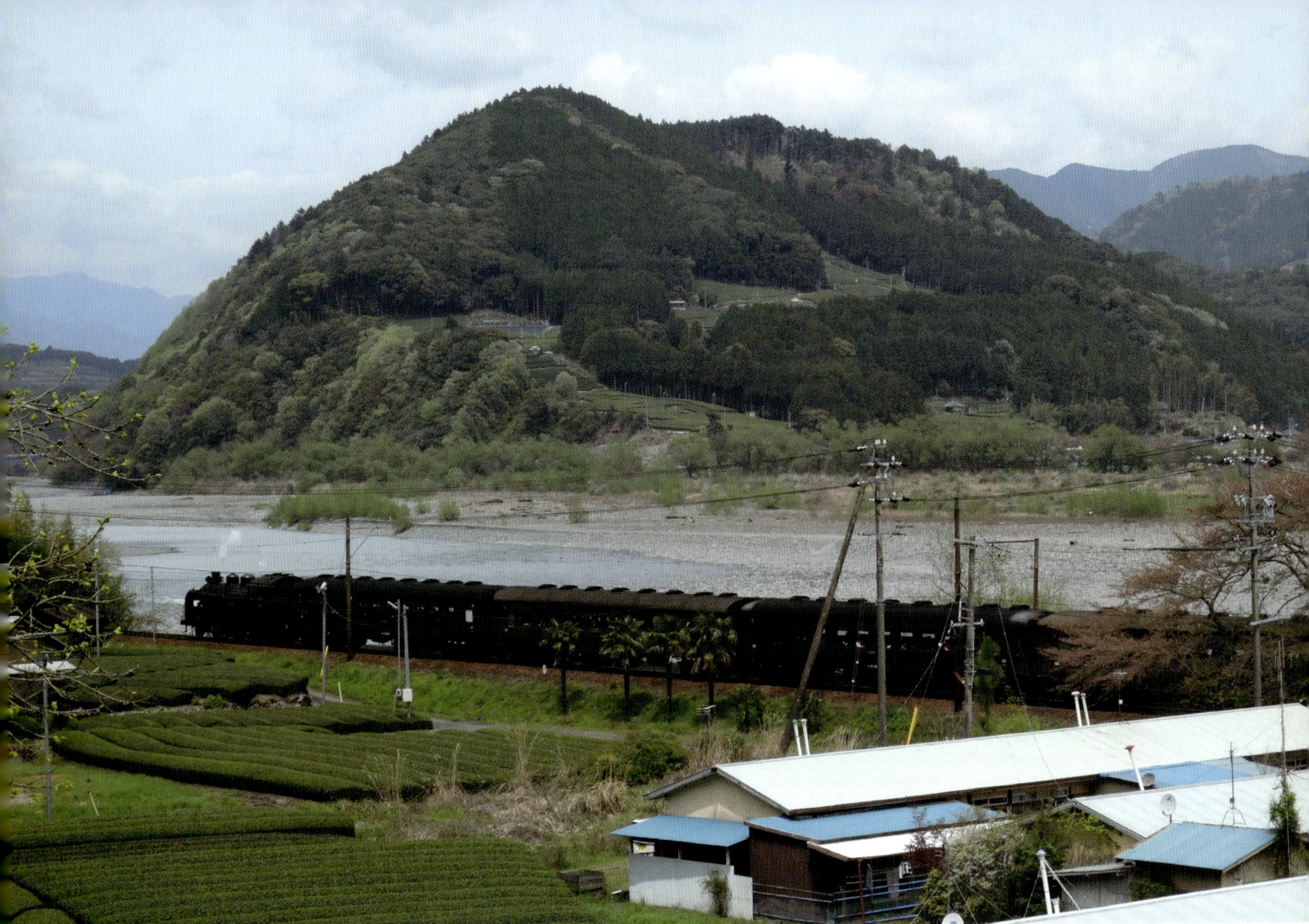

Above: On the Oigawa, No C11 227 (Nippon 1108/1942) heads a northbound train past one of the Gawa valley's many tea plantations on 12 April 2015. The railway has always been privately-owned and began its heritage service on 9 July 1976, only a few months after Japanese mainline steam working finished. At its inland terminus at Senzu, locos are turned on a 50ft Ransomes & Rapier turntable, another reminder of British influence on Japan's early railways.

Opposite above: On 26 May 2016 No C11 325 runs through paddy fields near Aizu-Wakamatsu. Japan probably chose the 3ft 6ins gauge because its first engineer had previously worked in New Zealand, a similarly mountainous country where the gauge had just been adopted.

Opposite below: On 14 April 2015, 2-8-2 No D51 498 (Takatori 26/1940) heads for Aizu-Wakamatsu over the Ban'etsu West line which dates from 1898. She is passing Mount Bandai, at 1,816 metres the highest mountain in this part of the country and a not wholly dormant volcano which last erupted in 1888. The D51s were Japan's most numerous class with 1,115 members.

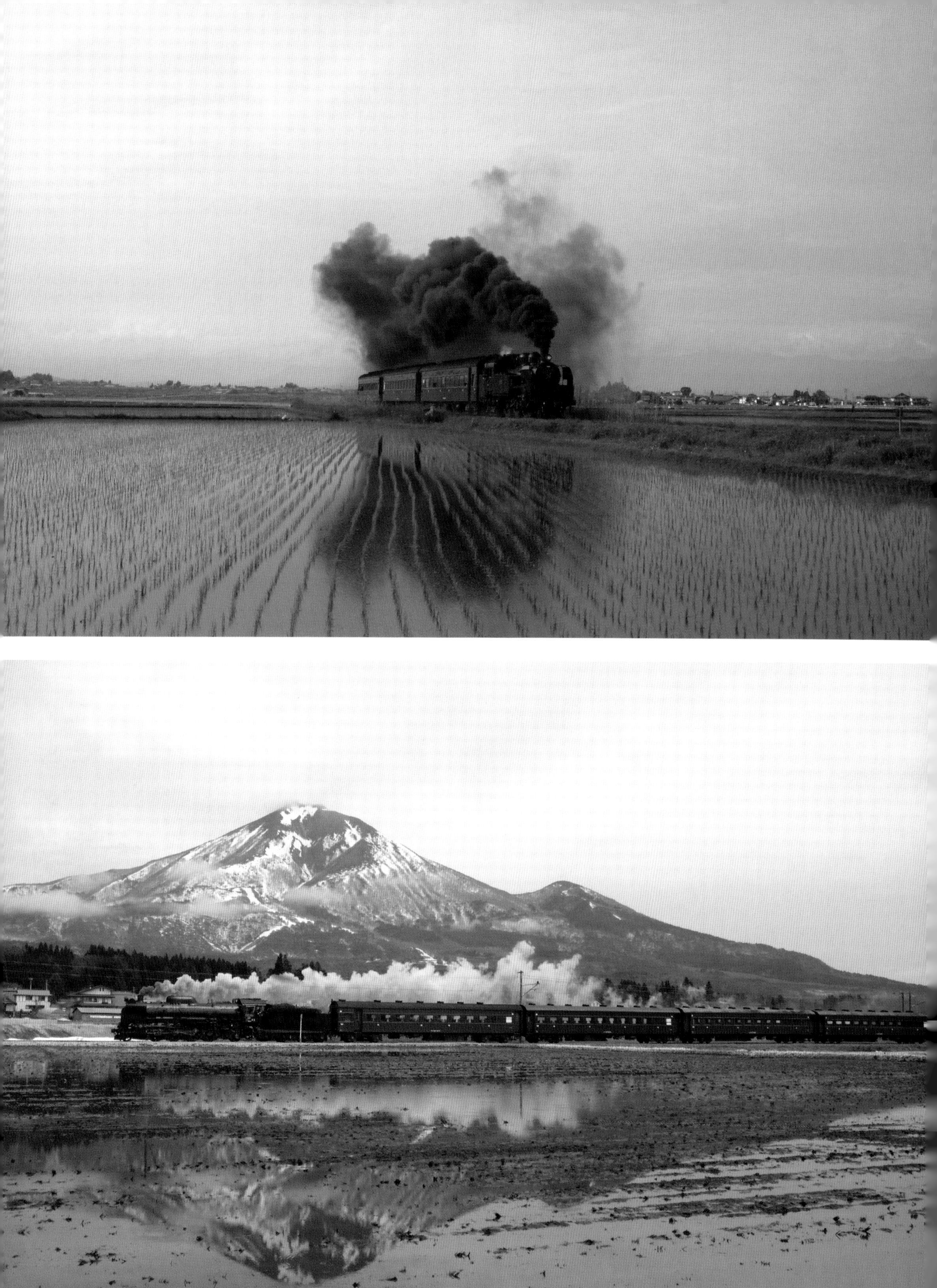

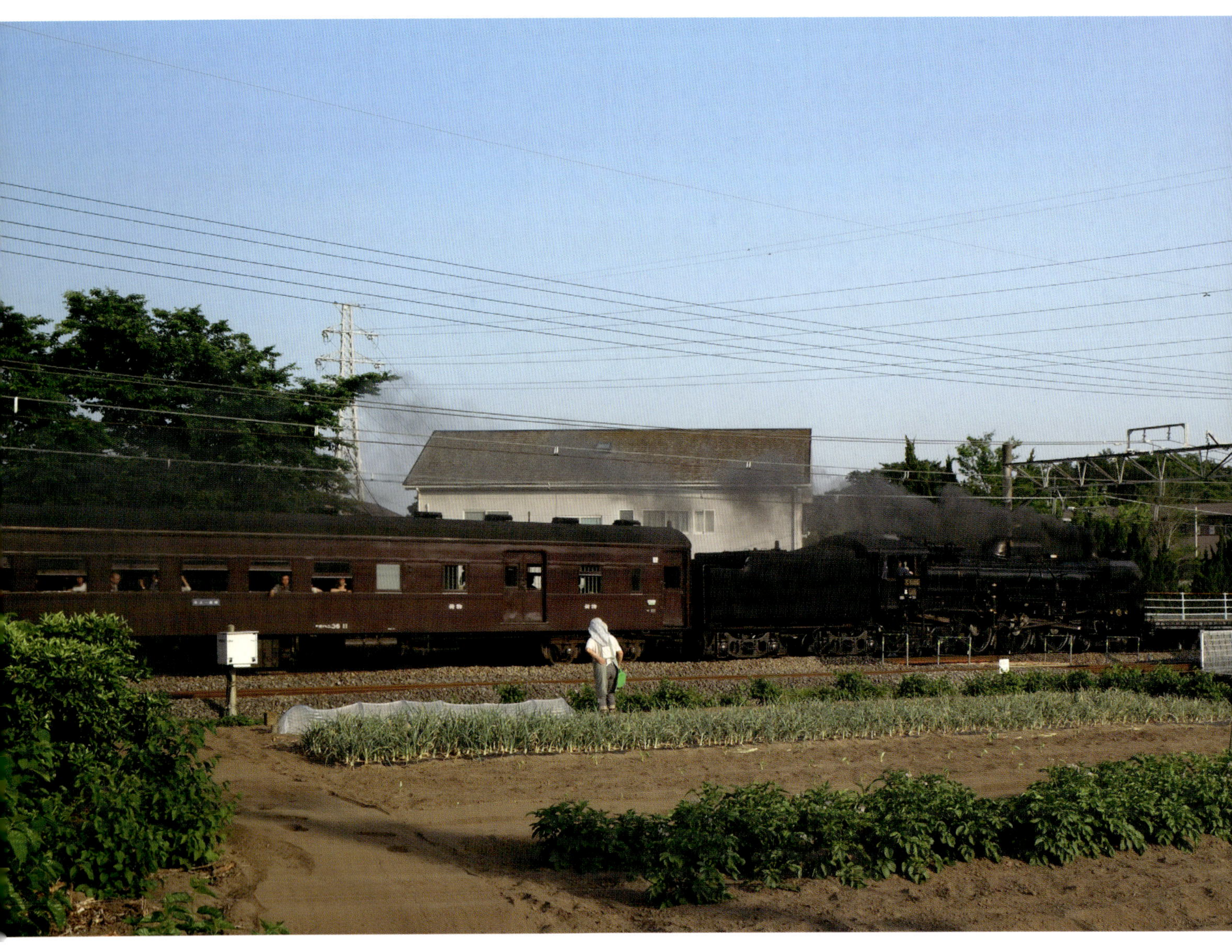

This lady looks up momentarily from watering her allotment as 4-6-4 No C61 20 (Mitsubishi 659/1949) runs through the outskirts of Takasaki on 22 May 2016. Freight traffic in Japan collapsed towards the end of the Second World War with the destruction of much of its heavy industry but peacetime brought a surge in passenger numbers and the boilers and other parts of surplus freight and mixed traffic machines were reused in the construction of new express locos. No C61 20 was rebuilt from No D51 1094.

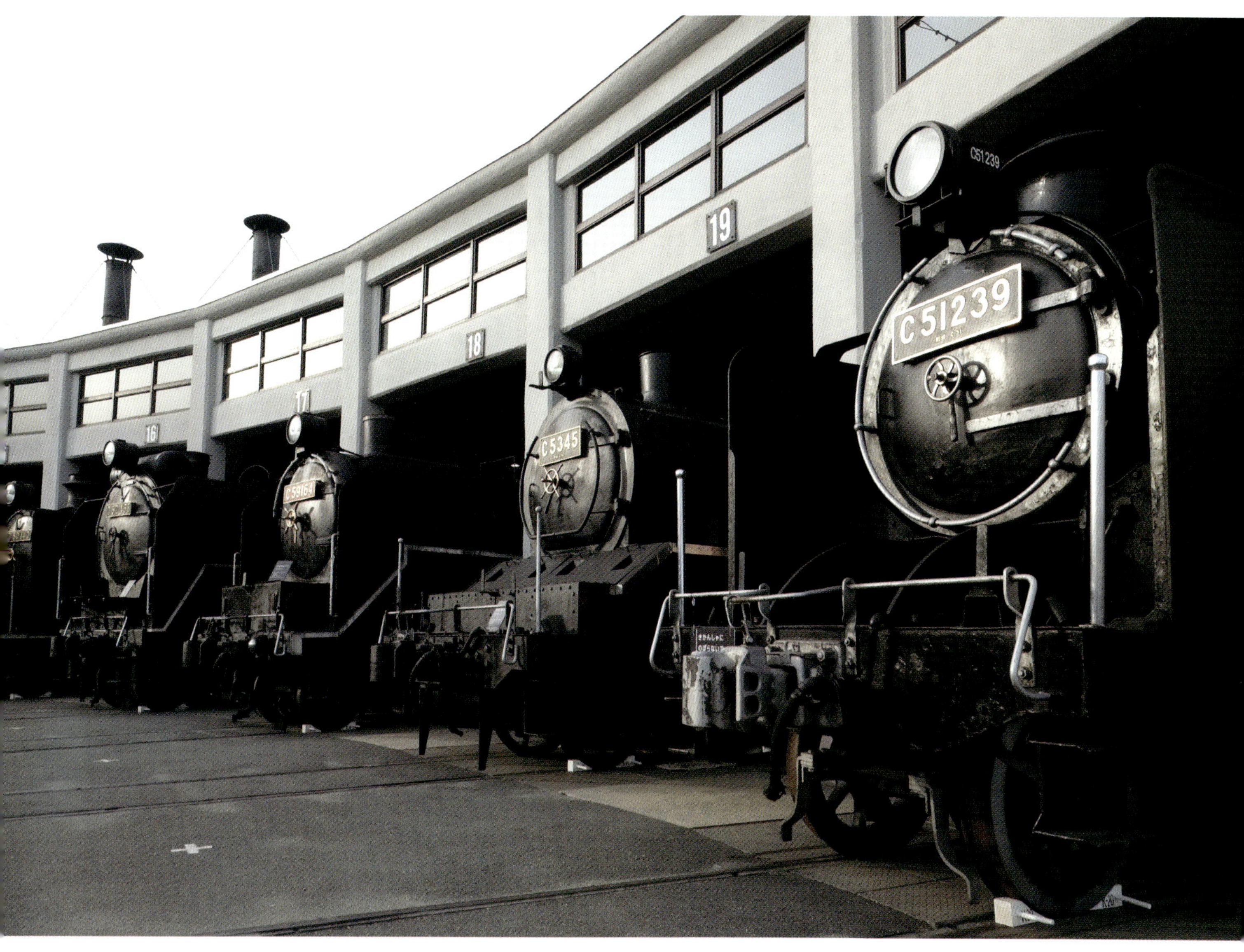

On 5 May 2016, five of Kyoto Railway Museum's twenty-two steam locos stand at the old Umekoji roundhouse, built in 1916 and now a listed structure. Pacific No C51 239 (Kisha 936/1927) was once a royal loco and hauled the emperor's train on 104 occasions. She was withdrawn in 1963 and, like the Finnish loco at Pereslavl, was lucky to survive severe earthquake damage, in her case in 1964. The C51s, built from 1919, were Japan's earliest domestically-produced express locos. No C53 45 (Kisha 1040/1928) is the sole surviving member of the only three-cylinder Pacific class constructed there. The C59 two-cylinder Pacifics were built from 1941 to replace them and No C59 164 (Hitachi 1999/1946), withdrawn in 1970, is one of three preserved examples. No D52 468 (Mitsubishi 502/1946) was the youngest of 285 heavy freight 2-8-2s built from 1943. No D50 140 (Hitachi 199/1925) was one of 276 members of Japan's first class of 2-8-2s which were built between 1923 and 1931.

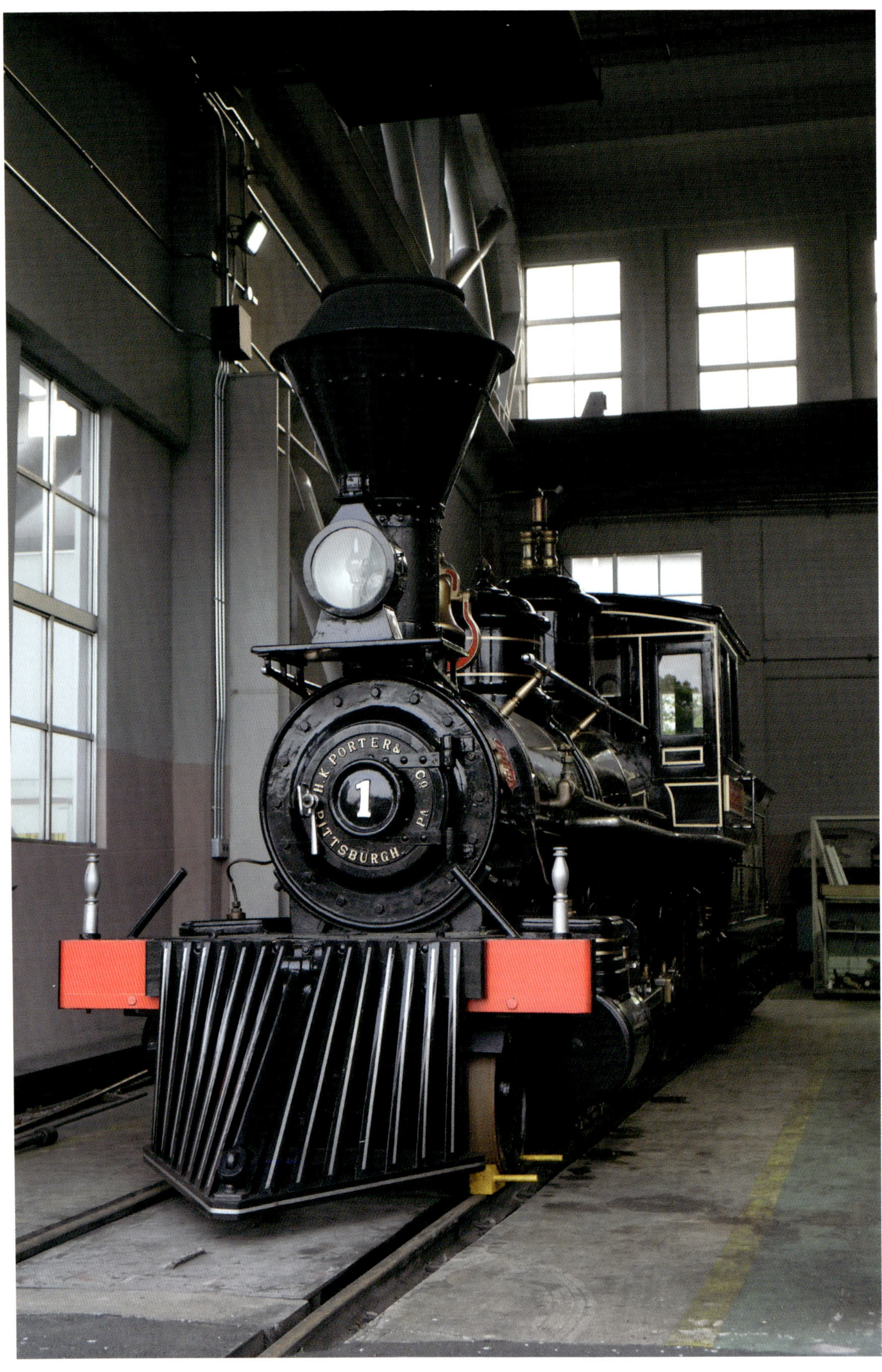
H.K. PORTER & CO
1
PITTSBURGH PA

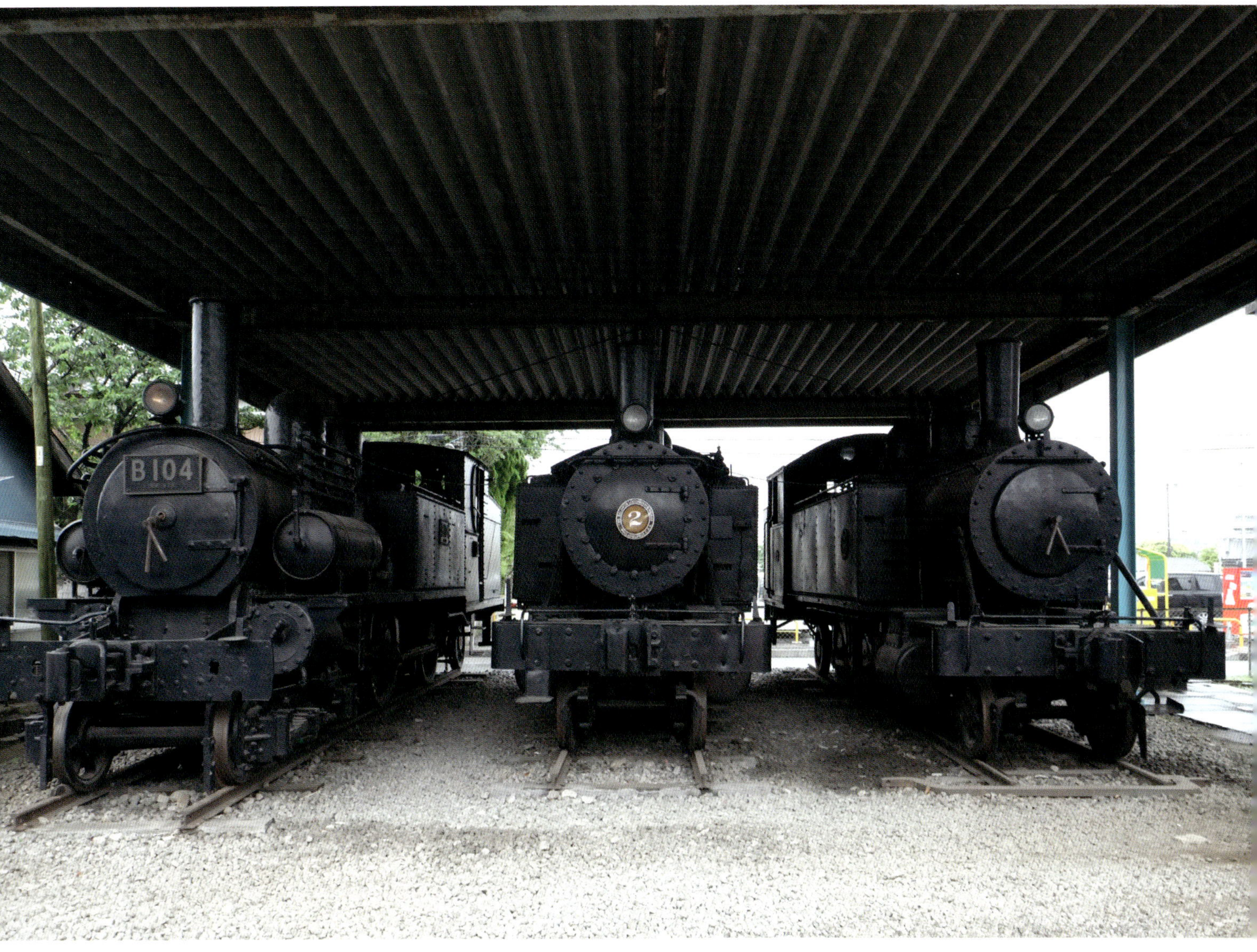

Above: The three engines of Goi! The little Kominato Railway, serving the Boso peninsula on the eastern side of Tokyo Bay, was built between 1925 and 1928 from a junction at Goi and was worked by two 2-6-2T's, Nos 1 and 2 (Baldwin 57776 and 57777/1924). In 1949, they were joined by a former state railway 4-4-2T No B10 4 (BP 3641/1894) but she only worked there for two years and was then just set aside at Goi depot, as were Nos 1 and 2 when steam operation finished in 1962. They were still there on 27 May 2016. The ten B10s were rebuilt in 1929 and 1930 from 5500 class 4-4-0s, seventy-two of which were built between 1893 and 1898 for the Nippon Railway. No B10 4 served the Japanese military from 1936 until moving to Goi.

Opposite: Hokkaido Railway No 1 *Yoshitune* (Porter 368/1880), later the state railway's No 7105, stands in the Umekoji roundhouse, the heart of the Kyoto museum, on 5 May 2016. She was the first loco to run on Japan's large northern island, was sold to the Umebachi-Tettksyo Railway in 1923 and entered preservation in 1952. She's the oldest of several working locos at Kyoto.

AUSTRALIA

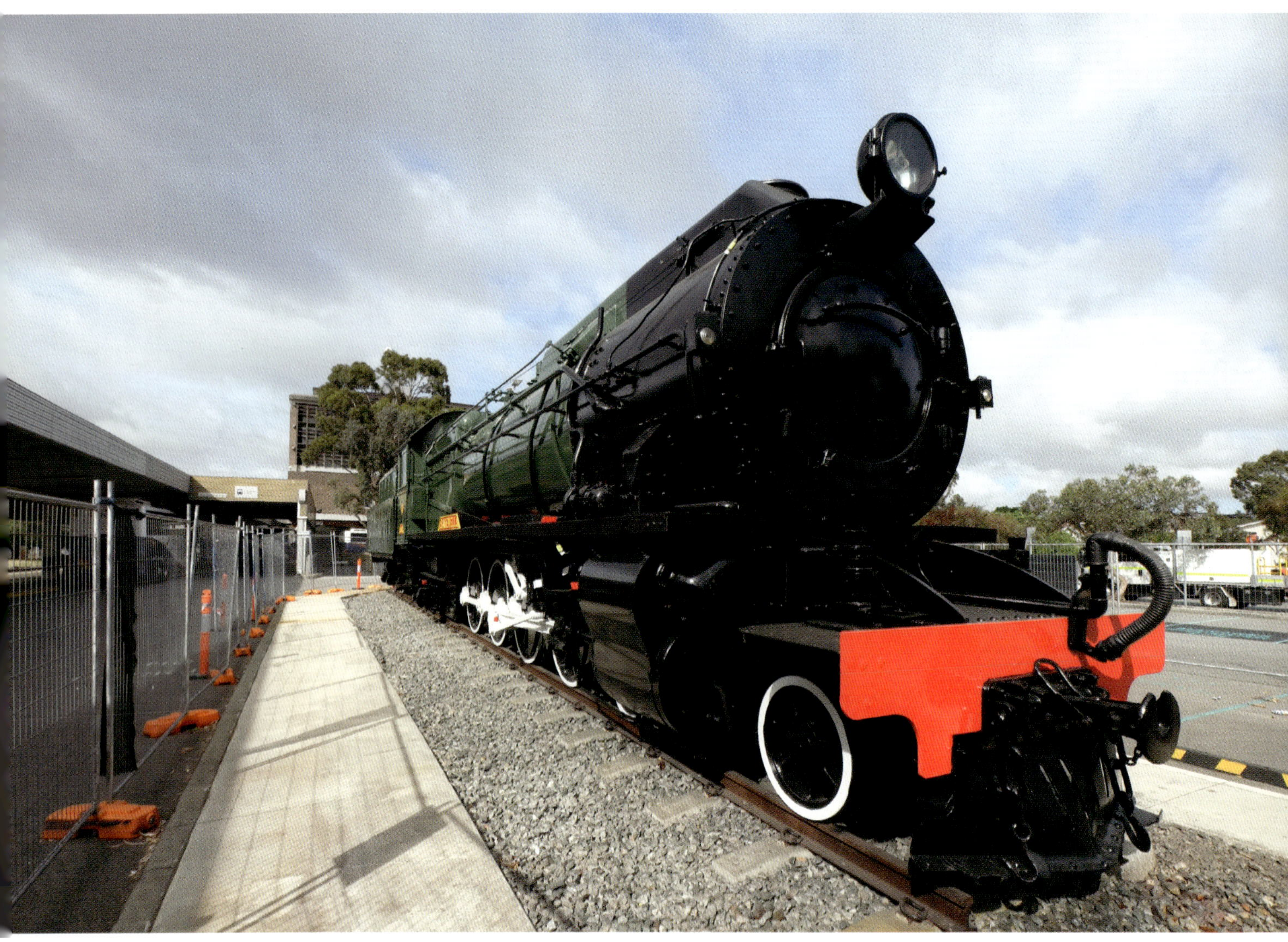

Railways came to Western Australia even later than Japan and the Western Australian Government Railways' first 3ft 6ins gauge line didn't open until 1879. Lessons were learned and its mainlines never suffered from the light axleloading limit which bedevils the 3ft 6ins railways in Queensland nor the tight loading gauge which has always been a problem in New Zealand. Western Australian locos could be seriously big! S class 4-8-2 No 542 *Bakewell* (Midland, 1943) is one of the biggest of all. She's a member of the only class to be designed and built entirely within the state and spends her retirement in the car park at East Perth station where she greets travellers arriving on the transcontinental trains from Sydney. She looks very smart on 3 October 2015 and has just been repainted in the larch green colour introduced on WAGR in 1951.

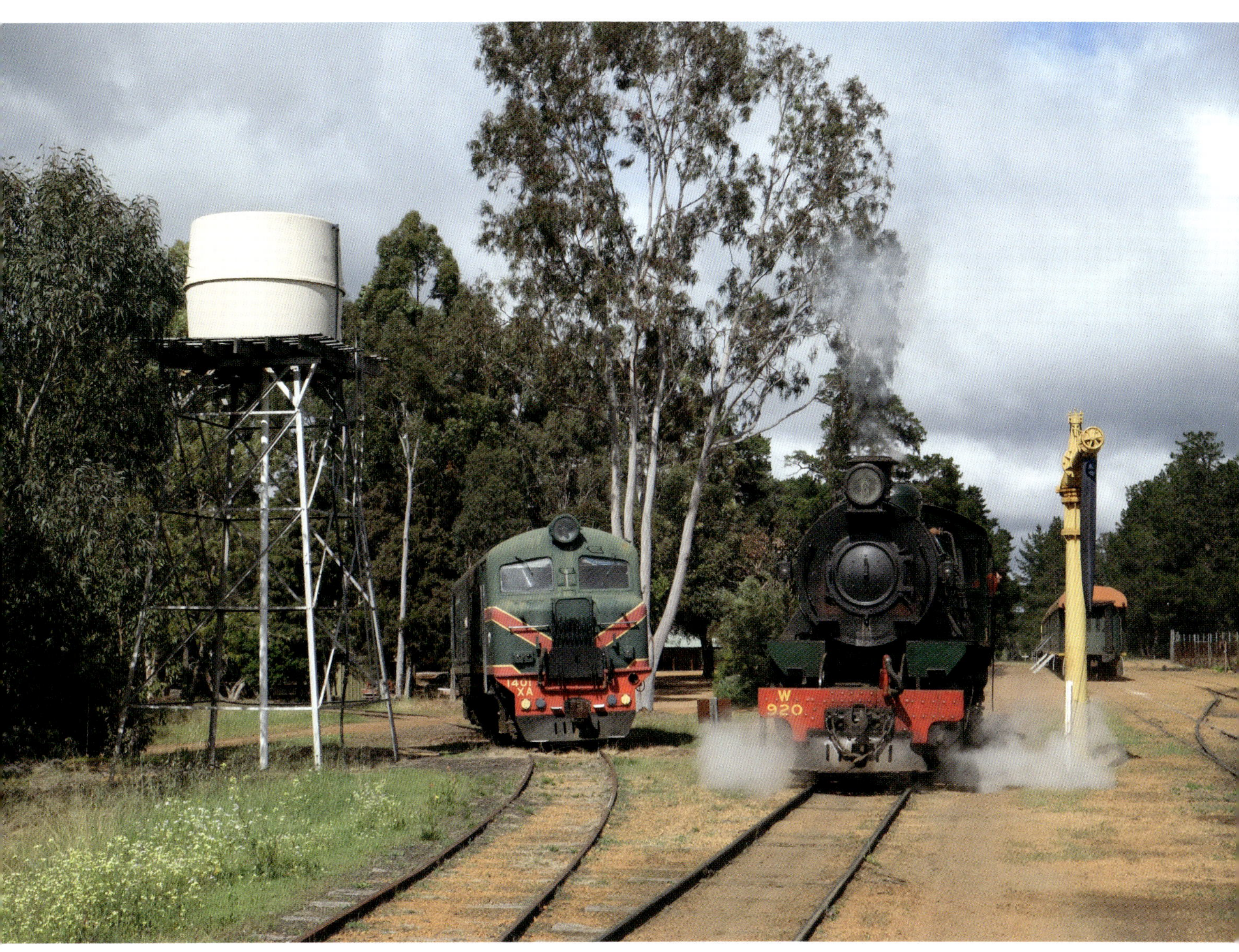

W class 4-8-2 No 920 (BP 7397/1951) stands with XA class diesel electric No 1401 *Pedong* (BP and MV 862/1956) at Dwellingup station on the preserved Hotham Valley Railway on 4 October 2015. The sixty lightweight Ws, introduced in 1951, were amongst Australia's most successful steam locos and all worked until 1971, WAGR's last full year of steam operation. The forty-eight X and XA class locos were its first main line diesels. They had an unusual 2-Do-2 wheel arrangement and were distinctly unsuccessful; it's reckoned that their failings prolonged steam operation on WAGR by several years.

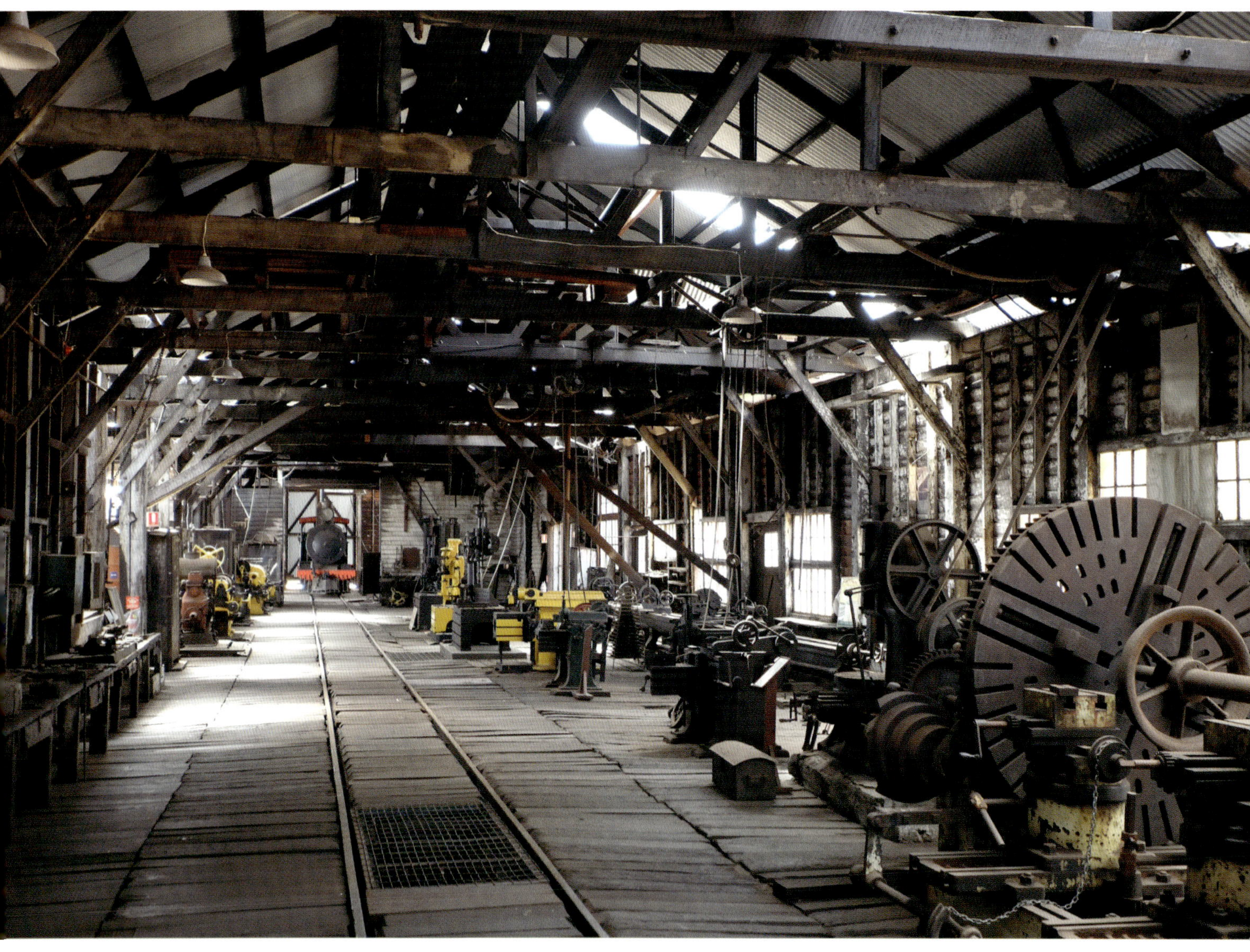

Western Australia possessed many logging railways. One of the biggest operators was the Millars group which ran central workshops at Yarloops, able to undertake full overhauls of locos and other heavy machinery. A large range of timber buildings housed machine, boiler, blacksmiths, casting and pattern shops, all powered by no fewer than eight stationary steam engines via belts and overhead shafting. The complex became a museum after it closed in 1978. I visited on 3 October 2015. It was highly atmospheric and must have been even more so on its monthly steaming days. Very sadly it was completely destroyed by a bushfire three months later. In happier times, former South Australian Railways Y class No 176 (Martin 178/1898) stands in the workshops. She enjoyed a long second life in the Western Australian logging industry after being withdrawn in 1929.

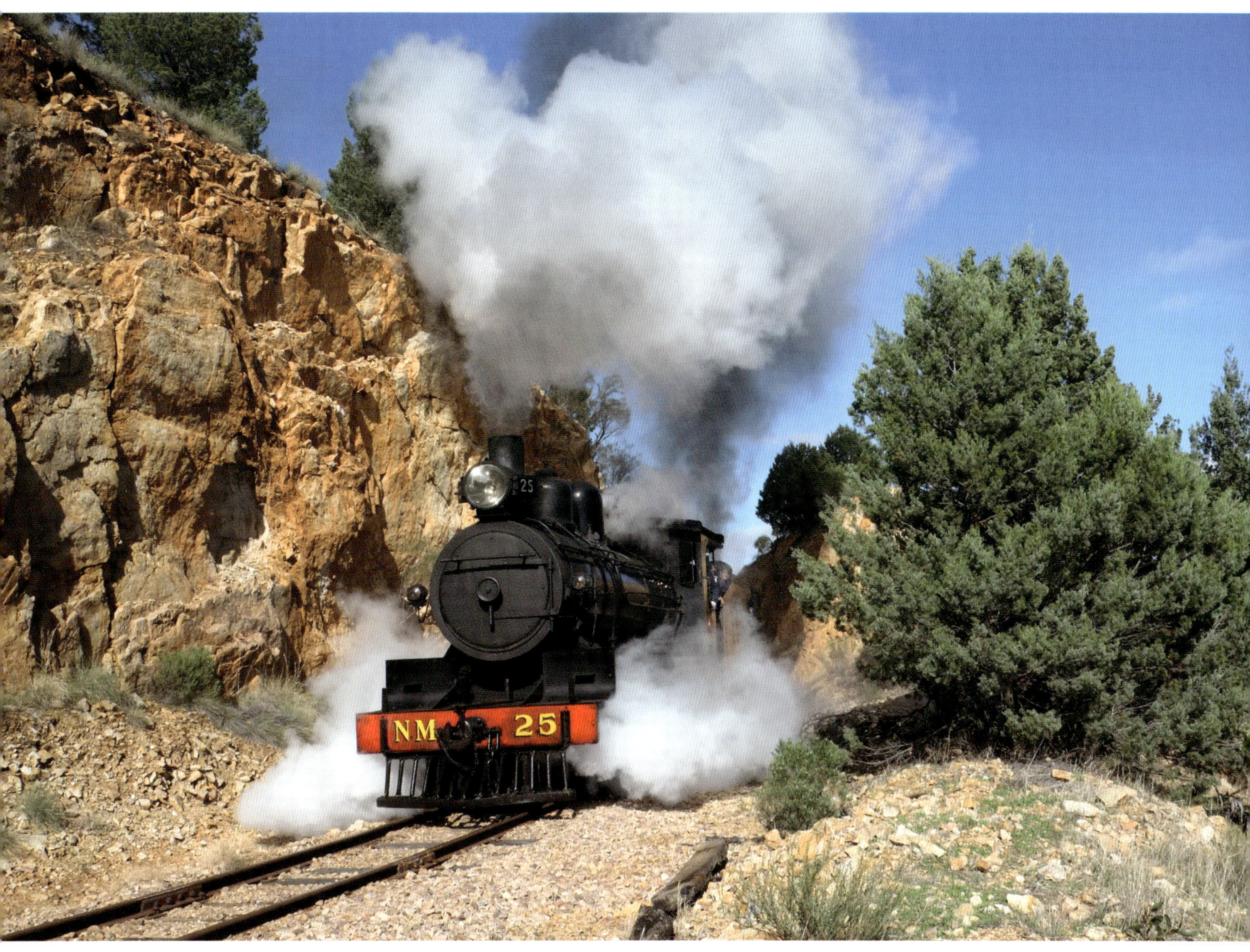

Back in the nineteenth century, South Australia's territory extended all the way to the continent's north coast. Construction of 5ft 3ins gauge railways around Adelaide began in 1854 but when its government decided in 1878 to build a transcontinental line to Darwin it chose the 3ft 6ins gauge. The first section, from Port Augusta through the scenic Flinders Ranges and the Pichi Richi Pass to Quorn, 38kms away, opened on 15 December 1879. The Northern Territory was handed over to the Commonwealth government in 1911 and they became responsible for the railway though SAR ran it for them until 1926. In 1956, it was replaced by a new route and the Quorn line is now one of the most attractive heritage railways anywhere in the country. Here, Commonwealth Railways NM class 4-8-0 No 25 (Thompson 51/1925) works hard north of Woolshed Flat on 12 June 2016.

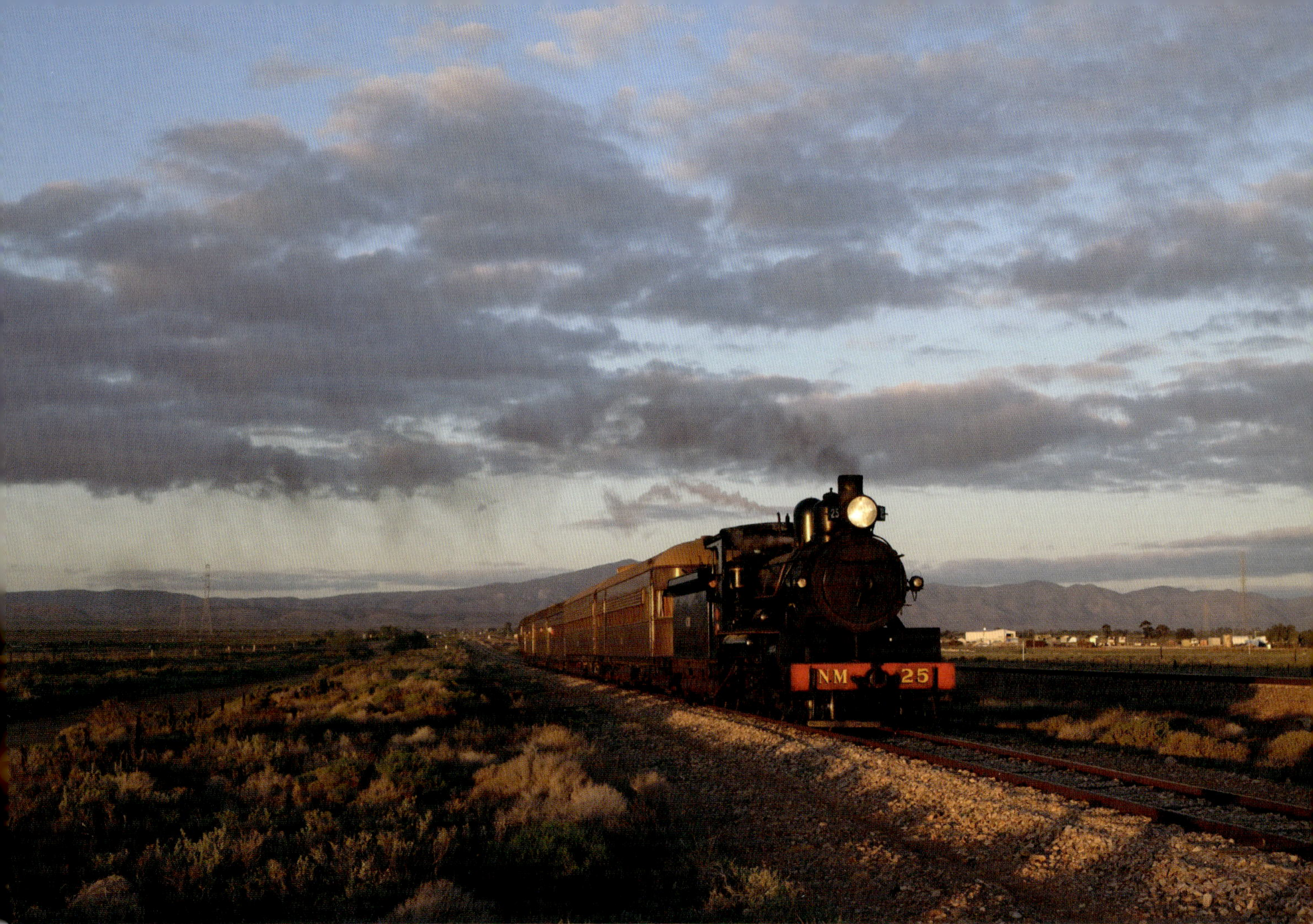

Above: It's just before sunset on 12 June 2016 and No 25 with her train of period CR coaches has left the Flinders Ranges behind and races across the flat land near Port Augusta, very much reminiscent of the old narrow gauge *Ghan* when it passed this way. The twenty-two NMs were built to the Queensland Railways' C17 design except that their tenders were larger. No 25 is one of two survivors.

Opposite above: The Pichi Richi Railway bought five WAGR W class 4-8-2s in its early years. They work many trains though perhaps look a little out of place in the Flinders Ranges which don't much resemble the countryside of Western Australia! Four similar locos, Nos W22-25, were built for the Silverton Tramway, effectively an extension of SAR's 3ft 6ins system eastwards over the state border to Broken Hill in New South Wales. The main difference was that they carried a boilertop cowling. The railway also has No W22 *Justin Hancock* but she needs major boiler work and in view of her local connections it has transferred her cowling and plates to WAGR No 916 (BP 7393/1951). She looks much more at home in this form as she approaches Summit station with a train of SAR coaches on 13 June 2016.

Opposite below: SAR steam railmotor No 1 (Kitson 4356/1905) crosses Woolshed Flat viaduct on 13 June 2016. Her survival is little short of miraculous. She spent her entire working life based at Quorn and often worked over the Pichi Richi line. CR bought her when they took over operations in 1926. She was withdrawn in 1931 after which she spent nearly thirty years in store at Quorn shed. In 1960, she was put on show at Alice Springs but later returned and first ran again in 1984. Virtually all the woodwork in her Birmingham-built body is original.

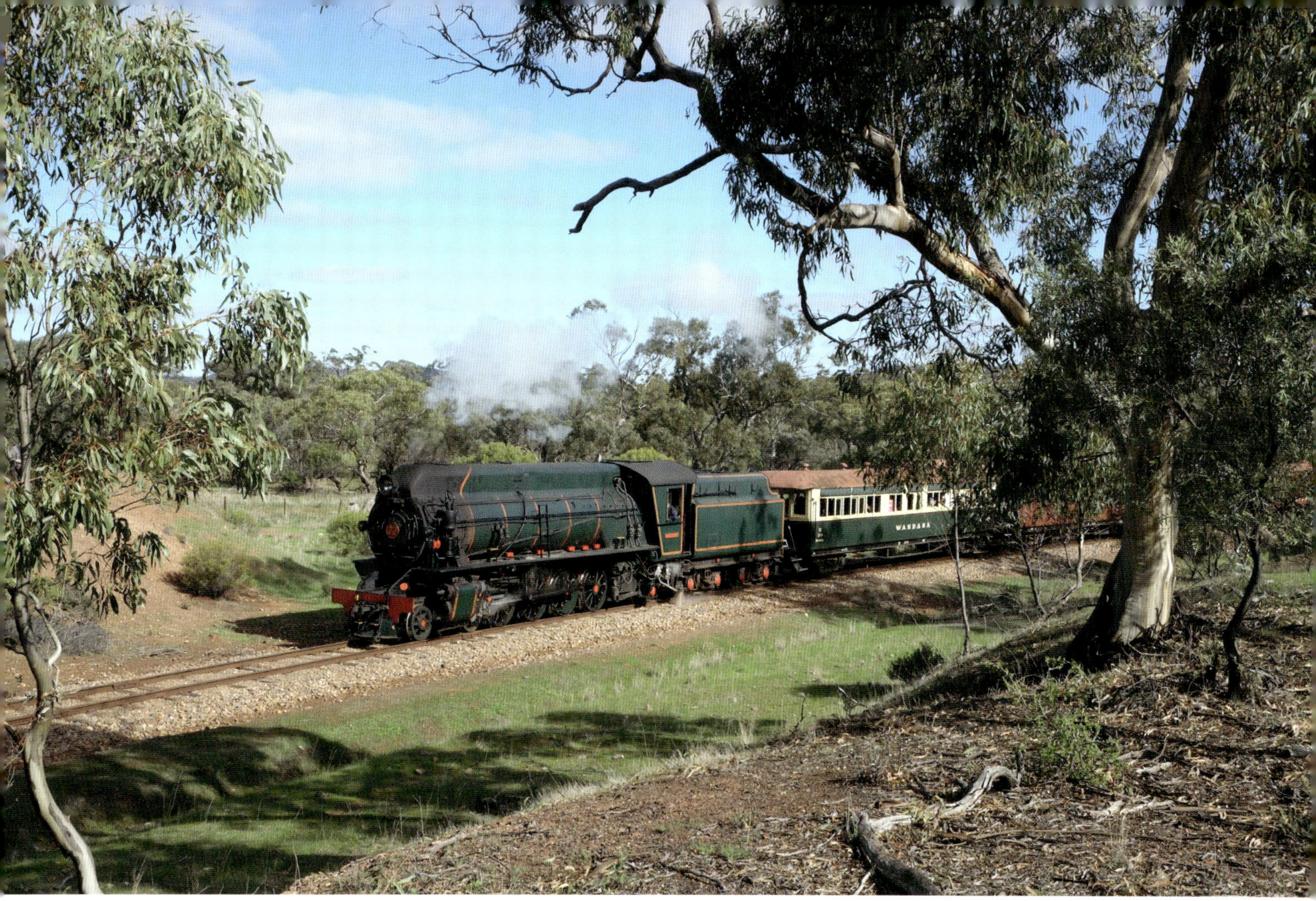

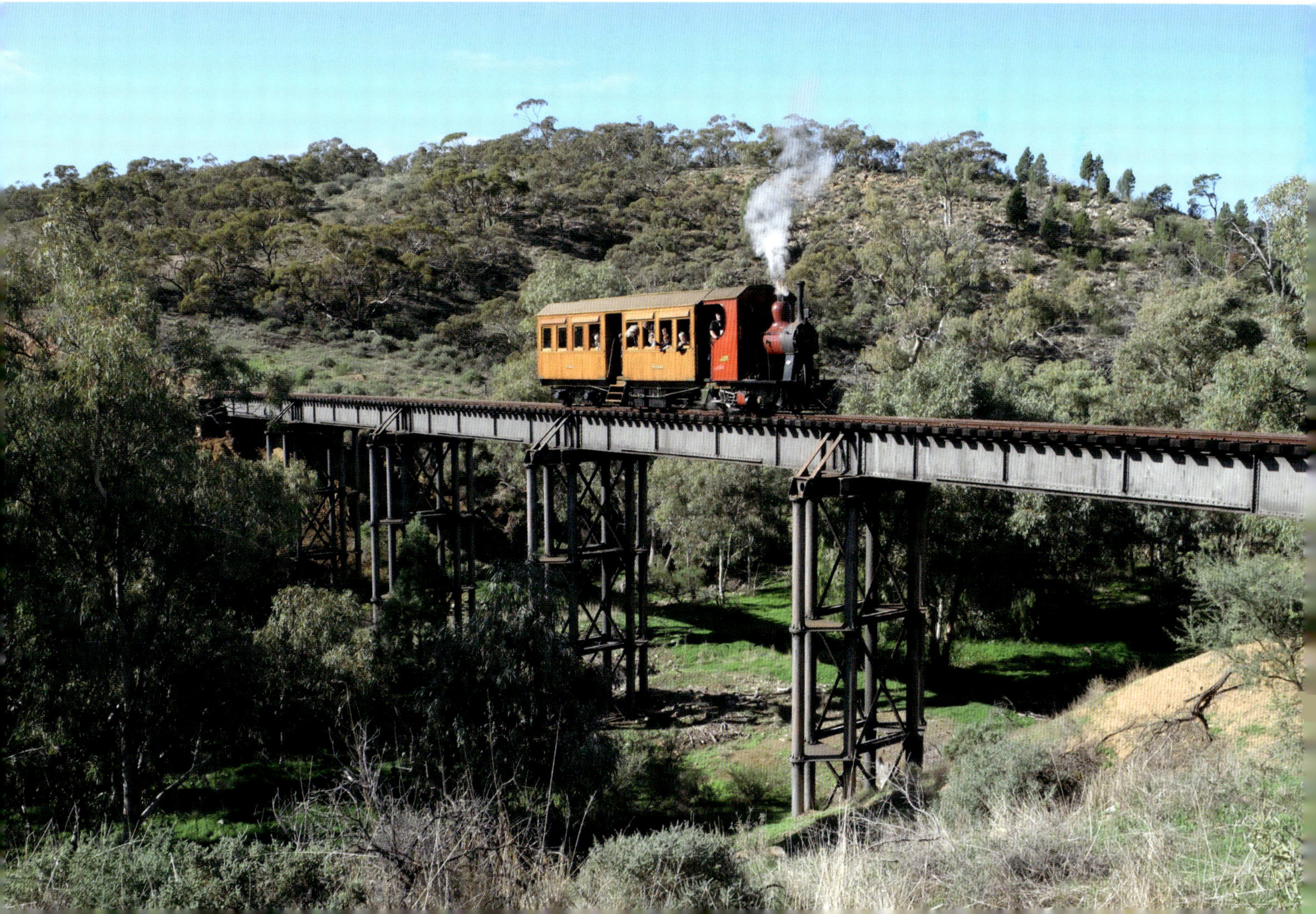

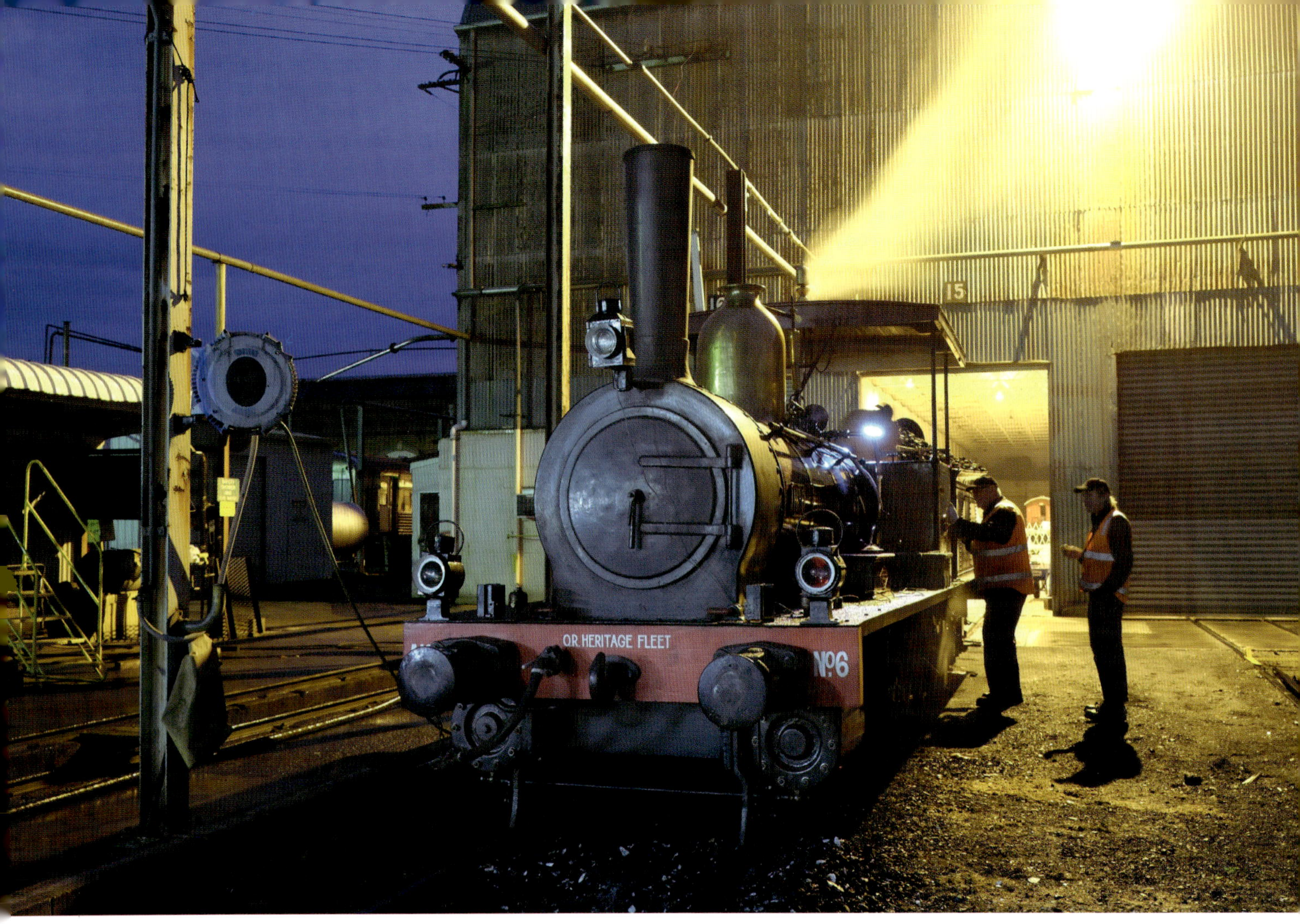

Above: In 2015, Queensland Rail, as it's now called, celebrated its 150th anniversary in style. At 4.00am on 26 July the weather wasn't just dismal – there was a hard frost on the ground and the forecast was bleak. Why does Queensland call itself the sunshine state?! A10 class 0-4-2 No 6 (Neilson 1170/1865) was due to work over the earliest section between Ipswich and Grandchester and I headed over to Ipswich works in the hope that I could see her raising steam. I wasn't confident of gaining entry but by great good fortune arrived at the same time as Paul Slater, the works manager and a great enthusiast. He welcomed me in, very kindly let me explore the yard and turned on the lights in the restoration shop while I was dodging the showers – and even lent me his tripod!

Opposite above: QR was only the world's second loco-worked 3ft 6ins gauge system after Norway's and is much the most heritage-minded of Australia's mainline railways. AC16 class 2-8-2 No 221A (Baldwin 69456/1943) was one of the MacArthur-type locos built in the USA for service around the world during the Second World War. She frequently hauls steam specials and during my early morning visit waits in the restoration shop for her next trip. Behind her is DD17 class 4-6-4T No 1051 (Ipswich 210/1952) and to the right BB18¼ class Pacific No 1089 (Walkers 557/1958), both receiving heavy overhauls.

Opposite below: Beyer Garratt 4-8-2+2-8-4 No 1009 (BP 7349/1950), standing nearby, is another member of QR's heritage fleet but now needs major boiler work. She's one of thirty developed from the War Department Garratts like the one at Guwahati which in turn had their origin in locos designed for the Great Western of Brazil in the 1930s, though not built until much later. Their weight was considerably reduced to suit conditions in Queensland.

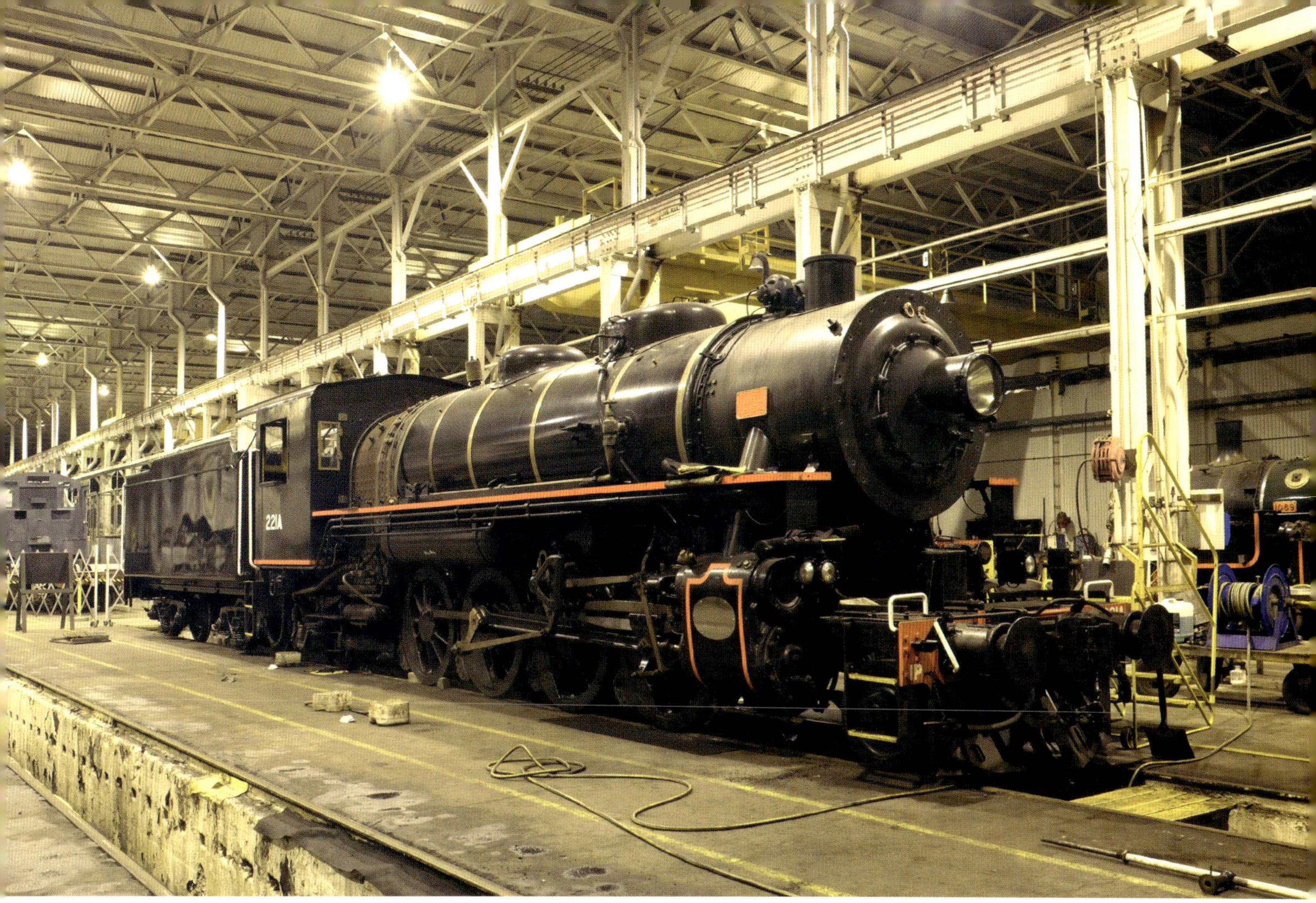

221A

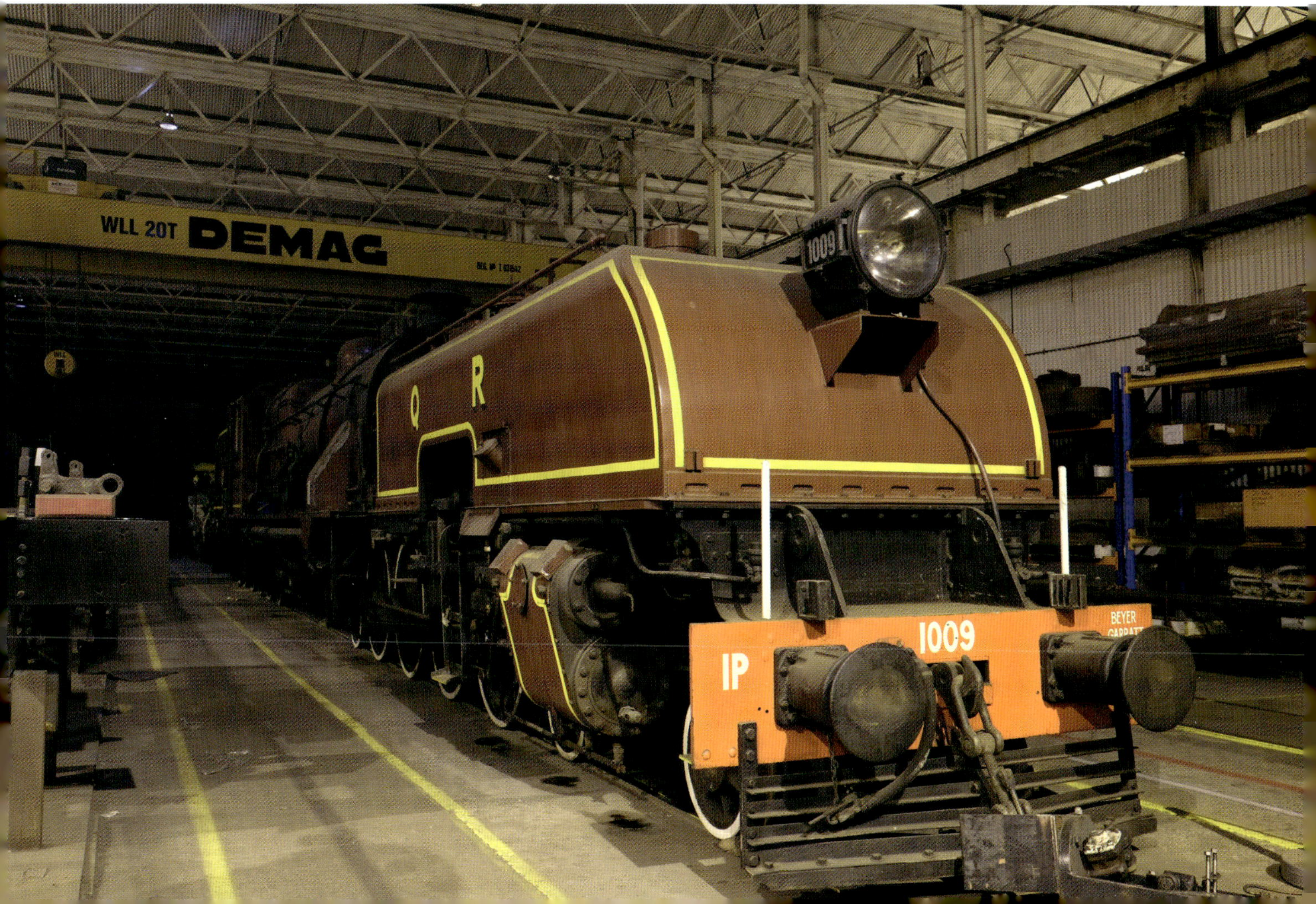

WLL 20T
DEMAG
Q
R
1009
IP
1009
BEYER GARRATT

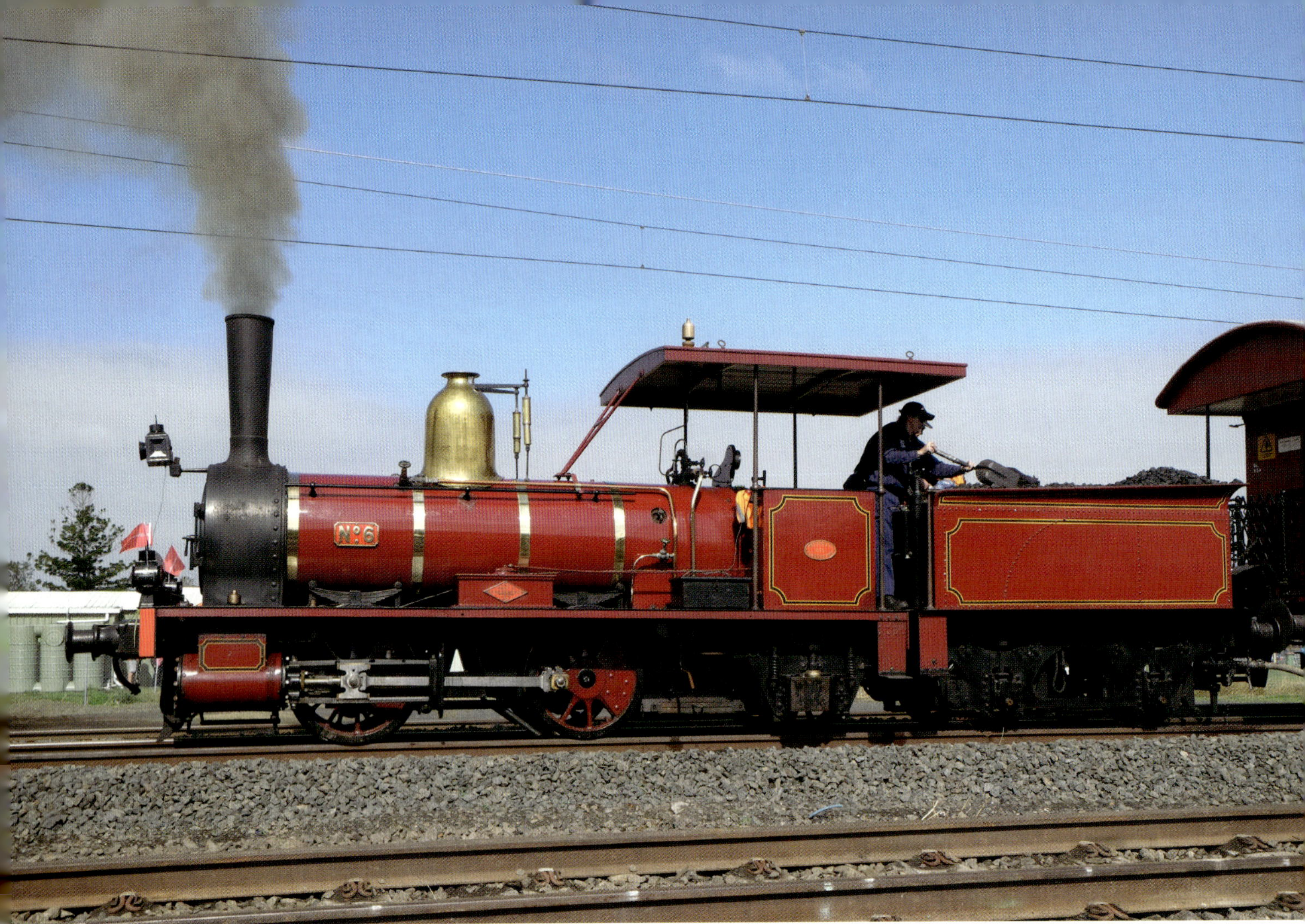

Above: Two anniversary trains ran to Grandchester on 26 July 2015, one with No 6 and one with BB18¼ class Pacific No 1079 (Walkers 547/1956). On her return journey No 6, one of the world's oldest working locos, pauses at Rosewood for water during a brief sunny spell.

Opposite above: In the hills above Rosewood later that afternoon, C17 class 4-8-0 No 720 (Walkers 348/1922) waits to leave Cabanda station on the preserved Rosewood Railway with her QR steam-era train. From the early 1950s, QR painted its modern locos a variety of colours – blue for the DD17s, green for the Pacifics, brown for the C17s and crimson for its Beyer Garratts, the latter reportedly inspired by the contemporary East African machines.

Opposite below: No 1079 is in steam at Brisbane's Roma Street station with QR's heritage train on 27 July 2015, another part of the celebration. On 31 July, the anniversary date, she made a surprise appearance at the head of a commuter train from Ipswich to Roma Street before taking another excursion out to Grandchester. Earlier in the year the two Pacifics made a two-month round trip from Brisbane to Cairns and beyond in Queensland's tropical north and No 1079 subsequently toured the south and west of the state. With numerous steam specials and the superb Rail Workshops Museum at Ipswich Queensland's enthusiasts are lucky that their state's railway heritage is so well cherished.

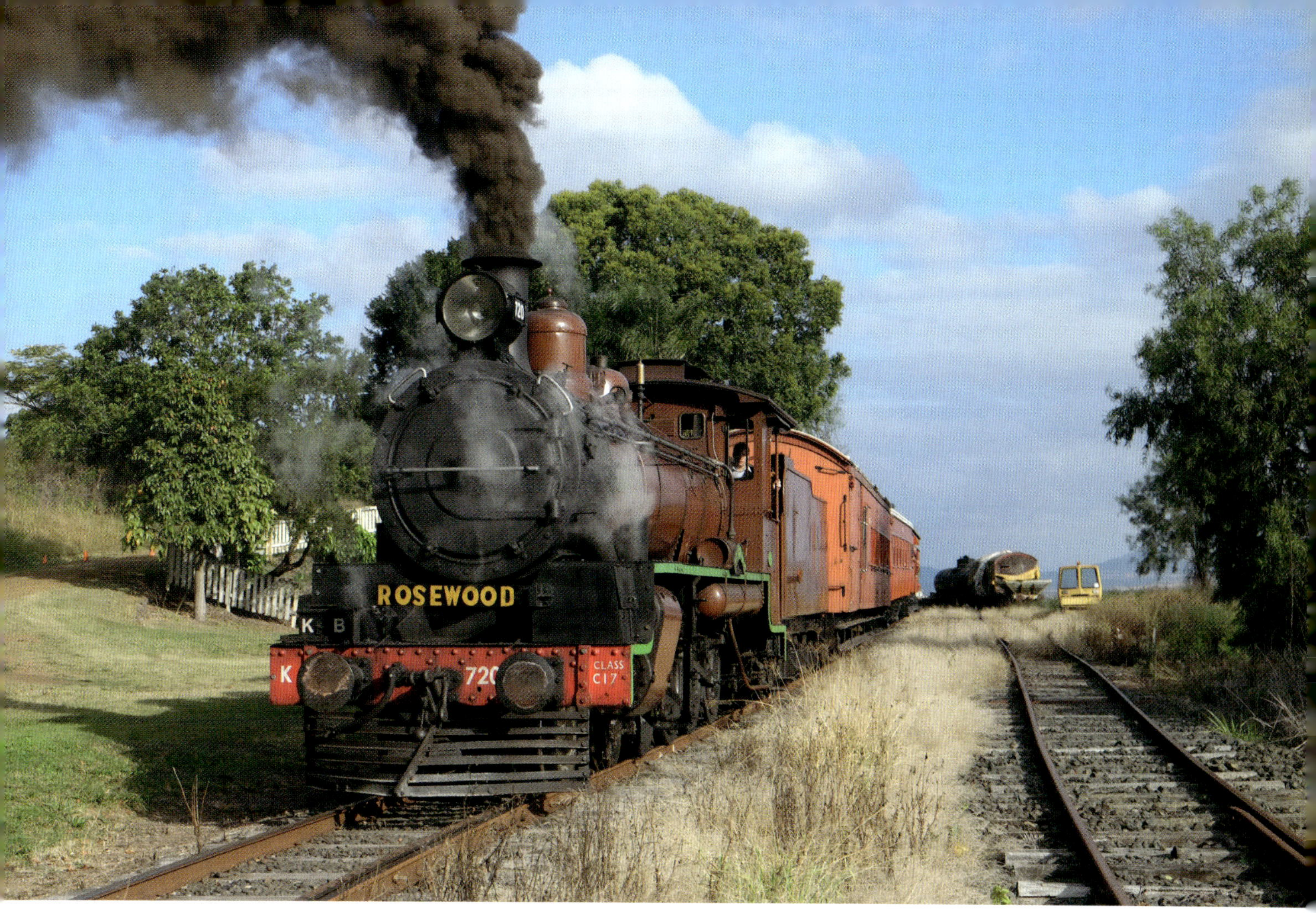

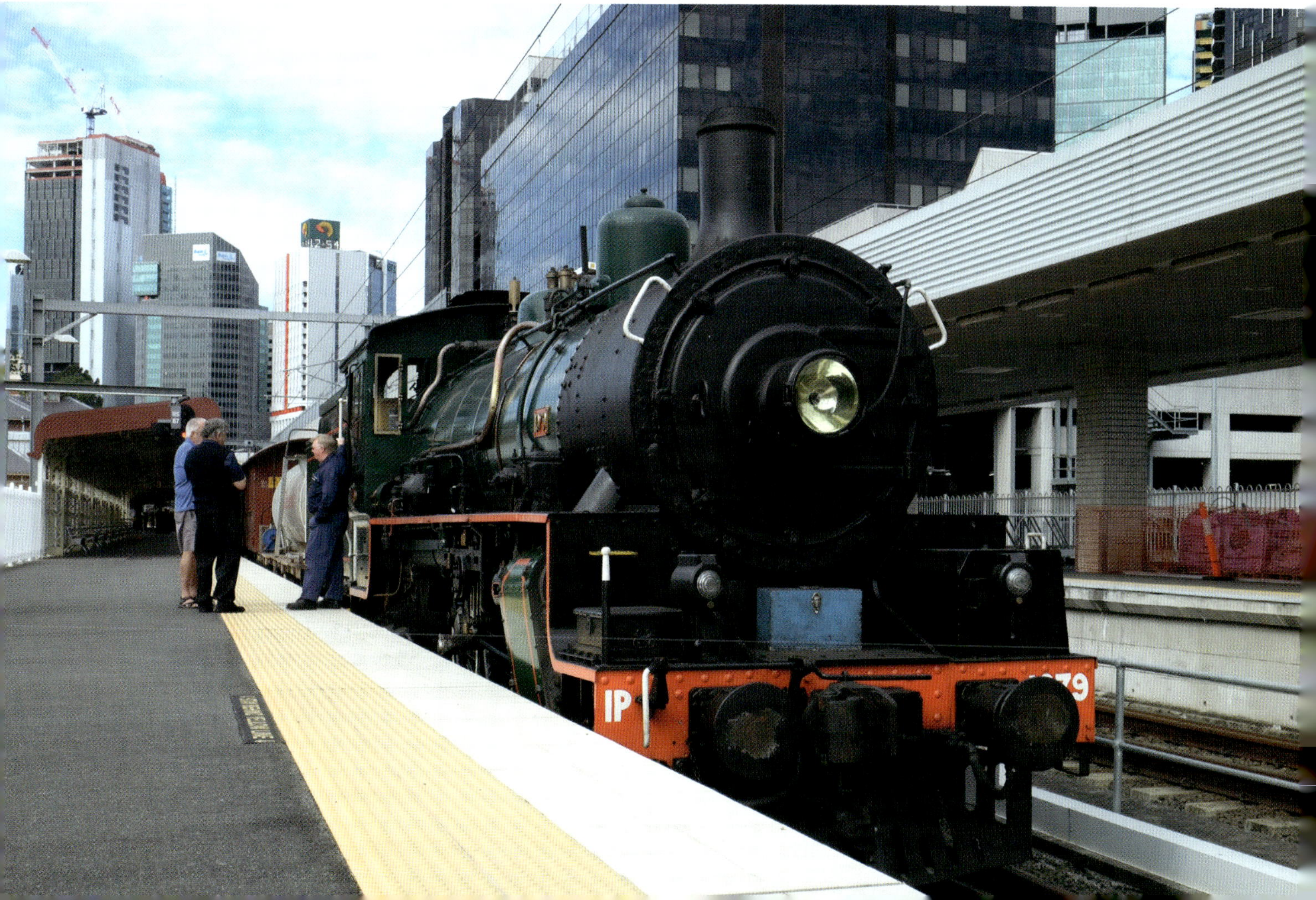

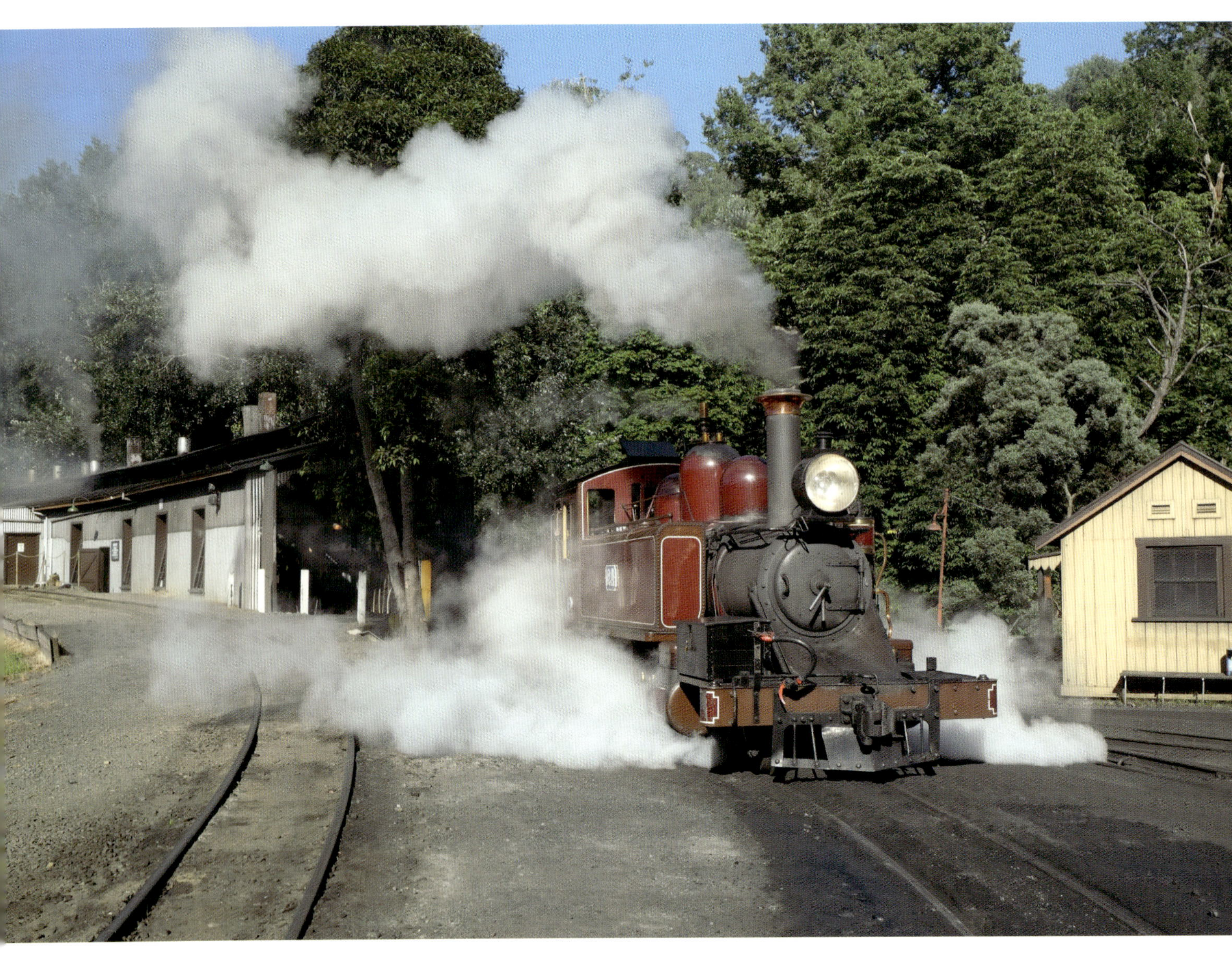

Early in the morning of 28 January 2017, Victorian Railways NA class 2-6-2T No 12A (Newport, 1912) leaves Belgrave shed on the 2ft 6ins gauge Puffing Billy Railway which runs to Gembrook through the Dandenong hills to the east of Melbourne. She's been restored in the colour she carried when she was built – copied from the Canadian Pacific. The Puffing Billy is a survivor of four 2ft 6ins lines whose origins lie in an economic depression which afflicted Australia in the 1890's during which the Victorian government sought an inexpensive way to develop the state's poorest districts. Today it carries enormous numbers of visitors and must be the most popular heritage railway anywhere in the southern hemisphere. Lengthy trains are commonplace and there's often gridlock on the narrow local roads as tour coaches jostle for position to pick up their passengers.

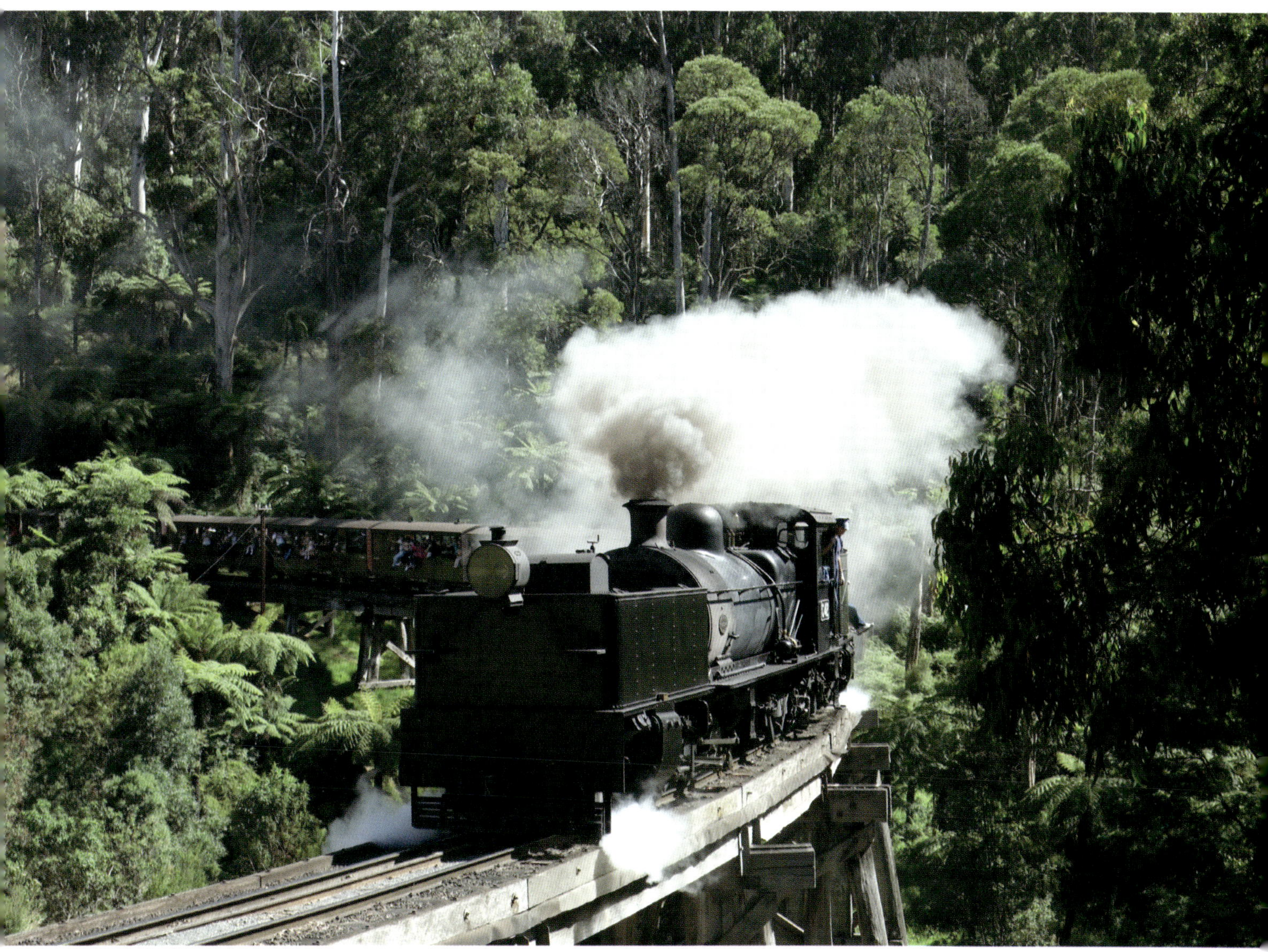

Shortly afterwards 2-6-0+0-6-2 Beyer Garratt No G42 (BP 6268/1926) crosses Monbulk Creek trestle bridge near Belgrave. Passengers have been dangling their legs from these open coaches since 1919! VR bought two 2ft 6ins Garratts for service on its lines to Crowes and Walhalla. Their design was based on WAGR's Ms class 3ft 6ins locos. No G42's boiler was worn out but fortunately there were two redundant Ms-type 3ft 6ins Garratts at Fyansford cement factory in Victoria and the restored loco now carries one of their boilers. She's been operational since 2004 and is especially useful in the peak summer holiday season. There's a small duck-billed platypus population in Clematis Creek which joins the Monbulk stream, but don't hold your breath looking for them as on average they're only sighted once every four years! An even rarer resident is an endemic freshwater crustacean which looks like a small prawn. After a sighting as long ago as 1911 it was believed to have become extinct until one turned up recently.

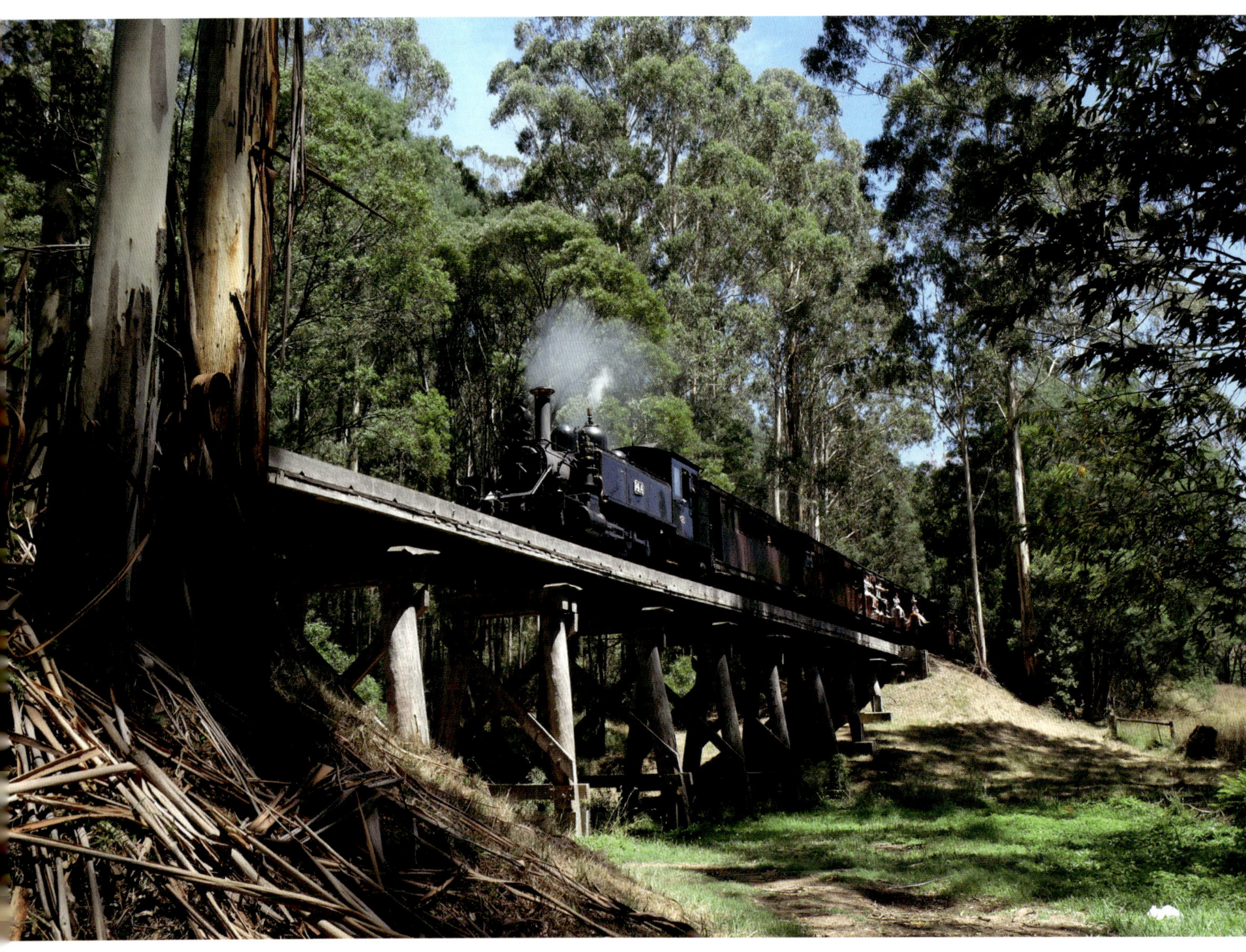

Later that morning NA class 2-6-2T No 14A (Newport, 1914) crosses Cockatoo Creek bridge with the daily train to Gembrook. The Puffing Billy line closed to regular traffic in 1953. The present heritage railway reopened in stages between 1962 and 1998 after a huge reconstruction effort, rebuilding this bridge being one of the largest tasks. Apart from the Garratts, the seventeen NAs were VR's only 2ft 6ins locos. The first two were built by Baldwin in 1898 to one of their standard designs, essentially an elongated version of their small 2-4-2T's like *Lyn* on the Lynton & Barnstaple. The other fifteen were built by VR between 1900 and 1915. Six have survived at the Puffing Billy.

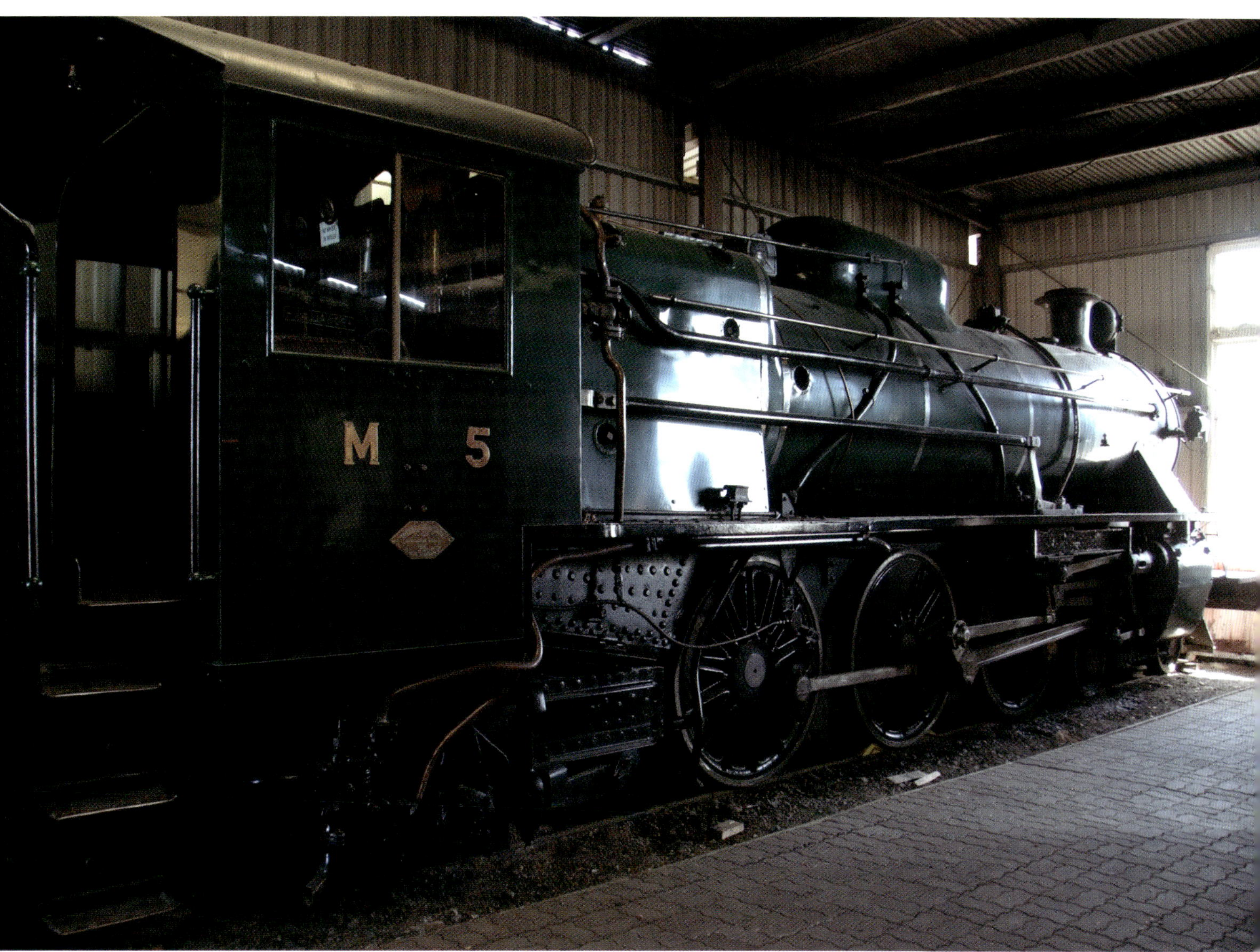

Time hasn't been kind to the old Tasmanian Government Railways which became 3ft 6ins after starting out on the 5ft 3ins gauge. The system was taken over by the federal government in March 1978 and only three months later became the only one in Australia to lose all its passenger services. Back in happier times, ten of these beautiful M class Pacifics were the last steam locos to be built though ominously two of the X class diesels which helped replace them arrived on board the same ship. They were withdrawn in 1971 and have all been preserved. No M5 (RSH 7425/1951) is in working order at the Tasmanian Transport Museum near Hobart. She once hauled mainline specials but is now confined to the museum and on 26 March 2013 was awaiting her next running day. Their design was based on the Indian standard YB's which in turn were developed from the Ab class Pacifics in New Zealand.

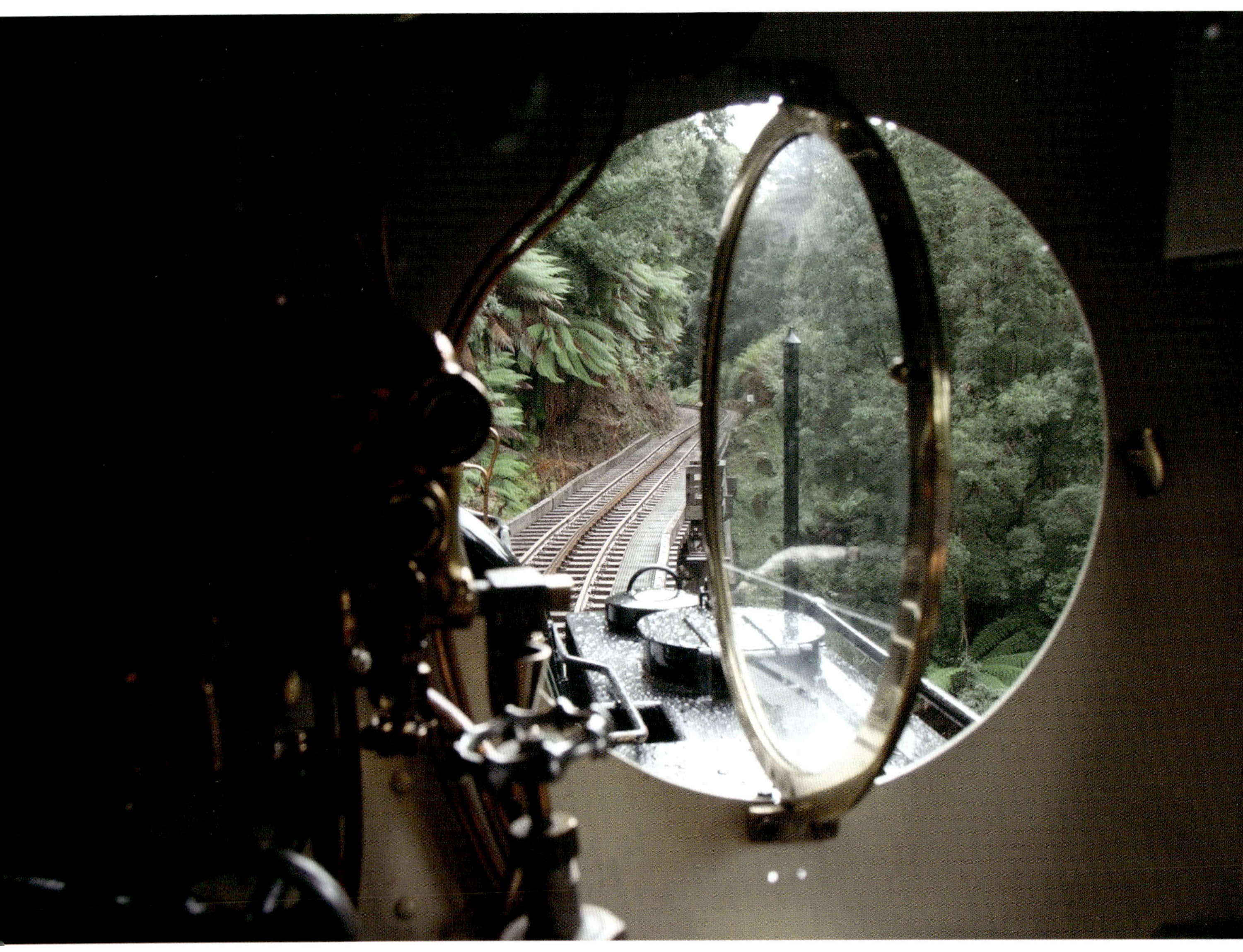

The 3ft 6ins Mount Lyell Railway, opened in 1896, connected the rich metal mines at Queenstown with the TGR at Strachan. It runs through the wild King River gorge, very difficult country. The sections up to Rinadeena and back down to Dubbil Barril use the Abt rack and there are numerous trestle bridges. By the 1960's the glory days of the mine and the town were over. The railway was worn out and closed in 1963. Closure of the mine and smelters came in 1993. The town's future looked bleak and the state and federal governments rebuilt the line to attract tourists. It was an enormous undertaking as much of the trackbed had been washed away and few of the bridges were capable of reuse. Three of the original five locos returned and the revived railway opened in 2002. On 23 March 2013 I was treated to a cab ride on 0-4-2RT No 3 (Dubs 3730/1898) and here she crosses bridge No 9 on the climb from Dubbil Barril to Rinadeena. The line provides one of the world's great heritage railway rides.

NEW ZEALAND

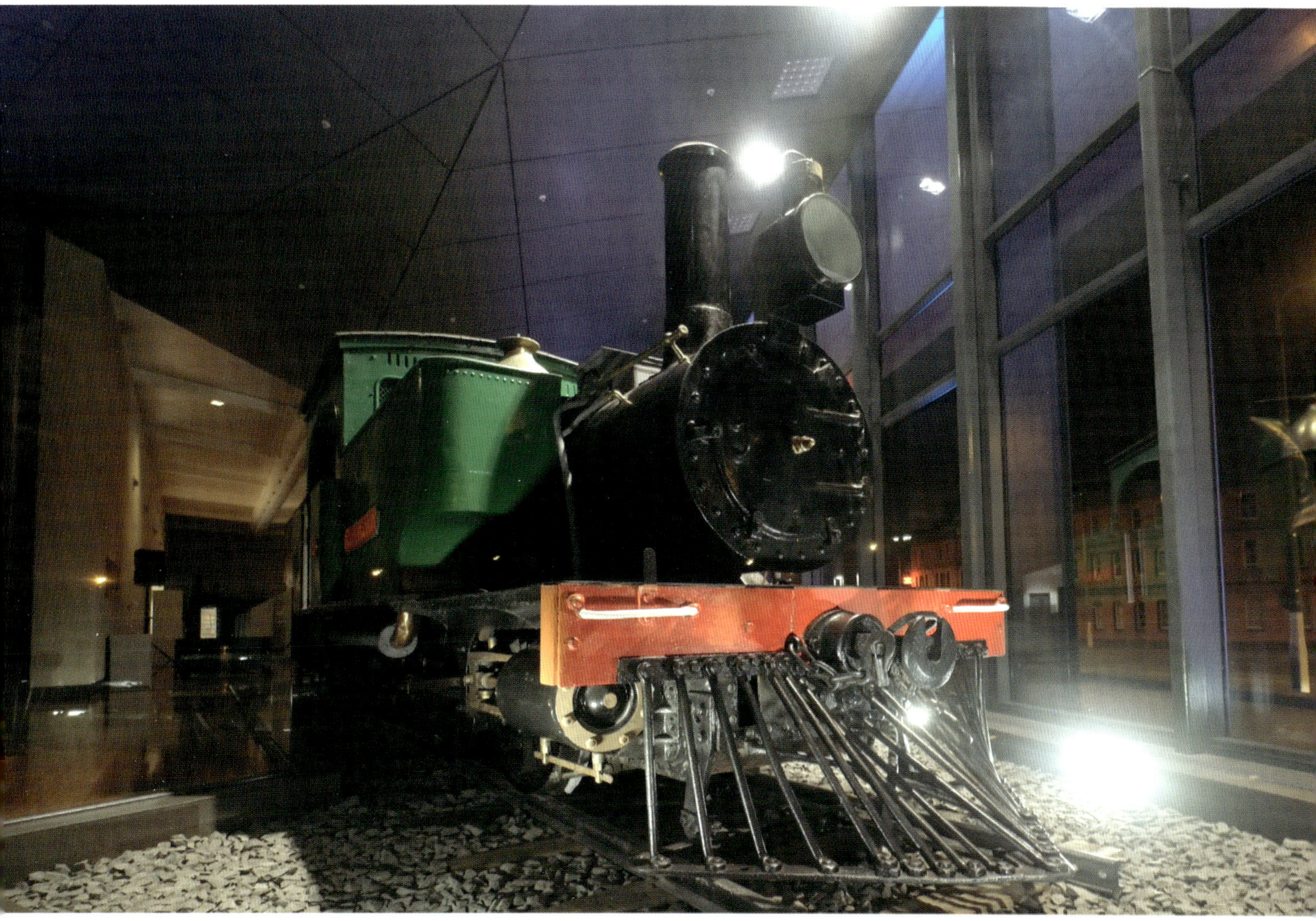

In New Zealand, a law was passed in 1870 to facilitate construction of a nationwide 3ft 6ins gauge system. Dunedin, then the commercial capital, was quick off the mark. A standard gauge line to Port Chalmers had already been proposed using two Double Fairlies. Plans were duly changed and 0-4-4-0 *Josephine* (VF637/1872) became the first 3ft 6ins loco to run in the country. She was designated as New Zealand Railways' E class No 175 in 1890 and moved to the government's Public Works Department in 1899, being renumbered 504. She helped build several of the country's mainlines including the scenic Arthur's Pass railway until being sold for scrap in 1917. Happily, her buyers took pity on her. In 1925 she was exhibited in Dunedin alongside No 608 *Passchendaele* (Addington 163/1915), the first of the Ab class Pacifics and NZR's First World War memorial loco, after which she moved to what is now the Toitū Otago Settlers Museum and has looked out over Dunedin station ever since. Here she is on 26 October 2015, the only remaining British-built Double Fairlie not constructed at Boston Lodge.

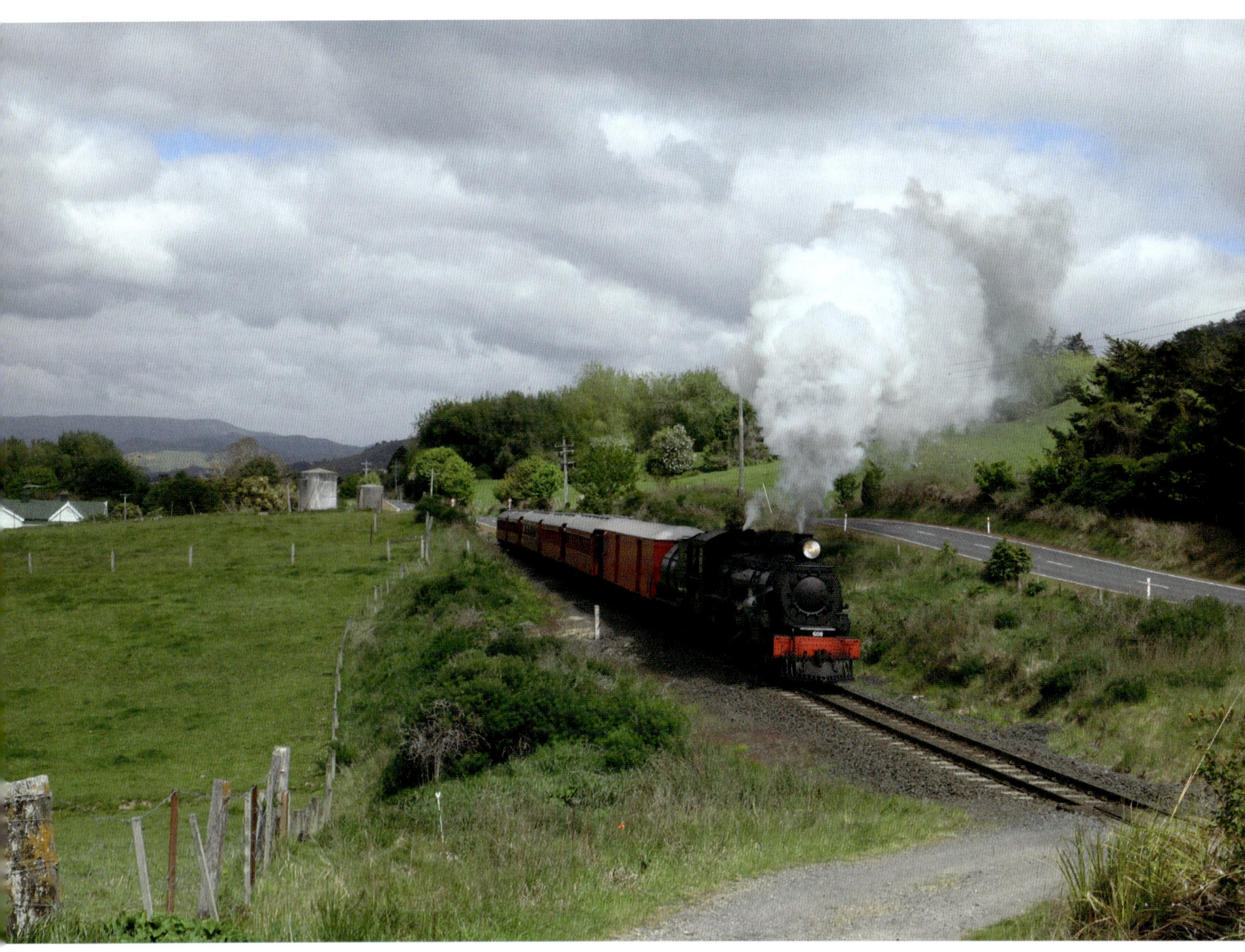

Nowadays passenger traffic at Dunedin is almost non-existent and its magnificent Edwardian station building now mostly has non-railway uses. The entire mainline south of Christchurch lost its regular passenger services in 2002 – a victim of a spectacularly unsuccessful attempt at privatisation which ended when the railways were taken back into public ownership in 2008. *Josephine* no longer has much to watch but the melodious sound of a chime whistle will have told her that the cold morning of 27 October 2015 was different. Ab class Pacific No 608 *Passchendaele*, her old friend from 1925, was back in town ready to haul a train of superbly restored period carriages along the hilly main line to Oamaru and on over the plains to Christchurch. Here's the train about 40kms out from Dunedin.

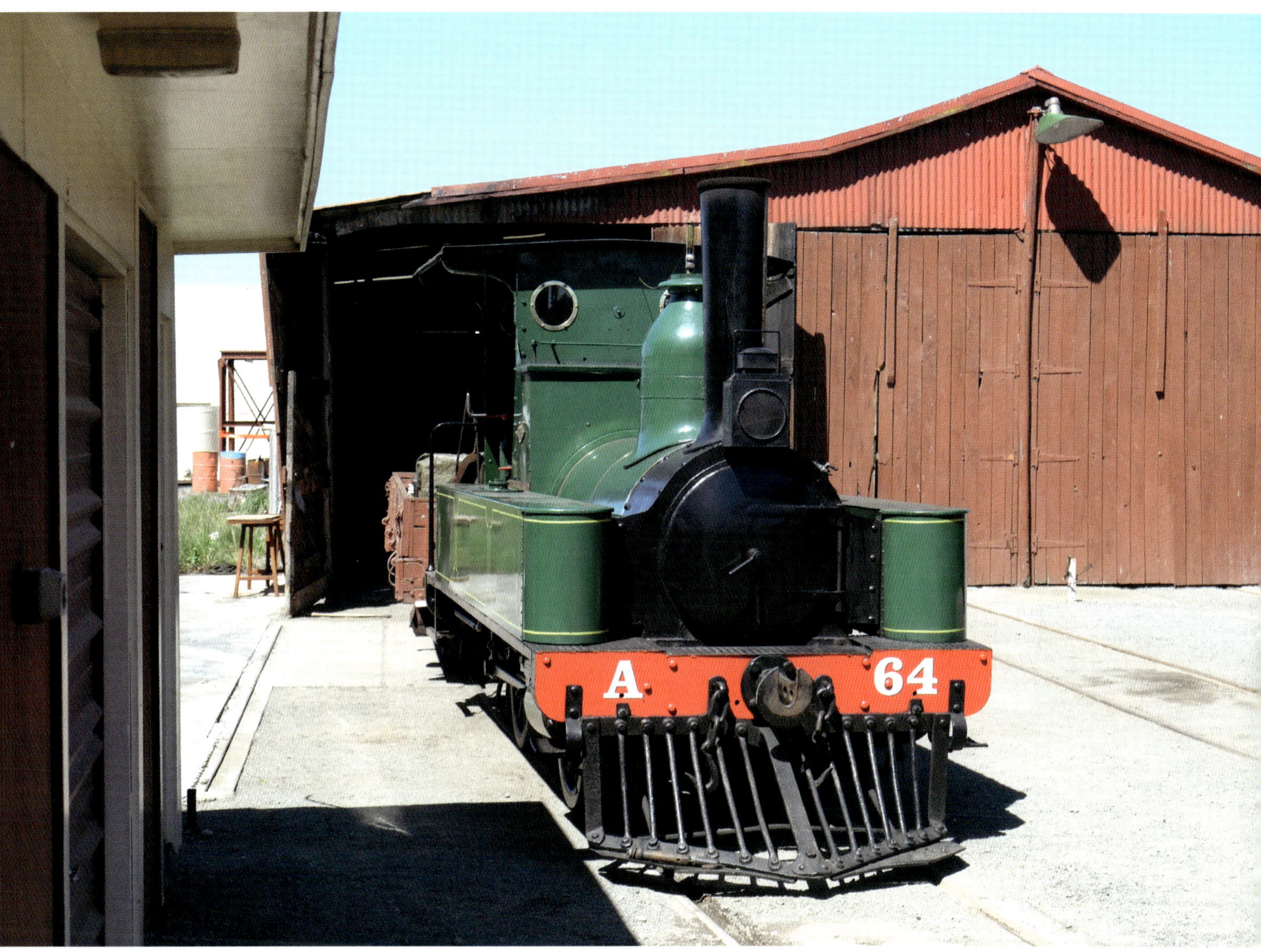

On 26 October 2015, A class 0-4-0T No 64 (Dübs 651/1873) stands outside the loco shed at the volunteer-run Plains Railway. In 1870 that decision to adopt the 3ft 6ins gauge was accompanied by a belief that the country's railways could be operated on light railway principles. Numerous small tank locos were acquired and the loading gauge, with a width of 8 feet and height of 11 feet 6 inches, was the most restrictive among the world's main 3ft 6ins systems. *Josephine* treated it with disdain from the start – her cab is 9ft 6ins wide! Traffic soon outgrew these little machines but the tight loading gauge was a lasting legacy. The fourteen As were the smallest of all. The last was withdrawn in 1906 but several spent long second lives in industrial service. Out of four which have survived two, including No 64, are usually in working order.

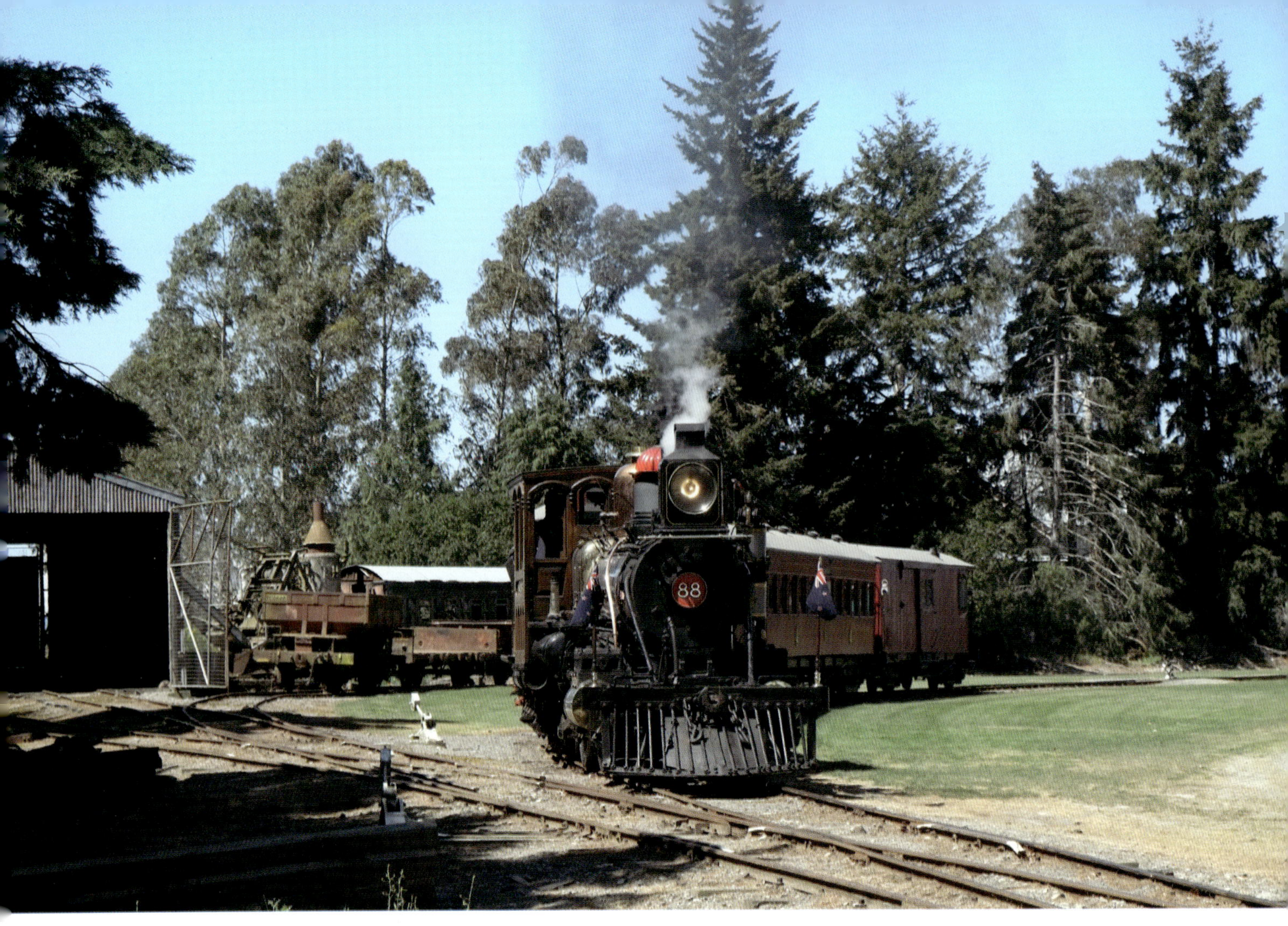

Above: 2-4-2 No K88 *Washington* (Rogers 2454/1877) hauled the very first train from Oamaru to Dunedin in September 1878. *Josephine* went along too as a pilot engine but misbehaved herself and broke down – which somehow she or her friends successfully attributed to the 2-4-2's excessive speed. It wasn't for nothing that one of New Zealand's railway historians has described her as a flighty old lady! When *Washington* was withdrawn in 1926 and dumped in the Oteri River *Josephine* must have thought she'd seen the last of her. However, the 2-4-2 had the last laugh as she was rescued in 1974 and steamed again in 1981, whereas *Josephine* hasn't run for more than one hundred years. On 26 October 2015 *Washington* sets off on the Plains Railway. Her restoration was a most impressive achievement for a small society.

Opposite: F class 0-6-0ST No 13 *Peveril* (Neilson 1672/1872), with her distinctive ogee-shaped tank, is the country's oldest working loco. Here she stands on shed at the volunteer-run Ferrymead Railway near Christchurch on 28 October 2015. The Fs were the first 3ft 6ins gauge locos to be ordered by the government. They were conceived as mixed traffic machines but ended up on local and shunting work. Eighty-eight had been built by the time production ended in 1888. The design was influential as three were built for the Rio Tinto line in Spain and two as WAGR's first locos, their No 1 now being preserved at the excellent Bassendean museum in Perth. No 13 was one of three prototypes and one of the last two to be withdrawn in 1963. To the right is Wd class 2-6-4T no 357 (Baldwin 19261/1901).

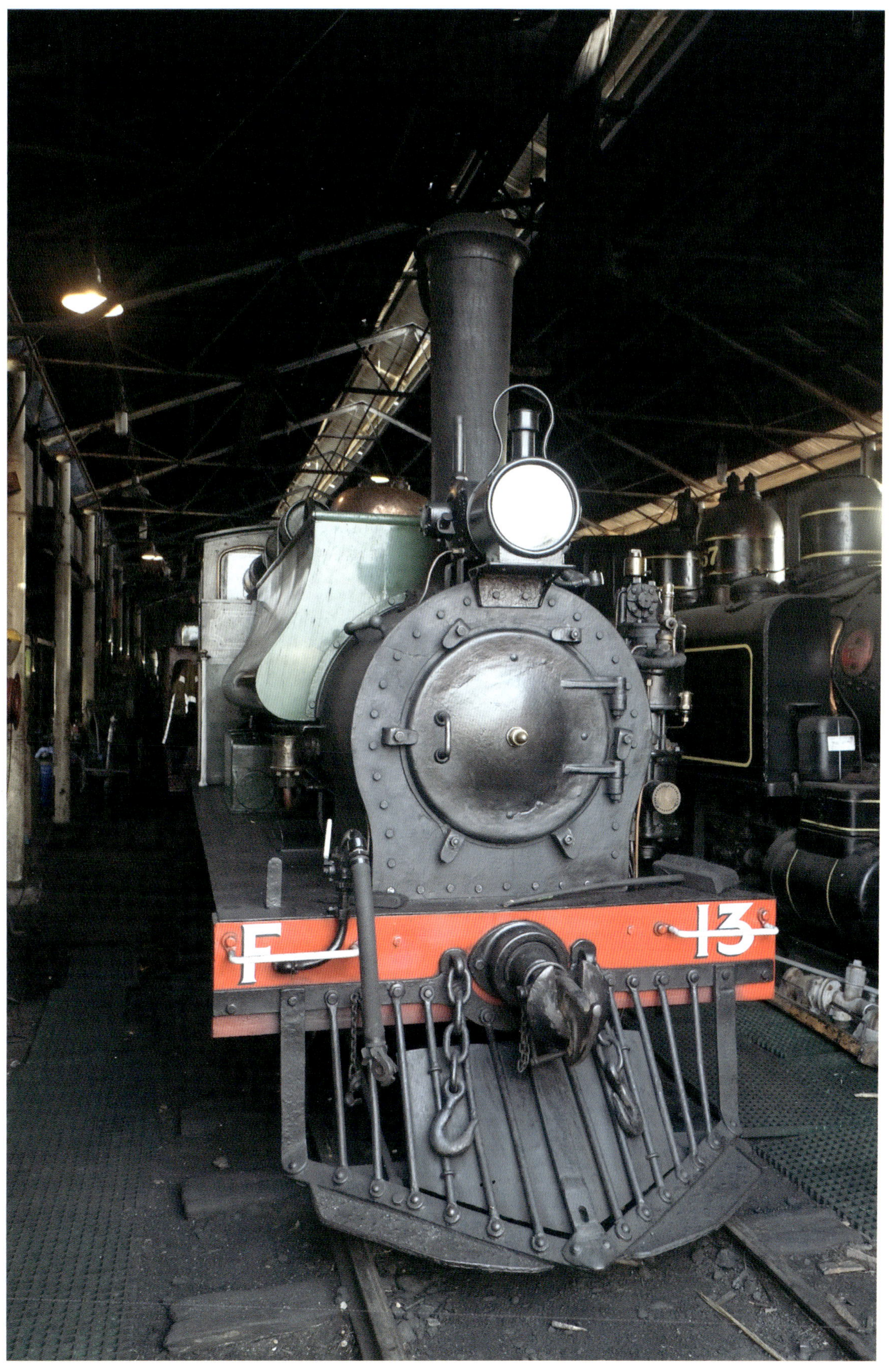
F
13

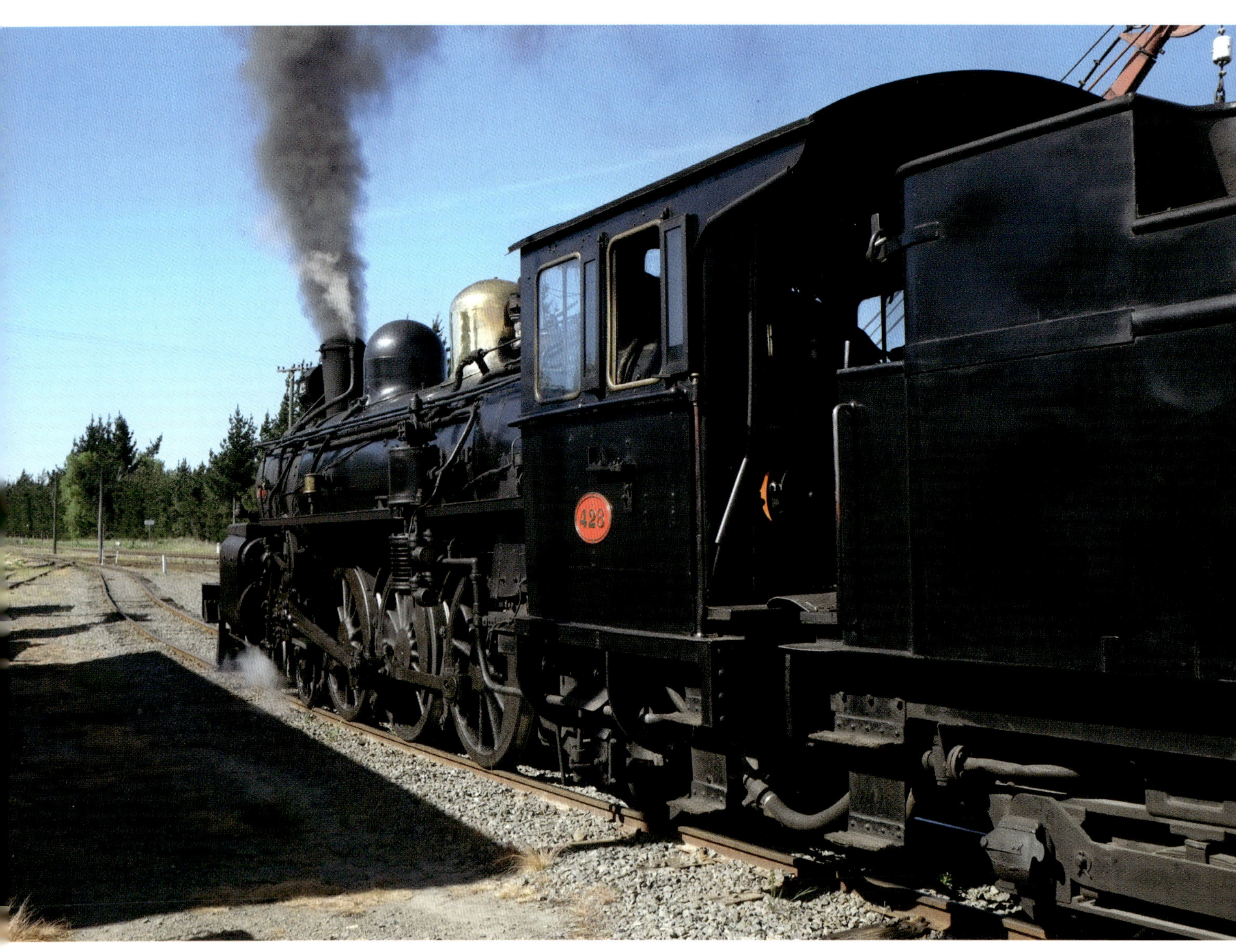

NZR designed their own locos after the mid-1880s and were notable for introducing the world's first wide-firebox Pacific type with their Baldwin-built Q class Pacifics in 1903. These were followed by the fifty-eight A class 4-cylinder de Glehn compounds in 1906, often considered to be the country's finest looking locos and quite a contrast in size to the previous A class! They were rebuilt much later as 2-cylinder simples. No 428 (Price 31/1909) stands at Waipara on the Weka Pass Railway on 26 October 2015.

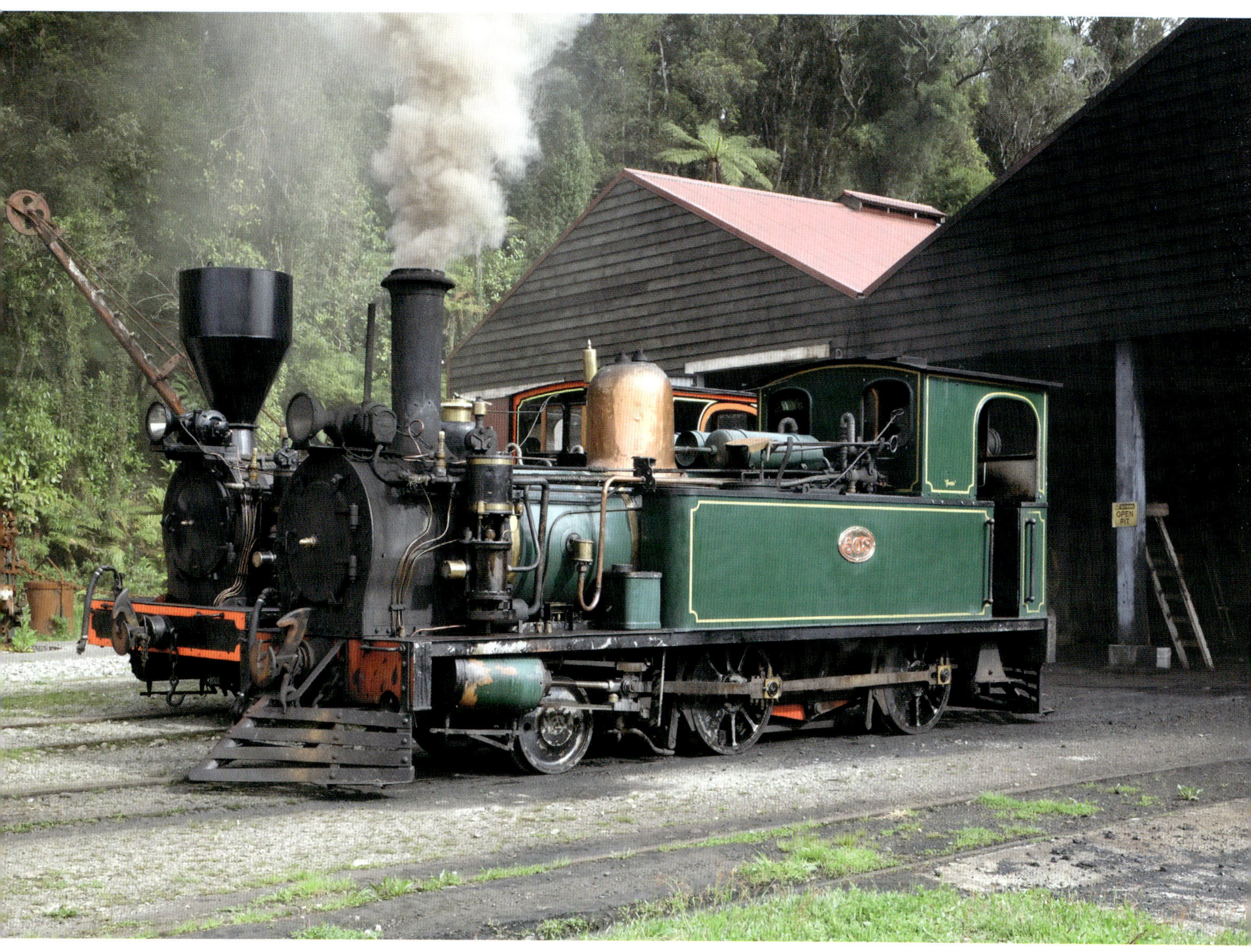

The shed at the Shantytown theme park near Greymouth on South Island's west coast originally stood at the nearby Blackball colliery. This work-stained 2-4-0T was NZR's L class No 208 (Avonside 1206/1877) which became the PWD's No 508 in 1901 and is preserved wearing their attractive lined green livery. On 30 October 2015, she makes one of her last appearances in steam before being withdrawn for overhaul. Behind her is 0-6-0T *Kaitangata* (SS 4270/1896), built to NZR's Fa class design but always owned by the Kaitangata Coal & Railway Company. She passed her boiler inspection the previous day after overhaul and was about to take over operations at Shantytown's old bush tramway.

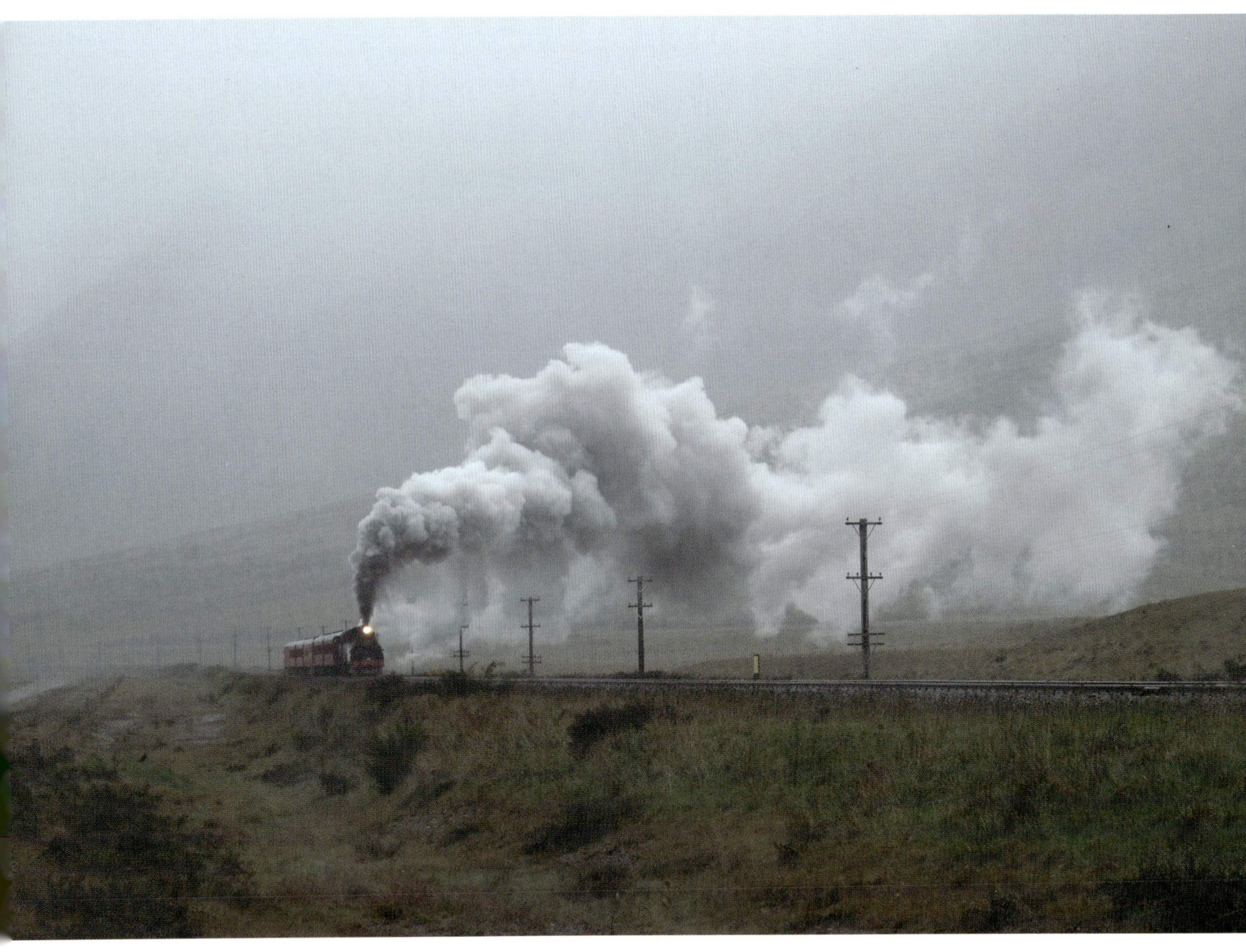

The mountains of South Island are on the receiving end of the Roaring Forties and storms coming up from Antarctica. Ab class Pacific No 608 makes her way through one of these on 29 October 2015 as she climbs towards Arthur's Pass on her way to Greymouth. NZR's distinctive blend of British and US practice was clearly seen in the Abs which were one of their great success stories. No fewer than 149 were built and several lasted until the twilight of steam in the late 1960s. They were equally at home on passenger and freight work and, with only a 10-ton axleload, could run almost anywhere. As we've already seen their influence reached far beyond New Zealand.